A BIBLIOGRAPHY OF
D. H. LAWRENCE

Second Edition

WARREN ROBERTS

CAMBRIDGE UNIVERSITY PRESS

Cambridge

London   New York   New Rochelle

Melbourne   Sydney

Published by the Press Syndicate of the University of Cambridge
The Pitt Building, Trumpington Street, Cambridge CB2 1RP
32 East 57th Street, New York, NY 10022, USA
296 Beaconsfield Parade, Middle Park, Melbourne 3206, Australia

© Warren Roberts 1963
Second edition © Warren Roberts 1982

First published by Rupert Hart-Davis, London, 1963
Second edition published by Cambridge University Press, 1982

Printed in Great Britain at the University Press, Cambridge

Library of Congress catalogue card number: 81–10149

British Library Cataloguing in publication data

Roberts, Warren
A bibliography of D. H. Lawrence–2nd ed.
1. Lawrence, D. H.–Bibliography
I. Title
016.828′912   PR6023.A93Z/
ISBN 0 521 22295 8

A BIBLIOGRAPHY OF
D. H. LAWRENCE

Charcoal sketch for portrait of D. H. Lawrence by Jan Juta. Humanities
Research Center, The University of Texas at Austin

FOR
MATTHEW, KATHERINE AND JUSTIN

CONTENTS

ILLUSTRATIONS

PREFACE TO THE FIRST EDITION

D. H. Lawrence's literary career offers an exceptional opportunity for the bibliographical study of a writer in the twentieth century; Lawrence was a prolific and versatile writer whose restless travels provided the background and motivation for much of his writing. The intricacies of Lawrence bibliography lead to Italy, Australia, Ceylon and Mexico, as well as to England and America.

Lawrence wrote in almost every literary genre, novels, short stories, plays, poetry, essays and travel books; his work was published in a variety of formats, frequently in ephemeral pamphlets and periodicals or in limited editions by private presses, and his difficulties with censorship further complicate Lawrence bibliography. All of these factors add materially to the interest and usefulness of a bibliography of D. H. Lawrence.

References to the published texts of Lawrence's work should be viewed with caution. This is particularly true of his early periodical appearances. Frequently, he revised between publications, and many times before a work was finally included in one of his own collected volumes, Lawrence found an opportunity to alter the text. Much of his early poetry was printed in different versions. It was customary for Lawrence to publish the same work in periodicals in both England and the United States, often with a change of title or text, and many Lawrence items were published after his death from variant manuscript sources which adds to the difficulties of establishing the Lawrence canon. Lawrence was a voluminous letter writer, and the account of his published letters recorded here does not pretend to be exhaustive.

An attempt has been made to identify all first appearances in print of the works of D. H. Lawrence, both in periodical and book form, with sufficient cross references to permit the student to follow each work through its significant publications. As many copies as possible of each book in the A and B sections were examined, but for some books, such as the Duffield *White Peacock*, there were not enough copies available to provide certain evidence for adequate descriptions. Many publishing records were lost in England during the Second World War, and records

ix

are unavailable for many of Lawrence's early American publishers. Thus, many bibliographical questions remain unanswered, but nonetheless, each description will serve as a basis for determining those irregularities which must inevitably come to light as a result of the publication of a bibliography.

Although textual considerations have supplied the primary criterion for deciding which books to describe after the first edition has been dealt with, this work is intended for the bibliophile and collector as well as for the student; and consequently, many examples have been described and variants listed, for which no textual or other significant problem exists, but which, for one reason or another, are of interest to the book fancier.

While it was not possible, or indeed desirable in a work of this sort, to compare all published texts, revisions and changes are frequently indicated, and the system of cross references provides a convenient machinery for investigating textual differences.

In order to preserve a simple arrangement for the bibliography and to provide a rational format for the complexities of Lawrence's literary career, all books for which D. H. Lawrence was primarily responsible are placed in the A section; this includes his translations. Although it is probable that other collaborations between D. H. Lawrence and Koteliansky logically belong in the A section, there is no evidence for Lawrence's extensive revision of any Koteliansky translation apart from Leo Shestov's *All Things Are Possible*, for which there exists a complete holograph manuscript in Lawrence's hand.

Although this work is based largely on the extensive collection of Lawrence books in the University of Texas Humanities Research Center, use has been made of books from the collections of George Lazarus, the Library of Congress, the University of New Mexico and the University of Kansas.

No work of this sort is ever accomplished without immense obligation to those who have gone before, and my debt to Mr E. D. McDonald's earlier bibliographical studies must remain obvious; I am equally grateful for Mr E. W. Tedlock's manuscript study, Mr Harry T. Moore's *Intelligent Heart* and Mr Edward Nehl's *Composite Biography*, all of which have made my task immeasurably lighter.

I shall be as much in debt to those who can remedy the deficiencies in this work as to those who find some reward in its use.

Austin   WARREN ROBERTS
August 1962

PREFACE TO THE SECOND EDITION

Since the first publication of this bibliography, interest in D. H. Lawrence has continued to increase to an extent which only a few dedicated Lawrentians might have thought possible twenty years ago. Perhaps the best indication of this growing concern for Lawrence and his work is the fact that more than one hundred and thirty new books and pamphlets about Lawrence have been added to the F section.

The *D. H. Lawrence Review*, founded by Dr James Cowan at the University of Arkansas, has become one of the more distinguished of the periodicals devoted to a single author. Of greater importance are the projects undertaken by the Cambridge University Press under the direction of Mr Michael Black. The first of a seven volume edition of Lawrence's letters edited by Professor James Boulton of the University of Birmingham has been published (A121), and the Cambridge Press is also publishing a critical edition of the works of Lawrence which will eventually consist of more than thirty volumes, the first of which, *Apocalypse and the Writings on Revelation* (A57b), was published in 1980.

As these various projects have progressed it has become evident that a revision of the bibliography will be useful for all Lawrence students and particularly helpful for those concerned with the development of Lawrence's texts. As stated in the preface for the first edition this bibliography does not pretend to compare all relevant texts or to indicate the textual changes in all the various publications of a given work, but the cross references and the publishing history should make it possible to trace the evolution of a text.

For the revised bibliography it has been thought expedient to preserve the original entry numbers as they appeared in the first edition of the bibliography; a system of decimal numbering has been employed for entries which had to be interpolated in the original chronological sequence. A new feature is a brief note about dust-jackets which have become increasingly important for collectors.

Entries in the A section consist of first editions and subsequent printings and editions of special interest to the student or the collector. Textual research with the Hinman Collator has revealed that many important

xi

textual differences exist in printings or issues which are not described in separate entries; however, notes frequently indicate changes in the state of the text for major works, and usually sufficient information is given to identify a book with a particular textual state.

Both scholars and collectors should be aware of the importance of subsequent printings of a text during Lawrence's lifetime. Often second, third and fourth printings are more difficult to find than the first, and these can be of critical significance for the textual editor or for the Lawrence student interested in the influences at work which alter the text from its original state. Subsequent editions of individual works are not always mentioned in the notes, particularly for books published after Lawrence's death.

It is not customary in descriptive bibliographies to include extensive lists of secondary materials, and the lists of reviews are not intended to be definitive, although enough reviews are recorded for the major works to enable the student to learn something of the reception of the work when it was first published. Dr James Cowan of the *D. H. Lawrence Review* has just completed an annotated bibliography of writings about Lawrence which will contain about 3,500 items including reviews and articles.

Only first appearances in print are given separate entries in the B and C sections, but frequently later appearances in periodicals or books are mentioned, usually in the entry identifying the first printing in each category. The D section lists only the first appearance of each translation; translations in periodicals are not included. Lists of translations are likely to be incomplete and must on occasion be viewed with caution because it has not always been possible to examine the books. Transliterations from languages not using the Roman alphabet may be inconsistent because the entries are sometimes derived from different sources.

The E section has been expanded considerably as a result of the efforts of Mrs Lindeth Vasey to gather information about the location of Lawrence manuscripts for the Cambridge editorial projects. A large number of previously unrecorded manuscripts have been added to the list from the collection of the late Mr Harold Smith of Bermuda.

The question of publication dates can be very confusing; there are several significant dates associated with the publication of a book: the date it was printed, the date copies were delivered to the publisher, the date review copies are sent out, the date copies are released to dealers, the date copies first become available to the public and finally the official publication date. It has been my contention that the publication date is when the publisher says it is, and that date is customarily recorded in the *U.S. Copyright Register* and the *English Catalogue of Books*. The notes in entry A7 about the American publication of *The Rainbow* illustrate the complexities which can occur. If the various dates that are part of the publication history are significant for some research purpose, the scholar must examine the situation himself and determine the relevance of these dates for his problem.

It is my sincere hope that those who use this work will find it serves them well as a guide through the uncertainties and complexities of Lawrence bibliography.

Austin   WARREN ROBERTS

March 1981

ACKNOWLEDGEMENTS FOR THE FIRST EDITION

So many kind people all over the world took the time and trouble to reply to my inquiries about D. H. Lawrence that it is impossible in the small space available to mention all their names.

Of these Mr John Hayward is due special thanks for his care in watching the development of the bibliography and for the invaluable advice and attention he gave so unfailingly. Special mention must also be made for Mr John G. Pattisson of Martin Secker and Warburg, who supplied an inordinate amount of information about the Secker publications of Lawrence's works; Mr E. D. McDonald, who very kindly made available his library of Lawrence books and all the papers concerned with his two bibliographical studies; Mr George Lazarus, who most hospitably opened his library of books and manuscripts to my use; Mr Bertram Rota, who never failed to respond with just the information needed to solve some crux or other; Mr Edward Nehls and Mr Harry T. Moore, who were most generous of their vast experience of Lawrence's works; Mr W. Forster, who very carefully studied my list of periodical appearances and made many useful suggestions; Mr Kenneth Hopkins, who read the galley proofs; and for Mr Angie Ravagli and the late Mrs Frieda Lawrence Ravagli, whose memories, books and papers were of invaluable assistance.

Special thanks must also go to Mr Harry Ransom for unfailing advice and inspiration and to the staff of the University of Texas Humanities Research Center, who suffered my long presence underfoot with kindness and patience.

Mr Rupert Hart-Davis' quiet confidence in the outcome of my labours has been the object of constant gratitude, and for this undeserved kindness, I offer my sincere if inadequate thanks.

Many librarians, publishers, friends and Lawrence scholars everywhere will recognize in these pages their contributions. They will know, I hope, how deeply I am indebted for all the unselfish help they gave.

Austin   WARREN ROBERTS
August 1962

ACKNOWLEDGEMENTS FOR THE SECOND EDITION

Once again the international community of Lawrence scholars has been the source of more help than anyone could reasonably expect, and my debt to the host of persons who responded to my inquiries or who sent vital information for the revision of the bibliography is one which cannot be discharged by the mere mention of a name; nevertheless it is my hope that all those who see in these pages their own special contributions will know how sincerely I appreciate the assistance they so unselfishly gave.

Much of my work was done in the D. H. Lawrence Collection in the Humanities Research Center at the University of Texas at Austin, and my obligation to those who were my colleagues there must be especially recognised. Dr David Farmer, my former assistant and Mrs Lindeth Vasey who headed the Lawrence research unit were immeasurably helpful. Lindeth Vasey was responsible for collecting detailed information about the location of Lawrence manuscripts and letters which was translated into a useful format for the editors of volumes in the various Cambridge University Press projects. Dr Gerald Lacy's pioneer work in compiling the first calendar of Lawrence letters provided much of the motivation for all that has come afterwards.

There are many Lawrence collections in private hands, and Mr George Lazarus, Mr W. Forster, Mr John Martin, the late Mr Harold Smith and the late Mr John Baker were typically generous both of their collections and their time. Mr Gerald Pollinger, the agent for the Lawrence estate, has responded consistently with the precise information I needed and has been particularly helpful in providing liaison with publishers. Book dealers usually know more about the intricacies of Lawrence books than the scholars who work with them, and I must give special thanks to Mr Anthony Rota, Mr Andreas Brown, Mr William Pieper and Mr Peter Howard.

All of the editors and scholars working on the various Cambridge University Press projects have provided valuable information; Dr Brian Finney has found much new information about the early publication of Lawrence's short fiction and invariably wrote to me about his discoveries. Professor James Boulton, Dr Keith Sagar, Dr Carl Baron, Dr Andrew

ACKNOWLEDGEMENTS FOR THE SECOND EDITION

Robertson, indeed everyone associated with the Cambridge projects have all contributed something to this revision.

Scholars working in languages other than English have made it possible to add many new and interesting entries for the translation section of the bibliography. For their persistent efforts in finding new translations and offering suggestions for corrections in the earlier lists, I am grateful to Bengt Altenberg, Miroslav Beker, Chongwha Chung, Simonetta de Filippis, Jacqueline Gouirand, Konrad Gross, Sandanobu Kai, Lászlo Kéry, Masakasu Koga, Hans Lundquist, Horst E. Meyer, Chaman Nahal, Cornelia Neuhäusel, Yasuichirô Ôhashi, Taiji Okada, Brita Seyersted and Krystina Stamrowska.

For almost twenty years persons interested in Lawrence have been sending me notes about bibliographical matters, and many names must necessarily have been inadvertently omitted from the list of those to whom I owe thanks. It is not possible to acknowledge properly here the unfailing cooperation which publishers of Lawrence books and the librarians who care for them have given my persistent and often tiresome efforts to elicit one more fact which they on occasion quite understandably find irrelevant, but I am grateful to them all.

Austin
March 1981

WARREN ROBERTS

xvii

A. BOOKS AND PAMPHLETS

A. BOOKS AND PAMPHLETS

a. *first edition*

THE | WHITE PEACOCK | *A NOVEL* | BY | D. H. LAW-
RENCE | [*publisher's device*] | NEW YORK | DUFFIELD &
COMPANY | 1911

Light blue cloth boards, printed in white on upper cover: [*a spread peacock
in white and dark blue*] | [*dark blue rule*] | [*ornamental rule in dark blue*] |
THE WHITE PEACOCK | D. H. LAWRENCE | [*within a single rule border in dark
blue*]; printed in white on spine: THE | WHITE | PEACOCK | [*short rule*]
| LAWRENCE | DUFFIELD The leaves measure $7\frac{5}{16}'' \times 5''$. All edges trimmed.

[i]–[viii] + [1]–496, as follows: [i]–[ii] blank; [iii] half-title; [iv] blank;
[v] title page as above; [vi] COPYRIGHT, 1910, BY | DUFFIELD &
COMPANY | [*short rule*] | THE TROW PRESS, NEW YORK; [vii] table of
contents; [viii] blank; [1] fly-title: PART 1; [2] blank; 3–187 text; [188]
blank; [189] fly-title: PART 11; [190] blank; 191–357 text; [358] blank;
[359] fly-title: PART 111; [360] blank; 361–496 text.

Published 19 January 1911 at $1.30; number of copies unknown.

VARIANTS: (1) copy described above.
          (2) as (1) but with cancel title and copyright date 1911.

b. *first edition, English impression*

The | White Peacock | By | D. H. Lawrence | [*publisher's device*] |
London | William Heinemann | 1911

Dark blue cloth boards, printed in black and white on upper cover:
[*rule in black*] | THE WHITE | PEACOCK | ··· | D. H. | LAWRENCE | [*rule
in black*] | [*four vertical rules combined with two horizontal rules form three
panels, the centre panel with lettering in white and the side panels with rosebush
designs in black*]; stamped in gold on spine: [*thick rule*] | THE WHITE |

3

PEACOCK │ ··· │ D. H. │ LAWRENCE │ [*two thick rules*] │ HEINEMANN │ [*thick rule*]; blind stamped on lower cover: [*publisher's device*] The leaves measure $7\frac{9}{16}''$ × $4\frac{7}{8}''$. Top and fore edges trimmed; bottom edges untrimmed.

[i]–[iv] + [1]–496, as follows: [i] half-title; [ii] list of Heinemann publications; [iii] title page as above; [iv] *Copyright, London, 1911, by William Heinemann, and Washington, U. S. A., │ by Duffield and Company*; [1] fly-title: PART I; [2] blank; 3–187 text; [188] blank; [189] fly-title: PART II; [190] blank; 191–357 text; [358] blank; [359] fly-title: PART III; [360] blank; 361–496 text.

Published 20 January 1911 at 6*s*.; the first printing consisted of 1500 copies.

VARIANTS: (1) as (3) but with original title page and 1910 copyright notice on page [iv]; original text on pages 227–230; no copy known.
(2) as (1) but with cancel title and 1911 copyright notice.
(3) copy described above, with cancel title, 1911 copyright notice and cancel pages 227–230 with modified text.
(4) as (3) but with pages [i]–[iv] reprinted and pasted in.
(5) as (4) but with pages 227–230 integral with signature.
(6) as (5) but without publisher's device blind stamped on lower cover.

Mr Bertram Rota very kindly supplied the list of variants with the exception of (4); Mr Rota also called attention to the probable existence of (1) which is assumed from a copy of (2) in Mr George Lazarus's library in which page [1] bears an offset from the original page [iv] showing a 1910 copyright date.

c. *colonial issue*

THE WHITE PEACOCK │ BY │ D. H. LAWRENCE │ LONDON │ WILLIAM HEINEMANN │ 1911

Tan cloth boards, printed in brown on upper cover: THE WHITE │ PEACOCK │ ··· │ D. H. │ LAWRENCE│ The upper cover is decorated with a series of vertical and horizontal rules forming panels. The upper left and lower right panels show the Heinemann windmill on a darker background; the upper right and lower left panels show a ship in full sail on a darker background. The spine is printed in black: THE WHITE │ PEACOCK │ [*ship in full sail on darker background*] │ D. H. │ LAWRENCE │

[*the Heinemann windmill on darker background*] | HEINEMANN'S | ·COLONIAL· | ·LIBRARY· The leaves measure $7\frac{1}{8}''$ × $4\frac{3}{4}''$. All edges trimmed.

[i]–[iv] + [1]–496, as follows: [i] Heinemann's Colonial Library of Popular Fiction | [*rule*] | *Issued for sale in the British* | *Colonies, and India, and not* | *to be imported into Europe or* | *the United States of America*; [ii] quotations from reviews of *The White Peacock* in *The Morning Post* and *The Observer*; [iii] title page as above; [iv] All rights reserved. [1]–496, as for (A1a) and (A1b).

Pages [i]–[iv] have been reprinted and pasted in and pages 227–230 are integral with the revised text.

d. *colonial issue, Duckworth binding*

This is the same as the Heinemann Colonial Edition described above except for the binding:
Blue cloth boards, printed in white on upper cover: THE WHITE PEACOCK |...D. H. LAWRENCE... | [*enclosed within a double rule forming a border for the upper cover*]; printed in white on spine: [*double rule*] | THE | WHITE | PEACOCK | D. H. | LAWRENCE | DUCKWORTH | [*double rule*]; printed in white on lower cover: [*publisher's device with motto*] The leaves measure $7\frac{3}{16}''$ × $4\frac{3}{4}''$. All edges trimmed.

NOTES: Lawrence began writing his first published novel while he was teaching as an uncertificated teacher in the British School at Eastwood and continued to work on the manuscript during his years at Nottingham University College. The final version was not completed until early in 1910. Although the book was not published until the month following his mother's death, Lawrence obtained an advance copy of the Heinemann edition which he put into her hands before she died. For an explication of the persons and places in the novel one may consult Ada Lawrence's *Young Lorenzo* (B34) and Jessie Chambers's *A Personal Record* (B43).

The Duffield *White Peacock* is given priority over the Heinemann edition for several reasons. Edward McDonald in his *Bibliography* (B16) appears to be correct in stating that although the book was intended to appear simultaneously on both sides of the Atlantic, Duffield actually published one day earlier than the English firm. Of greater importance is the fact that Heinemann imported the Duffield plates for the English edition, and after some of the copies were bound, Heinemann asked Lawrence to rewrite a paragraph on page 230 which they felt might be considered objectionable.

Lawrence complied with this request and as a consequence the English edition contains cancel leaves while the American text remains unaltered. Another change was effected in the Heinemann text on page 227, where the phrase "the miserable brute has dirtied that angel" was substituted for "the dirty devil's run her muck over that angel." The original text for page 230, as given in the American edition, reads in part:

"God!—we were a passionate couple—and she would have me in her bedroom while she drew Greek statues of me—her Croton, her Hercules! I never saw her drawings. She had her own way too much—I let her do as she liked with me.

"Then gradually she got tired—it took her three years to have a real bellyful of me."

For Heinemann Lawrence rewrote the passage as follows:

"Lord!—we were an infatuated couple—and she would choose to view me in an aesthetic light. I was Greek statues for her, bless you: Croton, Hercules, I don't know what! She had her own way too much—I let her do as she liked with me.

"Then gradually she got tired—it took her three years to be really glutted with me."

Several states of the Heinemann *White Peacock* exist. Copies are seen with no cancel leaves; some copies have only the cancel pages 229–230, while others are found with both cancel leaves. McDonald notes a copy with both the cancel pages 229–230 and the original pages 229–230 intact. According to the publisher there were two binding orders for the Heinemann edition, each for 750 copies; the copies in the first order have the Heinemann windmill blind stamped on the back cover; those in the second order do not.

The White Peacock has been reprinted frequently; Heinemann reprinted the original edition in March 1911, and Duckworth (who took the title over from Heinemann in 1915) issued a third impression of their edition in May 1921. Secker's thin paper pocket edition appeared in September 1927. Cheap English language editions include the Albatross Modern Continental Library No. 32, Leipzig, 1932; the Everyman edition in March 1935; Penguin Books No. 760, August 1950 with an introduction by Richard Aldington, whose essay also prefaced the Heinemann pocket edition of March 1951.

REVIEWS: *The White Peacock* was reviewed in the *Athenaeum*, 10 February 1911; the *Saturday Review*, 13 May 1911; by Violet Hunt in the *Daily Chronicle*, 10 February; by Frederic Tabor Cooper in the *Bookman* (New

York), April 1911; by Catherine Jackson (later Catherine Carswell whose *Savage Pilgrimage* (B37) defended Lawrence against John Middleton Murry) in the *Glasgow Herald*, 18 March; by Henry Savage in the *Academy* (London), 18 March and in the *English Review*, May 1911.

NOTES (2): Dr Andrew Robertson, editor for the Cambridge edition of *The White Peacock*, gives in his introduction a detailed account of the textual and typographical differences between the Duffield and Heinemann first printings, and he reveals a curious fact bearing on the authority of the texts of the two impressions. The galley proofs which Lawrence revised existed in two copies, one of which was returned to Heinemann; the other, on which Lawrence partly entered duplicate revisions, was sent to Louie Burrows. When Lawrence sent the last lot of duplicate proofs to her, he noted that galley 59 was missing; this set has survived and is now at the University of California at Los Angeles with galley 59 still missing. See (E430e). Unfortunately the fully corrected set of galleys has disappeared. It was noted earlier in this entry that the Heinemann *White Peacock* was printed from plates imported from Duffield in New York. This is true, but the Duffield copy was set from the corrected proofs Lawrence had returned to Heinemann. Thus as Robertson correctly points out, Lawrence had no control over the text of his work after releasing the proofs to Heinemann.

Here a word must be said about variant (1) of *The White Peacock* (A1b) as set forth in the first edition of this bibliography. As yet no copy has turned up, and Robertson reports that the George Lazarus copy seems to read 1911 in the offset impression, and I must confess that I have not been able to identify a copy, including the Lazarus copy, in which the offset 1910 can be seen clearly.

There are, however, additional variants for which no logical reasons can be adduced to justify a precise sequence.

VARIANTS: (2a) as (2) but with pp. [i]–[iv] reprinted and pasted in; p. [iv] reads *Copyright, London, 1911, by William Heinemann.*

(3a) as (3) but without the publisher's device on the lower cover.

(4a) as (4) but without the publisher's device on the lower cover.

(4b) as (4) but with pp. 227–228 cancelled and pp. 229–230 integral with the signature and with the altered text.

Mr John Martin has reported a copy of *The White Peacock*, with the text of a later variant, bound in blue cloth on which only the title and the name of the author are blind stamped on the spine; this may be a trial Duckworth binding.

REVIEWS (2): Additional reviews of *The White Peacock* appeared in *The Times Literary Supplement*, 26 January; the *Observer*, 29 January; *Daily Mail*, 3 February; *Standard*, 3 February; *Manchester Guardian*, 8 February by Allan Monkhouse; *Morning Post*, 9 February; *Scotsman*, 9 February; *Eastwood and Kimberley Advertiser*, 10 February by William Hopkin; *Daily News*, 14 February; *Yorkshire Post*, 15 February; *Nottingham Guardian Literary Supplement*, 21 February; *Westminster Gazette*, 4 March; *Nation* (London), 1 April; *Vanity Fair* (London) by Richard Middleton; *Birmingham Daily Post*, 3 April; *New York Times*, 9 June; *Sheffield Daily Telegraph*, 11 May.

A2 THE TRESPASSER 1912

first edition

THE TRESPASSER | BY | D. H. LAWRENCE | [*publisher's device*] | LONDON: DUCKWORTH & CO. | HENRIETTA STREET, COVENT GARDEN | 1912

Dark blue cloth boards, blind stamped on upper cover: [*thick rule*] | [*thin rule*]; stamped in gold: THE | TRESPASSER | By the Author of | "THE WHITE | PEACOCK" | [*the lettering within a gold circle*]; blind stamped: [*thin rule*] | [*thick rule*]; blind stamped on lower cover: [*publisher's device*]; stamped in gold on spine: [*thick rule*] | [*thin rule*] | THE | TRESPASSER | D. H. | LAWRENCE | DUCKWORTH | [*thin rule*] | [*thick rule*] The leaves measure $7\frac{1}{4}'' \times 4\frac{3}{4}''$. All edges trimmed.

[i]–[iv] + [1]–292 and 20 pp. advertisements, as follows: [i] half-title; [ii] blank; [iii] title page as above; [iv] *All rights reserved.*; [1]–292 text, at bottom of page 292: [*short rule*] BILLING AND SONS, LTD., PRINTERS, GUILDFORD; 20 pp. of advertisements.

Published 23 May 1912 at 6s.; number of copies unknown.

VARIANTS: (1) copy described above.
    (2) as (1) except bound in green cloth boards with upper cover printed in black: D. H. | LAWRENCE | The | Trespasser | [*the preceding two lines within a series of blind stamped rules*]. Stamped on spine in gold as (1) except for DUCKWORTH, which is printed in black.

It has been conjectured that the green cloth copies may have been the result of a trial binding, and a member of the Duckworth staff informed Mr McDonald that he remembered as much, although it has been reported as well that the green copies were a "colonial" issue.

NOTES: *The Trespasser* is related to the author's association with Miss Helen Corke, who wrote *Lawrence and Apocalypse* (F27); Lawrence took the theme of his novel from autobiographical papers belonging to her. In the BBC broadcast "Son and Lover" Miss Corke recalls lending Lawrence some notes in the form of a diary in which she had recorded the experiences of a previous summer. He took the notes home with him and eventually suggested that he might "expound them and make what he called a long poem." This was the beginning of the book called *The Trespasser*. Miss Corke's own novel, *Neutral Ground*, written in 1918 but not published until 1934, is a variation of the same theme developed from these papers. Among other titles considered for the novel before its publication were "The Saga of Siegmund," "Trespassers in Cythera" and "A Game of Forfeits." Lawrence began rewriting "The Saga of Siegmund" early in 1912 while recovering from the severe illness which forced him to give up teaching; the final draft was completed by early spring, for he received the proofs from Duckworth at Eastwood in April. Although the novel was offered to Heinemann first, who agreed to publish it, adverse criticism by Hueffer caused Lawrence to decide against publication; Hueffer considered the book too "erotic." Edward Garnett, then a reader for Duckworth, received the manuscript in December of 1911 and responded with letters of encouragement which led to its ultimate publication with the Duckworth imprint.

Mitchell Kennerley of New York published the first American issue of *The Trespasser* in May 1912 from the Duckworth sheets. Duckworth reprinted it several times; Secker published a pocket edition in October 1927, and Heinemann issued a cheap edition in 1936. It was published as No. 98 in the Albatross Library, 1934.

REVIEWS: *The Trespasser* was reviewed in the *Athenaeum*, 1 June 1912; the *Saturday Review*, 22 June 1912 and the *New York Times Book Review*, 17 November 1912.

NOTES (2): Variant (2) is the colonial issue of *The Trespasser*. Several additional copies in the green binding have turned up, but all have the words AUSTRALASIAN EDITION printed on the spine in black between LAWRENCE and DUCKWORTH. Dr Elizabeth Mansfield has noted in her introduction for the Cambridge edition of *The Trespasser* that the copy originally described as variant (2) from the Edward McDonald Collection at the University of Texas appears to have had some printed words erased from the spine where AUSTRALASIAN EDITION appears in other copies. An examination of the copy under oblique illumination reveals that this is indeed the case; the impression of the words AUSTRALASIAN EDITION is clearly to be seen.

REVIEWS (2): Additional reviews of *The Trespasser* appeared in the *Manchester Guardian,* 5 June by Basil de Selincourt; *Westminster Gazette,* 8 June; *Evening Standard,* 12 June; *Morning Post,* 17 June; *Daily News and Leader,* 21 June; *Standard,* 21 June; *Outlook* (London), 29 June; *English Review,* July; *Nottingham Guardian Literary Supplement,* 2 July; *Sheffield Daily Telegraph,* 4 July by A. N. C. L.; *Eye-Witness,* 11 July; *Free-woman,* 11 July by Rebecca West; *Birmingham Daily Post,* 12 July; *Rhythm,* October by Frederick Goodyear; *Academy* (London), 5 October; *Nation* (London), 19 October; *New York Herald,* 20 July; *New York Tribune,* 21 December.

A3   LOVE POEMS AND OTHERS   1913

first edition

LOVE [dot] POEMS | AND [dot] OTHERS | BY [dot] D. H. LAW-RENCE | AUTHOR OF "THE WHITE PEACOCK" "THE TRESPASSER" | DUCKWORTH [dot] AND [dot] CO. | COVENT [dot] GARDEN [dot] LONDON | MCMXIII

Blue cloth boards, stamped in gold on upper cover: LOVE POEMS | AND OTHERS | By | D. H. LAWRENCE | [*within a blind stamped rule*]; blind stamped on the bottom left corner of lower cover: [*publisher's device*]; stamped in gold on the spine: [*thick rule*] | [*thin rule*] | LOVE | POEMS | AND | OTHERS | [*short thin rule*] | D. H. | LAWRENCE | DUCKWORTH | [*thin rule*] | [*thick rule*]. The leaves measure $8\frac{5}{8}'' \times 6''$. Top edges trimmed and gilt; fore edges trimmed; bottom edges rough-trimmed.

[i]–[viii] + i–[lxiv], as follows: [i]–[ii] blank; [iii] half-title; [iv] blank; [v] title page as above; [vi] acknowledgements; [vii]–[viii] table of contents; i–[lxiv] text; at bottom of page [lxiv]: [*short rule*] | TURNBULL AND SPEARS, PRINTERS, EDINBURGH

Published in February 1913 at 5s.; number of copies unknown.

VARIANTS: (1) copy described above.
             (2) as (1) but with "i" omitted from the word "is" in line 16, page xlv.

(3) as (1) but bound in a darker blue, coarser cloth.

(4) as (3) but with the "i" omitted from page xlv.

CONTENTS

Wedding Morn—Kisses in the Train (printed in the Smart Set, September 1913)—Cruelty and Love (as "Love on the Farm" in Collected Poems (A43))—Cherry Robbers—Lilies in the Fire—Coldness in Love—End of Another Home-Holiday—Reminder—Bei Hennef—Lightning (first appeared in the Nation (London), 4 November 1911 (C8))—Song-Day in Autumn (not in Collected Poems (A43) but in Complete Poems (A98))—Aware—A Pang of Reminiscence—A White Blossom—Red Moon-Rise—Return—The Appeal—Repulsed—Dream-Confused (first appeared in the English Review, April 1910 (C4) as "Wakened")—Corot—Morning Work—Transformations—Renascence—Dog-Tired—Michael-Angelo—Violets (first appeared in the Nation (London), 4 November 1911 (C8); also in the Smart Set, September 1913)—Whether or Not—A Collier's Wife—The Drained Cup—The Schoolmaster—I. A Snowy Day in School (first appeared in the Saturday Westminster Gazette, 1 June 1912 (C15))—II. The Best of School (first appeared in the Saturday Westminster Gazette, 1 June 1912 (C15))—III. Afternoon in School (first appeared in the Saturday Westminster Gazette, 18 May 1912 (C12), as "The Last Lesson"; as "The Last Lesson of the Afternoon" in Collected Poems (A43)).

NOTES: These are the poems of Lawrence's youth, the Nottingham and Croydon years, and in them one sees the women he knew before he went away with Frieda. Jessie Chambers, Helen Corke, Louie Burrows and perhaps others unnamed appear in the poetry. At least one is concerned with Frieda, "Bei Hennef" written at Hennef am Rhein in 1912. Lawrence placed this poem in the Look! We Have Come Through! (A10) cycle for the Collected Poems (A43). "Wedding Morn" is the poem which Amy Lowell quoted to Lawrence when he denied to her that he was an imagist. In spite of this denial Lawrence continued to appear in Amy Lowell's imagist anthologies. In August of 1912 Lawrence wrote Edward Garnett that Heinemann had returned the poems; subsequently Garnett read and accepted them for publication by Duckworth.

Some writers have advanced the opinion that the first issue of Love Poems is distinguished by having the "i" missing from the word "is" in line 16 of page xlv, but Mr Bertram Rota argues that the printing probably began with the word properly set, after which the "i" either broke down or was pulled out by the inking roller, hence the conclusion that at least some of the copies without the "i" were actually printed later than some copies with the "i" intact. Mr Rota has seen copies in both states, each with the publisher's review stamp announcing the date of publication on the title page.

According to McDonald (B16) Mitchell Kennerley published the first American issue in 1913 from the Duckworth sheets; Duckworth reprinted the collection in February 1914 and November 1923. Secker issued a cheap edition in June 1934.

REVIEWS: *Love Poems* was reviewed by Ezra Pound in *Poetry*, July 1913, and by Edward Thomas in the article "More Georgian Poetry" in the *Bookman* (London), April 1913.

NOTES (2): In an effort to establish some pattern in the dropped "i" on page xlv, thirteen copies of the first edition were examined in the collection at the University of Texas; the copies were about equally divided, and no pattern was discernible. The first American edition from the English sheets measured the same as the original Duckworth edition. Kennerley issued another edition in 1915, which was smaller, measuring $7\frac{1}{4}'' \times 5''$. The dust-jacket of the Duckworth book is printed in blue on grey paper covered with thin vertical and horizontal lines simulating a linen weave. For the versions of "The Schoolmaster," "Violets," "Lightning," "Michael-Angelo" and "Whether or Not" published here, see (A104).

REVIEWS (2): Additional reviews of *Love Poems* appeared in the *English Review*, April; *New York Times*, 26 October; *Nineteenth Century*, January 1914 by Darrell Figgis; *Poetry and Drama*, June 1913 by John Alford; 6 March 1913 in the *Morning Post*; the *Daily News* for 6 March 1913 by Max Plowman; the *New Freewoman*, 1 September 1913 by Ezra Pound.

A4   SONS AND LOVERS   1913

first edition

SONS AND LOVERS | BY | D. H. LAWRENCE | AUTHOR OF | "LOVE POEMS," "THE WHITE PEACOCK," "THE TRESPASSER" | [*publisher's device*] | LONDON: DUCK-WORTH & CO. | HENRIETTA STREET, COVENT GARDEN | 1913

Dark blue cloth boards, stamped in gold on upper cover: SONS AND LOVERS | ···D. H. LAWRENCE··· | [*the whole enclosed within a double rule, blind stamped*]; stamped in gold on spine: [*double rule*] | SONS | AND |

LOVERS | D. H. | LAWRENCE | DUCKWORTH | [*double rule*]; blind stamped on bottom left corner of lower cover: [*publisher's device*] The leaves measure $7\frac{1}{4}'' \times 4\frac{3}{4}''$. All edges trimmed.

[i]–[viii] + [1]–[424] and 20 pp. of advertisements, as follows: [i] half-title; [ii] blank; [iii] title page as above; [iv] *All rights reserved*; [v] dedication to Edward Garnett; [vi] blank; vii table of contents; [viii] blank; [1]–423 text, at bottom of page 423: [*short thin rule*] | BILLING AND SONS, LTD., PRINTERS, GUILDFORD; [424] blank; 20 pp. of advertisements.

Published May 1913 at 6*s*., number of copies unknown.

VARIANTS: (1) copy described above with cancel title.
(2) as (1) but with integral title.
(3) as (2) but without date on title page.

NOTES: Lawrence's autobiographical novel, *Sons and Lovers*, was written during 1911 and 1912 although the final draft was prepared in Gargnano, Italy, after the elopement with Frieda. The novel relates the story of the mother–son–girl triangle in almost classic form. The girl is identified with Jessie Chambers, the childhood friend who lived on a farm near Eastwood. Her own story of the relationship is told in *A Personal Record* (B43) published under the pseudonym E.T. A more specific commentary by Jessie Chambers is found in an interesting group of manuscript papers now in the T. E. Hanley Library at the University of Texas. These papers consist of portions of an early version of the novel in the handwriting of both Jessie Chambers and of Lawrence. The Lawrence portion contains interlinear corrections and comments by Jessie Chambers. Harry T. Moore discusses these papers in the appendix to his *Life and Works* (F57). Helen Corke, who knew both Lawrence and Jessie, gives more useful information in her memoir of Jessie Chambers, *D. H. Lawrence's Princess* (F59) published by the Merle Press, Thames Ditton, Surrey, 1951. Ada Lawrence's *Early Life* (B34) is another important secondary source.

During the composition of the novel Lawrence was assisted by Jessie Chambers, who helped him recall events of the years covered by the book; *Sons and Lovers* was long known to them as "Paul Morel," hence the many references in the secondary material to "Paul Morel" rather than the title by which the book is commonly known.

Heinemann had first refusal of the manuscript, and Lawrence always thought he did not accept the book because he considered it "unclean."

Edward Garnett, to whom the novel is dedicated, read and accepted the manuscript for Duckworth.

About the early issues of the first edition of *Sons and Lovers* there has been much debate. McDonald (B16) describes the first issue as bound in dark blue cloth with the date of publication on the title page, and he cautions that a later issue bound in light blue cloth without the date on the title page is not to be confused with the true first issue. Dr Schwartz, in *1100 Obscure Points*, lists three states of the first edition: the first issue with a bound-in title without the date; the second issue with a tipped-in title with the date; and the third state with the date on the title which is an integral part of the signature. Although McDonald in his *Bibliographical Supplement* (B31) is not convinced, he does concede that some sort of error was made when the book was first published. Review copies have been noted both with the bound-in title without date and the tipped-in title with date; there is then the possibility that Dr Schwartz's theory is correct. Inasmuch as Duckworth's records were destroyed during the war, a final solution to these bibliographical problems may be impossible.

The first American edition of *Sons and Lovers* was published from new plates by Mitchell Kennerley in New York on 17 September 1913. A Modern Library edition with an introduction by John Macy appeared in 1922. Seltzer published an edition in New York in 1923. Boni and Liveright published the novel as a Bonibook in 1931, and Harper issued a new edition with an introduction by Mark Schorer in July of 1951. In England, Secker published a thin paper pocket edition in August 1927. Heinemann issued a cheap edition in October 1935 and a pocket edition in January 1949.

Tauchnitz published the novel in two volumes (Nos. 4879 and 4880) in 1929; it appeared as No. 292 in the Albatross Library in 1936 and in the Penguin Books (No. 668) during November 1949.

The following figures are indicative of the wide distribution this book has received; in 1929 Secker made an initial printing of a cheap edition of 4220 copies, and in 1930, 1931, 1932 and 1933 respectively reprinted 5000, 4100, 5500 and 10,000 copies.

Chapter XV of *Sons and Lovers* was published as "Derelict" in *Forum*, September 1913.

REVIEWS: Reviews of *Sons and Lovers* appeared in the *Saturday Review*, 21 June 1913; the *Athenaeum*, 21 June 1913; in "A Novel of Quality" by Perceval Gibbon in the *Bookman* (London), August 1913; by Louise Maunsell Field in the *New York Times Book Review*, 21 September 1913;

in "A Fair Page of Life" in the *Independent* (New York), 9 October 1913; the *Outlook* (New York), 6 December 1913; the *Nation* (New York), 11 December 1913; and in the *New Republic*, 10 April 1915 by Alfred Kuttner.

NOTES (2): All nine copies in the Lawrence Collection at the University of Texas have the cancel title page with the date and the 20 pp. catalogue; although the other two variants have been reported by various sources, none has been located or examined by me. Two different dust-jackets have been identified for the Duckworth *Sons and Lovers*: one is printed in blue on gray paper, and the other is printed in blue on paper with the simulated linen weave like that for *Love Poems* (A3). The Kennerley dust-jacket is cream paper printed in black.

REVIEWS (2): Additional reviews appeared in the *English Review*, August 1913; the *Nineteenth Century*, October; *Sunday Times*, 1 June; *Daily News* by Robert Lynd, 7 June; *Observer*, 8 June; *Times Literary Supplement*, 12 June; *Westminster Gazette*, 14 June; *Daily Chronicle* by Howard Massingham, 17 June; *Daily Telegraph*, 18 June; *Evening Standard*, 24 June; *Academy*, 28 June; *Manchester Guardian* by Lascelles Abercrombie, 2 July; *Glasgow Herald*, 3 July; *Irish Times*, 4 July; *New Statesman* by Hubert Bland, 5 July; *Blue Review*, July; *Nation* (London) by E. C. Mayne, 12 July; *Yorkshire Post*, 23 July; *Standard* (London), 30 May.

A5   THE WIDOWING OF   1914
MRS. HOLROYD

first edition

THE WIDOWING OF | MRS. HOLROYD | A DRAMA IN THREE ACTS | BY | D. H. LAWRENCE | [*publisher's device*] | NEW YORK | MITCHELL KENNERLEY | MCMXIV

Dark red cloth boards, blind stamped on upper cover: THE MODERN DRAMA SERIES | EDITED BY EDWIN BJÖRKMAN | [*enclosed within a single rule, blind stamped*]; stamped in gold on spine: D. H. | LAW- | RENCE | [*printer's ornament*] | THE | WIDOW- | ING | OF MRS. | HOL- | ROYD | MITCHELL | KENNERLEY The leaves measure $7\frac{3}{8}'' \times 5''$. All edges trimmed.

[i]–[iv] + [i]–x + [1]–[98], as follows: [i]–[iv] blank; [i] half-title; [ii] blank; [iii] title page as above; [iv] COPYRIGHT 1914 BY | MITCHELL KENNERLEY | THE · PLIMPTON · PRESS | NORWOOD · MASS · U.S.A; [v] table of contents; [vi] blank; [vii]–x introduction; [1] fly-title: THE WIDOWING OF MRS. HOLROYD; [2] list of characters; [3]–93 text; [94]–[98] blank.

Published 1 April 1914 at $1.50; the first printing consisted of 1000 copies, 500 of which were sold to Duckworth as sheets.

NOTES: Lawrence completed the final draft of *The Widowing of Mrs. Holroyd* at Fiascherino in Italy during his second stay on the Continent, but a version had existed much earlier, for he showed a copy to Jessie Chambers while he was living at Croydon. The play has had at least two stage productions, the first by a group of experienced amateurs in 1920 at Altrincham in Cheshire. Catherine Carswell, who saw both performances, gives an account in *Savage Pilgrimage* (B37). The second performance was directed by Esmé Percy for the Stage Society and took place at the Kingsway Theatre, in London, in December 1926. The first English issue of the book was published by Duckworth 17 April 1914 from the Kennerley sheets. Thomas Seltzer issued another edition in New York in 1921.

REVIEWS: Reviews of the book itself appeared in the *Independent* (New York), 25 May 1914; the *Nation* (New York), 23 July 1914, under the title "The Black Country"; the *New York Times Book Review*, 4 October 1914; the *Dial*, 16 January 1915, by H. E. Woodbridge; and a criticism by J. R. Crawford in the *Yale Review*, April 1915.

The State Society production was reviewed in the *Nation* (London), 18 December 1926, by "Omicron"; the *New Statesman*, 18 December 1926, by Desmond MacCarthy; the *Saturday Review*, 18 December 1926, by Ivor Brown; the *Outlook* (London), 24 December 1926; the *Graphic* (London), 25 December 1926; and by H. Shipp in the *English Review*, January 1927.

NOTES (2): The Kennerley dust-jacket is cream paper printed in black. All copies of the dust-jacket examined had the price, $1.00, blacked out on the spine and then rubber-stamped with the new price, $1.50.

REVIEWS (2): A review of *Widowing of Mrs. Holroyd* appeared in the *Times* for 24 April 1914, which was reprinted in the *Times Literary Supplement*, 30 April.

A6　　　THE PRUSSIAN OFFICER　　　1914

first edition

THE | PRUSSIAN OFFICER | AND OTHER STORIES | BY | D. H. LAWRENCE | [*publisher's device*] | LONDON | DUCKWORTH & CO. | 3 HENRIETTA STREET, COVENT GARDEN

Blue cloth boards, stamped in gold on upper cover: THE PRUSSIAN OFFICER | ···D. H. LAWRENCE ···| [*enclosed within a double rule, blind stamped*]; blind stamped on bottom left corner of lower cover: [*publisher's device*]; stamped in gold on spine: [*double rule*] | THE | PRUSSIAN | OFFICER | D. H. | LAWRENCE | DUCKWORTH | [*double rule*] The leaves measure $7\frac{5}{16}'' \times 4\frac{3}{4}''$. All edges trimmed.

[i]–[viii] + [1]–[312] and 20 pp. of advertisements, as follows: [i]–[ii] blank; [iii] half-title; [iv] list of books by D. H. Lawrence; [v] title page as above; [vi] *Published December 1914*; [vii] table of contents; [viii] blank; [1]–310 text, at bottom of page 310: WILLIAM BRENDON AND SON, LTD. | PRINTERS, PLYMOUTH; [311]–[312] advertisements of books by D. H. Lawrence; 20 pp. of advertisements.

Published 26 November 1914 at 6*s*.; number of copies unknown.

VARIANTS: (1) copy described above.
      (2) as (1) but with 16 page catalogue at end.
      (3) as (2) but bound in light blue cloth boards; all printing on cover including rules and publisher's device in dark blue.

CONTENTS

The Prussian Officer (first appeared in the *English Review*, August 1914, as "Honour and Arms" (C34); also in *Pearsons*, February 1922)—The Thorn in the Flesh (first appeared in the *English Review*, June 1914, as "Vin Ordinaire" (C33))—Daughters of the Vicar (an early version appeared in *Time and Tide*, 24 March 1934, as "Two Marriages" (C214))—A Fragment of Stained Glass (first appeared in the *English Review*, September 1911 (C7))—The Shades of Spring (first appeared in the *Forum*, March 1913, as "The Soiled Rose" (C18))—Second Best (first appeared in the *English Review*, February 1912 (C9))—The Shadow in the Rose Garden (first appeared in the *Smart Set*, March 1914 (C31))—Goose Fair (first appeared in the *English Review*, February 1910 (C3))—The White Stocking (first appeared in the *Smart Set*, October 1914 (C34.5))—A Sick Collier (first appeared in the *New Statesman*, 13 September 1913 (C25))—The Christening (*Smart Set* (C30.5))—Odour of Chrysanthemums (first appeared in the *English Review*, June 1911 (C6)).

NOTES: Lawrence's first volume of short stories was seen through the press for Duckworth by Edward Garnett who changed the title of "Honour and Arms" to "The Prussian Officer" much to Lawrence's displeasure. "The White Stocking" was one of the three stories submitted for the Christmas contest held by the *Nottinghamshire Guardian* in 1907. See (C1) and (C7). Lawrence corrected most of the printer's proofs at Chesham in Buckinghamshire.

McDonald (B16) notes two "issues" of the first edition of *The Prussian Officer*, distinguished by the different number of pages in the publisher's catalogues bound in at the end of the book. Although McDonald gives priority to the copies with the sixteen-page catalogue, the library of the University of Texas has a copy with the twenty-page catalogue which has the publisher's review stamp giving the date of publication as 26 November 1914; hence it may be assumed that the copies with the twenty-page catalogue are earlier.

The first American issue of *The Prussian Officer* was published in New York from the Duckworth sheets by Huebsch in 1916. Duckworth reprinted the collection in November 1924, and Secker published a pocket edition in October 1927. The Penguin *Prussian Officer* appeared in October 1945.

REVIEWS: *The Prussian Officer* was reviewed in the *Outlook* (London), 19 December 1914; the *Saturday Review*, 9 January 1915; the *Athenaeum*, 23 January 1915; *English Review*, January 1915; the *Bookman* (London), March 1915; the *Bookman* (New York), 6 February 1917 by H. W. Boynton; and the *Nation* (New York), 15 March 1917.

NOTES (2): Variant (3) bound in light blue cloth boards has a 16 page catalogue bound at the end, but the text is different from the catalogue distinguishing variant (2) and page 16 of the catalogue bears only the familiar publisher's device. Two additional variants have been examined:

(4) as (1) but bound in red cloth boards.
(5) as (1) but bound in coarse dark blue cloth printed in black on covers and spine with a 24 page catalogue bound at the end; the catalogue is numbered with lower case Roman numerals at the bottom of the page, rather than with Arabic numerals at the top of the page as in the other variants.

The following two variants have been reported:

(6) as (2) but with a 20 page catalogue.
(7) as (3) but with the 24 page catalogue.
See (C256).

The dust-jacket of the Duckworth *Prussian Officer* is grey paper printed in blue with the publisher's emblem on the lower cover.

a. *first edition*

THE RAINBOW | BY | D. H. LAWRENCE | AUTHOR OF
"SONS AND LOVERS" | METHUEN & CO. LTD. | 36
ESSEX STREET W. C. | LONDON

Dark blue-green cloth boards, blind stamped on upper cover: THE
RAINBOW | D. H. LAWRENCE | [*enclosed within a single rule*] ; stamped in gold
on spine: [*printer's ornament*] | THE | RAINBOW | [*printer's ornament*] | D. H.
| LAWRENCE | [*printer's ornament*] | METHUEN The leaves measure
$7\frac{1}{2}'' \times 4\frac{7}{8}''$. Top and fore edges trimmed; bottom edges untrimmed.

[i]–[viii] + [1]–[464] and 4 pp. of advertisements, as follows: [i] half-
title; [ii] blank; [iii] title page as above; [iv] *First Published in 1915*; [v]
dedication: TO ELSE; [vi] blank; vii table of contents; [viii] blank;
[1]–463 text; [464] PRINTED IN GREAT BRITAIN | BY HAZELL, WATSON
AND VINEY, LD., | LONDON AND AYLESBURY.; and 4 pp. of advertisements.

Published 30 September 1915 at 6*s.*; the first printing consisted of 2500
copies, of which the majority, presumably, were destroyed as a result
of the court action against the book.

b. *colonial issue*

THE RAINBOW | BY | D. H. LAWRENCE | AUTHOR OF
"SONS AND LOVERS | METHUEN & CO. LTD | 36
ESSEX STREET W. C. | LONDON | *Colonial Library*

Brown cloth boards, stamped in gold on spine: [*decorative ornament of
leaves*] | THE | RAINBOW | D. H. LAWRENCE [*the preceding three lines enclosed
within a single rule*] | [*decorative ornament of leaves*] | METHUEN; blind stamped
on lower cover: METHUEN'S COLONIAL LIBRARY The leaves measure
$7\frac{1}{2}'' \times 5''$. Top and fore edges trimmed; bottom edges untrimmed.

[i]–[viii] + 1–[464] and 4 pp. of advertisements, as follows: [i] Methuen
Colonial Library | [*rule*] | THE RAINBOW; [ii] blank; [iii] title page as
above; [iv] *First Published in 1915*; [v] TO ELSE; [vi] blank; vii contents;
[viii] blank; 1–463 text; [464] PRINTED IN GREAT BRITAIN | BY HAZELL,
WATSON AND VINEY, LD., | LONDON AND AYLESBURY.; 4 pp. advertisements.

VARIANTS: (1) copy described above.
       (2) as (1) except bound in red cloth.
       (3) as (1) except issued in paper covers.

NOTES: In a letter dated March 1913 Lawrence told Edward Garnett that he was more than half through with a new novel which was "quite unlike" *Sons and Lovers*. For the next two, almost three, years he was busy working and reworking a mass of material which eventually became *The Rainbow* and *Women in Love* (A15). The novel shaping itself during this time was known variously as "The Sisters" or "The Wedding Ring." On occasion, Lawrence did not so much correct early versions as literally rewrite them, beginning anew each time. He wrote A. W. McLeod, a fellow teacher at Croydon and a friend for many years, in February 1914, that he was beginning his novel for "about the seventh time." The final draft of *The Rainbow* was prepared sometime during the first months of 1915.

The Rainbow was destined to provide the occasion for Lawrence's first real trouble with the problem of censorship, a difficulty which plagued him frequently afterwards. Methuen objected to parts of the book when it was being prepared for publication, and Lawrence agreed to alter or remove sentences and phrases, but he refused to delete whole paragraphs or pages. Court action was taken against *The Rainbow* about five weeks after its publication; a moving force in the prosecution was the National Purity League. The action was taken under Lord Campbell's Obscene Publications Act, which dated from 1857. Records of the Bow Street Magistrate's Court show that the decision against *The Rainbow* was an order for the books "to be destroyed at the expiration of seven days." As late as 1954 a member of Methuen's staff wrote that a legend survived in the office to the effect that the confiscated copies "were burnt by the public hangman outside the Royal Exchange."

Several literary people of importance spoke out against the proceedings, including John Drinkwater, Arnold Bennett and Hugh Walpole. Philip Morrell, M. P., husband of Lady Ottoline and Lawrence's friend, asked a question in Parliament, but all such protests availed nothing. Richard Aldington and others, notably Gilbert Cannan, in "A Defense of D. H. Lawrence" in the *New York Herald Tribune* for 10 January 1920, have remarked that the real reason for the suppression of *The Rainbow* was political rather than moral, i.e., Lawrence's anti-war stand. His dedication of the book to Frieda's sister, Else, could have attracted such chauvinistic criticism.

The *English Catalogue* gives the date of publication for *The Rainbow* as October, but the publishers report the date as 30 September, which agrees with McDonald. The first American edition was published by Huebsch in New York on 30 November 1915, the text for which was the "expurgated" form to which Lawrence referred in "The Bad Side of Books," the prefatory essay to McDonald's *Bibliography* (B16). Harry T. Moore's *Intelligent Heart* (B57) gives the changes for the Huebsch edition in a previously unpublished letter from Lawrence to the agent J. B. Pinker.

Huebsch published a more expensive edition of *The Rainbow* in 1916 and Seltzer issued the book in a new format in 1924; Boni and Liveright published a Uniform Edition in 1931. In England Secker issued a pocket edition in June 1929 and Heinemann a cheap edition in June 1935. *The Rainbow* appeared as a Penguin Book in February 1949.

REVIEWS: Discussions and reviews of *The Rainbow* may be found in the *Sphere*, 23 October 1915 by Clement Shorter; the *Athenaeum*, 13 November 1915; a letter by G. W. de Tunzelmann in the *Athenaeum*, 20 November 1915; and in an article about the suppression of the book in *Current Opinion*, February 1916.

NOTES (2): Much additional interesting information has become available about the publication of *The Rainbow*, much of it derived from the Methuen ledger sheets now in the Lilly Library at the University of Indiana. Apparently Methuen ordered 2500 sets of sheets from Hazell, Watson and Viney on 16 August 1915. Mr W. Forster has in his collection a letter from Methuen stating that a total of 2516 copies were printed. Of these 1250 copies were bound for the domestic market and 500 were designated for colonial distribution, 300 hard bound (A7b) and 200 in paper covers. The letter also states that 766 sets of sheets were destroyed. This agrees with the Methuen records at the Lilly Library. Professor Mark Kinkead-Weekes, editor of *The Rainbow* for the Cambridge University Press Edition, says that other records at Methuen indicate that in addition to the 766 sets of sheets noted to have been destroyed, the police confiscated 245 copies of the domestic edition on 3 and 5 November, and that Methuen subsequently recalled and destroyed another 184 copies. If all these figures are correct, then some 821 copies of the book were finally distributed in England, including file copies, etc.

The American edition officially published by B. W. Huebsch on 30 November 1915 also has a curious history. The title page for the American edition, as noted in the copyright registration, bears the date 1916. Mr Huebsch explained the circumstances surrounding the publication of his *Rainbow* in a letter to Richard Aldington, now in the Huebsch papers at the Library of Congress.

While the book was being manufactured, Mr Huebsch accepted an invitation to accompany the Ford Peace Expedition which departed for Europe in December. Because of his absence from the United States and for fear the Society for the Suppression of Vice would cause trouble, Mr Huebsch distributed only enough copies to establish the validity of the American copyright and gave instructions to lock up the remaining stock until his return which he expected to be in January. Unfortunately he did not return until March, and when additional copies were released, he instructed his salesmen to "let the book dribble out to the trade without talking too much about it." There was no advertising, and no review copies were sent out according to Mr Huebsch. In a letter to Mrs Belloc Lowndes of 17 December 1915 Lawrence mentions having received a copy of the American *Rainbow* that day.

Although Lawrence wrote Pinker in December that the omissions in the American edition were not very many, more than sixty lines were cut by Huebsch, enough to impair seriously the text. The omissions that Lawrence noticed were:

Methuen edition	*Huebsch edition*
p. 220: lines 20–24 (3 lines)	p. 222
(He wished he were a cat...her flesh)	
p. 300: line 18 (1 line)	p. 303
(let me come—let me come)	
p. 318: (lines 7–10) (4 lines)	p. 321
(Ursula lay still...about her mistress)	
p. 425: lines 4–26 (24 lines)	p. 429
(But the air was cold...always laughing)	
p. 446: lines 10–40 (31 lines)	p. 450
(She let him take her...house felt to her)	

Subsequent American editions followed the Huebsch text including the Seltzer 1924 edition and its reprints. Although Martin Secker in a letter to *The Times Literary Supplement*, 3 November 1966, claimed that he fulfilled a promise to Lawrence to bring out *The Rainbow* "without the alteration of a single word" by the publication of a crown octavo edition in February 1926, his edition was in fact published from the Seltzer sheets. Consequently all the following Secker issues of *The Rainbow* contained the abridged text. It was not until the publication of the Penguin *Rainbow* in 1949 that the original text of the Methuen edition became available.

The dust-jacket for the Methuen *Rainbow* was printed in blue on white paper; the upper cover was illustrated with a painting in colour of a man and woman by Frank Wright. The same dust-jacket was used for the colonial issue. The Huebsch dust-jacket was printed in black on cream paper.

REVIEWS (2): Additional reviews of *The Rainbow* appeared in the *Glasgow Herald* by Catherine Carswell, 4 November 1915; *Daily News and Leader* by Robert Lynd, 5 October; *Star* by James Douglas, 22 October; *New Statesman* by Soloman Eagle (J. C. Squire), 20 November; *Globe*, 5 October; *Westminster Gazette* by Walter de la Mare, 9 October; *Evening Standard*, 21 October; *New Statesman* by Gerald Gould, 23 October; *Manchester Guardian* by Mrs H. M. Stanwick, 28 October; *World*, 26 October; *Nation* (London), 20 November.

A8 TWILIGHT IN ITALY 1916

first edition

TWILIGHT IN ITALY | BY | D. H. LAWRENCE | [*publisher's device*] | LONDON | DUCKWORTH AND CO. | 3 HENRIETTA STREET, COVENT GARDEN, W. C.

Dark blue cloth boards, stamped in gold on upper cover: TWILIGHT IN ITALY | ···D. H. LAWRENCE··· [*within a double rule, blind stamped*]; blind stamped on bottom left corner of lower cover: [*publisher's device*]; stamped in gold on spine: [*double rule*] | TWILIGHT | IN | ITALY | D. H. | LAWRENCE | DUCKWORTH | [*double rule*] The leaves measure $7\frac{1}{4}'' \times 4\frac{3}{4}''$. All edges trimmed.

[i]–[viii] + 1–[312] and 32 pp. of advertisements, as follows: [i] half-title; [ii] list of works by D. H. Lawrence; [iii] title page as above; [iv] *First published* 1916; v acknowledgements; [vi] blank; vii table of contents; [viii] blank; 1 fly-title: THE CRUCIFIX ACROSS THE | MOUNTAINS; [2] blank; 3–26 text; 27 fly-title: ON THE LAGO DI GARDA; [28] blank; 29–221 text; [222] blank; [223] fly-title: ITALIANS IN EXILE; [224] blank; 225–261 text; [262] blank; [263] fly-title: THE RETURN JOURNEY; [264] blank; 265–[311] text, at bottom of page [311]: *Printed by* R. & R. CLARK, LIMITED, *Edinburgh.*; [312] blank; and 32 pages of advertisements consisting of two 16-page catalogues.

Published 1 June 1916 at 6*s.*, the first printing consisted of 1500 copies.

CONTENTS

The Crucifix Across the Mountains (first appeared in the *Saturday Westminster Gazette*, 22 March 1913, as "Christs in the Tirol" (C20))— On the Lago di Garda: The Spinner and the Monks; The Lemon Gardens; The Theatre (the first three essays under the "Lago di Garda" section first appeared in the *English Review*, September 1913, as "Italian

Studies: By the Lago di Garda" (C23)); San Gaudenzio; The Dance; Il Duro; John—Italians in Exile—The Return Journey.

NOTES: *Twilight in Italy* consists of a series of travel sketches and is Lawrence's first book of non-fiction prose; it describes many of the people and places he and Frieda knew in Italy during their first months there. Arrangements were completed during the summer of 1915 with Duckworth to publish the book as "Italian Studies," and Lawrence corrected the proofs while convalescing at Portcothan on the Cornwall coast, where they lived in an old farmhouse for the first months of 1916.

The first American issue was published by B. W. Huebsch from the Duckworth sheets in 1916. Duckworth reprinted the first edition in October 1924, and the book was issued in the Traveller's Library by Jonathan Cape in October 1926. Secker published a cheap edition in the New Adelphi Library in 1934, and the book has been included in Heinemann's pocket series with an introduction by Richard Aldington.

REVIEWS: *Twilight in Italy* was reviewed in *The Times Literary Supplement*, 15 June; by Francis Bickley in the *Bookman* (London), October 1916; in the *Review of Reviews*, February 1917; and in the *Nation* (New York), 15 March 1917.

NOTES (2): A variant of the Duckworth *Twilight in Italy* has been reported by Mr W. Forster.

VARIANTS: (1) copy described above.
(2) as (1) except bound in light blue cloth.

The dust-jacket for the Duckworth *Twilight in Italy* is cream paper printed in black with quotations from reviews of previous Lawrence books. The Huebsch dust-jacket is cream paper printed in black with a quotation from the *Pall Mall Gazette*.

REVIEWS (2): An additional review appeared in *English Review*, July 1916.

A9   AMORES   1916

a. *first edition*

AMORES | POEMS | BY | D. H. LAWRENCE | [*publisher's device*] LONDON | *Duckworth and Company* | 3 HENRIETTA STREET, W. C.

Dark blue cloth boards, stamped in gold on spine: [*double rule*] | AMORES

| POEMS | D. H. | LAWRENCE | DUCKWORTH | [*double rule*]; blind stamped on bottom left corner of lower cover: [*publisher's device*] The leaves measure $7\frac{1}{4}'' \times 4\frac{7}{8}''$. All edges trimmed.

[i]–[viii] + 1–[140] and 16 pp. of advertisements, as follows: [i] title page as above; [ii] blank; [iii] dedication to Ottoline Morrell; [iv] blank; v–vii table of contents; [viii] blank; 1–[138] text, at bottom of page [138]: [*short thin rule*] | Printed by T. and A. CONSTABLE, Printers to His Majesty | at the Edinburgh University Press; [139]–[140] blank; and sixteen pages of advertisements.

Published July 1916 at 5s.; the first printing consisted of 900 copies.

VARIANTS: (1) as (2) except fore and bottom edges untrimmed.
                (2) copy described above.
                (3) as (2) but without the 16 pages of advertisements.

It is probable that some copies, perhaps advance copies, were not trimmed on all edges; there is a copy of (1) in the library of Mr George Lazarus in which the publisher's review stamp appears.

b. *first American edition*

AMORES | POEMS | BY | D. H. LAWRENCE | [*publisher's device*] | NEW YORK | B. W. HUEBSCH | 1916 | [*enclosed within a quadruple rule*]

Brown cloth boards, stamped in gold on upper cover: AMORES | D. H. LAWRENCE; stamped in gold on spine: AMORES | LAWRENCE | HUEBSCH The leaves measure $7\frac{3}{8}'' \times 5''$. Top edges gilt; all edges trimmed.

[i]–[xii] + 1–[116], as follows: [i] AMORES; [ii] list of books by D. H. Lawrence; [iii] title page as above; [iv] Copyright, 1916, by | D. H. LAWRENCE; [v] TO | OTTOLINE MORRELL | IN TRIBUTE | TO HER NOBLE | AND INDEPENDENT SYMPATHY | AND HER GENEROUS UNDER-STANDING | THESE POEMS | ARE GRATEFULLY DEDICATED; [vi] blank; [vii]–[ix] table of contents; [x] blank; [xi] AMORES; [xii] blank; 1–[113] text; [114]–[116] blank.

Published 25 September 1916 at $1.00; number of copies unknown.

CONTENTS

Tease (first appeared in *Poetry and Drama*, December 1914, as "Teasing" (C36))—The Wild Common—Study—Discord in Childhood—Virgin Youth—Monologue of a Mother (first appeared in *Poetry*, January 1914

(C29), as "The Mother of Sons")—In a Boat (first appeared in *English Review*, for October 1910, as "Tired of the Boat" (C5))—Week-Night Service—Disagreeable Advice (as "Irony" in the American edition of *Amores* (A9b); not in *Collected Poems* (A43) but included in *Complete Poems* (A98))—Dreams Old (first appeared in *English Review*, November 1909 (C2))—Dreams Nascent (first appeared in *English Review*, November 1909 (C2))—A Winter's Tale (first appeared in the *Egoist*, 1 April 1914 (C32))—Epilogue (as "Forecast" in *Collected Poems* (A43))—A Baby Running Barefoot (first appeared in *English Review*, November 1909 (C2))—Discipline (first appeared in *English Review*, November 1909 (C2))—Scent of Irises (first appeared in *Some Imagist Poets* (B2))—The Prophet (first appeared as a part of "Discipline" in *English Review*, November 1909 (C2))—Last Words to Miriam (also in the *Poetry Journal*, December 1916)—Mystery—Patience (as "Suspense" in *Collected Poems* (A43))—Ballad of Another Ophelia (first appeared in *Some Imagist Poets* (B2))—Restlessness (not in *Collected Poems* (A43) but included in *Complete Poems* (A98))—A Baby Asleep After Pain (first appeared in the *English Review*, November 1909 (C2), as "Trailing Clouds")—Anxiety (as "Endless Anxiety" in *Collected Poems* (A43))—The Punisher (first appeared in the *Saturday Westminster Gazette*, 25 May 1912 (C13))—The End (first appeared in *Poetry*, December 1914 (C35), as "Memories")—The Bride (included in *Young Lorenzo* (B34), as "The Dead Mother")—The Virgin Mother—At the Window (first appeared in the *English Review*, April 1910 (C4); first collected in *Some Imagist Poets* 1916 (B4))—Drunk—Sorrow (first appeared in *Poetry*, December 1914 (C35), as "Weariness") —Dolor of Autumn—The Inheritance—Silence—Listening—Brooding Grief (first appeared in *Some Imagist Poets* (B4))—Lotus Hurt by the Cold (as "Lotus and Frost" in *Collected Poems* (A43))—Malade—Liaison (as "The Yew Tree on the Downs" in *Collected Poems* (A43))—Troth with the Dead—Dissolute (as "At a Loose End" in *Collected Poems* (A43)) —Submergence—The Enkindled Spring—Reproach (as "Release" in *Collected Poems* (A43))—The Hands of the Betrothed—Excursion (first appeared in the *Egoist*, 1 April 1914 (C32), as "Honeymoon"; as "Excursion Train" in *Collected Poems* (A43))—Perfidy (first appeared in the *Egoist*, 1 April 1914 (C32), as "Fooled"; as "Turned Down" in *Collected Poems* (A43); first collected in *Some Imagist Poets* (B4))—A Spiritual Woman (as "These Clever Women" in *Collected Poems* (A43))— Mating (as "Come Spring, Come Sorrow" in *Collected Poems* (A43))—A Love Song—Brother and Sister (included in *Young Lorenzo* (B34) as "To Lettice, My Sister")—After Many Days—Blue (as "Shadow of Death" in *Collected Poems* (A43))—Snap-Dragon (first appeared in the *English*

Review, June 1912 (C14); first collected in *Georgian Poetry 1911–1912* (B1))—A Passing Bell—In Trouble and Shame (first appeared in *Some Imagist Poets* (B4))—Elegy (as "Call into Death" in *Collected Poems* (A43))—Grey Evening—Firelight and Nightfall (from the *English Review*, February 1914 (C30), as "Twilight," a longer version)—The Mystic Blue (as "Blueness" in *Collected Poems* (A43)).

NOTES: The poems in *Amores* are largely early work, and they portray Lawrence's relationships with Jessie Chambers, Helen Corke and his mother. "Excursion" records a train trip which he and Helen Corke made returning to London from Nottinghamshire in the Autumn of 1910. The three poems "The End," "The Bride" and "The Virgin Mother" were given to Jessie Chambers to read the day before his mother's funeral. "Study" was written at Nottingham University College while Lawrence was a student there; he submitted the poem to the college paper and it was rejected.

On 24 May 1916 he wrote Lady Ottoline Morrell that he had returned the proofs to the publisher with a dedication to her, but that he had crossed out everything but her name because "people are as they are, so jeering and shallow." The dedication appeared in full in the American edition of the poems (A9b). There apparently was some jeering, for Catherine Carswell (B37) records that an unnamed publisher returned the poems in February 1916 with a letter which gave "instructions as to how to write poetry," and John Middleton Murry tells the story upon which the "Pompadour Café" incident in *Women in Love* (A15) is based. Late in 1916 Katherine Mansfield was in the Café Royal in London with S. S. Koteliansky and Mark Gertler, a young painter friend of the Lawrences; near by were sitting several people who had visited Frieda and Lawrence at Byron Villas. These persons had on the table before them a copy of *Amores* which they read aloud by turns, making fun of the poems, when Katherine Mansfield, in anger, went to the table, seized the copy of *Amores* and marched out of the café.

The copies of the first edition of *Amores* which do not contain the publisher's catalogue were a "remainder issue" released years later according to Mr Bertram Rota. Secker issued a cheap edition in June 1934.

REVIEWS: *Amores* was reviewed in *The Times Literary Supplement*, 10 August 1916; by Francis Bickley in the *Bookman* (London), October 1916; in the *New York Times Book Review*, 26 November 1916; in the *Review of Reviews*, December 1916; by Eunice Tietjens in *Poetry*, February 1917; and by William Bradley in the *Dial*, 19 April 1917.

NOTES (2): The following variant of the Duckworth *Amores* is in the collection of Mr W. Forster.

> (4) as (3) except the note at the bottom of page 138 reads: Printed in Great Britain by Ebenezer Baylis & Son, Ltd., The Trinity Press, Worcester. Thinner paper is used, and the book measures about $\frac{1}{4}''$ less in thickness.

The Duckworth dust-jacket is white printed in black; on the upper cover appear quotations from reviews of previously published Lawrence books.

For the versions of "Virgin Youth," "Dreams Old and Nascent," "A Baby Running Barefoot," "Last Words to Miriam," "Dissolute," "Liaison" and "A Spiritual Woman" published here, see (A104).

A10 LOOK! WE HAVE COME THROUGH! 1917

a. *first edition*

LOOK! WE HAVE | COME THROUGH! | BY | D. H. LAWRENCE | PUBLISHED BY CHATTO & WINDUS | LONDON MCMXVII

Salmon-red cloth boards, white paper label on spine printed in red: Look! | We Have | Come | Through! | D. H. | LAWRENCE The leaves measure $8\frac{3}{8}'' \times 6\frac{5}{8}''$. Top edges trimmed; fore edges rough-trimmed; bottom edges untrimmed.

[1]–[168], as follows: [1] half-title; [2] blank; [3] title page as above; [4] acknowledgements; [5] foreword; [6] blank; [7]–[9] table of contents; [10] argument; 11–[163] text; [164] PRINTED AT | THE COMPLETE PRESS | WEST NORWOOD | LONDON; [165]–[167] advertisements; [168] blank.

Published 26 November 1917 at 5*s.*; the first printing consisted of 1000 copies, of which 500 were sold to Huebsch as sheets for the American edition.

b. *first illustrated edition, English issue*

LOOK! WE HAVE COME [*in red*] | THROUGH! [*in red*] *A Cycle of Love* | *Poems by* D. H. LAWRENCE | [*drawing of the phoenix*] | *With an Introduction by* FRIEDA LAWRENCE | *& with illustrations by* MICHAEL ADAM. *Out of* | THE ARK PRESS *Marazion Cornwall England*

Black cloth boards, stamped in gold on upper cover: [*drawing of a sheaf of wheat*]; stamped in gold on spine, reading from top to bottom: D. H. LAWRENCE *Look! We Have Come Through!* THE ARK PRESS The leaves measure $8\frac{3}{8}'' \times 5\frac{5}{16}''$. All edges trimmed.

[1]–[112], as follows: [1] half-title; [2] blank; [3] title page as above; [4] Printed in Great Britain by | WORDEN (PRINTERS) LTD. MARAZION CORNWALL; [5]–[6] foreword by Warren Roberts; [7] table of contents; [8] blank; 9–16 introduction by Frieda Lawrence; [17] fly-title: LOOK! WE HAVE COME THROUGH!; [18] blank; 19 foreword and argument by D. H. Lawrence; [20] blank; 21–103 text; [104] blank; [105] fly-title: APPENDIX I; [106] blank; 107–108 notes; [109] fly-title: APPENDIX II; [110]–[111] facsimile reproduction of a manuscript by Frieda Lawrence; 112 THESE POEMS *are printed with permission of the* | *Executor of D. H. Lawrence and William Heinemann* | *Limited in whom all rights are vested and reserved.* | [*drawing*] | *Printed by Worden (Printers) Ltd. Marazion, Corn-* | *wall, in Monotype Bembo on Basingwerk Parchment* | *paper. Blocks by Garratt &* *Atkinson, London. Binding* | *by The Pitman Press, Bath. Out of* THE ARK 1958

Published October 1958 at 21*s.*; 180 English copies were printed and bound with specially illustrated end-papers.

c. *first illustrated edition, American issue*

LOOK! WE HAVE COME [*in red*] | THROUGH! [*in red*] *A Cycle of Love* | *Poems by* D. H. LAWRENCE | [*drawing of the phoenix*] | *With an Introduction by* FRIEDA LAWRENCE | *& with illustrations* by MICHAEL ADAM. *Out of* | THE ARK PRESS *Cornwall for The Rare Books* | *Collection of* THE UNIVERSITY OF TEXAS

The American copies are identical with (b) except that the end-papers are plain and the title page reads as above.

Published March 1959 at $3.00; 420 American copies were printed.

CONTENTS

Moonrise (in *Poetry* for July 1918)—Elegy—Nonentity—Martyr à la Mode—Don Juan (first appeared in *Poetry*, December 1914 (C35))—The Sea (first appeared in the *English Review*, September 1917 (C51))—Hymn to Priapus (first appeared in the *English Review*, September 1917 (C51), as "Constancy of a Sort")—Ballad of a Wilful Woman—First Morning— "And Oh–That the Man I Am Might Cease To Be—"—She Looks Back—On the Balcony (first appeared in *Poetry*, January 1914 (C29), as "Illicit"; first collected in *Some Imagist Poets* (B2) as "Illicit"; also in *Lyric*, August 1917)—Frohnleichnam—In the Dark—Mutilation—Humiliation—A Young Wife—Green (first appeared in *Poetry*, January 1914 (C29); first collected in *Some Imagist Poets* (B2))—River Roses (first appeared in *Poetry*, January 1914 (C29), as a part of "All of Roses")—Gloire de Dijon (first appeared in *Poetry*, January 1914 (C29), as a part of "All of Roses")—Roses on the Breakfast Table (first appeared in *Poetry*, January 1914 (C29), as a part of "All of Roses")—I Am Like a Rose—Rose of all the World—A Youth Mowing (first appeared in *The Smart Set*, November 1913 (C27), as "The Mowers"; first collected in *Some Imagist Poets* (B2) as "The Mowers")—Quite Forsaken—Forsaken and Forlorn—Fireflies in the Corn (first appeared in *Poetry*, January 1914 (C29); first collected in *Some Imagist Poets* (B2))—A Doe at Evening—Song of a Man who is Not Loved—Sinners—Misery—Sunday Afternoon in Italy—Winter Dawn—A Bad Beginning—Why Does She Weep?— Giorno dei Morti (first appeared in the *New Statesman*, 15 November 1913 (C28), as "Service of All the Dead," first collected in *Georgian Poetry 1913–1915* (B3) as "Service of All the Dead")—All Souls—Lady Wife—Both Sides of the Medal—Logger-heads—December Night—New Year's Eve—New Year's Night—Valentine's Night—Birth Night—Rabbit Snared in the Night—Paradise Re-entered—Spring Morning—Wedlock—History—Song of a Man Who Has Come Through—One Woman to All Women—People (also in *Poetry*, July 1918)—Street Lamps (first appeared in the *Egoist*, January 1917 (C41.5))—"She Said as Well to Me"—New Heaven and Earth (first appeared in *Some Imagist Poets* (B6) as "Terra Nuova")—Elysium—Manifesto—Autumn Rain (first appeared in the *Egoist*, February 1917 (C42))—Frost Flowers (first appeared in the *English Review*, September 1917 (C51))—Craving for Spring—Illustrated Edition Only: Bei Hennef (first appeared in *Love Poems* (A3))—All of Roses (first appeared in *Poetry*, January 1914 (C29))—Meeting Among the Mountains (first appeared in the *English Review*, February 1914 (C30); first collected in *Georgian Poetry 1913–1915* (B3))—Everlasting Flowers (first appeared in *New Poems* (A11))—Coming Awake (first appeared in *New Poems* (A11))—Song of a Man Who is Loved (first appeared in *Collected Poems* (A43)).

NOTES: This group of poems, like the sonnet cycles of earlier poets, tells the story of the love conflict between a man and woman; they are, of course, autobiographical poems and form Lawrence's poetic account of his life with Frieda which she has told from her own viewpoint in *Not*

I, But the Wind (B40). Many of the poems are set in the beautiful mountain country through which Lawrence and Frieda walked on the trip to Italy in 1912.

Lawrence rewrote and collected the poems for publication in January and February of 1917. In *The Savage Pilgrimage* (B37) Catherine Carswell tells of reading the completed manuscript which was then called "Man and Woman."

The book was accepted for publication by Chatto and Windus in August but with reservations; they insisted that two of the poems be omitted from the sequence, "Song of a Man Who is Loved" and "Meeting Among the Mountains," which consequently do not appear in the first printing of the book. Long afterwards when the Ark Press edition (A10b) was in preparation, Frieda recalled that the objection to the poems was based on the feeling that "you cannot mix religion and love." When he was preparing the manuscript for his *Collected Poems* (A43) Lawrence took advantage of the opportunity for replacing "Song of a Man Who is Loved," but it was a watered-down version, perhaps less effective than the original, and for some reason he did not include "Meeting Among the Mountains" with the collected poetry. In *Not I, But the Wind* Frieda reprinted the original version of the former poem which she preferred and "Meeting Among the Mountains." The *Look! We Have Come Through!* cycle in the *Collected Poems* also contains the titles "Bei Hennef," "Everlasting Flowers" and "Coming Awake" in accordance with Lawrence's rearrangement for *Collected Poems*.

B. W. Huebsch published the first American issue from the Chatto and Windus sheets in 1918. The collection was not reprinted separately until the Ark Press book in 1958.

REVIEWS: *Look! We Have Come Through!* was reviewed in *The Times Literary Supplement*, 22 November 1917; the *New Statesman*, 26 January 1918; the *Athenaeum*, February 1918; by John Gould Fletcher in *Poetry*, August 1918; the *New York Times Book Review*, 20 April 1919, and in "The Melodic Line" by Conrad Aiken in the *Dial*, 9 August 1919.

NOTES (2): The dust-jacket for the Chatto and Windus *Look! We Have Come Through!* is white paper printed in black and pink; the upper cover reproduces a drawing by E. McKnight Kauffer. The Ark Press published another illustrated edition of *Look! We Have Come Through!* in 1971 with woodcuts by Felix Hoffman. The format is quite different, but the text is the same as for (A10b), the first illustrated edition also designed by Kim Taylor, proprietor of The Ark Press. The book was printed by

Wordens of Cornwall, Ltd. The Ark Press was then located in Dulverton, Somerset, but has since removed to Cornwall.

REVIEWS (2): An additional review appeared in *English Review*, April 1918.

A11   NEW POEMS   1918

a. *first edition*

NEW POEMS | BY | D. H. | LAWRENCE | LONDON | MARTIN SECKER | MCMXVIII

Grey paper covers, printed in blue on upper cover: *NEW* | *POEMS* | *BY* | *D. H.* | *LAWRENCE* | *LONDON* | *MARTIN SECKER* | *MCMXVIII* | [*enclosed within a double rule with two vertical rules enclosing the lettering within the double rule*]; printed in blue on lower cover: [*publisher's device*] | xvii Buckingham Street | Adelphi The leaves measure $7\frac{1}{2}'' \times 5''$. Top edges trimmed; fore edges rough-trimmed; bottom edges untrimmed.

[1]–64, as follows: [1] half-title; [2] list of books of poetry by D. H. Lawrence; [3] title page as above; [4] dedication to Amy Lowell; PRINTED IN ENGLAND BY THE WESTMINSTER PRESS | 411A, HARROW ROAD, LONDON; 5–6 table of contents; 7–64 text.

Published October 1918 at 2*s*. 6*d*.; the first printing consisted of 500 copies.

b. *first American edition*

NEW POEMS | BY | D. H. LAWRENCE | [*publisher's device*] | NEW YORK | B. W. HUEBSCH | INC. | MCMXX | [*enclosed within a quadruple rule*]

Blue paper boards, blind stamped on upper cover: [*publisher's device*]; cream paper label on spine printed in black: [*single rule*] | D. H. | LAWRENCE | [*double rule*] | *New* | *Poems* | [*double rule*] | HUEBSCH | [*single rule*] The leaves measure $7\frac{5}{16}'' \times 5''$. All edges trimmed.

[i]–[vi] + i–[xii] + 1–78, as follows: [i] half-title; [ii] list of books of poetry by D. H. Lawrence; [iii] title page as above; [iv] COPYRIGHT, 1920 | BY B. W. HUEBSCH | INC.; [v] dedication to Amy Lowell; [vi] acknowledgements; i–x preface by D. H. LAWRENCE; [xi]–[xii] table of contents; 1–78 text.

Published 11 June 1920 at $1.60; number of copies unknown.

CONTENTS

Preface (first appeared in *Playboy*, Nos. 4 and 5, 1919 (C69) and (C70), as "Poetry of the Present"; collected in *Phoenix* (A76))—Apprehension (as "Noise of Battle" in *Collected Poems* (A43))—Coming Awake—From a College Window—Flapper (first appeared in the *Egoist*, 1 April 1914 (C32), as "Song")—Birdcage Walk—Letter from Town: The Almond Tree—Flat Suburbs, S. W., In the Morning—Thief in the Night—Letter from Town: On a Grey Evening in March (as "Letter from Town: On a Grey Morning in March" in *Collected Poems* (A43))—Suburbs on a Hazy Day—Hyde Park at Night: Clerks (first appeared in the *English Review* (C4) as "Yesternight")—Gipsy—Two-Fold—Under the Oak—Sigh no More (first appeared in the *English Review*, October 1910 (C5))—Love Storm—Parliament Hill in the Evening—Piccadilly Circus at Night: Street Walkers (first appeared in the *English Review*, April 1910 (C4) as "To-Morrow Night")—Tarantella—In Church—Piano—Embankment at Night: Charity—Phantasmagoria (as "Late at Night" in *Collected Poems* (A43))—Next Morning—Palimpsest of Twilight (as "Twilight" in *Collected Poems* (A43))—Embankment at Night: Outcasts—Winter in the Boulevard—School on the Outskirts—Sickness—Everlasting Flowers—The North Country—Bitterness of Death (first appeared in *Poetry*, January 1914 (C29), as "A Woman and Her Dead Husband," as "A Man Who Died" in *Collected Poems* (A43); first collected in *Some Imagist Poets* (B2) as "A Woman and Her Dead Husband")—Seven Seals—Reading a Letter—Twenty Years Ago—Intime (as "A Passing Visit to Helen" in *Collected Poems* (A43))—Two Wives—Heimweh (as "At the Front" in *Collected Poems* (A43))—Débâcle (as "Reality of Peace, 1916" in *Collected Poems* (A43))—Narcissus—Autumn Sunshine (first appeared in the *Egoist*, 1 April 1914 (C32), as "Early Spring")—On That Day (first appeared in *Poetry*, January 1914 (C29), as "Birthday").

NOTES: Although this volume was given the name "New Poems," most of the poetry was early Lawrence verse; he collected the poems and prepared them for publication during the summer of 1918. *New Poems*, the first of Lawrence's books to appear with Secker's imprint, was the only Lawrence book to appear that year.

The first American edition of *New Poems* was published by B. W. Huebsch in 1920 and is of particular interest because it contains a prefatory essay by Lawrence which did not appear in the English edition. This essay appeared in the magazine *Playboy*, Nos. 4 and 5 for 1919

(C69) and (C70) as "Poetry of the Present" and in *Voices*, October 1919, as "Verse Free and Unfree."

REVIEWS: *New Poems* was reviewed in the *New Statesman*, 14 December 1918; the *Athenaeum*, February 1919; *The Times Literary Supplement*, 6 February 1919; by H. S. Gorman in the *New York Times Book Review*, 4 July 1920; by John Gould Fletcher in *Freeman*, 21 July 1920; by R. M. Weaver in the *Bookman* (London), September 1920; in the *Nation* (New York) *Supplement Number 414*, 13 October 1920; by Babette Deutsch in the *Dial*, January 1921; and by N. A. Crawford in *Poetry*, September 1921.

NOTES (2): The dust-jacket for the Huebsch *New Poems* is cream paper printed in black.

A12   BAY   1919

a. *first edition (hand-made paper copies)*

BAY··A BOOK | OF··POEMS··BY | D: H: LAWRENCE

Decorative paper boards with a dark green cloth backstrip, stamped in gold on spine, reading upwards: [*printer's ornament*] | BAY·D. H. LAWRENCE | [*printer's ornament*] The leaves measure $7\frac{3}{8}'' \times 5''$. All edges untrimmed.

[1]–[48] and a tipped-in dedication page, as follows: [1] half-title; [2] This is the eighth book issued by the Beaumont Press | and the fourth printed by hand 30 copies have been | printed on Japanese vellum signed by the author and | artist and numbered 1 to 30 50 copies on cartridge | paper numbered 31 to 80 and 120 copies on hand-made | paper numbered 81 to 200. | 155 [*autograph number in black ink*]; [3] title page as above; [4] blank; tipped-in leaf, dedication to Cynthia Asquith; verso blank; [5]–[7] table of contents; [8] blank; 9–43 text; 44 blank; [45] HERE ENDS BAY A BOOK OF POEMS BY | D. H. Lawrence The Cover and the Decorations | designed by Anne Estelle Rice The Typography | and Binding arranged by Cyril W. Beaumont | Printed by Hand on his Press at 75 Charing | Cross Road in the City of Westminster | Completed November the Twentieth | MDCCCCXIX | [*printer's device*] | Pressman Charles Wright | Compositor C. W. Beaumont; [46]–[48] blank.

Published 20 November 1919 at 12s. 6d.; 200 copies were printed on hand-made paper.

b. *first edition (cartridge paper copies)*

BAY·· A BOOK | OF·· POEMS·· BY | D: H: LAWRENCE

The cartridge paper copies are identical with (a) except for hand-coloured illustrations and the paper stock.

Published simultaneously with (a) at 21*s.*; 50 copies were printed on cartridge paper, of which about 25 were destroyed before binding.

c. *first edition (vellum copies)*

BAY·· A BOOK | OF·· POEMS·· BY | D: H: LAWRENCE

The vellum copies are identical with (b) except for the paper stock, a vellum backstrip and the signature of the author and artist on page [1], which reads: BAY | D. H. Lawrence [*autograph signature in black ink*] | Anne Estelle Rice [*autograph signature in black ink*].

Published simultaneously with (a) and (b) at 30*s.*; 30 copies were printed on Japanese vellum.

CONTENTS

Guards!: A Review in Hyde Park 1913, The Crowd Watches, Evolutions of Soldiers—The Little Town at Evening (first appeared in the *Monthly Chapbook*, July 1919 (C66))—Last Hours—Town (first appeared in the *English Review*, June 1918 (C54); as "Town in 1917" in *Collected Poems* (A43))—After the Opera (first appeared in the *English Review*, June 1918 (C54))—Going Back—On the March—Bombardment—Winter-Lull—The Attack—Obsequial Ode (first appeared in *Poetry*, February 1919 (C59), as "Obsequial Chant")—Shades (first appeared in *Poetry*, February 1919 (C59), as "Pentecostal")—Bread Upon the Waters (first appeared in *Poetry*, February 1919 (C59))—Ruination—Rondeau of a Conscientious Objector (first appeared in *Voices*, July 1919 (C68))—Tommies in the Train (first appeared in *Poetry*, February 1919 (C59))—War-Baby (first appeared in the *English Review*, June 1918 (C54))—Nostalgia (first appeared in *Poetry*, February 1919 (C59)).

NOTES: These poems, with those published in *Poetry* for July 1919 (C67) under the collective title of "War Films," and the "Nightmare" chapter of *Kangaroo* (A26), comprise the greater part of Lawrence's literary reaction to the war. He collected the poems for *Bay* in the summer of 1918 at the same time he was arranging the manuscript for *New Poems* (A11). Several references to *Bay* and to Cyril Beaumont in Lawrence's letters of the period indicate that he was rather perturbed at Beaumont's delay in bringing out the book. *Bay* was supposed to have been dedicated to Lady Cynthia Asquith, and when Lawrence received a copy at Capri which did not contain the dedication, he was further enraged. The dedication was later tipped-in after page four.

Bay was the first of many Lawrence books to be issued in an expensive format from a private press, and while he commended the printing and the paper, Lawrence seemed to consider the woodcuts illustrating the book unsuitable. The book was designed by Cyril Beaumont and illustrated by Anne Estelle Rice, an American, who, Lawrence said, belonged to the "Matisse" crowd in Paris.

According to Mr Beaumont only about half of the cartridge paper copies were issued because of an accident. When the Lawrence manuscripts were exhibited at the University of Texas in 1955 Frieda had in her possession a copy of *Bay* in which she herself had coloured the illustrations; this was copy number 176.

NOTES (2): At least two copies of the cartridge paper copies have been reported without the tipped-in dedication leaf; a copy in the collection of Mr George Lazarus, which also lacks the dedication leaf, is slightly taller than the copy described here. Apparently some of the cartridge paper copies were bound so the printing on the spine is somewhat higher than the other copies. Mr Lazarus has pointed out that the illustration for "Last Hours", p. 14, is printed upside down.

A13   ALL THINGS ARE POSSIBLE   1920

first edition

ALL THINGS ARE POSSIBLE | BY LEO SHESTOV | AUTHORIZED TRANSLATION | BY S. S. KOTELIAN-SKY | WITH A FOREWORD BY | D. H. LAWRENCE | LONDON: MARTIN SECKER

Blue cloth boards, cream paper label on spine printed in violet: ALL | THINGS ARE | POSSIBLE | · | SHESTOV The leaves measure $7\frac{1}{2}'' \times 5''$. Top edges trimmed; fore and bottom edges untrimmed.

[1]–[248], as follows: [1] half-title; [2] blank; [3] title page as above; [4] *First published in England, 1920*; [5] note on Leo Shestov; [6] blank; 7–12 foreword by D. H. Lawrence; [13] quotation from Heine; [14] blank; 15–[244] text, at bottom of page [244]: [*short rule*] | THE LONDON AND NORWICH PRESS, LIMITED, LONDON AND NORWICH, ENGLAND; [245]–[248] blank.

Published April 1920 at 7*s*. 6*d*.; the first printing consisted of 1000 copies.

NOTES: Although Lawrence is credited only with the "Foreword" for this translation of Shestov's *All Things Are Possible*, Bertram Rota reports that S. S. Koteliansky named D. H. Lawrence as a full collaborator in the translation. Koteliansky was a member of the Lawrence coterie during the war years in England, and he remained a friend and literary associate of Lawrence's. Apparently Koteliansky felt that he did not write English well enough to carry through the work of translation without assistance. John Middleton Murry collaborated with him on several translations before Lawrence agreed to work on *All Things Are Possible*. The final translation was effected through a complete revision by Lawrence of Koteliansky's version. Koteliansky's original manuscript was so heavily revised that Lawrence eventually rewrote the entire translation in his own handwriting; this was the manuscript from which Secker printed the present edition.

In a memorandum dated 28 April 1952, Mr Rota writes, "Koteliansky says the reason why Lawrence's name does not appear as a collaborator in the translation of this book, or of Dostoevsky's *Grand Inquisitor* or other translations which they did together, is that Lawrence felt it would be damaging to his reputation with publishers as a creative writer if he should appear as a translator." The holograph manuscript of the "Foreword" and of the complete translation, entirely in Lawrence's handwriting, are now in the collection of Mr George Lazarus. The "Foreword" is collected in *Phoenix* (A76).

NOTES (2): The dust-jacket for the Secker *All Things Are Possible* is cream or light tan paper printed in black.

A14   TOUCH AND GO   1920

first edition

Touch and Go | *A Play in Three Acts by* | *D. H. Lawrence* | LONDON: C. W. DANIEL, LTD. | Graham House, Tudor Street, E. C. 4 | 1920

Orange paper boards, blue paper label on upper cover printed in blue: TOUCH | & GO | D. H. LAWRENCE | [*enclosed within a decorative rule*]; blue paper label on spine printed in blue, reading upwards: TOUCH AND GO—D. H. Lawrence. The leaves measure $7\frac{5}{8}'' \times 5''$. All edges untrimmed.

[1]– 96, as follows: [1] half-title; [2] *Copyright in the United States of America.* THE performing rights of this play are fully protected, | and

permission to perform it, whether by amateurs or | professionals, must
be obtained in advance from the author's | sole agent, R. GOLDING
BRIGHT, of 20 Green Street, | Leicester Square, London, from whom all
particulars can | be obtained.; [3] title page as above; [4] list of "Plays
for a People's Theatre": "The Fight for Freedom" by Douglas Goldring;
"Touch and Go" by D. H. Lawrence; "The Kingdom, the Power and
the Glory" by Hamilton Fyfe; followed by a quotation from Bela Kun.;
5–12 preface; [13] blank; 14 list of characters; 15–96 text, at bottom
of page 96: [*short rule*] | PRINTED IN GREAT BRITAIN BY NEILL AND CO.,
LTD., EDINBURGH.

Published May 1920 at 3s. 6d.; number of copies unknown.

NOTES: Lawrence finished *Touch and Go* some time before November
1918, for he wrote of it as recently completed in a letter to Amy Lowell
dated in November. *Touch and Go* was to be the first play in a series
known as "Plays for a People's Theatre"; according to Douglas Goldring,
the originator of the scheme, there was to be a People's Theatre Society
which would produce the plays which were to be published by
C. W. Daniel of London. Lawrence's preface to *Touch and Go* written in
the summer of 1919 was designed as an announcement of and a plea
for the "People's Theatre." Catherine Carswell tells of Lawrence's anger
when he learned that Douglas Goldring had published a play of his
own as the first of the series with its own inaugural preface; *Touch and
Go* then became the second of the series. See *Odd Man Out* (B41) by
Douglas Goldring.

The first American edition was published by Thomas Seltzer from
new plates on 5 June 1920.

REVIEWS: Reviews of *Touch and Go* were printed in *The Times Literary
Supplement*, 13 May 1920; in the *Athenaeum* as "Mr. Lawrence and the
People" by T. Moult, 11 June 1920; the *Dial* by Gilbert Seldes, August
1920; by Amy Lowell in the *New York Times Book Review*, 22 August
1920; the *Spectator*, 28 August 1920; the *Survey*, 20 August 1920; by
Ludwig Lewisohn in the *Nation* (New York), 11 September 1920; the
New York Evening Post Literary Review, 27 November 1920 by J. R. Towse;
and in the *Freeman*, 15 December 1920 by Elva de Pue.

NOTES (2): The C. W. Daniel *Touch and Go* dust-jacket is tan paper
printed in black and green; the lower cover has a list of "Plays for a
People's Theatre." The Seltzer dust-jacket is off-white printed in green;
the upper cover is decorated with theatrical masks for comedy and
tragedy.

Touch and Go was produced by The Questors Theatre Company at the Questors Theatre, Matlock Lane, Ealing on Saturday, 6 October 1973.

A14.5 FOREWORD TO WOMEN IN LOVE 1920

first edition

Privately Printed and Sold Only to Subscribers | *[single rule]* | WOMEN IN LOVE | By D. H. Lawrence | *[advertising matter]* | *[single rule]* | *This first, and complete definitive edition, for sub-* | *scribers only, strictly limited to 1250 copies, each copy* | *numbered, was set up in Monotype, and printed on* | *Olde Style watermarked rag paper, and bound with* | *pages untrimmed in blue buckram, stamped with gold.* | *The type has been distributed after printing* | *and this edition will never* | *be duplicated.*

Without covers; first page serves as title page. The leaves measure 9″ × 6″. Probably not trimmed.

[1]–[4], as follows: [1] title page as above; [2]–[3] text, signed: D. H. LAWRENCE | *Hermitage, 12 September 1919.*; [4] quotations from Douglas Goldring and B. F. Edgett about Lawrence, an advertisement for the forthcoming limited edition of *Psychoanalysis and the Unconscious* and the subscription form for ordering copies of *Women in Love*.

Printed and distributed in the autumn of 1920, not for sale; number of copies unknown.

NOTES: This was an advertising leaflet prepared by Thomas Seltzer for his first printing of *Women in Love* (A15a). The text is that published in 1936 (A74) and reprinted in *Phoenix II* (A107). The leaflet exists in two forms. An earlier trial printing has Lawrence's name and the title of *Women in Love* in green, and omits the advertisement for *Psychoanalysis and the Unconscious*; the quotations are also different.

A15   WOMEN IN LOVE   1920

a. first edition

WOMEN IN LOVE | BY | D. H. LAWRENCE | NEW YORK | PRIVATELY PRINTED FOR SUBSCRIBERS ONLY | 1920

Dark blue cloth boards, stamped in gold on spine: *[double rule]* | *[double rule, blind stamped]* | WOMEN | IN | LOVE | *[short rule]* | D. H. LAWRENCE

| [*double rule, blind stamped*] | [*double rule, blind stamped*] | [*double rule, blind stamped*] | [*double rule*] The leaves measure $9\frac{1}{2}'' \times 6\frac{1}{4}''$. All edges rough-trimmed.

[i]–[iv] + [1]–[540], as follows: [i] half-title; [ii] *1250 copies of this book have been* | *printed of which this is* | *No. 92.* [*autograph number in blue ink*]; [iii] title page as above; [iv] Copyright, 1920, by | D. H. Lawrence | [*short rule*] | All rights reserved; [1] fly-title: WOMEN IN LOVE; [2] blank; [3]–536 text; [537]–[540] blank.

Published 9 November 1920 at $15.00; the first printing consisted of 1250 copies, of which 50 were sold to Martin Secker as sheets and published as (A15b).

VARIANTS: (1) as (2) but autographed by D. H. Lawrence.
(2) copy described above.

NOTE: In a letter to Edward McDonald dated September 1924, Thomas Seltzer wrote that Lawrence had autographed "16 or 18" copies of this edition. Mr McDonald noted in his bibliography (B16) that the copies were numbered in red ink; however, all copies examined, with the exceptions of Mr McDonald's own copy and Mr W. Forster's, were numbered in blue ink. Apparently the earlier copies were numbered in blue ink.

b. *first edition, English issue*

WOMEN IN LOVE | BY | D. H. LAWRENCE | NEW YORK | PRIVATELY PRINTED FOR SUBSCRIBERS ONLY | 1920

Dark brown cloth boards, blind stamped on upper and lower covers: [*thick rule enclosed within a thin rule*]; stamped in gold on spine: [*thin rule*] | [*thick rule*] | WOMEN IN | LOVE | · | D. H. | LAWRENCE | 1920 | [*thick rule*] | [*thin rule*] The leaves measure $9\frac{1}{8}'' \times 6\frac{1}{4}''$. Top edges trimmed and stained dark green; fore edges untrimmed; bottom edges rough-trimmed.

[i]–[iv] + [1]–[540] as follows: [i] blank; [ii] *Fifty copies have been* | *signed by the Author,* | *of which this is No.* 25 [*autograph number in black ink*] D. H. Lawrence [*autograph signature in black ink*]; [iii] title page as above; [iv] Copyright, 1920, by | D. H. Lawrence | [*short rule*] | All rights reserved; [1] fly-title: WOMEN IN LOVE; [2] blank; [3]–536 text; [537]–[540] blank. Pp. [i]–[ii] form a cancel leaf.

Published June 1922 at 63*s*.; these 50 copies were made up from American sheets (A15a).

c. *first trade edition*

WOMEN IN LOVE | BY D. H. LAWRENCE | LONDON |
MARTIN SECKER | NUMBER FIVE JOHN STREET
ADELPHI

Chocolate brown cloth boards, blind stamped on upper cover: [*double
rule forming a border*]; blind stamped on lower cover: [*double rule forming
a border*]; stamped in gold on spine: [*thin rule*] | [*thick rule*] | WOMEN IN
| LOVE | · | D. H. | LAWRENCE | SECKER | [*thick rule*] | [*thin rule*] The
leaves measure $7\frac{9}{16}''\times4\frac{15}{16}''$. Top and fore edge trimmed; bottom edge
untrimmed.

[1]–[512], as follows: [1] half-title; [2] blank; [3] title page as above;
[4] LONDON: MARTIN SECKER (LTD.), 1921; 5 table of contents; [6] blank;
7–508 text, at bottom of page 508: [*short rule*] | PRINTED IN GREAT BRITAIN
BY | THE DUNEDIN PRESS LIMITED, EDINBURGH; [509]–[512] advertise-
ments.

Published June 1921 at 9*s.*; the first printing consisted of 1500 copies.

NOTES: *Women in Love* was the first Lawrence novel to appear in print
after *The Rainbow* (A7) fiasco five years before; it is related textually to
The Rainbow and was in part reworked from the material left over from
"The Sisters." The final version was completed in 1916 while the
Lawrences were living in Cornwall; Catherine Carswell records her
reactions after reading a typescript in November of that year. Mrs
Carswell says that almost every publisher in London refused the
manuscripts. Methuen cancelled their contract with Lawrence after
reading it, and Duckworth also refused to accept the novel for publication. Lawrence anticipated the trouble he would have and wrote Lady
Cynthia Asquith asking her to suggest a patron who would accept a
"serious dedication" and thus afford the book protection which could
prevent the sort of trouble *The Rainbow* experienced. These efforts were
in vain, however, for publication had to wait for almost five years, and
then it was privately printed in New York.

The printing of the private edition in New York was done under the
supervision of Thomas Seltzer. Some 16 or 18 of the copies were signed
by Lawrence, and these copies were the first numbered according to
McDonald (B16).

Martin Secker, who had published the first trade edition of *Women
in Love* in June 1921, imported fifty sets of the sheets from Thomas Seltzer
and issued a limited autographed edition (A15b) in June 1922. The

English trade edition contained chapter headings written by Lawrence which the original edition did not have.

Women in Love has been one of Lawrence's more popular novels; Lawrence wrote from Del Monte ranch at Taos in December 1922 that the Seltzer trade edition published the previous October would run to 15,000 copies. Boni and Liveright issued the title in the Uniform Edition in 1931, and Grosset and Dunlap printed it in the Novels of Distinction series in 1933. The Modern Library edition was published in 1937 with a "Foreword" by Lawrence, also published separately as *Foreword to Women in Love* (A74) in 1936. The Secker trade edition was reprinted three times by 1925, and Heinemann issued a Cheap Edition in January 1936 and a Pocket Edition in 1946 which was reprinted with an introduction by Richard Aldington in March 1950. The book also appears as No. 303 in the Albatross Modern Continental Library.

REVIEWS: *Women in Love* was reviewed in the *Nation* (New York), 26 January 1921, in an article called "Hungry" by Carl Van Doren; in "Philosopher of the Erotic" by Evelyn Scott in the *Dial*, April 1921; by Rebecca West in the *New Statesman*, 9 July 1921; by John Middleton Murry in "The Nostalgia of Mr. D. H. Lawrence" in the *Nation and Athenaeum*, 13 August 1921; a letter of Murry's concerning his review appears in the 27 August issue of the *Nation and Athenaeum*; by Edward Shanks in the *London Mercury*, August 1921; and in the *Nation* (New York), 17 January 1923 by B. L. Burman.

NOTES (2): The publishing history of the English *Women in Love* is considerably more complicated than the notes for the first edition of the bibliography indicate. Sometime after the appearance of the first English trade edition Philip Heseltine took legal advice about the description of the characters Halliday and Pussum in the book which he considered a gross libel of himself and his mistress. Because of his objections the text was changed, e.g., the name Pussum became Minette, and her colouring and the description of Halliday's apartment were altered to make the resemblance less obvious. The English publisher, Secker, also persuaded Lawrence to make changes in the text because of his fear of adverse reactions by the lending libraries.

In November 1921 Secker issued the novel with the words, "Second Impression" on the verso of the title page; this issue incorporated the changes required by Heseltine's threatened libel action, but apparently changes in the text of the novel had been made progressively before November 1921, because copies exist with changes in the text which have no indication that a separate issue is involved and which in all other respects are the same as the first English trade edition of June 1921. A careful comparison of many copies of the first English trade edition will be necessary before accurate conclusions can be made about the various states of the novel. Dr David Farmer who has done considerable work on the textual problems of *Women in Love* has identified the copies with textual changes before the "Second Impression" as a "hidden impression."

The following variants of (A15c) may be listed:

VARIANTS: (1) copy described above.

(2) as (1) except for various textual changes; this issue can be identified by the following:

page 61, line 31 reads "come round and see" instead of "come round to the flat, and see" as in (1).

page 63, line 19 reads "girl with bobbed, blond hair" instead of "girl with dark, soft, fluffy hair" as in (1).

(3) as (1) except for the words "SECOND IMPRESSION" on the title page and various textual changes:

page 66, line 37 reads "Minette" instead of "Pussum" as in (1) and (2).

page 66, line 26 reads "Gerald watched her fair, close hair" instead of "Gerald watched her dark, soft hair" as in (1) and (2).

The dust-jacket for the Secker trade edition is cream paper printed in red. The Seltzer dust-jacket is cream paper printed in black and red; the upper cover is illustrated with the head of a woman with streaming hair. This is the dust-jacket which Lawrence considered "terrible."

REVIEWS (2): Additional reviews of *Women in Love* appeared in *The Times Literary Supplement*, 9 June 1921; the *Observer*, 26 June; *Saturday Westminster Gazette*, 2 July; *Manchester Guardian* by Frank Swinnerton, 15 July; *Outlook* (London), by H. C. Harwood, 13 August; *English Review*, September; *John Bull* by Charles W. Pilley, 17 September.

A16 THE LOST GIRL 1920

first edition

THE LOST GIRL | BY D. H. LAWRENCE | LONDON | MARTIN SECKER | NUMBER FIVE JOHN STREET ADELPHI

Dark brown cloth boards, blind stamped on upper and lower covers:

[*thick rule enclosed within thin rule*]; stamped in gold on spine: [*thin rule*] | [*thick rule*] | THE LOST | GIRL |·| D. H. | LAWRENCE | SECKER | [*thick rule*] | [*thin rule*] The leaves measure $7\frac{1}{2}'' \times 5''$. Top edges trimmed; fore edges rough-trimmed; bottom edges untrimmed.

[1]–[372], as follows: [1] half-title; [2] blank; [3] title page as above; [4] LONDON: MARTIN SECKER (LTD.), 1920; 5 table of contents; [6] blank; 7–371 text; [372] [*short rule*] | PRINTED IN GREAT BRITAIN BY | THE DUNEDIN PRESS LIMITED, EDINBURGH

Published November 1920 at 9*s*.; the first printing consisted of 4000 copies.

VARIANTS: (1) copy described above.
(2) as (1) except with cancel pages 255–256 and 267–268 and modified text.
(3) as (2) except pages 255–256 and 267–268 are integral with the signature.

NOTES: Secker's first edition of *The Lost Girl* appeared in London the same month the privately printed *Women in Love* (A15) came off the press in New York, giving English readers their first chance at a Lawrence novel since the ill-fated *Rainbow* (A7) in 1915. In reality, *The Lost Girl* was of quite early vintage, for it was begun in Gargnano, Italy, in 1913; Lawrence mentions "The Insurrection of Miss Houghton," an early title for the book, in a letter to Edward Garnett from Irschenhausen in which he says he has finished two hundred pages of the novel. The finishing touches were probably done at Fontana Vecchia in Taormina; Lawrence announced in a letter to Lady Cynthia Asquith, written 7 May 1920, that he had just completed the book. *The Lost Girl* received the James Tait Black Prize of Edinburgh University in 1921.

Although Lawrence considered the book quite "moral," some passages were changed to satisfy demands of the "libraries." Thus it is that the first edition of the *The Lost Girl* is distinguished by three states involving textual changes on pages 256 and 268. In the first state the unaltered text beginning on line 15 of page 256 reads:

White, and mute, and motionless, she was taken to her room. And at the back of her mind all the time she wondered at his deliberate recklessness of her. Recklessly, he had his will of her—but deliberately, and thoroughly, not rushing to the issue, but taking everything he wanted of her, progressively, and fully, leaving her stark, with nothing, nothing of herself—nothing.

The original text on page 268 reads:

Once more it was about the sleeping accommodation—whether the landlady heard anything in the night—whether she noticed anything in the bedrooms, in the beds.

The second state has pages 255–256 and 267–268 tipped-in, and the text is changed to read as follows:

White, and mute, and motionless, she let be. She let herself go down the unknown dark flood of his will, borne from her old footing forever.

Page 268 is changed to read:

Once more it was about the sleeping accommodation—whether the landlady heard anything in the night—whether she noticed anything.

The third state has changed text with both pages 255–256 and 267–268 as integral parts of the signature. It should be noted, however, that copies have been recorded which have the text changed on one page only, that is with only one tipped-in leaf, so it is likely the corrections were not made all at once but progressively.

Martin Secker reprinted *The Lost Girl* in 1925 in an edition of 1500 copies, 841 of which were remaindered in 1930. Secker also issued the Thin Paper Pocket Edition in 1927; Heinemann published the Cheap Edition in May 1935 and the Pocket Edition with an introduction by Richard Aldington in 1950.

The first American edition of *The Lost Girl*, published by Thomas Seltzer from new plates in January 1921, has the unaltered text of the first English copies. Boni and Liveright issued both a paper-covered Bonibook and the Uniform Edition in 1931, and Grosset and Dunlap published it in the Novels of Distinction Series in 1933. It appeared as No. 295 in the Albatross Continental Library in 1936.

REVIEWS: Reviews of *The Lost Girl* appeared in *The Times Literary Supplement*, 2 December 1920 by Virginia Woolf; as "The Decay of Mr. D. H. Lawrence" by John Middleton Murry in the *Athenaeum*, 17 December 1920; by Edward Shanks in the *London Mercury*, December 1920; in the *Spectator*, 29 January 1921; in the *Nation* (London), 22 January 1921; by B. F. Edgett in the *Boston Transcript*, 16 February 1921; by L. M. Robinson in the *Publisher's Weekly*, 19 February 1921; as "The Surplus Woman" by Francis Hackett in the *New Republic*, 16 March 1921; by John Macy in the *New York Evening Post Literary Review*, 19 March 1921; by L. M. Field in the *New York Times Book Review*, 27 March 1921; by Evelyn Scott in "The Philosopher of the Erotic" in the *Dial*, April; in "The Quality of Mr. D. H. Lawrence" by Mary Colum in the *Freeman*, 22 June 1921; and as "Frustrate Ladies" in the *Nation* (New York), 7 September 1921.

NOTES (2): A slight mystery concerning the textual changes in *The Lost Girl* has surfaced since the first edition of the bibliography. In a letter to Lawrence dated 9 October 1924 Martin Secker says the cancel pages were printed and inserted in a number of copies as a temporary expedient to secure library circulation and that later when the library demand ceased, the cancel pages were ignored and subsequent binding orders presented the book as originally published. Lawrence repeated this information in a letter to Edward McDonald, but McDonald did not mention Secker's story in his account of *The Lost Girl* (B31). Variant (3) does have the new text integral with the signatures, so it seems likely that Secker did not want to admit to Lawrence that he had authorized changes in the text for reasons of censorship. This seems even more likely in view of additional changes made in variant (3). When the pages were reset, Secker took advantage of the opportunity to make other changes in the text on pages 45 and 223. Page 45, lines 1 and 2, in variant (1) read:

> liberties. They pinched her haunches and attacked her in | unheard-of ways. Sometimes her blood really came up in...

In variant (3) these lines were changed to read:

> liberties. Somehow her blood really came up in | the fight, and she felt as if, with her hands, she could tear...

On page 223, lines 10–14, in variant (1) read:

> If for one moment she could have escaped from that black | spell of his beauty, she would have been free. But she | could not. He was awful to her, shameless so that she died | under his shamelessness, his smiling, progressive shameless- | ness.

In variant (3) these lines are changed to read:

> If for one moment she could have escaped from that black | spell of his beauty, she would have been free. If | only she could, for one second, have seen him | ugly, he would not have killed her and made her | his slave as he did. But the spell was on her,...

When Secker made the additional changes on page 45 and 232, several lines of type were accidentally transposed on page 242 so that variant

(3) can be additionally identified by the first line on page 242 which reads, "'What do you want?' said Cicio, rising." instead of, "Miss Pinnegar went away into the scullery." A detailed account of the differences in the text of the various issues has been included in the Cambridge edition of *Lost Girl* edited by John Worthen, as well as "Elsa Culverwell," the hitherto unpublished opening of the first version of the novel, published 29 October 1981.

Some copies of *The Lost Girl* appear to have been trimmed to a size larger that the $4\frac{7}{8}''$ noted for the copy described here; a few copies are fully 5″ wide.

A copy of variant (1) is in the collection at the University of Texas in which Martin Secker has written, "...only about 90 or so [copies] were so issued."

The Lost Girl dust-jacket is cream paper printed in red.

REVIEWS (2): Additional reviews of *The Lost Girl* appeared in the *Star* by H. T. for 30 November 1920; the *Glasgow Herald*, 2 December 1920; the *Observer*, 5 December; the *Manchester Guardian* by Edward Garnett, 10 December; the *Westminster Gazette*, 11 December; the *Morning Post*, 24 December; the *Daily Mail* by Hamilton Fyfe, 13 December; the *Tatler* by Richard King, 29 December; the *Bookman* (New York) by Marguerite Arnold, April 1921; the *New York Evening Post Literary Review* by H. S. Canby, 3 June 1922.

A17   MOVEMENTS IN   1921
EUROPEAN HISTORY

a. first edition

MOVEMENTS IN | EUROPEAN HISTORY | BY | LAWRENCE H. DAVISON | HUMPHREY MILFORD | OXFORD UNIVERSITY PRESS | LONDON, EDIN- BURGH, GLASGOW | TORONTO, MELBOURNE, CAPE TOWN, BOMBAY | 1921

Light-brown cloth boards, printed in black on spine: MOVEMENTS | IN| EUROPEAN | HISTORY | DAVISON | MILFORD The leaves measure $7\frac{3}{16}'' \times 4\frac{7}{8}''$.

[i]–[ii] + [i]–[x] + [1]–306 and 14 plates at end of text, as follows: [i]–[ii] blank; [i] half-title; [ii] blank; [iii] title page as above; [iv] blank; v–viii introduction for the teacher; ix table of contents; [x] list of maps; [1]–306 text, at bottom of page 306: [*short thin rule*] | Edinburgh: Printed by T. and A. CONSTABLE LTD.; 14 plates of maps.

Published February 1921 at 4s. 6d.; the first printing consisted of 2000 copies.

VARIANTS: (1) copy described above.

(2) as (1) except issued in light-blue cloth boards.

The brown cloth binding is given priority because a copy has been noted with a review stamp, and an official of the Oxford University Press reports that to the best of his memory the brown cloth binding was used first.

b. *first illustrated edition (large-paper copies)*

MOVEMENTS IN | EUROPEAN HISTORY | BY | D. H. LAWRENCE | [*publisher's device*] | OXFORD UNIVERSITY PRESS | HUMPHREY MILFORD | 1925

Dark blue cloth boards, stamped in gold on upper cover: [*publisher's device enclosed within a single rule*]; stamped in gold on spine: [*single rule*] | MOVEMENTS | IN | EUROPEAN | HISTORY | LAWRENCE | [*publisher's device*] | OXFORD | [*single rule*] The leaves measure $7\frac{7}{8}'' \times 5\frac{1}{2}''$. All edges trimmed.

[i]–[xiv] + [1]–[370], as follows: [i] blank; [ii] frontispiece; [iii] title page as above; [iv] BIBLIOGRAPHICAL NOTE | This is the first illustrated edition of a | work which was first published in 1921 as | *Movements in European History*, by Lawrence | H Davison. It is issued both in a crown 8vo | and in a large-paper edition. | Printed in England; [v] table of contents; [vi]–ix list of illustrations; [x]–xiii introduction; [xiv] illustration; [1]–344 text; [345]–354 index; [355]–[369] maps; [370] PRINTED IN ENGLAND | AT THE OXFORD UNIVERSITY PRESS

Published 21 May 1925 at 7s. 6d.; 2000 large-paper copies were printed.

VARIANTS: (1) copy described above with the caption for the illustration on page 271 mistakenly identifying the Old South Church in Boston as the building in which Patrick Henry made his "Give me liberty or give me death" speech.

(2) as (1) but with the view of Boston harbour on page 271.

In all copies examined of variant (2) of both (b) and (c), although the illustration on page 271 has been replaced with the view of Boston harbour, the list of illustrations still gives the original caption.

c. *first illustrated edition (ordinary copies)*

MOVEMENTS IN | EUROPEAN HISTORY | BY | D. H.
LAWRENCE | [*publisher's device*] | OXFORD UNIVERSITY
PRESS | HUMPHREY MILFORD | 1925

The ordinary copies were identical with (b) except that they were issued
in grey cloth boards printed in black on upper cover: MOVEMENTS IN
| EUROPEAN | HISTORY | [*publisher's device*] | D. H. LAWRENCE | [*enclosed
within a double ornamental rule*]; printed in black on spine: [*ornamental rule*] |
MOVEMENTS | IN | EUROPEAN | HISTORY | [*printer's ornament*] | LAWRENCE
| OXFORD | [*ornamental rule*] The leaves measure $7\frac{1}{2}''\times 5\frac{1}{16}''$. The printing
notice on page [370] of (b) is found in (c) on page 354 and reads:
Printed in England at the Oxford University Press.

VARIANTS: (1) copy described above.
(2) as (1) but with the view of Boston harbour on page 271.

Published 21 May 1925 at 3s. 6d.; 6000 ordinary copies were
printed.

d. *Irish edition*

MOVEMENTS | IN EUROPEAN HISTORY | BY D. H.
LAWRENCE | NEW AND REVISED EDITION, SPECIAL-
LY PREPARED | FOR IRISH SCHOOLS, WITH THE
ADDITION OF | THE FOLLOWING APPENDICES: (*a*)
INTRODUCTORY | SKETCH OF EARLY MEDITERRA-
NEAN HISTORY; | (*b*) IRELAND AND THE NORMANS;
(*c*) IRELAND AND | FOREIGN COUNTIRES | [*publisher's
device*] | THE EDUCATIONAL COMPANY | OF IRELAND
: :   : : LIMITED | DUBLIN & CORK

Green cloth boards, printed in black on upper cover: MOVEMENTS IN |
EUROPEAN | HISTORY | IRISH | SCHOOL | EDITION | [*publisher's device*] |
[*the preceding four lines enclosed within a decorative rule*] | D. H. LAWRENCE |
[*enclosed within a double decorative rule*]; printed in black on spine: [*decorative
rule*] | MOVEMENTS | IN | EUROPEAN | HISTORY | [*printer's ornament*] |
LAWRENCE | EDUCATIONAL | COMPANY | [*decorative rule*] The leaves
measure $7\frac{1}{4}''\times 4\frac{13}{16}''$. All edges trimmed.

[1]–400, as follows: [1] half-title; [2] frontispiece; [3] title page as
above; [4] *Special Edition authorized by* | *The Oxford University Press* |
[*bracket*] *Printed in Ireland* [*bracket*]; 5 table of contents; 6 list of illustrations

and maps; 7–347 text; 348 map of Ireland; 349–374 appendices; 375–383 index; [384] blank; 385–399 maps; [400] blank.

Published September 1926 at 4s. 6d.; the first printing consisted of 3000 copies.

e. *first edition with epilogue*

Movements in European History | [*double rule*] | D. H. LAWRENCE | OXFORD UNIVERSITY PRESS | 1971

Dark blue cloth boards; stamped in gold on spine: [*rule*] | Movements | in | European | History | LAWRENCE | [*publisher's device*] | OXFORD | [*rule*] The leaves measure 8″ × 5¼″. All edges trimmed.

[i]–xxviii + [1]–[356], as follows: [i] half-title; [ii] blank; [iii] title page as above; [iv] *Oxford University Press, Ely House, London W. 1* | [*list of cities for Oxford University Press imprint*] | Epilogue © D. H. Lawrence Estate 1971 | Introduction © Oxford University Press 1971 | Original edition first published 1921 | Illustrated edition 1925 | This edition 1971 | PRINTED IN GREAT BRITAIN | AT THE UNIVERSITY PRESS, OXFORD | BY VIVIAN RIDLER | PRINTER TO THE UNIVERSITY; [v] table of contents; [vi] blank; [vii]–xxiv introduction to the new edition by James T. Boulton; [xxv]–xxviii introduction; [1]–[306] text; [307]–321 epilogue; [322] blank; [323]–336 index; [337]–[351] maps; [352]–[356] blank.

Published 24 February 1972 at £3.50; the first printing consisted of 2000 copies.

NOTES: *Movements in European History* was referred to by Catherine Carswell as the one piece of work Lawrence did satisfactorily to order. He told Cecil Gray in a letter dated July 1918 that he was to do a school book of history for the Oxford University Press; the book was finished in the spring of the following year. According to Harry T. Moore (B57), the idea for the book was suggested to Lawrence by H. Vere Collins, who then persuaded his superior at the Oxford University Press, Humphrey Milford, to consider the book for publication. Lawrence, perhaps understandably, agreed to publish under a pseudonym, and thus *Movements in European Literature* appeared with the name, Lawrence H. Davison on the title page. It is a moot question as to what Lawrence contributed to the illustrations in the illustrated edition of the *Movements*. Although McDonald states that Lawrence had nothing to do with the illustrations, a diary transcribed in Tedlock (B51) records that Lawrence sent an "epilogue" and "illustrations" to the Oxford University Press on 30 September 1924. These illustrations may have been the maps which appeared in the book.

An interesting state of the illustrated edition exists which can be identified by the picture on page 271 of Boston's Old South Church with a caption stating that Patrick Henry made his famous "Give me liberty or give me death" speech there. This, of course, is in error, for Patrick Henry's speech was delivered in Virginia. The illustration was later suppressed.

The Irish edition (A17d) was published by the Educational Company of Ireland, Ltd., of which 500 sets of sheets were imported by the Oxford University Press, bound and published in January 1927. This Irish edition was revised for consumption in Ireland; in 1954 when Jake Zeitlin appraised Mrs Lawrence's collection of Lawrence manuscripts, she still had in her possession a copy of the Oxford edition, "corrected and censored in blue pencil by the Irish Catholic Church."

Oxford's first edition was reprinted in March 1923 in an edition of 2000 copies, and the illustrated edition was reprinted in the smaller format in an edition of 3000 copies in 1931. There has been no American edition of the book.

REVIEWS: Critical notices and reviews of *Movements in European History* appeared in the *New Statesman*, 26 November 1921; the *Nation* (New York), 16 December 1925; and by Kenneth Pickthorn in the *London Mercury*, August 1926.

NOTES (2): Priority was assigned to the brown binding of *Movements* because a letter from the Oxford University Press dated 14 April 1959 quoted the deputy publisher as remembering the first binding to have been that in the brown cloth. Mr George Lazarus has in his collection a copy in the blue cloth binding which belonged to Vere H. G. Collins who states in an accompanying letter that the copy was of the first "impression." Although Mr Collins may have meant the first copies were bound in blue cloth, it seems equally likely that he was referring to the copy as being of the first impression; both bindings were used for the first impression. The Oxford Press records are reported to have been destroyed, and it may be impossible to decide which binding was first. There is a copy of the book in the brown binding at the University of Texas which is inscribed by Lawrence to Vere Collins; however in his memoir *A Young Man's Passage* published under the pen-name of Mark Teller and quoted earlier in Nehls (B60), Collins states categorically about 500 copies were bound in blue cloth, and no more being available, the binders asked to be allowed to continue binding in brown cloth.

Two additional states of (A17c) variant (2) have been reported in the John Martin Collection at the University of Tulsa; one has 4 pp. of advertisements, and the other has 8 pp.; both are presumably later issues.

The 500 sets of sheets from the Irish edition (A17d) imported by the Oxford Press were issued in the binding format of (A17c) with a cancel title page reading:

MOVEMENTS IN | EUROPEAN HISTORY | *By* D. H. LAWRENCE | Revised Edition for Irish Schools, with | appendices on Early Mediterranean | History, Ireland and the Normans, | Ireland and Foreign Countries | 1926 | OXFORD UNIVERSITY PRESS LONDON: HUMPHREY MILFORD

The verso of the title page reads: ISSUED BY ARRANGEMENT WITH | THE EDUCATIONAL COMPANY OF IRELAND | DUBLIN AND CORK Mr George Lazarus has a copy of this book in his collection which according to the title page was issued in 1926. Mr Philip Crumpton in his article, "D. H. Lawrence's Mauled History" in the *D. H. Lawrence Review*, 13 (Summer 1980), 105–118, gives a complete account of the Irish edition; he notes that there are textual differences between the first Oxford edition of 1921 (A17a) and the illustrated edition of 1925 (A17b,c) which was revised for the Irish edition. The marked copy in Mrs Lawrence's possession in 1954 was the illustrated edition.

(A17e) includes a previously unpublished "Epilogue" derived from a manuscript in the library of The University of California at Los Angeles. Some copies of (A17a) appear to be trimmed to a size slightly smaller than the $4\frac{7}{8}''$ noted for the copy described above.

VARIANTS: A17c (3) as (2) except with four pages of advertisements following the text.

(4) as (2) except with eight pages of advertisements.

REVIEWS (2): Additional reviews of *Movements in European History* appeared in the *Bookman's Journal and Print Collector*, 13 May 1921 and in the *Reader*, February 1926.

first edition

Psychoanalysis | and the | Unconscious | BY | D. H. LAW-RENCE | [*publisher's device*] | NEW | YORK | THOMAS SELTZER | 1921

Grey paper boards, printed in dark blue on upper cover: PSYCHOANALYSIS | AND THE | UNCONSCIOUS | [*short rule*] | D. H. LAWRENCE; printed in dark blue on spine: PSYCHO- | ANALYSIS | AND THE | UNCON- | SCIOUS | [*short rule*] | D. H. | LAWRENCE | THOMAS | SELTZER The leaves measure $7\frac{3}{8}'' \times 5''$. All edges trimmed.

[i]–[iv] + [1]–[124], as follows: [i]–[iv] blank; [1] half-title; [2] blank; [3] title page as above; [4] Copyright, 1921, by | THOMAS SELTZER, INC. | [*short rule*] | All rights reserved | PRINTED IN THE UNITED STATES OF AMERICA; [5] table of contents; [6] blank; [7] fly-title: PSYCHOANALYSIS | AND THE | UNCONSCIOUS; [8] blank; 9–120 text; [121]–[124] blank.

Published 10 May 1921 at $1.50; the first printing consisted of 2000 copies.

VARIANTS: (1) copy described above.
          (2) as (1) except issued in oyster-white paper boards, printed in black; the leaves measure $7\frac{5}{16}'' \times 5''$; a statement of limitation on page [2] reads: *Special Issue of the First Edition | Limited to 250 copies of which this is | No* . . . .

Variant (2) is reputed to have been released some time after (1) appeared; there are no known numbered or signed copies.

NOTES: *Psychoanalysis and the Unconscious* was apparently written after the departure from England in 1919 and during the Mediterranean residence. Few references to the book appear in the Lawrence letters or other Lawrence literature with the exception of *Son of Woman*, where Murry draws heavily on the psychological writings.

The Seltzer first edition of *Psychoanalysis and the Unconscious* exists in the two forms described here; evidently there was to have been a specially numbered large-paper issue of 250 copies, but no copy examined was numbered, and there is no record of plans for the special issue being brought to completion. When the first edition was exhausted, Seltzer reprinted with a cloth-bound issue.

Secker published the first English edition of the book in July 1923 and reprinted it in the New Adelphi Library in June 1931.

REVIEWS: *Psychoanalysis and the Unconscious* was reviewed in *Survey*, June 1921; by L. L. Buermeyer in the *New York Evening Post Literary Review*, 16 July 1921; in "A Novelist as Psychoanalyist" by George Soule in the *Nation* (New York), 27 July 1921; by Francis Hackett in the *New Republic*, 17 August 1921; as "The Science of the Unconscious" by Adrian Stephen in the *Nation and Athenaeum*, 25 August 1923; and in "Artist Turned Prophet" by Alyse Gregory in the *Dial*, January 1924.

NOTES (2): Mr George Lazarus has in his collection a copy of variant (2) which is inscribed by Lawrence to S. S. Koteliansky, which could be evidence for arguing that it was released before variant (1) on the assumption that Lawrence would give one of the earliest copies to his friend Koteliansky.

Apparently Heinemann took over some of the sheets for *Psychoanalysis and the Unconscious* because an English bookseller has reported a copy with the Heinemann imprint on the title page and the spine, dated 1923.

The Seltzer dust-jacket is grey paper printed in black; the Secker dust-jacket is also grey paper printed in black.

A19   TORTOISES   1921

first edition

TORTOISES | BY | D. H. LAWRENCE | [*publisher's device in orange*] | NEW YORK | THOMAS SELTZER | 1921

Greenish-brown decorative paper boards, upper cover decorated with a colour print of Fujiyama by Hiroshige for the background; a huge tortoise is suspended from a scaffolding by a rope secured around his middle; at the bottom of the scaffolding in pseudo-oriental lettering: TORTOISES | [*double rule marking the base of the scaffolding*] | by | D. H. LAWRENCE; white paper label on spine, printed in black, reading upwards: [*single rule*] | TORTOISES [*short rule forming a dash*] D. H. LAWRENCE | [*single rule*] The leaves measure $9'' \times 6\frac{1}{4}''$. Top edges trimmed; fore and bottom edges untrimmed.

[1]–50, as follows: [1] half-title; [2] blank; [3] title page as above; [4] COPYRIGHT, 1921, BY | THOMAS SELTZER, INC. | [*short rule*] | All rights reserved | *Printed in the United States of America*; [5] table of contents; [6] blank; [7] fly-title: BABY TORTOISE; [8] blank; 9–13 text; [14] blank; [15] fly-title: TORTOISE-SHELL; [16] blank; 17–19 text; [20] blank; [21]

fly-title: TORTOISE FAMILY CONNECTIONS; [22] blank; 23–26 text; [27] fly-title: LUI ET ELLE; [28] blank; 29–35 text; [36] blank; [37] fly-title: TORTOISE GALLANTRY; [38] blank; 39–41 text; [42] blank; [43] fly-title: TORTOISE SHOUT; [44] blank; 45–50 text.

Published 9 December 1921 at $1.00; number of copies unknown.

CONTENTS

Baby Tortoise—Tortoise-Shell—Tortoise Family Connections—Lui et Elle—Tortoise Gallantry—Tortoise Shout.

NOTES: These poems were probably written in Italy during the period when most of the poems in *Birds, Beasts and Flowers* (A27) were composed, and Moore (B57) suggests that they were written at San Gervasio near Florence on the basis of a previously unpublished letter to Catherine Carswell in which Lawrence told her that he wrote in Florence a little book of poetry he liked. This evidence places the composition of the poems in September of 1920 or shortly before.

Tortoises was never published separately in England; there the poems appeared in the Secker edition of *Birds, Beasts and Flowers* (A27b) in November 1923.

REVIEWS: *Tortoises* was reviewed briefly in the *Bookman* (New York), March 1922.

NOTES (2): *Tortoises* was issued in a glassine wrapper.

A20   SEA AND SARDINIA   1921

first edition

SEA AND SARDINIA | BY | D. H. LAWRENCE | WITH EIGHT PICTURES | IN COLOR BY | JAN JUTA | [*publisher's device in orange*] | NEW YORK | THOMAS SELTZER | 1921

Green paper boards with a cream-coloured cloth backstrip, green paper label on spine, printed in blue: SEA | AND | SARDINIA | [*printer's ornament*] | By | D. H. Lawrence | [*printer's ornament*] | THOMAS SELTZER | [*enclosed within a single rule border*] The leaves measure $9\frac{1}{4}''\times 6\frac{1}{4}''$. Top edges trimmed; fore and bottom edges untrimmed.

[1]–[356] with frontispiece and eight illustrations facing pages 44, 100, 148, 180, 204, 236, 268 and 300, as follows: [1] half-title; [2] blank; [3] title page as above; [4] COPYRIGHT, 1921, BY | THOMAS SELTZER, INC.

| [*short rule*] | *All rights reserved* | *Printed in the United States of America* ; [5] table of contents; [6] blank; [7] list of illustrations; [8] blank; [9] fly-title: SEA AND SARDINIA; [10] blank; 11–355 text; [356] blank.

Published 12 December 1921 at $5.00; number of copies unknown.

VARIANTS: (1) copy described above.

(2) as (1) but with brown paper label and backstrip of a slightly more orange colour.

CONTENTS

As Far as Palermo (first appeared in the *Dial*, October 1921 (C85))—The Sea—Cagliari (first appeared in the *Dial*, November 1921 (C86))—Mandas—To Sorgono—To Nuovo—To Terranova and the Steamer—Back.

NOTES: In her book *Lorenzo in Taos* (B35), Mabel Dodge Luhan says it was after reading *Sea and Sardinia* that she wrote Lawrence inviting him to come to New Mexico; his descriptions of the island had convinced her that he was the only one who could adequately portray the Taos country. Lawrence and Frieda made the trip to Sardinia in January 1921, and Lawrence wrote Eleanor Farjeon after their return that he liked the island very much but not as a place to live. In April he wrote Catherine Carswell listing "A Diary of a Trip to Sardinia" among the manuscripts he had ready for placing with publishers. Lawrence considered illustrations necessary for the book and wrote to Cagliari to obtain photographs, but this effort apparently failed, and paintings were eventually used instead. The paintings were done during the summer of 1921 by Jan Juta, a young painter from South Africa, who with his sister had accompanied Lawrence and other friends on a trip to Syracuse in April. At one time Lawrence considered calling the book "Sardinian Films," a possible title he suggested to Curtis Brown in a letter from Florence during negotiations for the illustrations. Unfortunately the manuscript of *Sea and Sardinia* met an ignominious end; Frieda (B40) tells of finding it in the W. C. at Fontana Vecchia.

The illustration facing page 44 in the Seltzer *Sea and Sardinia* is a map drawn by Lawrence; this map appears in the English edition printed in brown on the end-papers.

The first English edition of the book was published by Secker in April 1923, who issued the title in the New Adelphi Library in April 1927. Boni and Liveright published a Uniform Edition in 1931, and it appeared in the Dollar Travel Books with the imprint of McBride in 1931.

Heinemann published the Pocket Edition in 1950, and the Penguin *Sea and Sardinia* was published in 1944.

REVIEWS: *Sea and Sardinia* was reviewed in the *Nation* (New York), 4 January 1922, by Carl Van Doren; as "A Week in D. H. Lawrence" by Francis Hackett in the *New Republic*, 11 January 1922; by I. W. L. in the *Boston Transcript*, 21 January 1922; by J. F. in the *Bookman* (New York), February 1922; by Padraic Colum in the *Dial*, February 1922; the *Review of Reviews*, February 1922; as "Sardinian Days" by H. B. Fuller in the *Freeman*, 1 March 1922; in the *Nation and Athenaeum*, 12 May 1923, as "Mr. Lawrence's Spiritual Home"; and in the *London Mercury*, October 1923, by Clennell Wilkinson.

NOTES (2): All copies of (A20) examined have line 3 on page 127 upside down. Both the English and American editions of *Sea and Sardinia* have a white paper dust-jacket printed in black with a colour illustration of "Fonni" by Jan Juta reproduced on the upper cover.

A21   AARON'S ROD   1922

first edition

AARON'S ROD | BY | D. H. LAWRENCE | [*publisher's device*] | NEW YORK | THOMAS SELTZER | 1922

Light blue-grey cloth boards, printed in black on upper cover: AARON'S | ROD | by | D. H. LAWRENCE | [*enclosed within a blind stamped single rule border; horizontal and vertical rules divide the upper cover; the horizontal rule is broken at the word "by" of the title*]; printed in black on spine: AARON'S | ROD | [*short rule*] | D. H. LAWRENCE | THOMAS | SELTZER The leaves measure $7\frac{5}{16}'' \times 5''$. All edges trimmed.

[1]–[348], as follows: [1] half-title; [2] blank; [3] title page as above; [4] Copyright, 1922, by | THOMAS SELTZER, INC. | [*short rule*] | *All rights reserved* | PRINTED IN THE UNITED STATES OF AMERICA; [5] table of contents; [6] blank; 7–347 text; [348] blank.

Published 14 April 1922 at $2.00; number of copies unknown.

VARIANTS: (1) copy described above.
           (2) as (1) except stamped in gold on upper cover and spine.

NOTES: It was the reading of *Aaron's Rod* as well as *Fantasia of the Unconscious* (A22) which determined John Middleton Murry to found the *Adelphi* as a vehicle for Lawrence's "message." *Aaron's Rod* was apparently begun in Berkshire in 1918, but it was not finished until 1921 in Italy; Lawrence wrote Curtis Brown from Baden-Baden in June 1921 that his American agent, Mountsier, had the first part of *Aaron's Rod*, which he would have to get back and revise before Brown could have it. Lawrence did say the novel was quite finished.

He wrote Donald Carswell from Fontana Vecchia in November that everyone, even Frieda, hated the book except Seltzer, who had written from America that the book was wonderful. Secker apparently had some difficulty in accepting the manuscript as it was and begged Lawrence to make alterations, which Lawrence refused to do.

Lawrence received his copies of the book from Seltzer in June 1922 at Thirroul, New South Wales, Australia, whence he sent Catherine Carswell a copy. Selections from Chapter 14 of *Aaron's Rod* appeared before book publication as "An Episode" in the *Dial*, February 1922 (C89).

The first English edition of *Aaron's Rod* was published by Secker in a printing of 3000 copies in June 1922; Secker also issued the Thin Paper Pocket edition in September 1927. Heinemann published the title in the Cheap Edition in May 1935, and it also appeared as a Guild Book in London in June 1948. Boni and Liveright published the Uniform Edition in 1930, and Grosset and Dunlap issued the title in the Novels of Distinction series in 1933. *Aaron's Rod* is No. 326 of the Albatross Modern Continental Library.

REVIEWS: *Aaron's Rod* was reviewed by L. M. Field in the *New York Times Book Review*, 30 April 1922; by H. W. Boynton in the *Independent*, 27 May 1922; by Dorothy Ogden in the *New York Evening Post Literary Review*, 3 June 1922; as "Love's Exasperations" by Joseph Wood Krutch in the *Nation* (New York), 7 June 1922; in *The Times Literary Supplement*, 22 June 1922; in the *Spectator*, 1 July 1922; by Rebecca West in the *New Statesman*, 8 July 1922; by Gerald Gould in the *Saturday Review*, 15 July 1922; by L. M. R. in the *Freeman*, 26 July 1922; by John Middleton Murry in the *Nation and Athenaeum*, 12 August 1922; by Edward Shanks in the *London Mercury*, October 1922; *English Review*, August 1922; and in *The Chapbook* No. 33, January 1923.

NOTES (2): It is apparent from Lawrence's correspondence with Thomas Seltzer that some concern existed for the possible identification of Argyle in *Aaron's Rod* with Norman Douglas, and for this reason Lawrence authorized Seltzer to make changes in the text depicting Argyle, and in a letter dated 29 December 1921 to Martin Secker Lawrence said he was making "some modifications" in *Aaron's Rod* for Seltzer. However, someone, perhaps without Lawrence's knowledge, excised sections from the Secker text which remained in the American first edition and in all texts descending from the Seltzer publication, and which have not been replaced in any English edition of the novel.

One omission occurs on page 119 on the Secker edition following line 31; the original text appears on page 132, lines 5–11 of the Seltzer edition, and reads:

"But I like children. Very different from the Battenbergs. Oh!—" he wrinkled his nose. "I can't stand the Battenbergs."

"Mount Battens," said Lilly.

"Yes! Awful mistake, changing the royal name. They were Guelfs, why not remain it. Why, I'll tell you what Battenberg did. He was in the Guards, too—"

A more substantial omission of almost three pages of text occurs in Chapter XVII of the Secker edition, the title for which has been changed to "Nel Paradiso" from "High Up Over the Cathedral Square" in the Seltzer book. The text between line 35, page 279 and line 13, page 283 of the Seltzer edition is omitted from the Secker text following line 40 on page 252.

The dust-jacket for the Seltzer *Aaron's Rod* is cream paper printed in black and red; the upper cover is decorated with a flute and leaves. The Secker dust-jacket is cream paper printed in red.

| A22 | FANTASIA OF THE UNCONSCIOUS | 1922 |

first edition

FANTASIA | of the | UNCONSCIOUS | BY | D. H. LAWRENCE | [*publisher's device*] | NEW YORK | THOMAS SELTZER | 1922

Bright blue cloth boards, stamped in gold on upper cover: FANTASIA | OF THE | UNCONSCIOUS | [*short rule*] | D. H. LAWRENCE | [*enclosed within single rule blind stamped border*]; stamped in gold spine: FANTASIA | OF THE | UNCONSCIOUS | [*short rule*] | D. H. LAWRENCE | THOMAS | SELTZER The leaves measure $7\frac{3}{8}'' \times 5''$.

[i]–[xvi] + 1–[300], as follows: [i] half-title; [ii] blank; [iii] title page as above; [iv] Copyright, 1922, by | THOMAS SELTZER, INC. | [*short rule*] | All Rights Reserved | PRINTED IN THE UNITED STATES OF AMERICA; [v]

table of contents; [vi] blank; vii–xv foreword; [xvi] blank; 1–297 text, just below the last line of text: [*short rule*]; [298]–[300] blank.

Published 23 October 1922 at $2.50; number of copies unknown.

NOTES: With *Aaron's Rod* (A21), *Fantasia* was one of the Lawrence books which caused John Middleton Murry to seek to renew their friendship after a long estrangement; Murry had reacted violently over *Women in Love* (A15) in particular. After reading *Fantasia* Murry wrote Lawrence that the *Adelphi* would be held in trust for Lawrence himself, if only he would come back to England. For the first issue of the *Adelphi* in June 1923 Murry reprinted Chapter Four of *Fantasia*, "Trees and Babies and Papas and Mamas", and continued to reprint other chapters in succeeding issues. The last issue of the magazine edited by Murry, the Lawrence memorial issue, June–August 1930 (C202), printed portions of *Fantasia of the Unconscious*.

The first English edition of *Fantasia* was published by Secker in a printing of 1000 copies in September 1923; this English edition did not contain the Epilogue present in the Seltzer *Fantasia* inasmuch as Lawrence had addressed the Epilogue particularly to America. Secker issued the book in the New Adelphi Library in April 1930, and Boni and Liveright in America published the Uniform Edition in 1930.

REVIEWS: Reviews of *Fantasia* appeared in *Survey*, 15 December 1922; by Paul Shorey in the *Independent*, 23 December 1922; by B. L. Burman in the *Nation* (New York), 17 January 1923; by Will Cuppy in the *New York Herald Tribune Books*, 14 January 1923; as "Artist Turned Prophet" by Alyse Gregory in the *Dial*, January 1923; in the *Bookman* (New York), March 1923; and as "Relevancy" by John Middleton Murry in the *Nation and Athenaeum*, 31 March 1923.

NOTES (2): After the first issue of the *Adelphi* in June 1923, which contained Chapter Four of *Fantasia of the Unconscious*, Murry printed Chapter Eight, "Education and Sex in Man, Woman and Child" under the title, "Education and Sex" in the issue for July. The *Adelphi* for September contained excerpts from Chapters Eleven and Twelve under the title "On Love and Marriage."

A variant of the Seltzer *Fantasia* has been identified; there is no evidence to establish its priority, but of the six copies at the University of Texas, only one copy is without the blind stamped border on the upper cover.

VARIANTS: (1) copy described above.
    (2) as (1) but without the blind stamped border on the upper cover.

The Seltzer dust-jacket for *Fantasia* is light grey paper printed in black; the Secker dust-jacket is dark grey paper printed in black.

A23   ENGLAND, MY ENGLAND   1922

first edition

ENGLAND | MY ENGLAND | AND OTHER STORIES | BY | D. H. LAWRENCE | [*publisher's device*] | NEW YORK | THOMAS SELTZER | 1922

Blue-grey cloth boards, stamped in gold on upper cover: ENGLAND | MY | ENGLAND | by | D. H. LAWRENCE | [*enclosed within single rule blind stamped border; horizontal and vertical blind stamped rules divide the upper cover; the horizontal rule is broken at the word "by" in the lettering*]; stamped in gold on spine: ENGLAND | MY | ENGLAND | [*short rule*] | D. H. LAWRENCE | THOMAS | SELTZER The leaves measure $7\frac{3}{8}'' \times 5''$. All edges trimmed.

[i]–[vi] + [1]–[274], as follows: [i] half-title; [ii] blank; [iii] title page as above; [iv] Copyright, 1922, by | THOMAS SELTZER, INC. | [*short rule*] | *All Rights Reserved* | PRINTED IN THE UNITED STATES OF AMERICA; [v] table of contents; [vi] blank; [1] fly-title: ENGLAND, MY ENGLAND; [2] blank; 3–47 text; [48] blank; [49] fly-title: TICKETS, PLEASE; [50] blank; 51–68 text; [69] fly-title; THE BLIND MAN; [70] blank; 71–97 text; [98] blank; [99] fly-title: MONKEY NUTS; [100] blank; 101–119 text; [120] blank; [121] fly-title: WINTRY PEACOCK; [122] blank; 123–144 text; [145] fly-title: YOU TOUCHED ME; [146] blank; 147–171 text; [172] blank; [173] fly-title: SAMSON AND DELILAH; [174] blank; 175–197 text; [198] blank; [199] fly-title: THE PRIMROSE PATH; [200] blank; 201–221 text; [222] blank; [223] fly-title: THE HORSE DEALER'S DAUGHTER; [224] blank; 225–249 text; [250] blank; [251] fly-title: FANNY AND ANNIE; [252] blank; 253–273 text; [274] blank.

Published 24 October 1922 at $2.00; number of copies unknown.

CONTENTS

England, My England (first appeared in the *English Review*, October 1915 (C38))—Tickets, Please (first appeared in the *Strand*, April 1919 (C62))—The Blind Man (first appeared in the *English Review*, July 1920 (C72))—Monkey Nuts (first appeared in the *Sovereign*, August 1922 (C97))—Wintry Peacock (first appeared in the *Metropolitan*, August 1921 (C34); first collected in *The New Decameron III* (B10))—You Touched Me (first appeared in *Land and Water*, 29 April 1920 (C71))—Samson

and Delilah (first appeared in the *English Review*, March 1917 (C43))—
The Primrose Path—The Horse Dealer's Daughter (first appeared in
the *English Review*, April 1922 (C91))—Fanny and Annie (first appeared
in *Hutchinson's Magazine*, 21 November 1921 (C87)).

NOTES: Lawrence wrote Martin Secker from Taos in September 1922
that Seltzer was calling a projected volume of stories *England, My England*,
the first collected volume of short stories since *The Prussian Officer* (A6)
eight years before. In accordance with Lawrence's usual practice, most
of these stories had prior publication in periodicals before being collected
in book form, and in fact it was customary for Lawrence to publish a
story in magazines in both the United States and England at about the
same time, and occasionally a story appeared in an anthology as well.
He frequently rewrote these stories between publications; consequently
it is quite possible for the student to be faced with the problem of some
three separate versions of a story, all of which were circulating in print
at approximately the same time.

The story "The Primrose Path," the only one in *England, My England*
for which a previous printing has not been traced, is a very early story,
one which Lawrence had submitted to Edward Garnett for criticism,
probably before he left England for the first time. He wrote Garnett
asking for the return of the manuscript in 1913 and sent another letter
eight years later asking for the same manuscript. The completed
"Primrose Path" was forwarded to Curtis Brown with other stories for
England, My England in December 1921.

Secker published the first English edition in January 1924 and the
Pocket Edition in February 1928; Heinemann issued a Pocket Edition,
and in the United States Boni and Liveright published a Uniform Edition
in 1930. *England, My England* is No. 4825 in the Tauchnitz Collection
of English and American Authors, 1933.

REVIEWS: *England, My England* was reviewed in the *New York Times Book
Review*, 19 November 1922; by L. Kantore in the *New York Herald Tribune
Books*, 24 December 1922; by B. L. Burman in the *Nation* (New York),
17 January 1923; as "English Types and Settings" by Arthur W. Colton
in the *New York Evening Post Literary Review*, 10 February 1923; by
E. B. C. Jones in the *Nation and Athenaeum*, 23 February 1924; by
J. B. Priestley in the *London Mercury*, March 1924; and in the *Literary
Digest International Book Review*, March 1923.

NOTES (2): Although it was quite usual for Lawrence to make changes
in the text of his work whenever an opportunity presented itself, his
treatment of "Wintry Peacock" is a good illustration of the difficulties

which lay in wait for the unwary Lawrence scholar. The story was originally published in the *Metropolitan* (C84); for the *New Decameron* (B10) Lawrence chose to alter the character of Alfred, making him a chauffeur who travelled with his employer on the continent, but for *England, My England*, a collection of stories related to the war, he restored the original reading of the *Metropolitan* in which Alfred was a soldier recently come from France to recover from a wound.

The dust-jacket for the Seltzer *England, My England* is tan paper printed in black; the Secker dust-jacket is cream paper printed in red.

REVIEWS (2): Additional reviews of *England, My England* appeared in the *New York Times Book Review* for 10 February 1924 by Filson Young; the *Weekly Westminster* for February 23 by Humbert Wolfe; and *Yale Review* for July 1923 by Rebecca West.

A24 THE LADYBIRD 1923

a. *first edition*

THE LADYBIRD | THE FOX: THE CAPTAIN'S DOLL | BY D. H. LAWRENCE | LONDON | MARTIN SECKER | NUMBER FIVE JOHN STREET ADELPHI

Chocolate-brown cloth boards, blind stamped on upper and lower cover: [*thick rule enclosed within thin rule forming border*]; stamped in gold on spine: [*thin rule*] | [*thick rule*] | THE | LADYBIRD |·| D. H. | LAWRENCE | SECKER | [*thick rule*] | [*thin rule*] The leaves measure $7\frac{1}{2}'' \times 4\frac{7}{8}''$. Top and fore edges trimmed; bottom edges rough-trimmed.

[1]–[256], as follows: [1] half-title; [2] list of books by D. H. Lawrence; [3] title page as above; [4] LONDON: MARTIN SECKER (LTD.), 1923; 5 table of contents; [6] blank; [7] fly-title: THE LADYBIRD; [8] blank; 9–82 text; [83] fly-title: THE FOX; [84] blank; 85–159 text; [160] blank; [161] fly-title: THE CAPTAIN'S DOLL; [162] blank; 163–255 text, at bottom of page 255: [*short rule*] | PRINTED IN GREAT BRITAIN BY | THE DUNEDIN PRESS LIMITED, EDINBURGH; [256] excerpts from reviews of *The Lost Girl, Women in Love* and *Aaron's Rod*.

Published March 1923 at 7s. 6d.; the first printing consisted of 3000 copies.

b. *first American edition*

THE | CAPTAIN'S DOLL | THREE NOVELETTES | BY | D. H. LAWRENCE | [*publisher's device*] | NEW YORK | THOMAS SELTZER | 1923

Blue-grey cloth boards, stamped in gold on upper cover: THE | CAPTAIN'S | DOLL | by | D. H. LAWRENCE | [*lettering appears in the right of two equal panels formed by a vertical blind stamped rule; horizontal blind stamped rule crosses upper cover at line four of lettering; blind stamped rule encloses all of above forming border*]; stamped in gold on spine: THE | CAPTAIN'S | DOLL | [*short rule*] | D. H. LAWRENCE | THOMAS | SELTZER The leaves measure $7\frac{3}{8}'' \times 5''$. All edges trimmed.

[i]–[vi] + [1]–[326], as follows: [i] half-title; [ii] list of books by D. H. Lawrence; [iii] title page as above; [iv] Copyright, 1923, by | THOMAS SELTZER, INC. | [*short rule*] | *All rights reserved* | PRINTED IN THE UNITED STATES OF AMERICA; [v] table of contents; [vi] blank; [1] fly-title: THE CAPTAIN'S DOLL; [2] blank; 3–123 text; [124] blank; [125] fly-title: THE FOX; [126] blank; 127–224 text; [225] fly-title: THE LADYBIRD; [226] blank; 227–323 text; [324]–[326] blank.

Published 14 November 1923 at $2.00; number of copies unknown.

CONTENTS

The Ladybird—The Fox (appeared in the *Dial*, May (C92), June (C93), July (C95) and August 1922 (C96); see (C73.5))—The Captain's Doll.

NOTES: Lawrence wrote Jan Juta, the artist who illustrated *Sea and Sardinia*, from Fontana Vecchia in January 1922 that he had just sent off three manuscripts to Curtis Brown, who arranged for their publication in England as *The Ladybird* and in the United States as *The Captain's Doll* (A24b). Lawrence also told Jan Juta that he thought the three long stories would make a "really interesting" book. "The Ladybird" was the last of the three stories to be made ready for publication according to a letter to Curtis Brown from Fontana Vecchia in December 1921 in which Lawrence said he was writing a third "longish" story to go with "The Fox" and "The Captain's Doll." It is a longer version of "The Thimble" (C44).

"The Captain's Doll" was written in part at least in Austria but completed in Italy; a note in the diary transcribed by Tedlock (B51) records that Lawrence had almost finished with the story on 21 October 1921. Catherine Carswell tells about some authentic information concerning Scottish tartans which her husband supplied Lawrence while he was writing the story. Lawrence wrote to Secker from Taos in September 1922 that Hearst was paying him a thousand dollars for "The Captain's Doll" for the *International*; however, there seems to be no record of its publication in the Hearst magazine.

Secker published *The Ladybird* in the Pocket Edition in February 1928, and Boni and Liveright issued *The Captain's Doll* as a Bonibook in 1930 and in the Uniform Edition in 1931.

REVIEWS: Reviews of *The Ladybird* and *The Captain's Doll* appeared in *The Times Literary Supplement*, 22 March 1923; by Raymond Mortimer in the *New Statesman*, 31 March 1923; by Gerald Gould in the *Saturday Review*, 31 March 1923; the *Spectator*, 14 April 1923; in the *New York Times Book Review*, 22 April 1923; by Heywood Broun in the *New York World*, 22 April 1923; by H. W. Boynton in the *Independent*, 26 May 1923; by Burton Rascoe in the *New York Herald Tribune Books*, 27 May 1923; by J. B. Priestley in the *London Mercury*, May 1923; by A. W. Colton in the *New York Evening Post Literary Review*, 2 June 1923; by John Macy in the *Nation* (New York), 6 June 1923; and by Leo Markun in the *Literary Digest International Book Review*, July 1923.

NOTES (2): Dr Brian Finney, who is editing a volume of the short fiction for the Cambridge edition of Lawrence, has discovered from the manuscript (E187) that two pages of text for "The Ladybird" were inadvertently omitted from all published versions of the story. See (C265).

An odd copy of *The Ladybird* has been reported by a London bookseller; apparently because of requirements for exporting copies of the book, the following statement was rubber stamped on page [4]: MADE AND PRINTED | IN GREAT BRITAIN.

For the first periodical publication of "The Fox" see (C73.5).

The dust-jacket for *The Ladybird* is cream paper printed in red. The dust-jacket for *The Captain's Doll* was designed by Knud Merrild, see (B47); it is of white paper printed in red, blue and black, and the upper cover has drawings in colour of a doll, a fox and the figure of a toy soldier.

A25   STUDIES IN CLASSIC   1923
AMERICAN LITERATURE

a. *first edition*

STUDIES IN | CLASSIC AMERICAN | LITERATURE | BY D. H. LAWRENCE | [*publisher's device*] | NEW YORK | THOMAS SELTZER | 1923

Dark blue cloth boards, stamped in gold on upper cover: STUDIES IN CLASSIC | AMERICAN LITERATURE | [*short rule*] | D. H. LAWRENCE | [*enclosed within single rule, blind stamped border*]; stamped in gold on spine: STUDIES

| IN | CLASSIC | AMERICAN | LITERATURE | D. H. | LAWRENCE | THOMAS | SELTZER | The leaves measure 9″ × 6¼″. Top edges trimmed and stained blue; fore and bottom edges rough-trimmed.

[i]–[x] + 1–[266], as follows: [i] half-title; [ii] list of works by D. H. Lawrence; [iii] title page as above; [iv] Copyright, 1923, by | THOMAS SELTZER, INC. | [*short rule*] | *All Rights Reserved* | PRINTED IN THE UNITED STATES OF AMERICA; [v] table of contents; [vi] blank; vii–ix foreword; [x] blank; 1–264 text; [265]–[266] blank.

Published 27 August 1923 at $3.00; number of copies unknown.

b. *first edition, early version*

D. H. LAWRENCE | [*ornamental rule*] | The Symbolic | Meaning | The uncollected versions of | *Studies in Classic American Literature* | Edited by | ARMIN ARNOLD | with a Preface by | HARRY T. MOORE | CENTAUR PRESS LIMITED

Black cloth boards, stamped in gold on spine: The | Symbolic | Meaning | D. H. | LAWRENCE | Armin | Arnold | [*preceding seven lines on a white background enclosed within an oval rule*] | CENTAUR | PRESS The leaves measure 8½″ × 5⅜″. All edges trimmed; top edges stained purple.

[i]–[xii] + 1–264, as follows: [i] half-title; [ii] list of books by Armin Arnold; [iii] title page as above; [iv] [*copyright notices*] | *First published in 1962 by the Centaur Press Ltd. of* | *Fontwell, Arundel, and printed in Great Britain by* | *T. J. Winterson, London, in 11 on 13 pt. Baskerville*; [v] contents; [vi] blank; vii acknowledgements; [viii] blank; ix–xi preface; [xii] blank; 1–11 introduction; [12] quotation from "The Spirit of Place"; [13] fly-title: 1. THE SPIRIT | OF PLACE; [14] blank; 15–31 text; [32] blank; [33] fly-title: 2. BENJAMIN | FRANKLIN; [34] blank; 35–49 text; [50] blank; [51] fly-title: 3. HECTOR ST. JOHN | DE CREVECOEUR; [52] blank; 53–70 text; [71] fly-title: 4. FENIMORE COOPER'S | ANGLO-AMERICAN | NOVELS; [72] blank; 73–87 text; [88] blank; [89] fly-title: 5. FENIMORE COOPER'S | LEATHERSTOCKING NOVELS; [90] blank; 91–111 text; [112] blank; [113] fly-title: 6. EDGAR ALLAN POE; [114] blank; 115–130 text; [131] fly-title: 7. NATHANIEL HAWTHORNE I; [132] blank; 133–158 text; [159] fly-title: 8. NATHANIEL HAWTHORNE II; [160] blank; 161–172 text; [173] fly-title: 9. THE TWO | PRINCIPLES; [174] blank; 175–189 text; [190] blank; [191] fly-title: 10. DANA'S TWO YEARS | BEFORE THE MAST; [192] blank; 193–214 text; [215] fly-title: 11. HERMAN MELVILLE'S | TYPEE AND OMOO.; [216] blank; 217–229 text; [230] blank; [231]

fly-title: 12. HERMAN MELVILLE'S | MOBY DICK; [232] blank; 233–250 text; [251] fly-title: 13. WHITMAN; [252] blank; 253–264 text.

Published 7 May 1962 at 35s.; 2000 copies were printed.

CONTENTS

Foreword—The Spirit of Place (first appeared in the *English Review*, November 1918 (C55))—Benjamin Franklin (first appeared in the *English Review*, December 1918 (C56))—Hector St. John Crèvecoeur (first appeared in the *English Review*, January 1919 (C57))— Fenimore Cooper's White Novels (first appeared in the *English Review*, February 1919 (C58), as "Fenimore Cooper's Anglo-American Novels")—Fenimore Cooper's Leatherstocking Novels (first appeared in the *English Review*, March 1919 (C60))—Edgar Allan Poe (first appeared in the *English Review*, April 1919 (C61))—Nathaniel Hawthorne and "The Scarlet Letter" (first appeared in the *English Review*, May 1919 (C64) as "Nathaniel Hawthorne")—Hawthorne's "Blithedale Romance"— Dana's "Two Years Before the Mast"— Herman Melville's "Typee" and "Omoo"—Herman Melville's "Moby Dick"—Whitman (first appeared in the *Nation and Athenaeum*, 23 July 1921 (C83)). Early version only: The Two Principles (first appeared in the *English Review*, June 1919 (C65)).

NOTES: Lawrence's project for his *Studies in Classic American Literature* was conceived in January 1917, and he began to write them during the following months. While he was in Cornwall, Lawrence wrote the agent Pinker several letters in which he spoke of his desire to go to America to write a series of essays on American literature and perhaps lecture in the United States. In March 1918 from Berkshire he wrote Cecil Gray that the American essays were in their final form, and a letter to Mrs S. A. Hopkin in June revealed that he was working on "Whitman," the last of them. Although all twelve of the essays included in the published *Studies* were completed in an early version by February 1919, for some reason the two essays on Melville, the one on Dana and "Hawthorne's Blithedale Romance" were not published in magazines as were the others; Lawrence wrote Harriet Monroe in February that all twelve were finished and noted that he had worked hard on them for four years and wanted to see them appear in book form in the United States. However, all of the published essays were considerably rewritten before publication in book form.

The first English edition was published by Martin Secker in a printing of 1000 copies in June 1924; the Secker *Studies* did not contain the "Foreword," which was designed especially for the American edition.

Studies in Classic American Literature was issued by Boni and Liveright in the Uniform Edition in 1931 and by Secker in the New Adelphi Library in April 1933.

REVIEWS: The *Studies* were reviewed in "On the Sin of Being an American" by Maurice Francis Egan in the *Literary Digest International Book Review*, September 1923; as "D. H. Lawrence Bombs Our Literary Shrines" in *Current Opinion*, September 1923; by I. Brock in the *New York Times Book Review*, 16 September 1923; in "The American Spirit" by John Macy in the *Nation* (New York), 10 October 1923; in the *New York Evening Post Literary Review*, 20 October 1923, as "America is Discovered" by Stuart P. Sherman; in "Mr. Lawrence on American Literature" by K. L. Daniels in the *New Republic*, 24 October 1923; in "Mr. D. H. Lawrence's Criticism" by Newton Arvin in the *Freeman*, 31 October 1923; by R. M. Weaver in the *Bookman* (New York), November 1923; in "Artist Turned Prophet" by Alyse Gregory in the *Dial*, January 1924; in "Mr. Lawrence Sensationalist" by Conrad Aiken in the *Nation and Athenaeum*, 12 July 1924; in *The Times Literary Supplement*, 24 July 1924, as "Mr. Lawrence's American Studies"; in "Mr. Lawrence's Criticism" by J. E. H. in the *New Statesman*, 2 August 1924; by Edward Shanks in the *London Mercury*, October 1924; and in *Life and Letters*, 10 August 1924.

NOTES (2): As was the case with several other Lawrence books, when Heinemann purchased the rights to Lawrence's work from Secker, a number of sets of the Secker sheets were included in the sale and subsequently were issued with a cancel title page in a Heinemann binding.

The Seltzer dust-jacket for *Studies in Classic American Literature* is cream paper printed in black and red; the Secker dust-jacket is dark grey-green paper printed in black.

A26　　　　　KANGAROO　　　　　1923

first edition

KANGAROO | BY | D. H. LAWRENCE |LONDON | MARTIN SECKER | NUMBER FIVE JOHN STREET ADELPHI

Chocolate-brown cloth boards, blind stamped on the upper and lower covers: [*thick rule within thin rule forming border*]; stamped in gold on spine:

[*thin rule*] | [*thick rule*] | KANGAROO | · | D. H. | LAWRENCE | SECKER |
[*thick rule*] | [*thin rule*] The leaves measure $7\frac{1}{2}'' \times 4\frac{15}{16}''$. Top and fore edges
trimmed; bottom edges untrimmed.

[i]–[ii] + [i]–[vi] + 1–[408], as follows: [i]–[ii] blank; [i] half-title; [ii]
blank; [iii] title page as above; [iv] LONDON: MARTIN SECKER (LTD.),
1923.; v table of contents; [vi] blank; 1–402 text, at bottom of page
402: [*short rule*] | PRINTED IN GREAT BRITAIN BY | THE DUNEDIN PRESS
LIMITED, EDINBURGH; [403]–[408] lists of works by Secker authors.

Published September 1923 at 7*s.* 6*d.*; the first printing consisted of 3000
copies.

NOTES: *Kangaroo* is Lawrence's Australian novel; at one time he expressed
the desire to write a novel for each of the world's continents, and he
might have accomplished this ambition had he been permitted a few
more years of work. He wrote Catherine Carswell in June 1922 from
Thirroul, New South Wales, that he was half through with a novel on
Australia. The manuscript was sent to Mountsier for the preparation
of a typescript for which Lawrence was still waiting after his arrival in
Taos. The printer's proofs were corrected in August 1923 according to
a letter to Middleton Murry dated that month from New York.

The first American edition of *Kangaroo* was published by Thomas
Seltzer from new plates on 17 September 1923. Secker reprinted the
first edition in an issue of 1000 copies in 1923 and published the Pocket
Edition in April 1950. The Heinemann Pocket Edition appeared in
April 1950 with an introduction by Richard Aldington. *Kangaroo* is
No. 354 in the Albatross Modern Continental Library.

Chapter XII of *Kangaroo* was published as "The Nightmare" in
J. P. Cooney's quarterly, *Phoenix*, Autumn 1940.

REVIEWS: *Kangaroo* was reviewed in *The Times Literary Supplement*, 20
September 1923; by Raymond Mortimer in the *New Statesman*, 29
September 1923; by P. B. W. in the *Boston Transcript*, 13 October 1923;
as "An Australian Reformer and an English Vicar" by F. W. Stokes in
the *Nation and Athenaeum*, 13 October 1923; the *New York Times Book
Review*, 14 October 1923; as "Wasteland" by Joseph Wood Krutch in
the *Nation* (New York), 7 November 1923; by H. W. Boynton in the
Independent, 10 November 1923; by H. J. Seligmann in the *New York
Herald Tribune Books*, 14 October 1923; by Henry Seidel Canby in the
New York Evening Post Literary Review, 17 November 1923; by J. B. Priestley in the *London Mercury*, November 1923; in "Some Autumn Novels"
by J. D. Beresford in the *Nation and Athenaeum*, 8 December 1923; in the

Literary Digest International Book Review, December 1923; and in "Artist Turned Prophet" by Alyse Gregory in the *Dial,* January 1924.

NOTES (2): Although the first edition of the bibliography gave precedence to the Secker *Kangaroo,* Lawrence insisted in letters to Martin Secker and Curtis Brown that the English edition of the novel was not to be published until the Seltzer edition appeared. Thus the American edition may have been published first, but both the English and the American editions are important because their texts differ radically.

These differences occur throughout the text, but those concerning the war in the Nightmare Chapter are particularly significant, and to complicate matters the English edition of *Kangaroo* has some four substantial paragraphs at the end of the book which do not appear in the American edition.

F. P. Jarvis in *Papers of the Bibliographical Society of America,* 59 (1965) pp. 400–424, notes differences in the two editions and concludes that the American text is the more reliable; however, a complete explanation of the circumstances responsible for the differences will probably have to wait for results of the study now being done for the Cambridge Press edition of *Kangaroo.*

From Lawrence's correspondence it is clear that he finished a first draft of the novel in Australia and posted the manuscript to Robert Mountsier in New York via the S. S. *Makura* on 20 July 1922. Sometime in October Mountsier returned a typescript to Lawrence in Taos. By 16 October Lawrence wrote both Seltzer and Mountsier that he had gone over the typescript making many changes, added a new last chapter and that the book was now as he wanted it. The corrected typescript was posted to Mountsier on 25 October. From this point onwards the history of the text is somewhat vague. Mr John Grover, who is preparing a proposal for editing the Cambridge *Kangaroo,* has suggested that Lawrence also had a carbon of the corrected typescript which he returned to Mountsier who then prepared two new typescripts by combining unchanged pages from the corrected typescript with retyped pages incorporating Lawrence's corrections and additions, one intended for Thomas Seltzer, the other for Martin Secker.

It is known that Lawrence corrected proofs of *Kangaroo* for Seltzer in New York in July 1923 and that he sent a copy of the corrected proofs to Curtis Brown before the end of July which apparently did not reach Secker in time for the English printer to make the alterations in accordance with Lawrence's corrections. The Secker edition would then have been set from the corrected typescript prepared by Mountsier rather than from the corrected Seltzer proofs as Lawrence probably intended.

Thus as Mr Grover maintains most of the differences in the English and American texts represent corrections and additions made by Lawrence on the Seltzer proofs. The omission of several passages in the Nightmare Chapter and elsewhere in the English edition evidently result from Martin Secker's efforts to censor passages he considered unsuitable.

The matter of the additional paragraphs at the end of the English text remains to be explained. Lawrence wrote Seltzer on 4 January 1923 and Curtis Brown on 10 February that he was enclosing the last page of *Kangaroo*, carefully warning both of them not to lose it. Perhaps the page sent to Seltzer was lost.

The dust-jacket of the Secker *Kangaroo* is cream paper printed in red; the Seltzer dust-jacket is off-white printed in color showing a ship leaving port.

REVIEWS (2): Additional reviews of *Kangaroo* appeared in the *Spectator* (London) for 6 October 1923 by Martin Armstrong; by Gerald Gould in the *Saturday Review* for 29 September; the *Baltimore Evening Sun* for 13 October by Amy F. Greif, and in *Observer* for September by J. C. Squire.

A27   BIRDS, BEASTS AND FLOWERS   1923

a. *first edition*

BIRDS, BEASTS | AND FLOWERS | BY | D. H. LAW-RENCE [*publisher's device*] | PUBLISHED BY THOMAS SELTZER | NEW YORK MCMXXIII

Strawberry-pink cloth boards, white paper label on spine, printed in red: *Birds,* | *Beasts* | *and* | *Flowers* | D. H. | LAWRENCE The leaves measure $8\frac{1}{4}'' \times 6\frac{1}{4}''$. Top edges trimmed; fore and bottom edges rough-trimmed.

[i]–[xii] + 1–180, as follows: [i] half-title; [ii] blank; [iii] title page as above; [iv] Copyright, 1923, by | THOMAS SELTZER, INC. | [*short rule*] | *All rights reserved* | PRINTED IN THE UNITED STATES OF AMERICA; [v] acknowledgements; [vi] blank; vii–ix table of contents; [x] blank; [xi] fly-title: BIRDS, BEASTS | AND FLOWERS; [xii] blank; 1–180 text.

Published 9 October 1923 at $2.50; number of copies unknown.

b. *first English edition*

BIRDS, BEASTS | AND FLOWERS | POEMS BY | D. H. LAWRENCE | LONDON | MARTIN SECKER | NUMBER FIVE JOHN STREET | ADELPHI

Yellow paper boards with a black cloth backstrip, yellow paper label
on spine, printed in black: [*single rule*] | BIRDS, BEASTS | AND FLOWERS
| POEMS | BY | D. H. LAWRENCE | [*short rule*] | SECKER | [*single rule*] The
leaves measure $8\frac{3}{4}'' \times 5\frac{5}{8}''$. Top edges trimmed and stained black; fore
and bottom edges untrimmed.

[1]–[208], as follows: [1] half-title; [2] list of books by D. H. Lawrence;
[3] title page as above; [4] Printed in Great Britain | by The Riverside
Press Limited | Edinburgh | LONDON: MARTIN SECKER (LTD.) 1923; [5]
acknowledgements; [6] blank; 7–8 table of contents; [9] fly-title: FRUITS;
[10] blank; 11–33 text; [34] blank; [35] fly-title: TREES; [36] blank;
37–47 text; [48] blank; [49] fly-title: FLOWERS; [50] blank; 51–70 text;
[71] fly-title: THE EVANGELISTIC BEASTS; [72] blank; 73–86 text; [87]
fly-title: CREATURES; [88] blank; 89–110 text; [111] fly-title: REPTILES;
[112] blank; 113–138 text; [139] fly-title: BIRDS; [140] blank; 141–151
text; [152] blank; [153] fly-title: ANIMALS; [154] blank; 155–193 text;
[194] blank; [195] fly-title: GHOSTS; [196] blank; 197–207 text; [208]
blank.

Published November 1923 at 10s. 6d.; the first printing consisted of 1000
copies.

c. *first illustrated edition* (*ordinary copies*)

BIRDS, BEASTS | AND FLOWERS | Poems by D. H. LAW-
RENCE [*printed in red*] | WITH WOOD-ENGRAVINGS BY |
BLAIR HUGHES-STANTON | THE CRESSET PRESS
LTD. | LONDON MCMXXX

Decorative marbled paper boards with vellum backstrip, stamped in
gold on upper and lower covers: [*vertical rule at edge of vellum backstrip*];
stamped in gold on spine: [*decorative rule*] | Birds | Beasts | and | Flowers |
[*five-pointed star*] | D. H. | Lawrence | Cresset | Press | [decorative rule]
The leaves measure $13\frac{3}{8}'' \times 8\frac{5}{8}''$. Top edges trimmed and gilt; fore and
bottom edges untrimmed.

[i]–[viii] + [1]–[196], as follows: [1] half-title; [ii] *This edition is limited
to 500 copies on* | *mould-made paper numbered 1–500,* | *and to 30 copies on
Batchelor's hand-* | *made paper, of which numbers A,* | *B, and C will be accompan-*
| *ied by a separate set* | *of signed proofs* | *This copy is No.* 376 [*autograph
number in black ink*]; [iii] blank; [iv] frontispiece ; [v] title page as above;
[vi] PRINTED IN ENGLAND | AT THE SHENVAL PRESS; [vii]–[viii] table of
contents; [1] blank; [2] illustration; [3] fly-title: FRUITS | [*preface for*

fruits]; [4] blank; 5–25 text; [26]–[27] blank; [28] illustration; [29] fly-title: TREES | [*preface for trees*]; [30] blank; 31–38 text; [39] *blank*; [40] illustration; [41] fly-title: FLOWERS | [*preface for flowers*]; [42] blank; 43–59 text; [60]–[61] blank; [62] illustration; [63] fly-title: THE EVANGELISTIC BEASTS | [*preface for evangelistic beasts*]; [64] blank; 65–77 text; [78]–[79] blank; [80] illustration; [81] fly-title: CREATURES | [*preface for creatures*]; [82] blank; 83–101 text; [102]–[103] blank; [104] illustration; [105] fly-title: REPTILES | [*preface for reptiles*]; [106] blank; 107–128 text; [129] blank; [130] illustration; [131] fly-title: BIRDS | [*preface for birds*]; [132] blank; 133–142 text; [143] blank; [144] illustration; [145] fly-title: ANIMALS | [*preface for animals*]; [146] blank; 147–180 text; [181] blank; [182] illustration; [183] fly-title: GHOSTS | [*preface for ghosts*]; [184] blank; 185–[195] text; [196] Printed at | The Shenval Press | mcmxxx

Published June 1930 at 30*s.*; 500 ordinary copies were printed.

d. *first illustrated edition* (*hand-made paper copies*)

BIRDS, BEASTS | AND FLOWERS | Poems by D. H. LAWRENCE [*printed in red*] | WITH WOOD-ENGRAVINGS BY | BLAIR HUGHES-STANTON | THE CRESSET PRESS LTD. | LONDON MCMXXX

The same as (c) except printed on Batchelor's hand-made paper and bound in tan pigskin; stamped in gold on spine: BIRDS | BEASTS | AND | FLOWERS | D. H. | LAWRENCE | CRESSET | PRESS

VARIANTS: (1) copy described above, accompanied by a separate set of proofs not signed.

(2) as (1) except numbered A, B and C and accompanied by separate set of signed proofs of the illustrations; three copies only, bound in black pigskin.

Published June 1930 at 63*s.*; 30 copies were printed on hand-made paper.

CONTENTS

Fruits: Pomegranate (first appeared in the *Dial*, March 1921 (C78)); Peach; Medlars and Sorb-Apples (first appeared in the *New Republic*, 5 January 1921 (C75)); Figs; Grapes—The Revolutionary (first appeared in the *New Republic*, 19 January 1921 (C76))—The Evening Land (first appeared in *Poetry*, November 1922 (C99))—Peace (first appeared in *Nation*, 10 Oct 1923 (C112.5))—Trees: Cypresses (C111); Bare Fig-Trees;

Bare Almond-Trees (C112.5)—Tropic (C112.5)—Southern Night—Flowers: Almond Blossom (first appeared in the *English Review*, February 1922 (C90)); Purple Anemones; Sicilian Cyclamens; Hibiscus and Salvia Flowers—The Evangelistic Beasts: St. Matthew (first appeared in *Poetry*, April 1923 (C106)); St. Mark (first appeared in the *Dial*, April 1921 (C79)); St. Luke (first appeared in the *Dial*, April 1921 (C79)); St. John (first appeared in the *Dial*, April 1921 (C79))—Creatures: Mosquito (first appeared in the *Bookman* (New York), July 1921 (C81)); Fish (first appeared in the *English Review*, June 1922 (C94)); Bat (first appeared in the *English Review*, November 1922 (C98); also in the *Literary Review*, 30 December 1922); Man and Bat—Reptiles: Snake (first appeared in the *Dial*, July 1921 (C82); first collected in *Georgian Poetry 1920–1922* (B11))—Birds: Turkey-Cock (first appeared in *Poetry*, November 1922 (C99)); Humming-Bird (first appeared in the *New Republic*, May 1921 (C80)); Eagle in New Mexico; The Blue Jay—Animals: The Ass; He-Goat; She-Goat; Elephant (first appeared in the *English Review*, April 1923 (C104)); Kangaroo; Bibbles; Mountain Lion; The Red Wolf—Ghosts: Men in New Mexico; Autumn at Taos (appeared in *Palms*, Autumn 1923 as "Autumn in New Mexico"); Spirits Summoned West (appeared in the *Adelphi*, October 1923; see (C111))—The American Eagle.

NOTES: In a way, *Birds, Beasts and Flowers* forms a literary bridge between Europe and America; most of the poems were written in Sicily, but some of the later ones were written at Taos, New Mexico. These "New Mexico" poems were offered to Harriet Monroe for *Poetry* in a letter written from Del Monte Ranch in February 1922. Lawrence began to collect the poems for publication before he left Fontana Vecchia, for he offered them to Curtis Brown in April 1921 at the time he asked Brown to represent him as his literary agent. The manuscript was sent to Seltzer from Taos, and Lawrence corrected the proofs while he was in New York in August 1923. The group of poems called "Animals" is particularly interesting for they form almost a zoological map of the Lawrence travels; "The Ass," "He-Goat" and "She-Goat" are European; "Elephant" was written in Ceylon, and "Kangaroo" is Australian, while the last three poems are of New Mexican origin.

The contents of the Secker edition (A27b) include the "Tortoise" poems, which were separately published in the United States by Seltzer (A19) but not in England. The Cresset Press illustrated edition (A27c) contains prefaces for each of the groups of poems which were not printed elsewhere until the appearance of *Phoenix* (A76) in 1936, where they are called "Notes for *Birds, Beasts and Flowers*." Secker reprinted the English edition in 1931.

REVIEWS: *Birds, Beasts and Flowers* was reviewed by Mark Van Doren as "In the Image of Bigness" in the *Nation* (New York), 5 December 1923; by H. S. Gorman in the *New York Times Book Review*, 9 December 1923; in the *Times Literary Supplement*, 13 December 1923; by J. C. Squire in the *London Mercury*, January 1924; by Edwin Muir in "Poetry in Becoming" in the *Freeman*, 2 January 1924; by Richard Hughes in the *Nation and Athenaeum*, 5 January 1924; by F. L. Lucas in the *New Statesman*, 8 March 1924; in "Strained Intensities" by Louis Untermeyer in the *Bookman* (New York), April 1924; and in "The Disintegration of Modern Poetry" by Conrad Aiken in the *Dial*, June 1924.

NOTES (2): The dates given above for the publication of the illustrated edition of *Birds, Beasts and Flowers* are by authority of a statement from the publisher; the *English Catalogue* gives April for the 30 copies on hand-made paper which sold for 30 gns; the ordinary illustrated copies were published in May according to the *English Catalogue*.

The University of Texas has one of four hand rubbed proofs of the illustration on page [62], facing the preface for "Evangelistic Beasts." The final version of this illustration as published is different. In a letter of March 1972 to David Farmer, Mr Hughes-Stanton explained why the alteration of the sexual organ of the male figure was considered necessary. It was not until proofs were available that both Lawrence and Hughes-Stanton noticed the suggestive positioning of the male organ with reference to the female figure; both Lawrence and the artist realized the awkward relationship of the figures, and in view of the fact that no such significance was intended, they thought it best to change the illustration.

The prefaces for the various groups of poems published for the first time in the illustrated edition were derived from John Burnet's *Early Greek Philosophy*, Third Edition, published by A. and C. Black in 1920. Most of the text for the prefaces was taken verbatim from the Burnet text.

The dust-jacket for the Seltzer *Birds, Beasts and Flowers* is tan paper printed in black; the upper cover is decorated with drawings of animals, leaves, a bird, a fish and the figure of a woman standing under a tree. The Secker dust-jacket is green paper printed in black.

The special copies bound in tan pigskin were issued in a tan paper covered slip case; the copies in black pigskin were issued in a black cloth covered slip case.

a. *first edition*

MASTRO-DON GESUALDO | BY | GIOVANNI VERGA | *Translated by* | D. H. LAWRENCE | [*publisher's device*] | NEW YORK | THOMAS SELTZER | 1923

Orange cloth boards, purple paper label on upper cover, printed in white: MASTRO- | DON | GESUALDO | by | GIOVANNI | VERGA | [*enclosed within single rule, blind stamped border; horizontal and vertical blind stamped rules divide upper cover; horizontal rule intersects paper label*]; purple label on spine, printed in white: MASTRO- | DON | GESUALDO | [*short rule*] | VERGA; printed in black on lower part of spine: THOMAS | SELTZER The leaves measure $7\frac{3}{8}"\times 5"$. All edges trimmed; top edges stained orange.

[i]–[xii] + [1]–456, as follows: [i] half-title; [ii] list of works by D. H. Lawrence; [iii] title page as above; [iv] Copyright, 1923, by | THOMAS SELTZER, INC. | [*short rule*] | *All Rights Reserved* | PRINTED IN THE UNITED STATES OF AMERICA; v–vii biographical note; viii bibliography; ix–[x] list of characters; [xi] table of contents; [xii] blank; [1] fly-title: FIRST PART; [2] blank; 3–162 text; [163] fly-title: SECOND PART; [164] blank; 165–267 text; [268] blank; [269] fly-title: THIRD PART; [270] blank; 271–350 text; [351] fly-title: FOURTH PART; [352] blank; 353–454 text; [455]–[456] blank.

Published 13 October 1923 at $2.50; number of copies unknown.

b. *first edition in* The Travellers' Library

MASTRO-DON GESUALDO | by | GIOVANNI VERGA | *Translated by* | D. H. LAWRENCE | [*publisher's device*] | LONDON | JONATHAN CAPE 30 BEDFORD SQUARE

Blue cloth boards, stamped in gold on spine: [*ornamental rule*] | MASTRO | DON | GESUALDO | [*printer's ornament*] | GIOVANNI | VERGA | [*publisher's device*] | JONATHAN | CAPE | [*ornamental rule*] The leaves measure $6\frac{3}{4}"\times 4\frac{1}{2}"$. All edges trimmed.

[i]–[xxviii] + 3–454 and a 40 page catalogue, as follows: [i] half-title; [ii] list of books from The Travellers' Library; [iii] title page as above; [iv] FIRST PUBLISHED 1925 | RE-ISSUED IN THE TRAVELLERS' LIBRARY 1928 | PRINTED IN GREAT BRITAIN; v–xx introduction by D. H. Lawrence; xxi–xxii biographical note; xxiii list of books by Giovanni Verga; [xxiv] blank; xxv–xxvi list of characters; xxvii contents; [xxviii] blank; 3–454

text, at bottom of page 454: PRINTED BY BUTLER AND TANNER LTD., FROME AND LONDON, and a 40 page catalogue of books in The Travellers' Library.

Published March 1928 at 3s. 6d.; number of copies unknown.

NOTES: *Mastro-don Gesualdo* is one of the stories about which Lawrence wrote Catherine Carswell in October 1921 asking if she knew of any English translations of Verga's work. The following month he appealed to Edward Garnett for the same information. An undated letter from Taormina, probably written in February 1922, to Curtis Brown told the agent that the story was half-finished, but the translation was not completed until the Lawrences were in Kandy, Ceylon, according to a note appended to a manuscript described by Tedlock (B51). Lawrence also translated other Verga stories published as *Little Novels of Sicily* (A30) and *Cavalleria Rusticana* (A39).

Jonathan Cape published the first English issue from the Seltzer sheets in March 1925; the first edition in *The Travellers' Library* (A28b) contains a longer introductory essay by D. H. Lawrence, a different version of that collected in *Phoenix* (A76).

REVIEWS: Reviews of *Mastro-don Gesualdo* appeared in the *Nation* (New York), 10 October 1923, by Ernest Boyd; by Leo Markun in the *New York Herald Tribune Books*, 4 November 1923; the *New York Times Book Review*, 11 November 1923; by J. F. Carter in the *New York Evening Post Literary Review*, 12 January 1924; and by Herbert J. Seligmann in the *Dial*, February 1924.

NOTES (2): Mr W. Forster reported a copy of *Mastro-don Gesualdo* with an extra blank leaf at each end of the pagination as given in the description above. An examination of the copies at the University of Texas revealed two copies with the extra leaf as reported by Mr Forster and one copy with three extra blank leaves at either end of the pagination; all other copies were as described above. The extra blank leaves in each case were not integral and were of slightly heavier stock than the paper on which the text was printed.

A second copy of the Cape Travellers' Library in the Texas collection is bound in straw coloured cloth with the publisher's device at the foot of the spine rather than the words JONATHAN CAPE. The publisher's device referred to in the original description consisted of a satyr bearing a vase filled with fruits and flowers. The publisher's device on the straw coloured binding is in addition and consists of the familiar vase of flowers and the initials J C on either side. There is no catalogue of the Travellers'

Library at the end of the copy in straw coloured binding. There is no positive evidence for establishing priority, but few of the books in the series are bound in straw coloured cloth.

A complicating factor is that the catalogue in the copy described above (A28b) lists books in the series; *Mastro-don Gesualdo* is No. 71, and the last of the series listed is No. 206, published after the first edition in the Travellers' Library; thus it seems that the copy with the 24 page catalogue reported by Mr Forster and noted below may indeed be the first issue.

VARIANTS: A28a (1) copy described above.
     (2) as (1) but with an extra blank leaf at each end of the pagination, not integral.
     (3) as (1) but with three extra leaves at each end of the pagination, not integral.
   A28b (1) copy described above.
     (2) as (1) but a 24 page catalogue.
     (3) as (1) except bound in straw coloured cloth and without a catalogue.

The Seltzer dust-jacket for *Mastro-don Gesualdo* is white paper printed in orange and black; on the upper cover is a reproduction in colour of a painting of a Sicilian scene by Kai Götzsche (see B47). The Cape dust-jacket is cream paper printed in green and black.

REVIEWS (2): An additional review of *Mastro-don Gesualdo* appeared in the *Yale Review* for January 1925 by Robert Herrick.

A29 THE BOY IN THE BUSH 1924

first edition

THE | BOY IN THE BUSH | BY | D. H. LAWRENCE | AND | M. L. SKINNER | LONDON | MARTIN SECKER | NUMBER FIVE JOHN STREET ADELPHI

Straw coloured cloth boards, printed in black on upper and lower covers: [*thick rule within thin rule forming border*]; printed in black on spine: [*thin rule*] | [*thick rule*] | THE BOY | IN THE BUSH | · | D. H. LAWRENCE | AND | M. L. SKINNER | SECKER | [*thick rule*] | [*thin rule*] The leaves measure $7\frac{3}{8}'' \times 4\frac{15}{16}''$. Top edges trimmed and stained black; fore edges trimmed; bottom edges untrimmed.

[i]–[ii] + [i]–vi + 1–[376], as follows: [i]–[ii] blank; [i] half-title; [ii] list of works by D. H. Lawrence; [iii] title page as above: [iv] LONDON:

MARTIN SECKER (LTD.), 1924; v–vi table of contents; 1–369 text, at bottom of page 369: [*short rule*] | PRINTED IN GREAT BRITAIN BY | THE DUNEDIN PRESS LIMITED, EDINBURGH; [370]–[376] advertisements of books published by Secker.

Published August 1924 at 7s. 6d.; the first printing consisted of 2000 copies.

NOTES: In May 1922 at Darlington, West Australia, Frieda and Lawrence stayed with a nurse, Mollie Skinner, who showed Lawrence the manuscript of a novel she was writing. He suggested changes which she incorporated into a new draft and forwarded to him for reading. He received the manuscript in California in September 1923 and rewrote it, changing the end a "good deal" as he wrote Miss Skinner in a letter from Guadalajara, Mexico, in November. He also suggested that her title "The House of Ellis" be changed to *The Boy in the Bush*. Miss Skinner liked the title, but she wrote in *Meanjin* in after years that she "wept" about the changed ending. Her statement is perhaps not to be taken too seriously, for the collaboration was a happy one from all accounts.

Seltzer published the first American edition from new plates on 30 September 1924, and Boni and Liveright issued the title in the Uniform edition in 1931. Secker reprinted the novel three times in 1924 for a total of 3500 copies, 750 of which were remaindered in 1930.

REVIEWS: Reviews of *The Boy in the Bush* appeared in *The Times Literary Supplement*, 28 August 1924; by Gerald Gould in the *Saturday Review*, 6 September 1924; by L. P. Hartley in the *Spectator*, 13 September 1924; in "Mr. Lawrence Speeded Up" by Edwin Muir in the *Nation and Athenaeum*, 20 September 1924; in "Mr. Lawrence in the Wilderness" by Humbert Wolfe in the *Weekly Westminster*, 27 September 1924; by J. Franklin in the *New Statesman*, 27 September 1924; by John Macy in the *New York Herald Tribune Books*, 19 October 1924; in "Mr. Lawrence on the Frontiers of Civilization" by Lloyd Morris in the *New York Times Book Review*, 26 October 1924; by J. W. C. in the *New York World*, 26 October 1924; by A. Donald Douglas in the *New York Post*, 8 November 1924; by Matthew Josephson in "Precocious Superman" in the *Saturday Review of Literature*, 29 November 1924; by R. M. Lovatt in the *New Republic*, 24 December 1924; by Joseph Wood Krutch in "A Nietzschean Novel" in the *Nation* (New York), 24 December 1924; by Elizabeth McDowell Jacobs in the *Literary Digest*, June 1925; and in the *Dial*, June 1925.

NOTES (2): The dust-jacket for the Secker edition of *The Boy in the Bush* is cream paper printed in red. The Seltzer dust-jacket is of special interest because it was designed by Dorothy Brett (see F26). It is white paper printed in blue and black; the upper cover reproduces Brett's drawing of the figures of a kangaroo and a man.

REVIEWS (2): A review of *The Boy in the Bush* appeared in the *Philadelphia Public Literary Review* for 9 November 1924.

A30   LITTLE NOVELS OF SICILY   1925

first edition

LITTLE NOVELS | OF SICILY | *by* | GIOVANNI VERGA | *Translated by* | D. H. LAWRENCE | [*publisher's device*] | NEW YORK | THOMAS SELTZER | 1925

Dark-red cloth boards, yellow paper label on spine printed in red: *Giovanni* | *Verga* | [*single rule*] | LITTLE | NOVELS | *of* | SICILY | [*single rule*] | *Translated by* | *D. H. Lawrence* The leaves measure $7\frac{1}{4}'' \times 5''$. All edges trimmed; top edges stained red.

[i]–x + [11]–[228], as follows: [i] half-title; [ii] note on translations by D. H. Lawrence; [iii] title page as above; [iv] Copyright 1925, by | THOMAS SELTZER, INC. | [*short rule*] | *All rights reserved* | PRINTED IN THE UNITED STATES OF AMERICA; [v] table of contents; [vi] blank; vii–x note on Giovanni Verga; [11] fly-title: LITTLE NOVELS OF SICILY; [12] blank; 13–226 text; [227]–[228] blank.

Published 9 March 1925 at $2.00; number of copies unknown.

VARIANTS: (1) copy described above.
         (2) as (1) except in purple cloth boards.
         (3) as (1) except in light-blue cloth boards.
         (4) as (1) except in dark-blue cloth boards.
         (5) as (1) except in light-green cloth boards.
         (6) as (1) except in dark-green cloth boards.
         (7) as (1) except in yellow cloth boards.
         (8) as (1) except in orange cloth boards.

This list of variants binding is from McDonald (B31), who gave priority to the dark-red binding, and there is no reason to think that he was not correct. Only the copies in the dark-red binding had the top edges stained.

In all copies examined the final "e" of the title "His Reverence" in the table of contents on page [v] was missing.

CONTENTS

Note on Giovanni Verga—His Reverence—So Much for the King—Don Licciu Papa—The Mystery Play—Malaria—The Orphans—Property—Story of the Saint Joseph's Ass (first appeared in the *Adelphi*, September 1923 (C109), as "St. Joseph's Ass")—Black Bread—The Gentry—Liberty (first appeared in the *Adelphi*, May 1924 (C119))—Across the Sea (first appeared in the *Adelphi*, November 1923 (C112)).

NOTES: Lawrence completed the translation of *Mastro-don Gesualdo* (A28) in Ceylon in March 1922, and work on the *Little Novels of Sicily* must have been begun soon after for the first eight stories were written in notebooks of Japanese manufacture purchased in Ceylon. These notebooks were perhaps given to Lawrence by Harwood, the young daughter of the Brewsters, whose book *D. H. Lawrence, Reminiscences and Correspondence* (B39) describes him at work on the Verga translations. The Lawrences had met the Brewsters in Capri and visited them in Ceylon on the way to Australia.

The first English edition, published by Basil Blackwell in 1925, has a somewhat shorter introduction than the Seltzer edition, and the title of "Story of the Saint Joseph's Ass" appears as "History of the Saint Joseph's Ass." Blackwell reprinted the book in 1929; Secker issued the book in the New Adelphi Library in March 1928, and Heinemann published a Pocket Edition in September 1937. McDonald (B31) notes that the Seltzer *Little Novels of Sicily* was bound in cloth of various colours "dark red, purple, light blue, dark blue, light green, dark green and yellow."

REVIEWS: *Little Novels of Sicily* was reviewed in the *New York Times Book Review*, 29 March 1925; by Eliseo Vivas in the *New York Herald Tribune Books*, 19 April 1925; by John T. Smertenko in the *Nation* (New York), 22 April 1925; by J. Ferris in the *New York Evening Post Literary Review*, 9 May 1925; by D. B. Woolsey in the *New Republic*, 20 May 1925; by Edwin Muir in the *Nation and Athenaeum*, 23 May 1925; by P. C. Kennedy in the *New Statesman*, 20 June 1925; in the *Dial*, July 1925; and in the *Saturday Review of Literature*, 15 August 1925.

NOTES (2): In 1977 a California bookseller offered for a sale a copy of *Little Novels of Sicily* bound in beige cloth which provides another variant: (9) as (1) except bound in beige cloth boards. As McDonald reported in the 1931 supplement to his bibliography, "Only the fanatic will ever get to the end of this rainbow." Mr George Lazarus has in his collection a copy of variant (3) with the top edges stained.

The Seltzer *Little Novels of Sicily* was issued in a yellow paper dust-jacket printed in red. The Blackwell edition was issued in a white paper dust-jacket printed in blue and black with a painting in colour on the upper cover of figures with a donkey by Ray Melòtual.

REVIEWS (2): Additional reviews of *Little Novels of Sicily* appeared in the *Adelphi* for July 1925 and in the *Calendar of Modern Letters* for November.

A31   ST. MAWR   1925

a. *first edition*

ST. MAWR | *Together with* THE PRINCESS | BY D. H. LAW-RENCE | LONDON | MARTIN SECKER | NUMBER FIVE JOHN STREET ADELPHI

Chocolate-brown cloth boards, blind stamped on upper and lower covers: [*thick rule enclosed within thin rule forming border*]; stamped in gold on spine: [*thin rule*] | [*thick rule*] | ST. MAWR | · | D. H. LAWRENCE | SECKER | [*thick rule*] | [*thin rule*] The leaves measure $7\frac{1}{2}'' \times 4\frac{7}{8}''$. Top and fore edges trimmed; bottom edges untrimmed.

[1]–[240], as follows: [1] half-title; [2] list of books by D. H. Lawrence; [3] title page as above; [4] LONDON: MARTIN SECKER (LTD.), 1925; [5] table of contents; [6] blank; 7–186 text; [187] fly-title: THE PRINCESS; [188] blank; 189–238 text; [239] [*short rule*] | *Printed in Great Britain by* | *The Dunedin Press, Limited, Edinburgh.*; [240] blank.

Published 14 May 1925 at 7s. 6d.; the first printing consisted of 4000 copies.

VARIANTS: (1) copy described above; seven-eighths of an inch thick excluding covers.

           (2) as (1) except in light-brown cloth boards; three-fourths of an inch thick excluding covers.

           (3) as (2) except table of contents correctly gives page 7 for the beginning of the text instead of page 9 as in (1) and (2).

Variants (2) and (3) are from McDonald (B31) and have not been examined; all copies of the book examined appeared to be (1) and measured about seven-eighths of an inch thick exclusive of covers.

b. *first separate edition*

ST. MAWR | *by* | D. H. LAWRENCE | [*enclosed within decorative rule forming border which incorporates the publisher's device at the bottom, in violet*] | *New York* | ALFRED A. KNOPF | 1925

Violet-blue cloth boards with a purple-red cloth backstrip, stamped in gold on spine: *St.* | *Mawr* | *by* | *D. H.* | *Lawrence* | *Alfred A. Knopf* The leaves measure $7\frac{1}{2}'' \times 5\frac{1}{8}''$. Top edges trimmed and· stained violet; fore and bottom edges rough-trimmed.

[1]–[224], as follows: [1] half-title; [2] list of works by D. H. Lawrence; [3] title page as above; [4] COPYRIGHT, 1925, BY ALFRED A. KNOPF, INC. | MANUFACTURED IN THE UNITED STATES OF AMERICA; [5] fly-title: ST. MAWR; [6] blank; 7–222 text; [223] blank; 224 [*note on the type in which book is set*] | [*publisher's device*] | SET UP, ELECTROTYPED, PRINTED AND | BOUND BY THE VAIL-BALLOU PRESS, | BINGHAMPTON, N. Y. · ESPARTO PAPER | MANUFACTURED IN SCOTLAND AND | FURNISHED BY W. F. ETHERING- | TON & CO., NEW YORK. ·

Published 5 June 1925 at $2.00; the first printing consisted of 3000 copies.

NOTES: These two stories as well as "The Woman Who Rode Away" (A41) are built around the Taos country. "St. Mawr" was written during the summer of 1924 in New Mexico and sent to Curtis Brown with several other manuscripts from Taos on 30 September. "The Princess" first appeared in the *Calendar of Modern Letters* for March, April and May 1925 (C128), (C129) and (C130).

The Knopf *St. Mawr* (A31b) did not include "The Princess." Secker issued *St. Mawr* in the pocket edition in February 1928, and the two stories together are No. 4953 in Tauchnitz's Collection of British and American Authors and No. 252, in the Albatross Library.

REVIEWS: Reviews of *St. Mawr Together with the Princess* or of *St. Mawr* appeared in the *Saturday Review*, 13 May 1925, by Gerald Bullett; by Edwin Muir in the *Nation and Athenaeum*, 30 May 1925; by Stuart P. Sherman in the *New York Herald Tribune Books*, 14 June 1925; in the *New York Times Book Review*, 14 June 1925; by P. C. Kennedy in the *New Statesman*, 20 June 1925; by Donald Douglas in the *New York Evening Post Literary Review*, 27 June 1925; by Milton Waldman in the *London Mercury*, June 1925; in the *Independent*, 4 July 1925; by J. W. Crawford in the *New York World*, 5 July 1925; by Robert Littell in the *New Republic*, 8 July 1925; by L. Kronenberger in the *Saturday Review of Literature*, 1 August 1925; and in the *Dial*, November 1925·

NOTES (2): It has been suggested that the measurements for variant (1) of (A31a) should measure $\frac{15}{16}''$ rather than the $\frac{7}{8}''$ given above. Thirteen copies of the Secker first edition at the University of Texas were measured carefully, and seven copies seemed to be closer to $\frac{15}{16}''$, but the other copies were closer to $\frac{7}{8}''$. It seems obvious that a slight difference occurs in the various copies of the first edition. The two copies bound in the light brown cloth of variant (2) clearly measured the same as variant (1); no copies examined measured $\frac{3}{4}''$. One copy was bound in straw coloured cloth similar to that of *The Boy in the Bush* (A29). No copies of variants (2) and (3) were identified, but presuming that they do in fact exist, the following additional variants may be listed.

VARIANTS: (4) as (1) except bound in straw coloured cloth.
(5) as (2) except measuring $\frac{7}{8}''$ to $\frac{15}{16}''$ excluding the covers.

Dr Brian Finney reports a letter from Martin Secker to W. H. Smith, the booksellers, in which the publisher agrees to omit a line on page 65 in 200 copies of the book. The line to which the bookseller objected is a sentence on lines 25–26 of page 65 reading: "Even our late King Edward." No copy of the first edition with the line omitted has been identified, but subsequent texts derived from the Secker first edition do omit the sentence, e.g., the Secker thin paper edition of 1930 and the Phoenix edition published by Heinemann. Although all 13 copies of the first edition at the University of Texas have the original text, it seems likely that another variant of *St. Mawr* exists.

The dust-jacket for the Secker first edition is cream paper printed in red. The Knopf dust-jacket is yellow paper printed in red and black; the upper cover has a drawing of D. H. Lawrence.

REVIEWS (2): Additional reviews appeared in the *Adelphi* for November 1925; *Calendar of Modern Letters*, June 1925 by H. C. Harwood; *Chicago Daily Tribune*, 27 June by Sidney Dark; *Empire Review*, July by John Sydenham; *Manchester Guardian*, 29 May by A. N. M.; *Observer*, 24 May; *Queen*, 29 July by Ida A. R. Wylie; *G. K.'s Weekly*, 30 May by Louis J. McQuilland; *Times Literary Supplement*, 28 May; and *Vogue* (London), June by Raymond Mortimer.

A32   REFLECTIONS ON THE DEATH   1925
OF A PORCUPINE

first edition

REFLECTIONS ON THE | DEATH OF A PORCUPINE | AND OTHER ESSAYS | *By* | D. H. LAWRENCE | [*publisher's device*] | THE CENTAUR PRESS | PHILADELPHIA | 1925

Decorative paper boards with a natural cloth backstrip, printed in black on spine: REFLECTIONS | ON | THE DEATH | OF A | PORCUPINE | [*printer's ornament*] | LAWRENCE | THE CENTAUR | PRESS The leaves measure $7\frac{7}{8}'' \times 5\frac{1}{2}''$. Top edges trimmed and stained blue; fore edges unopened; bottom edges rough-trimmed.

[i]–[x] + 1–[246], as follows: [i] half-title; [ii] blank; [iii] title page as above; [iv] COPYRIGHT, 1925 | THE CENTAUR PRESS; [v] table of contents; [vi] blank; [vii] fly-title: THE CROWN; [viii] blank; [ix]–[x] note to *The Crown*; 1–100 text; [101] fly-title: THE NOVEL; [102] blank; 103–123 text; [124] blank; [125] fly-title: HIM WITH HIS TAIL IN HIS MOUTH; [126] blank; 127–141 text; [142] blank; [143] fly-title: BLESSED ARE THE POWERFUL; [144] blank; 145–158 text; [159] fly-title: ... LOVE WAS ONCE A LITTLE BOY; [160] blank; 161–189 text; [190] blank; [191] fly-title: REFLECTIONS ON THE DEATH OF A PORCUPINE; [192] blank; 193–219 text; [220] blank; [221] fly-title: ARISTOCRACY; [222] blank; 223–240 text; [241] THE SECOND BOOK OF THE | CENTAUR PRESS | THE EDITION IS LIMITED | TO NINE HUNDRED AND | TWENTY-FIVE COPIES FOR | SALE OF WHICH THIS | IS NUMBER | 522 [*autograph number in blue ink*]; [242]–[246] blank.

Published 7 December 1925 at $4.00; the first printing consisted of 925 copies.

CONTENTS

The Crown (first appeared in the *Signature*, 4 October, 18 October and 1 November 1915 (C39), (C40) and (C41))—The Novel—Him With His Tail in His Mouth (a poem from this essay appeared in the *Adelphi*, February 1926 as "Creative Evolution")—Blessed Are the Powerful—Love Was Once a Little Boy (an excerpt from this essay appeared in the *Laughing Horse*, No. 15, March–July 1928, as "Susan the Cow")—Reflections on the Death of a Porcupine—Aristocracy.

NOTES: With the exception of "The Crown" associated with the *Signature* and the war years in London, all the essays in this volume were probably written in New Mexico, and several are the result of experiences at the ranch in the mountains above Taos. Both Mabel Dodge Luhan, in *Lorenzo in Taos* (B35), and Dorothy Brett, in *Lawrence and Brett* (F26), give an account of the killing of a porcupine by Tony Luhan, Mabel's Indian husband, which inspired the title essay.

Lawrence probably arranged for publication of the essays by the Centaur Press before he left the United States for Europe in September 1925. In December he wrote Dorothy Brett from Spotorno that the book was overdue; he did receive copies in January and wrote Middleton Murry asking if his copies had come. Another letter later in the month commented to Dorothy Brett about an "impudent" review in the *New York Times*. The Centaur Press also published the two McDonald bibliographies of Lawrence (B16) and (B31).

The first English edition of the collection was published in 1934 by Secker, who issued the title in the New Adelphi Library in February.

REVIEWS: *Reflections on the Death of a Porcupine* was reviewed in the *New York Times Book Review*, 27 December 1925; by Donald Douglas in the *Nation* (New York), 17 March 1926; in the *Bookman* (New York), April 1926; in the *Dial*, April 1926; by Edward Sackville-West in the *New Statesman*, 10 July 1926; and by Dudley Carew in the *London Mercury*, August 1926.

NOTES (2): Although the colophon of the copy described above states that the edition consisted of 925 copies, apparently 475 copies were especially prepared for distribution in England. On these copies page [241] reads:

THE SECOND BOOK OF THE | CENTAUR PRESS | THE EDITION IS LIMITED | TO FOUR HUNDRED AND | SEVENTY-FIVE COPIES FOR | SALE IN ENGLAND OF | WHICH THIS IS | NUMBER | 384 [*autograph number in black ink*]

It seems likely that the 475 copies for England were in addition to the 925 copies described above because one copy of the American issue is numbered 639, and other copies are numbered to indicate the total was more than 925. Some of the English copies had a slip pasted on the title page which noted that Simpkin, Marshall, Hamilton, Kent & Company, Ltd. were sole agents for Great Britain and Ireland.

There were also special copies which had the words "Presentation Copy" written in black ink in place of the number on page [241]. These presentation copies also have a slip pasted on the recto of the front free end-paper, printed in green, reading: With the compliments of | The Centaur Press | 1224 Chancellor Street | PHILADELPHIA

The following variants may be listed:

VARIANTS: (1) copy described above.
            (2) as (1) except with the special colophon for the English copies quoted above.
            (3) as (1) except with the words "Presentation Copy," instead of being numbered in the colophon.

The book was issued in a black slip case with a green paper label on the spine reading: REFLECTIONS | ON | THE DEATH | OF A | PORCUPINE | [*printer's device*] | LAWRENCE

A33 THE PLUMED SERPENT 1926

first edition

THE | PLUMED SERPENT | (QUETZALCOATL) | BY D. H. LAWRENCE | LONDON | MARTIN SECKER | NUMBER FIVE JOHN STREET ADELPHI

Chocolate-brown cloth boards, blind stamped on upper and lower covers: [*thick rule enclosed within thin rule forming border*]; stamped in gold on spine: [*thin rule*] | [*thick rule*] | THE PLUMED | SERPENT | · | D. H. | LAWRENCE | SECKER | [*thick rule*] | [*thin rule*] The leaves measure $7\frac{5}{16}'' \times 4\frac{7}{8}''$. All edges trimmed.

[1]–480, as follows: [1] half-title; [2] list of works by D. H. Lawrence; [3] title page as above; [4] LONDON: MARTIN SECKER (LTD.), 1926.; 5 table of contents; [6] blank; 7–476 text, at bottom of page 476: [*short rule*] | *Printed in Great Britain by* | *The Dunedin Press Limited, Edinburgh.*; [477]–[480] excerpts of reviews of books by D. H. Lawrence.

Published January 1926 at 7s. 6d.; the first printing consisted of 3000 copies.

NOTES: Lawrence wrote *The Plumed Serpent* for the most part in Mexico at Oaxaca and on Lake Chapala. Frieda Lawrence in *Not I, But the Wind* (B40) gives an account of their life there. The first mention of the novel occurs in a letter from Lawrence to Curtis Brown from Chapala in May 1923, in which he wrote that he had begun a new novel set in Mexico. He expected to have a rough draft finished by the end of July, but the manuscript was evidently put aside, for Lawrence wrote Curtis Brown from Paris in February 1924 that he would get the manuscript from New York and return to Oaxaca to finish it. The book was not completed until February of 1925; Lawrence considered the novel, then, his most important work.

The first American edition was published by Knopf from new plates on 5 February 1926. Secker reprinted the first edition in a printing of 500 copies in the year of its first publication and issued a Thin Paper Pocket Edition in March 1927. Penguin Books published a double volume in March 1950 with an introduction by Richard Aldington, and Heinemann issued a Pocket Edition with the Aldington introduction the same month. A new edition with an introduction by William York Tindall appeared with Knopf's imprint in March 1950. The "songs" from *The Plumed Serpent* were reprinted in *Selected Poems* (A83).

REVIEWS: *The Plumed Serpent* was reviewed in *The Times Literary Supplement*, 21 January 1926; in the *Spectator*, 30 January 1926; by L. P. Hartley in the *Saturday Review*, 30 January 1926; by P. C. Kennedy in the *New Statesman*, 30 January 1926; by J. W. Crawford in the *New York World*, 7 February 1926; by P. A. Hutchison in the *New York Times Book Review*, 7 February 1926; by M. H. in the *New Republic*, 17 February 1926; by Edwin Muir in the *Nation and Athenaeum*, 20 February 1926; by Landon Robinson in the *New York Evening Post Literary Review*, 20 February 1926; by Katherine Anne Porter in the *New York Herald Tribune Books*, 9 March 1926; by Donald Douglas in the *Nation* (New York), 17 March 1926; in "Many Mysteries" by Isabel Paterson in the *Bookman* (New York), March 1926; in "D. H. Lawrence Revives Mexico's Ancient Gods" by L. Moore in the *Literary Digest International Book Review*, March 1926; in the *Living Age*, 4 April 1926; by E. S. Sergeant in the *Saturday Review of Literature*, 24 April 1926; by H. C. Harwood in the *Outlook* (London), April 1926; by Mabel Dodge Luhan in the *Laughing Horse* (April 1926); by Edward Shanks in the *London Mercury*, April 1926; and in the *Dial*, June 1926.

NOTES (2): In 1972 a London bookseller offered for sale a copy of *The Plumed Serpent* (A33) bound in straw coloured cloth; thus the following variants may be listed:

VARIANTS: (1) copy described above.
(2) as (1) except bound in straw coloured cloth.

The dust-jacket for the Secker edition is cream paper printed in red. The dust-jacket for the first American edition of the *Plumed Serpent* is especially interesting because it was designed by Dorothy Brett; the jacket is white paper printed in black and red with drawings of Mexican figures with large hats.

REVIEWS (2): Additional reviews of *The Plumed Serpent* appeared in the *Boston Evening Transcript* for 24 February 1926; the *Calendar* for April 1926; and in the *Adelphi* for August 1926.

first edition

DAVID | A PLAY | BY | D. H. LAWRENCE | LONDON | MARTIN SECKER | NUMBER FIVE JOHN STREET | ADELPHI | [*enclosed within double rule border consisting of thin rule within thick rule*]

Tan cloth boards, stamped in gold on spine: *David* | [*printer's ornament*] | *D. H.* | *Lawrence* | *Secker* The leaves measure $8\frac{3}{4}'' \times 5\frac{3}{4}''$. Top edges trimmed and stained dark green: fore and bottom edges untrimmed.

[1]–[128], as follows: [1] half-title; [2] NOTE | This edition is limited to | Five Hundred copies; [3] title page as above; [4] Printed in Great Britain | by The Riverside Press Limited | Edinburgh | LONDON: MARTIN SECKER (LTD.) 1926; 5 list of characters; [6] blank; 7–128 text.

Published March 1926 at 15*s.*; the first printing consisted of 500 copies.

NOTES: *David* was apparently written in New Mexico, for the first mention of the play occurs in a letter to Curtis Brown from Del Monte Ranch in May 1925, where Lawrence tells the agent he has done *David*, a biblical play, but does not care to publish it; however, a letter dated in June remarks that the agent must have the play "now" and an agreement was signed with Secker in November. Frieda translated *David* into German after the return to Europe while they were living at Spotorno. The manuscript in Frieda's handwriting is now in the library of the University of California at Berkeley.

During the last months of 1926 plans were under way for a stage production of *David*; in June Lawrence asked Miss Pearn, in Curtis Brown's office, to inquire about the performance, and rehearsals were to begin in August. The actual performance was given by the Stage Society, 22–23 May 1927.

The Secker first edition was completely sold out in the month it was published, and Secker reprinted an edition of 1500 copies in 1927; the title appeared in the New Adelphi Library in 1930. The first American edition was published from new plates by Alfred Knopf on 23 April 1926.

REVIEWS: *David* was reviewed by Bonamy Dobrée in "Mr. Lawrence's *David*" in the *Nation and Athenaeum*, 24 April 1926; by Edward Sackville-West in the *New Statesman*, 10 July 1926; by John Cournos in the *Literary Digest*, November 1926. The stage production was reviewed by "Omicron" in the *Nation and Athenaeum*, 28 May 1927 and by Richard Jennings in the *Spectator*, 28 May 1927.

a. first edition

SUN. | BY | D. H. LAWRENCE. | E. ARCHER, | 68, RED
LION STREET, LONDON, W. C. 1. | *September,* 1926.

Decorative paper wrappers, printed in black on upper cover: SUN. | BY
| D. H. LAWRENCE. | [*printer's ornament*] The leaves measure 10″ × 7½″.
Top edges unopened; fore and bottom edges trimmed.

[i]–[ii] + [1]–[22], as follows: [i] blank; [ii] ONE HUNDRED COPIES |
PRIVATELY PRINTED. | NO. 63 [*autograph number in black ink*]; [1] title page
as above; [2] blank; 3–[20] text, at bottom of page [20]: [*short rule*] |
Smith's Printing Company (London and St. Albans), Ltd., 22–24, Fetter
Lane, London, E. C. 4.; [21]–[22] blank.

Published September 1926 at 6*s.*; 100 copies were printed.

b. first unexpurgated edition (ordinary copies)

SUN [*in red*] | by | D. H. LAWRENCE | THE BLACK SUN
PRESS | ÉDITIONS NARCISSE [*in red*] | RUE CARDI-
NALE | PARIS [*in red*] | MCMXXVIII

Cream paper wrappers, printed in black and red on upper cover: SUN
[*in red*] | by | D. H. LAWRENCE | THE BLACK SUN PRESS | ÉDITIONS NARCISSE
[*in red*] | RUE CARDINALE | PARIS [*in red*] | MCMXXVIII; printed in black
on lower cover: [*sun rays outlining white sun*] The leaves measure 9½″ × 6⅜″.
Top edges trimmed; fore and bottom edges untrimmed.

[i]–[viii] + 1–[48], and a frontispiece of a drawing of the sun-god by
D. H. Lawrence, as follows: [i]–[iv] blank; [v] half-title; [vi] blank;
[vii] title page as above; [viii] blank; 1–[38] text; [39] [*sun rays outlining
white sun*]; [40] blank; [41] This unexpurgated edition of | Sun by
D. H. Lawrence with | a drawing by the author | printed in Paris
October 1928 | at the Black Sun Press | (Maître-Imprimeur Lescaret)
| for Harry and Caresse Crosby | is limited to 15 numbered | copies
on Japan Paper and | 150 copies on Holland Van | Gelder Zonen to
be sold at the | bookshop of Harry Marks | New York; [42]–[48] blank.

Published October 1928; 150 ordinary copies were printed.

c. first unexpurgated edition (Japanese vellum copies)

SUN [*in red*] | by | D. H. LAWRENCE | THE BLACK SUN

PRESS | ÉDITIONS NARCISSE [*in red*] | RUE CARDI-
NALE | PARIS [*in red*] | MCMXXVIII

The Japanese vellum copies were identical with (b) except that they
were numbered and printed on vellum.

Published October 1928; 15 copies were printed on Japanese vellum.

Apparently some of the Japanese vellum copies were not numbered;
neither the copy described here from the library of Mr George Lazarus
nor the copy in the University of Texas Library was numbered, but the
Texas copy is autographed by D. H. Lawrence.

NOTES: *Sun* was written at Villa Bernardo at Spotorno before the end
of 1925; a letter to Dorothy Brett in December asked if she had finished
reading the manuscript. Lawrence was trying to place the story by
February of the next year, but his efforts were unsuccessful with his
usual publishing outlets. Curtis Brown wrote that it was "too pagan"
except for the "highbrow" reviews. It was finally accepted by *New Coterie*,
where it was published in No. 4 for Autumn 1926 (C145).

The *New Coterie* was published by Charles Lahr, who conducted his
business under his wife's name, Esther Archer, hence the "E. Archer."
Apparently the Archer *Sun* was printed from the *New Coterie* type;
Lawrence noted in a letter to Nancy Pearn, in an attempt to locate the
manuscript of *Sun* for Harry Crosby, that the *Coterie* people had printed
100 extra copies of the story. Charles Lahr's Blue Moon Press also printed
the *Letter to Charles Lahr* (A55) and *The Life of John Middleton Murry* (A51).

Sometime early in 1928 Harry Crosby wrote Lawrence wanting to
buy manuscripts and expressing an especial interest in "Sun"; Lawrence
tried to locate the *New Coterie* manuscript, but was unsuccessful, for in
a letter from Villa Mirenda in April 1928 he told Harry Crosby that
he was sending the "final manuscript" of "Sun" and expressed the wish
that it could have been printed in its unexpurgated form. It was from
this manuscript that the Black Sun edition (A35b) was printed. Harry
T. Moore, in his *Intelligent Heart* (B57), gives an account of the purchase
of the manuscript. In payment the Crosbys sent Lawrence three pieces
of gold in a snuff box which had once belonged to the Queen of Naples.

"Sun" was pirated in the United States, and although the statement
of limitation records that the copies were numbered, no copies examined
were actually numbered. See Appendix II, p. 566.

The Archer text was collected in *The Woman Who Rode Away* (A41).

NOTES (2): Although the statement of limitation in (A35a) notes that

100 copies were printed, the Newberry Library reports a copy numbered 115. Apparently there were irregularities as well with the numbering of the Black Sun copies; Mr W. Forster has a copy of (A35b) numbered IV and marked *"hors commerce,"* a presentation copy to P. R. Stephensen from Lawrence. Of the three copies of (A35c) at the University of Texas, none is numbered, but one is lettered C; all copies are signed by Lawrence. A careful census of all copies might reveal a pattern for these different states.

The designation of (A35b) and (A35c) as "unexpurgated" may be misleading. According to the Lawrence correspondence, the manuscript from which (A35a) was published could not be located; hence the manuscript Lawrence sent to Harry Crosby could represent a later version rather than the original version from which the (A35a) text was derived.

The three copies of (A35c) at the University of Texas were apparently issued in a gold coloured cardboard folder in a gold coloured slip case; the only copy of (A35b) is in a gold coloured folder with pink ribbon ties. Both the Vellum and Van Gelder copies were issued in glassine wrappers.

A36   GLAD GHOSTS   1926

first edition

GLAD GHOSTS | *By* | D. H. LAWRENCE | 1926 | ERNEST BENN LIMITED | BOUVERIE HOUSE LONDON

Yellow paper wrappers, printed in black on upper cover: GLAD GHOSTS | *By* | D. H LAWRENCE | ERNEST BENN LIMITED | BOUVERIE HOUSE LONDON | [*enclosed within double rule*] The leaves measure $7\frac{1}{16}'' \times 4\frac{1}{8}''$. All edges trimmed.

[i]–[iv] + [1]–80, as follows: [i]–[iv] blank; [1] blank; [2] list of Yellow Books: [3] title page as above; [4] PRINTED IN GREAT BRITAIN | *This, the first Edition* | *of* GLAD GHOSTS, *is* | *limited to 500 copies* | *Richard Clay & Sons, Ltd., Printers, Bungay, Suffolk*; 5–[78] text; [79]–[80] blank.

Published November 1926 at 6*s.*; the first printing consisted of 500 copies.

NOTES: *Glad Ghosts* was the second of the Ernest Benn "Yellow Books." McDonald (B31) was informed that the original intention was to sign some of the copies of the first edition, but that Lawrence signed none before publication. Benn reprinted the little volume in November, the month of original publication, but without the certificate of issue which distinguished the Yellow Book first editions. The story has not been published separately in America, but it first appeared in the *Dial*, July and August 1926 (C143) and (C144). "Glad Ghosts" was first collected in *The Woman Who Rode Away* (A41).

REVIEWS (2): A review of *Glad Ghosts* appeared in the *New Adelphi* for September 1927 by M. R.

A37   MORNINGS IN MEXICO   1927

first edition

MORNINGS IN | MEXICO | By | D. H. LAWRENCE | LONDON: | MARTIN SECKER | 1927

Tan cloth boards, stamped in gold on spine: *Mornings | in | Mexico | [printer's ornament] | D. H. | Lawrence | Secker* The leaves measure $8'' \times 5\frac{5}{8}''$. Top edges trimmed and stained green; fore edges unopened; bottom edges untrimmed.

[1]–[180], as follows: [1] half-title; [2] [*acknowledgements*] | LONDON: MARTIN SECKER LIMITED | NUMBER FIVE JOHN STREET ADELPHI; [3] title page as above; [4] dedicated to Mabel Luhan; [5] table of contents; [6] blank; [7] fly-title: CORASMIN AND THE PARROTS; [8] blank; 9–23 text; [24] blank; [25] fly-title: WALK TO HUAYAPA; [26] blank; 27–52 text; [53] fly-title: THE MOZO; [54] blank; 55–76 text; [77] fly-title: MARKET DAY; [78] blank; 79–93 text; [94] blank; [95] fly-title: INDIANS AND ENTERTAINMENT; [96] blank; 97–118 text; [119] fly-title: THE DANCE OF THE SPROUTING CORN; [120] blank; 121–132 text; [133] fly-title: THE HOPI SNAKE DANCE; [134] blank; 135–169 text; [170] blank; [171] fly-title: A LITTLE MOONSHINE WITH LEMON; [172] blank; 173–[178] text, at bottom of page [178]: Printed in Great Britain at | *The Mayflower Press, Plymouth.* William Brendon & Son, Ltd.; [179]–[180] blank.

Published June 1927 at 7*s.* 6*d.*; the first printing consisted of 1000 copies.

CONTENTS

Corasmin and the Parrots (first appeared in the *Adelphi*, December 1925 (C134))—Walk to Huayapa (first appeared in *Travel*, November 1926 (C147), as "Sunday Stroll in Sleepy Mexico")—The Mozo (first appeared in the *Adelphi*, February 1927 (C151))—Market Day (first appeared in *Travel*, April 1926 (C140), as "The Gentle Art of Marketing in Mexico")—Indians and Entertainment (first appeared in the *New York Times Magazine*, 26 October 1924 (C126))—The Dance of the

Sprouting Corn (first appeared in *The Theatre Arts Monthly*, July 1924 (C122))—The Hopi Snake Dance (first appeared in *The Theatre Arts Monthly*, December 1924 (C127); also in the *Adelphi* for January and February 1925)—A Little Moonshine with Lemon (first appeared in *The Laughing Horse*, April 1926 (C139)).

NOTES: Although this collection of travel sketches is given to Mexico by its title, several of the essays were written as a result of Lawrence's experiences in the American Southwest. The first four sketches were written in Mexico, where the Lawrences went from Taos in October 1924. The following January Lawrence wrote Curtis Brown that he was sending four of them for placing, but they were not accepted immediately, because the London office was advised in April that the articles were still wandering on the American side of the Atlantic. Although Lawrence told Curtis Brown that he was not particularly eager to give the essays to Middleton Murry, two of them were published in the *Adelphi*. The Secker first edition was protected by a dust-jacket which was decorated with a drawing by Lawrence, "The Corn Dance," originally published with "The Dance of the Sprouting Corn" (C122).

Knopf published the first American edition from new plates on 5 August 1927, and issued a cheap edition in 1934. Secker reprinted the first edition in a printing of 1000 copies in the same year it was first published, and it appeared in Secker's New Adelphi Library in April 1930. Heinemann published *Mornings in Mexico* in the Pocket Edition with an introduction by Richard Aldington in 1950.

REVIEWS: *Mornings in Mexico* was reviewed in *The Times Literary Supplement*, 7 July 1927; by Peter Quennell in the *New Statesman*, 23 July 1927; in the *New York Evening Post Literary Review*, 6 August 1927; by Genevieve Taggard in the *New York Herald Tribune Books*, 7 August 1927; the *New York Times Book Review*, 7 August 1927; the *Nation and Athenaeum*, 13 August 1927; the *Saturday Review*, 27 August 1927; by Carleton Beals in the *Saturday Review of Literature*, 27 August 1927; in "Acknowledge the Wonder" by Carleton Beals in the *Nation* (New York), 14 September 1927; by Thomas Walsh in the *Commonweal*, 28 September 1927; by Conrad Aiken in the *Dial*, 15 October 1927; in the *Independent*, 15 October 1927; by Halle Schaffner in *Survey*, November 1927; and by Clennell Wilkinson in the *London Mercury*, December 1927.

NOTES (2): The Knopf *Mornings in Mexico* has a yellow dust-jacket printed in red, green and black; the upper cover and spine have a decorative design. See (A81.5).

A38 · [SELECTED POEMS]

first collected edition

*THE AUGUSTAN BOOKS OF | ENGLISH POETRY |
SECOND SERIES NUMBER TWENTY-TWO | [single rule] |
D. H. | LAWRENCE | [single rule] | LONDON: ERNEST
BENN LTD. | BOUVERIE HOUSE, FLEET STREET | [whole
enclosed within single border in turn enclosed within ornamental rule border in
turn enclosed within double rule border consisting of thin rule and thick rule]*

White paper covers, the upper cover serves as the title page as above.
On the lower cover is a list of the Augustan Books of English Poetry,
First Series. The leaves measure $8\frac{11}{16}'' \times 5\frac{5}{8}''$. Top edges trimmed; fore
and bottom edges untrimmed.

[i]–iv + 5–32, as follows: [i] title page and upper cover as above; [ii]
list of Augustan Books of English Poetry, Second Series; iii introduction
by Humbert Wolfe; iv contents; 5–30 text; 31 bibliography; [32] list
of Augustan Books of English Poetry, First Series. Page [32] also serves
as the lower cover.

Published 17 February 1928 at 6*d.*; number of copies unknown.

CONTENTS

Wedding Morn (from *Love Poems* (A3))—Kisses in the Train (A3)—
Cherry Robbers (A3)—Lilies in the Fire (A3)—Reminder (A3)—Song-
Day in Autumn (A3)—Aware (A3)—Return (A3)—Morning Work
(A3)—Dog-Tired (A3)—The Schoolmaster: A Snowy Day in School
(A3)—The Wild Common (from *Amores* (A9))—Monologue of a Mother
(A9)—Dreams Old (A9)—Dreams Nascent (A9)—A Winter's Tale (A9)
—Scent of Irises (A9)—Restlessness (A9)—The End (A9)—The Bride
(A9)—Drunk (A9)—After Many Days (A9)—A Passing Bell (A9)—
Elegy (A9).

NOTES (2): As described above this pamphlet is Number 22 in the Second
Series of Augustan Poets. Copies of the third impression published in
1934 reveal that the second impression was published in 1932. In the
third impression a list of pamphlets in the series apparently ignores the
earlier division into First and Second Series, and the Lawrence pamphlet
is given the number 78. The measurements of the first pamphlet as
described above are somewhat ambiguous. The pamphlet is stapled,
and the outer leaves are a bit wider than the inside leaves. One may

safely say the measurements fall within the limits of $8\frac{5}{8}'' \times 5\frac{1}{2}''$ and $8\frac{11}{16}'' \times 5\frac{5}{8}''$.

A39   CAVALLERIA RUSTICANA   1928

first edition

CAVALLERIA RUSTICANA | AND OTHER STORIES | by | GIOVANNI VERGA | *Translated and with an Introduction by* | D. H. LAWRENCE | [*publisher's device*] | JONATHAN CAPE | THIRTY BEDFORD SQUARE | LONDON

Dark-red cloth boards, stamped in gold on spine: CAVALLERIA | RUSTICANA | [*printer's ornament*] | VERGA | JONATHAN CAPE The leaves measure $7\frac{9}{16}'' \times 5''$. All edges trimmed.

[1]–224, as follows: [1] half-title; [2] note of translation by D. H. Lawrence; [3] title page as above; [4] FIRST PUBLISHED MCMXXVIII | PRINTED IN GREAT BRITAIN BY | BUTLER & TANNER LTD | FROME; 5 table of contents; [6] blank; 7–28 translator's preface; [29] fly-title: CAVALLERIA RUSTICANA; [30] blank; 31–224 text.

Published February 1928 at 6*s.*; the first printing consisted of 4500 copies.

CONTENTS

Translator's Preface—Cavalleria Rusticana—La Lupa—Caprice—Jeli the Herdsman—Rosso Malpelo, or the Red-Headed Brat—Gramigna's Lover—War of Saints—Brothpot—The How, When, and Wherefore.

NOTES: Lawrence's second book of translations from the Sicilian novelist Giovanni Verga was probably done during his travels from Italy through Australia and the East to Taos. Tedlock (B51) describes a manuscript notebook, containing some of the stories, which was in use in Australia. In May 1923 Lawrence wrote Middleton Murry from Chapala, Mexico, telling him to ask Curtis Brown to let him see the manuscript of "Novelle Rusticane" and offered to let him publish either "Cavalleria Rusticana" or "La Lupa" in the *Adelphi*, but none of the *Cavalleria Rusticana* stories appeared in the magazine, although several of the *Little Novels of Sicily* (A30) were published there.

Jonathan Cape reprinted *Cavalleria Rusticana* in June 1931 and published it in the Travellers' Library in April 1932. The first American edition was published by the Dial Press in 1928.

REVIEWS: Reviews of *Cavalleria Rusticana* appeared in *The Times Literary*

Supplement, 8 March 1928; by Edmund Blunden in the *Nation and Athenaeum*, 10 March 1928; in the *Spectator*, 2 June 1928; the *New Statesman*, 16 June 1928; the *New York Times Book Review*, 14 October 1928; by Vincent McHugh in the *New York Evening Post Literary Review*, 20 October 1928; and by H. Brickell in the *New York Herald Tribune Books*, 21 October 1928.

NOTES (2): Copies of *Cavalleria Rusticana* have been reported in an orange cloth binding, so an account of the variants should be:

VARIANTS: (1) copy described above.

(2) as above except bound in orange cloth; the leaves measure $7\frac{1}{2}'' \times 5''$.

It is probable that the orange cloth copies were later.

A40   RAWDON'S ROOF   1928

first edition

This is number seven of | the Woburn Books, being | Rawdon's Roof, a Story | by D. H. Lawrence: | published at London in | 1928 by Elkin Mathews & | Marrot | [*enclosed within decorative rule*] | [*publisher's device enclosed within decorative rule*]

Grey and blue decorative paper boards, printed in blue on upper cover: RAWDON'S | ROOF | BY | D. H. LAWRENCE | [*enclosed within decorative pattern*]; printed in blue on lower cover: THE WOBURN BOOKS The leaves measure $7\frac{5}{8}'' \times 5\frac{5}{8}''$. Top edges unopened; fore and bottom edges untrimmed.

[1]–32, as follows: [1] title page as above; [2] Five hundred and thirty | numbered copies of this story | have been set by hand in Im- | print Shadow, and printed by | Robert MacLehose & Co. Ltd., | at the University Press, Glas- | gow, of which Nos. 1–500 only | are for sale and Nos. 501–530 | for presentation. | This is copy No. 364 [*autograph number in blue ink*] D. H. Lawrence [*autograph signature in blue ink*]; 3–32 text.

Published March 1928 at 6*s.*; the first printing consisted of 530 copies.

NOTES: *Rawdon's Roof* was first collected in the posthumous *Lovely Lady* (A63).

NOTES (2): The dust-jacket for *Rawdon's Roof* is grey paper with decorations and lettering printed in blue.

a. *first edition*

THE WOMAN | WHO RODE AWAY | AND OTHER
STORIES | BY D. H. LAWRENCE | LONDON | MARTIN
SECKER | NUMBER FIVE JOHN STREET ADELPHI

Chocolate-brown cloth boards, blind stamped on upper and lower
covers: [*thick rule within thin rule forming border*]; stamped in gold on
spine: [*thin rule*] | [*thick rule*] | THE WOMAN | WHO RODE | AWAY | · |
D. H. | LAWRENCE | SECKER | [*thick rule*] | [*thin rule*] The leaves measure
$7\frac{1}{2}'' \times 4\frac{7}{8}''$. Top and fore edges trimmed; bottom edges untrimmed.

[1]–[296], as follows: [1]–[2] blank; [3] half-title; [4] blank; [5] title
page as above; [6] LONDON: MARTIN SECKER (LTD.), 1928; 7 table of
contents; [8] blank; [9] fly-title: TWO BLUE BIRDS; [10] blank; 11–29
text; [30] blank; [31] fly-title: SUN; [32] blank; 33–54 text; [55] fly-title:
THE WOMAN WHO RODE AWAY; [56] blank; 57–102 text; [103] fly-title:
SMILE; [104] blank; 105–110 text; [111] fly-title: THE BORDER LINE;
[112] blank; 113–136 text; [137] fly-title: JIMMY AND THE DESPERATE |
WOMAN; [138] blank; 139–168 text; [169] fly-title: THE LAST LAUGH;
[170] blank; 171–191 text; [192] blank; [193] fly-title: IN LOVE; [194]
blank; 195–211 text; [212] blank; [213] fly-title: GLAD GHOSTS; [214]
blank; 215–264 text; [265] fly-title: NONE OF THAT; [266] blank; 267–292
text; [293] PRINTED IN GREAT BRITAIN BY THE DUNEDIN PRESS LTD.,
EDINBURGH; [294]–[296] advertisements of Secker books.

Published 24 May 1928 at 7s. 6d.; the first printing consisted of 3000
copies.

b. *first American edition*

D. H. LAWRENCE | [*ornamental rule in orange*] | THE WOMAN |
WHO RODE AWAY | AND | OTHER STORIES | [*publisher's
device in orange*] | MCMXXVIII | NEW YORK: ALFRED·A·
KNOPF | [*enclosed within ornamental rule in orange in turn enclosed within
single rule in orange*]

Orange cloth boards, printed in black on upper cover: THE WOMAN |
WHO | RODE AWAY | [*short double rule*]; printed in green on lower cover:
[*publisher's device*]; printed on spine in black and green: [*thin rule*] | [*thick
rule*] | [*double thin rule*] | THE WOMAN | WHO | RODE AWAY | [*double short
rule*] | D. H. | LAWRENCE | [*double thin rule*] | [*the preceding ten lines on green

background] | [*thick rule*] | [*double thin rule on green background*] | [*series of decorative rules with vertical green stripe in centre*] | [*double thin rule on green background*] | [*thick rule*] | [*double thin rule*] | [*preceding three lines on green background*] | ALFRED · A · KNOPF | [*ornamental rule*] | [*double thin rule*] | [*preceding three lines on green background*] | [*thick rule*] | [*thin rule*] The leaves measure $7\frac{9}{16}'' \times 5\frac{1}{4}''$. Top edges trimmed and stained orange; fore edges untrimmed; bottom edges rough-trimmed.

[i]–[viii] + [1]–[312], as follows: [i]–[ii] blank; [iii] half-title; [iv] list of works by Lawrence; [v] title page as above; [vi] COPYRIGHT 1927, 1928 BY ALFRED A. KNOPF, INC. | MANUFACTURED IN THE UNITED STATES OF AMERICA; [vii] contents; [viii] blank; [1] fly-title: TWO BLUE BIRDS | [*short double rule*]; [2] blank; [3]–20 text; [21] fly-title: SUN | [*short double rule*]; [22] blank; [23]–43 text; [44] blank; [45] fly-title: THE WOMAN WHO RODE AWAY | [*short double rule*]; [46] blank; [47]–90 text; [91] fly-title: SMILE | [*short double rule*]; [92] blank; [93]–98 text; [99] fly-title: THE BORDER LINE | [*short double rule*]; [100] blank; [101]–122 text; [123] fly-title: JIMMY AND THE DESPERATE WOMAN | [*short double rule*]; [124] blank; [125]–154 text; [155] fly-title: THE LAST LAUGH | [*short double rule*]; [156] blank; [157]–177 text; [178] blank; [179] fly-title: IN LOVE | [*short double rule*]; [180] blank; [181]–197 text; [198] blank; [199] fly-title: THE MAN WHO LOVED ISLANDS | [*short double rule*]; [200] blank; [201]–230 text; [231] fly-title: GLAD GHOSTS | [*short double rule*]; [232] blank; [233]–280 text; [281] fly-title: NONE OF THAT | [*short double rule*]; [282] blank; [283]–307 text; [308] [*ornamental rule*] | [*note on the type*] | [*publisher's device*] | SET UP, ELECTROTYPED, PRINTED AND BOUND | BY THE VAIL-BALLOU PRESS, INC., | BINGHAMTON, N. Y. | PAPER MANUFACTURED BY S. D. WARREN CO., | BOSTON; [309]–[312] blank.

Published 25 May 1928 at $2.50; the first printing consisted of 2500 copies.

CONTENTS

Two Blue Birds (first appeared in the *Dial*, April 1927 (C154); first collected in *Great Stories of All Nations* (B22))—Sun (first appeared in the *New Coterie*, Autumn 1926 (C145); also separately published (A35))—The Woman Who Rode Away (first appeared in the *Dial*, July and August 1925 (C131) and (C132); first collected in *Best British Short Stories of 1926* (B20))—Smile (first appeared in the *Nation and Athenaeum*, June 1926 (C142))—The Border Line (first appeared in *Hutchinson's Magazine*, September 1924 (C123))—Jimmy and the Desperate Woman (first appeared in the *Criterion*, October 1924 (C125); first collected in

Best British Short Stories of 1925 (B17))—The Last Laugh (first appeared in *Ainslee's*, Jan 1926 (C136.5))—In Love (first appeared in the *Dial*, November 1927 (C162))—Glad Ghosts (first appeared in the *Dial*, July and August 1926 (C143) and (C144); also separately published (A36))—None of That—American edition only: The Man Who Loved Islands (first appeared in the *Dial*, July 1927 (C157)).

NOTES: All of the stories in this collection, the last before Lawrence's death, had been published previously with the exception of "None of That." Lawrence had tried unsuccessfully to find a place for it. In a letter to Dorothy Brett from Bandol in November 1928 he lamented the fact that no one would publish a story like "None of That" when the newspapers paid so well for the series of articles he did for London newspapers in 1928. The first American edition of *The Woman Who Rode Away* (A41b) contained the story "The Man Who Loved Islands," which was omitted from the Secker first edition, reportedly owing to the objection of Compton Mackenzie, who is said to have felt himself caricatured in the story.

Secker reprinted *The Woman Who Rode Away* in a Pocket Edition in March 1929; Chatto–Heinemann issued it as an Evergreen Book in May 1940, and Heinemann published a Pocket Edition with an introduction by Richard Aldington in April 1950. It is No. 758 in the Penguin series, published in March 1950; No. 244 in the Albatross Library and No. 4877 in the Tauchnitz Collection of British and American Authors; Tauchnitz published an abridged edition by Hans Schroder in the Students Series in 1948.

REVIEWS: *The Woman Who Rode Away* was reviewed in *The Times Literary Supplement*, 24 May 1928; by Henry Seidel Canby in "Too Soon and Too Late" in the *Saturday Review of Literature*, 2 June 1928; by L. P. Hartley in the *Saturday Review*, 2 June 1928; by R. A. Taylor in the *Spectator*, 2 June 1928; by G. W. Kennedy in the *New Statesman*, 2 June 1928; by J. R. Chamberlain in the *New York Times Book Review*, 3 June 1928; by Raymond Mortimer in the *Nation and Athenaeum*, 9 June 1928; by Mary Ross in the *New York Herald Tribune Books*, 10 June 1928; in the *Independent*, 16 June 1928; by Tess Slesinger in the *New York Evening Post Literary Review*, 22 June 1928; the *New York Times Book Review*, 24 June 1928; in the *Nation*, 4 July 1928; by William McFee in the *Bookman*, July 1928; by Herschell Brickell in the *North American Review*, July 1928; by D. B. Woolsey in the *New Republic*, 29 August 1928; by Ruth Suckow in the *Outlook* (New York), 29 August 1928; by Edward Shanks in the *London Mercury*, August 1928; in the *Dial*, August 1928.

REVIEWS (2): A review of *The Woman Who Rode Away* appeared in *Life and Letters* for August 1928.

A42   LADY CHATTERLEY'S LOVER   1928

a. *first edition*

LADY CHATTERLEY'S LOVER | BY | D. H. LAWRENCE | PRIVATELY PRINTED | 1928

Mulberry coloured paper boards, printed in black on upper cover: [*the Lawrence phoenix*]; white paper label on spine printed in black: LADY | CHATTERLEY'S | LOVER | D. H. | LAWRENCE | [*enclosed within single rule*] The leaves measure $8\frac{15}{16}'' \times 6\frac{3}{8}''$. Top edges rough-trimmed; fore and bottom edges untrimmed.

[i]–[iv] + 1–[368], as follows: [i] blank; [ii] This edition is limited | to One Thousand copies. | No 703 [*autograph number in blue ink*] | signed D. H. Lawrence [*autograph signature in blue ink*]; [iii] title page as above; [iv] Florence—Printed by the Tipografia Giuntina, directed by L. Franceschini.; 1–365 text; [366]–[368] blank.

Published July 1928 at £2; the first printing consisted of 1000 copies.

VARIANTS: (1) copy described above.
    (2) as (1) except printed on blue paper; two copies only.

b. *first edition (cheap paper issue)*

LADY CHATTERLEY'S LOVER | BY | D. H. LAWRENCE | PRIVATELY PRINTED | 1928

Mulberry coloured paper covers, printed in black on upper cover: [*the Lawrence phoenix*]; white paper label on spine, printed in black: LADY | CHATTERLEY'S | LOVER | D. H. | LAWRENCE | [*enclosed within single rule*] The leaves measure $8\frac{1}{2}'' \times 6\frac{3}{8}''$. Top edges rough-trimmed; fore and bottom edges untrimmed.

[i]–[iv] + 1–[368], as follows: [i] blank; [ii] Second edition | limited to 200 copies.; [iii] title page as above; [iv] Florence—Printed by the Tipografia Giuntina, directed by L. Franceschini.; 1–365 text; [366]–[368] blank.

Published November (?) 1928 at 21*s.*; the edition consisted of 200 copies.

c. *Paris popular edition*

THE AUTHOR'S UNABRIDGED POPULAR EDITION |
[*short rule*] | LADY CHATTERLEY'S LOVER | Including | MY
SKIRMISH WITH JOLLY ROGER | Written Especially and
Exclusively as an | Introduction to this Popular Edition | BY | D. H.
LAWRENCE | PRIVATELY PRINTED | 1929

Mulberry brown paper covers, printed in black on upper cover: 60 Frs
| [*short rule*] | [*the Lawrence phoenix*]; printed in black on lower cover:
LECRAM PRESS—PARIS; white paper label on spine printed in black: LADY
| CHATTERLEY'S | LOVER | D. H. | LAWRENCE | [*enclosed within single rule*]
The leaves measure $7\frac{1}{2}'' \times 5\frac{7}{16}''$. Top edges trimmed; fore and bottom
edges untrimmed.

[i]–[iv] + 1–VIII + 1–368, as follows: [i] title page as above; [ii] blank;
[iii] *Tous droits de reproduction, de | traduction et d'adaptation réservés | pour
tous pays y compris la Russie.* | Copyright by D. H. LAWRENCE.; [iv] blank;
1–VIII *My Skirmish With Jolly Roger* by D. H. Lawrence; 1–365 text;
[366]–[368] blank.

Published May 1929 at 60 fr; the first printing consisted of 3000 copies
reproduced photographically from (A42a).

d. *first authorized expurgated edition*

LADY CHATTERLEY'S | LOVER | BY D. H. LAWRENCE
| LONDON | MARTIN SECKER | NUMBER FIVE JOHN
STREET ADELPHI

Chocolate-brown cloth boards, blind stamped on upper and lower
covers: [*thick rule within thin rule forming border*]; stamped in gold on spine:
[*thin rule*] | [*thick rule*] | LADY | CHATTERLEY'S | LOVER |·| D. H. |
LAWRENCE | SECKER | [*thick rule*] | [*thin rule*] The leaves measure
$7\frac{7}{16}'' \times 4\frac{7}{8}''$. Top and fore edges trimmed; bottom edges untrimmed.

[1]–[328], as follows: [1]–[4] blank; [5] half-title; [6] blank; [7] title
page as above; [8] AUTHORIZED BRITISH EDITION | *First Published February
1932* | LONDON: MARTIN SECKER LTD., 1932; 9–327 text; [328] [*short rule*]
| PRINTED IN GREAT BRITAIN BY | THE DUNEDIN PRESS, LIMITED, EDINBURGH

Published February 1932 at 7s. 6d.; the first printing consisted of 3440
copies.

e. *first authorized expurgated edition, American impression*

D. H. LAWRENCE | [*short rule printed in orange*] | LADY CHAT-
TERLEY'S | LOVER | AUTHORIZED ABRIDGED EDI-
TION | [*publisher's device printed in orange*] | MCMXXXII | NEW
YORK: ALFRED·A·KNOPF | [*enclosed within decorative rule in
orange*]

Orange cloth boards, printed in black on upper cover: LADY CHAT-
TERLEY'S | LOVER | [*short double rule*]; printed in orange on lower cover
on a green background: [*publisher's device*]; printed in black on spine:
LADY | CHATTERLEY'S | LOVER | [*short double rule*] | D. H. | LAWRENCE |
ALFRED·A·KNOPF Spine is decorated with black and green horizontal
rules; title and author's name appear on a green panel background.
There is a vertical green and black decorative rule in the centre of the
middle portion of the spine. The leaves measure $7\frac{1}{2}'' \times 5\frac{1}{8}''$. Top edges
trimmed and stained orange; fore and bottom edges rough-trimmed.

[1]–[328], as follows: [1] blank; [2] list of books by and about
D. H. Lawrence; [3] half-title; [4] blank; [5] title page as above; [6]
FIRST AMERICAN EDITION | *All rights reserved—no part of this book may be
reprinted in* | *any form without permission in writing from the publishers* |
MANUFACTURED IN THE UNITED STATES OF AMERICA; [7] fly-title: LADY
CHATTERLEY'S LOVER; [8] blank; 9–327 text; [328] blank.

Published 1 September 1932 at \$2.50; the first printing consisted of
2000 copies.

f. *Odyssey Press edition*

LADY CHATTERLEY'S | LOVER | *by* | D. H. LAWRENCE
| THE ODYSSEY PRESS | HAMBURG·PARIS·BOLOGNA

Dark blue paper covers, printed in black on upper cover: LADY
CHATTERLEY'S | LOVER | BY | D. H. LAWRENCE |; printed in black on
spine: LADY | CHATTER | LEY'S | LOVER | BY | D. H. | LAWRENCE | THE
| ODYSSEY | PRESS; printed in black on lower cover: RM 2.80–FRS
18–LIRE 14 | NOT TO BE INTRODUCED INTO THE BRITISH EMPIRE OR THE
U.S.A. The leaves measure $7\frac{1}{16}'' \times 4\frac{5}{16}''$. All edges trimmed.

[i]–[viii] + 1–[364], as follows: [i]–[ii] blank; [iii] half-title; [iv] blank;
[v] title page as above; [vi] COPYRIGHT 1933 | BY THE ODYSSEY PRESS,
CHRISTIAN WEGNER, HAMBURG | IMPRIMÉ EN ALLEMAGNE; [vii]–[viii]

prefatory note by Frieda Lawrence; 1–[360] text; [361] blank; [362] THIS EDITION IS COMPOSED IN | BASKERVILLE TYPE CUT BY THE | MONOTYPE CORPORATION. THE | PAPER IS MADE BY THE PAPIER- | FABRIK BAUTZEN. THE PRINTING AND | THE BINDING ARE THE WORK OF | OSCAR BRANDSTETTER ·ABTEILUNG | JAKOB HEGNER·LEIPZIG; [363] advertisement of James Joyce's *Ulysses*; [364] blank.

Note: The description of the binding is taken from the second impression; the remainder of the description is taken from the first printing.

g. *first edition of first manuscript version*

The First Lady Chatterley | BY D. H. LAWRENCE | [*publisher's device*] Dial Press: New York

Blue-grey cloth boards, printed in black on spine: [*decorative rule*] | D. H. | LAWRENCE | [*printer's ornament*] | THE | First Lady | Chatterley | [*decorative rule*] Dial The leaves measure $7\frac{15}{16}'' \times 5\frac{5}{16}''$. All edges trimmed. Top edges stained blue.

[i]–xviii + [1]–322, as follows: [i] half-title; [ii] blank; [iii] title page as above; [iv] This book is complete and unabridged in contents, and | is manufactured in strict conformity with Government | regulations for saving paper. | Designed by William R. Meinhardt | Copyright, 1944, by The Dial Press, Inc. | Printed in the United States of America by | The Haddon Craftsmen, Inc., Scranton, Pa.; v–xiii foreword by Frieda Lawrence; [xiv] blank; xv–xviii a manuscript report by Esther Forbes; [1] fly-title: The First Lady Chatterley; [2] blank; 3–320 text; [321]–[322] blank.

Published 10 April 1944 at $2.75; the first printing consisted of 7500 copies.

h. *first edition of second manuscript version*

D. H. LAWRENCE | LE TRE [*printed in blue*] | "LADY CHAT-TERLEY" [*printed in blue*] | [*publisher's device in blue*] | ARNOLDO MONDADORI | EDITORE | [*enclosed within decorative rule*]

Rust-coloured cloth boards, stamped in gold on upper cover: [*publisher's device*]; stamped in gold on spine: VII | D. H. LAWRENCE | LE TRE | *LADY* | *CHATTERLEY* | MONDADORI | [*space between lines of lettering covered with decorative designs enclosed within thin rule in turn enclosed within thick rule forming border*] The leaves measure $7\frac{5}{8}'' \times 5\frac{1}{8}''$. All edges trimmed; top edges stained pink.

[i]–[xl] + [1]–[1060] and frontispiece facing title page, as follows: [i]–[ii] blank; [iii] I CLASSICI CONTEMPORANEI STRANIERI; [iv] blank; [v] TUTTE LE OPERE | DI DAVID HERBERT LAWRENCE | A CURA DI PIERO NARDI | [*short decorative rule*] | VOL. VII; [vi] blank; [vii] PIANO DELL' OPERA; [viii]–[ix] list of titles in *Tutte Le Opere Di David Herbert Lawrence*; [x] blank; [xi] title page as above; [xii] PROPRIETÀ LETTERARIA RISERVATA | [*short decorative rule*] | I EDIZIONE: GIUGNO 1954 | STAMPATO IN ITALIA—PRINTED IN ITALY | OFF. GRAF. VERONESI DELL'EDITORE ARNOLDO MONDADORI—VI—1954; [xiii] fly-title: INTRODUZIONE; [xiv] blank; [xv]–xxxviii introduction by Piero Nardi; [xxxix] fly-title: LE TRE | "LADY CHATTERLEY"; [xl] blank; [1] fly-title: I | LA PRIMA LADY CHATTERLEY | (*Traduzione di Carlo Izzo*); [2] blank; [3]–244 text; [245] fly-title: II | LA SECONDA LADY CHATTERLEY | (*Traduzione di Carlo Izzo*); [246] blank; [247]–627 text; [628] blank; [629] fly-title: III | L'AMANTE DI LADY CHATTERLEY | (*Traduzione di Giulio Monteleone*); [630] blank; [631]–1002 text; [1003] fly-title: A PROPOSITO DI | "L'AMANTE DI LADY CHATTERLEY" | (*Traduzione di Carlo Izzo*); [1004] blank; [1005]–1047 text; [1048] blank; [1049] fly-title: NOTA INFORMATIVA; [1050] blank; [1051]–1054 text; [1055] fly-title: INDICE; [1056] blank; [1057] index; [1058] QUESTO VOLUME, COMPOSTO CON CARATTERI | BEMBO, È STATO IMPRESSO SU CARTA TIPO | INDIA DELLE CARTIERE FEDRIGONI NEL | MESE DI GIUGNO DELL'ANNO MCMLIV NELLE | OFFICINE GRAFICHE VERONESI DELL'EDITORE | ARNOLDO MONDADORI | [*publisher's device in blue*]; [1059]–[1060] blank.

Published June 1954 at L. 5000; the first printing consisted of 2745 copies.

i. *first authorized unexpurgated American edition*

LADY | CHATTERLEY'S | LOVER | *by D. H. Lawrence* | With an Introduction by MARK SCHORER | GROVE PRESS INC. · NEW YORK

Cream-coloured cloth boards with a blue cloth backstrip; stamped in gold on spine, reading from top to bottom: LADY CHATTERLEY'S LOVER | *D. H. Lawrence* | GROVE | PRESS | [*preceding two lines read from left to right*] The leaves measure $8'' \times 5\frac{3}{8}''$. All edges trimmed.

[i]–[ii] + [i]–[xlii] + 1–[372], as follows: [i]–[ii] blank; [i] half-title;

A42

[ii] blank; [iii] title page as above; [iv] *Introduction by* Mark Schorer, | Copyright © 1957 by Grove Press, Inc. | *Letter from Archibald Macleish,* | Copyright © 1959 by Grove Press, Inc. | This edition is the third manuscript version, | first published by Giuseppe Orioli, Florence, 1928. | *Grove Press Books and Evergreen Books* | *are published by Barney Rosset at Grove Press, Inc.* | *795 Broadway New York 3, N. Y.* | MANUFACTURED IN THE UNITED STATES OF AMERICA; v–vii a letter by Archibald MacLeish; [viii] blank; ix–xxxix introduction by Mark Schorer; [xl] blank; [xli] fly-title: LADY CHATTERLEY'S LOVER; [xlii] blank; 1–365 text; [366] blank; 367–368 bibliographical note by Mark Schorer; [369]–[372] blank.

Published 4 May 1959 at $6.00; there were three printings of 15,000 copies each, before publication.

j. *first authorized unexpurgated English edition*

D. H. LAWRENCE | [*ornamental rule*] | *Lady Chatterley's Lover* | PENGUIN BOOKS

Orange paper covers, printed in black and orange on upper cover: PENGUIN BOOKS [*in orange*] | [*single rule*] | LADY | CHATTERLEY'S | LOVER | [*the Lawrence phoenix in black rising from orange flames*] | D. H. | LAWRENCE | [*single rule*] | COMPLETE AND 3/6 [*price in orange*] UNEXPURGATED | [*the preceding ten lines on white centre panel*] | [*publisher's device at right of Lawrence phoenix*]; printed in black on spine, reading from top to bottom: [*single rule*] | D. H. Lawrence | [*publisher's device in orange*] | Lady Chatterley's Lover | 1484 | [*single rule*]; on lower cover: [*portrait and biographical sketch of D. H. Lawrence*] The leaves measure $7\frac{1}{8}'' \times 4\frac{3}{8}''$. All edges trimmed.

[1]–[320], as follows: [1] half-title; [2] blank; [3] title page as above; [4] Penguin Books Ltd, Harmondsworth, Middlesex | AUSTRALIA: Penguin Books Pty Ltd, 762 Whitehorse Road, | Mitcham, Victoria | [*short rule*] | First printed 1928 | This complete text first published in | Great Britain 1960 | Made and printed in Great Britain | by Western Printing Services Ltd | Bristol; 5–[317] text; [318]–[320] blank.

Initially "published" on 16 August 1960, when twelve copies were handed to the police; copies were officially released to the public on 10 November 1960 at 3s. 6d.; the first printing consisted of 200,000 copies. Heinemann published a hard-cover edition from the Penguin text in July 1961.

k. *first English language edition of second manuscript version*

D. H. LAWRENCE | *John Thomas* | and | *Lady Jane* | (*the second version of 'Lady Chatterley's Lover'*) | [*publisher's device*] | HEINEMANN: LONDON

Brown cloth boards; stamped in gold on spine, reading from top to bottom: *John Thomas* | and | *Lady Jane* D. H. LAWRENCE | [*publisher's device*] The leaves measure $8\frac{1}{2}'' \times 5\frac{3}{8}''$. All edges trimmed.

[i]–[viii] + [1]–372, as follows: [i] half-title [ii] list of D. H. Lawrence books published by Heinemann; [iii] title page as above; [iv] William Heinemann Ltd | 15 Queen Street, Mayfair, London W1X 8BE | LONDON MELBOURNE TORONTO | JOHANNESBURG AUCKLAND | © Italian translation by Carlo Izzo, | Arnoldo Mondadori 1954 | © First publication in English, | The Frieda Lawrence Estate 1972 | 434 40737 2 | Printed in Great Britain by | Cox & Wyman Ltd., London, Fakenham and Reading; [v]–vii publisher's note; [viii] blank; [1]–372 text.

Published in August 1972 at £4.00; the first printing consisted of 2500 copies.

NOTES: Although Lawrence's *Lady Chatterley's Lover* in its time has been called many things, it is unquestionably one of the most interesting bibliographical specimens of the century. It has been pirated extensively, expurgated and bowdlerized, condemned and confiscated, translated into many languages, and published in a great variety of formats.

Frequently Lawrence wrote whole drafts anew rather than revise or correct early efforts, and because of this many of his writings exist in two or more manuscript versions. *Lady Chatterley's Lover* is unique among his novels in that three complete manuscript versions have been preserved. After Mrs Lawrence's death in 1956 the three manuscripts were sold to a private collector in California. Tedlock has appended to his *Bibliography* (B51) a study comparing the three versions, all of which were written between the autumn of 1926 and January 1928. The "Manuscript Report" which forms a portion of the prefatory pages of the *First Lady Chatterley* (A42g) is a comparison of the first manuscript version and the final version which supplied the text for the Florentine first edition in 1928. Piero Nardi comments on the three versions in his introduction to *Le Tre Lady Chatterley* (A42h) and in "Le Tre Radazioni dell'Amante di Lady Chatterley" in *Tre Venezie*, April–June 1949.

The earliest dating of the novel is derived from a note on the manuscript of the first version, in which Lawrence records the fact that some smudges on the manuscript were made by John, the dog, on 26 October 1926. John belonged to an Italian family on the estate of San Paolo Mosciano near Scandicci, where the Lawrences lived at the Villa Mirenda. There are various references to Lawrence's work on the novel in letters written in January and February of 1927, and he wrote Dorothy Brett in March that the novel was done, but that it would never be printed because it was improper according to the "poor unconventional fools." The second version must have been completed during the spring and summer of 1927, because Lawrence wrote Dorothy Brett from the Villa Mirenda in January 1928 that the third draft was completed except for the last chapter.

Several English publishers apparently saw the manuscript of *Lady Chatterley*; Secker decided not to publish the book, and Lawrence wrote Pollinger of Curtis Brown's office not to submit the manuscript to Chatto. This request presumably marked the surrender of hopes for English publication, but Knopf wrote from New York that they would try to get the novel "in shape" to offer to the public. Knopf eventually published an expurgated version (A42e), and the first English edition was also an expurgated version (A42d) published by Secker in 1932.

The first edition of *Lady Chatterley* was printed in the spring of 1928 as Lawrence's private business venture by the Tipografia Giuntina in Florence. He planned to dispose of the thousand numbered copies for two pounds each, and suggested to Aldous Huxley in April that "this procedure" was the solution for "us small-selling authors." Small order-forms were printed, and Lawrence sent them to his friends in Europe and America who were to act as his agents for the distribution of the book. These friends included the Huxleys, Harriet Monroe, Witter Bynner, Rolf Gardiner, Harry Crosby and many others. Enid Hilton, a friend from the Eastwood days, also helped him; during the trouble with officials in England over the selling of the novel, she kept several dozen copies ready in her flat for forwarding to customers.

English booksellers quickly placed orders with Lawrence for copies of *Lady Chatterley,* but as a result of rumours of police raids, many orders were cancelled in the summer of 1928, and it came about very soon that the author's avenue to the consumer was restricted to those friends who were willing to pass around the order forms. By December the price had risen to four pounds, and the novel was about to be suppressed in London and was stopped from entering the United States. In spite of all this difficulty, the first edition was sold out, or nearly so, by December 1928. In December Lawrence wrote Enid Hilton that he had done a small edition of 200 copies on "common paper" (A42b); this small edition was printed from the type used for the first edition, which was set by hand by the Tipografia Giuntina.

The only other edition of *Lady Chatterley* with which Lawrence had anything to do was the Paris Popular Edition (A42c), printed in Paris in May 1929; this is the edition for which Lawrence wrote the essay *My Skirmish With Jolly Roger* (A48) which discusses the various piracies of the novel which had come to Lawrence's attention. The Paris edition was promoted by Lawrence in an effort to combat the piracies, which, however, continued to appear. E. W. Titus, who printed the Paris edition, also distributed it for Lawrence; in a letter to the Huxleys from Baden-Baden in August 1929 Lawrence noted that Titus had sold the first 3000 copies and was reprinting.

In 1933 Frieda Lawrence authorized the Odyssey Press to publish a "definitive" edition of *Lady Chatterley* (A42f), correcting the many typographical errors present in the Florentine first edition.

The printers and type-setters in the Tipografia Giuntina knew no English, a situation which Lawrence characterized as one where "ignorance is bliss," but as a result there were a great many typographical errors, duplicated of course in the "common paper" copies, in the Paris Popular edition, actually a photographic facsimile, and in those piracies which were photographically reproduced from the original edition. The following selection of typographical errors may be used to identify the original text:

page 4, line 17	"yeld" for "yield"
page 6, line 3	"hnow" for "know"
page 6, line 10 from bottom	"agaim" for "again"
page 25, line 6 from bottom	"surroudings" for "surroundings"
page 78, line 14	"forme" for "for me"
page 219, line 3 from bottom	"overwhalming" for "overwhelming"

A complete account of the *Lady Chatterley* piracies would make a fascinating chapter of publishing history. Lawrence wrote from Baden-Baden in July 1929 of a rumour that an illustrated edition, the sixth piracy, was to be printed in Philadelphia. Lawrence's most complete discussion of the piracies is found in *A Propos of Lady Chatterley's Lover* (A48b), an extended version of *My Skirmish With Jolly Roger*.

The first pirated edition of the novel came to light in Paris in 1928; it was a close replica of the original and was marked "Imprimé en Allemagne." Some copies of this piracy were noted with Lawrence's forged signature. Another piracy, which apparently originated in New

York in 1928, was bound in black cloth; this printing had two title pages containing the vignette of an American eagle with six stars around its head and lightning coming from the claw. A second piracy appearing in New York the same year was a photographic facsimile of the original, bound in orange cloth boards with a green paper label; copies have been noted with a forged Lawrence signature.

Another photographic facsimile was selling in New York for fifteen dollars about a month after the first genuine copies arrived from Italy. This may be the piracy which booksellers still list occasionally; it looks very much like the original edition, but the mulberry-coloured paper boards are a slightly different shade and without the Lawrence phoenix on the upper cover. According to the statement of limitation in the forgery, 1500 copies were printed. The forgery is somewhat thicker than the genuine *Lady Chatterley*; the spurious copy measures $1\frac{1}{2}''$, while the genuine first edition measures only $1\frac{3}{16}''$ over the covers. Two other *Lady Chatterley*s, probably unauthorized, appeared in New York in 1930 under the imprints of William Faro and Nesor. See Appendix 1, pp. 563–565.

Lady Chatterley's Lover has been distinguished by several parodies, sequels and similar literary compliments. William Faro issued *Lady Chatterley's Husbands* in September 1931 in New York, and although the book was advertised as an anonymous sequel to the "celebrated novel," Samuel Roth is credited with the work. Faro also published a dramatization of the Roth novel in April 1931.

Sadie Catterley's Cover, A Leg Pull was published by Cranley and Day in London in November 1933; it was written by William S. Scott and published under the pseudonym Robert Leicester.

A serious sequel to *Lady Chatterley*, *Le Deuxième Mari de Lady Chatterley*, by Jehanne d'Orliac was published in Paris by Albin Michel in 1934 and an English translation by Warre Bradley Wells was published in New York in March 1935 under the title *Lady Chatterley's Second Husband*. The Wells translation was reviewed in the *Times Literary Supplement*, 21 February 1935 and in the *Springfield* (Massachusetts) *Republican*, 11 August 1935.

The Arthur Yeoman Press of Hollywood published *Lady Loverly's Chatter* under the pseudonym Mart Reb in May 1945, and what may have been a serious attempt to dramatize *Lady Chatterley*, a two-act play based on Lawrence's story, was copyrighted for oral delivery by Benjamin Capito in August 1951.

The Secker abridged *Lady Chatterley* (A42d) was reprinted in the Cheap Edition in July 1933 and in the Pocket Edition in February 1934. Heinemann published the book in 1935, in the Pocket Edition in 1950 and in the Vanguard Library in 1953. In the United States Grosset and Dunlap issued the novel in the Novels of Distinction series in 1934 and as a Madison Square Book in 1940. The first authorized unexpurgated edition of *Lady Chatterley's Lover* (A42i) published in either England or the United States was issued by the Grove Press in New York in 1959.

English language editions published abroad include the Pegasus book published at Paris in 1938; an edition by Jan-Forlag at Stockholm in 1942; one by Keimeisha of Tokyo in 1952 and a reprint of the Paris Popular edition by G. W. Breugel at The Hague in 1944. *Lady Chatterley* is No. 56 of the Albatross Library, and the *First Lady Chatterley* was published by Scherz in Bern as No. 53 of the Phoenix Books in 1946.

REVIEWS: Reviews and discussions of *Lady Chatterley* appeared in the *New York Sun*, 1 September 1928, by H. J. Seligmann; by Edmund Wilson in the *New Republic*, 3 July 1929; *The Times Literary Supplement*, 25 February 1932; by V. S. Pritchett in the *Fortnightly Review*, April 1932; in "Bowdlerized Lawrence" by H. Hazlitt in the *Nation* (New York), 7 September 1932; by Horace Gregory in the *New Republic*, 14 December 1932; in "Fine and Imprisonment for Selling Lawrence's Book" in the *Publisher's Weekly*, 30 November 1929; in editorial comment in the *Nation* (New York), 10 December 1930.

Reviews and comments on *The First Lady Chatterley* appeared in "The Unpublished Lady Chatterley" by T. M. Pearce in the *New Mexico Quarterly* No. 8, 1938; by Diana Trilling in the *Nation* (New York), 22 April 1944. The *Publisher's Weekly* published a five-part article called "The First Lady Chatterley Case" in the 6 May, 20 May, 27 May, 17 June and 11 November issues, 1944, which discussed the copyright aspects of *The First Lady Chatterley* publication.

NOTES (2): Speculation continues about the provenance of the so-called "Third Edition" of *Lady Chatterley* noted in item II of Section B, Appendix I of the first edition of the bibliography. The presence of the photograph of the bust of Lawrence by Jo Davidson would indicate the date of printing, 1929, to be false. Mr S. Vogelmann of the Tipografia Giuntina in a letter to me dated 25 January 1964 stated that an examination of a copy of the book in the National Library in Florence revealed that a different type face was used and that in his opinion the book was not printed by Tipografia Giuntina. The records of the firm had nothing about a 1929 edition of *Lady Chatterley*. Hence the original conclusion that the 1929 edition is spurious must stand.

Apparently there were in circulation before the publication of the Penguin edition of *Lady Chatterley* (A42j) a number of proof copies in white wrappers in which page 4 records the printer as Hazell, Watson and Viney Ltd., Aylesbury and Slough. George Watson of Bertram Rota, Ltd. has been quoted as saying the former printer withdrew for fear of prosecution.

There are two variants for (A42i):

VARIANTS: (1) copy described above, the first printing.

(2) as (1) but on page [iv] the following words are omitted: *Grove Press Books and Evergreen Books | are published by Barney Rosset at Grove Press, Inc. | 795 Broadway New York 3, N. Y.*

Mr W. Forster has in his collection a copy of (A42g) which was printed by Peter Huston, Sidney 1944; otherwise the description agrees with the copy described above. Mr George Lazarus has a copy of the "third edition" numbered 95 which is blank on the spine and upper cover, but has on the lower cover the Lawrence phoenix stamped in black, set diagonally in the lower left corner.

A43 COLLECTED POEMS 1928

a. *first edition (ordinary copies)*

VOL. I

THE COLLECTED POEMS OF | D. H. LAWRENCE | *VOLUME ONE* | RHYMING POEMS | LONDON | MARTIN SECKER | 1928

Dark-brown cloth boards, stamped in gold on upper cover: THE COLLECTED POEMS OF | D. H. LAWRENCE | [*five-pointed star*]; stamped in gold on spine: THE | COLLECTED | POEMS OF | D. H. | LAWRENCE | [*five-pointed star*] | SECKER The leaves measure 8″ × 5⅝″. Top edges trimmed and stained dark-green; fore and bottom edges untrimmed.

[1]–[232], as follows: [1] half-title; [2] blank; [3] title page as above; [4] LONDON: MARTIN SECKER (LTD.) | NUMBER FIVE JOHN STREET ADELPHI; 5–7 introductory note by D. H. Lawrence; [8] blank; 9–230 text; 231–[232] table of contents.

VOL. II

THE COLLECTED POEMS OF | D. H. LAWRENCE | *VOLUME TWO* | UNRHYMING POEMS | LONDON | MARTIN SECKER | 1928

Dark-brown cloth boards, stamped in gold on upper cover: THE

COLLECTED POEMS OF | D. H. LAWRENCE | [*two five-pointed stars*]; stamped in gold on spine: THE | COLLECTED | POEMS OF | D. H. | LAWRENCE | [*two five-pointed stars*] | SECKER The leaves measure 8″ × 5⅝″. Top edges trimmed and stained dark-green; fore and bottom edges untrimmed.

[1]–[304], as follows: [1] half-title; [2] blank; [3] title page as above; [4] LONDON MARTIN SECKER (LTD.) | NUMBER FIVE JOHN STREET ADELPHI; [5] fly-title: LOOK! WE HAVE COME | THROUGH!; [6]–118 text; [119] fly-title: BIRDS, BEASTS AND | FLOWERS; [120] blank; [121] fly-title: FRUITS; [122] blank; 123–143 text; [144] blank; [145] fly-title: TREES; [146] blank; 147–155 text; [156] blank; [157] fly-title: FLOWERS; [158] blank; 159–175 text; [176] blank; [177] fly-title: THE EVANGELISTIC BEASTS; [178] blank; 179–191 text; [192] blank; [193] fly-title: CREA-TURES; [194] blank; 195–213 text; [214] blank; [215] fly-title: REPTILES; [216] blank; 217–238 text; [239] fly-title: BIRDS; [240] blank; 241–250 text; [251] fly-title: ANIMALS; [252] blank; 253–287 text; [288] blank; [289] fly-title: GHOSTS; [290] blank; 291–301 text; [302] blank; 303–[304] table of contents, at bottom of page [304]: Printed in Great Britain | by The Riverside Press Limited | Edinburgh

Published September 1928 at 21*s*.; 1000 ordinary copies were printed.

b. *first edition (special copies)*

VOL. I

THE COLLECTED POEMS OF | D. H. LAWRENCE | *VOL-UME ONE* | RHYMING POEMS | LONDON | MARTIN SECKER | 1928

Grey paper boards with a white vellum paper backstrip. Top edges gilt; otherwise identical with the ordinary issue.

The limited issue of *Collected Poems* was identical with the ordinary issue with the exception of page [4] of Vol. I which reads: ONE HUNDRED SPECIAL COPIES | HAVE BEEN PREPARED, BEARING | THE AUTHOR'S SIGNATURE, OF | WHICH THIS COPY IS No. 55 [*autograph number in black ink*] D. H. Lawrence [*autograph signature in black ink*]

VOL. II

THE COLLECTED POEMS OF | D. H. LAWRENCE | *VOLUME TWO* | UNRHYMING POEMS | LONDON | MARTIN SECKER | 1928

Volume II of the limited issue of *Collected Poems* was identical with the ordinary issue except for the binding described above for Volume I.

Published September 1928 at 42*s.*; 100 special copies were printed.

Mr Bertram Rota has reported a copy of *The Collected Poems* which internally corresponds with the ordinary issue, but is bound with the vellum paper backstrip of the limited issue.

CONTENTS

VOL. I RHYMING POEMS

Autumn (A9)—The Inheritance (A9)—Silence (A9)—Listening (A9)—
Brooding Grief (A9)—Last Words to Miriam (A9)—Malade (A9)—
Lotus and Frost (from *Amores* as "Lotus Hurt by the Cold")—The
Yew-Tree on the Downs (from *Amores* as "Liaison")—Troth with the
Dead (A9)—At a Loose End (from *Amores* as "Dissolute")—Submerg-
ence (A9)—The Enkindled Spring (A9)—Excursion Train (from *Amores*
as "Excursion")—Release (from *Amores* as "Reproach")—These Clever
Women (from *Amores* as "A Spiritual Woman")—Ballad of Another
Ophelia (A9)—Kisses in the Train (A3)—Turned Down (from *Amores*
as "Perfidy")—After Many Days (A9)—Snap-Dragon (A9)—Come
Spring, Come Sorrow (from *Amores* as "Mating")—The Hands of the
Betrothed (A9)—A Love Song (A9)—Twofold (A11)—Tarantella
(A11)—Under the Oak (A11)—Brother and Sister (A9)—The Shadow
of Death (from *Amores* as "Blue")—Birdcage Walk (A11)—In Trouble
and Shame (A9)—Call into Death (from *Amores* as "Elegy")—Grey
Evening (A9)—Firelight and Nightfall (A9)—Blueness (from *Amores* as
"Mystic Blue")—A Passing-Bell (A9)—The Drained Cup (A3)—Late
at Night (from *New Poems* as "Phantasmagoria")—Next Morning
(A11)—Winter in the Boulevard (A11)—Parliament Hill in the Evening
(A11)—Embankment at Night, before the War: Charity (A11)—Em-
bankment at Night, before the War: Outcasts (A11)—Sickness (A11)—
In Church (A11)—Piano (A11)—The North Country (A11)—Love
Storm (A11)—Passing Visit to Helen (from *New Poems* as "Intime")—
Twenty Years Ago (A11)—Reading a Letter (A11)—Seven Seals
(A11)—Two Wives (A11)—Noise of Battle (first appeared in *New Poems*
as "Apprehension")—At the Front (first appeared in *New Poems* as
"Heimweh")—Reality of Peace, 1916 (first appeared in *New Poems* as
"Débâcle")—Narcissus (A11)—Tommies in the Train (A12)—On the
March (A12)—Ruination (A12)—The Attack (A12)—Winter-Lull (A12)
—Bombardment (A12)—Rondeau of a Conscientious Objector (A12)—
Obsequial Ode (A12)—Going Back (A12)—Shades (A12)—Town in
1917 (first appeared in *Bay: A Book of Poems* as "Town")—Bread Upon
the Waters (A12)—War-Baby (A12)—Nostalgia (A12)—Dreams Old
and Nascent: Nascent (A9)—On That Day (A11)—Autumn Sunshine
(A11).

VOL. II UNRHYMING POEMS

Look! We Have Come Through!

Note: The contents of this section are the same as for *Look! We Have
Come Through!* (A10) with the exception of the following titles which

were added by Lawrence when he prepared the *Collected Poems* for publication:

Bei Hennef (first appeared in *Love Poems* (A3))—Everlasting Flowers (first appeared in *New Poems* (A11))—Coming Awake (A11)—Song of a Man Who is Loved (previously unpublished; see (A10) and (B40)).

Birds, Beasts and Flowers

The contents of this section are the same as for *Birds, Beasts and Flowers* (A27b), which included the *Tortoise* (A19) poems not printed in the American edition of *Birds, Beasts and Flowers* (A27a).

NOTES: Lawrence began to prepare the manuscript for *The Collected Poems* as early as November 1927, for he wrote then to Aldous Huxley from the Villa Mirenda that he was typing out the old poems. A letter to Witter Bynner the following January from Switzerland told that he was busy collecting poems for the Secker edition, and by March he was correcting proofs back in Florence at the Villa Mirenda.

In the preface to *The Collected Poems* Lawrence noted that some of the earlier poems, such as "The Wild Common" and "The Virgin Youth," were a good deal rewritten; however, as McDonald (B31) notes, this is something of an understatement, and as a matter of fact, a good many of the poems were submitted to a rigorous revision. Lawrence also changed the titles of a number of the poems.

In general, the plan for *The Collected Poems* involved the inclusion of *Love Poems* (A3), *Amores* (A9), *New Poems* (A11) and *Bay* (A12) in Volume I as "Rhyming Poems" and the poems in *Look! We Have Come Through!* (A10) and *Birds, Beasts and Flowers* (A27) in Volume II as "Unrhyming Poems." Lawrence attempted to arrange the poems in Volume I in chronological order, omitting two poems from *Amores* and one from *Love Poems* which were replaced in the Phoenix *Complete Poems* (A98). Although he changed a few of the poems from *Look! We Have Come Through!* only slightly, Lawrence did take the opportunity to replace four poems in the cycle which he had intended for the original publication in 1917. The poem "Song of a Man Who is Loved" integral to the *Look! We Have Come Through!* sequence appears in print for the first time here in the collected edition. Frieda prints a different, probably earlier, version in *Not I, But the Wind* (B40). The text of the *Birds, Beasts and Flowers* is reproduced from the English edition of the book (A27b).

The first American impression of *The Collected Poems* was published by Jonathan Cape and Harrison Smith in July 1929; Secker reprinted the poems in a one-volume edition in August 1932 and the two-volume edition in December 1929.

REVIEWS: *Collected Poems* was reviewed by Edward Shanks in the *Saturday Review*, 6 October 1928; by Affable Hawk [Desmond MacCarthy] in the *New Statesman*, 20 October 1928; by J. C. Squire in the *Observer*, 1 October 1928; in the *Nation and Athenaeum*, 10 November 1928; *The Times Literary Supplement*, 15 November 1928; by E. G. Twitchett in the *London Mercury*, February 1929; by John Middleton Murry in the *Adelphi*, December 1928; by Percy Hutchison in the *New York Times Book Review*, 7 July 1929; by John Gould Fletcher in the *New York Herald Tribune Books*, 14 July 1929; by J. D. Tasker in the *Outlook* (New York), 17 July 1929; by Conrad Aiken in the *New York Evening Post*, 20 July 1929; in "Hot Blood's Blindfold Art" by Louis Untermeyer in the *Saturday Review of Literature*, 3 August 1929; in the *Spectator*, 29 September 1928; by Isidor Schneider in "Salvation Through Sex" in the *Book League Monthly*, October 1929; in the *Bookman* (New York), January 1930; in "Two English Poets" by Mark Van Doren in the *Nation* (New York), 15 January 1930; by Humbert Wolfe in the *Observer*, 14 August 1932; by Alan Pryce-Jones in the *London Mercury*, September 1932; in "Poetry of Fear" in the *Saturday Review*, 24 September 1932; *The Times Literary Supplement*, 29 September 1932; by V. S. Pritchett in the *Fortnightly Review*, October 1932.

NOTES (2): (A43a) the ordinary copies were issued in cream paper dust-jackets printed in brown; the special copies were issued in cream paper dust-jackets printed in red with the statement of limitation on the upper cover. The American edition published by Jonathan Cape and Harrison Smith was issued in a red paper covered slip case with a cream paper label on the spine printed in black.

REVIEWS (2) Additional reviews of the *Collected Poems* appeared in the *Springfield Republican* for 4 November 1928 by J. C. Squire; and in the *Boston Evening Transcript* for 20 July 1929 by E. B. Hall.

A44 SEX LOCKED OUT 1928

first edition

SEX LOCKED OUT | BY THE AUTHOR OF | "LADY CHATTERLEY'S LOVER" | REPRINTED, DECEMBER, 1928, FROM THE | SUNDAY DISPATCH, LONDON, NOVEMBER 25, 1928

Without wrappers but with protective tissue cover; tied together with white cord; title page as above serves as upper cover, page [12] as lower cover. The leaves measure $8\frac{3}{4}'' \times 5\frac{1}{2}''$. All edges untrimmed.

[1]–[12], as follows: [1] title page as above; [2] blank; 3–11 text; [12] PRIVATELY PRINTED DECEMBER, 1928

Published December 1928, probably not offered for sale; number of copies unknown.

NOTES: This small booklet was apparently an unauthorized reprint from the *Sunday Dispatch*, 25 November 1928 (C179); the article was collected in *Assorted Articles* (A53) as "Sex Versus Loveliness." McDonald (B31) suggests that someone in London had the article printed as a Christmas greeting and affirms that Lawrence was probably unaware of its publication; however, there is a copy in my library which has tipped in at page 3 a small slip which reads: "From Mitchell Kennerley Christmas 1928." It is of course possible that Lawrence did know about the printing.

A45 THE STORY OF DOCTOR MANENTE 1929

a. *first edition (ordinary copies)*

THE STORY OF DOCTOR MA- | NENTE BEING THE TENTH AND | LAST STORY FROM THE SUP- | PERS OF A. F. GRAZZINI CALLED | IL LASCA TRANSLATION AND INTRO- | DUCTION BY D. H. LAWRENCE | [*engraving*] | G. ORIOLI. 6 LUNGARNO CORSINI. FLORENCE.

Paper vellum boards, printed in black on upper cover: [*oval ornament with fleur-de-lis in centre*]; printed in black on spine reading upwards: D. H. LAWRENCE—THE STORY OF DOCTOR MANENTE BY LASCA The leaves measure $7\frac{11}{16}'' \times 5\frac{3}{8}''$. Top edges unopened; fore and bottom edges untrimmed.

[i]–xxiv + [1]–[122] with frontispiece and two plates facing pages [1] and [108], as follows: [i]–[ii] blank; [iii] half-title; [iv] PRINTED IN FLORENCE: all rights reserved. | 1929; [v] fly-title: LASCA | THE THIRD SUPPER; [vi] Twelve hundred copies have been printed of this edition: | Two hundred Special copies signed on Binda hand- | made paper, and one thousand numbered on Lombardy | paper, of which this is No. 445 [*autograph number in black ink*]; [vii] title page as above; [viii] blank; ix–xxiv foreword by D. H. Lawrence; [1]–108 text; 109–119 notes on

the text; [120] blank; [121] PRINTED | BY | TIPOGRAFIA L. FRANCESCHINI | 3, VIA DELLA SPADA | FLORENCE; [122] blank.

Published November 1929 at 10s.; 1000 ordinary copies were printed.

b. *first edition (special copies)*

THE STORY OF DOCTOR MA- | NENTE BEING THE TENTH AND | LAST STORY FROM THE SUP- | PERS OF A. F. GRAZZINI CALLED | IL LASCA TRANSLATION AND INTRO- | DUCTION BY D. H. LAWRENCE | [*engraving*] | G. ORIOLI. 6 LUNGARNO CORSINI. FLORENCE.

Paper vellum boards, printed in red on upper cover: [*oval ornament with fleur-de-lis in centre*]; printed in red on spine reading upwards: D. H. LAW-RENCE—THE STORY OF DOCTOR MANENTE BY LASCA The leaves measure $8\frac{7}{16}'' \times 5\frac{5}{8}''$. Top edges unopened; fore and bottom edges untrimmed.

[i]–xxiv + [1]–[122] with frontispiece and two plates facing pages [1] and [108], as follows: [i]–[ii] blank; [iii] half-title; [iv] PRINTED IN FLORENCE: all rights reserved. | 1929; [v] fly-title: LASCA | THE THIRD SUPPER; [vi] Twelve hundred copies have been printed of this edition: | Two hundred Special copies signed on Binda hand- | made paper, [*autograph parenthesis in blue ink*] and one thousand numbered on Lombardy | paper, [*autograph parenthesis in blue ink*] of which this is No. 178. [*autograph number in blue ink*] | D. H. Lawrence [*autograph signature in blue ink*]; [vii] title page as above; [viii] blank; ix–xxiv foreword by D. H. Lawrence; [1]–108 text; 109–119 notes on the text; [120] blank; [121] PRINTED | BY | TIPOGRAFIA L. FRANCESCHINI | 3, VIA DELLA SPADA | FLORENCE; [122] blank.

Published November 1929, price unknown; 200 special copies were printed.

VARIANTS: (1) copy described above.
(2) as (1) except printed on blue paper, two copies only.

NOTES: In the autumn of 1928 Lawrence suggested to Pino Orioli that they should collaborate in the publication of a series of Italian renaissance novelists and told him he was already translating the *Terza Cena* of Lasca. Lawrence continued to interest himself in the project and wrote to Maria Huxley in November asking if Aldous might like to do a title for the series; he also suggested to Pollinger that the Oxford University Press might be induced to publish them.

Although the statement of limitation gives the number of copies as 1200, Orioli in his *Adventures of a Bookseller*, the twelfth and last of the Lungarno Series, laments the fact that he overprinted the first Lungarno title, *Doctor Manente*, because of Lawrence's over-optimism and records that 2400 copies were printed. In 1957 the successor to Orioli's bookshop in Florence still had copies on hand.

Orioli continued the publication of the series, publishing translations by Richard Aldington and Harold Acton among others. Lawrence's *Apocalypse* (A57) and *Last Poems* (A62) were respectively Nos. 6 and 10 in the Lungarno Series.

REVIEWS: *The Story of Doctor Manente* was reviewed by Lyn St. Irvine in the *Nation and Athenaeum*, 14 December 1929.

NOTES (2): In all copies examined of both (A45a) and (A45b) in which the last leaf was present, i.e., pp. 121–122, the leaf was a cancel; some copies do not have the leaf. The dust-jacket for (A45a) is tan paper printed in black; no dust-jackets were observed for (A45b). There are two copies in the University of Texas library marked in Orioli's handwriting as "Review copies" with the price given as 12/6.

The foreword was reprinted in *Phoenix* (A76).

REVIEWS (2): A review of *The Story of Doctor Manente* appeared in *Life and Letters* for March 1930 by Peter Quennell.

A46   THE PAINTINGS OF   1929
D. H. LAWRENCE

a. *first edition* (*ordinary copies*)

The PAINTINGS of | D. H. LAWRENCE | [*Lawrence phoenix*] | *Privately printed for subscribers only* | THE MANDRAKE PRESS | 41 MUSEUM STREET | LONDON W. C. 1

Green cloth boards with brown morocco backstrip and corners, stamped in gold on upper and lower covers: [*Lawrence phoenix*]; stamped in gold on spine, reading upwards: THE PAINTINGS OF D. H. LAWRENCE The leaves measure $14\frac{3}{8}''$ × $10\frac{3}{4}''$. Top edges trimmed and gilt; fore and bottom edges untrimmed.

[1]–[148], as follows: [1] half-title; [2] blank; [3] title page as above; [4] blank; [5] table of contents; [6] blank; [7]–[39] introduction by D. H. Lawrence; [40] blank; [41]–[144] reproductions of the paintings, half-titles and reproductions are on alternate rectos, versos are blank;

[145] [*drawing of man and woman*] | THIS BOOK OF PAINTINGS BY D. H. LAWRENCE | is printed for the Mandrake Press at the Botolph | Printing Works Kingsway London [*printer's ornament*] Typography | and production arranged by P. R. Stephensen | Letterpress and colourwork under the super- | vision of William Dieper [*printer's ornament*] The edition | is limited to 510 copies, numbers 1–10 | being printed upon Japanese | vellum [*printer's ornament*] Numbers 11–510 on | Arches mouldmade paper | *This is number 107*; [146]–[148] blank.

Published June 1929 at 10 guineas; 500 ordinary copies were printed.

b. *first edition (special copies)*

The PAINTINGS of | D. H. LAWRENCE | [*Lawrence phoenix*] | Privately printed for subscribers only | THE MANDRAKE PRESS | 41 MUSEUM STREET | LONDON W. C. 1

Vellum boards, stamped in gold on upper and lower covers: [*Lawrence phoenix enclosed within single rule forming border*] The leaves measure $14'' \times 10\frac{1}{2}''$. All edges trimmed and gilt. Otherwise the limited issue was the same as the ordinary issue.

The special copies of *The Paintings of D. H. Lawrence* are identical with the ordinary copies with the exception of page [145] which reads: [*drawing of man and woman*] | THIS BOOK OF PAINTINGS BY D. H. LAWRENCE | is printed for the Mandrake Press at the Botolph | Printing Works Kingsway London [*printer's ornament*] Typography | and production arranged by P. R. Stephensen | Letterpress and colourwork under the super- | vision of William Dieper [*printer's ornament*] The edition | is limited to 510 copies, numbers 1–10 | being printed upon Japanese | vellum [*printer's ornament*] Numbers 11–510 on | Arches mouldmade paper | *This is out of Series* | D. H. Lawrence [*autograph signature in black ink*].

Published June 1929 at 50 guineas; 10 special copies were printed.

It will be seen that some special copies were "out of series" as was the case with the copy described here from the library of Mr George Lazarus.

CONTENTS

Introduction to These Paintings

The Oil Paintings: Resurrection (reproduced in *Sex, Literature and Censorship* (A92))—A Holy Family (reproduced in *Vanity Fair*, November

1929)—Red Willow Trees (reproduced in *Vanity Fair*, November 1929)—Finding of Moses (reproduced in *Creative Art*, July 1929 (C188), and *Sex, Literature and Censorship* (A92))—Contadini (reproduced in *Art News*, February 1957)—Rape of the Sabine Women (reproduced in *Art News*, February 1957)—Flight Back into Paradise—Boccaccio Story—Accident in a Mine—North Sea—Fight with an Amazon—Fauns and Nymphs (reproduced in *Vanity Fair*, November 1929, and in *Sex, Literature and Censorship* (A92))—Family on a Verandah—Close-Up (Kiss) (reproduced in *Art News*, Febuary 1957)—Dance-Sketch (reproduced in *Art News*, February 1957 as "Dance").

The Water Colours: Spring—Summer Dawn (actually in oils)—Fire-Dance—Under the Hay-Stack (reproduced in *Sex, Literature and Censorship* (A92))—Yawning—Leda—Renascence of Men (reproduced in *Art News*, February 1957, as "Renascence")—The Mango Tree—Throwing Back the Apple (reproduced in *Art News*, February 1957, as "Flinging Back the Apple")—The Lizard (reproduced in *Art News*, February 1957)—Singing of Swans.

NOTES: Perhaps less is known of Lawrence's work as a painter than of any other facet of his creative activity. Most of the paintings reproduced in this volume were done in Italy at the Villa Mirenda in 1928, although some were painted in Switzerland and other places to which the Lawrences journeyed during the period. Much information about Lawrence's painting activity is revealed in the correspondence with the Huxleys during 1928 and 1929; several of the paintings are mentioned by name.

A letter to Aldous Huxley from the Villa Mirenda in April 1928 lists seven of the watercolours, "Throwing Back the Apple" which Lawrence then called "Adam Throwing the Apple," "The Fire-Dance" then referred to as "Torch Dance," "The Mango Tree," "Yawning," "The Lizard" and "Under the Hay-Stack." Another letter to Aldous Huxley the same month spoke of "The Finding of Moses" and announced that he was doing a picture called "A Family in a Garden" which may be "Holy Family." In May Lawrence sent photographs of several of the paintings to Mark Gertler, the London painter friend; thus these pictures, "Resurrection," "Fauns and Nymphs" and "Fight with an Amazon" were painted by then. In a letter from Gsteig bei Gstaad to the Huxleys in August he mentioned that he had done the "Contadini"; "North Sea" and "Accident in a Mine" were painted in Gsteig.

Lawrence wrote Juliette, the wife of Julian Huxley, from the Villa Mirenda in April 1928 that Dorothy Warren wanted to exhibit his pictures in her Maddox Street Gallery, and he sent word to Dorothy Brett later in the month that the show was fixed for May or June; actually the show did not open until the following summer. At the same time Dorothy Brett in the United States was attempting to arrange an exhibition of the pictures at Alfred Stieglitz's gallery in New York. Lawrence suggested to Dorothy Brett in September that she could tell Stieglitz to expect the paintings after the Warren exhibition was over.

Unfortunately the paintings were not to reach America until after Lawrence's death, and then Frieda was allowed to bring them into the country only with the stipulation that she never exhibit them. The Warren exhibition opened on 14 June 1929 and was raided by the police on 5 July. Frieda tells an interesting story about the exhibition; she was in London, but Lawrence was not able to come from the Continent for the show. Just as the police were about to collect the pictures, the Aga Khan appeared, and the police obligingly waited while he viewed them before carrying out their orders. The police took thirteen of the pictures away, but they were eventually returned to Frieda. Harry T. Moore (B57) quotes from a previously unpublished letter in which Lawrence instructs Dorothy Warren to compromise with the police rather than suffer the paintings to be burned.

The night of the raid Frieda received at her hotel an invitation to dinner from a "Mr Khan" which she refused, unaware that the "Mr Khan" was the Aga Khan; they did, however, dine together the following night. The Aga Khan visited Lawrence in Vence during the last illness, where he saw the pictures again. After Lawrence's death he attempted to buy them from Frieda, but they could not come to an agreement about the purchase.

Another exhibition of the paintings was held in Vence in 1931; the show opened on 6 April at the Peasant Shop on the Place du Peyra, which was owned by Mrs Gordon Crotch, who met the Lawrences through Norman Douglas.

The Paintings of D. H. Lawrence was the first book of the Mandrake Press, the moving spirit of which was P. R. Stephensen, who had been associated with Jack and Norman Lindsay in the Fanfrolico Press in Bloomsbury Square. Lawrence mentioned the new press and Stephensen's part in its establishment in a letter to Curtis Brown from Bandol in January 1929. Lawrence was quite impressed with the proposal to reproduce the paintings in such an elaborate format and was especially struck with the ten copies on vellum which were to sell for fifty guineas.

The production of the book of paintings was quite successful. On 17 May Lawrence wrote Aldous Huxley from Palma de Mallorca that

Stephensen had orders for more than £2500 worth and that the ten copies on vellum were contracted for with subscribers at fifty guineas each. By June 300 copies had been sold at ten guineas each; by September the price of the ordinary copies had risen to twelve guineas in London, and Lawrence wrote Dorothy Brett that her copy was worth that. He also wrote her that an American dealer had received 125 copies safely.

After the exhibition in Vence, Frieda brought the pictures to the United States, and those which remained in her possession at the time of her death were hanging on the walls of her Taos home. In 1956 she still had "Red Willow Trees," "Rape of the Sabine Women," "Flight Back into Paradise," "Boccaccio Story," "Fight with an Amazon," "Fauns and Nymphs," "Close-Up (Kiss)," "Dance-Sketch" and "Summer Dawn." Many of the other paintings are owned by friends of the Lawrences. Dorothy Warren had "Leda," the Aldous Huxleys "The North Sea"; John Middleton Murry owned "Renascence of Men." Betty Cottam, a Taos friend, was given "Family on a Verandah"; "The Mango Tree" belonged to Mabel Dodge Luhan and Mary Christine Hughes owned "A Holy Family" before her death.

REVIEWS: Reviews of *The Paintings of D. H. Lawrence* and of the Warren exhibition appeared as "The Paintings of D. H. Lawrence" by H. Furst in *Apollo*, July 1929; in "Exhibition at the Warren Gallery" by R. McIntyre in the *Art Digest*, July 1929; in a news article "Paintings Seized by London Police as Indecent" in the *New York Times*, 6 July 1929; in "The Exhibition at the Warren Gallery" by R. McIntyre in the *Architectural Review*, August 1929; "Magistrate Orders Prints of D. H. Lawrence's Paintings to be Destroyed" in the London *Daily Express*, 5 August 1929; in "Mr. Lawrence on Painting" by T. W. Earp in the *New Statesman*, 17 August 1929; in "Letter from Abroad: D. H. Lawrence as Painter" by Rebecca West in the *Bookman* (New York), September 1929; in "D. H. Lawrence's Pictures" by Stuart Fletcher in *Sackbut*, October 1929; and in "The Censor" by Aldous Huxley in *Vanity Fair* (New York), November 1929. A critical article "Lady Chatterley's Painter" by Hubert Crehan with reproductions of several paintings was published in *Art News*, February 1957.

NOTES (2): There is a copy of (A46b) at the University of Texas with no border on the upper cover and the lower cover blank; it is out of series. Hence the following variants may be listed:

VARIANTS: (1) copy described above.

          (2) as (1) without border on upper cover and lower cover blank.

(3) as (1) but numbered.

REVIEWS (2): Additional reviews of *The Paintings* appeared in the *London Mercury* for July 1929; in *Everyman* for 27 June 1929 by Gwen John; in the *Daily Express* for 17 June 1929; and a story about the seizure of the paintings by the police in the *Daily News* for 6 July 1929.

A47   PANSIES   1929

a. *first edition (special copies)*

PANSIES | POEMS | BY | D. H. LAWRENCE | LONDON | MARTIN SECKER | NUMBER FIVE JOHN STREET | ADELPHI

Red and yellow decorative paper boards with a white paper backstrip, stamped in gold on spine reading downwards: PANSIES BY D. H. LAW-RENCE The leaves measure $8\frac{11}{16}'' \times 5\frac{3}{4}''$. Top edges trimmed and gilt; fore and bottom edges untrimmed.

[1]–[160] and tipped-in certificate of limited issue following page [4], as follows: [1] half-title; [2] blank; [3] title page as above; [4] LONDON: MARTIN SECKER (LTD.) 1929; tipped-in leaf bearing on recto: TWO HUNDRED AND FIFTY SPECIAL | COPIES HAVE BEEN PREPARED, | BEARING THE AUTHOR'S SIGNATURE, | OF WHICH THIS IS NO. 79 [*autograph number in blue ink*] | D. H. Lawrence [*autograph signature in blue ink*], verso blank; 5–6 foreword by D. H. Lawrence; 7–12 table of contents; [13] fly-title: PANSIES; [14] blank; 15–154 text; [155] blank; [156] Printed in Great Britain | by The Riverside Press Limited | Edinburgh; [157]–[160] blank.

Published July 1929 at 42s.; 250 special copies were printed.

b. *first edition (ordinary copies)*

PANSIES | POEMS | BY | D. H. LAWRENCE | LONDON | MARTIN SECKER | NUMBER FIVE JOHN STREET | ADELPHI

Blue and yellow decorative paper boards with a blue cloth backstrip, stamped in gold on spine reading downwards: PANSIES BY D. H. LAW-RENCE The leaves measure $8\frac{11}{16}'' \times 5\frac{3}{4}''$. Top edges trimmed and gilt; fore and bottom edges untrimmed.

[1]–[160], as follows: [1] half-title; [2] blank; [3] title page as above; [4] LONDON: MARTIN SECKER (LTD.) 1929; 5–6 foreword by D. H. Law-

rence; 7–12 table of contents; [13] fly-title: PANSIES; [14] blank; 15–154 text; [155] blank; [156] Printed in Great Britain | by The Riverside Press Limited | Edinburgh; [157]–[160] blank.

Published July 1929 at 10s. 6d.; 2600 ordinary copies were printed.

c. *definitive edition (ordinary copies)*

[*Lawrence phoenix in blue*] | *D. H. LAWRENCE* | *PANSIES* | *June, 1929* | [*printer's ornament in blue*] | [*printer's ornament in blue*] *This Edition is* | *limited to 500 copies* | *privately printed* | [*all lettering in blue, ornamental design in brown in shape of key encloses lettering*]

Stiff white paper wrappers, printed in red and black on upper cover: PANSIES [*in red*] | POEMS | BY | D. H. LAWRENCE | June, 1929; printed in black on lower cover: [*Lawrence phoenix*]; printed in red and black on spine: P|A|N|S|I|E|S| [*preceding word in red*] |D.|H.|L|A|W| R|E|N|C|E The leaves measure $8\frac{7}{8}'' \times 5\frac{3}{4}''$. Top edges trimmed; fore and bottom edges untrimmed.

[i]–[xviii] + 1–[128], as follows: [i]–[ii] blank; [iii] blank; [iv] frontispiece, portrait of D. H. Lawrence; [v] title page as above; [vi] Nº 327 [*autograph notation in blue ink*] | This limited edition is printed complete, | following the original manuscript, | according to my wish. | D. H. Lawrence [*autograph signature in blue ink*]; [vii]–[xi] introduction by D. H. Lawrence; [xii]–[xvi] table of contents; [xvii] fly-title: PANSIES [*in red*]; [xviii] blank; 1–125 text; [126] This Edition of 500 copies | is privately printed for | Subscribers only by | P. R. Stephensen, | 41 Museum Street, | London, W. C. 1; [127]–[128] blank.

Published August 1929 at 40s.; 500 ordinary copies were printed.

d. *definitive edition (special copies)*

[*Lawrence phoenix in blue*] | *D. H. LAWRENCE* | *PANSIES* | *June, 1929* | [*printer's ornament in blue*] | [*printer's ornament in blue*] *This Edition is* | *limited to 50 copies* | *privately printed* | [*all lettering in blue, ornamental design in brown in shape of key encloses lettering*]

Blue leather flexible boards, printed in blue and stamped in gold on upper cover: [*double rule with ornament at right*] | [*ornament*] | *PANSIES* [*in gold*] | *by* [*in gold*] | *D. H. LAWRENCE* [*in gold*] | [*ornament*] | [*double rule with ornament at right*]; printed in blue and gold on lower cover: [*double rule with ornament at left*] | [*Lawrence phoenix in gold*] | [*double rule *with ornament at left*]; printed in blue and stamped in gold on spine: [*double rule*] | *PANSIES* [*in gold reading from top to bottom*] | [*printer's ornament in gold*] | [*double rule*] The leaves measure $8\frac{7}{8}''$ × $5\frac{3}{4}''$. Top edges trimmed and gilt; fore and bottom edges untrimmed.

[i]–[xviii] + 1–[128], as follows: [i]–[iii] blank; [iv] frontispiece consisting of portrait of D. H. Lawrence; [v] title page as above; [vi] No. 20. [*autograph notation in blue ink*] | This limited edition of fifty copies is printed | complete, following the original manuscript, | according to my wish. | D. H. Lawrence [*autograph signature in blue ink*]; [vii]–[xi] introduction; [xii]–[xvi] table of contents; [xvii] fly-title: PANSIES [*in red*]; [xviii] blank; 1–125 text; [126] This Edition of 50 copies | is privately printed for | Subscribers only by | P. R. Stephensen, | 41 Museum Street, | London, W. C. 1.; [127]–[128] blank.

Presumably published August 1929; 50 special copies were printed.

e. *definitive edition (laid paper copies)*

PANSIES | POEMS | BY | D. H. LAWRENCE

Stiff pink paper covers, printed in black on upper cover: PANSIES | POEMS | BY | D. H. LAWRENCE; printed in black on lower cover: [*Lawrence phoenix*]; printed in black on spine reading from top to bottom: PANSIES [*printer's ornament*] | D. H. LAWRENCE The leaves measure $9\frac{1}{2}''$ × $5\frac{7}{8}''$. Top edges rough-trimmed; fore and bottom edges untrimmed.

[i]–[xvi] + 1–[128], as follows: [i]–[ii] blank; [iii] title page as above; [iv] blank; [v]–[ix] introduction by D. H. Lawrence; [x]–[xiv] table of contents; [xv] fly-title: PANSIES [*in red*]; [xvi] blank; 1–125 text; [126]–[128] blank.

Printed on laid paper from the same plates as (*c*) and (*d*); other data unknown.

f. *limited edition, autographed by Frieda Lawrence*

PANSIES | POEMS | D. H. LAWRENCE | [*drawing of flower and female figures*] | Privately Printed at the | PRESS OF THEO. GAUS' SONS, INC., | Brooklyn, New York

Blue-green cloth boards, stamped in gold on upper cover: PANSIES | Poems | [*printer's ornament*] | D. H. LAWRENCE; stamped in gold on spine: Pansies | [*printer's ornament*] | D. H. | LAWRENCE The leaves measure $8''$ × $5\frac{3}{8}''$. All edges trimmed.

[i]–[ii] + [i]–xiv + [1]–[208], as follows: [i]–[ii] blank; [i] half-title; [ii] list of works by D. H. Lawrence; [iii] title page as above; [iv] *Copyright 1929 by Alfred A. Knopf Inc.* | ALL RIGHTS RESERVED INCLUDING THE RIGHT TO REPRODUCE | THIS BOOK OR PARTS THEREOF IN ANY FORM | No 125 [*autograph notation in black ink*] | *Private Edition Limited to* | *1,000 Numbered Copies.* | Frieda Lawrence [*autograph signature in black ink*] | *Manufactured in the United States of America*; v–vii foreword by D. H. Lawrence, on page vii a note by Frieda Lawrence Ravagli; [viii] blank; ix–xiv table of contents; [1] fly-title: P | A | N | S | I | E | S; [2] blank; 3–202 text; [203]–[208] blank.

Published May 1954 at $3.00; the edition consisted of 1000 copies.

In 1953 Frieda Lawrence Ravagli purchased the plates of the Knopf edition of *Pansies* and printed this limited edition which she autographed and sold through the book shop in Taos, New Mexico. Altogether Frieda autographed about 250 copies of the book according to Angie Ravagli; most of the unsold copies were remaindered in 1956.

CONTENTS

The poems marked with an asterisk appeared only in the definitive edition of *Pansies* (A47c).

Our Day is Over—Hark in the Dusk!—Elephants in the Circus—Elephants Plodding—On the Drum—Two Performing Elephants—Twilight—Cups—Bowls—You—After Dark—To Let Go or to Hold On? (first appeared in the *Dial*, July 1929 (C189))—Destiny—How Beastly the Bourgeois Is—Worm Either Way—Natural Complexion—The Oxford Voice—True Democracy—To Be Superior—Swan—Leda—Give Us Gods—Won't It Be Strange?—Spiral Flame—Let the Dead Bury Their Dead—When Wilt Thou Teach the People?—A Living—When I Went to the Film—When I Went to the Circus (first appeared in the *Dial*, May 1929 (C186))—*The Noble Englishman—Things Men Have Made (first appeared in the *Dial*, July 1929 (C189))—Things Made by Iron—New Houses, New Clothes—Whatever Man Makes (first appeared in the *Dial*, July 1929 (C189))—We Are Transmitters—All That We Have is Life—Let Us Be Men—Work—Why?—What is He?—O! Start a Revolution—Moon Memory—There is Rain in Me—Desire Goes Down into the Sea—The Sea, The Sea—November by the Sea (first appeared in the *Dial*, July 1929 (C189))—Old Song—Good Husbands Make Unhappy Wives—Fight! O My Young Men—*Women Want Fighters for Their Lovers—It's

Either You Fight or You Die—Don'ts—The Risen Lord—The Secret Waters—Beware, O My Dear Young Men—Obscenity—Sex isn't Sin—The Elephant is Slow to Mate—Sex and Trust—The Gazelle Calf—Little Fish—The Mosquito Knows—Self-Pity—New Moon—Spray—Sea-Weed (first appeared in the *Dial*, July 1929 (C189))—My Enemy—Touch—Noli Me Tangere—Chastity—Let Us Talk, Let Us Laugh—Touch Comes—Leave Sex Alone—The Mess of Love—Climb Down, O Lordly Mind—Ego-Bound—Jealousy—*Ego Bound Women—Fidelity—Know Deeply, Know Thyself More Deeply—All I Ask—The Universe Flows—Underneath—The Primal Passions—Escape—The Root of Our Evil—The Ignoble Procession—No Joy in Life—Wild Things in Captivity—Mournful Young Man—*There is no Way Out—Money-Madness—Kill Money—Men Are Not Bad—Nottingham's New University—I Am in a Novel—No! Mr. Lawrence!—Red-Herring—Our Moral Age—*My Naughty Book—*The Little Wowser—*The Young and Their Moral Guardians—When I Read Shakespeare—Salt of the Earth—Fresh Water—Peace and War—Many Mansions—Glory—Woe—Attila (first appeared in the *Dial*, July 1929 (C189))—What Would You Fight For? (first appeared in the *Dial*, July 1929 (C189))—Choice— Riches—Poverty—Noble—Wealth—Tolerance—Compari—Sick—Dead People—Cerebral Emotions—Wellsian Futures—To Women, As Far As I'm Concerned—Blank—Elderly Discontented Women—Old People—The Grudge of the Old—Beautiful Old Age—Courage—Desire is Dead—When the Ripe Fruit Falls—Elemental—Fire—I Wish I Knew a Woman—Talk—The Effort of Love—Can't be Borne—Man Reaches a Point—Grasshopper is a Burden—Basta!—Tragedy—After All the Tragedies are Over—Nullus—Dies Irae—Dies Illa—Stop It—The Death of Our Era—The New World—Sun in Me—Be Still!—At Last—Nemesis—The Optimist—The Third Thing—The Sane Universe—Fear of Society is the Root of All Evil—God—Sane and Insane—A Sane Revolution—Always This Paying—Poor Young Things—A Played-Out Game—Triumph—The Combative Spirit—Wages—Young Fathers—A Tale Told by an Idiot—Being Alive—Self-Protection—A Man—Lizard (first appeared in the *Dial*, July 1929 (C189))—Relativity—Space—Sun-Men—Sun-Women—Democracy—Aristocracy of the Sun—Conscience—The Middle-Classes—Immorality—Censors (first appeared in the *Dial*, July 1929 (C189))—Man's Image—Immoral Man—Cowards—Think——!—Peacock—Paltry-Looking People—Tarts—Latter-Day Sinners—*What Matters—Fate and the Younger Generation—As for Me, I'm a Patriot—The Rose of England—England in 1929—Liberty's Old Old Story—New Brooms—

Police Spies—Now It's Happened—Energetic Women—Film Passion—
Female Coercion—Volcanic Venus—*What Does She Want?—
Wonderful Spiritual Women—Poor Bit of a Wench!—What Ails Thee?
—It's No Good!—*Don't Look at Me—Ships in Bottles—Know Thyself,
and That Thou Art Mortal—What Is Man Without an Income?—
Canvassing for the Election—Altercation—Finding Your Level—
Climbing Up—*To Clarinda—Conundrums—A Rise in the World—
Up He Goes!—The Saddest Day—Prestige—Have Done With
It—Henriette—Vitality—Willy Wet-Legs—Maybe—Stand Up!—
*Demon Justice—*Be a Demon—*The Jeune Fille—Trust.

g. *facsimile edition*

PANSIES | By | D H | LAWRENCE

Brown paper wrappers with white paper label on upper cover, hand
lettered in red: PANSIES | BY | D H | LAWRENCE The leaves measure
$8\frac{1}{2}'' \times 5''$. All edges untrimmed.

[1]–[56], as follows: [1]–[2] blank; [3] title page as above; [4] blank;
[5]–[25] introduction; [26]–[28] blank; [29]–[55] text; [56] blank.

Publication data and number of copies unknown.

CONTENTS

The Noble Englishman—Women Want Fighters for Their Lovers—Ego-
Bound Women—There Is No Way Out—My Naughty Book—The
Little Wowser—The Young and Their Moral Guardians—What Does
She Want—Don't Look at Me—To Clarinda—Demon Justice.

NOTES: The *Pansies* poems were characterized by Lawrence in a letter
to the Aldous Huxleys from Bandol in December 1928 in which he said
he had been writing a book of Pensées which he called "pansies," a sort
of loose little poem form. Frieda called them "real Doggerel." Lawrence
wrote Aldous Huxley in December that *Pansies* was finished and that
two typescripts were on their way to Curtis Brown. These typescripts
were seized by the postal authorities at the behest of the Home Office,
apparently as a result of the action against *Lady Chatterley*. Perhaps
because of this seizure Lawrence found it necessary to retype the poems,
for he wrote Rhys Davies in February that he had almost finished
retyping them. As he retyped, he revised, and some fourteen of the
poems were dropped from the Secker edition.

Lawrence arranged for the unexpurgated *Pansies* (A47c) to be privately printed in London in August 1929; P. R. Stephensen, who did the typography for *The Paintings* (A46), allowed his name to be used as the printer, but Lawrence in a letter to the Huxleys from Baden-Baden in August implied that Stephensen was not responsible for the book. Lawrence himself thought the book looked like "a cheap printed report" and the price of £2 caused Lawrence to pity the purchasers. Fifty copies of this edition were bound in flexible blue-grey leather, and later a so-called popular edition was printed from the same plates and issued in heavy pink covers for distribution on the Continent.

The introduction to the Secker edition of *Pansies* is somewhat different from that of the definitive edition. The introduction for the definitive edition is dated at Bandol in January 1929 and that for the expurgated *Pansies* at Bandol in March. Although the introduction to Frieda's autographed edition of *Pansies* (A47f) is signed at Palma de Mallorca in April 1929, the text is the same as that in the Secker edition (A47a).

The first American edition of *Pansies* was published by Knopf on 27 September 1929; the text follows that of the Secker edition. Secker published a "new edition" in April 1930 in a printing of 2800 copies and reprinted 2000 copies in 1932.

REVIEWS: *Pansies* was reviewed in *The Times Literary Supplement*, 4 July 1929; by Barrington Gates in the *Nation and Athenaeum*, 27 July 1929; by Peter Quennell in the *New Statesman*, 27 July 1929; by Richard Church in the *Spectator*, 3 August 1929; by Mark Van Doren in the *New York Herald Tribune Books*, 15 December 1929; and by Mark Van Doren in "Two English Poets" in the *Nation*, 15 January 1930.

NOTES (2): The portrait of Lawrence on page [iv] of (A47c) is a self-portrait done in 1929, see (B57b) and (A55).

It is doubtful if the whole truth about the various forms of the definitive *Pansies* will ever be known, and certainly the circumstances of their production will remain forever a mystery. Some new information has become available. The University of Texas library has one new variant of (A47d) which differs from the copy described above as follows:

Grey flexible leather boards, printed in blue and brown on upper cover: [*ornament in blue*] | PANSIES | *by* | D. H. LAWRENCE | [*ornament in blue*] There are also ornaments in blue at the outside corners of the upper cover and a vertical border of ornaments in blue at the left of the upper cover; printed in brown on the lower cover: [*Lawrence phoenix*]; printed in brown on spine: PANSIES [*reading from top to bottom*] | June | 1929

Another variant of (A47d) is reported by the University of Sussex. It is the same as (A47d) except that it is bound in green vellum with PANSIES stamped in gold on the spine. Underneath the statement on page 126 has been written, evidently by Charles Lahr: No. 10 of ten copies bound in vellum. C. L. Thus the following variants of (A47d) may be listed:

VARIANTS: (1) copy described above.
(2) as (1) except bound in grey leather.
(3) as (1) except bound in green vellum.

Perhaps the most interesting of the new forms of *Pansies* is that described above as (A47g). It is a facsimile edition of eleven manuscript poems not included in (A47a) and (A47b) but printed in the definitive edition. The handwriting is unidentified, but there is a note on the free front end-paper in the late David Garnett's hand which states, "privately printed edition containing poems omitted from Secker edition. There are other variants of this—one being signed by D. H. L." Nothing in the correspondence indicates that Lawrence was aware of this production. David Garnett had the book from his father's estate, and associated it with Charles Lahr. The paper is watermarked, A. Millburn & Co. BRITISH HAND MADE. The verso of all the leaves are blank. There are textual variations in both the introduction and the poems.

Mr George Lazarus has in his collection a copy of (A47e) without printing on the upper cover, and Mr W. Forster reports a copy which appears to be a trial binding in red cloth; this copy has on page [iii] a facsimile of a page of Lawrence's essay on tragedy. See (C202). Mr Forster also has a copy of (A47b) bound in blue cloth, probably a trial binding as well. Mr Lazarus has a copy of (A47d) in "plain white boards."

Both (A47c) and (A47d) were issued in glassine wrappers in slip cases; the slip cases for (A47c) are covered with white paper; those for (A47d) are covered with blue marbled paper. The dust wrapper for (A47a) is light tan paper printed in red and black; that for (A47b) the same printed in blue and black.

A48 MY SKIRMISH WITH JOLLY ROGER 1929

a. *first edition*

[*ornamental rule*] MY SKIRMISH WITH JOLLY ROGER | D. H. LAWRENCE | WRITTEN | AS | AN INTRODUC- TION TO | AND A MOTIVATION OF THE | PARIS

EDITION | OF | LADY CHATTERLEY'S LOVER | NEW
YORK·RANDOM HOUSE·MCMXXIX | [*ornamental rule*] |
[*triangular space on either side of lettering is blocked in with alternate ornamental
and thin single rules*]

Grey paper boards, grey paper label on upper cover printed in black:
[*ornamental rule*] | [*short rule*] MY [*short rule*] | [*short ornamental rule*] SKIRMISH
[*short ornamental rule*] | [*short rule*] WITH [*short rule*] | [*short ornamental rule*]
JOLLY ROGER [*short ornamental rule*] | [*short rule*] [*short rule*] | [*short ornamental
rule*] D. H. LAWRENCE [*short ornamental rule*] | [*short rule*] [*short rule*] | [*short
ornamental rule*] RANDOM HOUSE [*short ornamental rule*] | [*short rule*] N Y [*short
rule*] | [*ornamental rule*] The leaves measure $8\frac{1}{2}''$ × $5\frac{11}{16}''$. All edges trimmed.

[1]–[12], as follows: [1] title page as above; [2] FIRST COPYRIGHT EDITION
| [*ornamental rule*] | COPYRIGHT 1929, RANDOM HOUSE | MANUFACTURED
IN UNITED STATES | OF AMERICA; [3]–11 text, page 11 signed: Paris, 1929;
[12] [*ornamental rule*] OF [*ornamental rule*] | THIS | EDITION | SIX HUNDRED
COPIES | WERE PRINTED IN THE WEEK OF JULY 8 | NINETEEN HUNDRED
AND TWENTY-NINE | THE PYNSON PRINTERS, NEW YORK | THIS COPY BEING
| NUMBER | [*ornamental rule*] [*this copy not numbered*] [*ornamental rule*] An
erratum slip with an apology for misspelling the word "photography"
on page [3] is laid in.

Published 15 July 1929 at $3.50; the first printing consisted of 700 copies
according to the publisher.

b. *first revised edition* (*regular copies*)

[*heavy rule*] | [*light rule*] | A PROPOS OF LADY | CHATTER-
LEY'S LOVER | *being an essay extended from* | "*My Skirmish with Jolly
Roger*" | BY | D. H. LAWRENCE | [*Lawrence phoenix*] | London 1930
| MANDRAKE PRESS LTD. | 41 Museum Street.

Blue cloth boards, printed in red on upper cover: A PROPOS OF LADY |
CHATTERLEY'S LOVER | D. H. LAWRENCE | [*enclosed within single rule border*];
printed in red on spine, reading from bottom to top: A PROPOS OF LADY
CHATTERLEY'S LOVER | The leaves measure $7\frac{1}{2}''$ × $4\frac{3}{4}''$. Top and fore edges
trimmed; bottom edges untrimmed.

[1]–[64], as follows: [1] half-title; [2] blank; [3] title page as above;
[4] blank; 5–[63] text; [64] [*short rule*] | *Printed in England for Mandrake
Press Ltd.* | *by W. Graves Drummond Street London N. W.*

Published 24 June 1930 at 3s. 6d.; number of copies unknown.

c. *first revised edition (advance copies)*

A PROPOS OF | LADY CHATTERLEY'S LOVER | *being an essay extended from* | *"My Skirmish with Jolly Roger"* | BY | D. H. LAWRENCE | [*printer's ornament*] | London 1930 | MANDRAKE PRESS LTD. | 41 Museum Street.

Blue cloth boards, printed in dark red on upper cover: *A PROPOS OF* | LADY CHATTERLEY'S LOVER | [*printer's ornament*] | D. H. Lawrence | [*enclosed within single rule forming border*]; printed in dark red on spine reading from bottom to top: A PROPOS OF LADY CHATTERLEY'S LOVER LAWRENCE The leaves measure $7\frac{1}{2}'' \times 4\frac{3}{4}''$. Top and fore edges trimmed: bottom edges untrimmed.

[i]–[iv] + [1]–[68], as follows: [i]–[iv] blank; [1] half-title, with note: [*short thick rule*] | [*short thin rule*] | ADVANCE COPY | with compliments from Mandrake Press Ltd. | Date of Publication is | JUNE 24th. | Price 3s. 6d. | [*short thin rule*] | [*short thick rule*]; [2] blank; [3] title page as above; [4] blank; 5–63 text; [64]–[68] blank.

NOTES: This essay was first published as the introduction to the Paris edition of *Lady Chatterley's Lover* (A42c) and was subsequently published by Random House in the limited edition described here (A48a). Later in the year, probably at Bandol, Lawrence rewrote the essay making it considerably longer, and this extended version was that published by the Mandrake Press as *A Propos of Lady Chatterley's Lover* (A48b). The essay has since then always appeared by the latter title. Secker published an edition of 2000 copies in June 1931; and the essay was included in *Sex, Literature and Censorship* (A92) in 1953.

The statement of limitation in *My Skirmish with Jolly Roger* says that only 600 copies were printed, but the publishers state that actually 700 copies were issued.

The advance copies of *A Propos of Lady Chatterley's Lover* (A48b) differ from the ordinary issue textually as well, but only in a minor fashion, and it is apparent that these differences were due to typographical errors rather than to revision.

REVIEWS: A review of *A Propos of Lady Chatterley's Lover* appeared in the *New Statesman*, 30 August 1930.

NOTES (2): *My Skirmish with Jolly Roger* (A48a) has decorative end-papers, and each of the eight copies at the University of Texas has a different paper.

A49 PORNOGRAPHY AND OBSCENITY 1929

a. *first edition (paper wrapper copies)*

PORNOGRAPHY | AND | OBSCENITY | BY | D. H. LAWRENCE | LONDON | FABER & FABER LIMITED | 24 RUSSELL SQUARE

Orange paper wrappers, printed in black on upper cover: CRITERION MISCELLANY—NO. 5 | PORNOGRAPHY | AND | OBSCENITY | D. H. LAWRENCE | ONE SHILLING NET | FABER & FABER; printed in black on lower cover: This is No. 5 of the | CRITERION MISCELLANY | Published by Faber & Faber Limited | at 24 Russell Square, London W. C. 1 The leaves measure $7\frac{1}{4}'' \times 5\frac{1}{8}''$. Top and bottom edges trimmed; fore edges untrimmed.

[1]–32, as follows: [1] half-title; [2] blank; [3] title page as above; [4] FIRST PUBLISHED IN MCMXXIX | BY FABER AND FABER LIMITED | 24 RUSSELL SQUARE LONDON W. C. I | PRINTED IN GREAT BRITAIN | BY TREND AND COMPANY PLYMOUTH | ALL RIGHTS RESERVED; 5–32 text.

Published 14 November 1929 at 1*s.*; the first printing consisted of 5000 copies, which presumably included the copies issued in orange cloth boards (A49b).

b. *first edition (cloth copies)*

PORNOGRAPHY | AND | OBSCENITY | BY | D. H. LAW-RENCE | LONDON | FABER & FABER LIMITED | 24 RUSSELL SQUARE

Orange cloth boards, stamped in gold on upper cover: CRITERION MISCELLANY—NO. 5 | [*short decorative rule*] | PORNOGRAPHY | AND | OBSCENITY | [*five-pointed star*] | D. H. LAWRENCE The leaves measure $7\frac{1}{8}'' \times 5\frac{1}{16}''$. All edges trimmed.

[1]–32, as follows: [1] half-title; [2] blank; [3] title page as above; [4] FIRST PUBLISHED IN MCMXXIX | BY FABER AND FABER LIMITED | 24 RUSSELL SQUARE LONDON W. C. I | PRINTED IN GREAT BRITAIN | BY TREND AND COMPANY PLYMOUTH | ALL RIGHTS RESERVED; 5–32 text.

Published January 1930 at 2*s.* 6*d.*; number of copies unknown.

NOTES: This essay first appeared in print in *This Quarter*, July–September 1929 (C190); it was written in the autumn of 1929 at Rottach-am-Tegernsee, where Lawrence was the guest of Max Mohr. Lawrence wrote to the Curtis Brown office in September that he was surprised Faber would risk the "obscenity article," but he agreed to a suggestion that the names of Galsworthy and Barrie be omitted from the published version. The reference was to their novels being more pornographic than Boccaccio, who was "wholesome."

The publishers asked both Lawrence and Lord Brentford, Home Secretary at the time and prime mover in the action against *Pansies* and *Lady Chatterley*, to write essays giving their respective viewpoints on the question of censorship. Faber published Lord Brentford's *Do We Need a Censor?* as No. 6 of the Criterion Miscellany. Lawrence was quite elated when his pamphlet sold better than his rival's.

The first American edition was published by Knopf on 28 February 1930, and the Alicat Bookshop in New York published a new edition as the Outcast Chapbook No. 13 in 1948 with a preface by Florenz Arslen Hasratoff.

REVIEWS: Reviews and notices of *Pornography and Obscenity* appeared in "Pornography and the Censorship" in the *New Statesman*, 23 November 1929; in "Mr. D. H. Lawrence and Lord Brentford" in the *Nation*, 11 January 1930; in "Who's Obscene" in the *Nation* (New York), 26 February 1930; and in "Lawrence and Britannia" by Richard Rees in the *New Adelphi*, June–August 1930.

A50   THE ESCAPED COCK   1929

a. first edition (ordinary copies)

The Escaped Cock [*in red*] | *by* | *D. H. Lawrence* [*in red*] | With Decorations in Color by the Author | The Black Sun Press | Rue Cardinale [*in red*] | Paris | MCMXXIX [*in red*]

White paper wrappers, printed in red and black on upper cover: *The Escaped Cock* [*in red*] | *by* | *D. H. Lawrence* [*in red*] | The Black Sun Press | Rue Cardinale [*in red*] | Paris | MCMXXIX [*in red*] [*enclosed within single rule border*]; printed in red and black on spine: The | Escaped | Cock [*title in red*] | Lawrence; printed in black on lower cover: [*Lawrence phoenix*] The leaves measure $8\frac{1}{4}'' \times 6\frac{1}{2}''$. Top edges trimmed; fore and bottom edges rough-trimmed.

[i]–[xii] + 1–[104] and frontispiece consisting of a painting by D. H. Lawrence, as follows: [i]–[vi] blank; [vii] half-title; [viii] blank; [ix] title page as above; [x] blank; [xi] fly-title: Part I [*in red*]; [xii] blank; 1–[42] text; [43] fly-title: Part II [*in red*]; [44] blank; 45–[96] text;

[97] blank; [98] Tous droits de traduction et de reproduction | réservés pour tous pays.; [99] This first edition of The Escaped Cock | by D. H. Lawrence with water-color | decorations by the author, privately | published for subscribers only by Harry | and Caresse Crosby at their Black Sun | Press (Maître—Imprimeur Lescaret) | in September 1929, is limited to 450 | numbered copies on Holland Van Gelder | Zonen and 50 copies on Japanese Vellum | signed by the author. | 298 [*hand stamped number in black ink*]; [100] list of Black Sun publications; [101]–[104] blank.

Published September 1929; 450 ordinary copies were printed.

b. *first edition (special copies)*

The Escaped Cock [*in red*] | *by* | *D. H. Lawrence* [*in red*] | With Decorations in Color by the Author | The Black Sun Press | Rue Cardinale [*in red*] | Paris | MCMXXIX [*in red*]

The copies printed on Japanese vellum are the same as the ordinary copies except that page [vii] reads: *The Escaped Cock* | number five [*holograph notation in blue ink*] | D. H. Lawrence [*autograph signature in blue ink*].

Published September 1929; 50 special copies were printed.

c. *first English edition*

THE | MAN WHO DIED | *by* | D. H. LAWRENCE | *London*: | MARTIN SECKER | *Number Five John Street Adelphi* | 1931

Green cloth boards, stamped in gold on upper cover: [*Lawrence phoenix*]; stamped in gold on spine reading downwards: THE MAN WHO DIED | [*printer's ornaments*] LONDON | D. H. LAWRENCE [*printer's ornament*] MARTIN SECKER The leaves measure $9\frac{7}{8}'' \times 6\frac{1}{2}''$. Top edges trimmed and gilt; fore and bottom edges untrimmed.

[1]–[100], as follows: [1]–[2] blank; [3] half-title; [4] blank; [5] title page as above; [6] LONDON: MARTIN SECKER LTD.; [7] THIS EDITION IS LIMITED | TO 2000 COPIES FOR SALE | IN ENGLAND AND THE | UNITED STATES OF AMERICA. | THE TYPE HAS BEEN | DISTRIBUTED.; [8] blank; [9] NOTE | The original title of this story | was *The Escaped Cock*. The | present title was decided upon | by the author shortly before | his death.; [10] blank; [11] fly-title: PART I; [12] blank; 13–49 text; [50] blank; [51] fly-title: PART II; [52] blank; 53–97 text; [98] [*Lawrence*

phoenix] | PRINTED IN GREAT BRITAIN BY | THE BOTOLPH PRINTING WORKS | GATE STREET, KINGSWAY, LONDON; [99]–[100] blank.

Published March 1931 at 21*s.*; the edition consisted of 2000 copies.

d. *first illustrated edition*

The Man who Died | By D. H. Lawrence | With illustrations drawn and engraved | on the wood by JOHN FARLEIGH | Type format arranged by J. H. MASON | Printed by W. LEWIS at Cambridge | London 1935 Published by William | HEINEMANN

Decorative paper boards with a tan cloth backstrip, stamped in gold on spine: The Man who Died by D·H·LAWRENCE [*reading from bottom to top*] | HEINE- | MANN The leaves measure 11″ × 8″. Top edges trimmed; fore and bottom edges untrimmed.

[1]–[68], as follows: [1] title page as above; [2] blank; [3] half-title; [4] blank; [5] fly-title: PART ONE [*in red*] | [*drawing of cock*] | PART ONE [*in red*]; 6–[65] text; [66] fly-title: The Man who Died | THE [*in red*] | Man who Died The | MAN [*in red*] | who Died The Man | WHO [*in red*] | Died The Man who | DIED [*in red*] | The Man who Died; [67] THE MAN WHO DIED BY D. H. LAWRENCE | With illustrations drawn and engraved on the wood by John | Farleigh. Type format arranged by J. H. Mason. Printed by | W. Lewis at the Cambridge University Press. Published by | William Heinemann, 99 Great Russell Street, London, W. C. 1 | [*list of illustrations*] | THE MAN WHO DIED BY D. H. LAWRENCE; [68] blank.

Published 25 November 1935 at 10*s.* 6*d.*; the first printing consisted of 2000 copies.

e. *United States copyright edition*

The Escaped Cock | by | D. H. Lawrence | [*printer's ornament*]| HARRY F. MARKS, INC. | 21 West 47th Street | New York City

Pink paper covers, printed in black on upper cover as title page above. Twenty-eight separate leaves stapled together. The leaves measure $8\frac{7}{8}″ × 6″$. All edges trimmed.

[1]–[56], as follows: [1] title page as above; [2] Copyrighted, 1930 *By* HARRY F. MARKS, INC. MANUFACTURED IN UNITED STATES.; 3–54 text, at bottom of page 54: This first edition of The Escaped Cock | by D. H. Lawrence with water-color | decorations by the author, privately

| published for subscribers only by Harry | F. Marks, Inc., 21 West 47th Street. | New York City.; [55]–[56] blank.

Published 1 May 1930; the edition consisted of ten copies.

f. *first critical edition* (*paper covers*)

THE | ESCAPED | COCK | [*preceding three lines in red*] | *D. H. LAWRENCE* [*in blue*] | *edited* | *with a* | *commentary* | *by* | *Gerald M. Lacy* [*preceding five lines in red*] | [*the whole enclosed within a double rule, consisting of a thin rule and a thick rule printed in blue*] | BLACK SPARROW PRESS · [*in red*] LOS ANGELES · [*in red*] 1973

Cream paper covers: [*colour reproduction of a watercolour by D. H. Lawrence enclosed within a rule printed in red*] | D. H. LAWRENCE | [*short heavy rule*] | *The Escaped Cock* [*preceding three lines in red*]; printed in black on spine, reading from top to bottom: D. H. LAWRENCE *The Escaped Cock* BLACK SPARROW PRESS The leaves measure 9″ × 6″. All edges trimmed.

[1]–[172], as follows: [1]–[2] blank; [3] title page as above; [4] First published 1928. | Copyright © 1928 by | David Herbert Lawrence. | THE ESCAPED COCK, *The Forum* text, & previously unpublished let- | ters: Copyright © 1973 by Angelo Ravagli and C. Montague | Weekley, Executors of the Estate of Frieda Lawrence Ravagli. | COMMENTARY: Copyright © by Gerald M. Lacy. | [*reservations, acknowledgements, and Library of Congress cataloging information*]; [5] preface by Gerald M. Lacy; [6] acknowledgements to libraries; [7] a note on the text; [8] blank; [9] table of contents; [10] blank; [11] half-title; [12] blank; 13–61 text; [62] blank; [63] fly-title: LETTERS RELATING TO | *THE ESCAPED COCK*; [64] list of correspondents; 65–93 text of letters; [94] blank; 95–99 appendix; [100] blank; [101] fly-title: "The Escaped Cock" | Original Short Story Version of Part I | reprinted from | *The Forum*, February 1928; [102] blank; 103–120 text; [121] fly-title: COMMENTARY | by | Gerald M. Lacy; [122] table of contents; 123–170 text of commentary; [171] [*publisher's device*] | Printed September 1973 in Santa Barbara for | the Black Sparrow Press by Noel Young. | Design by Barbara Martin. This first edition | is published in paper wrappers; there are | 750 hardcover copies; & 126 numbered copies | have been printed on blue paper & | handbound in boards by Earle Gray.; [172] quotation from Catherine Carswell.

Published 10 September 1973 at $4.00; 2505 copies were issued in paper covers.

g. *first critical edition* (*hard cover copies*)

The hard cover copies are identical with (A50f) except for the binding consisting of cream paper covered boards with a green cloth backstrip; cream paper label on spine printed in black, reading from top to bottom D. H. LAWRENCE *The Escaped Cock*

Published simultaneously with (A50f) at $ 10.00; although the colophon notes 750 copies were printed, the publisher is authority for the statement that only 725 copies were actually issued in this binding.

h. *first critical edition* (*numbered copies*)

The numbered copies are identical with (A50g) except for the gold cloth backstrip and the blue paper on which they are printed.

Published simultaneously with (A50f) at $ 30.00; although the colophon notes that 126 copies were printed, the publisher is authority for the statement that only 100 copies were issued in this binding.

i. *first critical edition* (*lettered copies*)

The lettered copies are identical with (A50h) except for the blue leather backstrip.

Note: Twenty copies of (A50f) were bound in white paper wrappers and stamped on the upper cover in red: ADVANCE REVIEW COPY Both upper and lower covers were printed: D. H. LAWRENCE [*in red*] | [*short heavy rule in blue*] | *The Escaped Cock* [*in red*]; printed on spine, reading from top to bottom: D. H. LAWRENCE [*in red*] *The Escaped Cock* [*in red*] BLACK SPARROW PRESS [*in black*] All hard cover copies were issued in the same dust-jacket, that designed for (A50g) and were marked $10.00. The printed dust-jacket was used for the paper wrapper for the advance review copies described above.

NOTES: Part one of this story was published under the title *The Escaped Cock* in the *Forum* for February 1928 (C167). Earl Brewster in his *Reminiscences* (B39) tells of being with Lawrence in Grosseto on Easter morning of 1927 when they passed a small shop in the window of which was a toy white rooster escaping from an egg. Brewster remarked to Lawrence that the toy suggested the title for a story of the Resurrection, "The Escaped Cock," and later, in May, after he had written the story, Lawrence wrote Brewster recalling the incident and attributing the title to the toy they had seen, although Lawrence himself recalled that the incident took place in Volterra.

The second half of the story was finished in the latter part of August 1928 according to a letter to the Curtis Brown office; in September he sent the manuscript to Enid Hilton for typing, and it was still in her possession in August 1929 when he wrote her from Palma de Mallorca to forward the complete manuscript, both parts, to Caresse Crosby.

Lawrence feared that the uproar about his paintings in London might have made the Crosbys dubious about printing *The Escaped Cock* and wrote them from Baden-Baden not to bother about the thing for a minute if they didn't want to. Of course the Crosbys did not consider for a moment the possibility of abandoning their plans.

The first American edition was published from new plates by Alfred Knopf in 1931; this edition as well as all editions other than the Black Sun book appeared under the title *The Man Who Died*. Secker reprinted the first English edition in September 1931 and again in November 1932; Heinemann published it in the Pocket Edition in 1935, and New Directions published it as No. 18 of the New Classics in 1947. Continental English language editions include Tauchnitz's No. 5034 in the Collection of British and American Authors and the Albatross Library No. 380.

REVIEWS: *The Escaped Cock* and *The Man Who Died* were reviewed by Richard Sunne in the *New Statesman and Nation*, 28 March 1931; in *The Times Literary Supplement* for 2 April 1931; by H. M. in the *Spectator*, 2 May 1931; in the *New York Times Book Review*, 10 May 1931; by Lorine Pruette in the *New York Herald Tribune Books*, 24 May 1931; by Mary Colum in the *New Republic*, 15 July 1931; by W. N. G. in the *Churchman*, 18 July 1931; by Frederick Dupee in the *Bookman* (New York), 5 July 1931; by Basil Davenport in the *Saturday Review of Literature*, 1 August 1931; by L. A. G. Strong in the *Spectator*, 3 October 1931; by V. S. Pritchett in the *Fortnightly Review*, November 1931; in the *Adelphi*, October 1930; by John Middleton Murry in the *Criterion* in 1930; and by Joan Haslip in the *London Mercury*, November 1931.

NOTES (2): Although the first American trade edition of *The Escaped Cock* was published by Alfred Knopf in 1931, Harry F. Marks, a New York bookseller and distributor in the United States for the Black Sun Press, manufactured an edition of ten copies (A50e) published on 1 May 1930 according to the records at the Library of Congress and a notice in *Publisher's Weekly*, 25 April 1931. Two copies were sent to the Library of Congress with the copyright application; the remaining copies were not for sale. The book was printed and bound by the Peck Advertising Agency in Brooklyn.

Both (A50a) and (A50b) were issued in glassine wrappers in marbled paper covered slip cases, coloured brown and gold and tan and gold respectively.

REVIEWS(2): Additional reviews of *The Escaped Cock* appeared in the *Observer* for 26 April 1931 and in the *Manchester Guardian* for 20 May.

A51   THE LIFE OF J. MIDDLETON   1930
MURRY

first edition

D. H. LAWRENCE | *The Life of* | *J. MIDDLETON MURRY* | *By* J. C. | Privately Printed 1930

Without covers; first page serves as title page and cover. The leaves measure $8'' \times 5\frac{1}{8}''$. All edges trimmed.

[1]–[4], as follows: [1] title page as above; [2] blank; [3] John Middleton was born in the year | of the Lord 1891? It happened also | to be the most lying year of the most | lying century since time began, but what | is that to an innocent babe!; [4] blank.

Printed October 1929, not for sale; the edition consisted of 50 copies.

NOTES: In the autumn of 1929 Lawrence conceived the idea of the *Squib*, a little magazine "to put crackers under people's chairs," somewhat in the mood of his *Nettles* (A52). Charles Lahr, who produced the *New Coterie* and printed the Archer *Sun* (A35) was to print the *Squib*. Lawrence attempted to interest Aldous Huxley in the venture, but Huxley was a bit dubious. Charles Lahr writes of Lawrence: "In one of his letters he suggested we do imaginary reviews of books." Murry had just published *The Life of Jesus Christ*. So Lawrence wanted to do the "Life of M. M. by Jesus Christ." Lawrence's death came soon after, and the *Squib* never came to life; consequently *The Life of J. Middleton Murry* is the only remaining trace of Lawrence's efforts to father this little "lampooning" periodical.

NOTES (2): Although, from a source which cannot now be identified, the first edition of this bibliography noted that fifty copies of *The Life of J. Middleton Murry* were printed, Mr Alan Clodd reports a copy annotated by Charles Lahr to the effect that, "Herbert Jones printed about 30 copies on our press which had once belonged to William Morris. [signed] Charles Lahr."

a. *first edition (cloth copies)*

NETTLES | BY | D. H. LAWRENCE | LONDON | FABER &
FABER LIMITED | 24 RUSSELL SQUARE

Red cloth boards, stamped in gold on upper cover: CRITERION MISCEL-
LANY —No. 11 | [*short decorative rule*] | NETTLES | [*five-pointed star*] |
D. H. LAWRENCE The leaves measure $7\frac{7}{16}'' \times 5\frac{1}{8}''$. Top edges trimmed;
fore edges rough-trimmed; bottom edges untrimmed.

[i]–[iv] + [1]–[32], as follows: [i]–[iv] blank; [1] half-title; [2] blank;
[3] title page as above; [4] FIRST PUBLISHED IN MCMXXX | BY FABER AND
FABER LIMITED | 24 RUSSELL SQUARE LONDON W. C. I | PRINTED IN GREAT
BRITAIN | BY TREND AND COMPANY PLYMOUTH | ALL RIGHTS RESERVED;
[5]–[6] table of contents; 7–28 text; [29]–[32] blank.

Published 13 March 1930 at 2s.; the first printing consisted of 3000
copies, which included both the cloth bound copies and the copies issued
in paper wrappers.

b. *first edition (paper wrapper copies)*

NETTLES | BY | D. H. LAWRENCE | LONDON | FABER &
FABER LIMITED | 24 RUSSELL SQUARE

Salmon-pink paper wrappers, printed in black on upper cover: CRITE-
RION MISCELLANY —No. 11 | NETTLES | D. H. LAWRENCE | ONE SHILLING
NET | FABER & FABER; printed in black on lower cover: This is No. 11
of the | CRITERION MISCELLANY | Published by Faber & Faber Limited
| at 24 Russell Square, London, W. C. I The leaves measure $7\frac{5}{8}'' \times 4\frac{7}{8}''$.
Top edges rough-trimmed; fore edges trimmed; bottom edges untrim-
med.

[i]–[ii] + [1]–[30], as follows: [i]–[ii] blank; [1] half-title; [2] blank;
[3] title page as above; [4] FIRST PUBLISHED IN MCMXXX | BY FABER AND
FABER LIMITED | 24 RUSSELL SQUARE LONDON W. C. I | PRINTED IN GREAT
BRITAIN | BY TREND AND COMPANY PLYMOUTH | ALL RIGHTS RESERVED;
[5]–[6] table of contents; 7–28 text; [29]–[30] blank.

Published 13 March 1930 at 1s.; the first printing consisted of 3000
copies, which included both the cloth bound copies and the copies issued
in paper wrappers.

CONTENTS

A Rose is not a Cabbage—The Man in the Street—Britannia's Baby—
Change of Government—The British Workman and the Government—
Clydesider—Flapper Vote—Songs I Learnt at School: I Neptune's Little
Affair with Freedom; II My Native Land; III The British Boy—13,000
People—Innocent England—Give Me a Sponge—Puss-Puss!—London
Mercury—My Little Critics—Editorial Office—The Great Newspaper
Editor to his Subordinate—Modern Prayer—Cry of the Masses—What
have they done to You——?—The People—The Factory Cities—Leaves
of Grass, Flowers of Grass—Magnificent Democracy.

NOTES: Most of *Nettles* was written in answer to Lawrence's critics over
the censorship difficulties with the *Paintings* and *Pansies*. The Brewsters
(B39) were with Lawrence at the Villa Beau Soleil a few weeks before
his death and have left an account of the selection of the poems included
in *Nettles*. Some of the poems Lawrence turned through that day were
to be called "Dead Nettles" because they had no sting in them; these
were probably published in *Last Poems* (A62), which also contained
additional "Pansies." *Nettles* was reprinted in its entirety in *Pornography
and So On* (A75) and in the *Complete Poems* (A98); it has not been published
separately in the United States.

REVIEWS: *Nettles* was reviewed by Richard Rees in the *New Adelphi*,
June–August 1930.

NOTES(2): An examination of the dozen or so copies in the University
of Texas library reveals that not all the copies of either (A52a) or (A52b)
were trimmed alike, and consequently the measurements vary slightly.
For (A52a) some of the fore and bottom edges were unopened, but some
of the fore edges were trimmed. The measurements vary from $4\frac{7}{8}''$ to
$5\frac{1}{16}''$ in width and from $7\frac{3}{8}'' \times 7\frac{7}{16}''$. in height. For (A52b) some of the
fore edges were trimmed and some were untrimmed; some of the bottom
edges were unopened; the width varies from $4\frac{5}{16}''$ to $4\frac{15}{16}''$.

A53   ASSORTED ARTICLES   1930

first edition

ASSORTED ARTICLES | *By* | D. H. LAWRENCE |
LONDON: | MARTIN SECKER | 1930

Red cloth boards, stamped in gold on upper cover: D. H. Lawrence
[*facsimile reproduction of Lawrence's autograph signature*]; stamped in gold

on spine: ASSORTED | ARTICLES | [*five-pointed star*] | LAWRENCE | SECKER
The leaves measure 8″ × 5$\frac{9}{16}$″. Top edges trimmed; fore edges unopened;
bottom edges untrimmed.

[1]–[216], as follows: [1] half-title; [2] blank; [3] title page as above;
[4] D. H. LAWRENCE | *Born September* 11, 1885 | *Died March* 2, 1930 |
LONDON: MARTIN SECKER LTD. | NUMBER FIVE JOHN STREET ADELPHI; [5]
acknowledgements; [6] blank; [7] table of contents; [8] blank; 9–[216]
text, at bottom of page [216]: *Made and Printed in Great Britain by* | *The
Botolph Printing Works, Gate Street, Kingsway, W. C. 2.*

Published April 1930 at 6*s.*; the first printing consisted of 3700 copies.

CONTENTS

The "Jeune Fille" Wants to Know (first appeared in the *Evening News*,
8 May 1928 (C169), as "When She Asks Why?")—Laura Philippine
(first appeared in *T. P.'s Weekly*, 7 July 1928 (C170))—Sex Versus
Loveliness (first appeared in the *Sunday Dispatch*, 25 November 1928
(C179), as "Sex Locked Out"; also separately published (A44))—
Insouciance (first appeared in the *Evening News*, 12 July 1928 (C171),
as "Over-Earnest Ladies")—Give Her a Pattern (first appeared in
Vanity Fair for May 1929 (C187), as "Woman in Man's Image")
—Do Women Change? (first appeared in the *Sunday Dispatch*,
28 April 1929 (C185), as "Women Don't Change")—Ownership—Mas-
ter in His Own House (first appeared in the *Evening News*, 2 August
1928 (C174))—Matriarchy—Cocksure Women and Hensure Men (first
appeared in the *Forum*, January 1929 (C181))—Is England Still a Man's
Country? (first appeared in the *Daily Express*, 29 November 1928
(C180))—Dull London (first appeared in the *Evening News*, 3 September
1928 (C175))—Red Trousers (first appeared in the *Evening News*, 27
September 1928 (C176), as "Oh! For a New Crusade")—The State of
Funk—The Risen Lord (first appeared in *Everyman*, 3 October 1929
(C192))—Enslaved by Civilization (first appeared in *Vanity Fair*, Sep-
tember 1929 (C191), as "The Manufacture of Good Little Boys")—Men
Must Work and Women As Well (first appeared in the *Star Review*,
November 1929 (C193), as "Men and Women")—Autobiographical
Sketch (first appeared in the *Sunday Dispatch*, 17 February 1929 (C182)
as "Myself Revealed," and in the *Insel-Almanach*, 1931, as "D. H. Law-
rence: über sich Selbst")—Hymns in a Man's Life (first appeared in the
Evening News, 13 October 1928 (C178))—Making Pictures (first appeared in *Creative Art*, July 1929 (C188))—Pictures on the Walls (first

appeared in *Vanity Fair*, December 1929 (C195), as "Dead Pictures on the Wall")—On Being a Man (first appeared in *Vanity Fair*, June 1924 (C121))—On Human Destiny (first appeared in the *Adelphi*, March 1924 (C117)).

NOTES: During the last months of 1929, a little while before his death, Lawrence began to think of collecting his essays and newspaper articles into a book; in August he wrote Miss Pearn of Curtis Brown's office to ask if she could let him have copies of the essays he had written four or five years before for the *Adelphi* and suggested that Murry might have copies if she hadn't. The plans for the collection must have been complete or nearly so by the end of 1929, for he wrote Rhys Davies in December that he had thought of calling his book "Chips and Faggots." The title "Assorted Articles" was chosen soon afterwards, for he referred to the collection by that name in a letter to Martin Secker the following month.

Although Lawrence inquired about the essays written for Murry's *Adelphi*, only two of the several published there were included in the collection; the majority of the essays in *Assorted Articles* were written and published in 1928 and 1929. On 24 November 1928, in a letter to Dorothy Brett from Bandol, he remarked that he was being paid far better for writing newspaper articles and told her he was appearing regularly in the *Evening News*, the *Sunday Dispatch* and the *Daily News*. He was somewhat despondent over the fact that he could get £25 for a 2000-word article written in an "hour and a half" when no one would even publish a story like "None of That" (A41). Lawrence did not live to see the published *Assorted Articles*.

The first American edition was published from new plates by Alfred Knopf on 11 April 1930. Secker reprinted 1000 copies of the first edition before the end of the year and published the collection in the New Adelphi Library in September 1932. Heinemann published a Pocket Edition in January 1936.

REVIEWS: *Assorted Articles* was reviewed in *The Times Literary Supplement*, 10 April 1930; in the *Saturday Review*, 26 April 1930; by Edwin Sheaver in the *New York Evening Post Literary Review*, 26 April 1930; by Margery Latimer in the *New York World*, 27 April 1930; in "He Who Asked Why?" by Lorine Pruette in the *New York Herald Tribune Books*, 27 April 1930; in "Last Testament" by Henry Hazlitt in the *Nation* (New York), 30 April 1930; in the *Nation and Athenaeum*, 3 May 1930; in the *Spectator*, 3 May 1930; in the *New York Times Book Review*, 11 May 1930; by Arthur Colton in the *Saturday Review of Literature*, 17 May 1930; by

Sherwood Anderson in "A Man's Mind" in the *New Republic*, 21 May 1930; and there is an article by Lawrence Clark Powell in the *Saturday Review of Literature*, 14 June 1930 which objects to portions of Arthur Colton's review in the 17 May 1930 issue of the magazine.

NOTES (2): The first edition of *Assorted Articles* was issued in a cream dust-jacket printed in brown; the upper cover of the dust-jacket has a reproduction of a photograph of Lawrence.

REVIEWS(2): An additional review appeared in *English Review*, May 1930.

A54   THE VIRGIN AND THE GIPSY   1930

first edition

THE VIRGIN | AND THE GIPSY | BY | D. H. LAWRENCE | [*Lawrence phoenix*] | G. ORIOLI | FLORENCE | 1930

White paper boards, printed in red on upper cover: [*Lawrence phoenix*]; white paper label on spine printed in red: D. H. LAWRENCE | THE VIRGIN | AND THE GIPSY The leaves measure $8\frac{3}{8}'' \times 5\frac{3}{4}''$. Top edges unopened; fore and bottom edges untrimmed.

[1]–[220], as follows: [1] series-title; [2] blank; [3] half-title; [4] blank; [5] Of this limited edition, printed on | Binda hand-made paper, eight hundred | and ten copies have been printed, of | which eight hundred are for sale. | This is No. 109 [*autograph number in black ink*]; [6] blank; [7] title page as above; [8] blank; [9] dedication to Frieda; [10] blank; 11–216 text; [217] *This work lacks the author's final revision, | and has been printed from the manuscript exactly | as it stands.*; [218]–[220] blank.

Published 17 May 1930 at 21*s*.; the edition consisted of 810 copies.

VARIANTS: (1) copy described above.
          (2) as (1) except printed on blue paper; two copies only.

NOTES: *The Virgin and the Gipsy* was written during the last months of 1925 after the Lawrences had returned to Europe from the Taos ranch for the last time. Lawrence wrote Miss Pearn of Curtis Brown from the Villa Bernardo at Spotorno on 29 January 1926 that he would send the story the following week. Martin Secker intended at the time to publish another three-story volume like *The Ladybird* (A24) and wanted to include "The Virgin and the Gipsy" and "Glad Ghosts" (A36) as two of them.
    Lawrence did not prepare a final version for the printer, and all of

the various first publications bear the notation that the book was printed from a manuscript without the author's final revision. As with most of the Lawrence books published in collaboration with Orioli, two special copies were printed on blue paper.

The first English edition of *The Virgin and the Gipsy* was published in an edition of 5800 copies by Secker in October 1930; Alfred Knopf published the first American edition from new plates on 10 November 1930. Secker reprinted 2360 copies before the year was out and published a Pocket Edition in August 1931. McLeod and Greenberg published reprints in New York in 1934, and the World Publishing Company issued the title as a Forum book in 1944. No. 757 of the Penguin books contains both "St. Mawr" (A31) and "The Virgin and the Gipsy," and the latter is No. 60 in the Albatross Modern Continental Library.

REVIEWS: *The Virgin and the Gipsy* was reviewed by V. Sackville-West in the *Spectator*, 28 June 1930; in the *New Statesman*, 30 August 1930; in *The Times Literary Supplement*, 23 October 1930; by V. S. Pritchett in the *Spectator*, 23 October 1930; in the *Saturday Review*, 1 November 1930; by H. Hansen in the *New York World*, 21 November 1930; by Lorine Pruette in the *New York Herald Tribune Books*, 23 November 1930; by Percy Hutchison in the *New York Times Book Review*, 30 November 1930; by F. L. Robbins in the *Outlook*, 10 December 1930; by Robert Cantwell in the *New Republic*, 24 December 1930; by Lionel Trilling in the *Nation* (New York), 24 December 1930, as "Lawrence's Last Novel"; in the *Bookman* (New York), January 1931; and by Basil Davenport in the *Saturday Review of Literature*, 16 May 1931.

NOTES(2): Although Lawrence did not revise *The Virgin and the Gipsy* for the Orioli edition, the colophon is not strictly accurate in the statement that "This work lacks the author's final revision..." When Lawrence was writing the story in January 1926, Secker visited him at Spotorno and read and liked the beginning. While Lawrence awaited Secker's response to the completed work, he probably revised a copy of the typescript, which was prepared by Secker's office and is now unlocated; this revision would account for the differences between the holograph manuscript and the Orioli text. Secker's reaction is not recorded but must not have been favourable because the plan to publish *The Virgin and the Gipsy* in a volume of novelettes was dropped.

The Virgin and the Gipsy was issued in a green paper dust-jacket printed in black which is usually found to be faded to a brown colour.

REVIEWS (2): Additional reviews of *The Virgin and the Gipsy* appeared in the *English Review* for 6 December 1930 and the *London Mercury* for December 1930.

A55   LETTER TO CHARLES LAHR   1930

first edition

A single sheet measuring $12\frac{7}{16}'' \times 8\frac{3}{4}''$, printed on white paper watermarked: BASINGWERK PARCHMENT.

The text of the letter appears as follows:

PALMA DE MALLORCO. SPAIN | 15 June 1929 | Dear Lahr | MY WIFE will come to London, arrive there | probably saturday, July 22nd. We are due to leave on | Tuesday for Marseilles. I shall give her the drawings | and photographs, you can choose which you like. I like | best the big head in red chalk done by myself—I think | it is BASICALLY like me. But my wife thinks it is | awful—chiefly because she doesn't understand— and | prefers the seated figure drawings by Tom Jones. | Which I think rather trivial, and bad in the sticking on | of the head. But I don't really care which you choose |—use even a photograph if you wish —anyhow if you | use one of my sketches, don't say it's by me. D. H. L. | six copies printed by THE BLUE MOON PRESS

Although the note at the end of the sheet says six copies were printed, Mr Lahr writes that about ten or twelve copies were pulled in August 1930 and given to friends; it was never sold.

NOTES: In 1928 Charles Lahr bought a hand-press which had belonged to William Morris, and with his friend, Herbert Jones the typographer, printed "little things on it like Christmas cards and a catalogue of first editions." Herbert Jones wanted to try out a new type he had just purchased and Lahr handed him a letter from Lawrence which resulted in this broadside.

A56   LOVE AMONG THE HAYSTACKS   1930

a. *first edition*

LOVE | AMONG THE | HAYSTACKS | & OTHER PIECES | BY | D. H. LAWRENCE | WITH A REMINISCENCE | BY | DAVID GARNETT | [*publisher's device*] | LONDON·MCMXXX | THE NONESUCH PRESS

Yellow cloth boards with a natural cloth backstrip, black leather label on spine stamped in gold: [*single rule*] | LOVE | AMONG | THE HAY- | STACKS | · | LAWRENCE | [*single rule*] The leaves measure $9\frac{1}{4}'' \times 5\frac{3}{4}''$. Top edges unopened; fore and bottom edges untrimmed.

[i]–[iv] + [i]–[xiv] + [1]–[102], as follows: [i]–[iv] blank; [i] title page as above; [ii] blank; [iii] table of contents; [iv] blank; [v]–xiii reminiscence by David Garnett; [xiv] blank; [1]–96 text; [97] This edition of *Love Among the Haystacks* | and other pieces by D. H. Lawrence, | printed in Caslon Monotype on Auvergne | hand-made paper at The Curwen Press, is | limited to sixteen hundred copies, of which | five hundred and fifty are for sale in the | United States by Random House. | This is number | 64 [*autograph number in black ink*]; [98] *Printed and made in England*; [99]–[102] blank.

Published 25 November 1930 at 15*s*.; the edition consisted of 1600 copies.

b. *first American edition*

LOVE | AMONG THE | HAYSTACKS | & OTHER PIECES | D. H. LAWRENCE | [*Lawrence phoenix*] | With a Reminiscence | By DAVID GARNETT | THE VIKING PRESS·NEW YORK | 1933

Green cloth boards, stamped in gold on upper cover: [*Lawrence phoenix on darker green background with circular rule border*]; stamped on the spine in gold: LOVE | AMONG | THE | HAYSTACKS | D. H. | LAWRENCE | THE | VIKING | PRESS [*the preceding three words blind stamped*] The leaves measure $7\frac{1}{2}'' \times 5\frac{1}{16}''$. Top edges trimmed and stained yellow; fore edges trimmed; bottom edges rough-trimmed.

[i]–xvi + [1]–[112], as follows: [i] half-title; [ii] list of Lawrence books published by Viking; [iii] title page as above; [iv] COPYRIGHT, 1933, BY FRIEDA LAWRENCE | PRINTED IN U. S. A. | DISTRIBUTED IN CANADA BY THE MACMILLAN COMPANY OF CANADA, LTD.; [v] contents; [vi] blank; vii–xvi reminiscence by David Garnett; [1] fly-title: [*ornamental rule*] | Love among the Haystacks | [*single rule*]; [2] blank; 3–58 text; [59] fly-title: [*ornamental rule*] | A Chapel among the Mountains | and | A Hay Hut among the Mountains | [*single rule*]; [60] blank; 61–86 text; [87] fly-title: [*ornamental rule*] | Once | [*single rule*]; [88] blank; 89–102 text; [103] fly-title: [*ornamental rule*] | Christs in the Tirol | [*single rule*]; [104] blank; 105–111 text; [112] blank.

Published 30 October 1933 at $1.50; number of copies unknown.

NOTES: All the stories and sketches in this volume were apparently of very early vintage; in the introductory material David Garnett recalls that they were written in July and August 1912, after which they were sent to his father, who was unable to place them for publication. After Lawrence's death they were sent to David Garnett, who was associated with Francis Meynell in the Nonesuch Press. At the time some of the stories were being written the young David Garnett was visiting the Lawrences in the Tirol; they were joined briefly by Garnett's friend Harold Hobson, with whom he departed after walking down the mountain from Mayrhofen with Lawrence and Frieda.

Secker published an edition in 1933 and a Pocket Edition in 1934. Scherz published the title as No. 14 of the Phoenix books at Berne in 1943.

REVIEWS: *Love Among the Haystacks* was reviewed in *The Times Literary Supplement*, 18 December 1930; by Harry Hanson in the *New York World*, 27 December 1930; in the *New York Times Book Review*, 11 January 1931; in the *New Statesman*, 24 January 1931; by Lorine Pruette in the *New York Herald Tribune Books*, 8 February 1931; in the *Nation and Athenaeum*, 14 February 1931; and by Joan Haslip in the *London Mercury*, March 1931.

NOTES (2): Copies of (A56b), the Viking edition of *Love Among the Haystacks* have been reported with the words "Viking Press" stamped on the spine in gold, but the three copies at the University of Texas agree with that described above, i.e., with the words blind stamped.

The Nonesuch edition was issued in a grey paper dust-jacket printed in black; the Viking dust-jacket is tan paper printed in orange and green.

A57   APOCALYPSE   1931

a. *first edition*

APOCALYPSE | BY | D. H. LAWRENCE | [*Lawrence phoenix*] | G. ORIOLI | FLORENCE | 1931

Red paper boards, printed in black on upper cover: [*Lawrence phoenix*]; black leather label on spine, stamped in gold: [*double rule*] | D. H. LAWRENCE | [*five-pointed star*] | APOCALYPSE | [*double rule*] The leaves measure $8\frac{1}{2}'' \times 5\frac{7}{8}''$. Top edges unopened; fore and bottom edges untrimmed.

[1]–[308] and frontispiece consisting of a photograph of D. H. Lawrence taken at Chapala, Mexico, in 1922, as follows: [1] series-title; [2] PRINTED BY THE | TIPOGRAFIA GIUNTINA | FLORENCE; [3] half-title; [4] blank; [5] Of this limited edition, printed on Binda | paper, seven hundred and fifty copies | have been printed, of which seven hundred | are for sale. | This is No. 745 [*autograph number in blue ink*]; [6] blank; [7] title page as above; [8] blank; 9–[308] text.

Published 3 June 1931 at 30*s*.; the edition consisted of 750 copies.

VARIANTS: (1) copy described above.

(2) as (1) except printed on blue paper; three copies only.

b. *definitive edition*

APOCALYPSE | AND THE WRITINGS ON | REVELA-TION | D. H. LAWRENCE | EDITED BY | MARA KALNINS | CAMBRIDGE UNIVERSITY PRESS | CAMBRIDGE | LONDON NEW YORK NEW ROCHELLE | MELBOURNE SYDNEY

Red cloth boards, stamped in gold on spine, reading from top to bottom: *The Works of* | *D. H. Lawrence* | [*preceding two lines enclosed within a single oval rule*] APOCALYPSE AND THE WRITINGS ON REVELATION | CAMBRIDGE [*preceding line reading from left to right*] The leaves measure $8\frac{1}{2}'' \times 5\frac{3}{8}''$. All edges trimmed.

[i]–[xiv] + [1]–[250], as follows: [i] half-title: THE | CAMBRIDGE EDITION OF | THE LETTERS AND WORKS OF | D. H. LAWRENCE | [*Cambridge Press design of Lawrence phoenix*]; [ii] list of general editors and members of the editorial board for THE WORKS OF D. H. LAWRENCE; [iii] title page as above; [iv] publishing, copyright and cataloguing information; v contents; [vi] blank; vii–viii general editors' preface; ix acknowledgements; x–xii chronology; xiii list of cue-titles; [xiv] blank; [1] fly-title: INTRODUCTION; [2] blank; 3–38 text; [39] fly-title: A REVIEW OF | *THE BOOK OF REVELATION* | BY DR. JOHN OMAN; [40] note on the text; 41–42 text; [43] fly-title: INTRODUCTION TO | *THE DRAGON OF THE APOCALYPSE* | BY FREDERICK CARTER; [44] note on the text; 45–56 text; [57] fly-title: *APOCALYPSE*; [58] note on the text; 59–149 text; [150] blank; [151] fly-title: *APOCALYPSE*: APPENDIXES I, II, III; [152] note on the texts; 153–200 text; [201] fly-title: EXPLANATORY NOTES; [202]

blank; 203–240 text; [241] fly-title: TEXTUAL APPARATUS; [242] blank; 243–249 text; [250] blank.

Published 30 October 1980 at £12.50; the first printing consisted of 3042 copies.

NOTES: This is the book which grew out of Lawrence's interest in the "Book of Revelation," an interest stimulated by his efforts to write an introduction for Frederick Carter's "Revelation of St. John the Divine" (C204). The Brewsters (B39) tell the story of the typing of the manuscript by their daughter Harwood during the Christmas holidays 1929. The beginning of work on *Apocalypse* may tentatively be dated by a presentation note from Harwood Brewster in a notebook containing portions of an early version. The Brewster's daughter gave the notebook to Lawrence for his birthday on 11 September 1929 at the Villa Beau Soleil in Bandol.

Martin Secker published the first English edition in May 1932, and the first American edition was published by Viking in November 1931. Viking published another edition in February 1932 with an introduction by Richard Aldington. *Apocalypse* is No. 31 of the Albatross Modern Continental Library.

REVIEWS: *Apocalypse* was reviewed in *The Times Literary Supplement*, 25 June 1931; by Joan Haslip in the *London Mercury*, November 1931; by E. S. Bates in the *Saturday Review of Literature*, 13 February 1932; by Lorine Pruette in the *New York Herald Tribune Books*, 14 February 1932; by Percy Hutchison in the *New York Times Book Review*, 28 February 1932; by W. R. Brooks in the *Outlook* (New York), March; in *The Times Literary Supplement*, 5 May 1932; by D. Campkin in the *Week-End Review*, 7 May 1932; by I. M. Parsons in the *Spectator*, 14 May 1932; by Kenneth White in the *New Republic*, 1 June 1932; in the *American Mercury*, June 1932; by Humbert Wolfe in the *Observer*, 3 July 1932; by Osbert Burdett in the *Saturday Review*, 11 July 1931; by Geoffrey West in the *Yale Review*, Winter 1933 (published December 1932).

NOTES (2): The untrimmed fore and bottom edges of *Apocalypse* render the measurements somewhat uncertain; those given above seem satisfactory as an average size for the bound sheets. The book was issued in a green paper dust-jacket printed in black; the green is usually faded to a brown colour.

REVIEWS (2): Additional reviews of *Apocalypse* appeared by Max Plowman in the *Adelphi*, February 1933; by A. D. Emmart in *Baltimore Evening Sun*, 20 February 1932; by Nathan Haskell Dale in *Portland News*,

14 March 1932; in *Dayton Ohio Herald*, 26 March 1932; by Edwin H. Ford in *Minneapolis Journal*, 17 April 1932; *Plain Dealer* (Cleveland, Ohio), 21 February 1932; by Hugh Cotterell in *South California Trojan*, 1 March 1932; *Chicago News*, 2 March 1932.

A58 TRIUMPH OF THE MACHINE 1930

a. *first edition (large-paper copies)*

D. H. LAWRENCE | [*short decorative rule*] | THE TRIUMPH OF THE MACHINE | *Drawings by Althea Willoughby* | LONDON: FABER & FABER LTD | [*short decorative rule*] | 1930

Green paper boards, stamped in gold on upper cover: D. H. LAWRENCE [*three six-pointed stars arranged in triangle with apex pointing downward*] THE TRIUMPH | OF THE MACHINE The leaves measure $8\frac{9}{16}'' \times 5\frac{1}{2}''$. Top edges trimmed; fore and bottom edges untrimmed.

[1]–[16], as follows: [1] This large-paper edition, printed | on English hand-made paper, is | limited to four hundred copies | This is Number 17 [*autograph number in black ink*]; [2] blank; [3] half-title; [4] blank; [5] title page as above; [6] PRINTED IN ENGLAND AT THE CURWEN PRESS; [7] [*illustration*]; [8] blank; [9] text; [10] blank; [11] text; [12] blank; [13] This is No. 28 of | THE ARIEL POEMS | Published in London by Faber & Faber | Limited, at 24 Russell Square, W. C. 1; [14]–[16] blank.

Published October 1930 at 7s. 6d.; 400 large-paper copies were printed.

b. *first edition (ordinary copies)*

D. H. LAWRENCE | [*short decorative rule*] | THE TRIUMPH OF THE MACHINE | [*illustration*] | *Drawings by Althea Willoughby*

Green paper wrappers, printed in black on upper cover: [title page as above]; printed in black on lower cover: This is No. 28 of | THE ARIEL POEMS | Published by Faber & Faber Limited | at 24 Russell Square, London, W. C. 1 | Printed at The Curwen Press, Plaistow The leaves measure $7\frac{3}{8}'' \times 4\frac{3}{4}''$. All edges trimmed.

[1]–[8], as follows: [1]–[2] blank; [3] [*illustration*]; [4]–[5] text; [6]–[8] blank.

Published October 1930 at 1s.; number of copies unknown.

NOTES: "Triumph of the Machine" first appeared in the *London Mercury*,

June 1930 (C200), and was first collected in the *Best Poems of 1930* (B29). It was also included in *Last Poems* (A62).

NOTES (2): The publication data for *Triumph of the Machine* illustrates the dangers of bibliographical practice. The preface to this revision of the bibliography explains the compiler's somewhat arbitrary attitude toward publication dates, but this is an extreme case. The date for the publication of *Triumph of the Machine* in the original bibliography was 25 September 1931. This date was unequivocally supplied by the publisher, and despite the 1930 on the title page, the September 1931 date was given for the date of publication. However, the *English Catalogue of Books* gives October 1930. This might have been explained away, but the copy in the British Library is stamped 16 October 1930, and this suggests strongly, as Mr W. Forster points out, that the publication date should be in 1930 rather than 1931.

A59   A LETTER FROM CORNWALL   1931

first edition

A LETTER | FROM | CORNWALL | (*JANUARY 5, 1916*) | D. H. LAWRENCE | [*publisher's device*] | YERBA BUENA PRESS | *1931* | [*decorative vertical rule made with pen and red ink is at left of title page*]

Decorative cloth boards with a parchment paper backstrip, ivory paper label on upper cover printed in black: A LETTER FROM CORNWALL The leaves measure $8'' \times 6\frac{3}{4}''$. Top edges trimmed; fore and bottom edges untrimmed.

[1]–[12], as follows: [1] half-title; [2] frontispiece consisting of a tipped-in photograph of Lawrence; [3] title page as above; [4] blank; [5] THE ORIGINAL LETTER | HERE REPRINTED | IS IN THE | CHARLOTTE ASHLEY FELTON | MEMORIAL LIBRARY | STANFORD UNIVERSITY; [6] blank; [7]–[10] text; [11] THIS EDITION | CONSISTS OF FIVE COPIES | OF WHICH THIS | IS NO. XX [*holograph crosses in ink*]

Published in 1931, not for sale; the edition consisted of five copies.

NOTES: The letter printed here was written to J. D. Beresford from Padstow, Cornwall, on 5 January 1916. Mr Van Patten also published *D. H. Lawrence's Letter to the Laughing Horse* (A77) under the Yerba Buena imprint and wrote the preface to the *Foreword to Women in Love* (A74). The letter to Beresford is in the *Letters* (A61).

first edition

ETRUSCAN PLACES | *By* | D. H. LAWRENCE | 1932 | [*short decorative rule*] | London: Martin Secker

Blue cloth boards, blind stamped on upper cover: [*embossed design of horses and chariot with two human figures*]; stamped in gold on spine: ETRUSCAN | PLACES | [*five-pointed star*] | LAWRENCE | SECKER The leaves measure $8\frac{3}{4}'' \times 5\frac{3}{4}''$. Top edges trimmed and stained blue; fore and bottom edges untrimmed.

[1]–[200], with frontispiece and 19 plates facing pages 22, 24, 26, 30, 32, 56, 60, 68, 72, 74, 76, 78, 82, 114, 126, 176, 188, 190, and 192, as follows: [1] half-title; [2] blank; [3] title page as above; [4] LONDON: MARTIN SECKER LTD. | NUMBER FIVE JOHN STREET ADELPHI; 5 table of contents; [6] blank; 7 list of illustrations; [8] blank; [9] fly-title: I | CERVETERI; [10] blank; 11–35 text; [36] blank; [37] fly-title: II | TARQUINIA; [38] blank; 39–62 text; [63] fly-title: III | THE PAINTED TOMBS OF | TARQUINIA; [64] blank; 65–102 text; [103] fly-title: IV | THE PAINTED TOMBS OF | TARQUINIA; [104] blank; 105–137 text; [138] blank; [139] fly-title: V | VULCI; [140] blank; 141–169 text; [170] blank; [171] fly-title: VI | VOLTERRA; [172] blank; 173–[199] text; [200] Printed in Great Britain | by The Riverside Press Limited | Edinburgh.

Published September 1932 at 15*s.*; the first printing consisted of 3070 copies.

CONTENTS

Cerveteri (first appeared in *Travel*, November 1927 (C163), as "City of the Dead at Cerveteri")—Tarquinia (first appeared in *Travel*, December 1927 (C165), as "Ancient Metropolis of the Etruscans")—The Painted Tombs of Tarquinia I (first appeared in *Travel*, January 1928 (C166))— The Painted Tombs of Tarquinia II—Vulci—Volterra (first appeared in *Travel*, February 1928 (C168), as "Wind-Swept Strongholds of Volterra").

NOTES: A letter written from Fontana Vecchia to Catherine Carswell in October 1921 suggests that she instigated Lawrence's interest in the Etruscans. He asks her to let him know the secret of the Etruscans she saw written so plainly at the place she visited; the Etruscans puzzled and interested Lawrence. The first mention of a possible book of sketches on the Etruscans occurs in a letter to Curtis Brown from the Villa Bernarda at Spotorno at Easter 1926 in which he fancied he might do a book on them, half travel, half study. Lawrence visited all the Etruscan places in the spring of 1927 with Earl Brewster, who gives a detailed account of the trip in his book (B39). Letters written in April and May mention work on the sketches. By October he could write the Brewsters that half of the Etruscan sketches were done and that four of them were to appear in *Travel* beginning with the November issue. The text of the magazine articles is not identical with that of the book, which also contains additional material. Several letters mention a desire to do more on the Etruscans, but he was never to have the opportunity.

The first American issue of *Etruscan Places* was published by Viking in November 1932 from the Secker sheets. Secker published a Cheap Edition in October 1933, and Heinemann issued another Cheap Edition in February 1938.

REVIEWS: *Etruscan Places* was reviewed in the *New Statesman and Nation*, 22 October 1932; by T. E. Welby in the *Observer*, 23 October 1932; by Aldous Huxley in the *Spectator*, 4 November 1932; in the *Saturday Review*, 12 November 1932; by Lorine Pruette in the *New York Herald Tribune Books*, 13 November 1932; in the *New York Times Book Review*, 11 December 1932; by Horace Gregory in the *New Republic*, 14 December 1932; by E. C. Oppenheim in the *Spectator*, 23 December 1932; in "Lawrence in Etruria" by Arthur Hall in the *Bookman* (London), October 1932; by J. W. Lane in the *Bookman* (New York), January 1933; in the *Nation* (New York), 1 February 1933; in *The Times Literary Supplement*, 23 February 1933; and by Max Plowman in the *New Adelphi*, February 1933.

NOTES (2): *Etruscan Places* was issued in a cream paper dust-jacket printed in black; the upper cover of the dust-jacket has a reproduction of a photograph of Etruscan statuary.

A61   LETTERS   1932

a. *first edition (special copies)*

THE LETTERS | OF | D. H. LAWRENCE [*title in red*] | EDITED | AND WITH AN INTRODUCTION BY | AL-DOUS HUXLEY | LONDON: WILLIAM HEINEMANN, LTD. | NEW YORK: THE VIKING PRESS, INC.

Parchment paper boards, printed in black on upper cover: [*Lawrence*

phoenix]; printed in black on spine: LETTERS | OF | D. H. | LAWRENCE
The leaves measure 8$\frac{15}{16}$″ × 5$\frac{7}{8}$″. All edges trimmed.

[i]–[ii] + [1]–xxxiv + 1–[892] and four leaves, integral with the signatures, but not counted in the pagination, preceding pages, 1, 201, 477 and 589, as follows: [i]–[ii] blank; [i] half-title; [ii] *This edition is limited to 525 | copies, of which 250 are for sale | in Great Britain and 250 in the | United States of America. This | copy is No.* 440 [*autograph number in black ink*]; [iii] title page as above; [iv] 1932 | PRINTED IN GREAT BRITAIN | AT THE WINDMILL PRESS; [v] table of contents; [vi] blank; [vii] fly-title: THE LETTERS | OF | D. H. LAWRENCE; [viii] blank; ix–xxxiv introduction by Aldous Huxley; uncounted leaf, recto, fly-title: [*printer's ornament*] | EARLY DAYS | *"THE WHITE PEACOCK"* | GERMANY, AUSTRIA AND ITALY; verso blank; 1–200 text; uncounted leaf, recto, fly-title: [*printer's ornament*] | THE WAR | *"THE RAINBOW"* | CORNWALL AND DERBYSHIRE; verso blank; 201–476 text; uncounted leaf, recto, fly-title: [*printer's ornament*] | ITALY AGAIN | *"WOMEN IN LOVE"* | CEYLON, AUSTRALIA, | NEW AND OLD MEXICO; verso, blank; 477–588 text; uncounted leaf, recto, fly-title: [*printer's ornament*] | THE PHOENIX | *"Will the bird perish | Shall the bird rise?"* | BACK TO MEXICO | SPOTORNO: VILLA MIRENDA | *"LADY CHATTERLEY'S LOVER"* | THE PAINTINGS, "PANSIES" | BANDOL, VENCE, | DEATH; verso, blank; 589–853 text; [854] blank; 855–858 biographical note; 859–889 index; [890]–[892] blank.

Published 26 September 1932; 525 special copies were printed.

b. *first edition* (*ordinary copies*)

THE LETTERS | OF | D. H. LAWRENCE | [*title in red*] | EDITED | AND WITH AN INTRODUCTION BY | ALDOUS HUXLEY | [*publisher's device*] | LONDON | WILLIAM HEINEMANN LTD. | 1932

Chocolate-brown cloth boards, stamped in gold on upper cover: THE LETTERS OF | D. H. LAWRENCE | [*Lawrence phoenix*]; blind stamped on lower cover: [*publisher's device*]; stamped in gold on spine: THE | LETTERS OF | D. H. LAWRENCE | [*Lawrence phoenix*] | HEINEMANN The leaves measure 9″ × 6″. All edges trimmed.

[i]–[ii] + [i]–xxxiv + 1–[892] with frontispiece and 16 illustrations facing pages 26, 186, 216, 344, 408, 472, 534, 548, 552, 566, 596, 636, 652, 692, 772 and 852 and four leaves, integral with the signatures, but not counted in the pagination, preceding pages 1, 201, 477 and 589, as

follows: [i]–[ii] blank; [i] half-title; [ii] blank; [iii] title page as above; [iv] PRINTED IN GREAT BRITAIN | AT THE WINDMILL PRESS; [v] table of contents; [vi] blank; [vii] list of illustrations; [viii] blank; ix–xxxiv introduction by Aldous Huxley; uncounted leaf, recto, fly-title: [*printer's ornament*] | EARLY DAYS | "*THE WHITE PEACOCK*" | GERMANY, AUSTRIA AND ITALY; verso, blank; 1–200 text; uncounted leaf, recto, fly-title: [*printer's ornament*] | THE WAR | "*THE RAINBOW*" | CORNWALL AND DERBYSHIRE; verso, blank; 201–476 text; uncounted leaf, recto, fly-title: [*printer's ornament*] | ITALY AGAIN | "*WOMEN IN LOVE*" | CEYLON, AUSTRALIA, | NEW AND OLD MEXICO; verso, blank; 477–588 text; uncounted leaf, recto, fly-title: [*printer's ornament*] | THE PHOENIX | "*Will the bird perish* | *Shall the bird rise?*" | BACK TO MEXICO | SPOTORNO: VILLA MIRENDA | "*LADY CHATTERLEY'S LOVER*" | THE PAINTINGS, "*PANSIES*" | BANDOL, VENCE, | DEATH; verso, blank; 589–853 text; [854] blank; 855–858 biographical note; 859–889 index; [890]–[892] blank.

Published 26 September 1932 at 21*s.*; 10,500 ordinary copies were printed.

NOTES: Lawrence has proved to be one of the most voluminous English letter writers. The catholicity of his correspondence makes the letters an important source for study of the period, and the letters themselves are indispensable for an understanding of Lawrence. Unfortunately the letters printed in this volume are only a part of those in existence; as late as 1955 Harry T. Moore was able to quote from almost two hundred previously unpublished letters in his *Intelligent Heart* (B57).

Heinemann reprinted the *Letters* in June 1934, and the Albatross Library issued the *Letters* in three volumes, Nos. 390, 396 and 502 in 1938 and 1939. See (A102) and (A121).

REVIEWS: Reviews of the *Letters* appeared in the *New York Evening Post Literary Review*, 24 September 1932, by William Soskin; by Ivor Brown in the *Observer*, 25 September 1932; by Percy Hutchison in the *New York Times Book Review*, 25 September 1932; by Lorine Pruette in the *New York Herald Tribune Books*, 25 September 1932; in *The Times Literary Supplement*, 29 September 1932; in "The Whole Hive of Genius" by David Garnett in the *Saturday Review of Literature*, 1 October 1932; by Harold Nicolson in the *New Statesman and Nation*, 1 October 1932; by Gerald Bullett in the *Week-End Review*, 8 October 1932; by Lord David Cecil in the *Spectator*, 18 November 1932; by Ferner Nuhn in the *Nation* (New York), 19 October 1932; by Kyle S. Crichton in *Scribner's*, November 1932; in "The Creed of D. H. Lawrence" by C. H. Warren in the *Fortnightly Review*, November 1932; in "D. H. Lawrence in His Letters" by Catherine Carswell in *Nineteenth Century*, November 1932; by Henri Fluchère in *Cahiers du Sud*, November 1932; in "D. H. Lawrence d'après sa Correspondance" by Louis Gillet in the *Revue des Deux Mondes*, 1 December 1932; by Horace Gregory in the *New Republic*, December 1932; by Peter Quennell in *Life and Letters*, December 1932; by W. Troy in *Symposium*, January 1933; by E. B. Burgum in the *Sewanee Review*, January–March 1933; by Theodore Spencer in the *Atlantic Monthly*, March 1933; in the *American Mercury*, April 1933; by Geoffrey West in the *Criterion*, April 1933; the *Yale Review*, Winter 1933 (published December 1932); and in the *English Review*, 1 December 1932 by E. C. Chilton.

A62   LAST POEMS   1932

first edition

LAST POEMS | BY | D. H. LAWRENCE | EDITED | BY | RICHARD ALDINGTON | AND | GIUSEPPE ORIOLI | WITH AN INTRODUCTION | [*Lawrence phoenix*] | G. ORIOLI | FLORENCE | 1932

Mulberry-coloured paper boards, printed in black on upper cover: [*Lawrence phoenix*]; tan paper label on spine, printed in black: LAST POEMS | D. H. LAWRENCE | [*enclosed within single rule forming border*] The leaves measure $9\frac{5}{8}'' \times 6\frac{1}{2}''$. Top edges unopened; fore and bottom edges untrimmed.

[i]–xxii + [1]–320 including a frontispiece which is not integral with the signature but is counted in the pagination, as follows: [i] half-title; [ii] PRINTED BY THE | TIPOGRAFIA GIUNTINA | FLORENCE; [iii] fly-title: LAST POEMS; [iv] blank; [v] THIS EDITION IS LIMITED | TO 750 COPIES, 700 ARE | FOR SALE. | THIS IS NO. 4 [*autograph number in black ink*]; [vi] blank; [vii] blank; [viii] frontispiece consisting of a reproduction of Lawrence's last drawing, "A Crown of Thorns"; [ix] title page as above; [x] blank; xi–xxii introduction by Richard Aldington; [1] fly-title: LAST POEMS; [2] blank; 3–80 text; [81] fly-title: MORE PANSIES; [82] blank; 83–302 text; [303] fly-title: APPENDIX; [304] blank; 305–316 text; 317–320 table of contents.

Published 1 October 1932 at 32*s.*; the edition consisted of 750 copies.

VARIANTS: (1) copy described above.
    (2) as (1) except printed on blue paper; two copies only.

CONTENTS

The Greeks are Coming!—The Argonauts—Middle of the World—For
the Heroes are Dipped in Scarlet—Demiurge—The Work of Creation—
Red Geranium and Godly Mignonette—Bodiless God—The Body of
God—The Rainbow—Maximus—The Man of Tyre—They Say the Sea
is Loveless—Whales Weep Not!—Invocation to the Moon—Butterfly—
Bavarian Gentians—Lucifer—The Breath of Life—Silence—The Hands
of God—Pax—Abysmal Immortality—Only Man—Return of Returns
—Stoic—In the Cities—Lord's Prayer—Mana of the Sea—Salt—The
Four—The Boundary Stone—Spilling the Salt—Walk Warily—Mystic
—Anaxagoras—Kissing and Horrid Strife—When Satan Fell—Doors—
Evil is Homeless—What then is Evil?—The Evil World-Soul—The
Wandering Cosmos—Death is not Evil, Evil is Mechanical—Strife—The
Late War—Murder—Murderous Weapons—Departure—The Ship of
Death—Difficult Death—All Souls' Day—The Houseless Dead—
Beware the Unhappy Dead!—After All Saints' Day—Song of Death—
The End, The Beginning—Sleep—Sleep and Waking—Fatigue—Forget
—Know-All—Tabernacle—Temples—Shadows—Change—Phoenix.

More Pansies

Image-Making Love (first appeared in the *Imagist Anthology 1930*
(B27))—People—Desire—To a Certain Friend—The Emotional Friend
—Correspondence in After Years—The Egoists—Chimaera—Ultimate
Reality (first appeared in the *Imagist Anthology 1930* (B27))—Sphinx (first
appeared in the *Imagist Anthology 1930* (B27))—Intimates (first appeared
in the *Imagist Anthology 1930* (B27))—True Love at Last (first appeared
in the *Imagist Anthology 1930* (B27))—Andraitx-Pomegranate Flowers—I
Dare Do All—Battle of Life—There Are too Many People—The Heart
of Man—Moral Clothing—Behaviour—The Hostile Sun—The Church
—The Protestant Churches—Loneliness—The Uprooted—Delight of
Being Alone—Refused Friendship—Future Relationships—Future
Religion—Future State—Future War—Signs of the Times—Initiation
Degrees—Unhappy Souls—Full Life—People Who Care—Non-
Existence—All-Knowing—Salvation—Old Archangels—Lucifer (first
appeared in the *Imagist Anthology 1930* (B27))—The Mill of God—
Multitudes—Fallen Leaves—The Difference—The Breath of Life—
Vengeance is Mine—Astronomical Changes—Fatality—Free Will—In
a Spanish Tram-Car—Spanish Privilege—At the Bank in Spain—The
Spanish Wife—The Painter's Wife—Modern Problems—Dominant
Women—Men and Women—The Scientific Doctor—Healing—En

Masse—God and the Holy Ghost—Humility—Proper Pride—Humility Mongers—Tender Reverence—Absolute Reverence—Belief—Bells (first appeared in the *London Mercury*, March 1930 (C197))—The Triumph of the Machine (first appeared in the *London Mercury*, June 1930 (C200); first collected in *Best Poems of 1930* (B29))—Forte Dei Marmi—Sea-Bathers—Talk of Loyalty—Talk of Faith—Amo Sacrum Vulgus—Boredom, Ennui, Depression—The Deadly Victorian—What are the Wild Waves Saying?—Welcome Death—Dark Satanic Mills—We Die Together—What have They Done to You?—What is a Man to Do?—City-Life—13 Pictures—Auto da Fe—Shows—Rose and Cabbage—The Gulf—The Cross—Fellow-Men—The Sight of God—Souls to Save—When Most Men Die—Hold Back!—Impulse—Men Like Gods—Men and Machines—Masses and Classes—Give Us the Thebaïd—Side-Step, O Sons of Men!—On And On And On—Oh Wonderful Machine!—But I Say Unto You: Love One Another—Love Thy Neighbour—As Thyself!—Lonely, Lonesome, Loney-O!—Trees in the Garden—Storm in the Black Forest—Revolution as Such!—Robot Feelings—Real Democracy—Robot-Democracy—Worship—Classes—Democracy is Service—False Democracy and Real—Service—What are the Gods!—The Gods! The Gods!—Name the Gods!—There are no Gods—Food of the North—Retort to Whitman—Retort to Jesus—The Deepest Sensuality—Sense of Truth—Satisfaction—Vibration of Justice—Lies—Poison—Commandments—Emotional Lies—Laughter—Drawing-Room—Cabbage-Roses—Cold Blood—Sunset—Listen to the Band!—The Human Face—Portraits—Furniture—Children Singing in School—Keep it Up—Race and Battle—Nothing to Save—British Sincerity—The English are so Nice!—The Hills—Tourists—Seekers—Search for Love—Search for Truth—Lies about Love—Travel is over—Old Men—Death—Bourgeois and Bolshevist—Property and no-Property—Cowardice and Impudence—Lord Tennyson and Lord Melchett—Choice of Evils—Hard-Boiled Conservatives—Solomon's Baby—The Property Question—The Way Out—St. George and the Dragon—The Half-Blind—Minorities in Danger—If You are a Man—Terra Incognita—Climbing Down—Only the Best Matters—To Pino—Broadcasting to the G.B.P.—We Can't be too careful—Glimpses—All Sorts of Gods—For a Moment—Goethe and Pose—Men Like Gods—Thought—Be it So—Conceit—Man is More Than Homo Sapiens—Self-Conscious People—Two Ways of Living and Dying—So Let Me Live—Gladness of Death—Humanity Needs Pruning—Self-Sacrifice—Shedding of Blood—The Old Idea of Sacrifice—Self-Sacrifice—I Heard a Little Chicken Chirp—"Gross, Course, Hideous"—Dearly-

Beloved Mr. Squire—Let There Be Light!—God is Born—The White
Horse—Flowers and Men—Prayer.

Appendix
Ship of Death—The Ship of Death—Song of Death—Glory of Darkness
—Bavarian Gentians.

NOTES: The Brewsters (B39) tell of Lawrence's efforts to collect poems
for book publication a few weeks before his death; some of these
poems were included in *Nettles* (A52), but many poems remained in
manuscript and unpublished when Richard Aldington and Pino Orioli
began the job of editing them for *Last Poems*. In his introduction Richard
Aldington mentions that it was evident that Lawrence intended the
material in the manuscripts for two books of poems; accordingly the
editors arranged the poems into two sections which they labelled "Last
Poems" and "More Pansies." Lawrence had struck out some of the
poems in the manuscripts, and the editors wishing to follow Lawrence's
desires as much as possible left these out of the published book. After
seeing the proofs of Tedlock's bibliography (B51), Richard Aldington
wrote the author that the two notebooks from which he edited the *Last
Poems* were not in the collection and that the collection contained a
notebook never seen by him. The poems from *Last Poems* were reprinted
in *The Complete Poems* (A98).

Viking published the first American edition of *Last Poems* in March
1933; the first English edition was published by Secker in April, and
Heinemann issued an edition in December 1935.

REVIEWS: *Last Poems* was reviewed in *The Times Literary Supplement*, 27
October 1932; by H. W. in the *Observer*, 27 November 1932; by Alan
Pryce-Jones in the *London Mercury*, November 1932; by C. H. Warren
in the *Fortnightly Review*, December 1932; by R. P. in the *Christian Science
Monitor*, 25 March 1933; by Eda Lou Walton in the *New York Herald
Tribune Books*, 26 March 1933; by Geoffrey West in the *Criterion*, April
1933; in the *Nation* (New York), 5 April 1933; by Louis Untermeyer in
the *Saturday Review of Literature*, 8 April 1933; in *Commonweal*, 12 April
1933; in the *Saturday Review*, 20 May 1933; in "Lawrence's Last Poems"
by John Gould Fletcher in *Poetry*, June 1933; by Isidor Schneider in
the *New Republic*, 7 June 1933; by Theodore Morrison in the *Atlantic
Monthly*, July 1933; by Yvonne ffrench in the *London Mercury*, July 1933;
by Lord David Cecil in the *Spectator*, 4 August 1933; and by Eugene
Davidson in the *Yale Review*, Autumn 1933.

first edition

THE | LOVELY LADY | BY D. H. LAWRENCE | LONDON | MARTIN SECKER | NUMBER FIVE JOHN STREET ADELPHI

Chocolate-brown cloth boards, blind stamped on upper and lower covers: [*thick rule enclosed within thin rule forming border*]; stamped in gold on spine: [*thin rule*] | [*thick rule*] | THE LOVELY | LADY | · | D. H. | LAWRENCE | SECKER | [*thick rule*] | [*thin rule*] The leaves measure $7\frac{1}{4}'' \times 4\frac{7}{8}''$. All edges trimmed.

[1]–[248], as follows: [1]–[2] blank; [3] half-title; [4] blank; [5] title page as above; [6] LONDON: MARTIN SECKER LTD., 1932.; 7 table of contents; [8] blank; [9] fly-title: THE LOVELY LADY; [10] blank; 11–40 text; [41] fly-title: RAWDON'S ROOF; [42] blank; 43–60 text; [61] fly-title: THE ROCKING HORSE WINNER; [62] blank; 63–87 text; [88] blank; [89] fly-title: MOTHER AND DAUGHTER; [90] blank; 91–127 text; [128] blank; [129] fly-title: THE BLUE MOCCASINS; [130] blank; 131–157 text; [158] blank; [159] fly-title: THINGS; [160] blank; 161–177 text; [178] blank; [179] fly-title: THE OVERTONE; [180] blank; 181–202 text; [203] fly-title: THE MAN WHO LOVED ISLANDS; [204] blank; 205–246 text; [247] PRINTED IN GREAT BRITAIN BY THE DUNEDIN PRESS, LTD., EDINBURGH.; [248] blank.

Published January 1933 at 7s. 6d.; the first printing consisted of 5000 copies.

CONTENTS

The Lovely Lady (first appeared in *The Black Cap* (B23))—Rawdon's Roof (separately published as a Woburn Book (A40))—The Rocking-Horse Winner (*Harper's Bazaar*, July 1926 (C142.5))—Mother and Daughter (first appeared in the *New Criterion*, April 1929 (C184))—The Blue Moccasins (first appeared in *Eve*, 22 November 1928 (C178.5))—Things (first appeared in the *Bookman*, August 1928 (C173))—The Overtone—The Man Who Loved Islands (first appeared in the *Dial*, July 1927 (C157), see (A41b)).

NOTES: With the single exception of "The Overtone" all the stories in this posthumous collection were published previously. Catherine Carswell places "The Overtone" shortly after the Lawrences returned to England in 1923; according to *The Savage Pilgrimage* (B37) the story reflects Lawrence's displeasure at Frieda's friendship with John Middleton Murry; Frieda had come to England ahead of Lawrence and professed admiration for Murry and the *Adelphi* which he was then just beginning.

The first American edition of the collection was published by Viking in February 1933; Secker reprinted 1000 copies of the first edition in the year of its publication and published a Pocket Edition in February 1934. *The Lovely Lady* is No. 97 of the Albatross Library.

REVIEWS: *The Lovely Lady* was reviewed in *The Times Literary Supplement*, 19 January 1933; by Mercury Patten [David Garnett] in the *New Statesman and Nation*, 21 January 1933; by L. A. G. Strong in the *Spectator*, 27 January 1933; by L. P. Herring in the *New York Herald Tribune Books*, 12 February 1933; by Percy Hutchison in the *New York Times Book Review*, 12 February 1933; in the *New Outlook*, February 1933; by Ben Ray Redman in the *Saturday Review of Literature*, 11 March 1933; in "Lawrence and the Short Story" by Ferner Nuhn in the *Nation* (New York), 24 March 1933; by V. S. Pritchett in the *Fortnightly Review*, March 1933; by Dorothea Brande in the *Bookman* (New York), March 1933; by Geoffrey West in the *Criterion*, April 1933; in the *Forum*, April 1933; by Virginia Barney in the *North American Review*, May 1933; and by Isidor Schneider in the *New Republic*, 7 June 1933.

NOTES (2): The Secker *Lovely Lady* was issued in a cream paper dust-jacket printed in red. The American edition published by Viking in February did not contain "The Man Who Loved Islands" which had already been published in the American edition of *The Woman Who Rode Away* (A41b).

REVIEWS (2): Additional reviews of *The Lovely Lady* appeared in the *Adelphi* by John Middleton Murry, June 1933; *Observer*, 22 January by Gerald Gould; *Bookman* (London), February by Arthur Ball; *Chicago Daily Tribune*, 18 February by Fannie Butcher; *Daily Mail*, 2 February by Compton Mackenzie; *Manchester Guardian*, 3 February by T. M.

A64   WE NEED ONE ANOTHER   1933

first separate edition

WE NEED ONE ANOTHER | [*ornamental rule*] | by D. H. LAWRENCE | [*ornamental rule*] | WITH AN INTRODUCTORY NOTE BY HENRY HART | ILLUSTRATED WITH DRAWINGS BY JOHN P. HEINS | EQUINOX | NEW YORK · NINETEEN HUNDRED THIRTY-THREE

Red cloth boards, stamped in silver on upper cover: WE | NEED | ONE ANOTHER | [*short ornamental rule*]; stamped in silver on the spine, reading from top to bottom: [*ornamental rule*] | WE NEED ONE ANOTHER D. H. LAWRENCE | [*ornamental rule*] The leaves measure $7\frac{3}{4}''$ × $4\frac{3}{4}''$. All edges trimmed.

[1]–[72] with frontispiece and three illustrations facing pages 26, 42 and 50 which are counted in the pagination but are not integral with the signatures, as follows: [1] blank; [2] frontispiece; [3] half-title; [4] blank; [5] title page as above; [6] COPYRIGHT 1930 BY FRIEDA LAWRENCE; 1933 BY | EQUINOX COOPERATIVE PRESS · INC · NEW YORK | PRINTED BY L. F. WHITE CO · NEW YORK · U.S.A.; [7] [*publisher's device*]; [8] blank; 9–13 introduction by Henry Hart; [14] blank; 15–68 text; [69]–[72] blank.

Published 6 April 1933 at $2.00; number of copies unknown.

NOTES: The contents of this book consist of two essays, "We Need One Another" and "The Real Thing" published respectively in *Scribner's*, May 1930 (C198), and in *Scribner's*, June 1930 (C201). Both essays are collected in *Phoenix* (A76) under the original titles.

A65   PLAYS   1933

first collected edition

THE PLAYS OF | D. H. LAWRENCE | LONDON | MARTIN SECKER | 1933

Green cloth boards, white paper label on spine printed in black: THE PLAYS | OF | D. H. | LAWRENCE | [*short rule*] | SECKER | [*enclosed within ornamental rule border in green*] The leaves measure $7\frac{3}{8}''$ × $5''$. Top edges trimmed and stained green; fore and bottom edges rough trimmed.

[i]–[iv] + [1]–[316], as follows: [i]–[ii] blank; [iii] half-title; [iv] blank; [1] title page as above; [2] ALL RIGHTS RESERVED | APPLICATIONS REGARDING PERFORMING RIGHTS SHOULD BE | ADDRESSED TO THE AUTHOR'S EXECUTORS, CARE OF THE PUBLISHERS | LONDON: MARTIN SECKER LTD. | NUMBER FIVE JOHN STREET ADELPHI; [3] table of contents; [4] blank; [5] fly-title: THE WIDOWING OF MRS. HOLROYD | (1914); [6] list of persons in the play; 7–79 text; [80] blank; [81] fly-title: TOUCH AND GO | (1919); [82] list of characters; 83–90 preface; 91–182 text; [183] fly-title: DAVID | (1926); [184] list of characters; 185–312 text, at the bottom of page 312: *The Mayflower Press, Plymouth.* William Brendon & Son, Ltd.; [313]–[316] list of Lawrence's books published by Martin Secker.

Published July 1933 at 7s. 6d.; the first printing consisted of 2000 copies.

The Widowing of Mrs. Holroyd (separately published (A5))—Touch and Go (separately published (A14))—David (separately published (A34)).

NOTES: All of the plays in this volume had been previously published. For other Lawrence plays see *A Collier's Friday Night* (A69); "Altitude" in the *Laughing Horse*, Summer 1938 (C222); "The Married Man" in the *Virginia Quarterly Review*, Autumn 1940 (C226); "The Merry-Go-Round" in the *Virginia Quarterly Review*, Winter 1941 (C227); and "The Fight for Barbara" in *Argosy*, December 1933 (C213).

Walter Greenwood completed a play called "My Son's My Son" from an unfinished Lawrence manuscript which was performed at the Playhouse in London in June 1936. The production was reviewed in the *Illustrated London News*, 6 June 1936 and by A. V. Cookman in the *London Mercury*, July 1936.

Heinemann published an edition of the *Plays of D. H. Lawrence* in February 1938.

NOTES (2): The *Plays* were issued in a cream dust-jacket printed in green. See (A105).

A66   THE SHIP OF DEATH   1933

first collected edition

THE SHIP OF DEATH AND OTHER POEMS | BY D. H. LAWRENCE WITH WOOD | ENGRAVINGS BY BLAIR HUGHES-STANTON | [*engraving*] | LONDON: MARTIN SECKER | NUMBER FIVE JOHN STREET | ADELPHI

Red-brown paper boards with a black cloth backstrip, red leather label on spine stamped in gold: THE | SHIP | OF | DEATH | [*five-pointed star*] | LAWRENCE The leaves measure 10″ × 6⅜″. Top edges trimmed and stained red; fore edges rough-trimmed; bottom edges untrimmed.

[i]–[x] + 1–[106], as follows: [i] half-title; [ii] blank; [iii] title page as above; [iv] NOTE | *The Contents of this Volume* | *are selected from the Author's* | "*Last Poems.*" | LONDON: MARTIN SECKER LTD. 1933; [v]–[viii] table of contents; [ix] list of engravings; [x] blank; 1–104 text; [105] blank; [106] Printed in Great Britain by | The Surrey Fine Art Press, | Cavendish Road, Redhill

Published November 1933 at 10s. 6d.; the first printing consisted of 1500 copies.

CONTENTS

Image-Making Love—The Ship of Death—Difficult Death—All Souls'
Day—The Houseless Dead—Beware the Unhappy Dead!—Song of
Death—The End, The Beginning—Sleep—Sleep and Waking—Fatigue
—Forget—Know-all—Tabernacle—Temples—Shadows—Change—
Phoenix—Gladness of Death—Two Ways of Living and Dying—
Humanity needs pruning—Self-Sacrifice—Shedding of Blood—The Old
Idea of Sacrifice—Self-Sacrifice—Flowers and Men—Lord's Prayer—
Mana of the Sea—Salt—The Four—The Boundary Stone—Spilling the
Salt—Walk Warily—Kissing and Horrid Strife—When Satan Fell—
Doors—Evil is Homeless—What Then is Evil?—The Evil World-Soul—
The Wandering Cosmos—Death is not Evil, Evil is Mechanical—The
Triumph of the Machine—We Die Together—What is a Man To
Do?—City-Life—Give Us the Thebaïd—Stoic—In the Cities—Terra
Incognita—The Gulf—The Cross—God is Born—The Man of Tyre—
The Greeks are Coming—The Argonauts—Middle of the World—For
the Heroes are dipped in Scarlet—They Say the Sea is Loveless—Whales
Weep Not!—Demiurge—The Work of Creation—Red Geranium and
Godly Mignonette—Bodiless God—The Body of God—The Rainbow—
Maximus—Invocation to the Moon—Old Archangels—What are the
Gods?—Name the Gods!—There are no Gods—All Sorts of Gods—For
a Moment—The White Horse—The Breath of Life—Silence—The
Hands of God—Pax—Abysmal Immortality—Only Man—Return of
Returns—Fatality—Mystic—Anaxagoras—Butterfly—Andraitx-
Pomegranate Flowers—Trees in the Garden—Bavarian Gentians—
Prayer.

NOTES: The contents of this volume were reprinted from *Last Poems*
(A62); the book with the same title published by Faber and Faber in
May 1941 contains a different selection.

NOTES (2): In 1967 an English bookseller's catalogue offered a set of the
13 wood engravings by Blair Hughes-Stanton limited to 12 copies on
vellum, signed and numbered by the artist. The book itself was issued
in a cream dust-jacket printed in red.

A67   TALES   1934

first collected edition

THE TALES | OF | D. H. LAWRENCE | LONDON |
MARTIN SECKER | 1934

Chocolate-brown cloth boards, stamped in gold on upper cover: THE TALES | OF | D. H. LAWRENCE; stamped in gold on spine: THE TALES | OF | D. H. LAWRENCE | SECKER The leaves measure $8\frac{1}{2}'' \times 5\frac{7}{16}''$. Top edges trimmed and stained brown; fore and bottom edges trimmed.

[1]–[1140], as follows: [1] half-title; [2] D. H. Lawrence | 1885–1930; [3] title page as above; [4] LONDON: MARTIN SECKER (LTD.) | NUMBER FIVE JOHN STREET ADELPHI; [5] NOTE | This volume contains the whole of | Lawrence's shorter fiction from | *The Prussian Officer*, published in 1914, | to *The Man Who Died*, posthumously | published in 1931. The stories are | printed in chronological sequence.; [6] blank; 7–8 table of contents; 9–1138 text; [1139] Printed in Great Britain at | *The Mayflower Press, Plymouth.* | William Brendon & Son, Ltd.; [1140] blank.

Published April 1934 at 8s. 6d.; the first printing consisted of 10,000 copies.

CONTENTS

The Prussian Officer (from *The Prussian Officer* (A6))—The Thorn in the Flesh (A6)—Daughters of the Vicar (A6)—A Fragment of Stained Glass (A6)—The Shades of Spring (A6)—Second Best (A6)—The Shadow in the Rose Garden (A6)—Goose Fair (A6)—The White Stocking (A6)—A Sick Collier (A6)—The Christening (A6)—Odour of Chrysanthemums (A6)—England, My England (from *England, My England* (A23))—Tickets Please (A23)—The Blind Man (A23)—Monkey Nuts (A23)—Wintry Peacock (A23)—You Touched Me (A23)—Samson and Deliah (A23)—The Primrose Path (A23)—The Horse Dealer's Daughter (A23)—Fanny and Annie (A23)—The Ladybird (from *The Ladybird* (A24))—The Fox (A24)—The Captain's Doll (A24)—St. Mawr (from *St. Mawr and the Princess* (A31))—The Princess (A31)—Two Blue Birds (from *The Woman Who Rode Away* (A41))—Sun (A41)—The Woman Who Rode Away (A41)—Smile (A41)—The Border Line (A41)—Jimmy and the Desperate Woman (A41)—The Last Laugh (A41)—In Love (A41)—Glad Ghosts (A41)—None of That (A41)—The Man Who Loved Islands (A41)—The Lovely Lady (from *The Lovely Lady* (A63))—Rawdon's Roof (A63)—The Rocking-Horse Winner (A63)—Mother and Daughter (A63)—The Blue Moccasins (A63)—Things (A63)—The Virgin and the Gipsy (separately published (A54))—The Man Who Died (separately published (A50c)).

NOTES: Secker reprinted *The Tales of D. H. Lawrence* in 1934 and again in 1948; Heinemann issued a Cheap Edition in February 1949.

REVIEWS: The collected *Tales of D. H. Lawrence* was reviewed in the *Observer*, 1 April 1934; by Helen Moran in the *London Mercury*, May 1934; and in *The Times Literary Supplement* 29 March.

NOTES (2): *The Tales of D. H. Lawrence* was issued in a cream paper dust-jacket printed in red.

A68 SELECTED POEMS 1934

first collected edition

D. H. LAWRENCE | [*ornamental rule*] | SELECTED POEMS | [*printer's ornament*] | London | MARTIN SECKER | 1934

Red cloth boards, stamped in gold on upper cover: SELECTED POEMS OF D. H. LAWRENCE; stamped in gold on spine: SELECTED | POEMS | [*five-pointed star*] | LAWRENCE | SECKER The leaves measure $7\frac{1}{2}'' \times 4\frac{1}{2}''$. Top edges trimmed and stained red; fore edges trimmed; bottom edges untrimmed.

[1]–[148], as follows: [1] half-title; [2] This selection has been made by | RICHARD ALDINGTON; [3] title page as above; [4] LONDON MARTIN SECKER LTD | NUMBER FIVE JOHN STREET ADELPHI | Printed in Great Britain by SHERRATT & HUGHES, at the | St Ann's Press, Manchester; 5–7 table of contents; [8] blank; 9–[148] text.

Published May 1934 at 5s.; the first printing consisted of 2000 copies.

CONTENTS

Discord in Childhood (from *Collected Poems* (A43))—Renascence (A43)—Love on the Farm (A43)—The Collier's Wife (A43)—The Best of School (A43)—A Man who Died (A43)—Violets (A43)—End of Another Home Holiday (A43)—Transformations (A43)—Last Lesson of the Afternoon (A43)—Lilies in the Fire (A43)—Scent of Irises (A43)—Discipline (A43)—Mystery (A43)—The End (A43)—Reminder (A43)—Last Words to Miriam (A43)—Malade (A43)—Release (A43)—Ballad of Another Ophelia (A43)—Turned Down (A43)—Snap-Dragon (A43)—The Hands of the Betrothed (A43)—The Shadow of Death (A43)—In Trouble and Shame (A43)—The Drained Cup (A43)—Late at Night (A43)—The North Country (A43)—Obsequial Ode (A43)—Moonrise (A43)—Don Juan (A43)—Ballad of a Wilful Woman (A43)—On the Balcony (A43)—A Young Wife (A43)—Green (A43)—River Roses (A43)—Gloire de Dijon (A43)—A Youth Mowing (A43)—Fireflies in the Corn (A43)—Sinners (A43)—Everlasting Flowers (A43)—Giorno dei Morti (A43)—Lady Wife (A43)—Birth Night (A43)—Spring Morning (A43)—Wedlock (A43)—Song of a Man Who Has Come Through (A43)—New Heaven and Earth (A43)—Manifesto (A43)—Pomegranate (A43)—Grapes (A43)—Peace (A43)—Cypresses (A43)—Sicilian Cyclamens (A43)—Bat (A43)—Snake (A43)—Bibbles (A43)—Middle of the World (from *Last Poems* (A62))—Red Geranium and Godly Mignonette (A62)—The Man of Tyre (A62)—Invocation to the Moon (A62)—Bavarian Gentians (A62)—Pax (A62)—Lord's Prayer (A62)—The Ship of Death (A62)—Difficult Death (A62)—All Souls' Day (A62)—The Houseless Dead (A62)—Beware the Unhappy Dead! (A62)—The End, the Beginning (A62)—Fatigue (A62)—Shadows (A62)—Phoenix (A62) —So Let Me Live (A62)—Gladness of Death (A62)—Prayer (A62).

A69 A COLLIER'S FRIDAY NIGHT 1934

first edition

A COLLIER'S | FRIDAY NIGHT | By D. H. LAWRENCE | WITH AN INTRODUCTION | By EDWARD GARNETT | LONDON | MARTIN SECKER | 1934

Green cloth boards, cream paper label on spine printed in black reading downwards: A COLLIER'S | FRIDAY NIGHT [*enclosed within decorative rule border in green*] The leaves measure $7\frac{3}{8}'' \times 4\frac{7}{8}''$. Top edges trimmed and stained green; fore edges trimmed; bottom edges rough-trimmed.

[i]–[viii] + [1]–[88], as follows: [i] half-title; [ii] list of plays by D. H. Lawrence; [iii] title page as above; [iv] All rights in this play are reserved by the Proprietor, whose | agents are Messrs. Curtis Brown, Ltd., of 6 Henrietta Street, | Covent Garden, London, W. C. 2. | Copyright 1934 by Frieda Lawrence. | LONDON: MARTIN SECKER LTD. | NUMBER FIVE JOHN STREET ADELPHI; v–vii introduction by Edward Garnett; [viii] blank; [1] list of characters; [2] blank; 3–87 text; [88] *The Mayflower Press, Plymouth.* | William Brendon & Son, Ltd.

Published June 1934 at 5*s.*; the first printing consisted of 1500 copies.

NOTES: The play is a very early one; a completed draft was in existence as early as November 1909, for Lawrence showed it to Jessie Chambers during her visit to London then.

REVIEWS: *A Collier's Friday Night* was reviewed by Sean O'Casey in the *New Statesman*, 28 July 1934, and by Osbert Burdett in the *London Mercury*, August 1934.

NOTES (2): *A Collier's Friday Night* was produced by Peter Gill for the English Stage Society at the Royal Court Theatre on 8 August 1965. The performance was reviewed in the *Daily Telegraph* for 9 August by Eric Shorter and in the *Times* by the *Times* drama critic on the same day. The Colchester Theatre Group produced the play at St. Martin's Centre in Colchester on the evenings of 27–30 January 1971. See (A105).

A Collier's Friday Night was issued in a cream paper dust-jacket printed in green.

A70 AN ORIGINAL POEM 1934

first separate edition

AN ORIGINAL | POEM | BY | D·H·LAWRENCE | WITH A NOTE | BY | CATHERINE CARSWELL | AT THE | CHISWICK POLYTECHNIC | SCHOOL OF ART | 1934

Yellow paper covers, printed in black on upper cover: AN ORIGINAL | POEM | BY | D. H. LAWRENCE The leaves measure $8\frac{7}{8}'' \times 5\frac{5}{8}''$. Top edges trimmed; fore and bottom edges untrimmed.

[1]–[8], as follows: [1]–[2] blank; [3] title page as above; [4] Printed under the direction of John Charles Tarr, Chief In- | structor, at the Chiswick School of Printing, a department of | the Chiswick Polytechnic School of Art, Bath Road, W. 4. | Composed in the Weiss types, and printed on a Wharfedale | Press. Machine Instructor: Herbert Howe. February, 1934.; [5] text, at bottom of page: 1912; [6] blank; [7]–[8] note by Catherine Carswell.

Published 15 July 1934, price unknown; the edition consisted of 150 copies.

NOTES: The poem printed here is "The Wind, the Rascal," which Catherine Carswell apparently thought unpublished when she found it in 1934; however, the poem appeared in *Poetry*, January 1914 (C29), although it was not collected in any of the Lawrence volumes of poetry. Collected in (A104).

In her note on pages 7 and 8 Catherine Carswell tells of finding the poem in a little autograph book left in her house by Enid Hilton, who lived for a year in the Carswell home. Enid Hilton was Enid Hopkin, a friend from the Eastwood days, and the supposition is that Lawrence wrote the little poem in the book, choosing from the multi-coloured pages a yellow surface for his inscription. Mrs Carswell gave the book to her son John and it was Ivy Elstob, of the Davis and Orioli Bookshop, who noticed Lawrence's holograph contribution.

NOTES (2): The Swan Galleries catalogue dated 27 February 1975 offered in lot 178 a copy of *An Original Poem* with a manuscript notation that it was one of 12 copies signed by Catherine Carswell. Apparently Lawrence used this short poem, "The Wind, the Rascal," for more than one album. Harriet Cohen's *A Bundle of Time* published in London in 1969 reproduces the poem in facsimile with a note that Lawrence wrote it in her autograph album.

A71 A MODERN LOVER 1934

first edition

A | MODERN LOVER | BY D. H. LAWRENCE | LONDON | MARTIN SECKER | NUMBER FIVE JOHN STREET ADELPHI

Chocolate-brown cloth boards, blind stamped on upper cover: [*thick rule within thin rule forming border*]; blind stamped on lower cover: [*thick rule within thin rule forming border*]; stamped in gold on spine: [*thin rule*] | [*thick rule*] | A MODERN | LOVER | · | D. H. | LAWRENCE | SECKER | [*thick rule*] | [*thin rule*] The leaves measure $7\frac{3}{16}'' \times 4\frac{7}{8}''$. All edges trimmed.

[1]–312, as follows: [1] half-title; [2] blank; [3] title page as above; [4] LONDON: MARTIN SECKER LTD., 1934; 5 a note on the early work in the volume; [6] blank; 7 table of contents; [8] blank; [9] fly-title: A MODERN LOVER; [10] blank; 11–44 text; [45] fly-title: THE OLD ADAM; [46] blank; 47–71 text; [72] blank; [73] fly-title: HER TURN; [74] blank; 75–83 text; [84] blank; [85] fly-title: STRIKE-PAY; [86] blank; 87–100 text; [101] fly-title: THE WITCH *A LA MODE*; [102] blank; 103–128 text; [129] fly-title: NEW EVE AND OLD ADAM; [130] blank; 131–166 text; [167] fly-title: MR NOON; [168] blank; 169–312 text, at bottom of page 312: [*short rule*] | PRINTED IN GREAT BRITAIN BY THE DUNEDIN PRESS, LTD., EDINBURGH.

Published October 1934 at 7s. 6d.; number of copies unknown.

CONTENTS

A Modern Lover (first appeared in *Life and Letters*, September–November 1933 (C211))—The Old Adam—Her Turn (first appeared in the *Saturday Westminster Gazette*, 6 September 1913 (C24), as "Strike-Pay I,

Her Turn")—Strike-Pay (first appeared in the *Saturday Westminster Gazette*, 13 September 1913 (C26), as "Strike-Pay II, Ephraim's Half Sovereign")—The Witch à la Mode (first appeared in *Lovat Dickson's Magazine*, June 1934 (C215))—New Eve and Old Adam—Mr. Noon.

NOTES: Most of the stories in this last original collection of Lawrence's fiction were early ones and were probably collected from diverse sources for publication here. Of the previously unpublished stories at least the "Witch à la Mode" and "Mr. Noon" had been submitted to publishers around 1921, but for some reason were never printed.

The first American edition of *A Modern Lover* was published by Viking in October 1934. Heinemann published a Pocket Edition and a Cheap Edition in June 1936. *A Modern Lover* is No. 279 in the Albatross Library and was issued as the *Avon Modern Short Story Monthly* No. 49 in New York in 1948.

REVIEWS: *A Modern Lover* was reviewed in the *New York Herald Tribune Books*, 21 October 1934; by Ferner Nuhn in the *Nation*, 24 October 1934; in *The Times Literary Supplement*, 25 October 1934; by P. M. Jacks in the *New York Times Book Review*, 4 November 1934; by Currie Cabot in the *Saturday Review of Literature*, 10 November 1934; by H. J. Davis in the *Canadian Forum*, January 1935; and in "Lawrence's Last Book" by Dilys Powell in the *London Mercury*, February 1935.

NOTES (2): "Mr. Noon" has recently been discovered to be the first part of an unfinished novel. Lawrence put the manuscript aside when he went to Sardinia in January 1921 and never returned to it. Secker and Seltzer first planned to publish Part I separately, but both then decided to postpone publication until the novel was completed. The semi-autobiographical second part, twice as long as the first, will be published for the first time in the Cambridge edition to be edited by Lindeth Vasey.

A Modern Lover was issued in a cream paper dust-jacket printed in red.

A72 THE SPIRIT OF PLACE 1935

first collected edition

THE | SPIRIT OF PLACE | AN ANTHOLOGY COMPILED FROM | THE PROSE OF | D. H. LAWRENCE | EDITED AND WITH AN INTRODUCTION BY | RICHARD ALD-INGTON | [*publisher's device*] | [*short rule*] | WILLIAM HEINE-MANN LTD | LONDON : : TORONTO

Chocolate-brown cloth boards, blind stamped on upper cover: [*thin rule enclosed within thick rule forming border*]; blind stamped on lower cover: [*publisher's device*]; stamped in gold on spine: [*thin rule*] | [*thick rule*] | THE SPIRIT | OF | PLACE | · | D. H. | LAWRENCE | HEINEMANN | [*thick rule*] | [*thin rule*] The leaves measure $7\frac{1}{2}'' \times 5''$. All edges trimmed.

[i]–[ii] + [i]–x + [1]–[340], as follows: [i]–[ii] blank; [i] half-title; [ii] blank; [iii] title page as above; [iv] FIRST PUBLISHED 1935 | PRINTED IN GREAT BRITAIN | AT THE WINDMILL PRESS, KINGSWOOD, SURREY; v–x editor's note by Richard Aldington; [1] fly-title: *England*; [2] blank; 3–147 text; [148] blank; [149] fly-title: INTERLUDE: | *Leaving England*; [150] blank; 151–156 text; [157] fly-title: *Italy*; [158] blank; 159–187 text; [188] blank; [189] fly-title: *Germany and Austria*; [190] blank; 191–209 text; [210] blank; [211] fly-title: INTERLUDE: | *Leaving Europe*; [212] blank; 213–216 text; [217] fly-title: *Australia*; [218] blank; 219–265 text; [266] blank; [267] fly-title: *New Mexico and Mexico*; [268] blank; 269–326 text; [327] fly-title: *Index of First Lines*; [328] blank; 329–335 index; [336]–[340] blank.

Published 28 November 1935 at 7*s*. 6*d*.; the first printing consisted of 3000 copies.

CONTENTS

Note: For *The Spirit of Place* Mr Aldington chose excerpts from the following works of D. H. Lawrence: *The White Peacock* (A1)—*The Trespasser* (A2)—*Sons and Lovers* (A4)—The Prussian Officer (A6)—*The Rainbow* (A7)—*Women in Love* (A15)—*Lady Chatterley's Lover* (A42)—*Aaron's Rod* (A21)— Introduction to *Memoirs of the Foreign Legion* (B14)—The Ladybird (A24)—The Woman Who Rode Away (A41)—*Fantasia of the Unconscious* (A22)—Letter from *Not I, But the Wind* (B40)—*Kangaroo* (A26)—St. Mawr (A31)—*The Plumed Serpent* (A33)—*Apocalypse* (A57).

NOTES: As stated in the title, this book is an anthology compiled from the prose of D. H. Lawrence. Richard Aldington, who made the selections and edited the book, arranged the excerpts in chronological sequence to provide a description of the places where Lawrence lived and travelled. Heinemann reprinted the book in January 1938.

REVIEWS: *The Spirit of Place* was reviewed in *The Times Literary Supplement*, 14 December 1935, and a discussion of the book and the review appeared in *The Times Literary Supplement*, 28 December 1935; K. Arns reviewed the book in *Englische Studien* 1936.

NOTES (2): *Spirit of Place* was issued in a white dust-jacket printed in blue and red with the Lawrence phoenix on the upper cover.

A73 THE UNIVERSE AND ME 1935

first separate edition

THE | UNIVERSE | AND ME | D. H. LAWRENCE | [*single rule with ornamental device at centre point*] | HARVEY TAYLOR | 425 MADISON AVENUE–:–NEW YORK | 1935

Stiff black paper covers, white paper label on upper cover, printed in black: *The Universe and Me* | [*triple rule*] | D. H. LAWRENCE The leaves measure $8\frac{3}{4}'' \times 5\frac{7}{8}''$. All edges trimmed.

[1]–[8], as follows: [1] dedicated to George Fite-Waters; [2] blank; [3] title page as above; [4] COPYRIGHT 1935 BY HARVEY TAYLOR | PRINTED IN THE UNITED STATES; [5] text; [6] a note concerning the discovery of the text; at the end of the note: One hundred and fifty copies | have been privately printed by the Powgen Press. | no. 131. [*autograph number in black ink*] | Harvey Taylor. [*autograph signature in black ink*]; [7]–[8] blank.

Published 1935, price unknown; the edition consisted of 150 copies.

NOTES: This small booklet reproduces the eighth paragraph of the essay "Morality and the Novel" which first appeared in *The Calendar of Modern Letters*, December 1925 (C135), and was collected in *Phoenix* (A76). A note on page [6] tells of the discovery of the paragraph inscribed by Lawrence on the flyleaf of James Mason's *Fra Angelico* by Harry F. Marks, who disposed of the book to Harry K. Wells, in whose collection the book was at one time.

A74 FOREWORD TO WOMEN IN LOVE 1936

first edition

D. H. LAWRENCE'S | UNPUBLISHED FOREWORD TO | "WOMEN IN LOVE" | 1919 | [*drawing in black*] | 1936 | SAN FRANCISCO | GELBER, LILIENTHAL, INC. | [*lettering on title page is printed in orange*]

Orange paper boards, cream paper label on upper cover printed in orange: D. H. LAWRENCE'S | FOREWORD | TO "WOMEN IN LOVE" The leaves measure $9\frac{3}{4}'' \times 7\frac{1}{2}''$. Top edges trimmed; fore and bottom edges untrimmed.

[1]–[16], as follows: [1]–[2] blank; 3 title page as above; [4] blank; [5] GRATEFUL ACKNOWLEDGEMENT | IS MADE TO | FRIEDA LAWRENCE | FOR PERMISSION TO PUBLISH | THIS FOREWORD; [6] blank; [7]–[8] introduction by Nathan Van Patten; [9]–[12] text printed in orange; [13] ONE HUNDRED COPIES | PRINTED BY THE GRABHORN PRESS | SAN FRANCISCO | MARCH 1936; [14]–[16] blank.

Published March 1936 at $5.00; the edition consisted of 103 copies.

VARIANTS: (1) copy described above.
(2) as (1) except printed on pink paper; three copies only.

NOTES: This particular essay was apparently designed by Lawrence as a preface to the American edition of *Women in Love* (A15), but it was not originally published with the novel. Nathan Van Patten was the proprietor of the Yerba Buena Press, the imprint under which *A Letter from Cornwall* (A59) and *D. H. Lawrence's Letter to the Laughing Horse* (A77) appeared. The *Foreword* was published as an introduction to the Random House Modern Library edition of *Women in Love*.

NOTES (2): Apparently some of the copies of the *Foreword to Women in Love* were issued in an orange cloth folder and a slip case. The slip case had a cream paper label on spine printed in red: D. H. Lawrence Foreword to Women in Love. This was first published in 1920 in an advertising leaflet; see (A14.5).

A75   PORNOGRAPHY AND SO ON   1936
first collected edition

PORNOGRAPHY | AND SO ON | by | D. H. LAWRENCE | LONDON | FABER AND FABER LIMITED | 24 Russell Square

Blue-green cloth boards, stamped in gold on spine: [*ornamental design*] | PORNO- | GRAPHY | & SO ON | [*printer's ornament*] | D. H. | LAWRENCE | FABER | AND FABER | [*ornamental design*] The leaves measure $6\frac{15}{16}'' \times 4\frac{3}{8}''$. All edges trimmed.

[1]–176 as follows: [1]–[2] blank; [3] half-title; [4] blank; [5] title page as above; [6] FIRST PUBLISHED IN THIS EDITION | SEPTEMBER MCMXXXVI | BY FABER AND FABER LIMITED | 24 RUSSELL SQUARE LONDON W. C. I | PRINTED IN GREAT BRITAIN | BY LATIMER TREND AND CO PLYMOUTH | ALL RIGHTS RESERVED; 7–8 table of contents; [9] fly-title: PORNOGRAPHY AND | OBSCENITY; [10] blank; 11–53 text; [54] blank; [55] fly-title: INTRO-DUCTION TO | PAINTING; [56] blank; 57–136 text; [137] fly-title: NETTLES; [138] blank; 139–174 text; [175]–[176] blank.

Published 24 September 1936 at 3*s*. 6*d*.; the first printing consisted of 4000 copies.

CONTENTS

Pornography and Obscenity (separately published (A49))—Introduction to Painting (from *The Paintings of D. H. Lawrence* (A46))—Nettles (separately published (A52)).

NOTES: This collection was published as a Lawrentian statement on censorship and the subject of pornography; *Nettles* consisted of a number of little barbed poems written after the censorship trouble with *Pansies* (A47) and the *Paintings* (A46).

REVIEWS: *Pornography and So On* was reviewed in the *London Mercury*, October 1936.

NOTES (2): Some copies of *Pornography and So On* had the lettering on the spine stamped in silver; thus two variants are identified:

VARIANTS: (1) copy described above.
(2) as (1) except for lettering on spine in silver.

The book was issued in a purple dust-jacket printed in red and green.

A76 PHOENIX: POSTHUMOUS PAPERS 1936

first edition

Phoenix | The Posthumous Papers of | D. H. Lawrence | Edited and with an Introduction by | Edward D. McDonald | The Viking Press · New York | 1936 | [*enclosed within four rules, alternating thin, thick, thin, thick*]

Black cloth boards, stamped in gold and red on the upper cover: [*Lawrence phoenix in red on gold circular background enclosed within circular gold rule*]; stamped in gold on spine: Phoenix | The Posthumous | Papers of | D. H. Lawrence | The Viking Press The leaves measure $9\frac{1}{4}'' \times 6''$. Top edges stained red; all edges trimmed.

[i]–[xxviii] + [1]–852, as follows: [i] [*Lawrence phoenix*]; [ii] list of Lawrence's books published by Viking; [iii] title page as above; [iv] PUBLISHED IN OCTOBER 1936 | [*publisher's device*] | COPYRIGHT 1936 BY FRIEDA LAWRENCE | PRINTED IN U.S.A. BY VAIL-BALLOU PRESS | DISTRIBUTED IN CANADA BY THE MACMILLAN COMPANY | OF CANADA, LTD.; v–viii table of contents; ix–xxvii introduction by Edward D. McDonald;

[xxviii] blank; [1] fly-title: Nature and Poetical Pieces | [*list of contents*]; [2] blank; 3–68 text; [69] fly-title: Peoples, Countries, Races | [*list of contents*]; [70] blank; 71–147 text; [148] blank; [149] fly-title: Love, Sex, Men, and Women | [*list of contents*]; [150] blank; 151–211 text; [212] blank; [213] fly-title: Literature and Art | [*list of contents*]; [214] blank; 215–584 text; [585] fly-title: Education | [*list of contents*]; [586] blank; 587–665 text; [666] blank; [667] fly-title: Ethics, Psychology, Philosophy | [*list of contents*]; [668] blank; 669–771 text; [772] blank; [773] fly-title: Personalia and Fragments | [*list of contents*]; [774] blank; 775–836 text; [837] fly-title: Appendix; [838] blank; 839–841 appendix; [842] blank; [843] fly-title: Index; [844] blank; 845–852 index.

Published 19 October 1936 at $3.75; the first printing consisted of 3000 copies.

CONTENTS

I. Nature and Poetical Pieces

Whistling of Birds (first appeared in the *Athenaeum*, 11 April 1919 (C63))—Adolf (first appeared in the *Dial*, September 1920 (C73); first collected in *The New Keepsake for 1921* (B8))—Rex (first appeared in the *Dial*, February 1921 (C77); first collected in *Stories from the Dial* (B13))—Pan in America (first appeared in the *Southwest Review*, January 1926 (C136); also in *Phoenix* for Spring 1938)—Man is a Hunter—Mercury (first appeared in the *Atlantic Monthly*, February 1927 (C152))—The Nightingale (first appeared in the *Forum*, September 1927 (C158))— Flowery Tuscany (first appeared in the *New Criterion*, October, November and December 1927 (C159), (C161) and (C164))—The Elephants of Dionysus—David—Notes for *Birds, Beasts and Flowers* (first appeared in the Cresset Press edition of *Birds, Beasts and Flowers* (A27)).

II. Peoples, Countries, Races

German Impressions: I. French Sons of Germany (first appeared in the *Saturday Westminster Gazette*, 3 August 1912 (C16))—II. Hail in the Rhineland (first appeared in the *Saturday Westminster Gazette*, 10 August 1912 (C17))—Christs in the Tirol (first appeared in the *Saturday Westminster Gazette*, 22 March 1913 (C20))—America, Listen to Your Own (from the *New Republic*, 15 December 1920 (C74); first collected in *The New Republic Anthology* (B45))—Indians and an Englishman (first appeared in the *Dial*, February 1923 (C102))—Taos (first appeared in the *Dial*, March 1923 (C103))—Au Revoir, U.S.A. (first appeared in the *Laughing Horse*, December 1923 (C114))—A Letter from Germany (first appeared in the *New Statesman*, 13 October 1934 (C216))—See Mexico After, by Luis Q—Europe v. America (first appeared in the *Laughing Horse*, April 1926 (C139))—Paris Letter (first appeared in the *Laughing Horse*, April 1926 (C139))—Fireworks in Florence (first appeared in the *Nation and Athenaeum*, 16 April 1927 (C155), as "Fireworks")—[Germans and Latins] (this appeared in *La Cultura*, November 1934 (C217), as "Tedeschi e Inglese")—Nottingham and the Mining Countryside (first appeared in the *Adelphi*, June–August 1930 (C202))—New Mexico (first appeared in the *Survey Graphic*, 1 May 1931 (C206)).

III. Love, Sex, Men and Women

Love (first appeared in the *English Review*, January 1918 (C52))—All There—Making Love to Music—Women are so Cocksure—Pornography and Obscenity (separately published (A49))—We Need One Another (first appeared in *Scribner's*, May 1930 (C198); see (A64))—The Real Thing (first appeared in *Scribner's*, June 1930 (C201); see (A64))—Nobody Loves Me (first appeared in *Life and Letters*, July 1930 (C203)).

IV. Literature and Art

Prefaces and Introductions to Books: All Things Are Possible [by Leo Shestov] (first appeared in *All Things are Possible* (A13))—The American Edition of New Poems [by D. H. Lawrence] (first appeared in *Playboy*, Nos. 4 and 5, 1919 (C69) and (C70), as "Poetry of the Present")—[Mastro-don Gesualdo by Giovanni Verga] (A28b)—A Bibliography of D. H. Lawrence [by Edward D. McDonald (first appeared in *A Bibliography of the Writings of D. H. Lawrence* (B16))—Max Havelaar [by E. D. Dekker (Multatuli, pseud.)] (first appeared in *Max Havelaar* (B21))—Cavalleria Rusticana [by Giovanni Verga] (first appeared in *Cavalleria Rusticana* (A39))—The Collected Poems of D. H. Lawrence (a longer perhaps earlier version of the published introduction to the *Collected Poems* (A43))—Chariot of the Sun [by Harry Crosby] (first appeared in *Chariot of the Sun* (B33))—The Mother [by Grazia Deledda] (first appeared in *The Mother* (B25))—Bottom Dogs [by Edward Dahlberg] (first appeared in *Bottom Dogs* (B26))—The Story of Dr. Manente [by A. F. Grazzini] (first appeared in *The Story of Dr. Manente* (A45))—The Privately Printed Edition of Pansies (first appeared in *Pansies* (A47))—The Grand Inquisitor [by F. M. Dostoevsky] (first appeared in *The Grand Inquisitor* (B28))—The Dragon of the Apocalypse [by Frederick Carter] (first appeared in the *London Mercury*, July 1930 (C204), as "Introduction" for Carter's "Revelation of St. John the Divine").

Reviews of Books: Georgian Poetry: 1911–1912 (first appeared in *Rhythm*, March 1913 (C19))—German Books: Thomas Mann (first appeared in the *Blue Review*, July 1913 (C21))—Americans [by Stuart P. Sherman] (first appeared in the *Dial*, May 1923 (C107))—A Second Contemporary Verse Anthology (first appeared in the *New York Evening Post Literary Review*, 29 September 1923 (C110))—Hadrian the Seventh [by Baron Corvo] (first appeared in the *Adelphi*, December 1925 (C134))—The Origins of Prohibition [by J. A. Krout] (first appeared in the *New York Herald Tribune Books*, 31 January 1926 (C137))—In the American Grain [by William Carlos Williams] (first appeared in the *Nation* (New York), 14 April 1926 (C141))—Heat [by Isa Glenn]—Gifts of Fortune [by H. M. Tomlinson] (first appeared in *T. P.'s and Cassell's Weekly*, 1 January 1927 (C150))—The World of William Clissold [by H. G. Wells] (first appeared in the *Calendar of Modern Letters*, October 1926 (C146))—Saïd the Fisherman [by Marmaduke Pickthall] (*New York Herald Tribune*, 27 Dec 1925 (C133.5))—Pedro de Valdivia [by R. B. Cunninghame Graham] (first appeared in the *Calendar of Modern Letters*, January 1927 (C149))—Nigger Heaven [by Carl Van Vechten]; Flight [by Walter White]; Manhattan Transfer [by John Dos Passos]; In Our Time [by Ernest Hemingway] (first appeared in the *Calendar of Modern Letters*, April 1927 (C153))—Solitaria [by V. V. Rozanov] and The Peep Show [by Walter Wilkinson] (first appeared in the *Calender of Modern Letters*, July 1927 (C156))—The Social Basis of Consciousness [by Trigant Burrow] (first appeared in the *Bookman* (New York), November 1927 (C160)); The Station: Athos, Treasures and Men [by Robert Byron]; England and the Octopus [by Clough Williams-Ellis]; Comfortless Memory [by Maurice Baring]; Ashenden [by Somerset Maugham] (first appeared in *Vogue* (London), 20 July 1928 (C172))—Fallen Leaves [by V. V. Rozanov] (first appeared in *Everyman*, 23 January 1930 (C196))—Art Nonsense and Other Essays [by Eric Gill] (first appeared in the *Book Collector's Quarterly*, October–December 1933 (C212))—Study of Thomas Hardy (first appeared in the *Book Collector's Quarterly*, January–March 1932 (C207), as "Six Novels of Thomas Hardy and the Real Tragedy")—Surgery for the Novel–or a Bomb (first appeared in the *Literary Digest International Book Review*, April 1923 (C105))—Art and Morality (first appeared in the *Calendar of Modern Letters*, November 1925 (C133))—Morality and the Novel (first appeared in the *Calendar of Modern Letters*, December 1925 (C135))—Why the Novel Matters—John Galsworthy (first appeared in *Scrutinies* (B24))—Introduction to These Paintings (first appeared in *The Paintings of D. H. Lawrence* (A46)).

V. Education
Education of the People.

VI. Ethics, Psychology, Philosophy
The Reality of Peace (first appeared in the *English Review*, May, June and July 1917 (C45), (C46) and (C48))—Life (first appeared in the *English Review*, February 1918 (C53))—Democracy (also in *Phoenix*, Summer 1938)—The Proper Study (first appeared in the *Adelphi*, December 1923 (C113))—On Being Religious (first appeared in the *Adelphi*, February 1924 (C116))—Books—Thinking About Oneself—Resurrection—Climbing Down Pisgah—The Duc de Lauzun—[The Good Man]—The Novel and the Feelings—[The Individual Consciousness v. The Social Consciousness]—Introduction to Pictures.

VII. Personalia and Fragments
The Miner at Home (first appeared in the *Nation* (London), 16 March 1912 (C10))—The Flying Fish—Accumulated Mail (first appeared in the *Borzoi* (B18))—The Late Mr. Maurice Magnus: A Letter (first appeared in the *New Statesman*, 20 February 1926 (C138))—The Undying Man—Noah's Flood—[Autobiographical Fragment].

NOTES: Edward McDonald, Lawrence's first bibliographer (B16) and (B31), included in *Phoenix* not only a number of previously unpublished manuscripts, but also many rather obscurely published items.

Among the previously unpublished items the essay "Man is a Hunter" may be roughly assigned to Italy in 1926 or 1927; the subject is the hunting of small birds by the Italians which Lawrence commented on adversely in letters during those years. The notebook containing "Elephants of Dionysus" was a gift from Harwood Brewster and contains a presentation inscription dated September 1929. "David" is an essay on the Michaelangelo statue set in Florence on a rainy day; two notes written in 1919 and 1926 mention a Florence filled with torrents of rain, and Tedlock in his manuscript study (B51) supports the 1926 composition date. "See Mexico After, by Luis Q" was apparently reworked from an essay by the young Mexican poet Luis Quintanilla. Dorothy Brett's *Lawrence and Brett* tells of the meeting between Lawrence and Quintanilla at a P.E.N. supper in Mexico City. "All There," "Making Love to Music" and "Women are So Cocksure" are associated with the newspaper articles written in 1927 and 1928.

A different version of the "Introduction" for *Mastro-don Gesualdo* was published in The Travellers' Library edition of the book (A28b), and the "Introduction" to *Collected Poems* is not the same as that published with the Secker *Collected Poems* (A43). Apparently the review of *Heat* was not published in a periodical, and thus appears in print here for the first time; it was probably written in 1926, the year Isa Glenn's book was published. Only "Chapter III" of the "Study of Thomas Hardy" was previously published; "Why the Novel Matters" appears in print here for the first time.

Lawrence wrote Katherine Mansfield from Middleton in Derbyshire in December 1918 that he had written three little essays on "Education of the People" which Freeman of the London *Times* had asked him to do for its *Educational Supplement*; Freeman returned the essays with the advice that they were matter for a book rather than for periodical publication. Although Lawrence told Lady Cynthia Asquith later that he had done "four essays," the text here apparently comes from a later version written as a single piece. In the diary transcribed by Tedlock (B51) Lawrence noted that he began "Education of the People" at the Palazzo Ferraro in Capri on 15 June 1920. The original essays have disappeared.

"Democracy" is remembered by Mrs Lawrence as having been written in Cornwall in 1917. Most of the essays under "Ethics, Psychology, Philosophy" remained unpublished until the appearance of *Phoenix*. Richard Aldington in *Life for Life's Sake* tells of suggesting to Lawrence at Scandicci *c.* 1927 the possibility of doing an introductory essay for the duc de Lauzun's memoirs. From Lawrence's opinion of eighteenth-century French aristocrats in general, Aldington apparently concluded that whatever he might say would be unsuitable, and so discouraged the project and wrote the essay himself.

"Individual Consciousness *v.* Social Consciousness" was apparently an abandoned beginning of the "Scrutiny" on Galsworthy (B24); the "Introduction to Pictures" is an early version of the introduction to the *Paintings* (A46).

Of the pieces in the last section the "Flying Fish" is a fragment of a story written on paper which bears the stamp of a bookseller in Oaxaca, Mexico. The Brewsters (B39) tell about Lawrence reading from an unfinished novel in Switzerland during the summer of 1928; he had begun the novel on the way back from Mexico when he was ill. It was called "The Flying Fish," and a portion of the manuscript was in Frieda's handwriting. When asked about the novel afterwards Lawrence replied that he had an intuition that the novel would never be finished. "Noah's Flood" is an unfinished play which Lawrence abandoned in favour of another biblical subject which resulted in *David* (A34). The "Autobiographical Fragment" was written in 1927 or 1928; the manuscript is on leaves from a notebook which was also the source of a few pages of the third version of *Lady Chatterley's Lover*.

The first English impression of *Phoenix* was published by Heinemann in November 1936; Heinemann also issued a Cheap Edition in April 1938 and another edition in January 1961.

REVIEWS: *Phoenix* was reviewed by Theodore Spencer in "Is Lawrence Neglected?" in the *Saturday Review of Literature*, 31 October 1936; in "A Lawrence Budget" by Harry T. Moore in the *Nation* (New York), 24 October 1936; in "D. H. Lawrence as Messiah" by Granville Hicks in the *New Republic*, 28 October 1936; by Lorine Pruette in the *New York Tribune Books*, 1 November 1936; by S. C. Chew in the *Christian Science Monitor*, 4 November 1936; by Harry K. Wells in the *New Republic*, 18 November 1936; by David Garnett in the *New Statesman and Nation*, 21 November 1936; in *The Times Literary Supplement*, 21 November 1936; by Catherine Carswell in the *Spectator*, 27 November 1936; by P. M. Jacks in the *New York Times Book Review*, 29 November 1936; by C. H. Warren in the *Observer*, 13 December 1936; in "D. H. Lawrence, His Posthumous Papers" by Edward Garnett in the *London Mercury*, December 1936; by Mina Curtiss in the *Living Age*, December 1936; by E. Delavenay in *Etudes Anglaises*, March 1937; by Kerker Quinn in the *Yale Review*, Summer 1937; by A. D. Hawkins in the *Criterion*, July 1937; and by F. R. Leavis in *Scrutiny*, December 1937.

NOTES (2): *Phoenix* was issued in a cream dust-jacket printed in red and black with the Lawrence phoenix on the upper cover.

A77 LETTER TO *THE LAUGHING HORSE* 1936

first separate edition

D. H. LAWRENCE'S | LETTER | *to* | "THE LAUGHING HORSE" | [*hand lettered ornamental 8 in red*] | PRIVATELY PRINTED | 1936

White paper boards with decorative paper backstrip, white paper label on upper cover printed in black: D. H. LAWRENCE'S | LETTER | *to* | "THE LAUGHING HORSE" The leaves measure 10″ × 7¼″. Top edges trimmed; fore and bottom edges untrimmed.

[1]–18, as follows: [1]–[2] blank; [3] half-title; [4]–[6] blank; [7] title page as above; [8] blank; 9–13 text; [14] blank; [15] Twelve copies

only printed | and the type destroyed. | This is No. | 8. [*autograph number in black ink*]; [16]–[18] blank.

Printed in 1936, not for sale; the edition consisted of 12 copies.

NOTES: The text of this letter to Spud Johnson first appeared in print in the *Laughing Horse*, No. 4, 1922; it was also published in the *Letters* (A61) and in Witter Bynner's *Journey With Genius* (B55). Mr Nathan Van Patten acknowledged the *Letter to the Laughing Horse* as a product of his Yerba Buena Press in the *Papers of the Bibliographical Society of America*, Vol. 43, Second Quarter, 1949; the Yerba Buena Press imprint appears on the *Letter from Cornwall* (A59). Witter Bynner (B55) gives an account of the letter and the furor which followed its publication in the *Laughing Horse* on the campus of the University of California.

A78   POEMS   1939

first collected edition

VOL. I

D. H. LAWRENCE | [*short rule*] | POEMS | [*short rule*] | *VOL. I* | [*publisher's device*] | [*short rule*] | WILLIAM HEINEMANN LTD | LONDON :: TORONTO

Red cloth boards, stamped in gold on spine: [*thin rule*] | [*thick rule*] |. *D. H.* | *Lawrence* | · | POEMS | I | *Heinemann* | [*thick rule*] | [*thin rule*]; blind stamped on lower cover: [*publisher's device*] The leaves measure $6\frac{13}{16}'' \times 4\frac{7}{16}''$. All edges trimmed.

[i]–[vi] + 1–[278], as follows: [i]–[ii] blank; [iii] half-title; [iv] a list of the Heinemann pocket editions of D. H. Lawrence; [v] title page as above; [vi] FIRST PUBLISHED 1939 | PRINTED IN GREAT BRITAIN AT THE WINDMILL PRESS | KINGSWOOD, SURREY; 1–3 a note by D. H. LAWRENCE; [4] blank; [5] fly-title: *PART ONE* | RHYMING POEMS; [6] blank; 7–179 text; [180] blank; [181] fly-title: *PART TWO* | UNRHYMING POEMS; [182] blank; [183] fly-title: *LOOK !* | *WE HAVE COME THROUGH !*; [184] argument; 185–277 text; [278] blank.

VOL. II

D. H. LAWRENCE | [*short rule*] | POEMS | [*short rule*] | *VOL. II* | [*publisher's device*] | [*short rule*] | WILLIAM HEINEMANN LTD | LONDON :: TORONTO

Red cloth boards, stamped in gold on spine: [*thin rule*] | [*thick rule*] |

D. H. | *Lawrence* | · | POEMS | II | *Heinemann* | [*thick rule*] | [*thin rule*]; blind stamped on lower cover: [*publisher's device*] The leaves measure $6\frac{13}{16}'' \times 4\frac{7}{16}''$. All edges trimmed.

[i]–[vi] + 281–[498], as follows: [i] half-title; [ii] a list of the Heinemann pocket editions of D. H. Lawrence; [iii] title page as above; [iv] FIRST PUBLISHED 1939 | PRINTED IN GREAT BRITAIN AT THE WINDMILL PRESS | KINGSWOOD, SURREY; [v] fly-title: BIRDS, BEASTS AND FLOWERS; [vi] blank; 281–433 text; [434] blank; [435] fly-title: LAST POEMS; [436] blank; 437–497 text; [498] blank.

Published 11 April 1939 at 3*s*. 6*d*. for each volume; the first printing consisted of 2000 copies.

CONTENTS

VOL. I

Volume One contains the "Rhyming Poems" from the first volume of *Collected Poems* (A43) and the "Look! We Have Come Through!" sequence from the "Unrhyming Poems" of the second volume of *Collected Poems* (A43).

VOL. II

Volume Two contains the "Birds, Beasts and Flowers" poems from the "Unrhyming Poems" of the second volume of *Collected Poems* (A43) and "Last Poems" section of *Last Poems* (A62) with the five poems in the "Appendix" of *Last Poems*.

A79   STORIES, ESSAYS, AND POEMS   1939

first collected edition

STORIES, ESSAYS, AND POEMS | [*decorative design*] | D. H. LAWRENCE | LONDON: J. M. DENT & SONS LTD

Orange cloth boards, blind stamped on upper cover: [*decorative design*]; stamped in gold on spine: STORIES | ESSAYS | AND | POEMS | [*short rule*] | LAWRENCE | EVERYMANS | LIBRARY The leaves measure $6\frac{3}{4}'' \times 4\frac{1}{4}''$. All edges trimmed; top edges stained brown.

[i]–[ii] + [i]–[xiv] + [1]–412 + [1]–4 and a 16-page catalogue of Everyman's Library, as follows: [i]–[ii] blank; [i] quotation from

Everyman; [ii] This is No. 958 of Everyman's Library. [*note on the series and addresses of the publishers*]; [iii] half-title; [iv] a biographical note on D. H. Lawrence; [v] title page as above; [vi] *All rights reserved | Made in Great Britain | at the Temple Press Letchworth | and decorated by Eric Ravilious | for | J. M. Dent & Sons Ltd | Aldine House Bedford St London | This Collection First Published in 1939*; vii–xi introduction by Desmond Hawkins; xii bibliography; xiii table of contents; [xiv] blank; [1] fly-title: STORIES; [2] blank; 3–240 text; [241] fly-title: SKETCHES AND ESSAYS; [242] blank; [243]–318 text; [319] fly-title: POEMS; [320] blank; 321–359 text; [360] blank; [361] fly-title: LETTERS; [362] a note; 363–412 text, at bottom of page 412: MADE AT THE | TEMPLE PRESS | [*drawing of flower*] LETCHWORTH | IN GREAT BRITAIN; [1]–4 a note on Everyman's Library by Ernest Rhys; and a 16-page catalogue of Everyman's Library.

Published 7 December 1939 at 2*s.*; the first edition consisted of 10,000 copies.

CONTENTS

Odour of Chrysanthemums (from *The Tales of D. H. Lawrence* (A67))—The White Stocking (A67)—England, My England (A67)—The Fox (A67)—The Woman Who Rode Away (A67)—Things (A67)—The Lovely Lady (A67)—Adolf (from *Phoenix* (A76))—San Gaudenzio (from *Twilight in Italy* (A8))—Man is Hunter (A76)—Flowery Tuscany (A76)—A Letter from Germany (A76)—The Mozo (from *Mornings in Mexico* (A37))—Edgar Allan Poe (from *Studies in Classic American Literature* (A25))—Love on the Farm (from *Collected Poems* (A43))—Ballad of Another Ophelia (A43)—Violets (A43)—Baby Running Barefoot (A43)—Tease (A43)—After the Opera (A43)—Sorrow (A43)—On That Day (A43)—A Doe at Evening (A43)—Song of a Man Who Has Come Through (A43)—Peach (A43)—Grapes (A43)—Snake (A43)—Kangaroo (A43)—Turkey-Cock (A43)—To Let Go, Or To Hold On—? (from *Pansies* (A47))—We Are Transmitters (A47)—Don'ts (A47)—Fidelity (A47)—To Women, As Far As I'm Concerned (A47)—Old People (A47)—Beautiful Old Age (A47)—Desire Is Dead (A47)—Man's Image (A47)—Ultimate Reality (from *Last Poems* (A62))—Latter-Day Sinners (A47)—It's No Good! (A47)—Ships in Bottles (A47)—Thought (A62)—Mystic (A62)—Abysmal Immortality (A62)—Shadows (A62)—The Ship of Death (A62)—Letters (from *The Letters of D. H. Lawrence* (A61)).

first edition

FIRE AND OTHER POEMS | BY D. H. LAWRENCE | WITH A FOREWORD BY ROBINSON JEFFERS | AND A NOTE ON THE POEMS BY | FRIEDA LAWRENCE | [*design of Indian pueblo in red*] | PRINTED AT THE GRABHORN PRESS FOR | THE BOOK CLUB OF CALIFORNIA | MCMXXXX

Natural cloth boards, black paper label on spine stamped in gold reading upwards: FIRE & OTHER POEMS | By D. H. Lawrence The leaves measure $9\frac{1}{2}'' \times 6\frac{1}{2}''$. Top edges rough-trimmed; fore and bottom edges untrimmed.

[i]–[viii] + [i]–[xiv] + [1]–[46], as follows: [i]–[viii] blank; [i] title page as above; [ii] Copyright 1940 by Frieda Lawrence; iii–[viii] foreword by Robinson Jeffers; ix–[xii] note on the poems by Frieda Lawrence; [xiii] contents; [xiv] blank; 1–[37] text; [38] blank; [39] [*ornamental rule in red*] | THREE HUNDRED COPIES | PRINTED AT THE GRABHORN PRESS | OF SAN FRANCISCO | [*ornamental rule in red*]; [40]–[46] blank. Pagination includes inside leaf of the end papers which form pages [5] and [6] at the front and pages [41] and [42] at the back.

Published 1 November 1940 at $3.50; the edition consisted of 300 copies.

CONTENTS

Fire—Eagle in New Mexico (first appeared in the *New Mexico Quarterly*, November 1938 (C223), a different version of the poem by the same name in *Birds, Beasts and Flowers* (A27))—O! Americans! (first appeared in the *New Mexico Quarterly*, May 1938 (C221))—What Do I Care—Are You Pining?—Change of Life—Reach Over—Softly, Then, Softly!—Traitors.

NOTES: The brochure issued by the Book Club of California stated that all the poems in this collection were previously unpublished; however, two of them had appeared in the *New Mexico Quarterly*.

NOTES (2): *Fire* was issued in a plain white paper dust-jacket without printing. A California bookseller offered a copy of the book in a different binding in 1979, which he described as "red cloth over blue-grey boards." This may have been a trial binding; no other copies similarly bound have been reported.

first collected edition

FULL SCORE | [*short decorative rule*] | TWENTY TALES | *by* | D. H. LAWRENCE | THE REPRINT SOCIETY | LONDON

Wine-red cloth boards, black leather label on spine stamped in gold: FULL | SCORE | D. H. | LAWRENCE | [*enclosed within decorative rule*] The leaves measure $7\frac{1}{4}''\times 4\frac{13}{16}''$. All edges trimmed.

[i]–[vi] + [1]–606, as follows: [i] half-title; [ii] blank; [iii] title page as above; [iv] PUBLISHED BY THE REPRINT SOCIETY LTD | BY ARRANGEMENT WITH WILLIAM HEINEMANN LTD. | 1943 | PRINTED IN GREAT BRITAIN AT THE WINDMILL PRESS | KINGSWOOD, SURREY; [v] table of contents; [vi] blank; [1]–606 text.

Published in 1943; the first printing consisted of 60,000 copies.

CONTENTS

The Prussian Officer (from *The Tales of D. H. Lawrence* (A67))—Second Best (A67)—The White Stocking (A67)—Samson and Delilah (A67)—The Horse Dealer's Daughter (A67)—Fanny and Annie (A67)—The Ladybird (A67)—The Fox (A67)—Two Blue Birds (A67)—The Captain's Doll (A67)—The Princess (A67)—The Woman Who Rode Away (A67)—Jimmy and the Desperate Woman (A67)—None of That (A67)—The Man Who Loved Islands (A67)—Rawdon's Roof (A67)—The Rocking-Horse Winner (A67)—The Blue Moccasins (A67)—Adolf (from *Phoenix* (A76))—Things (A67).

NOTES: All the stories in this collection were reprinted from the *Tales of D. H. Lawrence* (A67) with the exception of "Adolf," which first appeared in print in the *Dial*, September 1920 (C73), from whence it was reprinted in *Phoenix* (A76).

A81.5   MORNINGS IN MEXICO   1945

first separate edition

[*decorative rule in green*] | MORNINGS | IN | MEXICO [*in green*] | *by D. H. Lawrence* | [*printer's device*] | Detroit | Privately Printed | 1945 | [*decorative rule in green*]

Green paper boards; white paper label on upper cover, printed in red:

MORNINGS | IN | MEXICO The leaves measure $7\frac{3}{8}'' \times 5''$. All edges trimmed.

[1]–[26] including the back free end-paper, as follows: [1] half-title: MORNINGS IN MEXICO; [2] blank; [3] title page as above; [4] blank; [5] fly-title: MARKET DAY; [6] blank; [7] *Acknowledgement is made to Alfred A. Knopf, | Inc., New York, for permission to use as a personal | Christmas greeting the chapter "Market Day" | from Mornings in Mexico by D. H. Lawrence*; [8] blank; 9–24 text; [25] *A limited number of copies of "Market Day" | by D. H. Lawrence have been privately printed | for | Bob Powers | 550 West Lafayette Boulevard | Detroit | Christmas, 1945 | [printer's device in green]*

Published Christmas 1945, apparently not for sale. Number of copies unknown.

NOTES: See (A37).

A82 THE PORTABLE D. H. LAWRENCE 1947

first collected edition

[*ornamental rule*] | THE PORTABLE | D. H. LAWRENCE | [*ornamental rule*] | EDITED AND | WITH AN INTRODUCTION | BY DIANA TRILLING | [*ornamental rule*] | NEW YORK · THE VIKING PRESS · MCMXLVII | [*ornamental rule*]

Orange cloth boards, printed in dark red on upper cover: [*Lawrence phoenix*]; printed in dark red on spine: [*thick rule*] | [*thin rule*] | [*five-pointed star*] | [*thin rule*] | D. H. | LAWRENCE [*stamped in gold on dark red background between preceding rule and following rule*] | [*thin rule*] | [*five-pointed star*] | [*thin rule*] | [*thick rule*] | THE | VIKING | PORTABLE | LIBRARY | [*thin rule*] | [*thick rule*] | EDITED | By | Diana | Trilling | [*thick rule*] | [*thin rule*] | THE | VIKING | PRESS | [*thin rule*] | [*thick rule*] The leaves measure $6\frac{1}{2}'' \times 4\frac{3}{16}''$. All edges stained brown and trimmed.

[i]–[viii] + 1–[696], as follows: [i] half-title; [ii] a note on the Viking Portable Library; [iii] title page as above; [iv] COPYRIGHT 1947 BY VIKING PRESS, INC. | [*prior copyright notices*] | PUBLISHED BY THE VIKING PRESS IN JANUARY 1947 | PUBLISHED ON THE SAME DAY IN THE DOMINION OF CANADA | BY THE MACMILLAN COMPANY OF CANADA LIMITED | [*acknowledgements*] | Printed in U.S.A. by The Colonial Press Inc.; v–vii table of contents; [viii] blank; 1–32 introduction by Diana Trilling; [33] fly-title: [*ornamental rule*] | STORIES | AND NOVELETTES | [*ornamental rule*]; 34–35 editor's preface; 36–305 text; [306] blank; [307] fly-title: [*ornamental rule*] | NOVELS | [*ornamental rule*]; 308–309 editor's preface;

310–470 text; [471] fly-title: [*ornamental rule*] | POEMS | [*ornamental rule*];
472–473 editor's preface; 474–498 text; [499] fly-title: [*ornamental rule*]
| TRAVEL | [*ornamental rule*]; 500–501 editor's preface; 502–554 text;
[555] fly-title: [*ornamental rule*] | LETTERS | [*ornamental rule*]; 556 editor's
preface; 557–601 text; [602] blank; [603] fly-title: [*ornamental rule*] |
ESSAYS | AND CRITICAL WRITING | [*ornamental rule*]; 604–605 editor's
preface; 606–692 text; [693]–[695] a partial list of titles in the Viking
Portable Library; [696] blank.

Published 6 January 1947 at $2.50; the first printing consisted of
15,000 copies.

CONTENTS

Stories and Novelettes: The Prussian Officer (from the *Tales of D. H.
Lawrence* (A67))—Tickets, Please (A67)—The Blind Man (A67)—Two
Blue Birds (A67)—The Lovely Lady (A67)—The Rocking-Horse
Winner (A67)—The Princess (A67)—The Fox (A67).

Novels: From *The Rainbow* (A7), Girlhood of Anna Brangwen—Wedding
at the Marsh. From *Women in Love* (A15), Man to Man—The Industrial
Magnate—Rabbit—Moony—Gladiatorial.

Poems: Sunday Afternoon in Italy (from *Collected Poems* (A43))—Baby
Tortoise (A43)—Tortoise-Shell (A43)—Snake (A43)—Elephant
(A43)—Won't It Be Strange——? (from *Pansies* (A47))—When I Went
to the Circus—(A47)—We are Transmitters (A47)—The Gods! The
Gods! (A62)—Retort to Whitman (A62)—Retort to Jesus (A62)—
Whales Weep Not! (A62).

Travel: To Sorgono (from *Sea and Sardinia* (A20))—The Theâtre (from
Twilight in Italy (A8))—The Mozo (from *Mornings in Mexico* (A37)).

Letters

Essays and Critical Writings: Christs in the Tirol (from *Phoenix* (A76))—
Nottingham and the Mining Countryside (A76)—Men Must Work and
Women As Well (from *Assorted Articles* (A53))—A Review of *Nigger
Heaven, Flight, Manhattan Transfer* and *In Our Time* (A76)—Pornography
and Obscenity (separately published (A49))—Edgar Allan Poe (from
Studies in Classic American Literature (A25)).

NOTES: Diana Trilling who edited *The Portable D. H. Lawrence* has
reviewed several Lawrence books and written articles about him; she
also edited *The Selected Letters of D. H. Lawrence* (A100).

REVIEWS: *The Portable D. H. Lawrence* was reviewed in the *New Yorker*, 4 January 1947; in the *New York Herald Tribune Books*, 9 February 1947; by Elizabeth Bowen in the *New York Times Book Review*, 9 February 1947; by Mabel Dodge Luhan in the *Chicago Sun Book Week*, 9 February 1947; and in "Some Notes on D. H. Lawrence" by W. H. Auden in the *Nation*, 26 April 1947.

A83   SELECTED POEMS   1947

first collected edition

D. H. LAWRENCE | SELECTED POEMS | *with an introduction by Kenneth Rexroth* | *The New Classics Series*

Grey cloth boards, printed in brown on spine, reading from top to bottom: SELECTED POEMS D. H. LAWRENCE The leaves measure $7'' \times 4\frac{3}{4}''$. All edges trimmed.

[i]–[x] + 1–[150], as follows: [i] half-title; [ii] list of *New Classics Series*; [iii] title page as above; [iv] [*prior copyright notices*] | COPYRIGHT 1947 BY NEW DIRECTIONS | [*acknowledgements*] | MANUFACTURED IN THE UNITED STATES | BY THE VAIL-BALLOU PRESS | *New Directions Books are published by James Laughlin* | NEW YORK OFFICE [*short rule*] 500 FIFTH AVENUE; v–viii table of contents; [ix] fly-title: THE SELECTED POEMS OF D. H. LAWRENCE; [x] blank; 1–23 introduction by Kenneth Rexroth; [24] blank; 25–144 text; 145–148 a Lawrence chronology; [149]–[150] blank.

Published 21 January 1948 at $1.50; the first printing consisted of 2016 copies.

CONTENTS

The Wild Common (from *Collected Poems* (A43))—Cherry Robbers (A43)—Twilight (A43)—Love on the Farm (A43)—Letter from Town: The Almond Tree (A43)—Wedding Morn (A43)—Lightning (A43)—Baby Running Barefoot (A43)—Aware (A43)—A White Blossom (A43)—After the Opera (A43)—Whether Or Not (A43)—A Winter's Tale (A43)—Suspense (A43)—The Bride (A43)—Sorrow (A43)—Silence (A43)—Brooding Grief (A43)—Troth with the Dead (A43)—At a Loose End (A43)—Release (A43)—Under the Oak (A43)—Piano (A43)—Passing Visit to Helen (A43)—Twenty Years Ago (A43)—Seven Seals (A43)—Moonrise (A43)—Hymn to Priapus (A43)—Bei Hennef (A43)—On the Balcony (A43)—A Young Wife (A43)—Green (A43)—River Roses (A43)—Gloire de Dijon (A43)—A Youth Mowing (A43)—Quite

Forsaken (A43)—Sinners (A43)—December Night (A43)—New Year's Eve (A43)—Coming Awake (A43)—Spring Morning (A43)—History (A43)—Song of a Man Who Has Come Through (A43)—New Heaven and Earth (A43)—Pomegranate (A43)—St. Mark (A43)—Fish (A43)— Bat (A43)—Snake (A43)—Tortoise Gallantry (A43)—Humming Bird (A43)—You (from *Pansies* (A47))—How Beastly the Bourgeois Is (A47)—To Be Superior (A47)—Swan (A47)—We Are Transmitters (A47)—November by the Sea (A47)—The Elephant is Slow to Mate (A47)—Little Fish (A47)—The Mosquito Knows (A47)—Self-Pity (A47)—Sick (A47)—Beautiful Old Age (A47)—When the Ripe Fruit Falls (A47)—Fire (A47)—I Wish I Knew a Woman (A47)— Latter-Day Sinners (A47)—Willy Wet-Legs (A47)—Image Making Love (from *Last Poems* (A62))—Andraitx-Pomegranate Flowers (A62)—Healing (A62) —City Life (A62)—Trees in the Garden (A62)—The Gods! The Gods! (A62)—The Deepest Sensuality (A62)—Nothing to Save (A62)—The English Are So Nice! (A62)—Search for Love (A62)—Terra Incognita (A62)—Thomas Earp (from *Last Poems* as "I Heard a Little Chicken Chirp")—Puss! Puss! (from *Nettles* (A52))—London Mercury (A52)— The White Horse (A62)—Prayer (A62)—Lords of the Day and Night (songs from the *Plumed Serpent* (A33))—Quetzalcoatl Looks Down on Mexico (A33)—Song of Huitzilopochtli (A33)—Huitzilopochtli's Watch (A33)—My Way Is Not Thy Way (A33)—Song of Death (A62)—Demiurge (A62)—Whales Weep Not! (A62)—Glory of Darkness (A62)—Bavarian Gentians (A62)—Death Is Not Evil, Evil Is Mechanical (A62)—The Ship of Death (A62)—The End, the Beginning (A62).

NOTES: This collection was reprinted in 1951 in an edition of 5000 copies. It may be interesting to note that the dust-jacket of the first printing contained advertising matter which began: "Had Lawrence not achieved pre-eminence as a novelist, he would surely have been known as the greatest English poet of his generation." The dust-jacket for the second printing was amended to read: "Lawrence's greatness as a novelist has overshadowed the worth of his poetry."

REVIEWS: *Selected Poems* was reviewed by F. W. Dupee in the *New York Times Book Review*, 7 March 1948; by Jean Starr Untermeyer in "Poet-Prophet-Problem" in the *Saturday Review of Literature*, 20 March 1948; by Louise Bogan in the *New Yorker*, 20 March 1948; in the *New York Herald Tribune Books*, 21 March 1948; and by R. Wilbur in the *Sewanee Review*, January 1950.

first edition

D. H. LAWRENCE'S LETTERS [*in red*] | TO | BERTRAND RUSSELL [*in red*] | EDITED BY HARRY T. MOORE | [*short rule in red*] | GOTHAM BOOK MART | NEW YORK

Dark blue cloth boards, stamped in gold on spine: D. H. LAWRENCE'S LETTERS TO BERTRAND RUSSELL [*reading downwards*] | EDITED BY | HARRY T. | MOORE | GOTHAM | BOOK | MART The leaves measure $9\frac{1}{4}'' \times 6\frac{1}{16}''$. All edges trimmed; top edges stained red.

[i]–[ii] + [i]–[x] + 1–[116] and two plates facing pages 53 and 88, as follows: [i]–[ii] blank; [i] half-title; [ii] blank; [iii] title page as above; [iv] *Copyright 1948 by Gotham Book Mart, Inc.* | The letters in this volume are published with the kind | permission of The Viking Press, holders of publication | rights in all letters of D. H. Lawrence. | PRINTED IN THE UNITED STATES OF AMERICA; v–vi foreword by Harry T. Moore; [vii] table of contents; [viii] blank; [ix] fly-title: D. H. LAWRENCE'S LETTERS | TO | BERTRAND RUSSELL; [x] blank; 1–26 introduction; [27] fly-title: D. H. LAWRENCE'S LETTERS | TO BERTRAND RUSSELL | [*note on text*]; [28] blank; 29–73 text; [74] blank; [75] fly-title: APPENDIX A | LAWRENCE'S CORRECTIONS ON | RUSSELL'S MANUSCRIPT | [*note on text*]; [76] blank; 77–96 text; [97] fly-title: APPENDIX B | A NOTE ON THE CHRONOLOGY | OF THE LETTERS; [98] blank; 99–111 text; [112] blank; [113] This first edition, designed by | Maurice Serle Kaplan, is limited | to 950 copies; [114]–[116] blank.

Published 1948 at $5.00; the edition consisted of 950 copies.

NOTES: Lawrence was probably introduced to Bertrand Russell sometime in 1915 although the two men were aware of each other as early as the first months of 1914. In his *Intelligent Heart* (B57) Harry T. Moore quotes from a letter to Gordon Campbell in which Lawrence tells of Lady Ottoline Morrell's plans to bring Russell to meet the Lawrences. After the meeting in 1915 the two men began the correspondence reproduced in this book. They soon began planning a series of joint lectures in London which never materialized. Lawrence visited Russell in Cambridge in March of 1915, and J. M. Keynes whom he met there at breakfast in Russell's rooms in Trinity College has given an account of Lawrence at Cambridge in his *Two Memoirs* (B53). Some of the letters to Bertrand Russell first appeared in the *Atlantic Monthly*, December 1948 (C230).

REVIEWS: *Lawrence's Letters to Bertrand Russell* was reviewed by Harvey Breit in the *New Times Book Review*, 23 January 1949, and in the *New Yorker*, 12 March 1949.

NOTES (2): The *Letters to Bertrand Russell* was issued in a tan paper dust-jacket printed in red and black.

A85   A PRELUDE   1949

first edition

A PRELUDE | By | D. H. LAWRENCE | His First and Previously Unrecorded Work | [*short decorative rule*] | With an Explanatory Foreword Dealing | With Its Discovery by | P. BEAUMONT WADS-WORTH | [*publisher's device*] | The Merle Press | 15 Speer Road, Thames Ditton, Surrey | 1949

Rust-coloured cloth boards with a brown leather backstrip, stamped in gold on spine reading upwards: D. H. LAWRENCE. A PRELUDE The leaves measure 8″ × 5⅜″. All edges trimmed.

[1]–[48], as follows: [1]–[2] blank; [3] half-title; [4] frontispiece consisting of: [*tipped-in portrait of Lawrence enclosed within single rule border*] | D. H. LAWRENCE | ON HIS TWENTY-FIRST BIRTHDAY | SEPT. 11, 1906.; [5] title page as above; [6] This story, which appears here for the first time | under the name of its author, D. H. Lawrence, | is published by kind permission of "The Notting- | hamshire Guardian." One hundred and sixty | copies have been printed, of which 150 only are | for sale. The type has been dispersed. | Copy No. 119. [*autograph number in black ink*]; 7–25 introduction by P. Beaumont Wadsworth; [26] blank; 27 fly-title: A PRELUDE | By | D. H. LAWRENCE; 28 note on Lawrence's life; 29–47 text; [48] T | S | M: | [*decorative initials*] | [*short rule*] | ALFRED ASHLEY SON & LTD., East Sheen, S. W. 14.

Published 15 August 1949 at 42s.; the edition consisted of 160 copies.

NOTES: This is a reprint from the *Nottinghamshire Guardian*, 7 December 1907 (C1) of a story, "A Prelude," which was Lawrence's first appearance in print. Introductory material tells how P. Beaumont Wadsworth, while working for the *Manchester Guardian* during the war, made a search of Midland papers for Lawrence material and in the process made the discovery of this story, the winning tale submitted for Lawrence by Jessie Chambers to a *Nottinghamshire Guardian* competition at Christmas 1907. The story appeared under the name of Jessie Chambers.

REVIEWS: *A Prelude* was reviewed in *The Times Literary Supplement*, 28 April 1950.

An account of Mr Wadsworth's discovery appeared in *The Nottinghamshire Guardian*, 29 October, 5, 12 and 19 November 1949, and the issue for 10 December reprinted "A Prelude" with the original illustrations.

A86   SELECTED ESSAYS   1950

first collected edition

D. H. LAWRENCE | [*ornamental rule*] | *Selected Essays* | PENGUIN BOOKS | IN ASSOCIATION WITH | WILLIAM HEINEMANN

Purple paper covers, printed in black and purple on upper cover: PENGUIN | BOOKS | [*preceding two lines enclosed within ornamental rules on white background*] | SELECTED | ESSAYS | [*short rule in purple*] | D. H. LAWRENCE | [*at left of preceding four lines, reading from bottom to top*] ESSAYS & BELLES LETTRES | [*at right of preceding four lines, reading from top to bottom*] ESSAYS & BELLES LETTRES | [*preceding four lines and lettering at right and left are on white background*] | [*publisher's device*] | 2/6; printed in black on spine, reading from bottom to top: 753 [*horizontal*] | [*publisher's device*] | VOLUME | A DOUBLE | 2/6 | SELECTED ESSAYS [on white background] D. H. LAWRENCE; on lower cover: [*portrait and biographical sketch of D. H. Lawrence*] The leaves measure 7″ × 4$\frac{5}{16}$″. All edges trimmed.

[1]–[352], as follows: [1] half-title; [2] blank; [3] title page as above; [4] THIS SELECTION | FIRST PUBLISHED IN PENGUIN BOOKS 1950 | MADE AND PRINTED IN GREAT BRITAIN | FOR PENGUIN BOOKS LTD, HARMONDSWORTH, MIDDLESEX | BY C. NICHOLLS AND COMPANY LTD; [5]–6 table of contents; [7]–10 introduction by Richard Aldington; [11] fly-title: *Love and Life*; [12] blank; [13]–106 text; [107] fly-title: *The Spirit of Place*; [108] blank; [109]–213 text; [214] blank; [215] fly-title: *Writing and Painting*; [216] blank; [217]–346 text; [347] fly-title: *Lawrence and Magnus*; [348] blank; [349]–351 text; [352] advertisement of Penguin Books.

Published March 1950 at 2*s*. 6*d*.; the first printing consisted of 40,000 copies.

CONTENTS

I. Love and Life

Sex Versus Loveliness (from *Assorted Articles* (A53))—Give Her a Pattern
(A53)—Love (from *Phoenix* (A76))—Cocksure Women and Hensure
Men (A53)—Nobody Loves Me (A76)—Books (A76)—Climbing Down
Pisgah (A76)—Reflections on the Death of a Porcupine (from *Reflections
on the Death of a Porcupine* (A32))—Democracy (A76)—The State of Funk
(A53)—Insouciance (A53).

II. The Spirit of Place

England

Whistling of Birds (A76)—Nottingham and the Mining Country (A76)
—Dull London (A53).

Italy

The Spinner and the Monks (from *Twilight in Italy* (A8))—Flowery
Tuscany (A76)—Man is a Hunter (A76).

Germany

The Crucifix Across the Mountains (A8)—Mercury (A76)—A Letter
from Germany (A76).

Mexico and New Mexico

New Mexico (A76)—Indians and an Englishman (A76)—Just Back
from the Snake Dance–Tired Out (originally published in the *Laughing
Horse*, September 1924 (C124), and reprinted in the *Letters* (A61))—
Corasmin and the Parrots (from *Mornings in Mexico* (A37))—A Little
Moonshine with Lemon (A37).

III. Writing and Painting

John Galsworthy (A76)—Benjamin Franklin (from *Studies in Classic
American Literature* (A25))—Moby Dick (A25)—Whitman (A25)—Gio-
vanni Verga (A76)—Preface to New Poems (A76)—Accumulated Mail
(A76)—Making Pictures (A53)—Introduction to His Paintings (A76).

IV. Lawrence and Magnus

The Late Mr. Maurice Magnus: A Letter (A76).

first collected edition

D. H. LAWRENCE | [*ornamental rule*] | *Letters* | SELECTED BY | RICHARD ALDINGTON | WITH AN INTRODUCTION BY | ALDOUS HUXLEY | PENGUIN BOOKS | IN ASSO-CIATION WITH | WILLIAM HEINEMANN LTD

Violet paper covers, printed in black and violet on upper cover: PENGUIN | BOOKS | [*preceding two lines enclosed within ornamental rule on white background*] | SELECTED | LETTERS | [*short rule in violet*] | D. H. LAWRENCE | [*at left of preceding four lines, in violet, reading from bottom to top*] ESSAYS AND BELLES LETTRES | [*at right of preceding four lines, reading from top to bottom*] | ESSAYS AND BELLES LETTRES | [*preceding four lines and printing at left and right are on white background*] | [*publisher's device*] | 1/6; printed in black on spine from bottom to top: 759 [*horizontal*] | [*publisher's device*] SELECTED LETTERS [*on white background*] D. H. LAWRENCE; on lower cover: [*portrait and biographical sketch of D. H. Lawrence*] The leaves measure $7\frac{1}{16}'' \times 4\frac{3}{8}''$. All edges trimmed.

[1]–[192], as follows: [1] half-title; [2] blank; [3] title page as above; [4] THIS SELECTION FIRST PUBLISHED 1950 | MADE AND PRINTED IN GREAT BRITAIN | FOR PENGUIN BOOKS LTD, HARMONDSWORTH, MIDDLESEX | BY HUNT, BARNARD AND CO LTD | LONDON AND AYLESBURY, BUCKS; [5]–[31] introduction by Aldous Huxley; [32] blank; 33–[183] text; [184]–[192] advertisements.

Published March 1950 at 1*s*. 6*d*.; the first printing consisted of 40,000 copies.

first collected edition

D. H. LAWRENCE | [*ornamental rule*] | *Selected Poems* | CHOSEN WITH AN INTRODUCTION | BY W. E. WILLIAMS | PENGUIN BOOKS | IN ASSOCIATION WITH | WILLIAM HEINEMANN LTD.

Blue paper covers, printed in black and blue on upper cover: PENGUIN | BOOKS | [*preceding two lines enclosed within ornamental rule on white background*] | SELECTED | POEMS | [*short rule in blue*] | D. H. LAWRENCE | [*at left of preceding four lines, in blue, reading from bottom to top*] POETRY | [*at right of preceding four lines, in blue, reading from top to bottom*] POETRY | [*preceding four lines and printing at right and left are on white background*] | [*publisher's device*] | 1/6; printed in black on spine from bottom to top: DII [*horizontal*] | [*publisher's device*] | SELECTED POEMS [*on white background*] D. H. LAWRENCE; on lower cover: [*portrait and biographical sketch of D. H. Lawrence*] The leaves measure $7\frac{1}{16}$" × $4\frac{3}{8}$". All edges trimmed.

[1]–[160], as follows: [1] half-title; [2] blank; [3] title page as above; [4] THIS SELECTION FIRST PUBLISHED IN | PENGUIN BOOKS 1950 | MADE AND PRINTED IN GREAT BRITAIN | FOR PENGUIN BOOKS LTD, HARMONDS-WORTH, MIDDLESEX | BY HUNT, BARNARD AND CO. LTD | LONDON AND AYLESBURY; [5]–[6] table of contents; 7–9 introduction by W. E. Williams; [10] blank; 11–[160] text.

Published March 1950 at 1s. 6d.; the first printing consisted of 40,000 copies.

CONTENTS

Rhyming Poems (from *Collected Poems* (A43)): Dog-Tired; Love on the Farm; Gipsy; The Collier's Wife; Monologue of a Mother; The Best of School; End of Another Home Holiday; A White Blossom; Morning Work; The End; Last Words to Miriam; Malade; Snap-Dragon; Piano—Look! We Have Come Through! (from *Collected Poems* (A43)): Bei Hennef: Sunday Afternoon in Italy; Giorno dei Morti; Manifesto—Fruits (from *Collected Poems* (A43)): Medlars and Sorb Apples; Figs; The Revolutionary; The Evening Land—Trees (A43): Cypresses; Bare Fig-Trees; Bare Almond-Trees—Flowers (A43): Hibiscus and Salvia Flowers—The Evangelistic Beasts (A43); St. Matthew; St. Mark; St. Luke; St. John—Creatures (A43): Fish; Man and Bat—Reptiles: Snake; Baby Tortoise—Birds (A43): Humming-Bird—Animals (A43): Kanga-roo; Mountain Lion—Ghosts (A43): Men in New Mexico; Autumn at Taos; The American Eagle—Last Poems (from *Last Poems* (A62)): The Argonauts; Red Geranium and Godly Mignonette; The Body of God; The Rainbow; The Man of Tyre; Bavarian Gentians; The Breath of Life; The Hands of God; Pax; Abysmal Immortality; Only Man; Lord's Prayer; Walk Warily; The Ship of Death; Shadows; Phoenix—Pansies (from *Pansies* (A47)): To Let Go or to Hold On—?; How Beastly the Bourgeois is—; The Oxford Voice; Give Us Gods; Spiral Flame; When wilt Thou Teach the People—?; Things Men have Made—; Things Made by Iron—; New Houses, New Clothes—; Whatever Man Makes—; We are Transmitters—; Let Us be Men—; Good Husbands Make Unhappy Wives—; The Mess of Love; Fidelity; All I Ask—;

Nottingham's New University; Peace and War; To Women, as Far as I'm Concerned; Courage; Elemental; I Wish I knew a Woman—; The Effort of Love; Basta!; God; A Sane Revolution; Lizard; Democracy; Ships in Bottles; Trust.

A89   ART AND PAINTING   1951

first collected edition

CURRENT AFFAIRS [*white on blue background*] | [*Lawrence phoenix*] | ART AND | PAINTING | D. H. Lawrence | [*preceding four lines in black on white panel*] | Number 137 21st July 1951 [*in black on blue background*] | THE BUREAU OF CURRENT AFFAIRS, 177 PICCADILLY, LONDON, W. 1 [*in white on blue background*] | Ninepence [*in black on blue background*] | [*blue background is enclosed within decorative rule of asterisks and blue squares, the whole printed on white paper cover*]

Paper covers, the upper cover is printed as above and serves also as the title page; lower cover contains teacher's notes. The leaves measure $9'' \times 6\frac{1}{2}''$. All edges trimmed.

[1]–[20], as follows: [1] title page and upper cover as above; [2] a note on D. H. Lawrence; 3–19 text; [20] lower cover, containing teacher's notes, at bottom of page [20]: Published fortnightly by the Bureau of Current Affairs, 117 Piccadilly, London, W. 1 (Telephone: Grosvenor 3901) | in whom copyright is vested. Printed by Staples Printers Limited at their Rochester, Kent, establishment.

Published 21 July 1951 at 9*d.*; number of copies unknown.

CONTENTS

Making Pictures (from *Assorted Articles* (A53))—Art and Morality (from *Phoenix* (A76))—Introduction to These Paintings (excerpts) (from *The Paintings of D. H. Lawrence* (A46))—Pictures on the Walls (A53).

A90   SELECTED POEMS   1951

first collected edition

D. H. LAWRENCE | [*short ornamental rule*] | SELECTED | POEMS | EDITED BY | JAMES REEVES | [*publisher's device*] | [*short rule*] | WILLIAM HEINEMANN LTD | MELBOURNE : : LONDON : : TORONTO

Blue cloth boards, stamped in gold on spine, reading from top to bottom: D. H. Lawrence [*short rule*] Selected Poems [*publisher's device*] The leaves measure 6⅝″ × 4¼″. All edges trimmed.

[i]–[ii] + [i]–xviii + 1–[80], as follows: [i]–[ii] blank; [i] half-title; [ii] blank; [iii] title page as above; [iv] David Herbert Lawrence 1885–1930 | FIRST PUBLISHED 1951 | PUBLISHED BY WILLIAM HEINEMANN LTD | 99, GREAT RUSSELL STREET, LONDON, W. C. 1 | PRINTED IN GREAT BRITAIN BY THE PUBLISHERS AT | THE WINDMILL PRESS, KINGSWOOD, SURREY; v–vi table of contents; vii–xviii introduction; 1–79 text; [80] blank.

Published 24 September 1951 at 4s.; the first printing consisted of 4000 copies.

CONTENTS

From *Collected Poems*, Vol. I (A43): Last Hours; Weeknight Service; Letter from Town: On a Grey Morning in March; Letter from Town: The Almond-Tree; Dog-Tired; Discord in Childhood; End of Another Home Holiday; Baby Running Barefoot; Aware; Corot; After the Opera; Morning Work; Last Lesson of the Afternoon; A Winter's Tale; Sorrow; Snap-Dragon; Firelight and Nightfall; A Passing-Bell; Piano —From *Collected Poems*, Vol. II (A43): On the Balcony; A Youth Mowing; Sunday Afternoon in Italy; Giorno dei Morti; Coming Awake; Peace—Hibiscus and Salvia Flowers (excerpt)—The Mosquito—Bat —Snake—Humming-Bird—The Blue Jay—Kangaroo—From *Pansies* (A47): Elephants in the Circus; A Living; Things Men Have Made—; Let Us Be Men; Spray; Many Mansions; Poverty; Talk; The Optimist; Lizard—From *Last Poems* (A62): The Argonauts; They Say the Sea is Loveless; Bavarian Gentians; Mystic; The Ship of Death; Intimates.

A91　THE LATER D. H. LAWRENCE　1952

first collected edition

[*Lawrence phoenix*] | THE | LATER | D. H. | LAWRENCE | NEW YORK | ALFRED A. KNOPF | 1952

Red cloth boards, printed in black on upper cover: [*black panel with Lawrence phoenix embossed in red*]; stamped in gold on spine: The LATER | D. H. | LAWRENCE | [*black panel with Lawrence phoenix embossed in red*] | Alfred A. Knopf The leaves measure 8⅜″ × 5⅝″. Top edges trimmed and stained yellow; fore and bottom edges rough-trimmed.

[i]–[iv] + [i]–xx + [1]–[456], as follows: [i]–[iii] blank; [iv] list of Knopf books by D. H. Lawrence; [i] half-title; [ii] *The Best Novels, Stories, Essays, 1925–1930* | ST. MAWR *and* THE MAN WHO DIED | *with complete sections from* | MORNINGS IN MEXICO | REFLECTIONS ON THE DEATH OF A PORCUPINE | THE WOMAN WHO RODE AWAY | *and* ASSORTED ARTICLES | *Selected with Introductions, by* | WILLIAM YORK TINDALL | [*publisher's device*]; [iii] title page as above; [iv] *L. C. catalog card number: 51–11982* | [*short thick rule*] | [*short thin rule*] | THIS IS A BORZOI BOOK, | PUBLISHED BY ALFRED A. KNOPF, INC. | [*short thin rule*] | [*short thick rule*] | [*short vertical decorative rules at either end between horizontal rules forming box*] | [*copyright notices*]; v–xvii introduction by William York Tindall; [xviii] blank; [xix]–xx table of contents; [1] fly-title: ST. MAWR; [2] blank; 3–4 introduction to *St. Mawr*; 5–166 text; [167] fly-title: FROM | REFLECTIONS | *ON THE* | DEATH | *OF A* | PORCUPINE; [168] blank; 169–170 introduction to *Reflections on the Death of a Porcupine* and *Mornings in Mexico*; 171–233 text; [234] blank; [235] fly-title: FROM | MORNINGS | *IN* | MEXICO; [236] blank; 237–296 text; [297] fly-title: FROM | *THE* | WOMAN | *WHO* | RODE AWAY; [298] blank; 299–300 introduction to *The Woman Who Rode Away* and *Sun*; 301–358 text; [359] fly-title: FROM | ASSORTED | ARTICLES; [360] blank; 361–362 introduction to *Assorted Articles*; 363–393 text; [394] blank; [395] fly-title: | *THE* | MAN | *WHO* | DIED ; [396] blank; 397–398 introduction to *The Man Who Died*; 399–449 text; [450] a note on the type, at bottom of note: *Composed, printed, and bound by* THE PLIMPTON | PRESS, *Norwood, Massachusetts, Designed by* HARRY | FORD. | [*publisher's device*]; [451]–[456] blank.

Published 19 February 1952 at $5.00; the first printing consisted of 5000 copies.

CONTENTS

St. Mawr (from *St. Mawr and the Princess* (A31))—Reflections on the Death of a Porcupine (from *Reflections on Death of a Porcupine* (A32))—The Novel (A32)—"... Love Was Once a Little Boy" (A32)—Aristocracy (A32)—Corasmin and the Parrots (from *Mornings in Mexico* (A37))—Market Day (A37)—Indians and Entertainment (A37)—The Dance of the Sprouting Corn (A37)—The Hopi Snake Dance (A37)—A Little Moonshine with Lemon (A37)—The Woman Who Rode Away (from *The Woman Who Rode Away* (A41))—Sun (separately published (A35))—Autobiographical Sketch (from *Assorted Articles* (A53))—Insouciance (A53)—Making Pictures (A53)—Hymns in a Man's Life (A53)—The Risen Lord (A53)—The Man Who Died (separately published (A50)).

REVIEWS: *The Later D. H. Lawrence* was reviewed by Harry T. Moore in the *New York Times Book Review*, 9 March 1952; by Mark Schorer in the *New Republic*, 7 April 1952; by G. F. Whicher in the *New York Herald Tribune Books*, 27 April 1952; and by Ben Ray Redman in the *Saturday Review of Literature*, 10 May 1952.

A92   SEX LITERATURE AND   1953
CENSORSHIP

a. *first collected edition*

D. H. Lawrence | [*drawing of Adam and Eve with snake and apple in garden of Eden*] SEX | LITERATURE | AND | CENSORSHIP | [*preceding word in white on black panel*] | Essays, edited by Harry T. Moore | *TWAYNE PUBLISHERS* | *NEW YORK* | [*larger drawing of Adam appears at top left behind lettering and Eve appears at lower right behind lettering*]

Orange cloth boards, printed in black on spine reading downwards: D. H. Lawrence SEX LITERATURE AND [*preceding three words in orange on black panel*] CENSORSHIP TWAYNE The leaves measure $8\frac{1}{2}'' \times 5\frac{7}{16}''$. All edges trimmed.

[1]–[128], as follows: [1] half-title; [2] blank; [3] title page as above; [4] *Copyright, 1953, by Harry T. Moore* | [*acknowledgements*] | *Manufactured in the United States of America.*; [5] table of contents; [6] blank; [7] quotation from *Studies in Classic American Literature*; [8] blank; 9–32 introduction by Harry T. Moore; 33–122 text; [123]–[128] blank.

Published October 1953 at $3.00; the first printing consisted of 3500 copies.

b. *first collected English edition*

SEX, LITERATURE AND | CENSORSHIP | *Essays by* | D. H. LAWRENCE | [*five-pointed star*] | *Edited by* | HARRY T. MOORE | With Introductions by | HARRY T. MOORE and H. F. RUBINSTEIN | [*publisher's device*] | [*short rule*] | WILLIAM HEINEMANN LTD | MELBOURNE :: LONDON :: TORONTO

Black cloth boards, blind stamped on lower cover: [*publisher's device*]; stamped in gold on spine: *Sex,* | *Literature* | *and* | *Censorship* | D. H. | LAWRENCE | HEINEMANN The leaves measure $7\frac{3}{4}'' \times 5\frac{1}{8}''$. All edges trimmed.

[i]–[x] + [1]–[270] with frontispiece consisting of the reproduction in colour of a painting by D. H. Lawrence and three plates between pages 166 and 167, as follows: [i]–[ii] blank; [iii] half-title; [iv] blank; [v] title page as above; [vi] FIRST PUBLISHED 1955 | PRINTED IN GREAT BRITAIN | AT THE WINDMILL PRESS | KINGSWOOD, SURREY; [vii] table of contents; [viii] list of illustrations; [ix] quotation from *Studies in Classic American Literature*; [x] blank; [1]–38 introduction by Harry T. Moore; [39]–54 introduction by H. F. Rubenstein; [55]–269 text; [270] blank.

Published 14 March 1955 at 15s.; the first printing consisted of 4500 copies.

CONTENTS

Love (from *Phoenix* (A76))—*The Novel (from *Reflections on the Death of a Porcupine* (A32))—*... Love Was Once a Little Boy (A32)—Making Love to Music (A76)—Cocksure Women and Hensure Men (from *Assorted Articles* (A53))—Sex Versus Loveliness (A53)—Introduction to Pansies (from the definitive edition of *Pansies* (A47c))—The State of Funk (A53)—*Introduction to His Paintings (from the *Paintings of D. H. Lawrence* (A46))—Pornography and Obscenity (A49)—A Propos of Lady Chatterley's Lover (A48b)—*The Finding of Moses (In colour) (A46)—*Resurrection: A painting (A46)—*Fauns and Nymphs: A painting (A46)—*Under-the-Haystack: A painting (A46).

Note: The items marked with an asterisk did not appear in the American edition of *Sex, Literature and Censorship*.

NOTES: Harry T. Moore's essay, "D. H. Lawrence and the 'Censor-Morons,'" was revised for the English edition to include comment on the additional textual material and the reproductions of the paintings. Rubenstein's essay, "The Law Versus D. H. Lawrence," was not in the American edition. Some copies of the American edition were bound in grey cloth printed in blue.

NOTES (2): Copies of the first edition of *Sex, Literature and Censorship* have been reported bound in dark blue cloth as well as the orange and grey bindings noted in the earlier edition of this bibliography. The publishers have stated that it is impossible to determine the various bindings because the bindery "used random colors that were in stock in order to achieve a lower binding cost."

first separate edition

LIFE [*in brown*] | D. H. LAWRENCE | *with engravings by* | RU VAN ROSSEM | [*drawing*] | THE ARK PRESS

Decorative paper boards in brown and cream, printed in black on upper cover: LIFE | *An essay by* D. H. LAWRENCE | *with engravings on wood by* | RU VAN ROSSEM | *out of* THE ARK PRESS The leaves measure $8\frac{1}{4}'' \times 5\frac{3}{16}''$. Top edges trimmed; fore and bottom edges untrimmed.

[1]–[16], as follows: [1]–[2] blank; [3] half-title; [4] blank; [5] title page as above; [6] blank; [7]–[14] text; [15] blank; [16] LIFE | *was first published* | *in the* ENGLISH REVIEW *in 1918* | *& in* PHOENIX *in 1936* | *among the posthumous papers of* | D. H. LAWRENCE | *It appears in this edition* | *of only 250 copies* | *with the consent of* | MRS FREIDA LAWRENCE | & WILLIAM HEINEMANN LTD | [*publisher's device*] | *Designed & printed* | *in Perpetua and Bembo types* | *on Abbey Mills Greenfield paper* | *by Kim Christen out of* | THE ARK PRESS | *Island Wastrel Saint Ives* | *in collaboration with* | WORDEN (PRINTERS) LTD | *Market Place Marazion* | *Cornwall* | 1954

Published 19 October 1954 at 7*s*. 6*d*.; the edition consisted of 250 copies.

NOTES: *Life* originally appeared in the *English Review*, February 1918 (C53). Kim Christen is the pseudonym of Kim Taylor, proprietor of the Ark Press, who also designed the Ark Press edition of *Look! We Have Come Through!* (A10b).

A94   COMPLETE SHORT STORIES   1955

first collected edition

VOL. I

THE COMPLETE | SHORT STORIES | *of* | D. H. LAW-RENCE | [*asterisk*] | *VOL. I* | [*publisher's device*] | [*short rule*] | WILLIAM HEINEMANN LTD | MELBOURNE :: LONDON :: TORONTO

Red cloth boards, stamped in silver on spine: D. H. | LAWRENCE | *The* | *Complete* | *Short* | *Stories* | VOL. I | [*Lawrence phoenix*] | HEINEMANN; blind stamped on lower cover: [*publisher's device*] The leaves measure $7\frac{1}{4}'' \times 4\frac{7}{8}''$. All edges trimmed.

[i]–[x] + 1–282, as follows: [i]–[ii] blank; [iii] half-title; [iv] list of works by D. H. Lawrence; [v] title page as above; [vi] FIRST PUBLISHED 1955

| PRINTED IN GREAT BRITAIN | AT THE WINDMILL PRESS | KINGSWOOD, SURREY; [vii]–[ix] table of contents; [x] blank; 1–282 text.

VOL. II

THE COMPLETE | SHORT STORIES | *of* | D. H. LAW-RENCE | [*asterisk*] | *VOL. II* | [*publisher's device*] | [*short rule*] | WILLIAM HEINEMANN LTD | MELBOURNE :: LONDON :: TORONTO

Red cloth boards, stamped in silver on spine: D. H. | LAWRENCE | *The* | *Complete* | *Short* | *Stories* | VOL. II | [*Lawrence phoenix*] | HEINEMANN; blind stamped on lower cover: [*publisher's device*] The leaves measure $7\frac{1}{4}'' \times 4\frac{7}{8}''$. All edges trimmed.

[i]–[viii] + 283–586, as follows: [i] half-title; [ii] list of works by D. H. Lawrence; [iii] title page as above; [iv] FIRST PUBLISHED 1955 | PRINTED IN GREAT BRITAIN | AT THE WINDMILL PRESS | KINGSWOOD, SURREY; [v]–[vii] table of contents; [viii] blank; 283–586 text.

VOL. III

THE COMPLETE | SHORT STORIES | *of* | D. H. LAW-RENCE | [*asterisk*] | *VOL. III* | [*publisher's device*] | [*short rule*] | WILLIAM HEINEMANN LTD | MELBOURNE :: LONDON :: TORONTO

Red cloth boards, stamped in silver on spine: D. H. | LAWRENCE | *The* | *Complete* | *Short* | *Stories* | VOL. III | [*Lawrence phoenix*] | HEINEMANN; blind stamped on lower cover: [*publisher's device*] The leaves measure $7\frac{1}{4}'' \times 4\frac{7}{8}''$. All edges trimmed.

[i]–[viii] + 587–[854], as follows: [i] half-title; [ii] list of works by D. H. Lawrence; [iii] title page as above; [iv] FIRST PUBLISHED 1955 | PRINTED IN GREAT BRITAIN | AT THE WINDMILL PRESS | KINGSWOOD, SURREY; [v]–[vii] table of contents; [viii] blank; 587–853 text; [854] blank.

Published 30 November 1955 at 10*s*. 6*d*. for each volume; the first printing consisted of 5000 copies of each volume.

CONTENTS

VOL. I

A Modern Lover (from *A Modern Lover* (A71))—The Old Adam (A71)—Her Turn (A71)—Strike-Pay (A71)—The Witch à la Mode

(A71)—New Eve and Old Adam (A71)—The Prussian Officer (from *The Tales of D. H. Lawrence* (A67))—The Thorn in the Flesh (A67)—Daughters of the Vicar (A67)—A Fragment of Stained Glass (A67)—The Shades of Spring (A67)—Second Best (A67)—The Shadow in the Rose Garden (A67)—Goose Fair (A67)—The White Stocking (A67)—A Sick Collier (A67)—The Christening (A67).

VOL. II

Odour of Chrysanthemums (A67)—England, My England (A67)—Tickets, Please (A67)—The Blind Man (A67)—Monkey Nuts (A67)—Wintry Peacock (A67)—You Touched Me (A67)—Samson and Delilah (A67)—The Primrose Path (A67)—The Horse-Dealer's Daughter (A67)—Fanny and Annie (A67)—The Princess (A67)—Two Blue Birds (A67)—Sun (A67)—The Woman Who Rode Away (A67)—Smile (A67).

VOL. III

The Border Line (A67)—Jimmy and the Desperate Woman (A67)—The Last Laugh (A67)—In Love (A67)—Glad Ghosts (A67)—None of That (A67)—The Man Who Loved Islands (A67)—The Overtone (from *The Lovely Lady* (A63))—The Lovely Lady (A67)—Rawdon's Roof (A67)—The Rocking-Horse Winner (A67)—Mother and Daughter (A67)—The Blue Moccasins (A67)—Things (A67).

A95 SELECTED LITERARY CRITICISM 1955

first collected edition

D. H. LAWRENCE | [*short thick rule*] | [*short thin rule*] | SELECTED LITERARY | CRITICISM | [*five-pointed star*] | EDITED BY ANTHONY BEAL | [*publisher's device*] | [*short rule*] | WILLIAM HEINEMANN LTD | MELBOURNE LONDON TORONTO

Red cloth boards, blind stamped on lower cover: [*publisher's device*]; stamped in gold on spine: D. H. | LAWRENCE | [*printer's ornament*] | SELECTED | LITERARY | CRITICISM | [*printer's ornament*] | HEINEMANN The leaves measure $8\frac{7}{16}'' \times 5\frac{1}{2}''$. All edges trimmed.

[i]–xii + 1–[436], as follows: [i] half-title; [ii] blank; [iii] title page as above; [iv] PUBLISHED BY WILLIAM HEINEMANN LTD | 99 GREAT RUSSELL STREET, LONDON W. C. I | PRINTED IN GREAT BRITAIN BY THE PUBLISHERS AT | THE WINDMILL PRESS, KINGSWOOD, SURREY | FIRST PUBLISHED 1955;

[v]–vii table of contents; [viii] blank; ix–xii introduction by Anthony Beal; 1–428 text; 429–435 index; [436] blank.

Published 16 January 1956 at 21*s.*; the first printing consisted of 4000 copies.

CONTENTS

I. *Autobiographical*

Autobiographical Sketch (from *Assorted Articles* (A53))—Hymns in a Man's Life (A53)—Extracts from Letters (from *The Letters of D. H. Lawrence* (A61)).

II. *Puritanism and the Arts*

Extracts from Letters (A61)—Introduction to Pansies (A76)—Extract from Letter (A61)—Pornography and Obscenity (A76)—Extract from Letter (A61)—Introduction to These Paintings (excerpt) (A76)—Study of Thomas Hardy (excerpt) (A76).

III. *Verse*

Review of *Georgian Poetry: 1911–1912* (A76)—Extracts from Letters (A61)—Introduction to *New Poems* (A76)—Chaos in Poetry (excerpt) (A76)—Review of *A Second Contemporary Verse Anthology* (A76)—The Nightingale (excerpt) (A76).

IV. *Contemporaries and the Importance of the Novel*

Why the Novel Matters (A76)—Morality and the Novel (A76)—Surgery for the Novel–Or a Bomb (A76)—John Galsworthy (A76)—Extracts from Letters (A61)—Review of *The World of William Clissold* by H. G. Wells (A76)—Extracts from Letters (A61)—Review of Four Contemporary Books (from *Phoenix* (A76) as A Review of *The Station* by Robert Byron, *England and the Octopus* by Clough Williams-Ellis, *Comfortless Memory* by Maurice Baring and *Ashenden or the British Agent* by Somerset Maugham)—Extracts from Letters (A61)—Review of *Hadrian the Seventh* by Baron Corvo (A76)—Introduction to *The Dragon of the Apocalypse* by Frederick Carter (A76)—Study of Thomas Hardy (excerpt) (A76).

V. *Continentals*

Extracts from Letters (A61)—Preface to *The Grand Inquisitor* by F. M. Dostoievsky (A76)—Extracts from Letters (A61)—Preface to *All Things are Possible* by Leo Shestov (A76)—Review of *Solitaria* by V. V.

Rozanov (A76)—Review of *Fallen Leaves* by V. V. Rozanov (A76)—
Extract from Letter (A61)—The Good Man (A76)—Thomas Mann
(A76)—Preface to *Max Havelaar* by E. D. Dekker (A76)—On *Mastro-don
Gesualdo* by Giovanni Verga (A76)—Introduction to *Cavalleria Rusticana*
by Giovanni Verga (A76)—Preface to *The Mother* by Grazia Deledda
(A76).

VI. Americans

The Spirit of Place (from *Studies in Classic American Literature* (A25))—
Fenimore Cooper's White Novels (A25)—Fenimore Cooper's Leather-
stocking Novels (A25)—Edgar Allan Poe (A25)—Nathaniel Hawthorne
and *The Scarlet Letter* (A25)—Herman Melville's *Typee* and *Omoo*
(A25)—Herman Melville's *Moby Dick* (A25)—Walt Whitman (A25)—
Review (sic) of *Bottom Dogs* by Edward Dahlberg (A76)—Review of
Americans by Stuart Sherman (A76)—Review of Four American Novels
(from *Phoenix* (A76) as A Review of *Nigger Heaven* by Carl Van Vechten,
Flight by Walter White, *Manhattan Transfer* by John Dos Passos and *In
Our Time* by Ernest Hemingway).

A96   THE SHORT NOVELS   1956

first collected edition

VOL. I

D. H. LAWRENCE | [*short ornamental rule*] | *The Short Novels* | *VOL. I*
| [*Lawrence phoenix*] | WILLIAM HEINEMANN LTD | MEL-
BOURNE : : LONDON : : TORONTO

Red cloth boards, stamped in silver on spine: D. H. | LAWRENCE | *The
Short* | *Novels* | VOL. I | [*Lawrence phoenix*] | HEINEMANN; blind stamped
on lower cover: [*publisher's device*] The leaves measure $7\frac{1}{4}'' \times 4\frac{7}{8}''$. All
edges trimmed.

[i]–[vi] + [1]–[40] + [1]–[70] + [1]–[70] + 1–[86], as follows: [i] half-
title; [ii] list of works by D. H. Lawrence; [iii] title page as above;
[iv] FIRST PUBLISHED 1956 | PRINTED IN GREAT BRITAIN | AT THE WINDMILL
PRESS | KINGSWOOD, SURREY; [v] table of contents; [vi] blank; [1] fly-title:
LOVE AMONG THE HAYSTACKS; [2] blank; 3–39 text; [40] blank; [1]
fly-title: THE LADYBIRD; [2] blank; 3–69 text; [70] blank; [1] fly-title:
THE FOX; [2] blank; 3–69 text; [70] blank; [1] fly-title: THE CAPTAIN'S
DOLL; [2] blank; 3–86 text.

VOL. II

D. H. LAWRENCE | [*short ornamental rule*] | *The Short Novels* | *VOL. II* | [*Lawrence phoenix*] | WILLIAM HEINEMANN LTD | MELBOURNE : : LONDON : : TORONTO

Red cloth boards, stamped in silver on spine: D. H. | LAWRENCE | *The Short* | *Novels* | VOL. II | [*Lawrence phoenix*] | HEINEMANN; blind stamped on lower cover: [*publisher's device*] The leaves measure $7\frac{1}{4}'' \times 4\frac{7}{8}''$. All edges trimmed.

[i]–[viii] + [1]–[148] + [1]–[82] + [1]–[50], as follows: [i]–[ii] blank; [iii] half-title; [iv] list of works by D. H. Lawrence; [v] title page as above; [vi] FIRST PUBLISHED 1956 | PRINTED IN GREAT BRITAIN | AT THE WINDMILL PRESS | KINGSWOOD, SURREY; [vii] table of contents; [viii] blank; [1] fly-title: ST. MAWR; [2] blank; 3–147 text; [148] blank; [1] fly-title: THE VIRGIN AND THE GIPSY; [2] blank; 3–81 text; [82] blank; [1] fly-title: THE MAN WHO DIED; [2] blank; 3–47 text; [48]–[50] blank.

Published 5 March 1956 at 10*s*. 6*d*.; the first printing consisted of 5000 copies.

CONTENTS

VOL. I

Love among the Haystacks (first appeared in *Love Among the Haystacks and Other Pieces* (A56))—The Ladybird (from *The Tales of D. H. Lawrence* (A67))—The Fox (A67)—The Captain's Doll (A67).

VOL. II

St. Mawr (first appeared in *St. Mawr and the Princess* (A31))—The Virgin and the Gipsy (separately published (A54))—The Man Who Died (separately published (A50)).

A97   EIGHT LETTERS TO RACHEL   1956
ANNAND TAYLOR

first edition

Eight Letters by | D. H. LAWRENCE | *to* | *Rachel Annand Taylor* | WITH A FOREWORD BY MAJL EWING | 1956 | *Printed by Grant Dahlstrom at the Castle Press* | *Pasadena, California*

Grey paper covers, printed in dark grey on upper cover: *Eight Letters*

by | D. H. LAWRENCE | *to* | *Rachel Annand Taylor* The leaves measure
8$\frac{15}{16}$″ × 6″. All edges trimmed.

[1]–[16], as follows: [1] title page as above; [2] *All rights reserved. These
letters are published with the kind permission of* | *The Viking Press, holders of
publication rights in all letters of D. H. Lawrence.* | *Inquiries about reprinting
them should be sent to Viking.*; [3]–[5] foreword by Majl Ewing; [6] blank;
[7]–[15] text; [16] blank.

Published 1956; the edition consisted of 500 copies.

NOTES: Lawrence met Rachel Annand Taylor at a dinner-party given
by Ernest Rhys in 1910, and later when asked to do a paper on some
contemporary poet for a Croydon study group, chose Mrs Taylor as his
subject. This paper was published in the first edition of *Young Lorenzo*
(B34a), Ada Lawrence's book about her brother, published by Orioli
in Florence. Seven of the eight letters reproduced here were written in
the autumn of 1910; the eighth was written in 1922 to thank Mrs Taylor
for her efforts in securing the James Tait Black Prize of Edinburgh
University for *The Lost Girl*. Majl Ewing in his foreword gives an account
of Lawrence's association with Mrs Taylor.

A98   COMPLETE POEMS   1957

first collected edition

VOL. I

D. H. LAWRENCE | [*short ornamental rule*] | *The Complete Poems* |
Vol. I | [*Lawrence phoenix*] | WILLIAM HEINEMANN LTD |
MELBOURNE : : LONDON : : TORONTO

Red cloth boards, stamped in silver on spine: D. H. | LAWRENCE
| *The* | *Complete* | *Poems* | *VOL. I* | [*Lawrence phoenix*] | HEINEMANN;
blind stamped on lower cover: [*publisher's device*] The leaves measure
7$\frac{1}{4}$″ × 4$\frac{7}{8}$″. All edges trimmed.

[i]–[xxxviii] + [1]–[270], as follows: [i] half-title; [ii] list of works by
D. H. Lawrence; [iii] title page as above; [iv] FIRST PUBLISHED 1957 |
PRINTED IN GREAT BRITAIN | AT THE WINDMILL PRESS | KINGSWOOD,
SURREY; [v] publisher's note; [vi] blank; vii–xiii table of contents of
volume one; [xiv] blank; xv–xxiii table of contents of volume two;
[xxiv] blank; xxv–xxxiv table of contents of volume three; xxxv–xxxvii
note by D. H. Lawrence; [xxxviii] blank; [1] fly-title: RHYMING POEMS;
[2] blank; 3–175 text; [176] blank; [177] fly-title: UNRHYMING POEMS

| LOOK! WE HAVE COME THROUGH!; [178] argument; 179–269 text; [270] blank.

VOL. II

D. H. LAWRENCE | [*short ornamental rule*] | *The Complete Poems* | Vol II | [*Lawrence phoenix*] | WILLIAM HEINEMANN LTD | MELBOURNE : : LONDON : : TORONTO

Red cloth boards, stamped in silver on spine: D. H. | LAWRENCE | *The* | *Complete* | *Poems* | *VOL II* | [*Lawrence phoenix*] | HEINEMANN; blind stamped on lower cover: [*publisher's device*] The leaves measure $7\frac{1}{4}'' \times 4\frac{7}{8}''$. All edges trimmed.

[i]–xxxvi + [1]–[300], as follows: [i] half-title; [ii] list of works by D. H. Lawrence; [iii] title page as above; [iv] FIRST PUBLISHED 1957 | PRINTED IN GREAT BRITAIN | AT THE WINDMILL PRESS | KINGSWOOD, SURREY; [v] publisher's note; [vi] blank; vii–xv table of contents for volume two; [xvi] blank; xvii–xxvi table of contents for volume three; xxvii–xxxiii table of contents for volume one; [xxxiv] blank; xxxv–xxxvi note by D. H. Lawrence [1] fly-title: UNRHYMING POEMS | BIRDS, BEASTS AND FLOWERS; [2] blank; 3–149 text; [150] blank; [151] fly-title: PANSIES; [152] blank; 153–299 text; [300] blank.

VOL. III

D. H. LAWRENCE | [*short ornamental rule*] | *The Complete Poems* | Vol. III | [*Lawrence phoenix*] | WILLIAM HEINEMANN LTD | MELBOURNE : : LONDON : : TORONTO

Red cloth boards, stamped in silver on spine: D. H. | LAWRENCE | *The* | *Complete* | *Poems* | *VOL. III* | [*Lawrence phoenix*] | HEINEMANN; blind stamped on lower cover: [*publisher's device*] The leaves measure $7\frac{1}{4}'' \times 4\frac{7}{8}''$. All edges trimmed.

[i]–xliv + [1]–[188], as follows: [i] half-title; [ii] list of works by D. H. Lawrence; [iii] title page as above; [iv] FIRST PUBLISHED 1957 | PRINTED IN GREAT BRITAIN | AT THE WINDMILL PRESS | KINGSWOOD, SURREY; [v] publisher's note; [vi] blank; vii–xvi table of contents for volume three; xvii–xxiii table of contents for volume one; [xxiv] blank; xxv–xxxiii table of contents for volume two; [xxxiv] blank; xxxv–xliv note by Richard Aldington; [1] fly-title: NETTLES; [2] blank; 3–23 text; [24] blank; [25] fly-title: MORE PANSIES; [26] blank; 27–124 text; [125] fly-title: LAST POEMS; [126] blank; 127–185 text; [186]–[188] blank.

Published 29 April 1957 at 12s. 6d.; the first printing consisted of 5000 copies of each volume.

CONTENTS

VOL. I

Volume I contains the poetry from Volume I of *Collected Poems* (A43) as reprinted, and in many instances revised, from *Love Poems* (A3), *Amores* (A9), *New Poems* (A11) and *Bay* (A12) and from Volume II of *Collected Poems* the poetry in *Look! We Have Come Through!* (A10a).

In addition the editor has included three poems from the earlier collections which Lawrence did not include in the *Collected Poems*; these are "Song Day in Autumn" from *Love Poems* and "Disgreeable Advice" and "Restlessness" from *Amores*.

VOL. II

Volume II contains the *Birds, Beasts and Flowers* (A27b) poems from Volume II of *Collected Poems* (A43) and the poems from the Secker edition of *Pansies* (A47a).

VOL. III

Volume III contains the poems from *Nettles* (A52) and *Last Poems* (A62).

A99 SELECTED POETRY AND PROSE 1957

first collected edition

D. H. LAWRENCE | [*short ornamental rule*] | *Selected Poetry* | *and Prose* | EDITED BY | T. R. BARNES | [*Lawrence phoenix*] | WILLIAM HEINEMANN LTD | MELBOURNE :: LONDON :: TORONTO

Red paper boards, stamped in silver on upper cover: D. H. LAWRENCE | Selected Poetry & Prose | EDITED BY T. R. BARNES; stamped in silver on spine, reading from top to bottom: D. H. LAWRENCE Selected Poetry & Prose | [*publisher's device*] The leaves measure $7\frac{1}{4}'' \times 4\frac{13}{16}''$. All edges trimmed.

[i]–[xvi] + 1–184, as follows: [i] half-title; [ii] list of other titles in the series; [iii] title page as above; [iv] FIRST PUBLISHED 1957 | INTRODUCTION © BY T. R. BARNES 1957 | PUBLISHED BY | WILLIAM HEINEMANN LTD | 99 GREAT RUSSELL STREET, LONDON, W. C. I | PRINTED IN GREAT BRITAIN BY THE PUBLISHERS AT | THE WINDMILL PRESS, KINGSWOOD,

SURREY; v table of contents; vi quotation; vii–xv introduction by T. R. Barnes; [xvi] blank; 1–184 text.

Published 25 November 1957 at 7s. 6d.; the first printing consisted of 5000 copies.

CONTENTS

Nottingham and the Mining Countryside (from *Phoenix* (A76))—Letters (excerpts) (from *The Letters of D. H. Lawrence* (A61))—Pornography and Obscenity (excerpt) (separately published (A49))—Introduction to These Paintings (excerpt) (from *The Paintings of D. H. Lawrence* (A46)) —Why the Novel Matters (excerpt) (from *Phoenix* (A76))—Flowery Tuscany (A76)—Man is a Hunter (A76)—Suburbs on a Hazy Day (from *Collected Poems* (A43))—After the Opera (A43)—At the Window (A43) —Sorrow (A43)—In Church (A43)—Piano (A43)—Giorno dei Morti (A43)—Baby Tortoise (A43)—Humming Bird (A43)—Stoic (from *Last Poems* (A62))—Mystic (A62)—Thought (A62)—Bavarian Gentians (A62)—A Rose is not a Cabbage (from *Nettles* (A52))—Odour of Chrysanthemums (from *The Tales of D. H. Lawrence* (A67))—The Prussian Officer (A67)— Fanny and Annie (A67)—Her Turn (from *A Modern Lover* (A71))—Things (A67)—You Touched Me (A67)—The Rocking Horse Winner (A67)—The Christening (A67).

A100   SELECTED LETTERS   1958

first collected edition

THE | SELECTED LETTERS OF | D. H. LAWRENCE | [*short rule*] | *EDITED WITH AN INTRODUCTION BY* | DIANA TRILLING | NEW YORK | FARRAR, STRAUS AND CUDAHY, INC.

Grey cloth boards, stamped in gold on spine: [*thin rule*] | THE | SELECTED | LETTERS | OF | D. H. | LAWRENCE | *TRILLING* | [*thick rule*] [*preceding nine lines on black background forming panel*] | FARRAR | STRAUS AND | CUDAHY The leaves measure $8\frac{1}{4}'' \times 5\frac{1}{2}''$. All edges trimmed.

[i]–[xliv] + [1]–324, as follows: [i] half-title; [ii] list of *Great Letters Series*; [iii] title page as above; [iv] copyright © 1958 by Diana Trilling | The letters in this edition are presented by arrangement with | The Viking Press, publishers of *The Letters of D. H. Lawrence,* | copyright 1932 by the Estate of D. H. Lawrence. Any requests | for reprinting the text of the letters should be addressed to | The Viking Press, New York. |

Library of Congress catalog card number 57–11489 | First Printing, 1958 | Printed in the United States of America | American Book-Stratford Press, Inc., New York; v–vii preface by Diana Trilling; [viii] blank; [ix] table of contents; [x] blank; xi–xxxvii a letter of introduction to Norman Podhonetz from Diana Trilling; [xxxviii] blank; xxxix–xliii list of correspondents; [xliv] blank; [1] fly-title: THE SELECTED LETTERS OF | D. H. Lawrence; [2] blank; 3–311 text; [312] blank; [313] fly-title: INDEX; [314] blank; 315–322 index; [323]–[324] blank.

Published 29 January 1958 at $4.50; number of copies unknown.

A101   D. H. LAWRENCE, 20 POEMS   1959

first collected edition

This is number 45 [*autograph number in black ink*] *of an original* [*in red*] | *edition limited to 65 copies.* [*in red*] | M. A. COTÉ | Hampstead, | 6th May 1959. [*the preceding three lines are autograph in black ink*]

Decorative paper covered slip case, yellow paper label on spine, printed in black: *D. H. Lawrence* | *20 poems* | *illustrated by M. A. Cote* In the slip case are a loose sheet of stiff paper, which serves as the title page as above, and 20 individual blue paper folders each containing a folio sheet with a poem by D. H. Lawrence and an illustration by M. A. Coté.

Published May 1959 at 9 guineas; the edition consisted of 65 copies.

CONTENTS

Future Religion (from *Last Poems* (A62))—Men Like Gods (A62)—Nothing to Save (A62)—After Dark (from *Pansies* (A47))—On the Drum (A47)—Peacock (A47)—Noble (A47)—Man Reaches a Point (A47)—Aware (from *Love Poems* (A3))—The Deepest Sensuality (A62)—The White Horse (A62)—Let Us Be Men (A47)—Change (A62)—Prophet (from *Amores* (A9))—Modern Prayer (from *Nettles* (A52))—Little Fish (A47)—Conscience (A47)—Salt (A62)—Men Are Not Bad (A47)—After All Saints' Day (A62).

A101.5   TUTTE LE POESIE   1959

first collected edition

VOL. I

D. H. LAWRENCE | TUTTE [*in blue*] | LE POESIE [*in blue*] | *Traduzione, introduzione e note* | di | PIERO NARDI | [*publisher's device in blue*] | ARNOLDO MONDADORI | EDITORE | [*the whole enclosed within decorative rules*]

Brown cloth boards, stamped in gold on upper cover: [*design of rose with leaves*] Stamped in gold on spine: II | D. H. LAWRENCE POESIE | [*five-pointed star*] | MONDADORI [*space between lines of lettering covered with decorative designs, the whole enclosed within a double rule forming a border*] The leaves measure $7\frac{1}{2}'' \times 5''$. All edges trimmed; top edges stained pink.

[i]–xl + [1]–1149 + [i]–[iii] and frontispiece, as follows: [i]–[iv] blank; [v] I CLASSICI CONTEMPORANEI STRANIERI; [vi] blank; [vii] TUTTE LE OPERE | DI DAVID HERBERT LAWRENCE | *A CURA DI PIERO NARDI* | [*short decorative rule*] | VOL. II; [viii] blank; [ix] PIANO DELL'OPERA; [x]–[xi] list of works in the edition; [xii] blank; [xiii] title page as above; [xiv] PROPRIETÀ LITTERARIA RESERVATA | © *Arnoldo Mondadori Editore: 1959* | I EDIZIONE: DICEMBRE 1959 | 7108-CCS [*enclosed within a single rule*]; [xv]–xl introduction and note by Piero Nardi; [1] TUTTE LE POESIE | *TOMO I*; [2]–1149 text; [i] blank; [ii] QUESTO VOLUME, COMPOSTO CON CARATTERI BEMBO, E| STATO IMPRESSO SU CARTA TIPO INDIA DELLE CARTIERE | FEDRIGONI NEL MESE DI DICEMBRE DELL'ANNO MCMLIX | NELLE OFFICINE GRAFICHE VERONESI DI | ARNOLDO MONDADORI EDITORE | [*publisher's device in blue*] | STAMPATO IN ITALIA [*short rule*] PRINTED IN ITALY; [iii] blank.

VOL.II

Title page and description as in Vol. I except for two five-pointed stars on the spine.

[i]–[xv] + 1150–[2330] and frontispiece, as follows; [i]–[iv] blank; [v] I CLASSICI CONTEMPORANEI | STRANIERI; [vi] blank; [vii] TUTTE LE OPERE | DI DAVID HERBERT LAWRENCE | *A CURA DI PIERO NARDI* | [*short decorative rule*] | VOL. II; [viii] blank; [ix] PIANO DELL'OPERA; [x]–[xi] list of works in the edition; xii blank; [xiii] title page as in Vol. I; [xiv] verso of title page as in Vol. I; [xv] TUTTE LE POESIE | *TOMO II*; 1150–2037 text; [2038] blank; [2039] APPENDICE PRIMA; [2040] blank; [2041] note; 2042–2075 text; [2076] blank; [2077] APPENDICE SECONDA; [2078] blank; [2079]–2207 text; [2208] blank; [2209] note; [2210] blank; [2211]–2241 text; [2242] blank; [2243] note; [2244] blank; [2245]–2261 text; [2262] blank; [2263] INDICI; [2264] blank; [2265]–2327 text; [2328] blank; [2329] colophon as in Vol. I; [2330] blank.

Published December 1959 at L. 12000; the first printing consisted of 3052 copies.

VOL. I

Collected Poems 1928 (A43)—*Pansies* (A47a)—through "Choice" p. 87.

VOL. II

Pansies (A47a)—*Nettles* (A52)—*Last Poems* (A62)—APPENDIX I: "The American Edition of *New Poems*" (A76) (A11b) —"The Collected Poems of D. H. Lawrence" (A76)—"Notes for *Birds, Beasts and Flowers*" (A76) (A27c)—"The Privately Printed Edition of *Pansies* by D. H. Lawrence" (A76) (A47c)—APPENDIX II: A Still Afternoon (C2)—Discipline (C2)—Rebuked (C4)—Ah! Muriel (C5)—The Schoolmaster: To One of My Boys and Morning (C11)—The Young Soldier with Bloody Spurs (A61)—Song of a Man who is Loved (B40)—Meeting Among the Mountains (B3)—Song-Day in Autumn (A3)—We Have Gone Too Far, Very Much Too Far (A61)—Erinnyes (B4)—Disagreeable Advice (A9)—Restlessness (A9)—Resurrection (C47)—Labour Battalion (B7) —No News (B7)—War Films: Mother's Son in Salonika—Casualty— Message to a Perfidious Soldier—The Jewess and the V. C.—Sighs—The Child and the Soldier—Zeppelin Nights—Daughter of the Great Man— Prisoner at Work in a Turkish Garden—Mourning—The Grey Nurse— Neither Moth Nor Rust (C67)—Mediterranean in January (C139)—Be- yond the Rockies (C139)—The Old Orchard (C153)—Rainbow (C153) —The Noble Englishman—Women Want Fighters for Their Lovers— Ego-Bound Women—There Is No Way Out—The Little Wowser—The Young and Their Moral Guardians—What Does She Want?—Don't Look at Me!—To Clarinda—Demon Justice—The Jeune Fille—Be a Demon!—What Matters—My Naughty Book (A47c)—The Triumph of the Machine (A58).

NOTES: This is volume II of *Tutti Gli Scritti Di D. H. Lawrence*.

A102 THE COLLECTED LETTERS 1962 OF D. H. LAWRENCE

VOL. I

The Collected | Letters of | D. H. Lawrence | *Edited with an Introduction by* | HARRY T. MOORE | VOLUME ONE [*enclosed within a single rule*] | THE VIKING PRESS·NEW YORK

Black cloth boards, stamped in gold on upper cover: D. H. Lawrence [*facsimile signature*]; stamped in gold on spine: 1 | The | Collected |

Letters of | D. H. | Lawrence | EDITED BY | HARRY T. | MOORE [*preceding eight lines enclosed within a single rule*] | VIKING The leaves measure $8\frac{5}{16}''\times5\frac{1}{2}''$. All edges trimmed.

[i]–[lviii] + 1–638, as follows: [i] [*publisher's device*]; [ii] blank; [iii] title page as above; [iv] Copyright © 1962 by Angelo Ravagli and C. Montague Weekley, | Executors of the Estate of Frieda Lawrence Ravagli | [*additional copyright and publication notices*] | ALL RIGHTS RESERVED | Published in 1962 by The Viking Press, Inc. | 625 Madison Avenue, New York 22, N.Y. | Published simultaneously in Canada by | The Macmillan Company of Canada Limited | Library of Congress catalogue card number: 62–9685 | Printed in the U.S.A. by The Murray Printing Company; [v] dedication; [vi] blank; [vii] contents; [viii] blank; ix–xxvii introduction; [xxviii] blank; xxix–lvi list of persons in the Lawrence letters; [lvii] fly-title: THE COLLECTED LETTERS | OF | D. H. LAWRENCE | VOLUME ONE; [lviii] blank; 1–638 text.

VOL. II

The Collected | Letters of | D. H. Lawrence | *Edited with an Introduction by* | HARRY T. MOORE | VOLUME TWO [*enclosed within a single rule*] | THE VIKING PRESS·NEW YORK

Black cloth boards, stamped in gold on upper cover: D. H. Lawrence [*facsimile signature*]; stamped in gold on spine: 2 | The | Collected | Letters of | D. H. | Lawrence | EDITED BY | HARRY T. | MOORE [*preceding eight lines enclosed within a single rule*] | VIKING The leaves measure $8\frac{5}{16}''\times5\frac{1}{2}''$. All edges trimmed.

[i]–[viii] + 639–[1310], as follows: [i] [*publisher's device*]; [ii] blank; [iii] title page as above; [iv] Copyright © 1962 by Angelo Ravagli and C. Montague Weekley, | Executors of the Estate of Frieda Lawrence Ravagli | [*additional copyright and publication notices*] | ALL RIGHTS RESERVED | Published in 1962 by The Viking Press, Inc. | 625 Madison Avenue, New York 22, N.Y. | Published simultaneously in Canada by | The Macmillan Company of Canada Limited | Library of Congress catalogue card number: 62–9685 | Printed in the U.S.A. by The Murray Printing Company; [v] contents; [vi] blank; [vii] fly-title: THE COLLECTED LETTERS | OF | D. H. LAWRENCE | VOLUME TWO; [viii] blank; 639–1246 text; 1247–1268 Appendix, Introduction to the 1932 edition of Lawrence's *Letters* (A61) by Aldous Huxley; 1269–1272 index to recipients of letters; 1273–1307 general index; [1308]–[1310] blank.

Published 19 March 1962 at $17.50; 4975 copies were printed.

REVIEWS: The *Collected Letters* was reviewed in the *Chicago Sunday Tribune* for 8 April 1962 by Warren Beck; in the *Christian Science Monitor* for 9 March by Rod Nordell; in the *Manchester Guardian* for 23 March by Raymond Williams; by Frank Kermode in the *New Statesman* for 23 March; in *New York Herald Tribune Books* by A. L. Prowse for 1 July; in the *New York Times Book Review* by Mark Schorer, 18 March; by Curt Gentry in the *San Francisco Chronicle*, 21 March; by Richard Aldington in the *Saturday Reviews* for 17 March; in the *Spectator* for 23 March by Tony Tanner; and in the *Times Literary Supplement* for 27 April 1962.

A103　　　　　SELECTED TALES　　　　1963

first collected edition

D. H. LAWRENCE | *Selected Tales* | INTRODUCED BY | IAN SERRAILLIER | [*publisher's device*] | HEINEMANN | LONDON MELBOURNE TORONTO

Brown and gray cloth boards with portrait of Lawrence in orange on upper cover, printed in white on upper cover: D. H. LAWRENCE | [*short rule*] | Selected Tales | Edited by Ian Serraillier Printed in white on spine: Selected | Tales | [*single rule*] | D. H. LAWRENCE [*reading from top to bottom*] | [*publisher's device*] The leaves measure $7\frac{1}{4}'' \times 4\frac{3}{4}''$. All edges trimmed.

[i]–[iv] + [i]–[xii] + 1–[240], as follows: [i]–[iv] blank; [i] half-title; [ii] list of Heinemann Educational Books; [iii] title page as above; [iv] Heinemann Educational Books Ltd | LONDON MELBOURNE TORONTO | SINGAPORE AUCKLAND | IBADAN | Introduction © Ian Serraillier 1963 | This selection first published 1963 | Published by | Heinemann Educational Books Ltd | 15–16 Queen Street, Mayfair, London W 1 | Printed in Great Britain by | Bookprint Limited, Kingswood, Surrey; [v] table of contents; [vi] acknowledgements; [vii]–xi introduction; [xii] blank; 1–236 text; [237]–240 blank. Note: The book consists of eight signed gatherings of 32 pages or 16 leaves each, but the first leaf of the first gathering forms the front pasted-down end-paper and is conjugate with 15–16; the final two leaves of the last gathering, signed H, [237]–[240], are not present, but have in some curious fashion been secured under the pasted-down end-paper which is not included in the gathering or counted in the pagination.

Published June 1963 at 7*s.* 6*d.*; number of copies unknown.

The Rocking-Horse Winner (A63)—Odour of Chrysanthemums (A6)—
Strike-Pay (A71)—The Christening (A6)—Tickets, Please (A23)—
Monkey Nuts (A23)—Fanny and Annie (A23)—You Touched Me
(A23)—The Man Who Loved Islands (A41b)—Things (A63)—Daughters of the Vicar (A6).

A104   THE COMPLETE POEMS OF   1964
D. H. LAWRENCE

a. *first collected edition*

VOL. I

THE COMPLETE POEMS OF | D. H. LAWRENCE | *Collected
and Edited with an | Introduction and Notes by* | Vivian de Sola Pinto | and
| Warren Roberts | VOLUME ONE | [*publisher's device*] | HEINEMANN: LONDON

Dark blue cloth boards, blind stamped on lower cover: [*publisher's device*];
stamped in gold on spine: The | Complete | Poems of | D. H. | LAWRENCE
| [*five-pointed star*] [*the whole enclosed within a double rule border, the inner
rule being decorative, both rules broken at the word Lawrence*] | HEINEMANN The
leaves measure 8$\frac{7}{16}$″ × 5$\frac{3}{8}$″. All edges trimmed; top edges stained purple.

[i]–[viii] + 1–[568], and frontispiece, as follows: [i] half-title; [ii] blank;
frontispiece, portrait of D. H. Lawrence at Del Monte Ranch by Kai
Gótzsche; [iii] title page as above; [iv] William Heinemann Ltd |
LONDON MELBOURNE TORONTO | CAPE TOWN AUCKLAND | First published,
1964 | Copyright © 1964 by Angelo Ravagli and C. M. Weekley, |
Executors of the Estate of Frieda Lawrence Ravagli. | Introduction and
Notes Copyright © by | William Heinemann Ltd. | *All rights reserved*
| All verse and poems by D. H. Lawrence in these volumes are | published
by arrangement with the Estate of D. H. Lawrence | Printed in Great
Britain | by Bookprint Limited | Kingswood, Surrey; [v]–[vi] table
of contents; [vii] acknowledgements; [viii] blank; 1–21 introduction by
Vivian de Sola Pinto; [22] blank; 23–26 a note on the text; 27–29
Lawrence's preface to the 1928 *Collected Poems*; [30] blank; [31] fly-title:
RHYMING POEMS; [32] blank; 33–180 text; 181–186 Lawrence's introduction to the American edition of *New Poems*; [187] fly-title: UNRHYMING
POEMS; [188] blank; [189] fly-title: LOOK! WE HAVE COME THROUGH!;
[190] blank; 191 Lawrence's foreword to the first edition of *Look! We
Have Come Through!*; [192] blank; 193–274 text; [275] fly-title: BIRDS,

BEASTS AND FLOWERS; [276] blank; 277–414 text; [415] fly-title: PANSIES; [416] blank; 417–421 Lawrence's introduction to *Pansies*, signed: D. H. L. | BANDOL, | January 1929; [422] blank; 423–424 Lawrence's foreword to *Pansies*, signed: D. H. LAWRENCE | BANDOL, | March 1929; 425–565 text; [566]–[568] blank.

VOL. II

THE COMPLETE POEMS OF | D. H. LAWRENCE | *Collected and Edited with an* | *Introduction and Notes by* | Vivian de Sola Pinto | and | Warren Roberts | VOLUME TWO | [*publisher's device*] | HEINE-MANN: LONDON

Dark blue cloth boards, identical with Volume I except for two five-pointed stars on spine.

[i]–[viii] + 569–1072, and frontispiece, as follows: [i] half-title; [ii] blank; frontispiece, facsimile reproduction of the manuscript of "Bavarian Gentians"; [iii] title page as above; [iv] identical with Vol. I; [v]–[vi] table of contents; [vii] fly-title: NETTLES; [viii] blank; 569–587 text; [588] blank; [589] fly-title: INTRODUCTION TO | *Last Poems* and *More Pansies* | By Richard Aldington | [*square bracket*] 1932 [*square bracket*]; [590] blank; 591–598 text; [599] fly-title: MORE PANSIES; [600] blank; 601–684 text; [685] fly-title: LAST POEMS; [686] blank; 687–728 text; [729] fly-title: UNCOLLECTED POEMS; [730] blank; 731–784 text; [785] fly-title: POEMS FROM *THE PLUMED* | *SERPENT*; 786–813 text; 814–820 text for additional uncollected poems; [821] fly-title: ADDITIONAL PANSIES; [822] blank; 823–846 text; [847] fly-title: APPENDIX I | Foreword to *Collected Poems*; [848] blank; 849–852 text, signed: *Scandicci.* 12 May 1928.; [853] fly-title: APPENDIX II | JUVENILIA: 1904–1912; 854–888 text; [889] fly-title: APPENDIX III | VARIANTS AND EARLY DRAFTS; [890] blank; 891–961 text; [962] blank; [963] fly-title: APPENDIX IV | NOTES AND GLOSSARY; [964] blank; 965–1040 text; 1041–1061 index of first lines; 1062–1072 index of titles.

Published 19 October £6 6s.; the first printing consisted of 2500 copies.

CONTENTS

VOL. I

RHYMING POEMS (A43)

To this section have been added the following poems which Lawrence did not include in *Collected Poems* (A43): Song-Day in Autumn (A3)—Disagreeable Advice (A9)—Restlessness (A9).

To this section have been added the following prose pieces: Poetry of the Present (A11b)—Foreword (A10)—and the poem: Meeting Among the Mountains (A10) which were not included in *Collected Poems*.

Birds, Beasts and Flowers (A27)

To this section have been added the short prose prefaces to the various sections which Lawrence included in the Cresset Press edition of *Birds, Beasts and Flowers* (A27c).

Pansies (A47c)

To this section has been added the Foreword to the trade edition of *Pansies* (A47a).

VOL. II

Nettles (A52)

To this section have been added two poems from a manuscript in the Library of Columbia University: Daddy-Do-Nothing (E83)—Question (E329).

MORE PANSIES (A62)

To this section have been added the following poems from a manuscript (E192) in the Library of the University of Texas: Emasculation—Lucky Little Britisher—The Working Man—The Gods.

Last Poems (A62)

The five variant drafts of poems in the appendix of *Last Poems* (A62) are reprinted in Appendix III of this volume.

Uncollected poems

Previously published poems except for those indicated as being from a Ms. source:
Rebuked (C4)—The Wind, the Rascal (A70)—The Young Soldier With Bloody Spurs (A61)—Ah, Muriel! (C5)—We Have Gone Too Far (A61)—Resurrection of the Flesh (C229)—Erinnyes (B4)—Eloi, Eloi, Lama Sabachthani? (C37)—Resurrection (C47)—Labour Battalion (B7)—No News (B7)—Bits: The Last Minute (E49)—Vicar's Son (E49)—Drill in the Heat (E49)—Mother's Son in Salonika (C67)—Casualty (C67)—Maiden's Prayer (E49)—Man Hauling a Wagon (E49)—Sighs (C67)—Daughter of the Great Man (C67)—The Child and the Soldier (C67)—Pietà (E49)—The Grey Nurse (C67)—Litany

of Grey Nurses (E49)—Message to a Perfidious Soldier (C67)—Dust in the East (E49)—The Girl in Cairo (E49)—The Jewess and the V. C. (C67)—Zeppelin Nights (C67)—Munitions (E49)—Land-Worker (E49)—Mourning (C67)—Mesopotamia (E49)—Tales (E49)—Foreign Sunset (E49)—Prisoner at Work in a Turkish Garden (C67)—Swing Song of a Girl and a Soldier (E49)—Prisoners at Work in the Rain (E49)—The Well in Africa (E49)—Neither Moth Nor Rust (C67); Apostrophe to a Buddist Monk (B39)—Him With His Tail in His Mouth (A32)—[Flat-Foot's Song] (A32)—Traitors (A80)—Reach Over (A80) —Softly, Then, Softly (A80)—Change of Life (A80)—What Do I Care? (A80)—Are You Pining? (A80)—O! Americans (A80)—Eagle in New Mexico (A80)—Fire (A80).

Poems from The Plumed Serpent (A33): [The Coming of Quetzalcoatl]— [Lord of the Morning Star]—[Someone Will Enter Between the Gates]—[My Name is Jesus]—Quetzalcoatl Looks Down on Mexico— What Quetzalcoatl Saw in Mexico—[Song to the Tune of *La Cucaracha*] —Jesus' Farewell—[The Song of Don Ramon]—[Son of the Morning Star]—[The Living Quetzalcoatl]—Welcome to Quetzalcoatl—[The Mid-Day Verse]—[The Dawn Verse]—[The Sunset Verse]—[Metal for Resistance]—[First Song of Huitzilopochtli]—[Second Song of Huitzilo-pochtli]—[Third Song of Huitzilopochtli]—The Song of the Grey Dog—[The Lords of Life Are the Masters of Death]—[Huitzilopochtli Gives the Black Blade of Death]—Huitzilopochtli's Watch—[Song of the Dead]—[Like the Green Candles of Malintzi]—[My Way is Not Thy Way].

Additional previously published poems: Mediterranean in January (C139)— Beyond the Rockies (C139)—The Old Orchard (C153)—Rainbow (C153).

Additional Pansies: Hymn to Nothingness (E164.9)—August Holidays (E29)—Bathing Resort (E40)—The Young Are Not Mean in Material Things (E302d)—The Young Want to Be Just (E302d)—The Gentle-man (E302d)—Roses (E302d)—The Young Are Not Greedy (E302d)— Middle-Class Children (E302d)—Know Thyself (E302d)—Night (E302d)—Love (E302d)—So There! (E302d)—Morality (E302d)— Immorality (E302d)—Censors (E302d)—Life and the Human Con-sciousness (E302d)—The Latent Desire (E302d)—For All That (E302d) —Love as an Escape (E302d)—What's To Be Done? (E302d)—Rallying-Point (E302d)—Today (E302d)—The Elements (E302d)—Gods (E302d)—Little-Boy Brilliant (E302d)—I Heard Her Say (E302d)— What's Wrong (E302d)—Money (E302d)—Sex Won't Work (E302d)

—Deeper Than Love (E302d)—[Bawdy Can Be Sane] (E302d)—[There Was a Gay Bird Named Christine] (E394.5)—A la Manière de D. H. Lawrence (El).

Appendix I: Foreword to *Collected Poems* (A76).

Appendix II: *Juvenilia*: Campions (C239)—Guelder Roses (C239)—The Fall of Day (E317)—Married in June (C239)—The Worm Turns (E317)—On the Road (E317)—The Death of the Baron (C239)—Love Comes Late (E317)—Song (E317)—A Failure (E317)—A Decision (E317)—A Train at Night (E317)—Baby Songs: Ten Months Old (C239)—Eve (E317)—After School (C239)—A Snowy Day at School (E317)—Reading in the Evening (E317)—A Man at Play on the River (E317)—Amour (E317)—Bereavement (E317)—Loss (E317)—Grief (E317)—A Love-Passage (E320.4)—[Ah, With His Blessing Bright on Thy Mouth and Thy Brow] (E320.4)—Aloof in Gaiety (E320.4)—And Jude the Obscure and His Beloved (E320.4)—A Drama (E320.4)—Separated (E320.4)—Assuming the Burden (E319.2)—The Chief Mystery (E319.2)—Erotic (E320.4)—Moon New-Risen (E320.4)—Red (E320.4)—She Was a Good Little Wife (E319.2)—Pear-Blossom (E319.2)—At the Cearne (E319.2)—A Kiss (E320.6)—[Other Women Have Reared in Me] (E319.2).

Appendix III: *Variants and Early Drafts*: The Wild Common (A9)—Renaissance (C239)—Virgin Youth (A9)—The Schoolmaster (A) (C11, C12, C13, C15)—The Schoolmaster (B) (A3)—Dreams Old and Nascent (C2)—Dreams Old and Nascent (A9)—Violets for the Dead (E317)—Violets (A3)—Lightning (A3)—Baby-Movements (C2)—A Baby Running Barefoot (A9)—Corot (B34)—Michael-Angelo (A3)—Night Songs (C4)—Whether or Not (A3)—Discipline (C2)—Last Words to Muriel (E317)—Last Words to Miriam (A9)—Liaison (A9)—Dissolute (A9)—Honeymoon (C32)—A Spiritual Woman (A9)—Another Ophelia (E320.4)—Snap-Dragon (E320.4)—To Lettice, My Sister (B34)—Grief (C35)—Twilight (C30)—The Piano (E317)—Birthday (C29)—Early Spring (C32)—All of Roses (C29)—The Mowers (C27)—Fireflies in the Corn (C29)—Song of a Man Who Is Loved (B40)—Religion (E302d)—[I Know a Noble Englishman] (E302d)—Work (E302d)—In Nottingham (E302d)—Morality (E302d)—Deeper Than Love (E302e)—What's Sane and What Isn't—(E302e)—The Triumph of the Machine (C200)—Glory of Darkness (A62)—Bavarian Gentians (A62)—Ship of Death (A62)—The Ship of Death (A62)—Song of Death (A62).

b. *first collected edition, second printing*

VOL. I

THE COMPLETE POEMS OF | D. H. LAWRENCE | *Collected and Edited with an* | *Introduction and Notes by* | Vivian de Sola Pinto | and | Warren Roberts | VOLUME ONE | [*publisher's device*] | HEINE-MANN: LONDON

Identical with (a) except for the leaves which measure $8\frac{1}{2}'' \times 5\frac{1}{2}''$ and the top edges which are stained red. Page [ii] contains a list of Lawrence books published by Heinemann, and page [iv] has an additional line after "First published, 1964," reading: Reprinted with minor revisions, 1967 | The printing notice at the bottom of page [iv] now reads: Printed and Bound in Great Britain by | Bookprint Limited, London and Crawley A prefatory note has been added on page 26.

VOL. II

THE COMPLETE POEMS OF | D. H. LAWRENCE | *Collected and Edited with an* | *Introduction and Notes by* | Vivian de Sola Pinto | and | Warren Roberts | VOLUME TWO | [*publisher's device*] | HEINE-MANN: LONDON

The title page and physical description are identical with (a) except for the leaves which measure $8\frac{1}{2}'' \times 5\frac{1}{2}''$ and the top edges which are stained red; the additional line appears on page [iv] as in Vol. I.

[i]–[viii] + 569–[1088], as follows: [i]–[viii] and 569–853 pagination is identical with (a); 854–894 text; [895] fly-title: APPENDIX III | VARIANTS AND EARLY DRAFTS; [896] blank; 897–968 text; [969] fly-title: APPENDIX IV | NOTES AND GLOSSARY; [970] blank; 971–1051 text; 1052–1073 index of first lines; 1074–1084 index of titles; [1085]–[1088] blank.

Published in May 1967 at £6 6s.; 1500 copies were printed.

CONTENTS

Appendix II:*Juvenilia*: The following poems have been added to Appendix II, pp. 870–876; they are from the Louie Burrows papers in the Library of the University of Nottingham: [Two Fragments on Sleep] (E229.5)—[To Toss the Troubled Night Long] (E319.3)—Love Message (E319.3)—The Witch I and II (E319.3)—Elixir (E319.3)—Good Night (E319.3)—Sympathy (E319.3)—[The Train] (E404.5)—At Midnight (E319.5)—Beloved (E319.5)—The Prophet in the Rose Garden (E319.5) —Moth and Rust (E319.5)—Irreverent Thoughts (E319.5)— Two-Fold (E319.5).

Appendix III: *Variants and Early Drafts*: Forty-one lines were added to the poem, "Deeper Than Love," p. 958; these lines are from a misplaced page in (E302b).

c. *first collected edition, second American printing*

THE COMPLETE POEMS OF | D. H. LAWRENCE | *Collected and Edited with an* | *Introduction and Notes by* | Vivian de Sola Pinto | and Warren Roberts | NEW YORK THE VIKING PRESS

Black cloth boards, stamped in silver and red-gold on spine, reading from top to bottom: Edited by Pinto and Roberts VIKING | THE COMPLETE POEMS OF | D. H. LAWRENCE [*the last line in red-gold*] The leaves measure $7\frac{3}{4}'' \times 5\frac{1}{4}''$. All edges trimmed; top edges stained orange.

[i]–[viii] + 1–[1080], as follows: [i] half-title; [ii] list of Lawrence books published by Viking; [iii] title page as above; [iv] Copyright © 1964, 1971 by Angelo Ravagli and C. M. Weekley, Executors | of The Estate of Frieda Lawrence Ravagli | Introduction and notes Copyright © 1964 by William Heinemann Ltd. | All rights reserved | Viking Compass Edition | Issued with corrections in 1971 by The Viking Press, Inc. | 625 Madison Avenue, New York, N.Y. 10022 | Distributed in Canada by | The Macmillan Company of Canada Limited | SBN 670–23472–9 (hardbound) | 670–00281–x (paperbound) | Library of Congress catalog card number: 64–11226 | Printed in U.S.A. | [*statement referring to previous copyrights and permission reservations*]; [v]–[vi] table of contents; [vii] acknowledgements; [viii] blank; 1–846 pagination is identical with (b), a prefatory note to the "third edition" has been printed on page 26 to replace the prefatory note to the "second edition" on page 26 of (b); [847] fly-title: APPENDIX | Appendix I: Foreword to *Collected Poems* | Appendix II: Juvenilia: 1904–1912 | Appendix III: Variants and Early Drafts | Appendix IV: Notes; [848] blank; 849–1046 text; 1047–1068 index of first lines; 1069–1079 index of titles; [1080] blank.

Published 30 November 1971; 1987 copies were issued in the black cloth binding at $12.50; 10,389 copies were issued in the paperback format at $4.50.

CONTENTS

A final stanza has been added to "Lightning" in Appendix III, and several final stanzas to "The Young Want to Be Just" in Uncollected Poems.

d. *first collected edition, third English printing*

VOL. I

THE COMPLETE POEMS OF | D. H. LAWRENCE | *Collected and Edited with an* | *Introduction and Notes by* | Vivian de Sola Pinto | and | Warren Roberts | VOLUME ONE | [*publisher's device*] | HEINE-MANN: LONDON

Brown cloth boards, stamped in gold on spine: identical with (b). The leaves measure $8\frac{1}{2}'' \times 5\frac{3}{8}''$. All edges trimmed; top edges stained red.

[i]–[viii] + 1–[568] and frontispiece, as follows: [i] half-title; [ii] list of Lawrence books published by Heinemann; [iii] title page as above; [iv] William Heinemann Ltd | 15 Queen Street, Mayfair, London W1X 8BE | LONDON MELBOURNE TORONTO | JOHANNESBURG AUCKLAND | First published 1964 | Reprinted with minor revisions 1967 | Reprinted with further minor revisions 1972 | Copyright © 1964, 1967, 1970, 1971 and 1972 by Angelo Ravagli, | C. M. Weekley and Laurence Pollinger Ltd, | Executors of the Estate of Frieda Lawrence Ravagli | Introduction and notes copyright © 1964 by | William Heinemann ltd | *All rights reserved* | 434 59250 1 | All verse and poems by D. H. Lawrence in these volumes are published | by arrangement with the Estate of D. H. Lawrence | Printed Offset Litho and bound in Great Britain | by Cox & Wyman Ltd, | London, Fakenham and Reading; [v]–[viii] and 1–21 pagination identical with (b); 22–25 a note on the text and the prefatory note to the "second edition"; 26 prefatory note to the "third edition"; 27–[568] pagination identical with (b).

VOL. II

THE COMPLETE POEMS OF | D. H. LAWRENCE | *Collected and Edited with an* | *Introduction and Notes by* | Vivian de Sola Pinto | and | Warren Roberts | VOLUME TWO | [*publisher's device*] | HEINE-MANN: LONDON

Brown cloth boards, identical with Vol. I except for the two five-pointed stars on spine.

[i]–[viii] and frontispiece + 569–[1104], as follows: [i]–[viii] and 569–853 pagination identical with (b); [854] blank; 855–903 text; [904] blank; [905] fly-title: APPENDIX III | VARIANTS AND EARLY DRAFTS; [906] blank; 907–980 text; [981] fly-title: APPENDIX IV NOTES AND GLOSSARY; 982–1065 text; [1066] blank; [1067] fly-title: INDEXES; [1068] blank;

1069–1090 index of first lines; 1091–1102 index of titles; [1103]–[1104] blank.

Published in November 1972 at £8.50; 4000 copies were printed.

CONTENTS

Appendix II: *Juvenilia*: For this printing the following poems have been added to Appendix II; they are from a manuscript notebook in the possession of Mr W. H. Clarke, the son of Lawrence's sister Ada, reprinted here from *Renaissance and Modern Studies*, 14 (1970) (C259): An Epistle from Thelma—An Epistle from Arthur—Epilogue from Thelma—School I. Morning—The Complaint of the Soul of a Worker— Late at Night Along the Home Road—Unwitting—Nocturne— Reproach—Transformations: Morning.
Appendix III: *Variants and Early Drafts*: The following two poems have been added to Appendix III from the same source: My Love, My Mother—A Beloved.

REVIEWS: *Complete Poems* was reviewed in *Book Week* by Louis Simpson, 13 December 1964; by Kenneth Rexroth in the *Nation* for 23 November; in the *New Statesman* for 30 October by D. J. Enright; in the *New York Review of Books* for 19 November by Christopher Ricks; in the *New York Times Book Review* by Horace Gregory, 15 November; in the *New Yorker* for 13 March 1965; in *Poetry* for June; and in the *Times Literary Supplement* for 26 August 1965.

A105   THE COMPLETE PLAYS   1965
OF D. H. LAWRENCE

first collected edition

The Complete Plays | *of* | D. H. LAWRENCE | [*publisher's device*] | HEINEMANN: LONDON

Gray-tan cloth boards, blind stamped on lower cover: [*publisher's device*]; stamped in gold on spine: *The* | *Complete* | *Plays of* | *D. H.* | *Lawrence* | HEINEMANN The leaves measure $8\frac{1}{2}'' \times 5\frac{1}{2}''$. All edges trimmed; top edges stained blue.

[1]–[560], as follows: [1] half-title; [2] list of D. H. Lawrence books published by Heinemann; [3] title page as above; [4] William Heinemann Ltd | LONDON MELBOURNE TORONTO | CAPE TOWN AUCKLAND | First published in this collected edition 1965 | The collection © 1965 by the Estate of the late | Mrs Frieda Lawrence | [*copyright*

notices for the plays in the volume] | All inquiries regarding performance rights of these plays should be | directed to Margery Vosper Ltd., 54A Shaftesbury Avenue, London, W. I | Printed in Great Britain | by Bookprint Limited | Kingswood, Surrey; [5] table of contents; [6] a note on the text; [7] fly-title: The Widowing of Mrs Holroyd | A PLAY IN THREE ACTS | (1914); [8] blank; [9] list of characters; [10] blank; [11]–61 text; [62] blank; [63] fly-title: David | A PLAY IN SIXTEEN SCENES | (1926); [64] blank; [65] list of characters; [66] list of scenes; [67]–154 text; [155] fly-title: The Married Man | A PLAY IN FOUR ACTS | (1912–revised 1926); [156] blank; [157] list of characters; [158] blank; [159]–201 text; [202] blank; [203] fly-title: The Daughter-in-Law | A PLAY IN FOUR ACTS | (1912); [204] blank; [205] list of characters; [206] blank; [207]–267 text; [268] blank; [269] fly-title: The Fight for Barbara | A COMEDY IN FOUR ACTS | (1912); [270] blank; [271] list of characters; [272] blank; [273]–319 text; [320] blank; [321] fly-title: Touch and Go | A PLAY IN THREE ACTS | (1920); [322] blank; [323] list of characters; [324] blank; [325]–386 text; [387] fly-title: The Merry-go-Round | A PLAY IN FIVE ACTS | (1912); [388] blank; [389] lists of characters and acts; [390] blank; [391]–467 text; [468] blank; [469] fly-title: A Collier's Friday Night | A PLAY IN THREE ACTS | (About 1909–first published 1934); [470] blank; [471] list of characters; [472] blank; [473]–530 text; [531] fly-title: Altitude: a fragment | (1924); [532] blank; [533] list of characters and scenes; [534] blank; 535–548 text; [549] fly-title: Noah's Flood: a fragment; [550] blank; [551] list of characters; [552] blank; [553]–558 text; [559]–[560] blank.

Published 6 December 1965 at 63*s*; the first printing consisted of 3000 copies.

CONTENTS

The Widowing of Mrs. Holroyd (A5)—David (A34)—The Married Man (C226)—The Daughter-in-Law (previously unpublished)—The Fight for Barbara (C213)—Touch and Go (A14)—The Merry-go-Round (C227)—A Collier's Friday Night (A6)—Altitude (C222)—Noah's Flood (A76).

NOTES: "The Daughter-in-Law" was produced by the Traverse Theatre Club, James Court, Lawnmarket, Edinburgh in January 1967; this performance was billed as the "World Premiere"; the play was also produced at the McCarter Theatre at Princeton in March 1974. The manuscript of "The Daughter-in-Law" was the source for the play which

Walter Greenwood adapted as "My Son's My Son" for the production at the Playhouse Theatre in London in 1936. See (A65). "The Fight for Barbara" was produced by The Mermaid Theatre Trust, Ltd. at The Mermaid Theatre, Puddle Dock, Blackfriars on 9 August 1967. The program reproduces a number of photographs of Lawrence, Frieda and his family as well as reproductions in black and white of several paintings by Lawrence.

"The Merry-Go-Round" was produced by the English Stage Company at The Royal Court Theatre on 7 November 1973. The program for "The Merry-Go-Round" makes note of the production as a trilogy in 1968 of "A Collier's Friday Night," "The Daughter-in-Law" and the "Widowing of Mrs Holroyd." See (A65).

In January 1970 Heinemann reprinted an impression of 1250 copies of *The Complete Plays of D. H. Lawrence.*

REVIEWS: The *Complete Plays* was reviewed in the *Times Literary Supplement* for 1 April 1966; in the *New York Times Book Review* for 10 April, by Anais Nin; by V. S. Pritchett in the *New Statesman* for 1 July; and in the *Nation* by D. J. Gordon, 6 June.

A106   D. H. LAWRENCE POEMS   1967
FOR YOUNG PEOPLE

first collected edition

D. H. LAWRENCE | Poems selected for young people | by WILLIAM COLE | [*drawing of a woman's face and a butterfly*] THE VIKING PRESS | *New York*

Blue cloth boards; stamped in gold on spine: D. H. LAWRENCE [*reading from top to bottom*] | Cole | Viking The leaves measure $8\frac{5}{16}'' \times 5\frac{1}{8}''$. All edges trimmed; top edges stained blue.

[1]–120, including fifteen full-page illustrations counted in the pagination, as follows: [1] half-title; [2] *Drawings by Ellen Raskin* [3] title page as above; [4] [*copyright notices on behalf of the Lawrence estate*] | Introduction and compilation Copyright © 1967 by William Cole | All rights reserved | First published in 1967 by The Viking Press, Inc. | 625 Madison Avenue, New York, N.Y. 10022 | Published simultaneously in Canada by | The Macmillan Company of Canada Limited | Library of Congress catalog card number: AC 67–10647 | 821 1. Lawrence, D. H. | Printed in U.S.A.; [5]–[7] table of contents; [8] blank; 9–14 introduction; [15] fly-title: *Animals* | [*drawing of birds*]; [16] blank; 17–[51] text; [52]

blank; [53] fly-title: *Man, Woman, Child* | [*drawing of woman at piano*]; [54] blank; 55–[67] text; [68] blank; [69] fly-title: *Celebrations and Condemnations* | [*at left drawing of a flower*]; [70] blank; 77–101 text; [102] blank; [103] fly-title: *Love* | [*drawing of a flower*]; [104] blank; 105–[117] text; [118] blank; 119–120 index of first lines.

Published 24 April 1967 at $3.95; 3884 copies were printed in the trade edition and 6209 in the Viking Library Edition.

CONTENTS

Animals

Humming-bird (A27)—Snake (A27)—The Elephant is Slow to Mate (A47)—Man and Bat (A27)—A Living (A47)—The Mosquito (A27)—Self-pity (A47)—Mountain Lion (A27)—Butterfly (A62)—Tortoise Family Connections (A19)—Kangaroo (A27)—The Blue Jay (A27).

Man, Woman, Child

Piano (A11)—Peach (A27)—Discord in Childhood (A9)—End of Another Home Holiday (A3)—The Best of School (A3)—The Collier's Wife (A3).

Celebrations and Condemnations

Conundrums (A47)—Thought (A62)—River Roses (A10)—How Beastly the Bourgeois Is (A47)—Reading in the Evening (A104)—Bare Fig-trees (A27)—The Great Newspaper Editor to His Subordinate (A52)—Elemental (A47)—At the Window (A9)—A Rose is Not a Cabbage (A52)—Things Made by Iron (A47)—All-knowing (A62)—Andraitx-Pomegranate Flowers (A62)—The Ignoble Procession (A47)—Last Hours (A12)—The Oxford Voice (A47)—When I Went to the Film (A47)—After the Opera (A12)—Sick (A47)—Bavarian Gentians (A62).

Love

Search for Love (A62)—Flapper (A11)—Green (A10)—Fidelity (A47)—Roses on the Breakfast Table (A10)—Intimates (A62)—Bei Hennef (A3)—In a Boat (A9)—Spring Morning.

A107   PHOENIX II   1968

first collected edition

PHOENIX II | Uncollected, Unpublished and Other Prose Works | by D. H. Lawrence | COLLECTED AND EDITED WITH AN |

INTRODUCTION AND NOTES BY | WARREN ROBERTS | AND | HARRY T. MOORE | [*publisher's device*] | HEINEMANN: LONDON

Red cloth boards, stamped in silver on upper cover: [*Lawrence phoenix*]; stamped in silver on spine: PHOENIX | II | [*short double rule*] | D. H. LAWRENCE | [*Lawrence phoenix*] | HEINEMANN The leaves $8\frac{1}{2}'' \times 5\frac{1}{2}''$. All edges trimmed.

[i]–[xvi] + [1]–640, as follows: [i] [*Lawrence phoenix*]; [ii] list of works in Phoenix edition of D. H. Lawrence; [iii] title page as above; [iv] William Heinemann Ltd | LONDON MELBOURNE TORONTO | CAPE TOWN AUCKLAND | First published 1968 | Copyright © 1968 by The Estate of Frieda Lawrence Ravagli | All rights reserved | Printed in Great Britain by | Western Printing Services Ltd, Bristol; [v]–vii table of contents; [viii] blank; [ix]–xv introduction by Warren Roberts and Harry T. Moore; [xvi] blank; [1] fly-title: Stories and Sketches | [*list of titles*]; [2] blank; [3]–191 text; [192] blank; [193] fly-title: Translation | [*title of piece*]; [194] blank; [195]–213 text; [214] blank; [215] fly-title: Essays | [*list of titles*]; [216] blank; [217]–266 text; [267] fly-title: Reviews and Introductions | [*list of titles*]; [268] blank; 269–296 text; [297] fly-title: Miscellaneous Pieces | [*list of titles*]; [298] blank; [299]–361 text; [362] blank; [363] fly-title: *Reflections on the Death of* | *a Porcupine* | [*list of titles*]; [364]–484 text; [485] fly-title: A Propos of | *Lady Chatterley's* | *Lover*; [486] blank; [487]–515 text; [516] blank; [517] fly-title: *Assorted Articles* | [*list of titles*]; [518] blank; [519]–629 text; [630]–635 notes; 636–640 index.

Published 15 January 1968 at 70s.; the first printing consisted of 5000 copies.

CONTENTS

I. Stories and Sketches

A Prelude (C1, A85)—A Fly in the Ointment (C22, B34 as "The Fly in the Ointment")—Lessford's Rabbits (E196.4)—A Lesson on a Tortoise (E196.5)—A Chapel Among the Mountains (A56a)—A Hay Hut Among the Mountains (A56a)—Once (A56b)—The Thimble (C44)—The Mortal Coil (C49)—Delilah and Mr. Bircumshaw (C225)—Prologue to *Women in Love* (C246)—Mr. Noon (A71).

II. Translation

The Gentleman from San Francisco by Ivan Bunin (B9, C88).

III. Essays
Rachel Annand Taylor (B34)—Art and the Individual (B34)—The Two Principles (C65, A25b)—Certain Americans and an Englishman (C100) —[Germans and English] (previously unpublished in English; see (C165.5) and (C217))—On Coming Home (C240, E290)—[Return to Bestwood] (E31).

IV. Reviews and Introductions
A Review of *The Oxford Book of German Verse*, edited by H. C. Fiedler (C8.5)—A Review of *The Minnesingers*, by Jethro Bithell (C8.5)—A Review of *The Book of Revelation*, by Dr. John Oman (C118)—Foreword to *Women in Love* (A74)—Note on Giovanni Verga (A30)—Introduction to *Mastro-don Gesualdo*, by Giovanni Verga (A28b)—Preface to *Touch and Go* (A14)—Preface to *Black Swans*, by M. L. Skinner (E49.5).

V. Miscellaneous Pieces
A Britisher Has a Word with an Editor (C115)—Autobiographical Sketch (B60, Vol. III)—Introduction to *Memoirs of the Foreign Legion* (A72).

VI. Reflections on the Death of a Porcupine
(from the separately published volume A32).

VII. A Propos of Lady Chatterley's Lover
(from the separately published volume A48).

VIII. Assorted Articles
(from the separately published volume A53).

REVIEWS: *Phoenix II* was reviewed in the *New Republic* for 23 March 1968 by Richard Gilman; in the *New Statesman* by Richard Hoggart for 14 June; in the *New York Review of Books* for 1 August by W. H. Gass; and in the *Times Literary Supplement* for 7 March.

A108 LAWRENCE IN LOVE 1968

first edition

Lawrence | in Love | [*decorative rule*] | Letters to | Louie Burrows | [*printer's ornament*] | Edited with introduction | and notes by | James T. Boulton | [*short double rule*] | *NOTTINGHAM* | University of Nottingham | 1968

Dark red cloth boards, stamped in gold on lower cover: 900572 00 0; stamped in gold on spine, reading from top to bottom: Lawrence in Love [*printer's ornament*] James T. Boulton | University | of | Nottingham [*the preceding three lines read from left to right*] The leaves measure $8\frac{3}{4}'' \times 5\frac{5}{8}''$. All edges trimmed.

[i]–xxviii + 1–[184] and frontispiece, as follows: [i] half-title; [ii] blank; frontispiece, reproduction of photograph of Louie Burrows; [iii] title page as above ; [iv] Lawrence's letters Copyright © 1968 | by Angelo Ravagli and C. M. Weekley | Executors of the Estate of | Frieda Lawrence Ravagli | Introduction and Notes | Copyright © 1968 | by James T. Boulton | All rights reserved | Letters by D. H. Lawrence in this volume | are published by arrangement | with the Estate of Frieda Lawrence Ravagli | and Laurence Pollinger Limited | First edition December 1968 | S.B.N. 900572 00 0; [v] table of contents; [vi] blank; vii–viii preface and a note on the text by James T. Boulton; ix–xxviii introduction; 1–172 text; 173–175 appendix; [176] blank; 177–182 index; [183] Composed in 11-point Ehrhardt 1-point leaded | and printed on Abbey Mills Process Cartridge | Made and printed in Great Britain by | William Clowes and Sons, Limited | London and Beccles | DESIGN BY M. CANE; [184] blank.

Published December 1968 at 40s.; the first printing consisted of 1500 copies.

NOTES: The upper cover of the dust-jacket has reproductions of photographs of D. H. Lawrence and Louie Burrows. In May 1969 1000 copies were reprinted.

A109   THE QUEST FOR RANANIM   1970

first edition

The | Quest for | Rananim | [*short rule*] | D. H. LAWRENCE'S | LETTERS TO | S. S. KOTELIANSKY | 1914 TO 1930 | [*short rule*] | EDITED WITH AN | INTRODUCTION BY | George J. Zytaruk | [*short rule*] | [*Lawrence phoenix*] | [*short rule*] | McGILL-QUEEN'S | UNIVERSITY PRESS | MONTREAL AND LONDON 1970

Grey cloth boards, stamped in gold on spine: Zytaruk [*on black panel*] | The | Quest | for | Ra | na | nim [*the preceding six lines on black panel*] | McGILL | QUEEN'S [*the preceding two lines on black panel*] The leaves measure $8\frac{1}{2}'' \times 5\frac{1}{2}''$. All edges trimmed.

[i]–[xxxviii] + 4 pp. illustrations + 1–[434], as follows: [i] half-title; [ii] blank; [iii] title page as above; [iv] Introduction and Notes by George J. Zytaruk | © 1970 McGill-Queen's University Press | [*copyright and reservation notices for D. H. Lawrence letters published in the volume*] | SBN 7735–0054–5 | Library of Congress Catalogue Card No. 79–96841 | Printed in Great Britain by | William Clowes and Sons, Limited | London and Beccles | Designed by Robert R. Reid; [v]–[vi] acknowledgements; [vii] table of contents; [viii] blank; four pages of illustrations not counted in the pagination; [ix] list of illustrations; [x] blank; xi–xxxvi introduction by George J. Zytaruk; xxxvii list of abbreviations; [xxxviii] blank; 1–405 text; [406] blank; 407–415 appendix; [416] blank; 417–433 index; [434] blank.

Published 6 March 1970 at $12.50; the first printing consisted of 2999 copies.

A110 LETTERS FROM D. H. LAWRENCE 1970 TO MARTIN SECKER

first edition

LETTERS FROM | D. H. LAWRENCE | *TO MARTIN SEC-KER* | *1911–1930* | MS [*decorative initials*] | [*Privately Published* | *1970*

Brown cloth boards; stamped in gold on upper cover: [*the Lawrence phoenix*]; stamped in gold on spine: LETTERS FROM D. H. LAWRENCE 1911–1930 [*reading from top to bottom*] | MS [*decorative initials*] The leaves measure $9\frac{15}{16}'' \times 6\frac{1}{4}''$. Top edges trimmed and stained purple; fore and bottom edges untrimmed.

[i]–[ii] + [1]–[136], as follows: [1] half-title: [ii] DAVID HERBERT LAWRENCE | *Born at Eastwood, Nottinghamshire* | September 23, 1885 | *Died at Vence, Alpes Maritimes* | March 2, 1930; [1] blank; [2] frontispiece, a reproduction of a photograph of D. H. Lawrence at Spotorno by Martin Secker; [3] title page as above; [4] copyright notice; [5] *500 copies only have been printed* | *for sale in England and America* | *and the type distributed. This* | *copy is No.* 125 [*number in black ink*]; [6] blank; [7] note by Martin Secker; [8] blank; [9] fly-title: THE LETTERS; [10] blank; 11–[125]; text; [126] blank; [127] fly-title: THE NOTES; [128] blank; 129–[133] notes to the letters; [134] Printed in Great Britain | by Clarke, Doble & Brendon Ltd., at | the Oakfield Press, Plymouth | and published by Martin Secker | at Bridgefoot Iver in the | County of Buckingham | mcmlxx.; [135]–[136] blank.

Published about October 1970 at 5 guineas; the first printing consisted of 500 copies.

A111   THE BODY OF GOD   1970
first collected edition

D. H. LAWRENCE | *the Body* | *of God* | *A sequence of poems* | *selected & arranged by* MICHAEL ADAM | *with woodcuts by* BARBARA WHITEHEAD | THE ARK PRESS [*the title page is decorated with a long-stemmed flower in brown arranged vertically in the centre of the page*]

Black cloth boards, stamped in gold on the upper cover: [*a long-stemmed flower arranged vertically in the centre of the cover*] Stamped in gold on the spine, reading from top to bottom: D. H. LAWRENCE THE BODY OF GOD THE ARK PRESS The leaves measure $8\frac{7}{8}'' \times 4\frac{5}{8}''$. All edges trimmed.

[1]–[48], as follows: [1] half-title; [2] blank; [3] title page as above; [4] *The poems have been taken from the Complete Poems of D. H.* | *Lawrence published in the Phoenix Edition by William Heinemann* | *Ltd., London. They are published here with the permission of the* | *Executors of D. H. Lawrence &* | *William Heinemann Ltd., in whom all* | *rights are vested and reserved* | *For* Warren Roberts *from M. A.* [*vertical rule*] K. T. | *Out of* | THE ARK PRESS | *Brushford Dulverton Somerset England* | 1970 | SBN: 9500510 1 2 | *Printed in Great Britain*; 5–6 introductory note; [7]–[8] table of contents; 9–46 text; [47] blank; [48] THE BODY OF GOD | *was printed in Monotype Bembo* | *by Wordens of Cornwall Limited, Penzance* | *on paper from Grosvenor Chater & Co. Ltd., Birmingham* | *Binding by The Pitman Press, Bath* | [*publisher's device*] | *Design by Kim Taylor* | 1970

Published March 1970 at £2 10s.; the first printing consisted of 2000 copies.

CONTENTS

The Heart of Man—The Church—The Protestant Churches—Future Religion—Absolute Reverence—Belief—Travel is Over—Terra Incognita—Pax—Flowers and Men—God is Born—Demiurge—The Body of God—Maximus—Name the Gods!—All Sorts of Gods—Be It So—The Man of Tyre—There Are No Gods!—What Are the Gods?—The Gods! The Gods!—Man is More than *Homo Sapiens*—For the Heroes Are Dipped in Scarlet—Glimpses—For a Moment—Lord's Prayer—The Hills—Nothing to Save—Know-All—Forget—Temples—The Breath of Life—The End, The Beginning—Sleep—Sleep and Waking—Shadows

—Phoenix—Two Ways of Living and Dying—So Let Me Live—Gladness of Death—Difficult Death—All Souls' Day—Song of Death—The Ship of Death—The Ship of Death (another version)—After All Saints' Day—Prayer.

NOTES: The text contains six full-page illustrations counted in the pagination. The end-papers and the dust wrapper are decorated with woodcuts; the illustrations on the dust wrapper are also in the text. Michael Adam is a pseudonym for Kim Taylor. All of the poems in this selection are from *Last Poems* (A62).

A112   D. H. LAWRENCE A SELECTION   1970

first collected edition

D. H. Lawrence: | *A Selection* | *Edited by* | R. H. Poole | Senior Lecturer in English | Wolverhampton Teachers' College for Day Students | *and* | P. J. Shepherd | Senior Lecturer in English | Eastbourne College of Education | [*publisher's device*] | HEINEMANN | LONDON

Black cloth boards. Stamped in gold on spine: D. H. | LAWRENCE | A | SELECTION | Edited by | R. H. Poole | and | P. J. Shepherd | HEINEMANN The leaves measure $8\frac{1}{2}'' \times 5\frac{1}{2}''$. All edges trimmed.

[i]–xviii + [1]–[302], as follows: [i] half-title; [ii] blank; [iii] title page as above; [iv] Heinemann Educational Books Ltd | [*list of cities for Heinemann imprint*] | ISBN 0 435 13730 1 (hardback) | ISBN 0 435 13731 X (paper) | Arrangement and Introductory Essays © R. H. Poole | and P. J. Shepherd 1970 | First published 1970 | Published by | Heinemann Educational Books Ltd | 48 Charles Street, London W1X 8AH | Printed in Great Britain by | Cox & Wyman Ltd, London, Fakenham and Reading; [v]–vi contents; [vii] references [viii] acknowledgements; [ix]–xii foreword; [xiii]–xviii biographical sketch; [1]–60 introductory essays; 61–297 text; [298] blank; [299]–301 bibliography; [302] blank.

Published 28 September 1970 at £2 25s.; the first printing consisted of 4000 copies.

CONTENTS

Letters: (A102).
Lawrence and Travel: Walk to Huayapa from *Mornings in Mexico* (A37)—Indians and Entertainment from *Mornings in Mexico*—extract from *Sea and Sardinia* (A20)—extract from The Crucifix Across the Mountains from *Twilight in Italy* (A8)—extract from *Etruscan Places* (A60).

Essays and Miscellaneous Works: Whistling of Birds (A76)—Morality and the Novel (A76)—Why the Novel Matters (A76)—extract from *A Propos of Lady Chatterley's Lover* (A106)—extract from Study of Thomas Hardy (A76)—Democracy (A76)—extract from Education of the People (A76) —Love was Once a Little Boy (A106)—extract from Introduction to *Memoirs of the Foreign Legion* (A106)—extract from *Fantasia of the Unconscious* (A22)—extract from *Apocalypse* (A57).

Short Stories (A67): The Christening—extract from The Blind Man— Sun.

Tales (A67): extract from *St. Mawr*—extract from *The Virgin and the Gipsy*—extract from *The Man Who Died.*

Novels: extract from *Woman in Love* (A15)—extract from *Aaron's Rod* (A21)—extract from *Kangaroo* (A26)—extract from *The Plumed Serpent* (A33)—extract from *Lady Chatterley's Lover* (A42).

Poems (A104): Dog-Tired—Violets—End of Another Home Holiday— Snap-Dragon—A Doe at Evening—The Song of a Man Who Has Come Through—Tortoise Shout—The Man of Tyre—Bavarian Gentians— The Ship of Death—Shadows.

Lawrence in Brief: a series of succinct quotations from Lawrence, various sources.

A113   THE CENTAUR LETTERS   1970

first edition

[*Centaur Press device in orange*] The Centaur Letters | *by* D. H. LAW-RENCE | INTRODUCTION BY EDWARD D. McDONALD

Tan paper boards with a white cloth backstrip; white paper label on upper cover in blind stamped panel: [*printer's ornament*] CENTAUR [*printer's ornament*] | [*Centaur Press device in orange*] | [*printer's ornament*] LETTERS [*printer's ornament*] On left of label, reading from bottom to top: D. H. LAWRENCE; on right of label, from top to bottom: D. H. LAWRENCE Stamped in gold on spine, reading from top to bottom: THE CENTAUR LETTERS *D. H. Lawrence* The leaves measure $9\frac{1}{2}'' \times 6''$. All edges trimmed.

[1]–[40], as follows: [1]–[3] blank; 4 Humanities Research Center. The University of Texas; [5] title page as above; [6] *Copyright © 1970 by Angelo Ravagli and C. Montague Weekley,* | *Executors of the Estate of Frieda Lawrence Ravagli.* | *L. C. Card Number: 75–110977* | *Distributed by The*

University of Texas Press; 7–10 foreword, signed: EDWARD D. MCDONALD | April 1969; [11] fly-title: THE CENTAUR LETTERS; [12] blank; 13–38 text; [39] [*Centaur Press device*] | *The Humanities Research Center in Austin issues eight hundred | and fifty copies of this book which is set in Intertype Baskerville | and the title in Centaur. The paper is Fabriano for the | binding and Curtis Rag for the text. The illustration of the centaur | has been taken from Edward D. McDonald's bibliography of | D. H. Lawrence's work which was published by Harold T. Mason's | Centaur Press of Philadelphia in 1925. | Design and Typography by William R. Holman, September 1970.*; [40] blank.

Published 23 December 1970 at $9.75; 850 copies were printed.

NOTES: The letters in this volume were all written to Edward McDonald, Lawrence's first bibliographer, and to Harold Mason and other personnel of the Centaur Bookshop in Philadelphia which published Professor McDonald's bibliographies of Lawrence (B16) and (B31) and *Reflections on the Death of a Porcupine* (A32). Most of the correspondence concerns these publications.

A114   THE PRINCESS AND   1971
                OTHER STORIES

first collected edition

D. H. LAWRENCE | [*short rule*] | *The Princess* | AND OTHER STORIES | Edited by Keith Sagar | [*publisher's device*] | PENGUIN BOOKS | *in association with William Heinemann Ltd*

White paper covers with orange spine, printed in pink and orange on upper cover: The Princess [*in pink*] [*publisher's device*] | and Other Stories [*in pink*] | D. H. Lawrence [*in orange*] | [*phoenix in gray*] | Printed in black and white on spine: D. H. Lawrence [*in black*] The Princess and Other Stories [*in white*] ISBN 0 14 | 00.3263 0 [*preceding two lines in black*] [*publisher's device*] The lower cover contains advertising matter concerning the book. The leaves measure $7\frac{1}{8}'' \times 4\frac{3}{8}''$. All edges trimmed.

[1]–[256], as follows: [1] half-title with biographical note about D. H. Lawrence; [2] blank; [3] title page as above; [4] Penguin Books Ltd, Harmondsworth, Middlesex, England | Penguin Books Australia Ltd, Ringwood, Victoria, Australia | [*short rule*] | [*notes on sources for the text*] | This collection published in Penguin Books 1971 | [*short rule*] | Made and printed in Great Britain by | Cox & Wyman Ltd, London, Reading and Fakenham | Set in Monotype Garamond | *D. H. Lawrence's complete short stories are also | available in Canada in a Viking* [*vertical rule*]

Compass edition | [*notice of conditions of sale*]; [5] table of contents; [6] blank; 7–12 introduction by Keith Sagar; [13] fly-title; [14] blank; 15–248 text; [249] note about *Penguinews and Penguins in Print*; [250] blank; [251]–[256] advertisements of other Penguin Books.

Published July 1971 at 30p; 25,000 copies were printed.

CONTENTS

The Wilful Woman (E432.6)—The Princess (A31)—The Overtone (A63)—The Flying Fish (A76)—Sun (A35b)—Mercury (A76)—The Man Who Was Through with the World (C241)—A Dream of Life (A76)—The Undying Man (A76)—The Blue Moccasins (A63)—Things (A63)—Mother and Daughter (A63).

NOTES: "The Man Who Was Through with the World," reprinted here from *Essays in Criticism* for July 1959 (C241), is derived from a manuscript (E227.4) in the library of the University of California at Berkeley. "The Wilful Woman" is from a manuscript also at the University of California at Berkeley, known previously as "The Luhan Story"; the manuscript is described in Tedlock (B46).

A115   THE MORTAL COIL AND   1971
         OTHER STORIES

first collected edition

D. H. LAWRENCE | [*rule*] | *The Mortal Coil* | AND OTHER STORIES | Edited by Keith Sagar | [*publisher's device*] | PENGUIN BOOKS | *in association with William Heinemann Ltd*

White paper covers with orange spine, printed in green and orange on upper cover: The Mortal Coil [*in green*] [*publisher's device*] | and Other Stories [*in green*] | D. H. Lawrence [*in orange*] | [*phoenix in gray*] Printed in black and white on spine, reading from top to bottom: D. H. Lawrence [*in black*] The Mortal Coil and Other Stories [*in white*] ISBN 014 | 00.3264 9 [*preceding two lines in black*] [*publisher's device*] The lower cover contains advertising material concerning the book. The leaves measure $7\frac{1}{8}'' \times 4\frac{3}{8}''$. All edges trimmed.

[1]–[240], as follows: half-title with biographical note about D. H. Lawrence; [2] blank; [3] title page as above; [4] Penguin Books Ltd, Harmondsworth, | Middlesex, England | Penguin Books Australia Ltd, Ringwood, | Victoria, Australia | [*notes on sources for the text*] | This

Collection published in Penguin Books 1971 | *D. H. Lawrence's complete | short stories are also available in Canada | in a Viking | [vertical rule]* Compass *edition* | Made and printed in Great Britain by | Richard Clay (The Chaucer Press), Ltd, | Bungay, Suffolk | Set in Monotype Garamond | [*notice of conditions of sale*]; [5] table of contents; [6] blank; 7–9 introduction; [10] blank; 11–236 text; [237] note about Penguin Books; [238] blank; [239]–[240] advertisements of other D. H. Lawrence books published by Penguin.

Published July 1971 at 30p; 25,000 copies were printed.

CONTENTS

Adolf (A76)—Rex (A76)—A Prelude (A107)—Lessford's Rabbits (A107)—A Lesson on a Tortoise (A107)—A Fly in the Ointment (C22)—The Old Adam (A71)—The Witch à la Mode (A71)—The Miner at Home (A76)—Her Turn (A71)—Delilah and Mr Bircumshaw (A107)—A Chapel and a Hay Hut among the Mountains (A107)—Once (A107)—New Eve and Old Adam (A71)—The Thimble (A107)—The Mortal Coil (A107).

NOTES: A note on the lower cover records the cover designer as Heather Mansell; the illustration of the phoenix on the upper cover was by Stephen Russ. This version of "The Fly in the Ointment" is from the *New Statesman* (C22), a slightly different version from that in *Phoenix II* (A107) and *Young Lorenzo* (B34).

A116   D. H. LAWRENCE   1972
SELECTED POEMS

first collected edition

D. H. LAWRENCE | [*rule*] | *Selected Poems* | EDITED, WITH AN INTRODUCTION | BY KEITH SAGAR | [*publisher's device*] | PENGUIN BOOKS

Decorative paper covers with a reproduction in colour on both upper and lower covers of the Jan Juta portrait of D. H. Lawrence in the National Portrait Gallery, printed in white on upper cover: [*publisher's device*] D. H. Lawrence | Selected Poems | Edited with an introduction | by Keith Sagar Printed in black on spine, reading from top to bottom: D. H. Lawrence Selected Poems ISBN 0 14 | 042.144 0 The lower cover contains advertising matter concerning the book. The leaves measure $7\frac{1}{8}'' \times 4\frac{3}{8}''$. All edges trimmed.

[1]–[272], as follows: [1] half-title with biographical note about D. H. Lawrence; [2] blank; [3] title page as above; [4] Penguin Books Ltd, Harmondsworth, Middlesex, England | Penguin Books Australia Ltd, Ringwood, Victoria, Australia | This selection first published by Penguin Books 1972 | Copyright © the Estate of D. H. Lawrence, 1972 | Introduction © Keith Sagar, 1972 | Made and printed in Great Britain by | Hazell Watson & Viney Ltd | Aylesbury, Bucks | Set in Monotype Garamond | [*notes about conditions of sale*]; 5–[10] table of contents; 11–[17] introduction; [18] blank; [19] fly-title: *Early Poems*; [20] blank; 21–61 text; [62] blank; [63] fly-title: '*Look! We Have Come Through!*'; [64] blank; 65–[90] text; [91] fly-title: *Birds, Beasts and Flowers*; [92] blank; 93–[190] text; [191] fly-title: *Pansies*; [192] blank; 193–[211] text; [212] blank; [213] fly-title: *Nettles* and *More Pansies*; [214] blank; 215–[231] text; [232] blank; [233] fly-title: *Last Poems*; [234] blank; 235–257 text; [258] blank; 259–264 index of first lines; 265–269 index of titles; [270] blank; [271]–[272] notes about Penguin Books.

Published 27 July at 40p; 20,000 copies were printed.

CONTENTS

Early Poems 1906–11 (A104)

Discord in Childhood—Piano—The Wild Common—Cherry Robbers—Renascence—Snap-Dragon—Cruelty and Love—Gipsy—A Collier's Wife—Violets—Dreams Old and Nascent—Afternoon in School: The Last Lesson—A Baby Running Barefoot—End of Another Home-Holiday—Corot—After the Opera—The Bride—Sorrow—Whether or Not—The Drained Cup—Ballad of Another Ophelia—Under the Oak—The North Country—Blue—The Mystic Blue—The Chief Mystery—Ballad of a Wilful Woman—Bei Hennef—First Morning—Multilation—Green—River Roses—Gloire de Dijon—A Doe at Evening—Misery—Meeting Among the Mountains—Giorno dei Morti—The Young Soldier with Bloody Spurs—New Year's Night—Rabbit Snared in the Night—Paradise Re-entered—Song of a Man Who has Come Through—'She Said as Well to Me'—Craving for Spring.

Birds, Beasts and Flowers 1920–23 (A104)

FRUITS: Pomegranate—Medlars and Sorb-Apples—Figs—Grapes—TREES: Cypresses—FLOWERS: Almond Blossom—Sicilian Cyclamens—THE EVANGELISTIC BEASTS: St Matthew—St Mark—St Luke—St John—CREATURES: Mosquito—Fish—Man and Bat—REPTILES: Snake—TORTOISES: Baby Tortoise—Tortoise-Shell

—Tortoise Family Connections—Lui et Elle—Tortoise Gallantry—
Tortoise Shout—BIRDS: Turkey-Cock—Humming-Bird—The Blue
Jay—ANIMALS: The Ass—He-Goat—She-Goat—Elephant—Kanga-
roo—Bibbles—Mountain Lion—The Red Wolf.

Pansies 1928 (A104)

Two Performing Elephants—Natural Complexion—The Oxford Voice
Swan—Leda—Give Us Gods—Won't it be Strange—?—When I Went
to the Circus—Whatever Man Makes—The Elephant is Slow to
Mate—The Gazelle Calf—The Mosquito Knows—Fidelity—
Nottingham's New University—No! Mr Lawrence!—Red-Herring—To
Women, as Far as I'm Concerned—Desire is Dead—Fire—Nemesis—
Wages—Self-Protection—Lizard—Relativity—What Ails Thee?—
Conundrums—Willy Wet-Leg.

Nettles and More Pansies 1929 (A104, except 'Fire')

Andraitx-Pomegranate Flowers—The Heart of Man—Moral Clothing
—The Church—In a Spanish Tram-Car—Bells—The Triumph of the
Machine—We Die Together—Innocent England—Modern Prayer—
Leaves of Grass, Flowers of Grass—Storm in the Black Forest—Name
the Gods!—There are No Gods—Retort to Whitman—Retort to
Jesus—Terra Incognita—For a Moment—Thought—God is Born—
Flowers and Men—Fire (C257).

Last Poems 1929 (A104)

The Greeks Are Coming!—The Argonauts—Middle of the World—For
the Heroes Are Dipped in Scarlet—Demiurge—Red Geranium and
Godly Mignonette—The Body of God—The Rainbow—The Man of
Tyre—They Say the Sea is Loveless—Whales Weep Not!—Bavarian
Gentians—Lucifer—Butterfly—Pax—Only Man—In the Cities—
Lord's Prayer—Mana of the Sea—Anaxagoras—Kissing and Horrid
Strife—When Satan Fell—Death is not Evil, Evil is Mechanical—The
Ship of Death—Shadows.

NOTES: The text for the last poem in the *Nettles* and *More Pansies* section,
"Fire" was taken from a manuscript in the library of the University of
California at Berkeley (E132); it was published in an article by
T. A. Smailes in the *D. H. Lawrence Review* (C257) for Spring 1970.
Mr Smailes arranged the text as verse, but Mr Sagar notes that the
piece is a prose poem and prints it as such in this selection.
The 1975 reprint included some minor revisions. "The Greeks Are

Coming!" was omitted; "Invocation to the Moon" was inserted after "Whales Weep Not!," and "Butterfly" was moved to precede "Bavarian Gentians."

A117 D. H. LAWRENCE ON EDUCATION 1973

first collected edition

D. H. Lawrence on | Education | Edited by Joy and Raymond Williams | Penguin Education

White paper covers, printed in brown, grey and black on upper cover: LAWRENCE [*in brown*] | ON [*in grey, the first letter containing a reproduction of a photograph of D. H. Lawrence taken from a group picture of his class at Beauvale Board School*] | EDUCATION [*in grey*] | EDITORS: JOY AND RAYMOND WILLIAMS [*in black*] [*publisher's device in grey*] Printed in black on spine, reading from top to bottom: LAWRENCE ON EDUCATION EDITORS: 014 08.1202 4 [*publisher's device in grey*] | JOY AND RAYMOND WILLIAMS The lower cover contains an advertisement for the book. The leaves measure $7\frac{13}{16}'' \times 5''$. All edges trimmed.

[1]–[248], as follows: [1] half-title; [2] blank; [3] title page as above; [4] Penguin Education | A Division of Penguin Books Ltd, | Harmondsworth, Middlesex, England | Penguin Books Inc, 7110 Ambassador Road, | Baltimore, Md 21207, USA | Penguin Books Australia Ltd, | Ringwood, Victoria, Australia | First published 1973 | This selection copyright © Joy and Raymond Williams, 1973 | Introduction and notes copyright © Joy and Raymond Williams 1973 | Made and printed in Great Britain by | Hazell Watson & Viney Ltd, Aylesbury, Bucks | Set in Linotype Times | [*note on the conditions of sale*]; [5] table of contents; [6] blank; [7]–13 introduction; [14] blank; [15] fly-title: *Starting Points*; [16] blank; [17]–35 text; [36] blank; [37] fly-title: *Experiences*; [38] blank; [39]–107 text; [108] blank; [109] fly-title: *Arguments*; [110] blank; [111]–222 text; [223] fly-title: *Reflections*; [224] blank; [225]–240 text; [241]–242 notes on sources; [243]–[246] notes on other books in the Penguin Education series; [247]–[248] blank.

Published October 1973 at £1.00; the first printing consisted of 10,000 copies.

CONTENTS

Starting Points

Autobiographical Sketch (A107)—The Proper Study (A76)—The Novel and the Feelings (A76)—Why the Novel Matters (A76).

Experiences

Schoolgirl (excerpt from chapter 12 of *The Rainbow* (A7))—Assistant
Teacher (excerpt from chapters 13 and 14 of *The Rainbow* (A7))—Class-
Room (excerpt from chapter 3 of *Women in Love* (A15))—Lessford's
Rabbits (A107)—A Lesson on a Tortoise (A107)—Last Lesson of the
Afternoon (A104).

Arguments

Men Must Work and Women as Well (A107)—Education of the People
(A76)—Education and Sex in Man, Woman and Child (excerpt from
Fantasia of the Unconscious (A22))—Letter to Lady Cynthia Asquith
(A102)—Benjamin Franklin (A25)—On Human Destiny (A107).

Reflections

Hymns in a Man's Life (A107)—Nottingham and the Mining Countryside (A76)—Return to Bestwood (A107).

A118   CONSCIOUSNESS   1974

first edition

CONSCIOUSNESS [*in blue*] | [*rule in grey*] | D. H. Lawrence | [*short
double rule in grey*] MCM LXXIV | [*short double rule in grey*] |
Privately Printed [*the whole enclosed within a rule in grey, with vertical rules
within forming a box on either side for elements of the Roman numerals in line
four above*]

Decorative marbled paper boards; grey paper label on upper cover,
printed in black: CONSCIOUSNESS [*enclosed within a decorative rule*] The
leaves measure $9\frac{15}{16}'' \times 6\frac{7}{16}''$. Top and bottom edges trimmed; fore edges
untrimmed.

[1]–[16], as follows: [1]–[2] blank; [3] title page as above; [4] Copyright
© 1974 by Angelo Ravagli and | C. Montague Weekley, Executors of
the Estate | of Frieda Lawrence Ravagli. All rights reserved. | Published
with the kind permission of | Laurence Pollinger Ltd.; [5] introductory
note; [6] blank; [7] fly-title; [8] blank; [9] text; [10] blank; [11] This
edition limited to fifty copies. | Printed for John Martin by the | Press
of the Pegacycle Lady.; [12]–[16] blank.

Published June 1974; not sold. The first printing consisted of 55 copies.

NOTES: The text of this small book is a letter written to Charles Wilson,
a freelance journalist who was active in the labor movement. Wilson

had asked Lawrence for a message to the miners at Willington Colliery; he was living at Willington, Durham at the time. Lawrence's message was incorporated in three short poems, "For God's Sake," "O! Start a Revolution" and "It's Either You Fight or You Die." These poems were published in (A61) and (A47).

A119   D. H. LAWRENCE LETTERS TO   1976
THOMAS AND ADELE SELTZER

a. *first edition (paper covers)*

D. H. LAWRENCE [*in yellow*] | LETTERS TO THOMAS | AND ADELE SELTZER [*preceding two lines in green*] | Edited by Gerald M. Lacy [*in blue*] [*the whole enclosed within a decorative rule in green*] | *Santa Barbara* | *BLACK SPARROW PRESS* | *1976*

Grey decorative paper covers: D. H. LAWRENCE [*in yellow*] | LETTERS | TO | THOMAS & ADELE | SELTZER [*in green*] | EDITED BY GERALD M. LACY [*in blue*] | [*stylized drawing of a pueblo in yellow and blue*] [*the whole enclosed within a decorative rule in green*]; printed on spine, from top to bottom: Letters To Thomas and Adele Seltzer [*in blue*] D. H. LAWRENCE [*in yellow*] BLACK SPARROW PRESS [*in blue*] The leaves measure $8\frac{15}{16}'' \times 5\frac{7}{8}''$. All edges trimmed.

[i]–xiv + [1]–[290], as follows: [i] blank; [ii] frontispiece, reproduction of a photograph of D. H. Lawrence by Edward Weston; [iii] title page as above; [iv] LETTERS TO THOMAS & ADELE SELTZER FROM D. H. LAWRENCE | copyright © 1976 by Angelo Ravagli and C. Montague | Weekly, Executors of the Estate of Frieda Lawrence | Ravagli. | THE SELTZERS & D. H. LAWRENCE: A BIOGRAPHICAL NARRATIVE | copyright © 1976 by Alexandra Lee Levin & Lawrence | L. Levin. | LETTERS FROM THOMAS & ADELE SELTZER copyright © 1976 | by the Estate of Thomas Seltzer. | INTRODUCTION & NOTES copyright © 1976 by Gerald M. Lacy. | [*reservations, acknowledgements and Library of Congress cataloguing information*]; [v] table of contents; [vi] blank; vii–xiv introduction by Gerald M. Lacy; [1] fly-title: Letters to Thomas | & Adele Seltzer | from | D. H. Lawrence; [2] illustrations; 3–155 text; [156] blank; 157–167 notes to the letters; [168] blank; [169] fly-title: The Seltzers & | D. H. Lawrence: | A Biographical Narrative | by | Alexandra Lee Levin & | Lawrence L. Levin; [170] illustrations; 171–198 text; 199–201 notes for the biographical narrative; [202] blank; [203] fly-title: The Letters from | Thomas & Adele Seltzer; [204] blank; 205–278 text; 279 list of books by D. H. Lawrence published by Thomas Seltzer; 280 list of locations of manuscripts and photographs; 281–282 acknowl-

edgements; 283–284 bibliography; [285] quotation from Catherine Carswell; [286] blank; [287] [*publisher's device*] | Printed June 1976 in Santa Barbara & Ann Arbor | for the Black Sparrow Press by Mackintosh & Young | and Edwards Bros. Inc. Design by Barbara Martin. | This edition is published in paper wrappers; there | are 1000 hardcover trade copies; & 126 numbered | copies handbound in boards by Earle Gray, each | containing a direct print of a previously unpublished | photograph of D. H. Lawrence; [288–290] blank.

Published 30 June 1976 at $5.00; 4043 copies were issued in paper covers.

b. *first edition* (*hard cover copies*)

The hard cover copies are identical with (a) except for the binding consisting of grey decorative paper boards with a green cloth backstrip; grey paper label on spine, reading from top to bottom: Letters To Thomas and Adele Seltzer [*in blue*] D. H. LAWRENCE [*in yellow*] The leaves measure 9″ × 6″.

Published simultaneously with (a) at $14.00; 745 hard cover copies were issued, and an additional 255 sets of unbound sheets were reserved by the publisher.

c. *first edition* (*numbered copies*)

The numbered copies are identical with (b) except for the blue cloth backstrip and a photographic print of D. H. Lawrence pasted on the recto of a separate leaf before page [i] sewn with the signature and pasted to the inner edge of page [22].

Published simultaneously with (a) at $30.00; 100 numbered copies were issued.

d. *first edition* (*lettered copies*)

The lettered copies were identical with (c) except for the yellow cloth backstrip.

Published simultaneously with (a) at $30.00; 26 lettered copies were issued.

NOTES: According to the publisher nine extra copies of (d) were issued out-of-series; one each for the publisher, the printer and the binder; one file copy; two for the editor; and three numbered copies marked for the D. H. Lawrence Estate. In all copies of the book pages [i]–[iv] were not integral with the first signature, but were tipped in to page [v].

A120　　SONS AND LOVERS　　1977

D. H. LAWRENCE | Sons and Lovers | A FACSIMILE OF THE MANUSCRIPT | Edited, with an Introduction by | MARK SCHORER | University of California Press | Berkeley · Los Angeles · London

Red cloth boards, stamped in gold on upper cover: Sons and Lovers | by | D. H. Lawrence [*preceding three lines facsimile of Lawrence's title and signature from the manuscript*] Stamped in gold on spine: D. H. LAWRENCE | Sons | and | Lovers | A Facsimile | of the | Manuscript | Edited by | Mark Schorer | California The leaves measure 14″ × 11″. All edges trimmed.

[i]–[viii] + 1–624, as follows: [1]–[ii] blank; [iii] half-title; [iv] blank; [v] title page as above; [vi] University of California Press | Berkeley and Los Angeles, California | University of California Press, Ltd. | London, England | Copyright © 1977 by | The Regents of the University of California | ISBN 0–520–03190–3 | Library of Congress Catalog Number: 75–46037 | Printed in the United States of America | Designed by Theo Jung | 123456789; [vii] contents; [viii] blank; 1–9 introduction; [10] blank; [11] fly-title: PAUL MOREL | A FACSIMILE OF SIX FRAGMENTS: [12] blank: [13] fly-title: FRAGMENT 1; [14]–[21] text; [22] fly-title: FRAGMENT 2; [23]–[33] text; [34] fly-title: FRAGMENT 3; [35]–[53] text; [54] fly-title: FRAGMENT 4; [55]–[56] text; [57] fly-title: FRAGMENT 5; [58]–[72] text; [73] fly-title: FRAGMENT 6; [74]–[76] text; [77] fly-title: Sons and Lovers | A FACSIMILE OF THE MANUSCRIPT; [78] blank; [79]–[608] text; 609–624 supplement, textual variants.

Published 17 April 1977 at $75.00; the first printing consisted of 1000 copies.

NOTES: The *Sons and Lovers* facsimile was issued in a red dust-jacket with white lettering.

A121 THE LETTERS OF D. H. LAWRENCE 1979

THE LETTERS OF | D. H. LAWRENCE | VOLUME I | *September 1901–May 1913* | EDITED BY | JAMES T. BOULTON

| CAMBRIDGE UNIVERSITY PRESS | CAMBRIDGE |
LONDON NEW YORK MELBOURNE

Red cloth boards, stamped in gold on spine: The | Letters of | D. H. |
Lawrence | I | 1901–13 | [the whole enclosed within a single oval rule]
| CAMBRIDGE The leaves measure $8\frac{1}{2}'' \times 5\frac{1}{2}''$. All edges trimmed.

[i]–[ii] + [i]–[xxxviii] + 1–[584] and frontispiece, as follows: [i]–[ii]
blank; [i] half-title; [ii] blank; [iii] list of members of editorial boards;
[iv] blank; frontispiece; [v] title page as above; [vi] Published by the
Syndics of the Cambridge University Press | The Pitt Building,
Trumpington Street, Cambridge CB2 1RP | Bentley House, 200 Euston
Road, London NW1 2DB | 32 East 57th Street, New York, NY 10022,
USA | 296 Beaconsfield Parade, Middle Park, Melbourne 3206,
Australia | [copyright notices] | First published 1979 | Printed in the
United States of America | Typeset at the University Press, Cambridge,
England | Printed and bound by Vail-Ballou Press Inc., Binghampton,
New York | [Library of Congress cataloguing data] | ISBN 0 521 22147 1;
vii table of contents; [viii] blank; ix list of illustrations; [x] blank; xi–xiv
preface; xv–xvii acknowledgements; xviii–xxiii rules of transcription
and cue-titles; [xxiv]–[xxv] Lawrence genealogy; xxvi–xxix chrono-
logy; [xxx]–[xxxvii] maps; [xxxviii] blank; 1–20 introduction; 21–554
text; [555]–579 index; [580]–[584] blank.

Published 10 September 1979 in the United States and 27 September
in the United Kingdom at £ 15.00; 5134 copies of the first impression
were printed for distribution in both countries.

NOTES: Immediately after publication a second impression of 2500 copies
was printed which can be distinguished by the top edges stained red
and the addition of the line: Reprinted 1979 added on page [vi]. The
dust-jacket is black printed in red and white; the upper cover has a
portrait in color of D. H. Lawrence from a miniature owned by Louie
Burrows. See (C272).

REVIEWS: The first volume of the Letters of D. H. Lawrence was reviewed
in the New York Review of Books for 27 September 1979 by John Gross;
in the New Republic, 1 and 8 September by Jack Beatty; the Listener for
27 September by P. N. Furbank; in the Birmingham Post for 27 September
by Norman Sanders; the Observer for 30 September by A. Alvarez; the
Sunday Telegraph for 30 September by Neville Braybrooke; the Daily
Telegraph for 4 October by Anthony Powell; the New Statesman for 5
October by Tom Paulin; in Now for 12 October by Stephen Spender;

in the *Economist* for 6 October; in the *Yorkshire Post* for 4 October by Norman Jeffares; in the *New York Times Book Review* for 9 September by Paul Delany; the *Chicago Tribune* in September by Daniel J. Cahill; in the *Financial Times* for 13 October by Peter Keating; in the *Chronicle for Higher Education* for 9 November by Eugene Goodheart; in *America* for 29 September by Paul H. Connolly; in the *Spectator* for 27 October by Jeffrey Meyers; in the *Los Angeles Times* for 21 October by Robert Kirsch; in the *Literary Review* for December by Stephen Gill; in the *Washington Post* for 4 November by Martin Green; in the *Times Educational Supplement* for 30 November by Myra Barrs; in the *Times Literary Supplement* for 7 December by Bernard Bergonzi; in the *Sunday Times* for 9 December by John Carey; in the *Times Higher Education Supplement* for 14 December by Patrick Parrinder; in *Country Life* for 10 January 1980 by Geoffrey Grigson; in the *Age* (Australia) for 19 January 1980 by Neville Braybrooke.

Fragment of an early manuscript version (E430c) of *The White Peacock* from which Helen Corke and others made a fair copy in 1910. From the editor's collection

The White Peacock, American (A1a) and English (A1b) first editions

Sons & Lovers

Paul Morel

CURTIS BROWN, LTD.,
6 Henrietta Street,
Covent Garden,
London, W.C.2

Chapter I.
Antecedents.

"The Breach" took the place of Hell Row. It was a natural succession. Hell Row was a block of some half dozen thatched, collapsing cottages which stood back in the brook-course by Greenhill Lane. Eastwood had scarcely gathered consciousness when the notorious Row was burned down. The village, was shrewed rather forlornly over hills and the valley. Since the seventeenth century the people of Eastwood have scratched at the earth for coal. The old cottage rows along Green-hill Lane were built to accommodate the workers in the old little gin-pits, which were scattered about among the fields, beside Derby Road, and Nottingham Road, and Mansfield Road. To these vanished pits the pasture land in many parts owes its queer configuration. But fifty years ago the pits were busy, and in the four square miles round Eastwood there were perhaps some two or three hundred of these miners cottages, old and mean, dabbed down

First page of "Paul Morel," an early manuscript version (E373d) of *Sons and Lovers*. Humanities Research Center Collections, University of Texas at Austin

The Rainbow, first English edition (A 7a)

Look! We Have Come Through! first English edition (A10a); *The Rainbow*, first American edition; *Women in Love*, first American trade edition; *Love Poems*, first English edition (A3)

B. CONTRIBUTIONS TO BOOKS

B. CONTRIBUTIONS TO BOOKS

B1   GEORGIAN POETRY 1911–1912   1912

first edition

GEORGIAN | POETRY | 1911–1912 | [*printer's ornaments*] | THE POETRY BOOKSHOP | 35 DEVONSHIRE ST. THEOBALDS RD. | LONDON W. C.

Tan paper boards, stamped in gold on upper cover: GEORGIAN POETRY | 1911–1912 | P [*printer's ornament*] B [*on red shield*] | THE POETRY BOOKSHOP; stamped in gold on spine: Georgian | Poetry | 1911–1912 $7\frac{9}{16}'' \times 5\frac{1}{8}''$. pp. [i]–[viii] + [1]–[200] Top edges trimmed and gilt; fore and bottom edges untrimmed. Published December 1912 at 3*s.* 6*d.*; number of copies unknown.

Contains: "Snapdragon," pp. 113–116; first appeared in the *English Review*, June 1912 (C14); collected in *Amores* (A9).

NOTES: The Georgian anthologies, most of which contained poetry by D. H. Lawrence, were edited by Edward Marsh, sometime secretary to Winston Churchill. Edward Marsh introduced the Lawrences to Lady Cynthia Asquith, visited them in Italy and in England and remained a friend through the years.

B2   SOME IMAGIST POETS   1915

first edition

SOME IMAGIST | POETS | AN ANTHOLOGY |[*publisher's device*] | BOSTON AND NEW YORK | HOUGHTON MIFFLIN COMPANY | The Riverside Press Cambridge | 1915

Green paper wrappers, printed in black on upper cover: Some Imagist Poets | An Anthology | THE NEW POETRY SERIES | [*publisher's device*] | HOUGHTON MIFFLIN COMPANY | Boston and New York | [*printer's ornament*]; printed in black on spine, reading from top to bottom: SOME IMAGIST POETS Top edges trimmed; fore and bottom edges rough-trimmed.

$7\frac{3}{4}'' \times 5\frac{5}{8}''$. pp. [i]–[ii] + [i]–[x] + [1]–96. Published 17 April 1915 at $0.75; the first printing consisted of 1000 copies.

Contains: "Ballad of Another Ophelia," pp. 67–68; collected in *Amores* (A9).

"Illicit," p. 69; first appeared in *Poetry*, January 1914 (C29); collected in *Look! We Have Come Through!* (A10) as "On the Balcony."

"Fireflies in the Corn," pp. 70–71; first appeared in *Poetry*, January 1914 (C29); collected in *Look! We Have Come Through!*

"A Woman and Her Dead Husband," pp. 72–74; first appeared in *Poetry*, January 1914 (C29); collected in *New Poems* (A11) as "Bitterness of Death."

"The Mowers," p. 75; first appeared in the *Smart Set*, November 1913 (C27); collected in *Look! We Have Come Through!* as "A Youth Mowing."

"Scent of Irises," pp. 76–77; collected in *Amores* (A9).

"Green," p. 78; first appeared in *Poetry*, January 1914 (C29); collected in *Look! We Have Come Through!*

NOTES: Lawrence met Amy Lowell, who edited the Imagist anthologies, in London in 1914; she attempted to identify him with the Imagist movement, and although he continued to allow his poetry to appear in her anthologies, he also continued to deny that he was an Imagist. At a dinner party in 1914 Amy Lowell quoted Lawrence's poem, "Wedding Morn," to its author in an effort to prove him an Imagist, but to no avail.

B3   GEORGIAN POETRY 1913–1915   1915

first edition

GEORGIAN | POETRY | 1913–1915 | [*printer's ornaments*] | THE POETRY BOOKSHOP | 35 DEVONSHIRE ST. THEOBALDS RD. | LONDON W. C. | MCMXV

Blue paper boards, stamped in gold on upper cover: GEORGIAN POETRY | 1913–1915 | THE POETRY BOOKSHOP; stamped in gold on spine: Georgian | Poetry | 1913–1915 | P [*printer's ornament*] B [*on red shield*] Top edges trimmed and gilt; fore edges rough-trimmed; bottom edges untrimmed. $7\frac{5}{8}'' \times 5\frac{3}{16}''$. pp. [i]–[x] + [1]–[246]. Published November 1915 at 3s. 6d.; number of copies unknown.

Contains: "Service of All the Dead," p. 153; first appeared in the *New Statesman*, 15 November 1913 (C28); collected in *Look! We Have Come Through!* (A10) as "Giorno dei Morti."

"Meeting Among the Mountains," p. 154; first appeared in the *English Review*, February 1914 (C30); reprinted in *Not I, But the Wind* (B40) and collected in the Ark Press *Look! We Have Come Through!* (A10b).

B4   SOME IMAGIST POETS   1916

first edition

SOME IMAGIST POETS | 1916 | [*short rule*] | AN ANNUAL ANTHOLOGY | [*publisher's device*] | BOSTON AND NEW YORK | HOUGHTON MIFFLIN COMPANY | The Riverside Press Cambridge | 1916

Green paper wrappers, printed in black on upper cover: Some Imagist Poets, 1916 | An Annual Anthology | THE NEW POETRY SERIES | [*publisher's device*] | HOUGHTON MIFFLIN COMPANY | Boston and New York | [*printer's ornament*]; printed in black on spine reading from top to bottom: SOME IMAGIST POETS, 1916 Top edges trimmed; fore and bottom edges rough-trimmed. $7\frac{3}{4}'' \times 5\frac{5}{8}''$. pp. [i]–[ii] + [i]–[xvi] + [1]–[98]. Published 6 May 1916 at $0.75; the first printing consisted of 1000 copies.

Contains: "Erinnyes," pp. 67–69.

"Perfidy," pp. 70–71; first appeared in the *Egoist*, 1 April 1914 (C32), as "Fooled"; collected in *Amores* (A9).

"At the Window," p. 72; first appeared in the *English Review*, April 1910 (C4); collected in *Amores*.

"In Trouble and Shame," p. 73; collected in *Amores*.

"Brooding Grief," p. 74; collected in *Amores*.

B5   THE NEW POETRY   1917

first edition

THE NEW POETRY | AN ANTHOLOGY | EDITED BY | HARRIET MONROE | AND | ALICE CORBIN HENDERSON | EDITORS OF POETRY | New York | THE MACMILLAN COMPANY | 1917 | *All rights reserved*

Green cloth boards, stamped in gold on upper cover: THE NEW

POETRY | [*printer's ornaments*] | AN ANTHOLOGY | [*enclosed within single rule, blind stamped, forming border*]; stamped in gold on spine: [*double rule*] | THE | NEW | POETRY | MONROE | [*printer's ornaments*] | HENDERSON | MACMILLAN | [*double rule*] Top edges trimmed; fore and bottom edges rough-trimmed. $7\frac{1}{2}'' \times 5\frac{1}{8}''$. pp. [i]–[xxxiv] + 1–[414]. Published 28 February 1917 at \$1.75; the first printing consisted of 4000 copies.

Contains: "Grief," p. 158; first appeared in *Poetry*, December 1914 (C35); a different version appeared in the *English Review*, February 1914 (C30), as "Twilight."

B6   SOME IMAGIST POETS   1917
first edition

SOME IMAGIST POETS | [*short rule*] | AN ANNUAL ANTHOLOGY | [*publisher's device*] | BOSTON AND NEW YORK | HOUGHTON MIFFLIN COMPANY | The Riverside Press Cambridge | 1917

Green paper wrappers, printed in black on upper cover: Some Imagist Poets, 1917 | [*short rule under 1917*] | An Annual Anthology | [*publisher's device*] | HOUGHTON MIFFLIN COMPANY | Boston and New York | [*printer's ornament*]; printed in black on spine reading from top to bottom: SOME IMAGIST POETS. 1917 [*short rule under 1917*] Top edges trimmed; fore and bottom edges rough-trimmed. $7\frac{3}{4}'' \times 5\frac{5}{8}''$. pp. [i]–[viii] + [1]–[92]. Published 14 April 1917 at \$0.75; the first printing consisted of 1000 copies.

Contains: "Terra Nuova," pp. 69–75; collected in *Look! We Have Come Through!* (A10) as "New Heaven and Earth."

B7   NEW PATHS   1918
first edition

NEW PATHS | VERSE·PROSE·PICTURES | 1917–1918 | Edited by | C. W. BEAUMONT AND M. T. H. SADLER | Decorated by | ANNE ESTELLE RICE | [*publisher's device*] | LONDON | C. W. BEAUMONT | 75 CHARING CROSS ROAD W. C. 2

Tan paper boards, printed in blue on upper cover: NEW PATHS | VERSE·PROSE·PICTURES | 1917–1918 | [*drawing of bowl of fruit*]; printed in blue on lower cover: [*drawing of woman's head*]; white paper label on spine printed in blue: NEW | PATHS | 1917–18 | [*printer's ornament*] | C. W. | Beaumont | [*enclosed within single rule border*] Top edges unopened; fore and bottom edges untrimmed. $8\frac{3}{4}'' \times 6\frac{3}{4}''$. pp. [i]–[xiv] + 1–[176]. Published May 1918 at 7s. 6d.; number of ordinary copies unknown; there were also 100 copies on cartridge paper and 30 copies on Japanese vellum, with the decorations handcoloured and the frontispiece in two states signed by the artist and decorator.

Contains: "Labour Battalion," pp. 37–38.
      "No News," p. 39.

NOTES: These poems were not collected in any of Lawrence's books of poetry, but were collected in (A104).

NOTES (2): Mr W. Forster reports that six copies of *New Paths* were printed on cartridge paper for presentation.

B8   THE NEW KEEPSAKE   1921

first edition

THE NEW [*short vertical double rule*] LE NOUVEAU | KEEP-SAKE | FOR POUR | THE YEAR L'ANNEE [*short vertical double rule separates the French and the English of the preceding two lines*] | 1921 | EDITED BY | X. M. BOULESTIN | WITH PLATES SE-LECTED BY | J. E. LABOUREUR | Published for X. M. BOULESTIN, 102, George Street | Portman Square, W., by the Chelsea Book Club | 65, Cheyne Walk, S. W. | LONDON [*short vertical double rule*] PARIS

Yellow cloth boards, printed in black on upper cover: THE NEW [*short vertical double rule*] LE NOUVEAU | KEEPSAKE | FOR POUR | THE YEAR L'ANNÉE [*short vertical double rule separates the French and English of the preceding two lines*] | 1921 | [*enclosed within single rule*] | [*drawing of leaf*]; printed in black on the spine: [*drawing of leaf*] Top edges trimmed; fore and bottom edges untrimmed. $7\frac{5}{8}'' \times 5\frac{5}{8}''$. pp. [1]–[128]. Published December 1920 at 18s. 6d.; 550 numbered copies were printed on hand-made paper. There were also 20 numbered copies on blue vellum in black cloth boards; 50 numbered copies on Japanese vellum in white cloth boards and an additional 31 copies on blue vellum numbered I–XXXI, not for sale.

Contains: "Adolf," pp. 19–33; first appeared in the *Dial*, September 1920 (C73); collected in *Phoenix* (A76).

first edition

THE | ENCHANTED YEARS | *A Book of Contemporary Verse* | DEDICATED BY POETS OF GREAT | BRITAIN AND AMERICA TO THE | UNIVERSITY OF VIRGINIA ON THE | OCCASION OF ITS ONE-HUNDREDTH | ANNI-VERSARY | EDITED BY | JOHN CALVIN METCALF | LINDEN KENT MEMORIAL PROFESSOR OF | ENG-LISH LITERATURE | AND JAMES SOUTHALL WILSON | EDGAR ALLAN POE PROFESSOR OF ENG-LISH | UNIVERSITY OF VIRGINIA | [*publisher's device*] | NEW YORK | HARCOURT, BRACE AND COMPANY | 1921

Blue cloth boards, stamped in gold on spine: [*double rule*] | *The* EN- | CHANTED | YEARS | [*printer's ornament*] | METCALF | *and* | WILSON | HARCOURT | BRACE | & CO | [*double rule*] All edges trimmed. $7\frac{3}{8}'' \times 4\frac{7}{8}''$. pp. [i]–[x] + [1]–[158]. Published June 1921.

Contains: "Slopes of Etna"; collected in *Birds, Beasts and Flowers* (A27) as "Peace."

"Tropic"; collected in *Birds, Beasts and Flowers.*

NOTES: There are textual differences in the versions published here and those included in later printings.

B9   THE GENTLEMAN FROM   1922
                SAN FRANCISCO

first edition

THE GENTLEMAN FROM | SAN FRANCISCO | *AND OTHER STORIES* | BY | I. A. BUNIN | TRANSLA-TED FROM THE RUSSIAN BY | S. S. KOTELIANSKY AND LEONARD WOOLF | PUBLISHED BY LEO-NARD & VIRGINIA WOOLF | THE HOGARTH PRESS, PARADISE ROAD, RICHMOND | 1922

Decorative paper boards, white paper label on upper cover printed in black: [*single rule*] | THE GENTLEMAN FROM | [*printer's ornament*] SAN FRANCISCO [*printer's ornament*] | AND OTHER STORIES. | [*printer's ornament*] | I. A. BUNIN. | [*single rule*]; white paper label on spine printed in black, reading downwards: THE GENTLEMAN FROM SAN FRANCISCO. I. A. BUNIN. All edges trimmed. $7\frac{3}{16}'' \times 4\frac{3}{4}''$. pp. [i]–[ii] + [i]–[vi] + 1–[88]. Pub-lished May 1922 at 4s.; the first edition consisted of about 1000 copies.

Contains: "The Gentleman from San Francisco," pp. 1–40; first appeared in the *Dial*, January 1922 (C88).

NOTES: According to the errata slip, Lawrence's name was omitted from the title page through an error; the title page of the first American edition, published by Thomas Seltzer in January 1923, correctly lists Lawrence as Koteliansky's collaborator for the translation of the title story.

Bio   THE NEW DECAMERON III   1922

first edition

THE NEW DECAMERON | THE THIRD VOLUME, CON-TAINING | STORIES BY | COMPTON MACKENZIE | J. D. BERESFORD | D. H. LAWRENCE | DESMOND COKE | MICHAEL SADLEIR | NORMAN DAVEY | STORM JAMESON | ROBERT KEABLE | V. SACKVILLE WEST | AND BILL NOBBS | OXFORD | BASIL BLACK-WELL | 1922

Blue paper boards with a grey cloth backstrip, white paper label on spine printed in black: THE NEW [*printer's ornament*] | DECAMERON | [*printer's ornament*] | COMPTON MACKENZIE | J. D. BERESFORD | D. H. LAWRENCE | MICHAEL SADLEIR | ROBERT KEABLE | and others | [*printer's ornament*] Top and fore edges unopened; bottom edges untrimmed. $7\frac{5}{8}'' \times 5\frac{1}{16}''$. pp. [i]–viii + [1]–[232]. Published 15 June 1922 at 7s. 6d.; the edition consisted of 2000 copies.

Contains: "The Wintry Peacock," pp. 123–46; first appeared in the *Metropolitan*, August 1921 (C84); collected in *England, My England* (A23).

B11   GEORGIAN POETRY 1920–1922   1922

first edition

GEORGIAN | POETRY | 1920–1922 | [*printer's ornaments*] | THE POETRY BOOKSHOP | 35 DEVONSHIRE ST. THEO-BALDS RD. | LONDON W. C. 1 | MCMXXII

Red paper boards, stamped in gold on upper cover: GEORGIAN POETRY | 1920–1922 | THE POETRY BOOKSHOP; stamped in gold on spine: Georgian | Poetry | 1920–1922 | P [*printer's ornament*] B [*on blue shield*] Top edges trimmed and gilt; fore and bottom edges untrimmed.

$7\frac{1}{2}'' \times 5''$. pp. [i]–[xiv] + [1]–[210]. Published November 1922 at 6*s.*; number of copies unknown.

Contains: "Snake," pp. 117–20; first appeared in the *Dial*, July 1921 (C82); collected in *Birds, Beasts and Flowers* (A27).

NOTES (2): Mr W. Forster has reported a copy of *Georgian Poetry 1920–1922* in his collection bound in red cloth and printed on hand-made paper. "Snake" also appeared in *A Miscellany of Poetry, 1920–1923*, edited by William Kean Seymour.

B12   THE NEW POETRY   1923

first revised edition

THE NEW POETRY | AN ANTHOLOGY | OF TWENTI-ETH-CENTURY VERSE IN | ENGLISH | NEW AND ENLARGED EDITION | EDITED BY | HARRIET MONROE | EDITOR OF *Poetry: A Magazine of Verse* | AND | ALICE CORBIN HENDERSON | New York | THE MACMILLAN COMPANY | 1923 | *All rights reserved*

Green cloth boards, blind stamped on upper cover: THE NEW POETRY | [*printer's ornaments*] | AN ANTHOLOGY | [*enclosed within single rule forming border*]; stamped in gold on spine: [*double rule*] | THE | NEW | POETRY | MONROE | [*printer's ornaments*] | HENDERSON | NEW AND | ENLARGED | EDITION | MACMILLAN | [*printer's ornaments*] | [*double rule*] Top edges trimmed; fore and bottom edges rough-trimmed. $7\frac{7}{8}'' \times 5\frac{7}{16}''$. pp. [i]–[liv] + [1]–[650]. Published 1 May 1923 at $3.50; during the publisher's first fiscal year 10,134 copies were printed. It is unknown how many printings this number included.

Contains: "Resurrection," pp. 238–40; first appeared in *Poetry*, June 1917 (C47).

B13   STORIES FROM THE DIAL   1924

first edition

[*short decorative rule*] | STORIES | *from* | THE DIAL | [*publisher's device*] | LINCOLN MACVEAGH | THE DIAL PRESS | NEW YORK · MCMXXIV | [*short decorative rule*]

Decorative paper boards with a dark blue cloth backstrip, stamped in gold on spine: STORIES | *from the* | DIAL | [*printer's ornament*] | [*publisher's device*] | THE DIAL PRESS Top edges trimmed and stained yellow; fore edges untrimmed; bottom edges rough-trimmed. $7\frac{9}{16}'' \times 5\frac{1}{4}''$. pp. [i]–[vi] + [1]–330. Published August 1924 at $2.50; number of copies unknown.

Contains: "Rex," pp. 37–52; first appeared in the *Dial*, February 1921 (C77); collected in *Phoenix* (A76).

B14 MEMOIRS OF THE FOREIGN 1924 LEGION

first edition

Memoirs of the | Foreign Legion | By | M. M. | With an Introduction by | D. H. Lawrence | 1924 | [*short rule*] | London: Martin Secker

Black cloth boards, stamped in gold on upper cover: MEMOIRS OF THE FOREIGN LEGION | *By* M. M.; stamped in gold on spine: MEMOIRS | *of the* | FOREIGN | LEGION | [*printer's ornament*] | M. M. | SECKER Top edges trimmed and stained pink; fore edges rough-trimmed; bottom edges untrimmed. $7\frac{9}{16}'' \times 5''$. pp. [1]–[320]. Published 1 October 1924 at 7s. 6d.; the first printing consisted of 2000 copies.

Contains: "Introduction," pp. 11–94.

NOTES: Maurice Magnus was an American wanderer about Europe who had enlisted in the French Foreign Legion during the First World War and subsequently deserted, making his way to Italy, where Lawrence met him in 1919 at Florence in the company of Norman Douglas. Magnus was to provide the major bone of contention for a rather lively quarrel between Lawrence and Douglas. Magnus, even in the midst of severe financial difficulties, would not forgo his gentlemanly standard of living, and this behaviour irritated Lawrence, who lived comfortably but economically. Lawrence loaned Magnus money, and several times made himself responsible for hotel bills run up by Magnus.

At Magnus's request Lawrence visited him at the ancient monastery of Monte Cassino, and for a time Magnus lived near the Lawrences in Taormina; they saw him again at Malta in 1920, where he committed suicide in November of that year. Magnus made Norman Douglas his literary executor, but two Maltese acquaintances of Lawrence refused to forward Magnus's manuscripts to Douglas, and instead, sent them to Lawrence, who, after some difficulty, arranged for the publication of the *Memoirs* in an effort to retrieve the money which Magnus owed to the two Maltese. It was the lengthy introduction to the *Memoirs* to which

Douglas took exception; he felt that Lawrence had not treated Magnus fairly.

Douglas's comments on the affair are recorded in *D. H. Lawrence and Maurice Magnus* (F2), which he published privately in Florence in 1924. Lawrence finally answered this attack in a letter to the *New Statesman*, entitled "The Late Mr. Maurice Magnus"; the letter appeared in the *New Statesman*, 20 February 1926 (C138). The first American edition of the *Memoirs of the Foreign Legion* was published by Knopf in January 1925.

NOTES (2): Bertram Rota offered a copy of *Memoirs of the Foreign Legion* in 1973 bound in red cloth. The dust-jacket for the first edition is tan paper printed in red.

B15   THE NEW DECAMERON IV   1925

first edition

THE NEW DECAMERON | THE FOURTH VOLUME, EDITED | BY BLAIR | AND | CONTAINING STORIES BY | J. D. BERESFORD | BLAIR | HORACE HORSNELL | STORM JAMESON | ROBERT KEABLE | D. H. LAWRENCE | EDGELL RICKWORD | MICHAEL SADLEIR | L. A. G. STRONG | OXFORD | BASIL BLACKWELL | 1925

Blue paper boards with a tan cloth backstrip, white paper label on spine printed in blue: THE NEW [*printer's ornament*] | DECAMERON | [*printer's ornament*] | D. H. LAWRENCE | J. D. BERESFORD | ROBERT KEABLE | MICHAEL SADLEIR | STORM JAMESON | and others | [*printer's ornament*] | EDITED BY BLAIR Top and fore edges unopened; bottom edges untrimmed. $7\frac{9}{16}"$ × 5". pp. [1]–[272]. Published 2 March 1925 at 7s. 6d.; the edition consisted of 2000 copies.

Contains: "The Last Laugh," pp. 235–61; collected in *The Woman Who Rode Away* (A41).

B16   A BIBLIOGRAPHY OF THE   1925
WRITINGS OF D. H. LAWRENCE

first edition

A Bibliography | of the Writings of | D. H. Lawrence [*in green*] | By | Edward D. McDonald | With a Foreword by D. H. Lawrence | [*publisher's device in green*] | PHILADELPHIA | THE CENTAUR BOOKSHOP [*in green*] | 1925

Blue paper boards with a natural cloth backstrip, white paper label on upper cover printed in blue: *The Centaur* | [*decorative rule*] | D. H. LAW-RENCE | *by* | EDWARD D. MCDONALD | [*decorative rule*] | *Bibliographies* | [*vertical double rules appear on either side of lettering above*]; white paper label on spine printed in blue: *The* | *Writings of* | D. H. LAWRENCE | [*decorative rule*] | *A* | *Bibliography* | *by* | E. D. MCDONALD | CBS Top edges trimmed; fore and bottom edges untrimmed. $7\frac{9}{16}'' \times 4\frac{3}{4}''$. pp. [i]–[vi] + [1]–[154] and one plate facing page 54. Published 23 June 1925 at $3.50; 500 ordinary copies were printed. There were also 100 large-paper copies signed by the author and compiler at $10.00.

Contains: "The Bad Side of Books," pp. 9–14; collected in *Phoenix* (A76).

NOTES: Professor McDonald, with the English Department at Drexel Institute for many years, also compiled the *Bibliographical Supplement* (B31) and edited *Phoenix: The Posthumous Papers of D. H. Lawrence* (A76). The last item described in the *Bibliography* was *The Boy in the Bush* (A29) and the *Bibliographical Supplement* (B31) published in 1931 continues the account through *The Man Who Died* (A50).

B17   THE BEST BRITISH   1925
SHORT STORIES OF 1925

first edition

THE BEST | BRITISH SHORT STORIES | OF 1925 | WITH AN IRISH SUPPLEMENT | EDITED BY | EDWARD J. O'BRIEN | AND | JOHN COURNOS | [*publisher's device*] | BOSTON | SMALL, MAYNARD & COMPANY, INC. | PUBLISHERS

Blue cloth boards, blind stamped on upper cover: [*single rule forming border*]; white paper label set in blind stamped panel on upper cover printed in blue: The Best British | Short Stories of 1925 | [*short rule*] | EDWARD J. O'BRIEN [*short rule*] JOHN COURNOS | [*enclosed within double rule*]; white paper label on spine printed in blue: The | Best British | Short | Stories | of 1925 | [*short rule*] | O'BRIEN | COURNOS | [*enclosed within double rule*] Top edges trimmed. $7\frac{5}{16}'' \times 5\frac{1}{16}''$. pp. [i]–[xxii] + [1]–346. Published 17 October 1925 at $2.50; number of copies unknown.

Contains: "Jimmy and the Desperate Woman," pp. 88–114; first appeared in the *Criterion*, October 1924 (C125); collected in *The Woman Who Rode Away* (A41).

first edition

THE | BORZOI | 1925 | [*publisher's device*] | *Being a sort of record* | *of ten years of* | *publishing* | ALFRED·A·KNOPF | NEW YORK | [*enclosed within double rule in turn enclosed within decorative rule*]

Decorative paper boards with a blue cloth backstrip, embossed lettering in blue on gold panel on spine: THE | BORZOI | 1925 Top edges trimmed and stained black; fore and bottom edges untrimmed. $7\frac{5}{8}'' \times 5\frac{3}{16}''$. pp. [i]–[iv] + [i]–[xiv] + 1–[356]. Published 24 December 1925 at $2.00; 5000 ordinary copies were printed. There were also 500 large-paper copies.

Contains: "Accumulated Mail," pp. 119–28; collected in *Phoenix* (A76).

NOTES: This essay is devoted to the discussion of a selection of mail Lawrence received, and was probably written during the latter part of 1925; in the essay Lawrence refers to an article in the *Nation* about him, written by Edwin Muir, which appeared in the 11 February 1925 issue of the magazine. Apart from some comment on the Maurice Magnus controversy with Norman Douglas, the essay is largely concerned with Muir's criticism of Lawrence.

B19   THE GHOST-BOOK   1926

first edition

The | GHOST- | BOOK | [*enclosed within ornamental rule with drawing of ghost as background*] | SIXTEEN NEW STORIES | OF THE UNCANNY | COMPILED BY | LADY CYNTHIA ASQUITH | LONDON | HUTCHINSON AND CO. (PUBLISHERS) LTD. | PATERNOSTER ROW

Blue cloth boards, printed in light blue on upper cover: The | GHOST- | BOOK | [*enclosed within ornamental rule with drawing of ghost as background*]; printed in light blue on spine: [*drawing of tree with hanged man*] | The | GHOST | BOOK | CYNTHIA | ASQUITH | HUTCHINSON Top edges trimmed; fore edges rough-trimmed; bottom edges untrimmed. $9\frac{5}{16}'' \times 6''$. pp. [i]–[viii] + 1–[320]. Published 28 September 1926 at 7s. 6d.; number of copies unknown.

Contains: "The Rocking-Horse Winner," pp. 167–88; collected in *The Lovely Lady* (A63).

NOTES: The "Rocking Horse Winner" was probably written at the Villa Bernardo, Spotorno, sometime during the first half of 1926, after it was decided that "Glad Ghosts" (C143) was unsuitable for Lady Cynthia Asquith's book. See (C142.5).

B20   **THE BEST BRITISH**   1926
         SHORT STORIES OF 1926

first edition

THE BEST | BRITISH SHORT STORIES | OF 1926 | WITH AN IRISH SUPPLEMENT | EDITED BY | EDWARD J. O'BRIEN | [*publisher's device*] | DODD, MEAD & COMPANY | NEW YORK 1926

Blue cloth boards, blind stamped on upper cover: [*single rule forming border*]; cream paper label on upper cover set in a blind stamped panel printed in black: The Best British | Short Stories of 1926 | [*short rule*] | EDITED BY | EDWARD J. O'BRIEN | [*enclosed within double rule*]; cream paper label on spine printed in black: The | Best British | Short | Stories | of 1926 | [*short rule*] | EDWARD J. | O'BRIEN | [*enclosed within double rule*] All edges trimmed. 7⅜″ × 5″. pp. [i]–[xii] + [1]–[428]. Published 6 November 1926 at $2.50; the first printing consisted of 4000 copies.

Contains: "The Woman Who Rode Away," pp. 161–201; first appeared in the *Dial*, July and August 1925 (C131) and (C132); collected in *The Woman Who Rode Away* (A41).

B21   **MAX HAVELAAR**   1927

first edition

MAX HAVELAAR [*in orange*] | *or* | THE COFFEE SALES OF THE | NETHERLANDS TRADING | COMPANY | *BY MULTATULI (1860)* | *Translated from the Dutch by* | W. SIEBENHAAR | *With an Introduction by* | D. H. LAWRENCE | [*publisher's device*] | *NEW YORK & LONDON* | ALFRED·A·KNOPF | 1927 | [*enclosed within decorative rule forming border*]

Orange cloth boards with a blue cloth backstrip, stamped in gold on spine: [*single rule*] | [*decorative rule*] | [*single rule*] | MAX | HAVELAAR | [*single rule*] | MULTATULI | [*single rule*] | [*decorative rule*] | ALFRED A. KNOPF | [*single rule*] | [*decorative rule*] | [*single rule*] Top edges trimmed and stained blue; fore and bottom edges rough-trimmed. 8⅛″ × 5½″. pp.

[i]–[xii] + [1]–[316]. Published 3 January 1927 at $3.00; the first printing consisted of 2000 copies.

Contains: "Introduction," pp. v–ix; collected in *Phoenix* (A76).

NOTES: Lawrence met W. Siebenhaar, the translator of *Max Havelaar*, in Australia and apparently promised help in finding a publisher for the manuscript. Siebenhaar sent the first part of his translation to Lawrence at Taos in the autumn of 1922, and Lawrence received the final manuscript and wrote his introduction at the Villa Mirenda in May 1926. Multatuli was the pseudonym of E. D. Dekker.

NOTES (2): There is a copy of *Max Havelaar* at the University of Texas identical with that described except that it is bound in brown cloth with a decorative spine printed in green and black. Knopf issued *Max Havelaar* in the Blue Jade Library, and the device indication for the Blue Jade Library is blind stamped on the upper cover of the copy described above. The copy bound in brown cloth is $8\frac{1}{16}$ inches high.

B22 GREAT STORIES OF ALL NATIONS 1927

first edition

[*thin rule*] | [*thick rule*] | [*thin rule*] | GREAT STORIES | OF ALL NATIONS | [*short ornamental rule*] | *One Hundred Sixty Complete Short* | *Stories from the Literatures of All* | *Periods and Countries* | [*short ornamental rule*] | EDITED BY | MAXIM LIEBER | & | BLANCHE COLTON WILLIAMS, PH.D. | *Head of Department of English,* | *Hunter College, New York* | [*publisher's device*] | NEW YORK | BRENTANO'S·PUBLISHERS | [*printer's ornament*] MCM-XXVII [*printer's ornament*] | [*thin rule*] | [*thick rule*] | [*thin rule*]

Blue cloth boards, stamped in gold on upper cover: GREAT STORIES | OF ALL NATIONS | [*short rule*] | LIEBER *and* WILLIAMS | [*enclosed within double rule in turn enclosed within ornamental rule in turn enclosed within single rule*]; stamped in gold on spine: [*thin rule*] | [*ornamental rule*] | [*thin rule*] | [*thick rule*] | GREAT | STORIES | OF ALL | NATIONS | [*short rule*] | LIEBER | *and* | WILLIAMS | [*thick rule*] | [*thin rule*] | [*ornamental rule*] | [*thin rule*] | BRENTANO'S Top edges trimmed; fore and bottom edges rough-trimmed. $8\frac{7}{16}'' \times 5\frac{5}{8}''$. pp. [i]–xii + [1]–[1122]. Published 17 September 1927 at $5.00; number of copies unknown.

Contains: "Two Blue Birds," pp. 425–38; first appeared in the *Dial*, April 1927 (C154); collected in *The Woman Who Rode Away* (A41).

B22.5 THE FIRST SCORE 1927

first edition

The First Score | BY | *CYRIL W. BEAUMONT* | [*short rule*] | An Account of the Foundation and | Development of the Beaumont Press | and its first Twenty Publications | [*short rule*] | [*ornament in blue*] | [*short rule*] | LONDON | The Beaumont Press | 1927 [*the whole enclosed within an ornamental border in blue*]

Decorative yellow, black and white paper boards with white vellum backstrip. Stamped in gold on spine, reading from bottom to top: THE FIRST SCORE ∴ C. W. BEAUMONT Top edges trimmed; fore and bottom edges untrimmed. $8\frac{7}{8}'' \times 5\frac{3}{4}''$. pp. [i]–[xii] + 1–100. Published about September 1927; the first printing consisted of 390 copies; 80 on handmade parchment vellum, signed by the author and numbered from 1 to 80, of which 5 were not for sale; 310 on handmade paper, numbered from 81 to 390, of which 10 were not for sale.

Contains: "Letters," to C. W. Beaumont.

NOTES: Cyril W. Beaumont was the proprietor of the Beaumont Press and published Lawrence's book of poems *Bay*, the eighth book to be issued under the imprint (A12). The colophon notes that the printing of the book was completed on 19 September 1927.

B23 THE BLACK CAP 1927

first edition

The | BLACK CAP | [*drawing of man with knife*] | NEW STORIES OF MURDER & MYSTERY | COMPILED BY | CYNTHIA · ASQUITH | HUTCHINSON & CO. (Publishers), LTD. | Paternoster Row [*short rule*] LONDON, E. C. 4.

Blue cloth boards, printed in light blue on upper cover: *The* | BLACK CAP | [*drawing of pistol, blackjack, etc.*] | NEW STORIES OF MURDER & MYSTERY | COMPILED BY | CYNTHIA · ASQUITH; printed in light blue on spine: *The* | BLACK CAP | NEW STORIES | OF | MURDER & MYSTERY | COMPILED BY | CYNTHIA | ASQUITH | HUTCHINSON All edges trimmed. $6'' \times 5\frac{1}{8}''$. pp. [i]–[viii] + 9–[320]. Published October 1927 at 7*s.* 6*d.*; number of copies unknown.

Contains: "The Lovely Lady," pp. 216–38; collected in *The Lovely Lady* (A63).

NOTES: This story was probably written at the Villa Mirenda early in 1927, as Lawrence sent the manuscript to Curtis Brown's office on 11 March; Lawrence referred to this particular collection of "unusual stories" as "murder stories."

B24   **SCRUTINIES BY**   1928
           VARIOUS WRITERS

first edition

SCRUTINIES | By VARIOUS WRITERS | Collected by | EDGELL RICKWORD | LONDON | WISHART & COMPANY | 1928

Blue cloth boards, stamped in gold on spine: [*thick rule*] | [*thin rule*] | SCRUTINIES | [*short rule*] | *Critical Essays* | *by* | VARIOUS | WRITERS | [*printer's ornament*] | [*within single rule which joins thick rule at top to form border*] | · | WISHART | [*thin rule*] | [*thick rule*] | [*enclosed within single rule which joins thick rule at bottom to form border*] Top and fore edges trimmed; bottom edges untrimmed. $7\frac{7}{16}'' \times 5\frac{3}{8}''$. pp. [i]–[x] + 1–[198]. Published March 1928 at 7s. 6d.; number of copies unknown. Some copies were bound in tan cloth boards printed in brown.

Contains: "John Galsworthy," pp. 51–72; collected in *Phoenix* (A76).

NOTES: Galsworthy met Lawrence at a luncheon in 1917 and recorded his impressions of the "provincial genius"; he found Lawrence interesting, but "a type I could not get along with." Galsworthy had been rather severely critical of *Sons and Lovers* and *The Rainbow* and indeed, had told Lawrence on one occasion that *The Rainbow* was a failure as a work of art. Lawrence wrote his Galsworthy essay for Edgell Rickword's *Scrutinies* at the Villa Mirenda in February 1927 and sent the manuscript to Miss Pearn in the Curtis Brown office on the 28th with a letter which remarked that he was ashamed of its untidy condition.

B25   **THE MOTHER**   1928

first edition in Travellers' Library

THE MOTHER | (*La Madre*) | by | GRAZIA DELEDDA | WINNER OF THE NOBEL PRIZE 1927 | Translated from the Italian by | MARY G. STEEGMANN | With an Introduction by | D. H. LAWRENCE | [*publisher's device*] | LONDON | JONATHAN CAPE 30 BEDFORD SQUARE

Blue cloth boards, stamped in gold on spine: [*decorative rule*] | *The* | MOTHER | [*printer's ornament*] | GRAZIA | DELEDDA | [*publisher's device*] JONATHAN | CAPE | [*ornamental rule*]; blind stamped on lower cover: [*publisher's initials*] All edges trimmed. $6\frac{13}{16}'' \times 4\frac{5}{8}''$. pp. [1]–[224]. Published April 1928 at 3*s*. 6*d*.; the first printing consisted of 4000 copies.

Contains: "Introduction," pp. 7–13; collected in *Phoenix* (A76).

NOTES: Lawrence's interest in the Sardinian writer Grazia Deledda was recorded as early as February 1919 when he wrote to Katherine Mansfield that Deledda was "very interesting"; in *Sea and Sardinia* Lawrence mentions that he has found what he believes to be the house of Deledda. The "Introduction" was probably written shortly before its publication; a note on the manuscript described by Powell and Tedlock indicates that he did the work by arrangement with Jonathan Cape.

B25.5   BUCH DES DANKES   1928
FUR HANS CAROSSA

first edition

BUCH DES DANKES | FÜR | HANS CAROSSA | [*short rule*] | *Dem 15. Dezember 1928* | [*short decorative rule*] | IM INSEL [*printer's device*] VERLAG·LEIPZIG [*the whole enclosed within a double rule*]

Orange cloth boards. Stamped in gold on upper cover: H C [*decorative initials with leaf spray*] Stamped in gold on spine: BUCH DES | DANKES | FÜR | HANS | CAROSSA [*the preceding five lines on black panel*] | [*rule*] | [*a series of vertical rules with decorative leaf sprays*] [*the whole enclosed within a single rule*] All edges trimmed; top edges stained yellow. $8'' \times 5''$. pp. [1]–[196]. Published about September 1928; number of copies unknown.

Contains: "Kirchenlieder im Leben Eines Mannes," a translation by Frieda Lawrence of "Hymns in a Man's Life"; see (A53) and (C178).

B26   BOTTOM DOGS   1929

first edition

EDWARD DAHLBERG | BOTTOM | DOGS | WITH AN INTRODUCTION BY | D. H. LAWRENCE | LONDON | G. P. PUTNAM'S SONS

Black cloth boards, stamped in gold on upper cover: BOTTOM DOGS; stamped in gold on spine: BOTTOM | DOGS | [*printer's ornament*] | EDWARD | DAHLBERG | PUTNAM Top edges trimmed and gilt; fore and bottom edges untrimmed. $7\frac{3}{8}'' \times 5\frac{1}{16}''$. pp. [i]–[xxiv] + [1]–[288]. Published November 1929 at 15*s*.; the edition consisted of 520 numbered copies, printed on cream paper. Regular copies printed on white paper without the certificate of limitation were published at the same time.

Contains: "Introduction," pp. vii–xix; collected in *Phoenix* (A76).

NOTES: Lawrence signed the "Introduction" at Bandol in 1929, and the book itself was signed by Dahlberg in Brussels on 10 October 1928; thus it is probable that Lawrence wrote the piece sometime during the early part of 1929, as the Lawrences left Bandol in March and returned in September.

B27 IMAGIST ANTHOLOGY 1930

first edition

[*printer's ornament*] | IMAGIST ANTHOLOGY 1930 | COVICI, FRIEDE * NEW YORK [*printing enclosed within single rule*] | [*printer's ornament*]

Light blue cloth boards, yellow paper label on spine printed in black: [*printer's ornament*] | [*single rule*] | Imagist | Anthology | 1930 | [*single rule*] | Covici | Friede | [*single rule*] | [*printer's ornament*] Top edges trimmed; fore and bottom edges untrimmed. $8\frac{3}{16}'' \times 5\frac{1}{2}''$. pp. [1]–[240]. Published 10 April 1930 at $3.50; the first edition consisted of 1000 copies.

Contains: "True Love at Last," pp. 183–84; collected in *Last Poems* (A62).
   "Lucifer," p. 185; collected in *Last Poems*.
   "Sphinx," p. 187; collected in *Last Poems*.
   "Intimates," p. 189; collected in *Last Poems*.
   "Image-Making Love," p. 191; collected in *Last Poems*.
   "Ultimate Reality," p. 193; collected in *Last Poems*.

NOTES: These poems were among those included in the "More Pansies" section of *Last Poems* (A62), which was edited by Richard Aldington and Pino Orioli from manuscripts left by Lawrence at his death.

first edition

The Grand Inquisitor [*initial letters of preceding three words in green*] | By F. M. Dostoevsky | Translated by S. S. Koteliansky | With an intro-duction by | D. H. Lawrence | Elkin Mathews & Marrot | 1930

Vellum boards, printed in black on upper cover: F. M. DOSTOEVSKY | [*design of inlaid blue and black morocco leather*] | The GRAND INQUISITOR | S. S. Koteliansky; printed in black on spine reading upwards: THE GRAND INQUISITOR Top edges trimmed and stained black; fore and bottom edges untrimmed. $9\frac{1}{2}'' \times 6\frac{5}{16}''$. pp. [i]–xvi + 1–[40]. Published July 1930 at 3 guineas; the edition consisted of 300 numbered copies.

Contains: "Introduction," pp. iii–xvi; collected in *Phoenix* (A76).

NOTES: Tedlock, in his manuscript study (B51), concludes that the "Introduction" to *The Grand Inquisitor* was one of the last things Lawrence wrote; this conclusion is reached on the basis of the similarity between the notebook in which the manuscript is found and that used by Lawrence for the review of Eric Gill's *Art Nonsense* (C212) written at Bandol in 1929. Apart from this evidence, one would suppose it to have been written earlier during the collaboration between Lawrence and Koteliansky, for according to Koteliansky's statement about the collabor-ation, Lawrence did share responsibility for the translation of *The Grand Inquisitor*; see (A13).

There was another issue of *The Grand Inquisitor*, obviously printed from the same type, internally exactly the same in every respect as the copy described here, with the exception of the title page, which bore the imprint of the Aquila Press. These copies were bound in decorative paper boards with an imitation vellum backstrip, stamped in gold on the spine. They were slightly taller than the copies described here.

B29   THE BEST POEMS OF 1930   1930

first edition

The | BEST POEMS | *of* 1930 | [*publisher's device*] | *Selected by* | THOMAS MOULT | *& decorated by* | ELIZABETH MONT-GOMERY | LONDON | *Jonathan Cape, Limited* | TORONTO

Decorative grey cloth boards, cream paper label on spine printed in black: The | BEST | POEMS | *of* | 1930 Top edges trimmed; fore and bottom edges untrimmed. $7\frac{7}{16}'' \times 5''$. [i]–[ii] + [i]–xiv + 1–[104].

Published 22 September 1930 at 6*s.*; the first printing consisted of 3500 copies.

Contains: "Triumph of the Machine," pp. 93–94; first appeared in the *London Mercury,* June 1930 (C200); collected in *Last Poems* (A62).

B30 SON OF WOMAN 1931

first edition

SON OF WOMAN | The Story of | D. H. LAWRENCE | *by* | JOHN | MIDDLETON | MURRY | [*publisher's device*] | [*quotation from D. H. Lawrence*] | London | JONATHAN CAPE | Toronto

Black cloth boards, stamped in gold on spine: [*triple rule joined at left and right by vertical rules*] | SON OF | WOMAN | THE STORY | OF | D. H. LAWRENCE | [*printer's ornament*] | J. MIDDLETON | MURRY | JONATHAN CAPE | [*triple rule joined at left and right by vertical rules*]; blind stamped on lower cover: [*publisher's device*] Top and fore edges trimmed; bottom edges rough-trimmed. $7\frac{7}{8}'' \times 5\frac{3}{8}''$. pp. [1]–[400]. Published 13 April 1931 at 10*s.* 6*d.*; number of copies unknown.

Contains: "Self-Portrait," frontispiece; also published in *D. H. Lawrence, A First Study* (F5) and in the definitive edition of *Pansies* (A47c).
"Drawing of the Phoenix," p. 206; with a facsimile reproduction of a holograph note to Murry.

NOTES: *Son of Woman* was the first movement in the Carswell–Murry controversy over Lawrence; its publication called forth Catherine Carswell's *Savage Pilgrimage* (B37) to which Murry replied with his *Reminiscences* (F24). *Son of Woman* was published with a new introduction by Murry in 1954.

B31 THE WRITINGS OF 1931
D. H. LAWRENCE 1925–1930

first edition

The Writings of | D. H. Lawrence [*in red*] | 1925–1930 | A Bibliographical Supplement | By | Edward D. McDonald | [*publisher's device in red*] | PHILADELPHIA | THE CENTAUR BOOKSHOP [*in red*] | 1931

Red paper boards with a natural linen backstrip, white paper label on upper cover printed in red: *The Centaur* | [*single rule*] | D. H. LAWRENCE | *A BIBLIOGRAPHICAL* | SUPPLEMENT | *by* | EDWARD D. MCDONALD | [*single rule*] | *Bibliographies* | [*double vertical rules on either side of label form box with horizontal rules enclosing five lines of lettering in centre*]; white paper label on spine printed in red: *The* | *Writings of* | D. H. LAWRENCE | 1925–1930 | [*ornamental rule*] | *A* | *Bibliographical* | *Supplement* | E. D. MCDONALD | CBS Top edges trimmed; fore and bottom edges rough-trimmed. 7$\frac{9}{16}$″ × 4$\frac{3}{4}$″. pp. [i]–[iv] + [1]–[144]. Published October 1931 at $3.50; 350 ordinary copies were printed. There were also 60 numbered large-paper copies signed by the compiler at $10.00.

Contains: "The Crown," frontispiece; a facsimile reproduction of the first page of manuscript with a drawing of the Lawrence phoenix.

NOTES: This *Bibliographical Supplement* continues the Lawrence bibliographical study begun with McDonald's *Bibliography of D. H. Lawrence* (B16); the last item described is *The Man Who Died* (A50), published in 1931. The essay, "The Crown," was first published in the *Signature* (C39), (C40) and (C41) and collected in *Reflections on the Death of a Porcupine* (A32).

B32   THE TRIAL OF JEANNE D'ARC   1931

first edition

THE TRIAL | OF | JEANNE D'ARC | And Other Plays | *by* | Edward Garnett | [*publisher's device*] | With a Foreword by | John Galsworthy | Jonathan Cape | Thirty Bedford Square, London

Green cloth boards, stamped in gold on spine: THE | TRIAL OF |JEANNE | D'ARC | [*printer's ornament*] | EDWARD | GARNETT | JONATHAN CAPE; blind stamped on lower cover: [*publisher's device*] Top and fore edges trimmed; bottom edges untrimmed. 7$\frac{1}{2}$″ × 4$\frac{7}{8}$″. pp. [1]–[304]. Published October 1931 at 6s.; number of copies unknown. There were also 100 specially bound copies signed by Mr Garnett.

Contains: "Letter," pp. 16–17; written to Edward Garnett in 1912 about *The Trial of Jeanne D'Arc*.

first edition

CHARIOT OF THE SUN [*in red*] | by | Harry Crosby [*in red*] | Introduction by D. H. Lawrence | The Black Sun Press | Rue Cardinale | Paris | MCMXXXI [*in red*]

White paper wrappers, printed in red and black on upper cover: CHARIOT OF THE SUN [*in red*] | by | Harry Crosby [*in red*] | The Black Sun Press | Rue Cardinale | Paris | MCMXXXI [*in red*]; printed in red on spine: C | H | A | R | I | O | T | O | F | T | H | E | S | U | N | 1931 Top edges trimmed; fore and bottom edges untrimmed. $9\frac{1}{16}'' \times 6\frac{7}{8}''$. pp. [i]–[viii] + I–[XXIV] + 1–[80]. Published November 1931 at $10.00; 500 copies were printed.

Contains: "Introduction," I–XVIII; first appeared in *Exchanges*, December 1929 (C194) as "Chaos in Poetry"; a slightly different version was collected in *Phoenix* (A76).

NOTES: According to the prospectus issued by Harry F. Marks in New York the copies on Holland paper were to sell for $40.00 the set of four volumes and the Navarre copies for $10.00 the set. The individual volumes of the Navarre copies were sold separately at $5.00 each, with the exception of volume two, which was only available with the sets.

There were several editions of Harry Crosby's poems before the one described here, but this, the *Edition de Luxe*, was the only one to contain the introduction by D. H. Lawrence.

Something of Lawrence's relations with the Crosbys is told in the entry for *Sun* (A35). According to Caresse Crosby, the essay was written for Harry Crosby at the Villa Mirenda on 1 May 1928; Lawrence sent the essay to the Crosbys and told Harry Crosby that he might do as he wished with it.

B34   YOUNG LORENZO   1931

a. *first edition*

YOUNG LORENZO | EARLY LIFE OF D. H. LAWRENCE | CONTAINING HITHERTO | UNPUBLISHED LETTERS, ARTICLES | AND REPRODUCTIONS OF PICTURES. | BY | ADA LAWRENCE AND G. STUART GELDER | [*Lawrence phoenix*] | G. ORIOLI | LUNGARNO DELLE GRAZIE | FLORENCE

Vellum paper boards, printed in red on upper cover: [*Lawrence phoenix*];
printed in red on spine: EARLY LIFE | OF | D. H. LAWRENCE | [*enclosed
within single rule forming box*] Top edges rough-trimmed; fore and bottom
edges untrimmed $8\frac{3}{8}'' \times 5\frac{3}{4}''$. pp. [i]–[ii] + [i]–[xiv] + [1]–[276]. Published 15 January 1932 at 25s.; the edition consisted of 740 copies.

b. *first English edition*

EARLY LIFE OF | D. H. LAWRENCE | TOGETHER
WITH | HITHERTO UNPUBLISHED | LETTERS AND
ARTICLES | BY | ADA LAWRENCE & | G. STUART
GELDER | *With Sixteen Illustrations* | LONDON: | MARTIN
SECKER | 1932 [*the whole enclosed within a single rule forming a box*]

Brown cloth boards, stamped in gold on upper cover: [*Lawrence phoenix*];
stamped in gold on spine: EARLY LIFE | OF | D. H. LAWRENCE | ADA |
LAWRENCE | & | STUART | GELDER | SECKER Top edges trimmed and
stained green; fore and bottom edges untrimmed. $7\frac{5}{16}'' \times 5''$. pp. [1]–
[220]. Published November 1932 at 7s. 6d.; 1440 copies were printed.

Contains: "Letters," to Ada Lawrence, 1911–1930, Gertrude Cooper
   and Ada's son.
   "Corot," pp. 67–69 (a poem); first appeared in *Love Poems*
      (A3).
   "To Lettice, My Sister," pp. 209–210 (a poem); first ap-
      peared in *Amores* (A9) as "Brother and Sister."
   "The Fly in the Ointment (A Blot)," pp. 215–230 (a story);
      although presumably included here as an unpublished
      story, "The Fly in the Ointment" first appeared in the *New
      Statesman*, 13 August 1913 (C22).
   "Rachel Annand Taylor," pp. 233–243 (an essay).
   "Art and the Individual," pp. 249–268 (an essay).
   Paintings, ff. p. 268:
   "A Vase of Flowers," reproduced in *Art News*, February 1957.
   "Still Life."
   "The Stick Gatherer."
      A copy of "A Lonely Life" by Hugh Cameron.
   "Autumn."
   "Tiger's Head," reproduced in *Art News*, February 1957.
      A copy of "Tiger's Head" by J. M. Swan.
   "An Idyll" (after M. Greiffenhagen).
   "Landscape."

A copy of "Fast Falls the Evening" by B. W. Leader.

"Landscape" (after Corot). A copy of "Summer Evening; Muthill" by J. Lawton Wingate.

"The Orange Market" (after Brangwyn).

English edition only:

"The Dead Mother," p. 161 (a poem); first appeared in *Amores* (A9) as "The Bride."

"Adolf," pp. 165–180; although presumably included here as an unpublished story or sketch, "Adolf" first appeared in the *Dial*, September 1920 (C73); it was first collected in the *New Keepsake for 1921* (B8) and included in *Phoenix* (A76).

NOTES: This book, actually a memoir of Lawrence by his sister, Lettice Ada, contains a number of letters, unpublished elsewhere, to Ada, her son Jack Clarke, and to Miss Gertrude Cooper, a member of the group of young people in Eastwood known as "The Pagans."

Ada's memoir covers approximately the same period of time as Jessie Chambers' *Personal Record* (B43), but from within the family circle. The reproductions of the paintings and the essay on Rachel Annand Taylor were not included in the Secker edition; Lawrence met Mrs Taylor at the house of Ernest Rhys in London and subsequently made her the subject of a talk before a Croydon study group. In 1956 Professor Majl Ewing of the University of California at Los Angeles edited *Eight Letters of D. H. Lawrence to Rachel Annand Taylor* (A97), and he gives an account of Lawrence's association with Mrs Taylor in his "Foreword" to the letters. The Stanford University Library owns the original corrected typescript of *Young Lorenzo*.

B35   LORENZO IN TAOS   1932

first edition

[*single rule*] | MABEL DODGE LUHAN | [*decorative rule*] | LORENZO [*in red*] | IN [*in red*] | TAOS [in red] | [*publisher's device*] | [*decorative rule*] | ALFRED·A·KNOPF | NEW YORK MCMXXXII | [*single rule*] | [*decorative rules run vertically on either side of lettering forming borders with horizontal rules*]

Orange cloth boards, printed in red on upper cover: [*series of horizontal decorative rules enclosed within double rule forming border*]; printed in red on lower cover: [*publisher's device*]; printed in red on spine: [*double rule*] | [*single rule*] | [*decorative rule*] | LORENZO | IN TAOS | [*printer's ornaments*] | MABEL DODGE | LUHAN [*preceding five lines stamped in gold*] | [*decorative rule*] | [*single rule*] | [*single rule*] | [*decorative rule*] | ALFRED · A · | KNOPF | [*decorative rule*] | [*single rule*] | [*double rule*] | [*decorative rules occupy spaces between lettering and horizontal rules*] Top edges trimmed and stained dark brown; fore and bottom edges rough-trimmed. $8\frac{5}{8}'' \times 5\frac{3}{4}''$. pp. [i]–[xii] + [1]–[356]. Published 15 February 1932 at $3.50; the first printing consisted of 2000 copies.

Contains: "Letters," to Mabel Dodge Luhan, 1921–1930.

NOTES: Mabel Dodge Luhan was a wealthy American woman who invited the Lawrences to come to the United States after reading *Sea and Sardinia* (A20), having become convinced that he was the proper person to write about the Taos country. Her book gives a detailed account of her association with Lawrence and contains many letters not available elsewhere. The life of the Lawrences in Taos is exceptionally well documented; apart from the Luhan book, memoirs of the residence in the United States and Mexico are found in Merrild's *A Poet and Two Painters* (B47), Dorothy Brett's *Lawrence and Brett* (F26) and in Witter Bynner's *Journey with Genius* (B55). *Lorenzo in Taos* is written in the form of a letter to Robinson Jeffers, the American poet, whom Lawrence never met, and Mrs Luhan's book is an attempt to present Lawrence to Jeffers. Mrs Luhan gave Frieda Lawrence the ranch near Taos where Lawrence is buried, receiving in exchange the manuscript of *Sons and Lovers*.

B36   D. H. LAWRENCE   1932
      AN UNPROFESSIONAL STUDY

first edition

ANAÏS NIN | D. H. LAWRENCE [*in red*] | *An Unprofessional Study* | *With two facsimile manuscript pages out of* | *Lady Chatterley's Lover* | [*publisher's device*] | Paris 1932 | EDWARD W. TITUS | *at the sign of the black manikin* | 4, RUE DELAMBRE, MONTPARNASSE

Black cloth boards, stamped in gold on upper cover: ANAÏS NIN | D. H. LAWRENCE; stamped in gold on spine: D. H. | LAWRENCE | [*short rule*] | ANAÏS NIN | E. W. TITUS | PARIS Top edges trimmed; fore edges rough-trimmed; bottom edges untrimmed. $7\frac{3}{4}'' \times 5\frac{3}{16}''$. pp. [i]–[xii] + 1–[148]. Published April 1932 at 12s. 6d.; the edition consisted of 550 numbered and signed copies.

Contains: "My Skirmish with Jolly Roger," pp. 76–77; a facsimile reproduction of two pages of the holograph manuscript.

NOTES: Although the title page of *An Unprofessional Study* states that the illustration consists of two pages from *Lady Chatterley's Lover*, actually the reproductions are of the first and last pages of the specially written "Introduction" to the Paris edition of *Lady Chatterley's Lover* (A42c). This is the essay later published separately as *My Skirmish with Jolly Roger* (A48a) and later revised as *A Propos of Lady Chatterley's Lover* (A48b). E. W. Titus also printed the Paris edition of *Lady Chatterley's Lover* for Lawrence.

B37   THE SAVAGE PILGRIMAGE   1932

first edition

THE | SAVAGE PILGRIMAGE | *A NARRATIVE OF* | D. H. LAWRENCE | BY | Catherine Carswell | *It has been a savage enough pilgrimage . . . . We* | *keep faith. I always feel death only strengthens* | *that—the faith between those who have it.* | D. H. LAWRENCE, 1923 | LONDON | Chatto and Windus | 1932

Orange cloth boards, stamped in gold on spine: [*ornamental rule*] | THE SAVAGE | PILGRIMAGE | [*printer's ornament*] | A NARRATIVE | OF | D. H. LAWRENCE | [*printer's ornament*] | Catherine | Carswell | CHATTO & WINDUS | [*ornamental rule*] Top edges trimmed and stained orange; fore edges trimmed; bottom edges rough-trimmed. 8″ × 5$\frac{3}{16}$″. pp. [i]–[ii] + [i]–[xiv] + 1–296. Published 23 June 1932 at 7s. 6d.; the first printing consisted of 3300 copies of which only about 1000 copies were sold.

Contains: "Letters," to Catherine Carswell.

NOTES: Catherine Carswell was a friend of Lawrence and an observer of his literary career almost from its beginning. She reviewed *The White Peacock* (A1) for the *Glasgow Herald*, and later her associations with that paper were terminated because of a favourable review she wrote of *The Rainbow* (A7). She did not meet Lawrence until he and Frieda returned from the Continent during the summer of 1914. The Lawrences were staying with Gordon Campbell in Kensington when they met Mrs Carswell, then Mrs Jackson, who knew Ivy Low, already a friend of the Lawrences.

Mrs Carswell wrote *The Savage Pilgrimage* as a refutation to Murry's *Son of Woman* (B30). Her strictures on Murry were objectionable to him, and a threatened lawsuit persuaded the publishers to withdraw *The Savage Pilgrimage*, but not before some thousand copies were sold. The edition published by Secker in December 1932 contains the text revised to conform with Murry's demands. The first American edition published by Harcourt in October 1932 contains the Secker text.

The Savage Pilgrimage was published in a French translation, *Le Pelerin Solitaire*, at Paris by Armand Colin in 1935.

NOTES (2): A new edition of the *Savage Pilgrimage* was published by Secker and Warburg in 1951 with a short note by John Carswell, Mrs Carswell's son.

B38 REMINISCENCES OF 1933
D. H. LAWRENCE

first edition

REMINISCENCES OF | D. H. LAWRENCE | BY | JOHN | MIDDLETON | MURRY | [*publisher's device*] | JONATHAN CAPE | THIRTY BEDFORD SQUARE | LONDON

Orange cloth boards, printed in blue on lower cover: [*publisher's device*]; printed in blue on spine: REMINIS- | CENCES OF | D. H. LAWRENCE | JOHN | MIDDLETON | MURRY | JONATHAN | CAPE Top edges trimmed and stained blue; fore edges trimmed; bottom edges rough-trimmed. $7\frac{7}{8}'' \times 5\frac{3}{8}''$. pp. [1]–[284]. Published January 1933 at 7s. 6d.; a first printing consisted of 3000 copies.

Contains: "Letters," to John Middleton Murry.

NOTES: Murry's *Reminiscences* is his counter-attack to Mrs Carswell's *Savage Pilgrimage* (B37); here Murry reprints the "Reminiscences," which appeared in the *Adelphi* from June 1930 (C202) to March 1931, and his criticism of Lawrence published during Lawrence's lifetime. The remainder of the book is devoted to an account of the Murry-Lawrence relationship and a point-by-point rejoinder to Mrs Carswell.

B38.5 LOOKING BACK 1933
first edition

LOOKING BACK | AN AUTOBIOGRAPHICAL | EXCURSION | *By* | NORMAN | DOUGLAS | Volume I | [*ornament*] | LONDON | CHATTO and WINDUS | 1933

Decorative red paper boards. Stamped in gold on spine: LOOKING | BACK | AN AUTOBIOGRAPHICAL | EXCURSION | NORMAN | DOUGLAS | VOLUME I Top edges trimmed and gilt; fore and bottom edges untrimmed.

$9\frac{1}{4}'' \times 6\frac{3}{8}''$. Vol I: pp. [i]–[xii] + 1–268 + [i]–[iv]. Vol II: pp. [i]–[viii] + 269–[532]. Published 27 April 1933; 532 sets were printed, numbered and signed by Norman Douglas, at three guineas. Five hundred were for sale. The one volume edition was published on 15 February 1934 in an edition of 3250 copies.

Contains: "Letter," to John Ellingham Brooks.

NOTES: Lawrence first knew Douglas when he was on the staff of the *English Review* (c. 1909) and later in Florence. See (B14). Brooks was a translator and poet who lived on Capri; Lawrence met him there during the winter of 1919. Although the colophon states that 535 copies were printed, the publisher reports that only 532 copies were issued.

B39   D. H. LAWRENCE REMINISCENCES 1934 AND CORRESPONDENCE

first edition

EARL AND ACHSAH BREWSTER | [*short ornamental rule*] | D. H. LAWRENCE | REMINISCENCES AND | CORRE-SPONDENCE | *London* | MARTIN SECKER | *Number Five John Street* | *Adelphi*

Brown cloth boards, stamped in gold on spine: D. H. LAWRENCE | REMINISCENCES | AND | CORRESPONDENCE | [*five-pointed star*] | BREWSTER | SECKER Top edges trimmed and stained brown; fore edges untrimmed; bottom edges rough-trimmed. $8\frac{5}{8}'' \times 5\frac{11}{16}''$. pp. [1]–[320]. Published 15 February 1934 at 10*s*. 6*d*.; the edition consisted of 1000 copies.

Contains: "Letters," to Earl and Achsah Brewster, 1921–30.
         "Apostrophe to a Buddhist Monk," p. 50 (a poem).

NOTES: The Brewsters were constant friends of the Lawrences after their first meeting in Capri in the summer of 1921. Earl Brewster was an American, a New Englander and a student of Oriental philosophy; the Brewsters were in Ceylon where Frieda and Lawrence visited them en route to Australia in 1922. They were all together again in Italy the last time that Lawrence came to Europe, and it was Earl Brewster who accompanied Lawrence on his tour of the Etruscan remains from which Lawrence drew material for his posthumous *Etruscan Places* (A60). Lawrence was very fond of the Brewsters' daughter, Harwood, and several of the notebooks containing his manuscripts are inscribed from her to "Uncle David." The Brewsters were among the friends who gathered in Vence when Lawrence was buried there.

a. *first edition*

"*Not I, But The Wind...*" | [*printer's ornament*] *By* [*printer's ornament*] | FRIEDA LAWRENCE | *geb. Freiin von Richthofen* | [*printer's ornament*] | [*printer's ornament*] | *Privately Printed by* | THE RYDAL PRESS | *Santa Fe, New Mexico*

Grey paper boards with a natural cloth blackstrip, grey paper label on spine printed in red: [*Lawrence phoenix*] | "NOT I, BUT | THE WIND" | Frieda | Lawrence | [*printer's ornament*] Top edges unopened; fore and bottom edges untrimmed. $9\frac{1}{2}'' \times 6\frac{5}{16}''$. pp. [1]–[312]. Published 17 July 1934 at $7.50; the edition consisted of 1000 copies.

Contains: "Letters," to Frieda Lawrence and the Baroness von Richthofen.

"Song of a Man who is Loved," p. 63; collected in the Ark Press *Look! We Have Come Through!* (A10b); the text is slightly different from that in *Collected Poems* (A43).

All of Roses," pp. 67–68; collected in the Ark Press *Look! We Have Come Through!*; the text here is a combination of "River Roses," "Gloire de Dijon" and "Roses on the Breakfast Table" (A10a) and (A43), but it is an earlier version preferred by Frieda.

"Meeting Among the Mountains," pp. 70–71; first appeared in the *English Review*, February 1914 (C30), but with a slightly different text.

"The Mother of Sons," pp. 76–77; first appeared in *Poetry*, January 1914 (C29); collected in *Amores* (A9) as "Monologue of a Mother."

"Essay on Painting," p. 206; a facsimile reproduction of a manuscript page of "notes for an essay on painting."

"The Nightingale," pp. 215–21; first appeared in the *Forum*, September 1927 (C158) and collected in *Phoenix* (A76).

b. *first German edition*

FRIEDA LAWRENCE | geb. Freiin von Richthofen | NUR DER WIND... | Mit neunzig Briefen und funf Gedichten von | D. H. LAWRENCE | MCMXXXVI | VERLAG DIE RABEN-PRESSE

Grey cloth boards. Printed in red-brown on the spine: [*double rule*] FRIEDA

| LAWRENCE | NUR DER | WIND... | [*a series of eighteen horizontal rules*]
All edges trimmed. Top edges stained red-brown. 8" × 5". pp. [1]–[358], including the front free end-paper which is counted in the pagination. Published 1936; number of copies unknown.

Contains: "Letters," in German to members of Frieda's family which did not appear in the English language editions of the book.

NOTES: Lawrence first met Frieda Weekley, *née* Frieda von Richthofen, during the first days of March 1912 when he went to the home of Professor Ernest Weekley in Nottingham to ask for advice and assistance in getting an appointment as a lecturer in a German university. Lawrence had studied French under Professor Weekley when he attended the old Nottingham University College, but he did not know the Professor's family then. The association between the Baron's daughter and the miner's son was perhaps a strange one, but the two had in common an individuality which could not be constrained by conventional social patterns.

They left for Germany from Charing Cross on 3 May 1912, and Frieda became the one important person for Lawrence until his death at Vence in 1930. Professor Weekley's divorce from his wife became final on 28 May 1914, and Frieda and Lawrence, then in Italy, immediately departed for England, where they were married on 13 July at the Kensington Registry Office with Katherine Mansfield, John Middleton Murry and Gordon Campbell as witnesses.

When Frieda chose to print Lawrence's poems in her memoir, she selected earlier versions of several, rather than the final texts which Lawrence included in *Look! We Have Come Through!* (A10) and the *Collected Poems* (A43). The prefatory essay by Giorgio Belloli does not reappear in later editions of the book. A French version of Frieda's book, *Lawrence et Moi*, was published in Paris in 1936. Selections from the letters and poetry in Frieda's book were printed in *Nuova Antologia* for 16 December 1935 and in the *Neue Rundschau* for December 1934.

B40.5   **THEN AND NOW**   1935

first edition

THEN AND NOW | A Selection of articles, stories & poems, taken from the first fifty | numbers of 'Now & Then' 1921–35 | together with | Some illustrations, and cer- | tain other works now printed | for the first time | [*drawing of a house*] | JONATHAN CAPE | Thirty Bedford Square London | 1935

Cream paper boards, printed in red and black. The upper cover reproduces the complete title in a decorative fashion; on the lower cover are printed the names of a selection of contributors to the volume. Printed in black and white on the spine: THEN | AND | NOW | 1921 | 1935 | THEN AND NOW [*in white reading from bottom to top*] | [*publisher's device*] All edges trimmed and stained black. $7\frac{3}{8}'' \times 4\frac{3}{4}''$. pp. [1]–124.

Contains: "Giovanni Verga," pp. 17–19; first appeared in *Now & Then* for Spring 1928 (C168.5).

B41   ODD MAN OUT   1935

first edition

ODD MAN OUT | THE AUTOBIOGRAPHY OF A | "PROPAGANDA NOVELIST" | *by* | DOUGLAS GOLDRING | LONDON | CHAPMAN AND HALL LTD | 11 HENRIETTA STREET, W. C. 2

Orange cloth boards, printed on spine in yellow: [*single rule*] | [*short double rule*] ODD | [*short triple rule*] MAN | [*short quadruple rule*] OUT | [*preceding three lines enclosed within single rule*] | By | Douglas Goldring | [*preceding five lines enclosed within single rule*] | CHAPMAN & HALL | [*double rule*] All edges trimmed; top and fore edges stained dark grey. $8\frac{9}{16}'' \times 5\frac{1}{2}''$. pp. [i]–[x] + [1]–[342]. Published 24 June 1935 at 15*s*.; the first printing consisted of 1500 copies.

Contains: "Letters," to Douglas Goldring.

NOTES: Douglas Goldring founded the People's Theatre Society, which was involved in the production of a series of plays "for a people's theatre," including Lawrence's *Touch and Go* (A14).

B42   AMY LOWELL, A CHRONICLE   1935

first edition

AMY LOWELL | *A Chronicle* | WITH EXTRACTS FROM HER CORRESPONDENCE | BY | S. FOSTER DAMON | [*publisher's device*] | *With Illustrations* | BOSTON AND NEW YORK | HOUGHTON MIFFLIN COMPANY | The Riverside Press Cambridge | 1935

Red cloth boards, blind stamped on upper cover: [*single rule forming border*]; stamped in gold on spine: [*single rule*] | AMY | LOWELL | S. FOSTER | DAMON | HOUGHTON | MIFFLIN CO. | [*single rule*] All edges trimmed. $8\frac{13}{16}'' \times 5\frac{15}{16}''$. pp. [i]–[xxii] + [1]–774. Published 1 November 1935 at $5.00; the first printing consisted of 2500 copies.

Contains: "Letters," to Amy Lowell.

NOTES: On 31 July 1914 Lawrence wrote Harriet Monroe that he had had dinner with Amy Lowell and the Aldingtons the night before; Amy Lowell had insisted that Lawrence was an "Imagist," but this he continued to deny in spite of her quotation of "Wedding Morn" to prove the contrary.

B43   **D. H. LAWRENCE**   1935
A PERSONAL RECORD

first edition

D. H. LAWRENCE | *A Personal Record* | *by* | E. T. | [*publisher's device*] | JONATHAN CAPE | THIRTY BEDFORD SQUARE | LONDON

Light-tan cloth boards, printed in violet on upper cover: D. H. LAW-RENCE; printed in violet on spine: D. H. LAWRENCE | [*three short rules*] | E. T. | JONATHAN | CAPE Top and fore edges trimmed; bottom edges untrimmed. $7\frac{9}{16}'' \times 5''$. pp. [1]–[224]. Published May 1935 at 5*s.*; the first printing consisted of 3750 copies.

Contains: "Letters," to Jessie Chambers.

NOTES: Jessie Chambers, the Miriam of *Sons and Lovers* (A4), was a childhood friend of Lawrence's; this is her own story of the relationship between Lawrence, Lawrence's mother and herself which formed the basis for much of the novel. The pseudonym, "E. T.," was taken from the name "Eunice Temple," the title of an unpublished novel by Jessie Chambers. Lawrence and Jessie attended the Congregational Sunday School in Eastwood together, and later were both student-teachers at the Ilkeston Pupil-Teacher Training Centre. Much of Lawrence's early writing is derived from his experiences with Jessie and her brothers in the Midland countryside, especially from the days Lawrence spent at the Chambers' farm, the Haggs.

Helen Corke, the Croydon friend from whose journal Lawrence obtained the inspiration and much of the material for *The Trespasser*

(A2), wrote a memoir of Jessie Chambers called *D. H. Lawrence's Princess* (F59). A letter from Jessie Chambers to Helen Corke about Lawrence appeared in *Arena*, No. 4, 1950. The American edition of *A Personal Record*, published by Knight in 1936, contained a special introduction by John Middleton Murry. Portions of *A Personal Record* first appeared in the *European Quarterly* in 1934.

B44 CONTACTS 1935

first edition

CONTACTS | [*short ornamental rule*] | CURTIS BROWN | [*publisher's device*] | CASSELL | and Company, Ltd. | London, Toronto, Melbourne | and Sydney

Dark blue cloth boards, stamped on spine in gold: [*double rule*] | CONTACTS | CURTIS | BROWN | CASSELL | [*double rule*] Top edges stained black; all edges trimmed. $8\frac{7}{16}'' \times 5\frac{7}{16}''$. pp. [i]–[xii] + 1–[268]. Published 11 October 1935; number of copies unknown.

Contains: "Letters," to Curtis Brown.

NOTES: Lawrence wrote Curtis Brown from Taormina in April 1921 asking if Brown would undertake to place his "stuff," and offering for immediate placement the manuscripts of *Birds, Beasts and Flowers* (A27), "Mr. Noon" (A71) and *Sea and Sardinia* (A20). The Curtis Brown agency represented Lawrence for many years.

B45 NEW REPUBLIC ANTHOLOGY 1936

first edition

The | NEW REPUBLIC | *Anthology* | 1915 : 1935 | · | Edited by | GROFF CONKLIN | Introduction by | BRUCE BLIVEN | [*publisher's device*] | DODGE PUBLISHING COMPANY | New York | [*enclosed within thin rule in turn enclosed within thick rule*]

Grey cloth boards, printed in black and red on upper cover: *The New* | REPUBLIC [*in red*] | Anthology | ··· [*in red*] | 1915–1935; printed in black and red on spine: *The New* | REPUBLIC | *Anthology* | · [*in red*] | 1915 : 1935 | · [*in red*] | GROFF | CONKLIN | DODGE Top edges stained red; all edges trimmed. $8\frac{3}{8}'' \times 5\frac{5}{8}''$. pp. [i]–xlii + [1]–566. Published 5 October 1936 at $3.00; number of copies unknown.

Contains: "America, Listen to Your Own," pp. 129–34; first appeared in the *New Republic*, 15 December 1920 (C74).

B45.5

notes: *The New Republic Anthology* also printed Walter Lippmann's answer to Lawrence's essay in "The Crude Barbarian and the Noble Savage," which originally appeared in the *New Republic* with the Lawrence essay.

B45.5 GOTHAM BOOK MART 1936
CATALOGUE 36

first edition

[*drawing of a man running by Jean Cocteau*] | GOTHAM BOOK MART | 51 WEST 47th STREET, N. Y. | CATALOGUE 36

Orange paper covers, upper cover serves as the title page, printed in black as above. All edges trimmed. $8'' \times 4\frac{7}{8}''$. pp. [1]–[40]. Published autumn 1936, probably not sold. Number of copies unknown.

Contains "Letter," to J. B. Pinker, printed on lower cover. See (B48).

B46 THE MANUSCRIPTS OF 1937
D. H. LAWRENCE

first edition

the manuscripts [*in blue*] | of d. h. lawrence [*in blue*] | *A Descriptive Catalogue* | [*formalized Lawrence phoenix in red and blue*] | *Compiled by* | LAWRENCE CLARK POWELL | *with a foreword by* | ALDOUS HUXLEY | LOS ANGELES | THE PUBLIC LIBRARY | 1937

Blue paper covers, printed in black on upper cover: the manuscripts | of d. h. lawrence Top edges trimmed; fore and bottom edges untrimmed. $9\frac{7}{16}'' \times 6\frac{5}{16}''$. pp. [i]–[ii] + [i]–[xiv] + 1–[80]. Published Autumn 1937, probably not sold; the edition consisted of 750 copies.

Contains: "The Rainbow," ff. p. 8; a facsimile reproduction of a page from the manuscript.

notes: This catalogue was written to accompany an exhibition of the Lawrence manuscripts held at the Los Angeles Public Library and also served as a "sales catalogue" for the Los Angeles bookseller, Jake Zeitlin. According to Mr Powell, there was no organized sale; copies of the catalogue were sent to interested persons, and several of the manuscripts were disposed of in this way.

The catalogue also contains a facsimile reproduction of a page of the manuscript of "Odour of Chrysanthemums," but E. W. Tedlock in his study (B51) concludes upon evidence from a handwriting expert that the manuscript in question was not written by Lawrence himself, but is rather a fair copy prepared by Jessie Chambers for submission to Ford Madox Hueffer of the *English Review*.

B47   A POET AND TWO PAINTERS   1938

first edition

Knud Merrild | A POET | AND TWO PAINTERS | *A Memoir of D. H. Lawrence* | GEORGE ROUTLEDGE & SONS LTD. | BROADWAY HOUSE: 68–74 CARTER LANE, E. C. | LONDON

Chocolate-brown cloth boards, stamped in gold on spine: A POET | & TWO | PAINTERS | · | KNUD | MERRILD | ROUTLEDGE Top edges stained yellow; all edges trimmed. $8\frac{7}{16}'' \times 5\frac{5}{16}''$. pp. [i]–[xx] + 1–[372]. Published 20 June 1938 at 12s. 6d.; number of copies unknown.

Contains: "Letters," to Knud Merrild and Kai Götzsche.

NOTES: Knud Merrild and Kai Götzsche were two Danish painters who made their way to Taos from New York in an old Ford Model T touring car in 1922; they had a letter of introduction to Walter Unfer, a member of the Taos art colony, who later introduced them to the Lawrences. During the winter of 1922–23 Merrild and Götzsche lived in a cabin near the Lawrences on the Del Monte Ranch in the foothills above Taos. The Del Monte Ranch was near Lobo Ranch, the property Frieda was to receive from Mabel Dodge Luhan in exchange for the manuscript of *Sons and Lovers*.

During the winter at the ranch Knud Merrild designed several dust-jackets for the American editions of Lawrence's books; although Seltzer, the American publisher, purchased designs for *Kangaroo, Studies in Classic American Literature* and *The Captain's Doll*, he used only one of them, that for *The Captain's Doll* (A24b). Viking published an American edition of *A Poet and Two Painters* in January 1939.

B48 THE BOOK-COLLECTORS' ODYSSEY 1938

first edition

THE BOOK-COLLECTORS' | ODYSSEY | *or* | "*TRAVELS in the REALMS OF GOLD*" | [*drawing of sailing vessel*] | GOTHAM

BOOK MART | 51 West 47th Street—New York | BR yant
9–5666–5667 | *Catalog 39 Winter '38*

Cream paper covers, upper cover serves as the title page which is printed
in blue as above. All edges trimmed. $7\frac{3}{4}'' \times 5\frac{1}{4}''$. pp. 3–82. Published
Winter 1938, probably not sold; 5000 copies were printed.

Contains: "Letter," to J. B. Pinker. See (B45.5).

NOTES: This catalogue offered a group of 17 early holograph letters from
Lawrence "to an agent," presumably J. B. Pinker.

B49   A NUMBER OF PEOPLE   1939

first edition

A NUMBER OF PEOPLE | A BOOK OF REMINISCENCES
| BY | EDWARD MARSH | LONDON | WILLIAM HEINE-
MANN LTD | IN ASSOCIATION WITH | HAMISH
HAMILTON LTD

Red cloth boards, stamped in gold on spine: A NUMBER | OF PEOPLE |
A BOOK OF | REMINISCENCES | EDWARD | MARSH | HEINEMANN | & | HAMISH
HAMILTON All edges trimmed. $8\frac{1}{2}'' \times 5\frac{1}{2}''$. pp. [i]–xii + 1–420. Published
March 1939 at 15*s*.; number of copies unknown.

Contains: "Letters," to Edward Marsh.

NOTES: Edward Marsh was an early friend of Lawrence's and editor of
the *Georgian Poetry* anthologies, most of which contained poetry by
Lawrence; see B1, B3 and B11. A portion of the Marsh memoir appeared
in *Harper's Magazine*, July 1939 (C224).

B49.5   MAGIC CASEMENTS   1941

first edition

P. E. N. BOOKS | *General Editor*: Hermon Ould | MAGIC
CASEMENTS | by | Eleanor Farjeon | *London* | GEORGE ALLEN
AND UNWIN LTD [*the whole enclosed within a double rule in gold ink*]

Printed in black on spine, reading from bottom to top: MAGIC
CASEMENTS All edges trimmed. $7\frac{1}{4}'' \times 4\frac{3}{4}''$. pp. [1]–[48]. Published
November 1941 at 2*s*., number of copies unknown.

Contains: "Letter," to Eleanor Farjeon.

NOTES: See (B62).

B49.7   DAVID EDER: MEMOIRS OF   1945
A MODERN PIONEER

first edition

DAVID EDER | MEMOIRS OF A MODERN PIONEER |
Edited by | J. B. HOBMAN | *Foreword by* | SIGMUND FREUD |
Special Contributions by | DR. EDWARD GLOVER, LEONARD
STEIN, | DR. HARRY ROBERTS, AND SIR WYNDHAM
DEEDES | LONDON | VICTOR GOLLANCZ LTD | 1945

Green cloth boards, stamped in gold on spine: DAVID | EDER | GOLLANCZ
$7\frac{3}{4}''$ × 5″. All edges trimmed. pp. [1]–[216] and frontispiece. Published
19 March 1945; number of copies unknown.

Contains: "Letters," to David Eder.

NOTES: Lawrence was introduced to David and Edith Eder by Ivy Low,
Mrs Eder's niece, who married Maxim Litvinov.

B50   THE NINETEEN TWENTIES   1945

first edition

THE | *NINETEEN TWENTIES* | A General Survey and some
Personal | Memories | by | Douglas Goldring | LONDON |
NICHOLSON & WATSON

Light-tan cloth boards, stamped in gold on spine: DOUGLAS | GOLDRING
| NINETEEN TWENTIES [*reading from top to bottom*] | NICHOLSON | AND |
WATSON All edges trimmed. $8\frac{5}{16}''$ × $5\frac{1}{2}''$. pp. [i]–[xxiv] + 1–[266].
Published December 1945 at 12*s*. 6*d*.; the first printing consisted of 7000
copies.

Contains: "Letters," to Douglas Goldring.

B51   THE FRIEDA LAWRENCE   1948
COLLECTION

first edition

THE FRIEDA | LAWRENCE COL- | LECTION OF | D. H.
LAWRENCE | MANUSCRIPTS | A DESCRIPTIVE [*in red*]
| BIBLIOGRAPHY [*in red*] | BY E. W. TEDLOCK, JR. | [*printer's
ornament in red*] | ALBUQUERQUE 1948 | UNIVERSITY OF
NEW MEXICO PRESS

Black cloth boards, stamped in gold on spine: [*single rule*] | [*ornamental rule*] | [*single rule*] | D. H. LAWRENCE | MANUSCRIPTS | A DESCRIPTIVE | BIBLIOGRAPHY | E. W. TEDLOCK | [*single rule*] | [*ornamental rule*] | [*single rule*] | [*all of foregoing on red panel*] | The University | of New | Mexico Press All edges trimmed. 9″ × 6″. pp. [i]–[xl] + [1]–[336]. Published 14 April 1948 at $3.50; the edition consisted of 1000 copies.

Contains: "The Second Lady Chatterley," p. 22; a facsimile reproduction of a page of the manuscript.

"The Blue Moccasins," p. 68; a facsimile reproduction of a page of the manuscript.

"Discipline," p. 80; a facsimile reproduction of a page of the manuscript.

"Repulsed," p. 84; a facsimile reproduction of a page of the manuscript.

"Diary," p. 88; a facsimile reproduction of a page of the manuscript.

"Diary 1920–1924," pp. 89–99.

"Cocksure Women and Hensure Men," p. 224; a facsimile reproduction of a page of the manuscript.

NOTES: Mr Tedlock completed his study at Taos in the summer of 1945 working from Frieda Lawrence's still impressive collection of manuscripts. It was substantially the same collection exhibited at the Los Angeles Public Library and for which Lawrence Clark Powell prepared the catalogue (B46). Many of the manuscripts were exhibited at the University of Texas Humanities Research Center during the winter of 1954–55.

B52   LIFE INTERESTS   1948

first edition

LIFE | INTERESTS | *by* | Douglas Goldring | *With a preface by Alec Waugh* | MACDONALD : LONDON

Blue cloth boards, stamped in gold on upper cover: [*drawing of paddlewheel steamer*]; stamped in gold on spine: [*thin rule*] | [*thick rule*] | [*thin rule*] | LIFE | INTERESTS | DOUGLAS | GOLDRING | [*thin rule*] | [*thick rule*] | [*thin rule*] MACDONALD All edges trimmed. $8\frac{1}{2}″ \times 5\frac{9}{16}″$. pp. [i]–[xvi] + 17–264. Published 12 December 1948 at 12s. 6d.; number of copies unknown.

Contains: "Letters," to Douglas Goldring.

first edition

TWO MEMOIRS | DR MELCHOIR: A DEFEATED
ENEMY | and | MY EARLY BELIEFS | by | JOHN
MAYNARD KEYNES | *Introduced by David Garnett* | [*publisher's
device*] | London RUPERT HART-DAVIS 1949

Black cloth boards, stamped in gold on spine: Two | Memoirs | [*printer's
ornament*] | J. M. | KEYNES | RHD Top edges stained grey; all edges
trimmed. 8″ × 5⅛″. pp. [1]–[108]. Published 20 May 1949 at 7s. 6d.;
the first printing consisted of 3350 copies.

Contains: "Letters," to David Garnett and Lady Ottoline Morrell.

NOTES: Lawrence met John Maynard Keynes at Cambridge in 1915
during his visit to Bertrand Russell; Harry T. Moore has discussed the
occasion of the visit in his introduction to *D. H. Lawrence's Letters to
Bertrand Russell* (A84).

B54   A CATALOGUE OF VALUABLE   1948
             BOOKS BY D. H. LAWRENCE

first edition

A CATALOGUE | OF | VALUABLE BOOKS | BY | D. H.
LAWRENCE | COMPRISING | SOME OF THE
AUTHOR'S OWN AND | FRIEDA LAWRENCE'S IN-
SCRIBED COPIES | MANUSCRIPTS | PROOF and
ASSOCIATION COPIES | RARE EDITIONS and
ENGLISH | and AMERICAN FIRST EDITIONS |
[*Lawrence phoenix*] | OFFERED FOR SALE BY |
MELVIN RARE BOOKS | 156, ST. JOHN'S ROAD,
| EDINBURGH, 12.

Grey paper covers, upper cover serves as title page which is printed in
black as above. All edges trimmed. 7$\frac{5}{16}$″ × 4$\frac{7}{8}$″. pp. 1–20. Published
sometime in 1948; number of copies unknown.

Contains: "An Inscription" in *Lady Chatterley's Lover*; a facsimile repro-
          duction of the holograph inscription.

NOTES: This catalogue listed some 46 items, many of which were D. H.
Lawrence's own copies of his books or other important association items,
the most important of which were probably a holograph manuscript of
an early version of Frieda Lawrence's *Not I, But the Wind* (B40) and one

of two blue paper copies of *Lady Chatterley's Lover* (A42) with an amusing inscription by Lawrence. Many of these items, including the blue paper copy of *Lady Chatterley's Lover*, were returned to the possession of Frieda Lawrence, who exhibited some of them at the University of Texas in 1954–55.

The inscription was on page ii and read as follows: [*device of circle and arrow drawn in ink*] | This edition is limited | to One Thousand copies [*preceding three words are crossed out in ink*] | only two copies | one for the master | one for the dame | [*preceding three lines are holograph*] | signed D. H. Lawrence [*autograph signature in ink*] | none for the little | boy | that lives down the lane | [*preceding four lines are holograph*]

NOTES (2): The Melvin Rare Books catelogue was not dated, but apparently it was issued in 1948. Mr W. Forster has in his collection an "interim" list which offered unsold items from the original catalogue at much reduced prices. Probably most of the items had by then been reclaimed by Frieda Lawrence.

B55   JOURNEY WITH GENIUS   1951

first edition

Journey with Genius | RECOLLECTIONS AND REFLECTIONS | CONCERNING THE D. H. LAWRENCES | *by Witter Bynner* | ILLUSTRATED | THE JOHN DAY COMPANY NEW YORK

Light-green cloth boards, printed in green on spine: *Journey* | *with* | *Genius* | RECOLLECTIONS | AND | REFLECTIONS | CONCERNING | THE D. H. | LAWRENCES | BY | WITTER | BYNNER | *John Day* All edges trimmed. $8\frac{5}{16}'' \times 5\frac{5}{8}''$. pp. [i]–[ii] + [i]–[xviii] + 1–[364]. Published 26 July 1951 at $4.00; the first printing consisted of 5000 copies.

Contains: "Letters," to Witter Bynner.

NOTES: Witter Bynner's *Journey with Genius* will probably prove to be the last of the personal memoirs written by people who knew Lawrence; he writes about the period when Lawrence was living and working in the southwestern United States and in Mexico. When Mabel Dodge Luhan met the Lawrences in the autumn of 1922 on the occasion of their first arrival in New Mexico, the first night was spent in Santa Fe on the way to Taos, and the party was unable to find accommodation in a hotel, so Mabel was forced to call upon her friends to put them up for the night. It fell to the lot of Witter Bynner to entertain the Lawrences.

Later Bynner accompanied the Lawrences to Mexico, and Bynner, himself a poet, reprints several of his poems about Lawrence in the memoir.

B56 VENUS IN THE KITCHEN 1952

first edition

VENUS IN | *THE KITCHEN* | [*enclosed within oval salmon-coloured decorative border of roses and leaves in outline; cupid at right is shooting arrow above border into salmon-coloured heart at left*] | or Love's Cookery Book [*preceding words on double pages of open book held by cupid at left*] | *By Pilaff Bey* | EDITED BY NORMAN DOUGLAS | INTRODUC-TION BY GRAHAM GREENE | [*cupid holding covered warming dish from which threads of steam rise forming semi-border for three lines immediately preceding*] | With decorations by *BRUCE ROBERTS* | [*salmon-coloured rose with leaves*] | WILLIAM HEINEMANN LTD | MELBOURNE : : LONDON : : TORONTO | [*enclosed within heavy salmon-coloured rule broken at cupid with bow and arrow; two thinner salmon-coloured rules cross page at cupid with dish and at open book*]

Rose-coloured cloth boards, blind stamped on upper cover: [*cupid holding covered dish*]; blind stamped on lower cover: [*publisher's device*]; stamped in gold on spine: VENUS | IN THE | KITCHEN | Edited by | NORMAN | DOUGLAS | HEINEMANN All edges trimmed; top edges stained blue-green. $8\frac{3}{8}'' \times 5\frac{1}{2}''$. pp. [i]–[xiv] + [1]–[194]. Published 28 November 1952 at 12s. 6d.; the first printing consisted of 7500 copies.

Contains: "Venus in the Kitchen" (a painting), frontispiece.

NOTES: The title for this posthumously published collection of aphrodisiac recipes by Norman Douglas was taken from the title of the painting which serves as a frontispiece. The painting in question, "Venus in the Kitchen," was probably painted by Lawrence in Italy in 1928 or 1929; it is not reproduced elsewhere.

NOTES (2): Mr W. Forster reports a secondary binding of *Venus in the Kitchen* with lettering on the spine in black.

B57 THE INTELLIGENT HEART 1955

a. *first edition*

THE | INTELLIGENT | HEART | *The Story of D. H. Lawrence* | *by* | HARRY T. MOORE | FARRAR, STRAUS AND YOUNG | NEW YORK:

Light-purple cloth boards, printed in black on spine: The | Intelligent | Heart | MOORE | F. S. Y. Top edges trimmed; fore edges untrimmed; bottom edges rough-trimmed. $8\frac{1}{8}'' \times 5\frac{5}{8}''$. pp. [i]–[xii] + 1–468. Published 3 January 1955 at $6.50; the first printing consisted of 7700 copies.

Contains: "Letters," to various people.
> "The Laughing Horse" (a drawing), ff. p. 308.
> "Rainbow" (a drawing), ff. p. 276.
> "Ah Muriel" (a poem), p. 97; first appeared in the *English Review*, October 1910 (C5).

b. *first revised edition*

THE PRIEST | OF LOVE | [*short rule*] | *A Life of D. H. Lawrence* | [*short rule*] | [*asterisk*] | REVISED EDITION | [asterisk] | HARRY T. MOORE | [*three asterisks arranged vertically*] | [*publisher's device*] | FARRAR, STRAUS AND GIROUX | *NEW YORK*

Yellow paper boards with a brown cloth backstrip. Stamped in gold on spine: [*rule*] | THE | PRIEST | OF | LOVE | [*asterisk*] | *Life of* | *D. H. Lawrence* | [*asterisk*] | [*double rule*] | HARRY T. | MOORE | [*five asterisks arranged vertically*] | [*publisher's device*] | FARRAR | STRAUS | GIROUX All edges trimmed. $8\frac{7}{8}'' \times 6''$. pp. [i]–[x] + [1]–550. Published 29 March 1974 at $15.00; 5523 copies were issued in this edition.

Contains: "Letters," previously unpublished to various persons.
> Reproductions of the following paintings and drawings: copy of Greiffenhagen's *Idyll*; portrait of David Garnett; "Rainbow" (see B79); map of Sardinia for *Sea and Sardinia*; sketch of Kiowa Ranch; "Villa Mirenda"; "Red Willow Trees"; "North Sea"; "Self-Portrait 1929" (A47c).

NOTES: According to Spud Johnson the drawing of the "Laughing Horse" was never actually used for the cover of the magazine, although Lawrence apparently designed it for issue No. 16, not 26, as there were only 21 numbers of the *Laughing Horse*. Edward Nehls gives an account of the drawing in his *Composite Biography* (B60). The drawing of the "Rainbow" was sent to Viola Meynell in March 1915.

In *The Intelligent Heart* Mr Moore quotes in part or completely some two hundred previously unpublished Lawrence letters; Mr Moore has also edited *Sex, Literature and Censorship* (A92) and *D. H. Lawrence's Letters to Bertrand Russell* (A84). Other Lawrence studies by Mr Moore include *The Life and Works of D. H. Lawrence* (F57), *Poste Restante* (F73) and *The*

Achievement of D. H. Lawrence (F67), edited with Frederick J. Hoffman. Frieda Lawrence reviewed *The Intelligent Heart* in the *New Statesman and Nation*, 13 August 1955 in "D. H. Lawrence as I knew Him."

B58 PREDILECTIONS 1955

first edition

[*thick rule*] | [*thin rule*] | MARIANNE MOORE | [*thin rule*] | [*thick rule*] | [*ornamental rules at either end form box for lettering*] | Predilections | 1955 | THE VIKING PRESS · NEW YORK

Blue cloth boards, blind stamped on upper cover: M | M; stamped in gold on the spine: MARIANNE | MOORE | Predilections [*reading from top to bottom*] | VIKING All edges trimmed. $8\frac{3}{8}'' \times 5\frac{5}{8}''$. pp. [i]–[viii] + [1]–[176]. Published 12 May 1955 at $3.50; number of copies unknown.

Contains: "Letters," to Marianne Moore.

NOTES: These letters were written to Miss Moore while she was editor of the *Dial* and are concerned with the publication of Lawrence's poetry in the magazine.

B59 THE FLOWERS OF THE FOREST 1955

first edition

DAVID GARNETT | THE FLOWERS | OF THE FOREST | *Being Volume Two of* | THE GOLDEN ECHO | 1955 | CHATTO & WINDUS | LONDON

Red cloth boards, stamped in gold on spine: THE | FLOWERS | OF THE | FOREST | [*printer's ornament*] | [*enclosed within double decorative rule*] | DAVID | GARNETT | CHATTO | & WINDUS Top edges stained red; all edges trimmed. $8\frac{1}{2}'' \times 5\frac{7}{16}''$. pp. [i]–[xii] + 1–[252]. Published 7 October 1955 at 21*s.*; number of copies unknown.

Contains: "Letters," to David Garnett.

NOTES: David Garnett visited the Lawrences in the Tyrol during the summer of 1912; his father, Edward Garnett, was an early friend and literary advisor to Lawrence; see *The Trespasser* (A2). David Garnett later edited some early manuscripts of Lawrence's for *Love Among the Haystacks* (A56), for which he wrote an introduction.

first edition

VOL. I

D. H. LAWRENCE: | A COMPOSITE BIOGRAPHY |
Gathered, arranged, and edited | by Edward Nehls | [*short rule*] | Volume
One, 1885–1919 | [*short rule*] | THE UNIVERSITY OF WIS-
CONSIN PRESS | *Madison*, 1957

Red cloth boards, stamped in gold on spine: D. H. Lawrence: | a
composite | biography | [*single rule*] | Volume I | 1885–1919 | NEHLS
| Wisconsin All edges trimmed. $9\frac{3}{16}'' \times 6\frac{1}{8}''$. pp. [i]–[xxvi] + [1]–614.
Published 12 August 1957 at $7.50; the first printing consisted of 3000
copies.

VOL. II

D. H. LAWRENCE: | A COMPOSITE BIOGRAPHY |
Gathered, arranged, and edited | by Edward Nehls | [*short rule*] | Volume
Two, 1919–1925 | [*short rule*] | THE UNIVERSITY OF WIS-
CONSIN PRESS | *Madison*, 1958

Grey cloth boards, stamped in gold on spine: D. H. Lawrence: | a
composite | biography | [*single rule*] | Volume II | 1919–1925 | NEHLS
| Wisconsin All edges trimmed. $9\frac{3}{16}'' \times 6\frac{1}{8}''$. pp. [i]–[xxii] + [1]–[538].
Published 28 March 1958 at $7.50; the first printing consisted of 3000
copies.

VOL. III

D. H. LAWRENCE: | A COMPOSITE BIOGRAPHY |
Gathered, arranged, and edited | by Edward Nehls | [*short rule*] | Volume
Three, 1925–1930 | [*short rule*] | THE UNIVERSITY OF WIS-
CONSIN PRESS | *Madison*, 1959

Black cloth boards, stamped in gold on spine: D. H. Lawrence: | a
composite | biography | [*single rule*] | Volume III | 1925–1930 | NEHLS
| Wisconsin All edges trimmed. $9\frac{3}{16}'' \times 6\frac{1}{8}''$. pp. [i]–[xxxii] + [1]–[768].
Published 6 February 1959 at $7.50; the first printing consisted of 3000
copies.

Contains in Vol. I:

"Letters," to various persons.

"Burns Novel," pp. 184–95.

"Burns Novel," p. 187; a facsimile reproduction of a page of the manuscript.

"Marginal Notes," pp. 66–70; in "Sur un exemplaire de Schopenhauer annoté par D. H. Lawrence"; first appeared in the *Revue Anglo-Américaine*, February 1936 (C220).

Contains in Vol. II:

"Letters," to various persons.

"A Britisher Has a Word with Harriett Monroe," pp. 268–69; first appeared in *Palms*, Christmas 1923 as "A Britisher Has a Word with an Editor" (C115).

Contains in Vol. III:

"Letters," to various persons.
"Autobiography," pp. 232–34;

Paintings, ff. p. 368:

"Dance-Sketch."
"Contadini."
"Rape of the Sabine Women."
"Throwing Back the Apple."
"Renascence of Men."
"The Lizard."

NOTES: All of the paintings appeared in *The Paintings of D. H. Lawrence* (A46). The "Burns Novel" consists of two fragments of an unfinished novel which Lawrence began some time before 1914 according to Else Jaffe-Richthofen from whom Mr Nehls acquired the manuscript. The "Autobiography" is from a manuscript in the possession of Mr Spencer Curtis Brown, originally written by Lawrence for a French publisher.

B61   D. H. LAWRENCE AN   1958
                  EXHIBITION

first edition

[*drawing of D. H. Lawrence*] | D. H. LAWRENCE | An Exhibition of First Editions, Manuscripts, | Paintings, Letters, and Miscellany | at | SOUTHERN ILLINOIS UNIVERSITY LIBRARY | April, 1958 | *Edited by Earl Tannenbaum* | Southern Illinois University Library | Carbondale, 1958

Yellow paper covers, printed in black and brown on upper cover: [*drawing of D. H. Lawrence in brown*] | D. H. LAWRENCE | An Exhibition of First Editions, Manuscripts, | Paintings, Letters, and Miscellany | [*preceding two lines on white background*] | at | SOUTHERN ILLINOIS UNIVERSITY LIBRARY | April, 1958; printed in brown on lower cover: [*Lawrence phoenix*] | [*white band appears on bottom half of lower cover and is continuation from upper cover*] All edges trimmed. 9" × 6". pp. [i]–[ii] + [i]–[xiv] + 1–64. Published 1 April 1938, not for sale; the ordinary issue consisted of 1500 copies. There was also a limited issue, consisting of 75 numbered and signed copies, published at the same time.

Contains: "Letters," ff. p. 24; a facsimile reproduction of a letter from Lawrence to Helmut von Erffa, dated 18 August 1925.

B62   EDWARD THOMAS   1958

first edition

EDWARD THOMAS | THE LAST FOUR YEARS | *Book One of* | *The Memoirs of* | *Eleanor Farjeon* | LONDON | OXFORD UNIVERSITY PRESS | 1958 | [*enclosed within single rule in turn enclosed within ornamental rule*]

Green cloth boards, stamped in gold on spine: [*ornamental rule*] | EDWARD | THOMAS | THE LAST | FOUR YEARS | *Book One of* | *The Memoirs of* | *Eleanor* | *Farjeon* | [*ornamental rule*] | OXFORD Top edges stained grey; all edges trimmed. 8½" × 5⅜". pp. [i]–[xvi] + 1–[272]. Published 9 October 1958 at 25*s.*; number of copies unknown.

Contains: "Letters," to Eleanor Farjeon.

NOTES: Eleanor Farjeon met the Lawrences in 1915 at Greatham, Sussex, through Viola Meynell. Miss Farjeon gives an account of her friendship with Lawrence in "Springtime with D. H. Lawrence" in the *London Magazine*, April 1955 (C235) where the "Letters" also appear. Portions of her memoir were printed in *Magic Casements*, published in London in 1941 by Allen and Unwin for the PEN club.

B63   A D. H. LAWRENCE   1959
             MISCELLANY

first edition

A | D. H. LAWRENCE | MISCELLANY | EDITED BY *Harry T. Moore* | *Southern Illinois University Press* | CARBONDALE, 1959

Red cloth boards, blind stamped on upper cover: [*design of triangle and half-moon*]; stamped in gold and white on spine, reading from top to bottom: *Harry T. Moore* [*in white*] A D. H. LAWRENCE MISCELLANY SOUTHERN ILLINOIS [*preceding two words in white*] Top edges stained red; all edges trimmed. $8\frac{7}{16}'' \times 5\frac{5}{16}''$. pp. [i]–xxvi + [1]–[398]. Published 16 November 1959 at $6.50; the first printing consisted of 3000 copies.

Contains: "Music for *David*," ff. p. 150; facsimile reproduction of the manuscript.

"Letter," to Robert Atkins, ff. p. 150; facsimile reproduction.

"Hymns in a Man's Life," ff. p. 282; facsimile reproduction of a page of the manuscript.

"The Fox," ff. p. 282; facsimile reproduction of a 22 page early version of the story.

B63.5 UNIVERSITY OF NEW MEXICO 1960 D. H. LAWRENCE FELLOWSHIP FUND

first edition

THE UNIVERSITY OF NEW MEXICO | d. h. lawrence | FELLOWSHIP FUND MANUSCRIPT COLLECTION | [*the Lawrence phoenix*] | HUMANITIES RESEARCH CENTER· THE UNIVERSITY OF TEXAS | AUSTIN·APRIL 1960

Cream paper covers. Printed in brown on upper cover: THE UNIVERSITY OF NEW MEXICO | d. h. lawrence | FELLOWSHIP FUND | [*the Lawrence phoenix*] HUMANITIES RESEARCH CENTER | THE UNIVERSITY OF TEXAS | APRIL 1960 | [*reproduction in colour of the Lawrence painting, "Kiowa Ranch"*] $8\frac{1}{8}'' \times 6\frac{1}{8}''$. Top and bottom edges trimmed; fore edges untrimmed. pp. [1]–[16]. Published 15 June 1960, not for sale; 1200 copies were printed, about half of which were sent to the University of New Mexico for distribution.

Contains: Colour reproduction of the painting "Kiowa Ranch" by D. H. Lawrence, Frieda Lawrence and Dorothy Brett. Collected in (B70).

NOTES: According to Dorothy Brett this painting was a joint effort by Lawrence, Frieda and her; Lawrence is supposed to have done the figures, Frieda the chickens, and Brett the landscape. The painting shows Lawrence and Brett on horseback with Frieda feeding the chickens.

first edition

D. H. LAWRENCE | AFTER THIRTY YEARS | 1930–1960 |
Catalogue of an Exhibition | held in the Art Gallery | of the University
of Nottingham | 17 June–30 July | 1960 | Edited by V. de S. Pinto

All edges trimmed. $9\frac{11}{16}'' \times 7\frac{1}{16}''$. pp. [1]–[56]. Published June 1960 at
7s. 6d.; the first printing consisted of 500 copies.

Contains: "Last Words to Muriel," ff. p. 16; facsimile reproduction of
the manuscript.
"The White Peacock," ff. p. 16; facsimile reproduction of a
page of the manuscript.
"Letter," to Mrs Margaret Needham, ff. p. 24; facsimile
reproduction, with sketch of the ranch at Taos.
"My Naughty Book," ff. p. 24; facsimile reproduction of the
manuscript.

B65   DAVID HERBERT LAWRENCE   1960
L'OEUVRE ET LA VIE

first edition

F. J. TEMPLE | *David Herbert Lawrence* | L'OEUVRE
ET LA VIE | *Préface de Richard ALDINGTON* | [*publisher's device*] |
SEGHERS, EDITEUR

Grey paper boards. Printed in red on upper cover: D. H. Lawrence
Printed in red on spine: F. J. | TEMPLE | [*asterisk*] | D. H. | LAWRENCE|
[*publisher's device*] $8\frac{1}{4}'' \times 5\frac{1}{4}''$. All edges trimmed. pp. [1]–[240]. Published
September 1960; number of copies unknown.

Contains: "Letter," to Adrian Berrington; facsimile reproduction of the
manuscript of a letter dated 18 November 1910.

B66   THE GARNETT FAMILY   1961

first edition

THE | GARNETT FAMILY | [*short decorative rule*] | Carolyn
G. Heilbrun | Ruskin House | GEORGE ALLEN & UNWIN LTD
| MUSEUM STREET LONDON.

Red cloth boards. Printed in silver on spine: *The | Garnett | Family |* CAROLYN | G. | HEILBRUN | *George | Allen | & | Unwin* All edges trimmed; top edges stained red. $8\frac{7}{16}'' \times 5\frac{3}{8}''$. pp. [1]–[216]. Published 6 July 1961 at 30s.; 2500 copies were printed.

Contains: "Letters," to Edward and Constance Garnett.

NOTES: See (A4) and (A56).

B66.5   INTERNATIONAL LITERARY   1961
ANNUAL NO. 3

first edition

INTERNATIONAL | LITERARY | ANNUAL | NO. 3 | edited by | ARTHUR BOYARS and PAMELA LYON | [*publisher's device*] | LONDON | JOHN CALDER

Green cloth boards, stamped in gold on spine: INTER- | NATIONAL | LITERARY | ANNUAL | [*printer's ornament*] | 3 | [*publisher's device*] | CALDER All edges trimmed. $7\frac{7}{8}'' \times 5\frac{1}{4}''$. pp. [1]–[232]. Published 25 February 1961 at 25s.

Contains: "Letter," to Eunice Tietjens dated 27 July 1917, with an introduction by A. Alvarez. Eunice Tietjens was an American poet and a friend of Harriet Monroe.

B67   CASTLE IN ITALY   1961

first edition

LINA WATERFIELD | Castle in Italy | AN AUTOBI-OGRAPHY | John Murray | FIFTY ALBEMARLE STREET LONDON

Red cloth boards, stamped in gold on spine: CASTLE | IN | ITALY | [*printer's ornament*] | Lina | Waterfield | John Murray All edges trimmed. $8\frac{1}{2}'' \times 5\frac{1}{2}''$. pp. [i]–[viii] + 1–280. Published 24 November at 28s.; 3500 copies were printed.

Contains: "Letter," to Lina and Aubrey Waterfield.

NOTES: Lina Duff Gordon Waterfield was the correspondent in Italy for J. L. Garvin's *Observer* during the twenties. She lived with her aunt, Janet Ross, in a Villa near Florence and married Aubrey Waterfield, a painter. The Lawrences visited them at the Fortress of Aulla, some miles inland from La Spezia, in the summer of 1914.

B68   FRIEDA LAWRENCE THE   1961
MEMOIRS AND
CORRESPONDENCE

first edition

[*short rule*] | FRIEDA LAWRENCE | The Memoirs and Correspond-ence | [*short rule*] | EDITED BY | E. W. TEDLOCK | [*publisher's device*] | HEINEMANN | LONDON MELBOURNE TORONTO

Black cloth boards. Stamped in gold on spine: FRIEDA | LAWRENCE | The Memoirs | and | Correspondence | HEINEMANN $8\frac{3}{8}'' \times 5\frac{1}{2}''$. All edges trimmed. pp. [i]–[xviii] + [1]–[438]. Published 20 November 1961 at 42s.; number of copies unknown.

Contains: "Notes" and "Letters" by Lawrence added to or included with letters from Frieda Lawrence Ravagli to various persons.

B69   D. H. LAWRENCE AND GERMAN   1963
LITERATURE

first edition

Armin Arnold | D. H. LAWRENCE AND GERMAN LITERA-TURE | with | Two Hitherto Unknown Essays | by | D. H. LAWRENCE | Montreal | Mansfield Book Mart: H. Heinemann | 1963

Brown cloth boards. All edges trimmed. $8\frac{11}{16}'' \times 5\frac{15}{16}''$. pp. 1–66. Published May 1963; the first printing consisted of 12 copies numbered from A to M and 375 copies numbered from 1 to 375.

Contains: "Reviews," of *The Oxford Book of German Verse* by H. G. Fiedler and *The Minnesingers* by Jethro Bithell (C8.5). Collected in (A107).

B70   PAINTINGS OF D. H. LAWRENCE   1964

first edition

PAINTINGS OF D. H. LAWRENCE [*name in red*] | EDITED BY MERVYN LEVY, WITH ESSAYS BY HARRY T.

MOORE, JACK LINDSAY & HERBERT READ | LONDON: CORY, ADAMS & MACKAY

Red cloth boards, printed in black on upper cover: D. H. Lawrence [*facsimile signature*] Printed in black on spine, reading from top to bottom: PAINTINGS OF D. H. LAWRENCE [*publisher's device*] All edges trimmed; top edges stained red. $11\frac{1}{4}'' \times 9\frac{5}{8}''$. pp. [i]–[ii] + [1]–104. Published 1 September 1964 at 75*s*.; the first printing consisted of 2000 copies.

Contains: Making Pictures (A53)—Coastal Scene with Figures, watercolour—Landscape with Figure, watercolour—Joachim and the Shepherds, watercolour copy from a print of the painting by Giotto—The Kiowa Ranch, New Mexico, oil (B63.5)—The Feast of the Radishes, oil—Resurrection, oil (A46)—Red Willow Trees, oil (A46)—Villa Mirenda, oil— Flight Back into Paradise, oil (A46)—Family on a Verandah, oil (A46)—Fauns and Nymphs, oil (A46)— Dance Sketch, oil (A46)—Rape of the Sabine Women, oil (A46)—Italian Landscape, oil—Jaguar Leaping at a Man, oil—Leda, watercolour (A46)—Nasturtiums, oil—A Vase of Flowers, watercolour (B34)—Italian Canal Scene, watercolour—Italian Scene, watercolour copy of "Pallanza, Lago Maggiore" by H. B. Brabazon—Evening Scene, watercolour—Two Apples, watercolour (B34 as "Still Life")—Wind on the Wold, watercolour copy of "The Wind on the Wold" by G. H. Mason—Sea scene, watercolour—An Idyll, watercolour copy of "An Idyll" by Maurice Greiffenhagen (B34)—Italian Scene with a Boat, watercolour—Fire Dance, watercolour (A46)—A Holy Family, oil (A46)—Men Bathing, oil—Boccaccio Story, oil (A46)—Fight with an Amazon, oil (A46)—Summer Dawn, oil (A46)—Close-Up Kiss, oil (A46)—Yawning, watercolour (A46)—The Lizard, watercolour (A46)—Under the Haystack, watercolour (A46)—Etruscan Design, embroi- dered canvas (A61)—Spring, watercolour (A46)— Renascence of Men, watercolour (A46)—Singing of Swans, watercolour (A46)—The Mango Tree, watercolour (A46)— Throwing Back the Apple, watercolour (A46)—Finding of Moses, oil (A46)—Contadini, oil (A46)—Accident in a Mine, oil (A46)—North Sea, oil (A46)—Venus in the Kitchen, watercolour (B56).

first edition

Word for Word | [*short decorative rule*] | A STUDY OF | AUTHORS'
ALTERATIONS | WITH | EXERCISES | [*short decorative rule*]
| *Wallace Hildick* | FABER AND FABER | 24 Russell Square |
London

Blue cloth boards. Stamped in gold on spine, reading from top to bottom:
Word for Word [*printer's ornament*] WALLACE HILDICK | *Faber* All edges
trimmed. $7\frac{1}{4}'' \times 4\frac{3}{4}''$. pp. [1]–[192]. Published 6 May 1965 at 21*s.*, the
school edition at 11*s.* 6*d.*; 4000 copies were printed.

Contains: Excerpts from early manuscript versions of *The White Peacock*
(A1), "Odour of Chrysanthemums" (A6) and *The Rainbow*
(A7).

first edition

MY LIFE | AND TIMES | OCTAVE FIVE | 1915–1923 |
Compton Mackenzie | 1966 | CHATTO & WINDUS | LONDON

Blue cloth boards. Stamped in gold on spine: MY LIFE | AND | TIMES |
[*short decorative rule*] | OCTAVE 5 | 1915–1923 | [*short decorative rule*]
| Compton | Mackenzie | CHATTO | & WINDUS All edges trimmed; top
edges stained blue. $8\frac{1}{2}'' \times 5\frac{1}{2}''$. pp. [1]–[272]. Published 24 February
1966 at 35*s.*; 7000 copies were printed.

Contains: "Letters," to Compton Mackenzie.

NOTES: The Lawrences resided near Compton Mackenzie at Chesham,
Buckinghamshire in 1914 and saw him later in Capri. It was Mackenzie
who felt himself caricatured in Lawrence's story, "The Man Who Loved
Islands" and objected to its publication in the Secker edition of *The
Woman Who Rode Away* (A41).

first edition

D. H. LAWRENCE: A FINDING LIST | [*short rule*] | Holdings
in the City, County and University | Libraries of Nottingham | Compiled

by: | Lucy I. Edwards, A. L. A. | Local History Librarian | Nottingham City Library | NOTTINGHAM | 1968

White paper covers. Printed in black on upper cover: [*photograph of D. H. Lawrence enclosed within a single rule*] D. H. Lawrence [*facsimile signature*] | A FINDING LIST Printed in black on lower cover: Printed by Nottinghamshire County Council All edges trimmed. $8\frac{1}{4}'' \times 5\frac{1}{4}''$. pp. [i]–[x] + 1–[126]. Published 16 September 1968; number of copies unknown.

Contains: "Letter," to Willie Hopkin, facsimile reproduction of a letter pasted in a copy of *Bay* (A12).

NOTES: William Edward Hopkin was a resident of Eastwood and a life-long friend of Lawrence. He was a member of the County Council and later a magistrate and an Alderman. He was an active Socialist and exerted considerable influence on the intellectual development of Lawrence during his youth.

B74   D. H. LAWRENCE: L'HOMME   1969 ET LA GENÈSE DE SON OEUVRE

first edition

UNIVERSITÉ DE PARIS | FACULTÉ DES LETTRES ET SCIENCES HUMAINES | [*large dot*] | D. H. LAWRENCE: L'HOMME | ET LA GENÈSE DE SON OEUVRE | LES ANNÉES DE FORMATION: | 1885–1919 | [*two decorative asterisks*] | DOCUMENTS | Thèse principale pour le doctorat ès-lettres | présentée à la Faculté des Lettres et Sciences Humaines | de l'Université de Paris par Emile DELAVENAY | Ancien Elève de l'Ecole Normale Supérieure | Agrégé de l'Université | Chargé d'enseignement à la Faculté des Lettres et Sciences Humaines | de l'Université de Nice | LIBRAIRIE C. KLINCKSIECK | PARIS

Tan paper covers, upper cover reproduces the title page as above. Printed in black on spine: EMILE | DELAVENAY | D. H. | LAWRENCE | L'HOMME | ET LA GENÈSE | DE SON OEUVRE | (1885–1919) | [*short rule*] | TOME 2 | KLINCKSIECK All edges trimmed. $8\frac{7}{16}'' \times 6\frac{1}{16}''$. pp. [647]–854. Published July 1969; the first printing consisted of 1200 copies.

Contains: "Letter," by D. H. Lawrence published in *The Teacher* for 25 March 1905, p. 655 (Co.5). See (F173).

first edition

A Return to [ornament] | PAGANY | *[single rule]* | *The History,*
Correspondence, and | *Selections from a Little Magazine 1929–1932* | *Edited*
by STEPHEN HALPERT | *with* RICHARD JOHNS | *Intro-*
duction by KENNETH REXROTH | BEACON PRESS *Boston*

Blue paper boards with red cloth backstrip, blind stamped on upper
cover: [*stylized impression of buildings in a town*] Printed in white on spine,
reading from top to bottom: HALPERT · JOHNS *A Return to* PAGANY BEACON
PRESS All edges trimmed. $9\frac{15}{16}'' \times 7''$. pp. [i]–[xx] + [1]–[522]. Published
11 September 1969; 400 copies were printed.

Contains: "Letter," to Richard Johns dated 10 October 1929.

NOTES: Soon after founding *Pagany* in 1929, Richard Johns wrote to
Lawrence asking for something to publish in the magazine; the letter
published here is Lawrence's answer.

B76   D. H. LAWRENCE AND *THE DIAL*   1970

first edition

D. H. LAWRENCE | *THE* | *AND* DIAL | *By* | Nicholas Joost and
Alvin Sullivan | *Southern Illinois University Press* CARBONDALE AND
EDWARDSVILLE | *Feffer & Simons, Inc.* LONDON AND
AMSTERDAM

Black paper boards with white cloth backstrip. Printed in red and black
on the spine, reading from top to bottom: D. H. Lawrence and the Dial
[*in red*] | By NICHOLAS JOOST and ALVIN SULLIVAN | Southern Illinois |
University Press [*the preceding two lines read from left to right*] All edges
trimmed. $9'' \times 6''$. pp. [i]–[xiv] + [1]–[242]. Published 22 June 1970 at
$8.50; 2324 copies were printed.

Contains: "Letters," from Lawrence to staff members of *The Dial*.

B77   IN THE DAYS OF MY YOUTH   1970

first edition

IN THE | DAYS | OF MY | YOUTH | by | GRACE LOVAT
FRASER | [*publisher's device*] | CASSELL · LONDON

Red cloth boards. Stamped in gold on spine, reading from top to bottom:

IN THE DAYS OF MY YOUTH | GRACE LOVAT FRASER Cassell [*the whole enclosed within a single rule*] 7$\frac{5}{16}$" × 5$\frac{1}{2}$". pp. [i]–[viii] + 1–[288]. Published 27 August 1970 at £2.50; 3700 copies were printed.

Contains: "Letters," to Grace Crawford, later Grace Lovat Fraser.

NOTES: Grace Crawford was a young American living in London with her mother; she met Lawrence through Ezra Pound in the autumn of 1909.

B78 ·THE FIFTH SPARROW 1972

first edition

THE FIFTH SPARROW | *An autobiography* | *M. L. SKINNER* | [*printer's ornament*] | With a foreword by | *MARY DURACK* | [*publisher's device*] | SYDNEY UNIVERSITY PRESS

Brown cloth boards with a horizontal white decorative strip dividing the top and bottom halves of the upper and lower covers. The top half of each cover is darker than the bottom half. Stamped in gold on spine, reading from top to bottom: M. L. SKINNER THE FIFTH SPARROW SYDNEY All edges trimmed. 8$\frac{3}{8}$" × 5$\frac{3}{8}$". pp. [i]–[xx] + 1–[172]. Published 22 March 1972; the first printing consisted of 2500 copies.

Contains: "Letters," to Mollie Skinner.

NOTES: Mollie Skinner was the Australian nurse with whom Lawrence collaborated on *The Boy in the Bush*. See A29.

B79 YOUNG BERT 1972

first edition

YOUNG BERT | *an exhibition of the early years of* | D. H. Lawrence | [*short rule*] | The Nottingham Festival Committee, with the assistance of the | Arts Council of Great Britain | 8 July to 29 August, 1972 | [*short rule*] | Castle Museum, Nottingham Castle, Nottingham NG1 6EL

White paper covers. Printed in yellow-brown on the upper cover: YOUNG | BERT | an Exhibition | of the early years of | D. H. Lawrence Printed in yellow-brown on lower cover: 50p | Nottingham Festival Committee | in association with | The Arts Council of Great Britain The cover is decorated with a drawing by Lawrence, titled, "I have finished my Rainbow" sent to Viola Meynell in 1915. See B57. 9$\frac{1}{2}$" × 5". All edges trimmed. pp. [1]–96. Published 8 July 1972 at 50p, the first printing consisted of 2000 copies.

Contains: Reproductions of the following paintings and drawings by Lawrence: Five untitled drawings from Emily Lawrence's Album; horses, a girl with flowers, flowers, leaves, a man's face—two untitled drawings to accompany entries by May and Jessie Chambers in Ethel Harris' Album; a wet cat, vine leaves with birds—untitled watercolour of a landscape with windmill from Grace Hardwick's Album—"Pauvre Fauvette," a copy in oil of a painting of the same name by Jules Bastien-Lepage—Seascape, a watercolour copy of "The Herring Market at Sea" by Colin Hunter—Trees, a watercolour copy of "Wintry March" by W. L. Picknell— Cottages and a Church, watercolour—River and Church, watercolour—Harvesting, a watercolour copy of "Harvest Scene" by Peter de Wint—Cows at Sunset, a watercolour copy of "The Herald of Night" by Arnesby Brown—River and Bridge, watercolour—Flowers in a Mug, oil—A Ginger Jar and Oranges, watercolour—Flowers in Vase, oil—An Idyll, a watercolour copy of the painting of the same name by Maurice Greiffenhagen (See B34)—Italian Lake Scene, watercolour—The Flight into Egypt, a copy in watercolour after the painting by Fra Angelico—Landscape with Figure, watercolour—Zurich, watercolour—a wooden box decorated by Lawrence with design of birds and flowers.

| B80 | PROSPECTUS FOR THE LETTERS OF D. H. LAWRENCE | 1973 |

first edition

PROSPECTUS AND NOTES FOR | VOLUME EDITORS | THE LETTERS OF | D. H. LAWRENCE | GENERAL EDITOR | JAMES T. BOULTON | [*publisher's device*] | TO BE PUBLISHED BY | CAMBRIDGE UNIVERSITY PRESS | FROM 1977 ONWARDS

Orange paper covers. Printed in black on upper cover: THE LETTERS OF | D. H. LAWRENCE 9″ × 6″. All edges trimmed. pp. [i]–[ii] + [1]–18. Published November 1973, not for sale; 350 copies were printed, of which only about 25 copies were bound in orange paper covers.

Contains: "Letters," to Louie Burrows, Ada Lawrence and Vere H. G. Collins, edited by James Boulton as examples for the volume editors.

B81   OTTOLINE AT GARSINGTON   1974

first edition

OTTOLINE | AT GARSINGTON | *Memoirs of* | *Lady Ottoline* *Morrell* | *1915–1918* | [*decorative rule*] | edited | with an introduction | by | ROBERT | GATHORNE-HARDY | FABER AND FABER | 3 Queen Square | London

Green cloth boards. Stamped in gold on spine: [*decorative rule*] | Ottoline | at Garsington [*the preceding two lines on a yellow background*] | [*decorative rule*] *Memoirs of* | *Lady Ottoline* | *Morrell* | *1915–1918* | *edited* | *with an introduction* | *by* | ROBERT | GATHORNE- | HARDY | FABER All edges trimmed. $9\frac{1}{8}'' \times 5\frac{3}{4}''$. pp. [1]–304 and frontispiece. Published 2 September 1974 at £4.95: 5000 copies were printed.

Contains: "Letters," to Lady Ottoline Morrell.

NOTES: Lawrence met Lady Ottoline Morrell sometime early in 1915 through Gilbert Cannan. A considerable correspondence resulted from Lawrence's association with Lady Ottoline who brought Lawrence and Bertrand Russell together. See (A84), (B83).

B82   IN OUR INFANCY   1975

first edition

IN OUR INFANCY | An Autobiography | Part I: 1882–1912 | HELEN CORKE | CAMBRIDGE UNIVERSITY PRESS | CAMBRIDGE | LONDON·NEW YORK·MELBOURNE

Brown cloth boards. Stamped in gold on spine: In Our | Infancy | [*double rule*] | HELEN | CORKE | Cambridge All edges trimmed. $8\frac{1}{2}'' \times 5\frac{3}{8}''$. pp. [i]–[xii] + 1–236. Published 2 October 1975 at £5.50; 3000 copies were printed.

Contains: "Letters," to Helen Corke.

NOTES: The dust-jacket contains a reproduction of a portrait of Helen Corke which does not appear in the book itself. For information about Lawrence's association with Helen Corke, see notes for *The Trespasser* (A2).

first edition

OTTOLINE | THE LIFE OF LADY OTTOLINE MOR-
RELL | Sandra Jobson Darroch | [*publisher's device*] | COWARD,
McCANN & GEOGHEGAN, INC. | New York

Brown paper boards with a red cloth backstrip. Stamped in gold on
upper cover: Ottoline [*facsimile signature*] Stamped in gold on spine:
Sandra | Jobson | Darroch | OTTOLINE [*previous line reads from top to
bottom*] | Coward, | McCann & | Geoghegan All edges trimmed.
$8\frac{7}{8}'' \times 6''$. pp. [1]–[320]. Published 26 November 1975 at $12.50; 7500
copies were printed.

Contains: "Letters," to Lady Ottoline Morrell. See (B81).

B84   PROSPECTUS FOR THE WORKS   1977 OF D. H. LAWRENCE

first edition

THE | CAMBRIDGE | EDITION OF | THE WORKS OF |
D. H. LAWRENCE | [*publisher's device*] | PROSPECTUS AND
NOTES FOR | VOLUME EDITORS | CAMBRIDGE
UNIVERSITY PRESS

Orange paper covers. Printed in black on upper cover: THE | CAMBRIDGE
| EDITION OF | THE WORKS OF | D. H. LAWRENCE | [*publisher's device*]
$8\frac{1}{2}'' \times 5\frac{1}{2}''$. All edges trimmed. pp. [1]–24. Published November 1977,
not for sale; 600 copies were printed of which 100 were bound in orange
covers.

Contains: Four pages of the definitive text of *The White Peacock* edited by
Andrew Robertson as a guide for the volume editors of the
Cambridge University Press critical edition of the works of
D. H. Lawrence, under the general editorship of James
Boulton and Warren Roberts.

B85   D. H. LAWRENCE COUNTRY   1979

first edition

ROY SPENCER | D. H. LAWRENCE COUNTRY | *A Portrait
of his Early Life and Background with* | *Illustrations, Maps and Guides* |
CECIL WOOLF·LONDON

Brown paper boards, stamped in gold on spine: D. H. LAWRENCE COUNTRY · ROY SPENCER WOOLF All edges trimmed. $7\frac{1}{4}'' \times 4\frac{3}{8}''$. pp. [1]–[112].

Contains: "Letter," reprinted from *Eastwood and Kimberley Advertiser* (Co.1).

C. CONTRIBUTIONS
TO PERIODICALS

C. CONTRIBUTIONS
TO PERIODICALS

CO.I LETTER

The Schoolmaster, 4 March 1905.

When Lawrence sat for the King's Scholarship Examination in December 1904, he passed "Division One of the First Class," and as a result the *Schoolmaster* asked him to write a letter about his success. He wrote about his tutors, text-books, study habits and recreational activities; "I always took the greatest care to let no spelling or grammatical error go unrectified in these notes, and thus acquired the habit of writing quickly and correctly." The *Eastwood and Kimberley Advertiser* for 10 March 1905, under the heading "A Distinguished Success" offered its congratulations to Lawrence and to the British Schools "for assisting to turn out so brilliant a student" and reprinted his letter. See (B85).

CO.5 LETTER to the editor

The Teacher (2:280–284), 25 March 1905.

When the results of the King's Scholarship Examination were published in *The Teacher* in March 1905, the top candidates were invited to write about the value of the periodical for their scholastic achievements; this letter was Lawrence's contribution. See (B74).

CI A PRELUDE

Nottinghamshire Guardian, 7 December 1907.

Separately published as *A Prelude* (A85).

This short story was written during the Autumn of 1907 while Lawrence was a student at Nottingham University College; he submitted three stories in a Christmas story competition held by the *Guardian*, and "A Prelude," actually submitted for him by Jessie Chambers, won first place. The other two stories were rewritten and eventually collected in *The Prussian Officer* (A6) as "A Fragment of

Stained Glass" and "The White Stocking." "A Prelude" is the "youthful story in the bad grey print of a provincial newspaper" which Lawrence mentioned to Edward D. McDonald (B16); Lawrence added "But, thank God, that has gone to glory in the absolute sense." P. Beaumont Wadsworth, in the foreword to *A Prelude* (A85), tells of its discovery during the war in the files of the *Nottinghamshire Guardian*. Jessie Chambers gives an account of the Christmas story competition in *D. H. Lawrence: A Personal Record* (B43); for this first published story Lawrence received a cheque for the sum of three guineas which of course was made out to Jessie Chambers, whose father cashed it and handed the money to Lawrence.

"A Prelude" was reprinted with the original illustrations in *The Nottinghamshire Weekly Guardian*, 10 December 1949.

C2 A STILL AFTERNOON

English Review (3: 561–565), November 1909.

DREAMS OLD AND NASCENT

I. OLD
Collected in *Amores* (A9) as "Dreams Old."

II. NASCENT
Collected in *Amores* as "Dreams Nascent."

BABY MOVEMENTS

I. RUNNING BAREFOOT
Collected in *Amores* as "A Baby Running Barefoot."

II. TRAILING CLOUDS
Collected in *Amores* as "A Baby Asleep After Pain."

DISCIPLINE
Collected in *Amores*.

On his first vacation home from teaching in Croydon, that for Christmas 1908, Lawrence showed Jessie Chambers and her family a copy of the *English Review* for which they subsequently subscribed. Later Jessie noted that the editor, Ford Madox Hueffer, was "prepared to welcome new talent," and this determined her to send some of Lawrence's work to the magazine. She looked through the poems he had sent from Croydon and copied out three of them which eventually became Lawrence's first professional appearance in print. Jessie placed "Discipline" first in her draft because she thought the "unusual title would attract attention"; she chose "Dreams Old and Nascent" because Lawrence was trying to explain himself to her, and she loved "Baby Movements" because it was about the baby in the house where Lawrence lived. Afterwards, Lawrence wrote of Jessie that she "had launched me, so easily, on my literary career, like a princess cutting a thread...." This prompted the title for a memoir of Jessie Chambers by Helen Corke published as *D. H. Lawrence's Princess* (F57). Ford Madox Hueffer, later Ford Madox Ford, told of his "discovery" of Lawrence in *Portraits from Life*. See also (A104).

C3 GOOSE FAIR

English Review (4: 399–408), February 1910.
Collected in *The Prussian Officer* (A6).

When Lawrence sent "Goose Fair" with the other stories in the collection to Edward Garnett in the summer of 1914, he suggested it as the title story; "Goose Fair" was revised for book publication.

C4 NIGHT SONGS

English Review (5: 4–8), April 1910.

WORKADAY EVENINGS

I. YESTERNIGHT
Collected in *New Poems* (A11) as "Hyde Park at Night: Clerks."

II. TO-MORROW NIGHT
Collected in *New Poems* (A11) as "Piccadilly Circus at Night: Street Walkers."

WAKENED
Collected in *Love Poems* (A3) as "Dream-Confused."

AT THE WINDOW
Collected in *Amores* (A9).

REBUKED
See also (A104).

C5 TIRED OF THE BOAT

English Review (6: 377–379), October 1910.
Collected in *Amores* (A9) as "In a Boat."

SIGH NO MORE
Collected in *New Poems* (A11).

AH MURIEL

Not included in any of the Lawrence collections, but reprinted in Harry T. Moore's *Intelligent Heart* (B57); Muriel was Lawrence's name for Jessie Chambers. Collected in (A104).

c6 ODOUR OF CHRYSANTHEMUMS

English Review (8: 415–433), June 1911.
Collected in *The Prussian Officer* (A6). See (C256).

c7 A FRAGMENT OF STAINED GLASS

English Review (9: 242–251), September 1911.
Collected in *The Prussian Officer* (A6).

Originally known as "Legend," this story was one of those submitted for the *Nottinghamshire Guardian* competition in 1907 and rejected; see (C1) and (A85). Also appeared in *Pearson's Magazine* for March 1922.

c8 LIGHTNING

Nation (London) (10:204), 4 November 1911.
Collected in *Love Poems* (A3).

VIOLETS

Collected in *Love Poems*.

c8.2 A REVIEW of *Contemporary German Poetry* edited by Jethro Bithell.

English Review (9: 721–724), November 1911. Also appeared in *Encounter* for August 1969. See (C33.5).

c8.5 A REVIEW of *The Oxford Book of German Verse*, ed. by H. G. Fiedler and *The Minnesingers*, ed. by Jethro Bithell.

English Review (10: 373–376), January 1912.

This review, published anonymously, was identified by Armin Arnold and reprinted with an introduction in his book, *D. H. Lawrence and German Literature* (B69). The review was also published in *PMLA* for March 1964. Collected in *Phoenix II* (A107).

c9 SECOND BEST

English Review (10: 461–469), February 1912.
Collected in *The Prussian Officer* (A6).

C10 THE MINER AT HOME

Nation (London), 16 March 1912.
Collected in *Phoenix* (A76).

C11 THE SCHOOLMASTER: TO ONE OF MY BOYS; MORNINGS;
SCRIPTURE LESSON

Saturday Westminster Gazette, 11 May 1912.

These verses are the first of a series of poems derived from Lawrence's teaching experience which appeared in consecutive issues of the *Saturday Westminster Gazette*; while the titles for these various poems differ in the several publications, the specific titles given here do not reappear. See (A104).

C12 THE SCHOOLMASTER

Saturday Westminster Gazette, 18 May 1912.

II. AFTERNOON, THE LAST LESSON

Collected in *Love Poems* (A3) as "Afternoon in School." See (A104).

C13 THE SCHOOLMASTER

Saturday Westminster Gazette, 25 May 1912.

III. EVENING

IV. THE PUNISHER

Collected in *Amores* (A9). See (A104).

C14 SNAP-DRAGON

English Review (11: 345–348), June 1912.
First collected in *Georgian Poetry 1911–1912* (B1) and included in *Amores* (A9).

Harry T. Moore has identified the person to whom this poem is addressed as Louie Burrows, an Ilkeston schoolteacher, whom Jessie Chambers refers to as "X" in *A Personal Record* (B43).

Other poems addressed to Louie Burrows include "The Hands of the Betrothed" in *Amores* and "Kisses in the Train" from *Love Poems* (A3).

C15 THE SCHOOLMASTER

Saturday Westminster Gazette, 1 June 1912.

V. A SNOWY DAY IN SCHOOL

Collected in *Love Poems* (A3).

VI. THE BEST OF SCHOOL

Collected in *Love Poems*. See (A104).

C16 GERMAN IMPRESSIONS: I. FRENCH SONS OF GERMANY

Saturday Westminster Gazette, 3 August 1912.
Collected in *Phoenix* (A76).

C17 GERMAN IMPRESSIONS: II. HAIL IN THE RHINELAND

Saturday Westminster Gazette, 10 August 1912.
Collected in *Phoenix* (A76).

C18 THE SOILED ROSE

Forum (49: 324–340), March 1913.
Collected in *The Prussian Officer* (A6) as "The Shades of Spring."

In a letter to Helen Corke in 1913 Lawrence says he wrote this story while he was sick in bed at Croydon; it also appeared in the *Blue Review*, May 1913.

C19 THE GEORGIAN RENAISSANCE: A review of *Georgian Poetry: 1911–1912*

Rhythm, March 1913.
Collected in *Phoenix* (A76).

It is interesting to note that this review by Lawrence is of a volume to which he himself contributed; see (B1). According to John Middleton Murry, who gives an account of the new movement in poetry in *Between Two Worlds*, *Rhythm* was largely subsidized by Edward Marsh, who edited the Georgian anthologies. The magazine was begun in the summer of 1911 and edited by John Middleton Murry and Katherine Mansfield through March 1912; Lawrence contributed only to the last number although he appeared later in the *Blue Review*, "an abortive continuation of *Rhythm*."

C20 CHRISTS IN THE TIROL

Saturday Westminster Gazette, 22 March 1913.
Collected in *Twilight in Italy* (A8) as "The Crucifix Across the Mountains."

This sketch was written from observations made during Lawrence and Frieda's walking trip through the Tirol after their elopement to Germany. Various versions of this essay have been published in the *Fortnightly Review*, July 1933, in the *Atlantic Monthly*, August 1933, in *Love Among the Haystacks* (A56b) and in *Phoenix* (A76).

C21 GERMAN BOOKS: THOMAS MANN

Blue Review, July 1913.
Collected in *Phoenix* (A76).

The *Blue Review* was edited and published by John Middleton Murry and Katherine Mansfield as a successor to *Rhythm* (C19); it appeared for three numbers only, during May, June and July 1913. In *The Georgian Literary Scene* Frank Swinnerton tells of a supper party that launched the *Blue Review* with high hopes.

C22 THE FLY IN THE OINTMENT (A BLOT)

New Statesman (1: 595–7), 16 August 1913.
Collected in *Young Lorenzo* (B34).

This story was included in *Young Lorenzo* as an example of Lawrence's early work; a note, presumably by Mr Gelder, records that the manuscript had an Eastwood address written by Lawrence and suggests that the story might have been written while he was staying with Ada during a holiday from Croydon. See (A107).

C23 ITALIAN STUDIES: BY THE LAGO DI GARDA

English Review (15: 202–234), September 1913.

I. THE SPINNER AND THE MONKS

II. THE LEMON GARDENS OF THE SIGNOR DI P.

III. THE THEATRE
Collected in *Twilight in Italy* (A8).

C24 STRIKE-PAY I, HER TURN

Saturday Westminster Gazette, 6 September 1913.
Collected in *A Modern Lover* (A71) as "Her Turn."
Also appeared in *Esquire* for August 1934 as "Turnabout is Fair."

C25 A SICK COLLIER

New Statesman (1: 722–4), 13 September 1913.

Collected in *The Prussian Officer* (A6).
Also appeared in *Pearson's Magazine* for February 1922.

C26 STRIKE-PAY II, EPHRAIM'S HALF SOVEREIGN

Saturday Westminster Gazette, 13 September 1913.
Collected in *A Modern Lover* (A71) as "Strike Pay."

The story also appeared in *Lovat Dickson's Magazine*, August 1934, and in *Esquire* for June 1934.

C27 THE MOWERS

Smart Set, November 1913.
First collected in *Some Imagist Poets* (B2); included in *Look! We Have Come Through!* (A10) as "A Youth Mowing."

C28 SERVICE OF ALL THE DEAD

New Statesman (Vol. 2), 15 November 1913.
First collected in *Georgian Poetry: 1913–1915* (B3) and included in *Look! We Have Come Through!* (A10) as "Giorno dei Morti," and with the same title in *The Book of Italy*, London, 1916.

The poem also appeared in *Poetry*, December 1914 (C35).

C29 GREEN

Poetry (3: 115–125), January 1914.
First collected in *Some Imagist Poets* (B2) and included in *Look! We Have Come Through!* (A10).

The poem "Green" was set to music by A. Walter Kramer and published as sheet music by the Boston Music Company in 1916.

ALL OF ROSES

Collected in *Look! We Have Come Through!* as three separate poems, "River Roses," "Roses on the Breakfast Table" and "Gloire de Dijon."

FIREFLIES IN THE CORN

First collected in *Some Imagist Poets* (B2) and included in *Look! We Have Come Through!*

A WOMAN AND HER DEAD HUSBAND

Collected in *New Poems* (A11) as "Bitterness of Death."

THE WIND, THE RASCAL

Separately published as *An Original Poem* (A70); collected in (A104).

THE MOTHER OF SONS

Collected in *Amores* (A9) as "Monologue of a Mother."

ILLICIT

First collected in *Some Imagist Poets* (B2); included in *Look! We Have Come Through!* as "On the Balcony."

BIRTHDAY

Collected in *New Poems* as "On That Day."

Frieda Lawrence included in her book *Not I, But the Wind* (B40) several early versions of poems which she preferred to the final form Lawrence chose for *Look! We Have Come Through!* (A10); among these were "All of Roses" and "The Mother of Sons." The original texts were used for the Ark Press *Look! We Have Come Through!* (A10b). "All of Roses" and "Illicit" appeared in *Lyric*, October and August 1917 respectively.

C30 TWILIGHT

English Review (16: 305–307), February 1914.
A shorter version was collected in *The New Poetry* (B5) as "Grief."
See "Firelight and Nightfall" in *Amores* (A9).

MEETING AMONG THE MOUNTAINS

Collected in *Georgian Poetry 1913–1915* (B3).

A shorter version of "Twilight" under the title "Grief" appeared in *Poetry*, December 1914 (C35); it was apparently designed as a Christmas greeting for Edward Marsh. The poem by the same name in *Collected Poems* (A43) is not this "Twilight." "Meeting Among the Mountains" was originally intended for the *Look! We Have Come Through!* sequence but was omitted in accordance with the wishes of the publisher; Frieda Lawrence printed it in *Not I, But the Wind* and the poem was replaced in the Ark Press *Look! We Have Come Through!* (A10b). For some reason Lawrence did not include it in *Collected Poems* (A43).

C30.5 THE CHRISTENING

The Smart Set, February 1914.
Collected in *The Prussian Officer* (A46).

C31 THE SHADOW IN THE ROSE GARDEN

Smart Set, March 1914.
Collected in *The Prussian Officer* (A6).
Also appeared in *Georgian Stories 1922*.

C32 SONG

Egoist (1: 134–135), 1 April 1914.
Collected in *New Poems* (A11) as "Flapper."

EARLY SPRING

Collected in *New Poems* as "Autumn Sunshine."

HONEYMOON

Collected in *Amores* (A9) as "Excursion."

FOOLED

Collected in *Amores* as "Perfidy."

A WINTER'S TALE

Collected in *Amores*.
"Song" appeared under the original title in *Poetry*, December 1914
(C35).

C33 VIN ORDINAIRE

English Review (17: 298–315), June 1914.
Collected in *The Prussian Officer* (A6) as "The Thorn in the Flesh."

C33.5 WITH THE GUNS

Manchester Guardian, 18 August 1914.

This essay was discovered by Carl Baron through a reference in the
Lawrence correspondence; the author was given as H. D.
Lawrence. Dr Baron published "With the Guns" and an early
anonymous review by Lawrence (C8.2) in an article in *Encounter* for
August 1969.

C34 HONOUR AND ARMS

English Review (18: 24–43), August 1914.
Collected in *The Prussian Officer* (A6) as "The Prussian Officer."

"Honour and Arms" was the original title for "The Prussian
Officer" to which Edward Garnett changed the title in 1914 when he
was supervising the publication of the collection of stories for

Duckworth. The story was written in Bavaria in 1913 according to a letter from Lawrence to Edward Garnett in which he said it was "the best short story" he had written. Despite Lawrence's dislike for the name chosen by Edward Garnett, it has always appeared as "The Prussian Officer" except in the *Metropolitan*, November 1914, where it had the original title.

C34.5 THE WHITE STOCKING

Smart Set (44: 97–108), October 1914.
Collected in *The Prussian Officer* (A6).

C35 GRIEF

Poetry (5: 102–106), December 1914.
Collected in *The New Poetry* (B5). See the *English Review*, February 1914 (C30).

MEMORIES

Collected in *Amores* (A9) as "The End."

WEARINESS

Collected in *Amores* as "Sorrow."

SERVICE OF ALL THE DEAD

Collected in *Look! We Have Come Through!* (A10) as "Giorno dei Morti." See the *New Statesman*, 15 November 1913 (C28).

DON JUAN

Collected in *Look! We Have Come Through!*

SONG

Collected in *New Poems* (A11) as "Flapper." See the *Egoist*, 1 April 1914 (C32).

A longer version of "Grief" appeared in the *English Review*, February 1914 (C30) as "Twilight"; the version here was printed in *Letters* (A61).

C36 TEASING

Poetry and Drama, December 1914.
Collected in *Amores* (A9) as "Tease."

C37 ELOI, ELOI LAMA SABACHTHANI?

Egoist (2: 75–76), 1 May 1915.

C38

This poem was discovered and brought to light in *Modern Language Notes*, June 1952, by E. W. Tedlock, Jr. This particular number of the *Egoist* was edited by Richard Aldington as a special "imagist" issue and was designed to reach the United States in time to advertise a forthcoming imagist anthology, but neither the magazine nor Lawrence's contribution met with Miss Amy Lowell's approval.

C38 ENGLAND, MY ENGLAND

English Review (21: 238–252), October 1915.
Collected in *England, My England* (A23).

This story was written about a year before its publication in the *English Review*, and its characters have been identified with the Meynells of Greatham in Sussex, where Lawrence and Frieda lived for a time during the war. In a letter to Catherine Carswell Lawrence regretted having written the story because it provided an unfavourable portrait of Percy Lucas, a Meynell son-in-law, who was killed in France shortly afterwards. "England, My England" also appeared in the *Metropolitan*, April 1917.

C39 THE CROWN I

Signature (No. 1: 3–14), 4 October 1915.
Collected in *Reflections on the Death of a Porcupine* (A32).

During the last half of 1915, while he and Frieda were living at Byron Villas in Hampstead, Lawrence was associated with John Middleton Murry and Katherine Mansfield in the publication of the short-lived *Signature*. Murry's *Reminiscences* (B38) gives an account of the magazine, and Lawrence's own story of the venture is found in the introduction he wrote for *Reflections on the Death of a Porcupine*. Lawrence gave Murry most of the credit for the inception of the magazine, but Murry says the *Signature* was begun to further Lawrence's doctrine for a revolutionary society. The "Crown" was Lawrence's sole contribution to the magazine, which appeared for three numbers only.

C40 THE CROWN II

Signature (No. 2: 1–10), 18 October 1915.
See C39.

C41 THE CROWN III

Signature (No. 3: 1–10), 1 November 1915.
See C39.

332

C41.5 STREET LAMPS

The Egoist, January 1917.
Collected in *Look! We Have Come Through!* (A10).

C42 AUTUMN RAIN

Egoist (4: 22), February 1917.
Collected in *Look! We Have Come Through!* (A10).

C43 SAMSON AND DELILAH

English Review (24: 209–224), March 1917.
Collected in *England, My England* (A23).

This story also appeared in the *Lantern* (San Francisco), June 1917.

C44 THE THIMBLE

Seven Arts (1: 435–448), March 1917.

A story of the war years in England, "The Thimble" is apparently based on an incident in the lives of the Asquiths; in a letter dated December 1916 Lawrence told Lady Cynthia Asquith that the story was being published in *Seven Arts*. The *Seven Arts* was a "little magazine" published in New York from November 1916 until October 1917, when it merged with the *Dial*. "The Thimble" was rewritten as "The Ladybird" (A24).

C45 THE REALITY OF PEACE I

English Review (24: 415–422), May 1917.
Collected in *Phoenix* (A76).

The first of four published instalments of the essay, this appearance introduces one of the mysteries of Lawrence bibliography. In March 1917 Lawrence wrote Catherine Carswell from Zennor in Cornwall that he had done seven short articles called "The Reality of Peace," and his agent, Pinker, was informed by letter in the same month that the seven essays were being forwarded to him. The last three parts have disappeared, and there is no record of publication or manuscripts beyond the four parts listed here.

C46 THE REALITY OF PEACE II

English Review (24: 516–523), June 1917.
See C45.

C47 RESURRECTION

Poetry (10: 139), June 1917.
Collected in *The New Poetry* (B12).

C48 THE REALITY OF PEACE III

English Review (25: 24–29), July 1917.
See C45.

C49 THE MORTAL COIL

Seven Arts (2: 280–305), July 1917.

While he was staying at Zennor, Cornwall, Lawrence wrote Pinker
that he had just received some "stuff" he had done before the war,
which included "the Mortal Coil." He wrote the story in October
1916 and called it one of his "purest creations."
Collected in *Phoenix II* (A107).

C50 THE REALITY OF PEACE IV

English Review (25: 125–132), August 1917.
See C45.

C51 THE SEA

English Review (25: 193–197), September 1917.
Collected in *Look! We Have Come Through!* (A10).

CONSTANCY OF A SORT

Collected in *Look! We Have Come Through!* as "Hymn to Priapus."

FROST FLOWERS

Collected in *Look! We Have Come Through!*

C52 LOVE

English Review (26: 29–35), January 1918.
Collected in *Phoenix* (A76).

C53 LIFE

English Review (26: 122–126), February 1918.
Collected in *Phoenix* (A76).

C54 WAR-BABY

English Review (26: 473–474), June 1918.
Collected in *Bay* (A12).

TOWN
Collected in *Bay*.

AFTER THE OPERA
Collected in *Bay*.
"War-Baby" appeared in *Poetry*, February 1919 (C59) and "After the Opera" in *Palms*, Christmas 1924.

C55 STUDIES IN CLASSIC AMERICAN LITERATURE

I. SPIRIT OF PLACE

English Review (27: 319–331), November 1918.
Collected in *Studies in Classic American Literature* (A25).

This first of the essays in *Studies in Classic American Literature* was completed by late summer 1918, for Lawrence enclosed the manuscript in a letter to the agent Pinker from Derbyshire on the third of August; all of the essays were considerably rewritten for book publication.

C56 STUDIES IN CLASSIC AMERICAN LITERATURE

II. BENJAMIN FRANKLIN

English Review (27: 397–408), December 1918.
See C55.

C57 STUDIES IN CLASSIC AMERICAN LITERATURE

III. HENRY ST. JOHN CRÈVECOEUR

English Review (28: 5–18), January 1919.
See C55.

"Henry" was changed to "Hector" for book publication.

C58 STUDIES IN CLASSIC AMERICAN LITERATURE

IV. FENIMORE COOPER'S ANGLO-AMERICAN NOVELS

English Review (28: 88–99), February 1919.
See C55.

For book publication Lawrence changed the title of this essay to "Fenimore Cooper's White Novels."

C59 TOMMIES IN THE TRAIN

Poetry (13: 258–264), February 1919.
Collected in *Bay* (A12).

WAR-BABY

Collected in *Bay*. See the *English Review*, June 1918 (C54).

OBSEQUIAL CHANT

Collected in *Bay* as "Obsequial Ode."

BREAD UPON THE WATERS

Collected in *Bay*.

PENTECOSTAL

Collected in *Bay* as "Shades."

NOSTALGIA

Collected in *Bay*.

"Nostalgia" and "Obsequial Chant" appeared in *Voices*, July 1919, and "Nostalgia" was reprinted in *Palms*, Midsummer 1923.

c60 STUDIES IN CLASSIC AMERICAN LITERATURE

V. FENIMORE COOPER'S LEATHERSTOCKING NOVELS

English Review (28: 204–219), March 1919.
See C55.

c61 STUDIES IN CLASSIC AMERICAN LITERATURE

VI. EDGAR ALLAN POE

English Review (28: 278–291), April 1919.
See C55.

c62 TICKETS PLEASE

Strand, April 1919.
Collected in *England, My England* (A23).

"Tickets Please" also appeared in the *Metropolitan*, August 1919, as "The Eleventh Commandment."

c63 WHISTLING OF BIRDS

Athenaeum (No. 4641: 167–168), 11 April 1919.
Collected in *Phoenix* (A76).

The appearance of this essay marks one of the few occasions when Lawrence published under a pseudonym; John Middleton Murry had just become the editor of the *Athenaeum*, and perhaps because of

Lawrence's somewhat dubious reputation, it was considered best to use the pseudonym "Grantorto."

C64 STUDIES IN CLASSIC AMERICAN LITERATURE

VII. NATHANIEL HAWTHORNE

English Review (28: 404–417), May 1919.
See C55.

C65 STUDIES IN CLASSIC AMERICAN LITERATURE

VIII. THE TWO PRINCIPLES

English Review (28: 477–489), June 1919.
See C55. This essay was not included in *Studies in Classic American Literature* (A25a), but was collected in *The Symbolic Meaning* (A25b).

C66 THE LITTLE TOWN AT EVENING

Monthly Chapbook (1: 13), July 1919.
Collected in *Bay* (A12).

This poem also appeared in *Palms*, Christmas 1924.

C67 WAR FILMS

Poetry (14: 178–182), July 1919.

MOTHER'S SON IN SALONIKA

CASUALTY

MESSAGE TO A PERFIDIOUS SOLDIER

THE JEWESS AND THE V. C.

SIGHS

THE CHILD AND THE SOLDIER

ZEPPELIN NIGHTS

DAUGHTER OF THE GREAT MAN

PRISONER AT WORK IN A TURKISH GARDEN

MOURNING

THE GREY NURSE

NEITHER MOTH NOR RUST

C68 RONDEAU OF A CONSCIENTIOUS OBJECTOR

Voices, July 1919.
Collected in *Bay* (A12).

NOSTALGIA

Collected in *Bay*. See *Poetry*, February 1919 (C59).

OBSEQUIAL ODE

Collected in *Bay*. See *Poetry*, February 1919 (C59).

c69 POETRY OF THE PRESENT I

Playboy (No. 4), 1919.

Printed as the introduction to the American edition of *New Poems* (A11) and collected in *Phoenix* (A76). Also in *Voices*, October 1919, as "Verse Free and Unfree" and reprinted from the American edition of *New Poems* in the *Evening Post Book Review* for 19 June 1920 as "Poetry of the Present."

c70 POETRY OF THE PRESENT II

Playboy (No. 5), 1919.
See C69.

c71 YOU TOUCHED ME

Land and Water (No. 3025), 29 April 1920.
Collected in *England, My England* (A23).

This story was originally known as "Hadrian" and is referred to several times by that name in the Lawrence letters. Tennessee Williams and Donald Windham wrote a play based on the plot of "You Touched Me" which was produced on Broadway in 1945 with Montgomery Clift and Katherine Willard playing the leading roles. This production was reviewed in the *Nation*, 6 October 1945, by Joseph Wood Krutch; in *Theatre Arts*, November, by Rosamond Gilder and in *Theatre World*, December. Samuel French published an acting edition of the play in February 1947 in an edition of 1006 copies, 506 of which were bound in cloth; it has been reprinted several times.

c72 THE BLIND MAN

English Review (31 : 22–41), July 1920.
Collected in *England, My England* (A23).

During the summer of 1918 Lawrence and Frieda visited the Carswells in the Forest of Dean near Lydbrook, where they had a "whole vicarage" to themselves; it was here that Lawrence conceived the idea for this story, and the vicarage in which they lived was the scene of its action. The story also appeared in the *Living Age*, 7 August 1920.

C73 ADOLF

Dial (69: 269–276), September 1920.
First collected in the *New Keepsake for the Year 1921* (B8) and included in *Phoenix* (A76) and *Young Lorenzo* (B34b).

"Adolf" is the story of a pet rabbit which the Lawrence children owned, and his sister Ada included it in the English edition of her book about Lawrence, *Young Lorenzo* (B34b).

C73.5 THE FOX

Hutchinson's Magazine (3: 477-490), November 1920.
For a discussion of Lawrence's letter in December of 1921 to Curtis Brown that "The Fox" had previously appeared in *Nash's Magazine*, see (C92); apparently Lawrence never did remember where the story had been published because earlier in December he wrote Robert Mountsier that the first part of "The Fox" had been published in the *Strand*.

C74 AMERICA, LISTEN TO YOUR OWN

New Republic (25: 68–70), 15 December 1920.
First collected in *The New Republic Anthology: 1915–1935* (B45) and included in *Phoenix* (A76).

This essay of admonition to America, signed in Florence in 1920, was answered by Walter Lippmann in "The Crude Barbarian and the Noble Savage" in the same issue of the magazine.

C75 MEDLARS AND SORB APPLES

New Republic (25: 169), 5 January 1921.
Collected in *Birds, Beasts and Flowers* (A27).

These verses, the first of the *Birds, Beasts and Flowers* poems to be published, were written at San Gervasio near Florence, where Lawrence stayed at the Villa Canovaia which belonged to a friend. "Medlars and Sorb Apples" also appeared in the *English Review*, August 1921.

C76 THE REVOLUTIONARY

New Republic (25: 231), 19 January 1921.
Collected in *Birds, Beasts and Flowers* (A27).

These verses also appeared in the *English Review*, September 1921, and in the *Literary Digest*, 29 October 1921.

C77 REX

Dial (70: 169–176), February 1921.
First collected in *Stories from the Dial* (B13) and included in *Phoenix* (A76).

"Rex" was the story of a dog which belonged to an uncle of the Lawrence children; when they were small, Mrs Lawrence permitted them to keep the dog for a while, and they were quite distressed when the uncle came to take their pet away. The story has been reprinted in many anthologies of dog stories and was published in *Jugend*, October 1928, in a German translation by Frieda's sister Else Jaffe-Richthofen.

C78 POMEGRANATE

Dial (70: 317–318), March 1921.
Collected in *Birds, Beasts and Flowers* (A27).

This poem to which Lawrence gave first place in the *Birds, Beasts and Flowers* collection was written near Florence in 1920. A note in the diary transcribed by E. W. Tedlock, Jr. (B51) records that Lawrence offered "Pomegranate" with some other verses to J. C. Squire for the *London Mercury*, but apparently they were not accepted. "Pomegranate" also appeared in the *English Review*, August 1921.

C79 APOSTOLIC BEASTS

Dial (70: 410–416), April 1921.

SAINT MARK

SAINT LUKE

SAINT JOHN

Collected in *Birds, Beasts and Flowers* (A27) with a fourth poem, "Saint Matthew" (C106) as "Evangelistic Beasts."

C80 HUMMING-BIRD

New Republic (26: 325), 11 May 1921.
Collected in *Birds, Beasts and Flowers* (A27).

"Humming-Bird" appeared in the *Nation* (New York), 10 October 1923, and in the *Bookman* (New York), January 1924.

c81 MOSQUITO

> *Bookman* (New York) (53: 430–431), July 1921.
> Collected in *Birds, Beasts and Flowers* (A27).

c82 SNAKE

> *Dial* (71: 19–21), July 1921.
> First collected in *Georgian Poetry: 1920–1922* (B11) and included in
> *Birds, Beasts and Flowers* (A27).

> One of Lawrence's most frequently reprinted poems, "Snake" was
> written in common with many other verses of *Birds, Beasts and Flowers*
> during the two years' residence at Fontana Vecchia in Taormina.
> Lawrence wrote the poem from an actual incident which he
> observed at the water trough near the house. "Snake" also appeared
> in the *London Mercury*, October 1921.

c83 WHITMAN

> *Nation and Athenaeum* (29: 616–618), 23 July 1921.
> See C55.

> Lawrence wrote Mrs S. A. Hopkin from Derbyshire in June 1918
> that he was just finishing the last of his book of American essays, the
> "Whitman." Also appeared in the *New York Call* for 21 August 1921.

c84 WINTRY PEACOCK

> *Metropolitan*, August 1921.
> First collected in *The New Decameron III* (B10) and included in
> *England, My England* (A23).

c85 SEA AND SARDINIA: selections from AS FAR AS PALERMO
and THE SEA

> *Dial* (71: 441–451), October 1921.
> Collected in *Sea and Sardinia* (A20).

> In a letter to Catherine Carswell from Taormina in April 1921,
> Lawrence mentioned a "diary" of a trip to Sardinia; these are the
> first of the *Sea and Sardinia* essays to appear in print.

c86 SEA AND SARDINIA: selections from CAGLIARI, MANDAS, TO
SORGONO and TO NUOVO

> *Dial* (71: 583–592), November 1921.
> Collected in *Sea and Sardinia* (A20).

c87 FANNY AND ANNIE

Hutchinson's Magazine, 21 November 1921.
Collected in *England, My England* (A23).

c88 THE GENTLEMAN FROM SAN FRANCISCO

Dial (72: 47–68), January 1922.
Collected in *The Gentleman from San Francisco and Other Stories* (B9).

Translated from the Russian by D. H. Lawrence and S. S. Koteliansky, this story was perhaps the first of their collaborations; see the discussion under *The Grand Inquisitor* (B28) and *All Things Are Possible* (A13).

c89 AN EPISODE

Dial (72: 143–146), February 1922.
This contains selections from Chapter XIV of *Aaron's Rod* (A21).

c90 ALMOND BLOSSOM

English Review (34: 101–104), February 1922.
Collected in *Birds, Beasts and Flowers* (A27).

c91 THE HORSE DEALER'S DAUGHTER

English Review (34: 308–325), April 1922.
Collected in *England, My England* (A23).

A note transcribed from the "Diary" by E. W. Tedlock, Jr. (B51), mentions that Lawrence sent the manuscript of this story to a Mrs Carmichael for typing on 26 October 1921, and he enclosed the typescript in a letter to Curtis Brown from Taormina in December. "The Horse Dealer's Daughter" was included in *The Best British Short Stories of 1923*.

c92 THE FOX I

Dial (72: 471–492), May 1922.
Collected in *The Ladybird* (A24).

When Lawrence sent his manuscripts to Curtis Brown for *England, My England* (A23) in December 1921, he included "The Fox." Although he noted that the "first part" had been published in *Nash's Magazine*, a search of *Nash's Pall Mall Magazine* for the years 1920 and 1921 revealed no trace of the story. "The Fox" was originally written in Derbyshire in December 1918 according to a letter to

Katherine Mansfield; apparently the story was rewritten several times and was considerably lengthened in its final form. See (C73.5).

C93 THE FOX II

Dial (72: 569–587), June 1922.
See C92.

C94 FISH

English Review (34: 505–510), June 1922.
Collected in *Birds, Beasts and Flowers* (A27).

Among the last of the poems to be included in the *Birds, Beasts and Flowers* collection, "Fish" was sent with a letter from Florence in September 1921 to Curtis Brown with instructions to place it in the "Beasts" section.

C95 THE FOX III

Dial (73: 75–87), July 1922.
See C92.

C96 THE FOX IV

Dial (73: 184–198), August 1922.
See C92.

C97 MONKEY NUTS

Sovereign, 22 August 1922.
Collected in *England, My England* (A23).

"Monkey Nuts" was returned to Lawrence from the agent Pinker in the summer of 1921 and forwarded to Mountsier, his American agent, with other manuscripts in December.

C98 BAT

English Review (35: 381–385), November 1922.
Collected in *Birds, Beasts and Flowers* (A27).

BABY TORTOISE

Collected in *Tortoises* (A19) and included in the English edition of *Birds, Beasts and Flowers* (A27b).

"Bat" was sent to Curtis Brown in September 1921 for inclusion in *Birds, Beasts and Flowers*, and according to Harry T. Moore the experience recorded in the poem may have occurred in the house where he was staying at the time, Nelly Morrison's flat at 32 Via dei Bardi in Florence, which legend says belonged to Romola. "Bat" also appeared in the *Literary Digest*, December 1930.

The "Tortoise" poems were separately published by Seltzer in the United States, and thus not included in the Seltzer edition of *Birds, Beasts and Flowers* (A27a).

C99 THE EVENING LAND

Poetry (21 : 59–67), November 1922.
Collected in *Birds, Beasts and Flowers* (A27).

TURKEY-COCK
Collected in *Birds, Beasts and Flowers*.

Lawrence wrote Harriet Monroe in September of 1922 saying that he was glad she could print the poems and noting that "Turkey-Cock" was a favourite of his; a few days later he sent another letter instructing her to make several small changes at the end of the poem.

C100 CERTAIN AMERICANS AND AN ENGLISHMAN

New York Times Magazine (4:1), 24 December 1922.

This is an article about the Pueblo Indians and the Bursum Land Bill.

C101 LETTER

Laughing Horse (No. 4), 1922.
Separately published as *D. H. Lawrence's Letter to the Laughing Horse* (A77) and included in the *Letters* (A61) and reprinted by Witter Bynner in *Journey with Genius* (B55).

The "letter" in question is to Willard Johnson, often referred to as "Spud" or "Spoodles" in the Lawrence correspondence, and actually is a review of Ben Hecht's *Fantazius Mallare* to which Lawrence took exception. The printing of the letter in the *Laughing Horse*, then published from the campus of the University of California, caused Spud Johnson's expulsion from school. An account of the incident is given in Witter Bynner's *Journey with Genius* (B55). Lawrence continued to contribute to the *Laughing Horse* and designed a cover which was never used on the magazine; this cover design is reproduced in Moore's *Intelligent Heart* (B57). Mr Johnson has told the story of his editorship of the magazine in the *New Mexico Quarterly*, Summer 1951.

C101.5 NIGHT LETTER to Thomas Seltzer in "Author Berates Justice John Ford"

New York Times (p. 18), 11 February 1923.
This night letter to Thomas Seltzer concerns the efforts of the Society for the Supression of Vice to ban *Women in Love* at the urging of Justice John Ford of the New York Supreme Court who objected to his daughter reading the novel. The case was decided in favor of the book in September. The text of the night letter is reprinted in an article, "Lawrence's Night Letter on Censorship and Obscenity" by Raymond W. Beirne in the *D. H. Lawrence Review* for Fall 1974. The letter was also published in the *Publisher's Weekly* for 24 February 1923.

C102 INDIANS AND AN ENGLISHMAN

Dial (74: 144–152), February 1923.
Collected in *Phoenix* (A76).

Lawrence wrote John Middleton Murry from Mexico in April 1923 suggesting that he might like the essay "Indians and an Englishman" which Curtis Brown then had in manuscript; Murry accepted it for the *Adelphi* where it appeared in the November issue in 1923 (C112).

C103 TAOS

Dial (74: 251–254), March 1923.
Collected in *Phoenix* (A76).

"Taos" is the third essay written and published as a result of Lawrence's experiences after his arrival in New Mexico in September 1922; it describes the Indian ceremonial dance of San Geronimo which takes place at the end of September. The essay also appeared in *Cassell's Weekly* (C108).

C104 ELEPHANT

English Review (36: 297–302), April 1923.
Collected in *Birds, Beasts and Flowers* (A27).

"Elephant" was written in Ceylon in March or April 1922 where Lawrence witnessed a ceremonial procession in which the Prince of Wales rode on an elephant's back.

C105 SURGERY FOR THE NOVEL, OR A BOMB

Literary Digest International Book Review, April 1923.
Collected in *Phoenix* (A76).

C106 ST. MATTHEW

Poetry (22: 27–31), April 1923.
Collected in *Birds, Beasts and Flowers* (A27).

Apparently all four of the "Apostolic Beasts" poems were written at about the same time, for Lawrence speaks of the four of them in a letter to Donald Carswell in November 1921, the year the other three were published in the *Dial* (C79). "St. Matthew" also appeared in the *Adelphi*, October 1923 (C111).

C107 MODEL AMERICANS: A review of Stuart Sherman's *Americans*

Dial (74: 503–510), May 1923.
Collected in *Phoenix* (A76).

This book review was written in Taos during the first months of 1923; Lawrence received the proofs from the *Dial* in February and mentioned them in a letter to Gilbert Seldes with the hope that the "Prof. Sherman criticism" would amuse him.

C108 AT TAOS, AN ENGLISHMAN LOOKS AT MEXICO

Cassell's Weekly (1: 535–536), 11 July 1923.
See (C103).

C108.5 AN INTERVIEW

New York Evening Post, 20 August 1923.

A few days before he left New York for Buffalo and the west coast Lawrence came to the city from the Seltzer cottage in New Jersey and was interviewed at length by the *New York Evening Post*.

C109 ST. JOSEPH'S ASS

Adelphi (1: 284–297), September 1923.
Collected in *Little Novels of Sicily* (A30).

Lawrence first became interested in the work of the Sicilian novelist, Giovanni Verga, at Fontana Vecchia in Taormina; he wrote Catherine Carswell and Edward Garnett from there in the Autumn of 1921 asking what translations of Verga had appeared in English and saying that he thought it would be fun to "do" him, that the language was fascinating. Other translations by Lawrence from Verga are found in *Cavalleria Rusticana and Other Stories* (A39), and *Mastro-don Gesualdo* (A28).

C 1 1 0 A SPIRITUAL RECORD: A review of *A Second Contemporary Verse Anthology*

New York Evening Post Literary Review, 29 September 1923.
Collected in *Phoenix* (A76).

C 1 10.5 PEACE

Nation (New York) (117: No. 3040), 10 October 1923.
Collected in *Birds, Beasts and Flowers* (A27).

BARE ALMOND TREES (A27)

TROPIC (A27)

C 1 1 1 CYPRESSES

Adelphi (1: 368–377), October 1923.
Collected in *Birds, Beasts and Flowers* (A27).

SAINT MATTHEW

Collected in *Birds, Beasts and Flowers* (A27). See *Poetry*, April 1923 (C106).

SPIRITS SUMMONED WEST

Collected in *Birds, Beasts and Flowers*.

C 1 1 2 ACROSS THE SEA

Adelphi (1: 466-475, 484-494), November 1923.
Collected in *Little Novels of Sicily* (A30).

INDIANS AND AN ENGLISHMAN

Collected in *Phoenix* (A76). See the *Dial*, February 1923 (C102).

C 1 1 3 THE PROPER STUDY

Adelphi (1: 584–590), December 1923.
Collected in *Phoenix* (A76).

Lawrence wrote John Middleton Murry from Los Angeles in September 1923 that he had asked Thomas Seltzer to send Murry "The Proper Study" for the *Adelphi*; the essay was written for the *Nation*, but Lawrence told Murry he had the *Adelphi* more in mind while he was writing it. Actually the essay never appeared in the *Nation*; its periodical publication in the United States was in *Vanity Fair*, where it appeared in the issue for January 1924 as "The Proper Study of Mankind."

C114 AU REVOIR, U. S. A.

>*Laughing Horse* (No. 8: 1–3), December 1923.
>Collected in *Phoenix* (A76). For additional information about Lawrence and the *Laughing Horse* see (C101).

C115 A BRITISHER HAS A WORD WITH AN EDITOR

>*Palms* (1: 153–154), Christmas 1923.
>Printed in *A Composite Biography*, Vol. II (B60).

>Edward Nehls identifies this anonymous contribution by Lawrence in Vol. II of his *Composite Biography*; the editor in question is Harriet Monroe, and the essay is a reply to her article "The Editor in England" which appeared in *Poetry*, October 1923.

C116 ON BEING RELIGIOUS

>*Adelphi* (1: 791–799), February 1924.
>Collected in *Phoenix* (A76).

C117 ON HUMAN DESTINY

>*Adelphi* (1: 882–891), March 1924.
>Collected in *Assorted Articles* (A53).

>This essay appeared in *Vanity Fair*, May 1924.

C118 A REVIEW of *The Book of Revelation* by Dr. J. Oman

>*Adelphi* (1: 1011–1013), April 1924.

>This review was published under the pseudonym L. H. Davidson; the topic of the book reviewed, the ideas in the article and the pseudonym under which it appeared all suggest D. H. Lawrence so strongly that Mr W. Forster of London addressed an inquiry about the review to John Middleton Murry in 1953, who replied that he was "reasonably certain" that it was written by D. H. Lawrence. In an undated note to Murry, written early in 1924, Lawrence mentions sending a review of the Oman book. Collected in *Apocalypse and the Writings on Revelation* (A57b).

C119 LIBERTY

>*Adelphi* (1: 1051–1059), May 1924.
>Collected in *Little Novels of Sicily* (A30).

C120 DEAR OLD HORSE, A LONDON LETTER

Laughing Horse (No. 10: 3–6, 19), May 1924.
Collected in the *Letters* (A61).

THE BAD GIRL IN THE PANSY BED (A drawing)

When he was in London in January 1924, Lawrence received a copy of the *Laughing Horse* from Spud Johnson, and this is the letter written in reply. The drawing, " The Bad Girl in the Pansy Bed," illustrates a poem by Mabel Dodge Luhan "The Ballad of a Bad Girl." Mrs Luhan is the author of *Lorenzo in Taos* (B35).

C121 ON BEING A MAN

Vanity Fair (22: 33–34), June 1924.
Collected in *Assorted Articles* (A53).

"On Being a Man" also appeared in the *Adelphi*, September 1924.

C122 THE DANCE OF THE SPROUTING CORN

Theatre Arts Monthly (8: 447–457), July 1924.
Collected in *Mornings in Mexico* (A37).

THE CORN DANCE (A drawing)

Printed on the dust-jacket of *Mornings in Mexico*.

The first of the *Mornings in Mexico* sketches to appear in print, this essay describes the Easter dance of the Taos Pueblo Indians which Lawrence witnessed in 1924. The essay also appeared in the *Adelphi*, August 1924.

C123 THE BORDER LINE

Hutchinson's Magazine, September 1924.
Collected in *The Woman Who Rode Away* (A41).

Harry T. Moore establishes the composition of "The Border Line" at Baden-Baden in February 1924 just before the Lawrences returned to Taos for the second stay. The story also appeared in the *Smart Set*, September 1924.

C124 JUST BACK FROM THE SNAKE DANCE—TIRED OUT

Laughing Horse (No. 11: 26–29), September 1924.
Reprinted in the *Letters* (A61).

Lawrence wrote an article about the Hopi snake dance which was published in the *Theatre Arts Monthly*, December 1924 (C127); this letter to Spud Johnson is apparently an early draft which Mabel Dodge Luhan disliked.

C125 JIMMY AND THE DESPERATE WOMAN

Criterion (3: 15–42), October 1924.

First collected in *The Best British Short Stories of 1925* (B17) and included in *The Woman Who Rode Away* (A41).

According to Catherine Carswell this story was written in Paris in 1924, where Lawrence stayed for a few days in January and February.

C126 INDIANS AND ENTERTAINMENT

New York Times Magazine (4: 3), 26 October 1924.
Collected in *Mornings in Mexico* (A37).

Lawrence noted in the diary transcribed by Tedlock (B51) that he had forwarded the manuscript of "Indians and Entertainment" to Curtis Brown in September 1924; the essay also appeared in the *Adelphi*, November 1924.

C127 THE HOPI SNAKE DANCE

Theatre Arts Monthly (8: 836–860), December 1924.
Collected in *Mornings in Mexico* (A37).

This article gives an account of a trip the Lawrences took with Mabel and Tony Luhan to the Hopi country of Arizona where they saw the Hopi Indians perform the snake dance. The letter to Spud Johnson in the *Laughing Horse*, September 1924 (C124), was apparently an early draft to which Mabel Luhan objected. Lawrence wrote her a note from Taos telling her that he would write another essay for the *Theatre Arts Monthly*, "not for the Horse to Laugh at." John Middleton Murry took it for the *Adelphi* as well, where it appeared in two parts for January and February 1925. A shorter version appeared in the *Living Age*, 4 April 1925.

C128 THE PRINCESS I

Calendar of Modern Letters (1: 1–22), March 1925.
Collected in *St. Mawr and the Princess* (A31).

Lawrence wrote to Curtis Brown from Taos in September 1924 that he was writing a story called "The Princess," and a note in the Tedlock Diary (B51) records that it was finished on 8 October. The story was not published with the American *St. Mawr* (A31b).

C129 THE PRINCESS II

Calendar of Modern Letters (1: 122–132), April 1925.
See C128.

C130 THE PRINCESS III

Calendar of Modern Letters (1: 226–235), May 1925.
See C128.

C131 THE WOMAN WHO RODE AWAY I

Dial (79: 1–20), July 1925.
First collected in *The Best British Short Stories of 1926* (B20) and included in *The Woman Who Rode Away* (A41).

"The Woman Who Rode Away" is set in the Taos country, and Mabel Dodge Luhan records that Lawrence showed her the manuscript around 1 July 1924; it was also about this time that Lawrence made a trip to a cave near the Arroyo Seco which supplied the scene for the story. The story also appeared in the *Criterion* in two parts for July 1925 and January 1926.

C132 THE WOMAN WHO RODE AWAY II

Dial (79: 121–136), August 1925.
See C131.

C133 ART AND MORALITY

Calendar of Modern Letters (2: 171–177), November 1925.
Collected in *Phoenix* (A76).

The essay also appeared in the *Living Age* for 26 December 1925.

C133.5 A REVIEW of Marmaduke Pickthall's *Säid the Fisherman*

New York Herald Tribune Books, 27 December 1925.
Collected in *Phoenix* (A76). See (C148).

C134 CORASMIN AND THE PARROTS

Adelphi (3: 480–489, 502–506), December 1925.
Collected in *Mornings in Mexico* (A37).

BARON CORVO, A review of Corvo's *Hadrian the Seventh*
Collected in *Phoenix* (A76).

C135 MORALITY AND THE NOVEL

Calendar of Modern Letters (2: 269–274), December 1925.
Collected in *Phoenix* (A76).

This essay also appeared in *Golden Book*, February 1926, and the eighth paragraph was published separately as *The Universe and Me* (A73).

C136 PAN IN AMERICA

Southwest Review, January 1926.
Collected in *Phoenix* (A76).

Evidence in Mabel Dodge Luhan's *Lorenzo in Taos* (B35) suggests that this essay was written in the summer of 1924.

C136.5 THE LAST LAUGH

Ainslee's (56: 55–65), January 1926.
Collected in *The New Decameron IV* (B15) and *The Woman Who Rode Away* (A41).

C137 A REVIEW of J. A. Krout's *Origins of Prohibition*
New York Herald Tribune Books, 31 January 1926.
Collected in *Phoenix* (A76).

A note on the manuscript of this review, described by Tedlock (B51), dates it in November 1925 at the Villa Bernarda at Spotorno; the note instructed Nancy Pearn in Curtis Brown's office to type the piece for the *Herald Tribune* to which Lawrence had promised it "ages ago."

C138 THE LATE MR. MAURICE MAGNUS (A letter)
New Statesman (26: 579), 20 February 1926.
Collected in *Phoenix* (A76).

Lawrence's introduction for Magnus' *Memoirs of the Foreign Legion* (B14) prompted a defense of Magnus in Norman Douglas' *D. H. Lawrence and Maurice Magnus, A Plea for Better Manners* (F2). The letter published here is Lawrence's refutation of Douglas' contention that he had treated Magnus unfairly. See (B14).

C139 A LITTLE MOONSHINE WITH LEMON

> *Laughing Horse* (No. 13: 1–15), April 1926.
> Collected in *Mornings in Mexico* (A37).

MEDITERRANEAN IN JANUARY (A poem)

EUROPE VERSUS AMERICA

> Collected in *Phoenix* (A76).

BEYOND THE ROCKIES (A poem)

PARIS LETTER

> Collected in *Phoenix* (A76).

PUEBLO INDIAN DANCE (A drawing)
> See *Mornings in Mexico* (A37) and *The Corn Dance* in *Theatre Arts Monthly*, July 1924 (C122).

Lawrence received a copy of this special D. H. Lawrence issue of the *Laughing Horse* at the Villa Mirenda in Florence in May or June of 1926 and sent it to Miss Pearn, describing it as a "little western magazine" which he thought would amuse her. The Tedlock diary (B51) dates the two poems at the Villa Bernarda in January 1926. "Mediterranean in January" also appeared in *Life and Letters*, March 1932.

C140 THE GENTLE ART OF MARKETING IN MEXICO

> *Travel* (46: 7–9, 44), April 1926.
> Collected in *Mornings in Mexico* (A37) as "Market Day."

This sketch appeared in the *New Criterion*, June 1926, as "Mornings in Mexico, Saturday."

C141 AMERICAN HEROES: A review of William Carlo Williams' *In the American Grain*

> *Nation* (New York) (122: 413–414), 14 April 1926.
> Collected in *Phoenix* (A76).

C142 SMILE

> *Nation and Athenaeum* (39: 319–320), 19 June 1926.
> Collected in *The Woman Who Rode Away* (A41).
> Also appeared in *New Masses* for June 1926.

C142.5 THE ROCKING HORSE WINNER

> *Harper's Bazaar* (pp. 97, 122, 124, 126), July 1926.

Dr Brian Finney records in *Notes and Queries* for February 1972 that the first publication of this story was in *Harper's Bazaar* rather than in *The Ghost Book* (B19) as noted in the earlier edition of this *Bibliography*. Collected in *The Lovely Lady* (A63).

C143 GLAD GHOSTS I

Dial (81: 1–21), July 1926.
Separately published as *Glad Ghosts* (A36) and collected in *The Woman Who Rode Away* (A41).

Written at the Villa Bernarda, Spotorno, during the winter of 1925–26, "Glad Ghosts" was originally intended for Lady Cynthia Asquith's *Ghost Book* (B19), to which, instead, Lawrence contributed "The Rocking-Horse Winner." Lawrence wrote Miss Pearn from Spotorno in January 1926 enclosing the manuscript of "Glad Ghosts," advising that it "might be unsuitable."

C144 GLAD GHOSTS II

Dial (81: 123–141), August 1926.
See C143.

C145 SUN

New Coterie (No. 4: 60–77), Autumn 1926.
Separately published as *Sun* (A35) and collected in *The Woman Who Rode Away* (A41).

The text here is the same as the Archer *Sun* (A35a), the short, early version; the *New Coterie* type was used to print the Archer edition. Charles Lahr published the *New Coterie* and used the imprint "Archer," which he derived from the name of his wife, Esther Archer. The expanded version of *Sun* is described in (A35b).

C146 A REVIEW of H. G. Wells' *The World of William Clissold*

Calendar (3: 254–257), October 1926.
Collected in *Phoenix* (A76).

C147 SUNDAY STROLL IN SLEEPY MEXICO

Travel (48: 30–35, 60), November 1926.
Collected in *Mornings in Mexico* (A37) as "Walk to Huayapa."

The essay also appeared in the *Adelphi*, March 1927.

C148 A REVIEW of Marmaduke Pickthall's *Saïd the Fisherman*

> *Adelphi* (4: 436–440), January 1927.
> Collected in *Phoenix*(A76).
> See (C133.5).

C149 A REVIEW of R. B. Cunninghame Graham's *Pedro de Valdivia*

> *Calendar* (3: 322–326), January 1927.
> Collected in *Phoenix* (A76).

> A typescript described by Tedlock (B51) is signed at the Villa Mirenda in Florence.

C150 COAST OF ILLUSION: A review of H. M. Tomlinson's *Gifts of Fortune*

> *T. P.'s and Cassell's Weekly* (7: 339–340), 1 January 1927.
> Collected in *Phoenix* (A76).

C151 MORNINGS IN MEXICO, THE MOZO

> *Adelphi* (4: 474–487), February 1927.
> Collected in *Mornings in Mexico* (A37).

> This essay appeared in the *Living Age*, 1 April 1927, as "Sons of Montezuma."

C152 MERCURY

> *Atlantic Monthly* (139: 197–200), February 1927.
> Collected in *Phoenix*(A76).

> In July 1926 Lawrence visited Baden-Baden where the hill, Mercury, the highest place in the region, is located. "Mercury" contains the description of a thunder storm, and Lawrence wrote Dorothy Brett from Baden-Baden in July that it was "pouring" with rain. The Brewsters (B39) tell of another visit when they all went to see the hill because of the "beautiful allegory" Lawrence had written about it. "Mercury" also appeared in the *Nation and Athenaeum*, 5 February 1927.

C153 A REVIEW of Carl Van Vechten's *Nigger Heaven*, Walter White's *Flight*, Dos Passos' *Manhattan Transfer* and Hemingway's *In Our Time*

> *Calendar* (4: 17–21, 67–73), April 1927.
> Collected in *Phoenix* (A76).

THE OLD ORCHARD (A poem)

RAINBOW (A poem)

C154 TWO BLUE BIRDS

Dial (82: 287–301), April 1927.
First collected in *Great Stories of All Nations* (B22) and included in *The Woman Who Rode Away* (A41).

This story was sent to Miss Pearn in the agent's office from the Villa Mirenda on 13 May 1926; it also appeared in *Pall Mall*, June 1928.

C155 FIREWORKS

Nation and Athenaeum (41: 47-49), 16 April 1927.
Collected in *Phoenix* (A76) as "Fireworks in Florence."

A sketch about St John's day in Florence, "Fireworks" may reasonably be dated in June 1926; Lawrence was in Florence on San Giovanni day in 1926 and wrote Dorothy Brett a letter about the festival. The essay also appeared in the *Forum*, May 1927.

C156 A REVIEW of Walter Wilkinson's *Peep Show* and V. V. Rozanov's *Solitaria*

Calendar (4: 157–161, 164–168), July 1927.
Collected in *Phoenix* (A76).

This review was probably written in May or June of 1927; Koteliansky's translation appeared in May. Although Lawrence's collaboration with Koteliansky has been shown to be more extensive than formerly supposed, there is no evidence to suggest that he collaborated on this translation. See (A13) and (C196).

C157 THE MAN WHO LOVED ISLANDS

Dial (83: 1– 25), July 1927.
Collected in *The Woman Who Rode Away* (A41), American edition only, and in *The Lovely Lady* (A63).

Harry T. Moore, in his *Intelligent Heart* (B57), quotes a previously unpublished letter from Lawrence to Orioli, written in July 1929, in which Lawrence tells of a projected expensive edition of "The Man Who Loved Islands" to be published by Heinemann. According to Moore, the plan was blocked because of the objections of Compton Mackenzie, who apparently saw himself as the central figure of the story. In any event Secker, who published the works of both men, omitted the story from the English edition of *The Woman Who Rode Away* (A41a), although it was included in the American volume (A41b). "The Man Who Loved Islands" also appeared in the *London Mercury*, August 1927.

C158 THE NIGHTINGALE

Forum (78: 382-387), September 1927.
Collected in *Phoenix* (A76).

While the Lawrences were living at the Villa Mirenda, he did much of his writing in the woods about the place and observed the nightingales of which he spoke in a letter to Martin Secker written in April 1927. The essay also appeared in the *Spectator*, 10 September 1927, and Frieda Lawrence printed it in her *Not I, But the Wind* (B40).

C159 FLOWERY TUSCANY I

New Criterion (6: 305–310), October 1927.
Collected in *Phoenix* (A76).

Catherine Carswell's *Savage Pilgrimage* (B37) tells of Lawrence's knowledge of wild flowers and records an experience related by Millicent Beveridge, with whom Lawrence went walking in Tuscany on the hills near Florence at the height of the Tuscan spring. Miss Beveridge said that Lawrence named at least thirty varieties of flowers and plants as they went through the countryside. The essay appeared in *Travel*, April 1929, as "A Year in Flowery Tuscany."

C160 A NEW THEORY OF NEUROSES: A review of Trigant Burrow's *The Social Basis of Consciousness*

Bookman (New York) (66: 314–317), November 1927.
Collected in *Phoenix* (A76).

Lawrence corresponded with Dr Burrow while he was at Del Monte Ranch near Taos before the Burrow book was published. There is a letter from Lawrence, written on Christmas Day 1926 from the Villa Mirenda, in which he thanks Dr Burrow for permitting him to read a paper called "Psychoanalysis in Theory and Life." Dr Burrow's book arrived at the Villa Mirenda on 1 August 1927, and Lawrence wrote the author three days later that he would write a review, remarking that the book was "most in sympathy with me of any book I've read for a long time."

C161 FLOWERY TUSCANY II

New Criterion (6: 403–408), November 1927.
See (C159).

C162 IN LOVE

Dial (83: 391–404), November 1927.
Collected in *The Woman Who Rode Away* (A41).

C163 CITY OF THE DEAD AT CERVETERI

Travel (50: 12–16, 50), November 1927.
Collected in *Etruscan Places* (A60) as "Cerveteri."

This essay, the first of the Etruscan pieces to appear in print, was also published in the *World Today*, February 1928. All four of the Etruscan sketches appeared first in the United States in *Travel* and then afterwards in the London *World Today*. Lawrence was accompanied on his tour of the Etruscan remains by Earl Brewster who gives an account of their experiences in his *Reminiscences and Correspondence* (B39).

C164 FLOWERY TUSCANY III

New Criterion (6: 516–522), December 1927.
See (C159).

C165 ANCIENT METROPOLIS OF THE ETRUSCANS

Travel (50: 20–25, 55), December 1927.
Collected in *Etruscan Places* (A60) as "Tarquinia."

Also published in *World Today*, March 1928, as "Sketches of Etruscan Places, Tarquinia." See (C163).

C165.5 EIN BRIEF VON D. H. LAWRENCE AN DAS INSELSCHIFF

Das Inselschiff (285–293), 1927.
Collected in *Phoenix II* (A107) as [Germans and English] from a typescript in the Humanities Research Center, the University of Texas at Austin. See (C217).

C166 PAINTED TOMBS OF TARQUINIA

> *Travel* (50: 28–33, 40), January 1928.
> Collected in *Etruscan Places* (A60).

Also appeared in *World Today*, April 1928, as "Sketches of Etruscan Places, Painted Tombs of Tarquinia." See (C163).

C167 THE ESCAPED COCK

> *Forum* (79: 286–296), February 1928.
> Published separately as *The Escaped Cock* (A50).

This is the earliest published form of the short novel which in its expanded form became known also as *The Man Who Died* (A50c). Earl Brewster (B39) tells of being with Lawrence in Grosseto on Easter morning in 1927 and seeing in a shop window a toy rooster emerging from an egg. Brewster remarked that the toy suggested the title for a story of the Resurrection, "The Escaped Cock." Afterwards, Lawrence wrote Brewster from the Villa Mirenda, in May, that he had done a story of the Resurrection and named it "The Escaped Cock" from the toy in the window, although Lawrence recalled that the incident took place in Volterra.

C168 THE WIND-SWEPT STRONGHOLD OF VOLTERRA

> *Travel* (50: 31–35, 44), February 1928.
> Collected in *Etruscan Places* (A60) as "Volterra."

Also published in *World Today*, May 1928, as "Sketches of Etruscan Places: Volterra." See (C163).

C168.5 GIOVANNI VERGA

> *Now & Then* (No. 27), Spring 1928.
> Collected in *Then and Now* (B40.5).

C169 WHEN SHE ASKS WHY?

> *Evening News*, 8 May 1928.
> Collected in *Assorted Articles* (A53) as "The 'Jeune Fille' Wants to Know."

This is the first of a number of essays and articles which Lawrence published in the London newspapers during 1928; "When She Asks Why?" appeared in the *Virginia Quarterly Review*, January 1929, as "Bogey Between the Generations."

C170 LAURA PHILIPPINE

T. P.'s and Cassell's Weekly, 7 July 1928.
Collected in *Assorted Articles* (A53).

C171 OVER-EARNEST LADIES

Evening News, 12 July 1928.
Collected in *Assorted Articles* (A53) as "Insouciance."

Earl Brewster (B39) places the composition of this essay during the summer of 1928 while Lawrence was staying in a hotel on Lake Geneva; several of the newspaper articles were written in Switzerland that summer.

C172 A REVIEW of Robert Byron's *The Station*, Clough Williams-Ellis' *England and the Octopus*, Maurice Baring's *Comfortless Memory* and W. S. Maugham's *Ashenden or the British Agent*

Vogue (London), 20 July 1928.
Collected in *Phoenix* (A76).

C173 THINGS

Bookman (New York) (67: 632–637), August 1928.
Collected in *The Lovely Lady* (A63).

In September 1928 Lawrence wrote Earl Brewster from Gsteig bei Gstaad that he was publishing an amusing story in the American *Bookman* which Brewster would identify with himself, but Lawrence assured Brewster that in truth he was not in the story. It was probably written after the Brewsters departed from Switzerland in August. "Things" also appeared in the *Fortnightly Review*, October 1928.

C174 MASTER IN HIS OWN HOUSE

Evening News, 2 August 1928.
Collected in *Assorted Articles* (A53).

Also appeared in *Vanity Fair* for November 1928 as "Deserted Battlefields."

C175 DULL LONDON

Evening News, 3 September 1928.
Collected in *Assorted Articles* (A53).

C176 OH! FOR A NEW CRUSADE

Evening News, 27 September 1928.
Collected in *Assorted Articles* (A53) as "Red Trousers."

C177 IF WOMEN WERE SUPREME

Evening News, 5 October 1928.
Collected in *Assorted Articles* (A53) as "Matriarchy."

C178 HYMNS IN A MAN'S LIFE

Evening News, 13 October 1928.
Collected in *Assorted Articles* (A53).

A reminiscent essay of Lawrence's youth, "Hymns in a Man's Life" was used as the basis for an article about Lawrence by Roger Detaller in the *Adelphi*, No. 28 for 1952. See (B25.5).

C178.5 THE BLUE MOCCASINS

Eve : The Lady's Pictorial Special Christmas Issue (35: 24, 25, 27, 70, 74), 22 November 1928.
See (C183).

C179 SEX LOCKED OUT

Sunday Dispatch, 25 November 1928.
Separately published as *Sex Locked Out* (A44) and collected in *Assorted Articles* (A53) as "Sex Versus Loveliness."

"Sex Locked Out" appeared in *Vanity Fair*, July 1929, as "Sex Appeal" and in *Golden Book*, December 1929, as "Men and Peacocks."

C180 IS ENGLAND STILL A MAN'S COUNTRY?

Daily Express, 29 November 1928.
Collected in *Assorted Articles* (A53).

C181 COCKSURE WOMEN AND HENSURE MEN

Forum (81), January 1929.
Collected in *Assorted Articles* (A53).

A note on the manuscript of this essay dates it in August 1928; someone had requested an article criticizing women, and apparently

Lawrence felt himself commissioned to do it. He wrote the Brewsters in November that the English newspapers had refused the article but that the *Forum* had purchased it for America.

C182 MYSELF REVEALED

Sunday Dispatch, 17 February 1929.
Collected in *Assorted Articles* (A53) as "Autobiographical Sketch."

C183 THE BLUE MOCCASINS

Plain Talk (4: 138–148), February 1929.
Collected in *The Lovely Lady* (A63).
See (C178.5).

This story was written in Switzerland during the summer of 1928; the Brewsters (B39) give an account of Lawrence reading the finished manuscript as they sat outdoors. He stopped before the denouement and asked them how it should end, and they all agreed on an ending, after which Lawrence told them he had first ended the story as they had decided but had changed the outcome. Both endings are preserved in manuscript form.

C184 MOTHER AND DAUGHTER

Criterion (8: 394–419), April 1929.
Collected in *The Lovely Lady* (A63).

"Mother and Daughter" was written between November 1928 when the Lawrences went to Bandol and 7 February 1929 when he wrote the Brewsters (B39) that the story was to appear in the next *Criterion*.

C185 WOMEN DON'T CHANGE

Sunday Dispatch, 28 April 1929.
Collected in *Assorted Articles* (A53) as "Do Women Change?"
Also appeared in *Vanity Fair* for April 1929.

C186 WHEN I WENT TO THE CIRCUS

Dial (86: 383–384), May 1929.
Collected in *Pansies* (A47).

C187 WOMAN IN MAN'S IMAGE

Vanity Fair, May 1929.
Collected in *Assorted Articles* (A53) as "Give Her a Pattern." Also

appeared in the *Daily Express* for 19 June 1929 as "The Real Trouble About Women."

C188 MAKING PICTURES

Creative Art (5: 466–471), July 1929.
Collected in *Assorted Articles* (A53).

THE FINDING OF MOSES (A painting)
Reprinted from *The Paintings of D. H. Lawrence* (A46).

A manuscript of the essay "Making Pictures" suggests that it may be dated in the autumn of 1928 or during the first months of 1929 while the Lawrences were at Ile de Port-Cros or Bandol, France. Lawrence's original holograph version of the essay was written on stationery from the Hotel de la Cité at Carcassonne. The essay also appeared in *Vanity Fair*, August 1929, and in the *Studio*, July 1929.

C189 TO LET GO OR HOLD ON—?

Dial (86: 543–548), July 1929.

THINGS MEN HAVE MADE

WHATEVER MAN MAKES—

WORK

WHAT WOULD YOU FIGHT FOR?

ATTILA

SEA-WEED

LIZARD

CENSORS

NOVEMBER BY THE SEA

All of the poems in this issue of *Dial* were collected in *Pansies* (A47).

C190 PORNOGRAPHY AND OBSCENITY

This Quarter (2: 17–27), July–September 1929.
Separately published as *Pornography and Obscenity* (A49) and collected in *Pornography and So On* (A75) and *Phoenix* (A76).

C191 THE MANUFACTURE OF GOOD LITTLE BOYS

Vanity Fair (33: 81), September 1929.
Collected in *Assorted Articles* (A53) as "Enslaved by Civilization."

C192 THE RISEN LORD

Everyman, 3 October 1929.
Collected in *Assorted Articles* (A53).

Lawrence wrote Miss Pearn from Germany in August 1929 that he was sending the article which *Everyman* had asked him to do for their series "A Religion for the Young." He told her this article was his idea of a religion for the young and indicated his uncertainty as to whether *Everyman* would actually print it.

C193 MEN AND WOMEN

Star Review (2: 614–626), November 1929.
Collected in *Assorted Articles* (A53) as "Men Must Work and Women as Well."

Apparently the *Star Review* asked Lawrence to do an article; he returned the proofs of a "*Star Review* article" to Miss Pearn in a letter from Bandol dated 4 October 1929.

C194 CHAOS IN POETRY

Echanges, December 1929.
Published as the introduction to *Chariot of the Sun* (B33) and collected in *Phoenix* (A76).

When Harry Crosby of the Black Sun Press was corresponding with Lawrence early in 1928 about the purchase of the manuscript of *Sun* (A35), he apparently sent Lawrence several of his poems for reading; Lawrence replied that if Crosby would send the complete book of poems, he would write an introduction of about two thousand words. Lawrence did not, however, wait for the complete manuscript and wrote Crosby on 29 April that the introduction was done.

C195 DEAD PICTURES ON THE WALL

Vanity Fair (3: 88, 108, 140), December 1929.
Collected in *Assorted Articles* (A53) as "Pictures on the Wall."
The essay also appeared in the *Architectural Review*, February 1930, as "Pictures on the Wall."

C196 A REMARKABLE RUSSIAN: A review of V. V. Rozanov's *Fallen Leaves*

Everyman, 23 January 1930.
Collected in *Phoenix* (A76).

Lawrence's friend and sometime collaborator Koteliansky translated *Fallen Leaves*, but as in the case of Rozanov's *Solitaria* (C156)
there is no evidence that Lawrence had anything to do with this
translation. See (A13).

C196.5 LETTERS to Lady Ottoline Morrell in "D. H. Lawrence,
1885–1930, By One of His Friends" by Lady Ottoline Morrell

Nation and Athenaeum (46: 859–860), 22 March 1930.
See (B81).

C197 BELLS

London Mercury (21: 93), March 1930.
Collected in *Last Poems* (A62).

"Bells" was intended for a volume of poetry Lawrence was planning
just before his death; Brewster (B39) tells of being with Lawrence a
few weeks before he died while Lawrence turned the pages of a
notebook selecting poems which he designated as "Nettles." A
selection of poems called *Nettles* (A52) was published by Faber, but
"Bells" remained to be collected in the "More Pansies" section of
Last Poems.

C198 WE NEED ONE ANOTHER

Scribner's Magazine (87: 479–484), May 1930.
Separately published as *We Need One Another* (A64) and collected in
Phoenix (A76).

This essay may be dated tentatively in the summer of 1928 by its
presence in a notebook described by Powell (B46) which contains
another essay "Nobody Loves Me," definitely dated then by a letter
to Mrs Aldous Huxley which quotes sentences from it. The essay also
appeared in the *Review of Reviews*, June 1930.

C199 LETTERS in "Comment: D. H. Lawrence" by Harriet Monroe

Poetry (36: 90–96), May 1930.

C200 THE TRIUMPH OF THE MACHINE

London Mercury (22: 106–107), June 1930.
Separately published as *The Triumph of the Machine* (A58); first
collected in *The Best Poems of 1930* (B29) and included in *Last Poems*
(A62).

C201 THE REAL THING

Scribner's Magazine (87: 587–592), June 1930.
Collected in *Phoenix* (A76).

A shorter version of "The Real Thing" appeared as a two-part article in the *Daily Herald*, 27 and 28 August 1930, as "Both Sides Lose in a Sex War" and "Love Among the Moderns."

C202 NOTTINGHAM AND THE MINING COUNTRYSIDE

New Adelphi (3: 255–263, 276–285, 286–297), June–August 1930.
Collected in *Phoenix* (A76).

NINE LETTERS TO KATHERINE MANSFIELD
SELECTED PASSAGES

Selected passages reprinted from *Psychoanalysis and the Unconscious* (A18), *Fantasia of the Unconscious* (A22), *Studies in Classic American Literature* (A25) and *Reflections on the Death of a Porcupine* (A32).

ON TRAGEDY

Facsimile reproduction of a manuscript page from an essay beginning "This is the whole condition of tragedy…"

This issue of the *Adelphi* was a special D. H. Lawrence number, devoted almost entirely to Lawrence as a memorial to his death. The autobiographical "Nottingham and the Mining Countryside" appeared in the *Architectural Review*, August 1930, as "Disaster Looms Ahead, Mining Camp Civilization, the English Contribution to Progress." The remainder of the issue was devoted to critical essays about Lawrence.

A folded sheet of four pages was inserted bearing a photograph of Lawrence and the facsimile reproduction of a manuscript page from an essay "On Tragedy." A note recorded that the essay "On Tragedy" was to have been published in forthcoming issues of the *Adelphi*, but it did not appear. The note gives the date of composition as 1915. See (E100).

C203 NOBODY LOVES ME

Life and Letters (5: 39–49), July 1930.
Collected in *Phoenix* (A76).

A letter from Lawrence to Mrs Aldous Huxley dates this essay in the summer of 1928; the essay was inspired by a visit from some friends when the Lawrences were living at Gsteig, Switzerland. "Nobody Loves Me" appeared in the *Virginia Quarterly Review*, July 1930.

C204 INTRODUCTION for Frederick Carter's "Revelation of St. John the Divine"

London Mercury (22: 217–226), July 1930.
Collected in *Phoenix* (A76).

The Brewster memoir (B39) dates the composition of this essay at the Villa Beau Soleil between September and Christmas of 1929. Lawrence had read a manuscript of Carter's as early as the summer of 1923 in Chapala, Mexico; this was an earlier version which Lawrence apparently preferred to the one for which he finally wrote the introduction. According to Brewster, the introduction which Lawrence began became too long for its original purpose and eventually became *Apocalypse* (A57). Frederick Carter's book was published by Desmond Harmsworth in 1932 as *Dragon of the Apocalypse* but without Lawrence's introduction, and although the publisher announced the book as an important collaboration between Lawrence and Carter, there is no evidence that either work is anything but an independent accomplishment. *The Dragon of the Apocalypse* was originally a project of the Mandrake Press, which, just before its suspension, announced a forthcoming book to be called "The Revelation of St. John the Divine" with an introduction by D. H. Lawrence, but of course the volume never materialized. Frederick Carter is the author of *D. H. Lawrence and the Body Mystical* (F19).

C205 A LETTER in *Reminiscences of D. H. Lawrence VI* by John Middleton Murry

New Adelphi (1(n.s.): 413–420), February 1931.

C206 NEW MEXICO

Survey Graphic (66: 153–155), 1 May 1931.
Collected in *Phoenix* (A76).

This is an essay written at Bandol in December 1928 in response to a request from Mabel Dodge Luhan; Lawrence wrote her from Bandol on 19 December saying that he would "have a shot" at the article for the *Graphic* mentioned in her last letter, and on Christmas Day wrote that the article was finished.

Book Collector's Quarterly (No. 5: 44–61), January–March 1932. Collected in *Phoenix* (A76) as "Study of Thomas Hardy."

Lawrence's study of Thomas Hardy was written in England during the war; he wrote to Edward Marsh from South Kensington in July 1914 asking for the loan of Lascelles Abercrombie's book on Hardy and any of the Hardy pocket editions Marsh might have. Lawrence was going to write a "little book" on the Hardy people; actually he began the book in September and told Edward Garnett in October that it was a third complete. Only chapter three appeared in the *Book Collector's Quarterly*; the entire essay is collected in *Phoenix*. An extra 100 copies of the January–March *Book Collector's Quarterly* were bound in decorative cloth boards and numbered as a limited issue. The essay also appeared in *John O'London's Weekly*, 12 and 19 March 1932.

c208 LETTERS in "On Love"

Saturday Review of Literature (9: 61–62), 27 August 1932. Extracts from *The Letters of D. H. Lawrence* (A61).

c208.4 LETTER to Robert Atkins dated 16 October 1926

New York Evening Post, 30 November 1932.

MUSIC for *David*

Both the letter to Atkins and the complete "Music" for *David* were published in *A D. H. Lawrence Miscellany* (B63). The letter is also in Nehls (B60), Vol. II and in Moore's *Letters* (A102).

c208.5 LETTER to Helen Thomas in "Two Pieces of Advice from D. H. Lawrence" by Helen Thomas

Times (London), 1 December 1932.

Helen Thomas was the wife of Edward Thomas, English poet who died in France in 1917. Lawrence visited her in the summer of 1919 at Forge House, Otford, Kent.

c209 LETTERS in "Two Letters of D. H. Lawrence, Written on the Way to Ceylon"

Twentieth Century (4: 1–3), January 1933.

A note records that these letters were written in German to Frau

Baronin von Richthofen and were translated by Frieda Lawrence
and Desmond Hawkins.

C210 LETTERS in "Briefe an Max Mohr"

Neue Rundschau (44: 527–540), April 1933.

Lawrence met Max Mohr, the German dramatist and physician, at
Irschenhausen in 1927 while visiting Frieda's sister. Mohr was one of
the few doctors Lawrence permitted to attend him during his
illnesses, and Mohr, his wife and child visited the Lawrences at
Bandol in the autumn of 1929. The Mohrs left Germany when the
Nazis came to power and went to Shanghai; Mohr mentioned in a
letter to Thomas Mann that one of his prized possessions when he
arrived in Shanghai was the letters of D. H. Lawrence. The letters
appeared in English in the *T'ien Hsia Monthly*, published by the Sun
Yat-Sen Institute at Shanghai, August and September 1935 (C218)
and (C219).

C211 A MODERN LOVER

Life and Letters (9: 257–286), September–November 1933.
Collected in *A Modern Lover* (A71).

C212 ERIC GILL'S ART NONSENSE: A review of Eric Gill's *Art Nonsense
and Other Essays*

Book Collector's Quarterly (12: 1–7), October–December 1933.
Collected in *Phoenix* (A76).

A note by Frieda Lawrence records that this review was the last thing
Lawrence wrote; it was completed a few days before his death at the
Villa Robermond, where he had been moved from the Ad Astra
Sanitorium in Vence.

C213 KEEPING BARBARA

Argosy (14: 68–90), December 1933.

This play is a very early piece written in 1912; in October of that
year Lawrence wrote Edward Garnett that he had done the play he
was sending as an interlude to "Paul Morel," and a bit later he wrote
again asking Garnett what he thought of it. According to Lawrence's
letters to Garnett, the play is largely autobiographical. Elsewhere
the play is known as "The Fight for Barbara."

C213.5 [THERE WAS A YOUNG MAN IN THE CORRIDOR]

Catalogue No. 297, 1933. Myers and Company, 102 New Bond Street, London.

This bookseller's catalogue offered a copy of *The Rainbow* on the title page of which Lawrence had written the following limerick. Apparently the limerick has not been printed elsewhere.

There was a young man in the corridor
Whose Conduct got horrider and horridor
He lit a cigar
And said, 'Europe is bar
Give me a ticket for Florida'.

C214 TWO MARRIAGES

Time and Tide, 24 March 1934. (Supplement)

An early version of "Daughters of the Vicar" published originally in *The Prussian Officer* (A6).

C215 THE WITCH À LA MODE

Lovat Dickson's Magazine, June 1934.
Collected in *A Modern Lover* (A71).

Also appeared in *Esquire* for September 1934.

C216 A LETTER FROM GERMANY

New Statesman and Nation (*Autumn Books Supplement*: 481–482), 13 October 1934.
Collected in *Phoenix* (A76).

According to a note in the *New Statesman and Nation*, the letter was written in 1928, but McDonald in *Phoenix* (A76) suggests the more probable date of 19 February 1924 for its composition.

C217 TEDESCHI E INGLESE

La Cultura (13: No. 9), November 1934.
Collected in *Phoenix II* (A107) as [Germans and English]. See (C165.5).

A note accompanying this essay in *La Cultura* states that it was written in the first spring days of 1927 in response to a request from Insel Verlag, who desired from Lawrence "a more or less personal article" for their *Almanach*; however, Insel Verlag, now at Wiesbaden, wrote that the only Lawrence item to appear in the *Insel Almanach* was "D. H. Lawrence Uber Sich Selbst" in the 1930 volume, but this was a translation into German by Kurt Fiedler of the "Autobiographical Sketch" from *Assorted Articles* (A53). The "Tedeschi e Inglese" of *La Cultura* must have been extant in a German version at one time, because it was translated into Italian from German by Emma Sole for the *La Cultura* publication.

C217.5 LETTERS to the Baroness Anna von Richthofen in "Unterwegs, Briefe von D. H. Lawrence"

Neue Rundschau (45: 702–717), December 1934.

These are Lawrence's German letters to his mother-in-law, several of which Frieda Lawrence included in English translation in *Not I, But the Wind* (B40a); the German texts of letters not used by Frieda were later published in *Nur der Wind* (B40b).

C218 LETTERS in "The Unpublished Letters of D. H. Lawrence to Max Mohr I"

T'ien Hsia Monthly (1: 21–36), August 1935.
See the *Neue Rundschau*, April 1933 (C210).

C219 LETTERS in "The Unpublished Letters of D. H. Lawrence to Max Mohr II"

T'ien Hsia Monthly (1: 166–179), September 1935.
See (C218).

C220 MARGINALIA in "Sur un exemplaire de Schopenhauer annoté par D. H. Lawrence" by Emile Delavenay

Revue Anglo-Américaine (13: 234-238), February 1936.

These notes in the margins of a book of Schopenhauer's essays were probably made while Lawrence was a student at Nottingham University College. M. Delavenay obtained the copy of Schopenhauer with the Lawrence annotations from Jessie Chambers; the notes are published in Edward Nehls' *Composite Biography* Vol. I (B60).

C221 O! AMERICANS!

New Mexico Quarterly (8: 75-81), May 1938.
Collected in *Fire and Other Poems* (A80).

C222 ALTITUDE

Laughing Horse (No. 20: 12–35), Summer 1938.

In "Altitude," an unfinished play which Lawrence wrote in Taos at Mabel Dodge Luhan's house in 1924, the characters are given their real names; those present in the script include Spud Johnson, Mabel Dodge Luhan and Mary Austin . Only the first scene was printed in the *Laughing Horse*, but a second scene exists in manuscript. A note in the *Laughing Horse* gives Spud Johnson's account of the writing of the play; the opening lines were scribbled on the back of a candy box one evening in Mabel Dodge Luhan's living-room, and the various guests made suggestions about the characters and speeches. It was not until several years later that the company knew that Lawrence had actually finished one scene and started another.

C223 EAGLE IN NEW MEXICO

New Mexico Quarterly (8: 215-218), November 1938.
Collected in *Fire and Other Poems* (A80).

C224 LETTERS in "A Number of People III" by Edward Marsh

Harper's Magazine (179: 171-179), July 1939.
Collected in *A Number of People* (B49).

C225 DELILAH AND MR. BIRCUMSHAW

Virginia Quarterly Review (16: 257–266), Spring 1940.

Frieda Lawrence dates the composition of this piece in 1912–13 according to Tedlock (B51), and Tedlock affirms that the manuscript itself resembles the early work. The published version is longer and presumably a revision of the manuscript described by Tedlock.

C225.5 LETTERS to Margaret Gardiner in "Meeting the Master" by Margaret Gardiner

Horizon (2:184–190), October 1940.

Margaret Gardiner was the sister of Rolfe Gardiner with whom Lawrence corresponded for several years before they met in London in 1926. Gardiner founded the Springhead Estate in Dorset for the youth groups with which he worked; he was sympathetic with the German Bünde movement and felt that his efforts fulfilled the Lawrentian version.

c225.6 LETTERS to Rhys Davies in "D. H. Lawrence in Bandol" by Rhys Davies

Horizon (2: 191–208), October 1940.

Lawrence met Rhys Davies through Charles Lahr, see (A55), the London bookseller. Davies visited Lawrence at Bandol in the latter part of 1928.

c226 THE MARRIED MAN

Virginia Quarterly Review (16: 523–547), Autumn 1940.

Lawrence mentioned this play by title in a letter to Edward Garnett written on 1 February 1913 in which he acknowledged receipt of three manuscript plays returned by Garnett. Lawrence told Garnett at the time the plays needed rewriting, but apparently they were never reworked.

c227 THE MERRY-GO-ROUND

Virginia Quarterly Review (*A Supplement to the Christmas Number*), Winter 1941.

Another of the early plays mentioned in a letter to Edward Garnett in 1912.

c228 LETTERS in "D. H. Lawrence to His Agent" by Theresa Coolidge

More Books (33: 23–24), January 1948.

The agent is Curtis Brown, and the letters were written in 1923 from Taos and Mexico City; for other letters to Curtis Brown see *Contacts* (B44).

c229 RESURRECTION OF THE FLESH (A poem)

Wake (No. 7: 26–27), 1948.

c230 LETTERS in "D. H. Lawrence's Letters to Bertrand Russell"

Atlantic Monthly (182: 92–102), December 1948.

Collected in *D. H. Lawrence's Letters to Bertrand Russell* (A48).

c230.5 LETTER to Charles Wilson

Swan Auction Catalogue No. 230, 14 April 1949.

See (A118).

C230.6 LETTERS to Lady Cynthia Asquith in "D. H. Lawrence as I knew Him" by Lady Cynthia Asquith

The Listener (42: 441–442), 15 September 1949.

C231 LETTERS in "D. H. Lawrence and The Boy in the Bush" by M. L. Skinner and in "Lawrence in Australia" by Katherine Susannah Prichard

Meanjin (9: 252–259, 260–263), Summer 1950.

Miss Skinner collaborated with Lawrence in writing *The Boy in the Bush* (A29), and Katherine Susannah Prichard is an Australian novelist with whom Lawrence corresponded while he was living at Thirroul and who later became a friend of Mollie Skinner.

C232 A FRAGMENT beginning "There is no real battle between me and Christianity..." in "About D. H. Lawrence" by Frieda Lawrence

New Mexico Quarterly (21: 155-158), Summer 1951.

C233 LETTERS in "Letters to S. S. Koteliansky"

Encounter (1: 29–35), December 1953.

These letters were written from 1915 to 1929; for other letters to Koteliansky see C236 and for an account of Lawrence's relations with Koteliansky see (A13).

C234 LETTERS in "D. H. Lawrence in Australia, Some Unpublished Correspondence" by H. E. Priday

Southerly (15: 2–7), 1954.

This article reproduces letters and postcards written to Mrs A. L. Jenkins, with whom the Lawrences travelled from Naples to the East on their way to Australia. Later Mrs Jenkins introduced them to Mollie Skinner, with whom Lawrence collaborated on *The Boy in the Bush* (A29). See Nehls, Vol. II (B60).

C235 LETTERS in "Springtime with D. H. Lawrence" by Eleanor Farjeon

London Magazine (2: 50–57), April 1955.
Collected in *Edward Thomas: The Last Four Years* (B62).

C236 LETTERS in "Rananim: D. H. Lawrence's Letters to S. S. Koteliansky" by K. W. Gransden

Twentieth Century (159: 22–32), January 1956.

These letters are from the letters and papers bequeathed to the British Museum by S. S. Koteliansky in 1955, in Add. 48966–48968.

C237 LETTERS in "I Will Send Address: New Letters of D. H. Lawrence" by Mark Schorer

London Magazine (3: 44–67), February 1956.

Contains letters from D. H. Lawrence to Lady Ottoline Morrell, Maria Cristina Chambers and others.

C238 LETTERS in "Conversations with D. H. Lawrence" by Brigit Patmore

London Magazine (4: 31–45), June 1957.

C239 LETTERS in "D. H. Lawrence Letter-Writer and Craftsman in Verse" by Vivian de Sola Pinto

Renaissance and Modern Studies (1: 5–34), 1957.

PIANO

Facsimile reproduction of an early manuscript version.

Poems:

GUELDER ROSES

CAMPIONS

THE DEATH OF THE BARON

MARRIED IN JUNE

BABY SONGS: TEN MONTHS OLD

AFTER SCHOOL

RENAISSANCE

LAST WORDS TO MURIEL

THE PIANO

PIANO

The letters reproduced here were written to Mrs Emily King, Lawrence's sister, and to her daughter, Mrs Margaret Needham; many of the poems are early drafts of published verse from a notebook which belonged to Mrs King.

C240 ON COMING HOME

Texas Quarterly (1: No. 3), Summer–Autumn 1958.

Facsimile reproduction of a page of the manuscript.

C241 THE MAN WHO WAS THROUGH WITH THE WORLD ed. by John R. Elliot

Essays in Criticism (9: 217–221), July 1959.

This fragment is published with an introduction by Elliot from a manuscript in the Library of the University of California at Berkeley (E227.4).

C242 LETTERS to Henry Savage in "D. H. Lawrence to Henry Savage: An Introductory Note" by Harry T. Moore

Yale University Library Gazette (34: 24–33), July 1959.

Henry Savage was an English editor and reviewer; he reviewed *The White Peacock* for the *Academy*, and Lawrence wrote to thank him. See (C260).

C243 LETTERS to Blanche Jennings in "D. H. Lawrence and Blanche Jennings" by Kenneth and Miriam Allott

Review of English Literature (1: 57–76), July 1960.

Blanche Jennings was a suffragist who corresponded with Lawrence during 1908–1910; they met only once, at Alice Dax's house late in 1907 or early 1908.

C243.5 LETTERS to various persons in "Excerpts from the Unpublished Letters of D. H. Lawrence"

Playboy (9: 107–110), January 1962.
See (A102).

C244 LETTER to Helen Corke in "Portrait of D. H. Lawrence: 1909–1910" by Helen Corke

Texas Quarterly (5: 168–177), Spring 1962.
See (B82).

C245 LETTERS to Arthur Gair Wilkinson and Frances Wilkinson in "Lawrence and the Wilkinsons" by Keith Sagar

Review of English Literature (3: 62–75), October 1962.

Gair Wilkinson was the brother of Walter Wilkinson who wrote *The Peep Show* about his travels in the west of England with a puppet show. Lawrence reviewed the book (C156) and the Wilkinsons were neighbors of the Lawrences when they lived at the Villa Mirenda near Florence in 1926–1928.

C246 PROLOGUE TO WOMEN IN LOVE

Texas Quarterly (6: 92–111), Spring 1963.

This is part of an early version of *Women in Love* (A15) edited by George Ford from a manuscript in the Library of the University of Texas (E441c).
Collected in *Phoenix II* (A107). See C248.

C247 LETTERS in "Die Deutscher Briefe von D. H. Lawrence" by Armin Arnold

Neue Zürcher Zeitung, 24 August 1963.

Letters to Friedel Jaffe (Frederick R. Jeffrey), Else Jaffe, and Baroness Anna von Richthofen. See (B40b). Armin Arnold also published an article on this subject in English, "The German Letters of D. H. Lawrence" in *Comparative Literature Studies*, 3 (1966).

C248 THE WEDDING in "The Wedding Chapter of D. H. Lawrence's *Women in Love*"

Texas Studies in Literature and Language (6: 134–147), Summer 1964.

This is part of an early version of *Women in Love* (A15) edited by George Ford. See (E441c) and (C246).

C249 LETTERS to Maria Cristina Chambers in "Afternoons in Italy with D. H. Lawrence" by Maria Cristina Chambers

Texas Quarterly (7: 114–120), Winter 1964.

Maria Cristina Chambers was an American, originally from Mexico, whose husband was editor of the *Literary Digest*; she corresponded with Lawrence about importing copies of *Lady Chatterley* into the United States and visited him at Forte dei Marmi in the summer of 1929.

C250 LETTERS to Francis Brett Young in "Three Separate Ways: Unpublished D. H. Lawrence Letters to Francis Brett Young" by Keith Sagar

Review of English Literature (6: 93–105), July 1965.

Lawrence met Francis Brett Young, British novelist and poet, on Capri in 1919; he helped the Lawrences find accomodation in Sicily at Fontana Vecchia. Some of the letter are to his wife, Jessica.

C251 LETTER to Anton Kippenberg in "Eine Ausstellung zur Geschichte des Verlags unter Anton und Katharina Kippenberg"

Die Insel (p. 214), 1965.

Anton Kippenberg was an official of Insel Verlag with whom Lawrence corresponded about various matters, including translations of his works. Among other titles, Insel Verlag published *The Rainbow* (D73), *Sons and Lovers* (D75) and *Women in Love* (D77) in German translations.

C252 LETTERS to S. S. Koteliansky in "D. H. Lawrence: Letters to Koteliansky" by George Zytaruk

Malahat Review (1: 17–40), January 1967.
See (A13) and (A109).

C253 LETTER to Carlo Linati in "Una Lettera Inedita di D. H. Lawrence" by Giuseppe Gadda Conti

English Miscellany (19: 335–338), 1968.

Lawrence corresponded with Carlo Linati in 1924 about an article the Italian critic was preparing for publication in Italy; Linati translated "The Fox" and "The Ladybird" into Italian. See (D112).

C254 LETTER to G. Herbert Thring in "The Rainbow Prosecution" by John Carter

Times Literary Supplement (No. 3496, p. 216), 27 February 1969.

Herbert Thring was Secretary for the Society of Authors; Lawrence wrote him concerning support for the protest against the banning of the *Rainbow*.

C255 LETTERS to Nancy Henry, Marie M. Meloney, Thomas Seltzer, A. D. Hawk, Richard Aldington, Arabella York, Jonathan Cape, Lady Ottoline Morrell in "D. H. Lawrence: Twelve Letters" by Paul Delany

D. H. Lawrence Review (2: 195–209), Fall 1969.

The letters published here are from the Alfred M. Hellman Collection in the Library of Columbia University.

C256 ODOUR OF CHRYSANTHEMUMS in "D. H. Lawrence's 'Odour of Chrysanthemums' An Early Version" by James T. Boulton

Renaissance and Modern Studies (13: 5–48), 1969.

This early version of the story is derived from the *English Review* galley proofs in the Louie Burrows papers in the Library of the University of Nottingham (E284c). These proofs were considerably revised and apparently still further revised for the version printed in the *English Review* (C6). The text collected in *The Prussian Officer* (A6) represents still another version.

C257 AMPHIBIAN in "D. H. Lawrence: Seven Hitherto Unpublished Poems" by T. A. Smailes

D. H. Lawrence Review (3: 42–46), Spring 1970.

SALT-LICKS

WIDDERSHINS

WAR

THE MALEFICENT TRIANGLE

BEAUTY AND TRUTH

FIRE

The first six poems are from a manuscript in the Library of the University of Texas (E192); the last poem is from a manuscript in the Library of the University of California at Berkeley (E132). All were excluded from *Complete Poems* (A104) because of editorial policy; "Fire" was reprinted in *Selected Poems* (A116) as a prose piece.

C258 INTRODUCTION TO PANSIES in "An Unpublished Version of D. H. Lawrence's Introduction to *Pansies*" by David Farmer

Review of English Studies (21: 181–184), May 1970.

This is an early version of the introduction to the definitive edition of *Pansies* (A47c) from a manuscript in the Library of the University of Texas (E303b).

C259 A BELOVED in "D. H. Lawrence, the Second 'Poetic Me': Some New Material" by Francis W. Roberts

Renaissance and Modern Studies (14:5–25), 1970.

AN EPISTLE FROM THELMA

AN EPISTLE FROM ARTHUR

EPILOGUE FROM THELMA

THE COMPLAINT OF THE SOUL OF A WORKER

SCHOOL I MORNING

LATE AT NIGHT ALONG THE HOME ROAD

UNWITTING

NOCTURNE

REPROACH

MY LOVE MY MOTHER

TRANSFORMATIONS: MORNING

These poems are from a manuscript notebook (E320.1) in the possession of Mr W. H. Clarke, the son of Lawrence's sister Ada; all are collected in *Complete Poems* (A104d). Through some curious circumstance, for which the editor of *Renaissance and Modern Studies* was in no way responsible, a number of errors appeared in the text of the poems as transcribed here. These errors were corrected in a subsequent article, "D. H. Lawrence, the Second 'Poetic Me': Corrigenda" in *Renaissance and Modern Studies* for 1971.

c260 LETTERS to Henry Savage in "D. H. Lawrence to Henry Savage: Two Further Letters" by Harry T. Moore

Yale University Library Gazette (46: 262-267), April 1972. See (C242).

c261 THE TURNING BACK in "D. H. Lawrence's 'The Turning Back': The Text and its Genesis in Correspondence" by David Farmer

D. H. Lawrence Review (5: 121–129), Summer 1972.

This poem was sent to Lady Cynthia Asquith in November 1915 and was published with the letter in Huxley's *Letters* (A61); however, the first two parts of the poem became separated from the letter, and only the third section appeared in Huxley. From there it was collected in *Complete Poems* (A104) with the first line of the third section as the title, "We Have Gone Too Far." The text printed here is from a manuscript (E411) in the Library of the University of Texas. Some verses are similar to "Erinnyes" (B4) and may be an early version of that poem.

c262 LETTERS to Sallie and William Hopkin in "The Letters of D. H. Lawrence to Sallie and Willie Hopkin" by Paulina S. Pollak

Journal of Modern Literature (3: 24–34), February 1973. See B73.

c263 LETTERS to Gordon and Beatrice Campbell in "D. H. Lawrence: Letters to Gordon and Beatrice Campbell" by Peter L. Irvine and Anne Kiley

D. H. Lawrence Review (6: 1–20), Spring 1973.

Lawrence was introduced to the Campbells by John Middleton Murry; Gordon Campbell was one of the witnesses at Frieda and Lawrence's marriage. See (B37).

c264 LETTERS to J. B. Pinker and Nancy Henry in "D. H. Lawrence and Nancy Henry: Two Unpublished Letters and a Lost Relationship" by Keith Cushman

D. H. Lawrence Review (6: 21–32), Spring 1973.

These letters are from the collection of Mr George Lazarus; J. B. Pinker was Lawrence's literary agent in London, 1914–1921, and Mrs Henry was the wife of Leigh Henry, whose poems, written while he was a prisoner of war in Germany, she sent to Lawrence. She was involved in the publication of *Movements in European History* (A17) as an employee of the Oxford University Press.

c265 THE LADYBIRD, two pages of text in "Two Missing Pages from 'The Ladybird'" by Brian Finney

Review of English Studies (24: 191–192), May 1973.

Finney discovered from the manuscript (E187) in the Berg Collection at the New York Public Library that two pages of the text had inadvertently been omitted from all published versions of the story.

c266 LETTER to W. H. Roberts in "D. H. Lawrence: Study of a Free Spirit in Literature, A Note on an Uncollected Article" by James T. Boulton

Renaissance and Modern Studies (18: 5–16), 1974.

W. H. Roberts was the author of an article about Lawrence, "Study of a Free Spirit in Literature" in the *Millgate Quarterly* for May 1928; Lawrence wrote to Roberts in the same month acknowledging receipt of copies of the article.

c267 LETTERS to Catherine Carswell in "D. H. Lawrence's Letters to Catherine Carswell" by Donald Gallup

Yale University Library Gazette (49: 253–260), January 1975. See (B37).

C268 LETTER to Thomas Seltzer in "The Composition of *Women in Love*: A History, 1913–1919" by Charles L. Ross

D. H. Lawrence Review (8: 198–212), Summer 1975.

Short excerpts from letters to various persons are quoted in the article; the text for the Seltzer letter is complete. See (A119).

C269 LETTERS to Dorothy Brett in "D. H. Lawrence and Frieda Lawrence: Letters to Dorothy Brett" by Peter L. Irvine and Anne Kiley

D. H. Lawrence Review (9: 1–116), Spring 1976.

The Hon. Dorothy E. Brett, daughter of Reginald Baliol Brett, 2nd Viscount Esher, came to America with the Lawrences in 1924. She was a student at the Slade School, became a painter and quondam member of the Bloomsbury group. She became a resident of Taos and lived near Frieda Lawrence's house in Taos until she died. See (F26).

C270 LETTERS to Harriet Monroe in "D. H. Lawrence and *Poetry*: The Unpublished Manuscripts" by Alvin Sullivan

D. H. Lawrence Review (9: 266–277), Summer 1976.

ECCE HOMO

The two letters and the poetry manuscripts discussed in this article are from the Harriet Monroe *Poetry* archive in the Library of the University of Chicago (E113.2). According to the article the poem "Ecce Homo" is an early version, at least in part, of "Eloi, Eloi Lama Sabachthani?" in Harriet Monroe's hand. See (B42).

C271 THROSTLES IN THE CHERRY TREE in "D. H. Lawrence: A Day in the Country and a Poem in Autograph" by Emily Gladys Potter Brooks

D. H. Lawrence Review (9: 278–282), Summer 1976.

In April 1909 Lawrence spent a day in the country with George Neville and Lilla Reynolds, friends of his, and Emily Gladys Potter who was introduced by Lilla Reynolds. Later Lawrence wrote this early version of "Cherry Robbers" (A3) in Miss Potter's autograph album.

C272 LETTERS in "Son and Lover: The Early Letters of D. H. Lawrence"

Harper's (258: 85–102), March 1979.

These letters are from the first volume of the Cambridge University Press edition of *The Letters of D. H. Lawrence*. This volume, edited by James T. Boulton, covers the period from September 1901–May 1913. See (A121).

D. TRANSLATIONS

D. TRANSLATIONS

ARABIC

DO.3 ... 'ABNĀ WA 'USHAQ ... Al-Qàhirah, Dàr al-Hilāl, 1970. pp. 186. A translation by Shafig Magàr of *Sons and Lovers*.

ASSAM

DO.5 ... LADY CHATTERLEYR PREM ... Calcutta, Sribhumi, 1973. pp. 404. A translation by Mustafiz-ur-Rahman of *Lady Chatterley's Lover*.

BENGALI

DI ... LEDI CHYATARLIER ... Calcutta, Signet Press, 1949. A translation by Hirendranath Datta of *Lady Chatterley's Lover*.

BURMESE

DI.3 ... NAIZAR KADAW NANKAYTHE ... Rangoon, 1967. pp. 273. A translation by Shwe Thway of *Lady Chatterley's Lover*.

CHINESE

DI.5 ... HSING YÜ K'O AI ... Taipei, Cactus Publishing Company, 1970. pp. 196. A translation by Ch'ên Ts'ang To of essays on sex and love.

DI.51 ... T'AI YANG ... Taipei, Morning Bell Publishing Company, 1970. pp. 146. A translation by Hsien Tai Wën Hsüeh of *Sun* and other pieces.

SERBO-CROATIAN AND SLOVENE

D2 ... SINOVI IN LJUBIMCI ... Ljubljana, Modra, 1934. pp. 495. A translation by Stanko Leben of *Sons and Lovers*.

D2.5 .. LADY CHATTERLEY I NJEZIN LJUBAVNIK ... Zagreb, Binoza, 1937. A translation by Iso Velikanović of *Lady Chatterley's Lover*.

D3..SINOVI I LJUBAVNICI...Beograd, Kosmos, 1939. 2 Vols. pp. 314 and 289. A translation by Mihailo Stojanović of *Sons and Lovers*.

D3.5...SINOVI I NJIHOVE LJUBAVI...Zagreb, Matica Hrvatska, 1943. 2 Vols. pp. 267 and 238. A translation by Mira Jurkić-Šunjić and Mirko Jurkić of *Sons and Lovers*.

D4...ZALJUBLENE ŽENE...Beograd, Omladina, 1954. 2 Vols. pp. 451 and 488. A translation by Nenad Jovanović of *Women in Love*.

D5...DUGA...Zagreb, Zora, 1955. pp. 526. A translation by Zlatko Gorjan of *The Rainbow*.

D6...SINOVI I LJUBAVNICI...Rijeka, Otokar Keršovani, 1955. pp. 550. A translation by Tatjana Blažeković of *Sons and Lovers*. With an introduction by Lovat Edwards.

D7...LJUBAVNIK LADY CHATTERLEY...Rijeka, Otokar Keršovani, 1956. pp. 389. A translation by Milivoj Mezzorana of *Lady Chatterley's Lover*.

D8...MAVRICA...Ljubljana, Slovenski Knjižni Zavod, 1956. pp. 573. A translation by Janko Moder of *The Rainbow*.

D9...BIJELI PAUN...Rijeka, Otokar Keršovani, 1957. pp. 529. A translation by Mladen Car of *The White Peacock*.

D10...ŽENA KOJA JE ODJAHALA OD KUĆE...Beograd, Narodna Knjižnica, n.d. pp. 71. A translation by B. Jovanović of "The Woman Who Rode Away."

D10.1...SENT MOR, DEVICA I CIGANIN...Sarajevo, Džepna Knjiga, 1959. pp. 334. A translation by Ranko Bugarski of *St. Mawr* and *The Virgin and the Gipsy*.

D10.11...ZALJUBLJENE ŽENE...Maribor, Obzorja, 1959. pp. 610. A translation by Jože Fistrovič of *Women in Love*.

D10.12...LISAC I DRUGE PRIČE...Sarajevo, Svjetlost, 1960. pp. 208. A translation by Aleksandar V. Stefanović of "The Fox" and other stories.

DIO.13 ... PREKRŠITELJ ... Rijeka, Otokar Keršovani, 1960. pp. 292. A translation by Milivoj Mezzorana of *The Trespasser*.

DIO.14 ... ARONOVA PALICA ... Rijeka, Otokar Keršovani, 1961. pp. 450. A translation by Omer Lakomica of *Aaron's Rod*.

DIO.15 ... ČOVJEK KOJI JE UMRO ... Rijeka, Otokar Keršovani, 1962. pp. 296. A translation by Mirjana and Dragon Vilke of *The Man Who Died*.

DIO.16 ... LJUBIMEC LADY CHATTERLEY ... Koper, Lipa, 1962. pp. 374. A translation by Anton Mejač of *Lady Chatterley's Lover*.

DIO.17 ... PRUSKI OFICIR, LISAC ... Beograd, Rad, 1963. pp. 122. A translation by Aleksandar V. Stefanović of "The Prussian Officer" and "The Fox."

DIO.18 ... IZGUBLJENKA ... Ljublana, Prešernova Družba, 1970. pp. 383. A translation by Michele Helps of *The Lost Girl*.

DIO.19 ... SNAHA ... Ljubljana, Prosevetni Servis, 1971. pp. 51. A translation by Dušan Tomše of "The Daughter-in-Law."

DIO.20 ... DJEVICA I GIGANIN ... Rijeka, Otokar Keršovani, 1975. pp. 355. A translation by Mirjana and Dragan Vilke of *The Virgin and the Gipsy*, *St. Mawr* and "The Fox."

DIO.21 ... PRVA LADY CHATTERLEY ... Zagreb, Naprijed, 1976. pp. 287. A translation by Ljerka Radović of *The First Lady Chatterley*.

DIO.22 ... ZALJUBLJENE ŽENE ... Zagreb, Naprijed, 1976. 2 Vols. pp. 310 and 315. A translation by Ljerka Radović of *Women in Love*.

CZECH

D11 ... SYNOVÉ A MILENCI ... Praha, Odeon, 1931. pp. 531. A translation by Zdeňka Vančura and René Wellek of *Sons and Lovers*.

D12 ... MILENEC LADY CHATTERLEYOVÉ ... Praha, Odeon, 1932. pp. 372. A translation by Staŝi Jílovské of *Lady Chatterley's Lover*.

D13 ... ZAMILOVANÉ ŽENY ... Praha, Odeon, 1932. pp. 607. A translation by L. Vymětal of *Women in Love*.

D14...PANNA A CIKÁN...Praha, Symposion, 1934. A translation by Hana Skoumalová of *The Virgin and the Gipsy*.

D15...TEN KTERÝ ZEMŘEL...Praha, Škeřik, 1936. pp. 158. A translation by E. A. Saudek of *The Man Who Died*. With a note by René Wellek.

D15.5...SYNOVÉ A MILENCI...Praha, SNKLU, 1962. pp. 468. A translation by Zdeněk Vančura and Anna Novotná of *Sons and Lovers*.

DANISH

D16...LADY CHATTERLEYS ELSKER ...København, Hasselbalchs Forlag, 1932 pp. 336. A translation by Christen Hansen of *Lady Chatterley's Lover*.

D17...SØNNER OG ELSKERE...København, Gyldendal, 1935. pp. 502. A translation by Tom Kristensen of *Sons and Lovers*.

D18...NAAR KVINDER ELSKER...København, Gyldendal, 1936. pp. 589. A translation by Elias Bredsdorff of *Women in Love*.

D19...ARONS STAV...København, Gyldendal, 1937. pp. 355. A translation by Per Lange of *Aaron's Rod*.

D20...KVINDEN SOM RED BORT OG ANDRE NOVELLER... København, Gyldendal, 1938. pp. 563. A translation by Tom Kristensen of "The Prussian Officer," "The Thorn in the Flesh," "Daughter of the Vicar," "Second Best," "The White Stocking," "The Christening," "Odour of Chrysanthemums," "The Fox," "Tickets Please," "The Blind Man," "Wintry Peacock," "You Touched Me," "Samson and Delilah," "The Primrose Path," "Two Blue Birds," "The Blue Moccasins," "The Rocking-Horse Winner," "Glad Ghosts," "Smile," "None of That" and "The Woman Who Rode Away." Selected and with an introduction by the translator.

D21...REGNBUEN...København, Westermanns Forlag, 1943. pp. 502. A translation by Ove Brusendorff of *The Rainbow*.

D22...MANDEN DER DØDE...København, Thaning and Appel, 1947. pp. 82. A translation by Elias Bredsdorff of *The Man Who Died*.

D23...LADY CHATTERLEYS ELSKER...København, Hasselbachs Forlag, 1950. pp. 362. A translation by Michael Tejn of *Lady Chatterley's Lover*.

D24...ELSKOV I HØST...København, Fønss Forlag, 1952. pp. 184. A translation by Lise Bang of *Love Among the Haystacks*.

D25...MARIEHØNEN, PRINSESSEN...København, Aschehoug, 1957. pp. 126. A translation by Mogens Boisen of "The Ladybird" and "The Princess."

D25.2...REJSE I ETRUSKERNES LAND...København, Vendelkaer, 1966. pp. 151. A translation by Poul Borum of *Etruscan Places*.

D25.3...APOKALYPSEN...København, Fremad, 1968. pp. 150. A translation by Karina Wendfeld-Hansen of *Apocalypse*.

DUTCH

D26...DE MAAGD EN DE ZIGEUNER...'s-Gravenhage, Servire, 1931. pp. 159. A translation by John Kooy of *The Virgin and the Gipsy*.

D27...DE MAN DIE GESTORVEN WAS...'s-Graveland, De Driehoek, 1939. pp. 167. A translation by Bert Honselaar of *The Man Who Died*.

D28...HET VERBLIJDE SPOOK...'s-Graveland, De Driehoek, 1941. pp. 64. A translation by Bert Honselaar of *Glad Ghosts*.

D29...DE REGENBOOG...'s-Graveland, De Driehoek, 1947. pp. 482. A translation by H. J. Balfoort and J. de Jong of *The Rainbow*.

D30...ALS VROUWEN LIEFHEBBEN...'s-Graveland, De Driehoek, 1948. pp. 266. A translation by J. de Jong of *Women in Love*.

D31...DE EERSTE LADY CHATTERLEY...'s-Graveland, De Driehoek, 1948. pp. 515. A translation by Jo Boer of *The First Lady Chatterley*.

D32...DE LATTSTE LACH...Amsterdam and Antwerpen, Contact, 1948. pp. 353. A translation by H. J. Scheepmaker of "The Prussian Officer," "The White Stocking," "England, My England," "The Blind Man," "Wintry Peacock," "The Ladybird," "The Woman

Who Rode Away," "The Last Laugh," "The Man Who Loved Islands" and "The Rocking-Horse Winner."

D33...DE VOS...Amsterdam and Antwerpen, Wereldbibliotheek, 1950. pp. 92. A translation by Inez van Dullemen of "The Fox."

D34...LADY CHATTERLEY'S MINNAAR...'s-Graveland, De Drie-hoek, 1950. pp. 301. A translation by J. A. Sandfort of *Lady Chatterley's Lover*. With an essay by E. du Perron.

D34.3...DE BEMINNELIJKE DAME...Amsterdam, Meulenhoff, 1961. pp. 159. A translation by Clara Eggink of "The Lovely Lady" and other stories.

D34.31..HET MEISJE EN DE ZIGEUNER..Amsterdam, Contact, 1962. pp. 119. A translation by Maurits Mok of *The Virgin and the Gipsy*.

D34.32...DE VROUW DIE WEGREED...Amsterdam, Contact, 1963. pp. 166. A translation by H. J. Scheepmaker and Hans Andreus of "The Woman Who Rode Away" and other stories.

D34.33...DE OUDE ADAM EN ZIJN NIEUWE EVA...Amsterdam, Contact, 1963. pp. 159. A translation by H. J. Scheepmaker and Hans Andreus of "New Eve and Old Adam" and other stories.

D34.34...DE HENGST ST. MAWR..Antwerpen, Contact, 1965. pp. 167. A translation by Jean Schalekamp of *St. Mawr*.

D34.35...ZONEN EN MINNAARS...Amsterdam, Contact, 1966. pp. 448. A translation by J. F. Kliphuis of *Sons and Lovers*.

D34.4...DE GEVEDERDE SLANG...Amsterdam, Contact, 1970. pp. 496. A translation by H. W. J. Schaup of *The Plumed Serpent*.

D34.41...DE KAPITEINSPOP...Amsterdam, Contact, 1971. pp. 104. A translation by Johan Fredrik of "The Captain's Doll."

FINNISH

D35...POJAT JA HEIDÄN RAKKAUTENSA...Porvoo, Werner Söderström Osakeyhtiö, 1934. pp. 584. A translation by Aune Brotherus of *Sons and Lovers*.

D36...SULKAKÄÄRME...Turku, Tammi, 1945. pp. 652. A translation by Jorma Partanen of *The Plumed Serpent*.

D37...LEPPÄKERTTU JA MUITA NOVELLEJA...Porvoo, Werner Söderström Osakeyhtiö, 1945. pp. 344. A translation by Aune Brotherus of "The Ladybird," "The Captain's Doll" and "The Woman Who Rode Away."

D38... LADY CHATTERLEY...Jyväskylä, K. J. Gummerus, 1950. pp. 346. A translation by Olli Nuorto of *The First Lady Chatterley*.

D39...LADY CHATTERLEY JA HÄNEN RAKASTAJANSA...Turku, Pohjolan Kirja, 1950. pp. 394. A translation of *Lady Chatterley's Lover* by Jorma Partanen. With a preface by the translator.

D39.3...MIES JOKA KUOLI..Helsinki, Welin and Groos, 1967. pp. 300. A translation by Elina Hytonen of *The Man Who Died* and *St. Mawr*.

D39.31...NOVELLEJA...Helsinki, Welin and Groos, 1968. pp. 442. A translation of the collected short stories, edited by Rauno Ekholm.

D39.32...JOHN THOMAS JA LADY JANE...Jyvaskyla, K. J. Gummerus, 1974. pp. 449. A translation by Risto Lehmusoksa of *John Thomas and Lady Jane*.

FRENCH

D40...LE RENARD...Paris, Librairie Stock, 1928. Le Cabinet Cosmopolite 27. pp. 127. A translation by L. A. Delieutraz of "The Fox." With a preface by John Charpentier.

D41...ÎLE, MON ÎLE... Paris, Editions du Sagittaire, 1930. pp. 123. A translation by Denyse Clairouin of *England, My England*.

D42...AMANTS ET FILS...Paris, Alexis Redier, 1931. Les Grands Etrangers 2. pp. 639. A translation by Jeanne Fournier-Pargoire of *Sons and Lovers*. With an introduction by Gérard de Catalogne.

D43...LE SERPENT À PLUMES...Paris, Librairie Stock, 1931. Le Cabinet Cosmopolite 56. A translation by Denyse Clairouin of *The Plumed Serpent*. With a preface by René Lalou.

D44...L'AMANT DE LADY CHATTERLEY...Paris, Gallimard, 1932. Collection du Monde Entier. pp. 429. A translation by Roger-Cornaz of *Lady Chatterley's Lover*. With a preface by André Malraux.

D45...DÉFENSE DE LADY CHATTERLEY...Paris, Gallimard, 1932. pp. 159. A translation by J. Benoist-Méchin of *A Propos of Lady Chatterley's Lover*. With a preface by J. Benoist-Méchin.

D46...FANTAISIE DE L'INCONSCIENT...Paris, Librairie Stock, 1932. pp. 247. A translation by Charles Mauron of *Fantasia of the Unconscious*.

D47...LA FEMME ET LA BÊTE...Paris, Editions du Siècle, 1932. Les Maîtres Étrangers 6. pp. 236. A translation by Jean Cabalé of *St. Mawr*. With an introduction by Eugène Marsan.

D48...FEMMES AMOUREUSES...Paris, Gallimard, 1932. pp. 603. A translation by Maurice Rancès and Georges Limbour of *Women in Love*.

D49...PAS DE ÇA...Paris, A. Fayard et Cie., 1932. Les Œuvres Libres 135. pp. 32. A translation by Jeanne Fournier-Pargoire of "None of That."

D50...LA FILLE PERDUE...Paris, Editions du Siècle, 1933. Les Maîtres Étrangers 17. pp. 411. A translation by Hélène and Roland Alix of *The Lost Girl*. With an introduction by René Lalou.

D51...LES FILLES DU PASTEUR...Paris, Gallimard, 1933. pp. 285. A translation by Colette Vercken of "Daughters of the Vicar" and other stories.

D52...L'HOMME ET LA POUPÉE...Paris, Gallimard, 1933. pp. 301. A translation by Mme A. Morice-Kerné and Colette Vercken of "The Captain's Doll," "The Ladybird," "A Fragment of Stained Glass," "A Sick Collier," "The Shadow in the Rose Garden," "Second Best" and "Goose Fair."

D53...L'HOMME QUI ÉTAIT MORT...Paris, Gallimard, 1933. pp. 187. A translation by Jacqueline Dalsace and Drieu la Rochelle of *The Man Who Died*. With a preface by Drieu la Rochelle.

D54...KANGOUROU...Paris, Gallimard, 1933. pp. 177. A translation by Maurice Rancès of *Kangaroo*.

D55...LE PAON BLANC...Paris, Calman-Levy, 1933. 2 vols. pp. 206 and 212. A translation by Jeanne Fournier-Pargoire of *The White Peacock*.

D56...LETTRES CHOISIES...Paris, Plon, 1934. Feux Croisés. 2 vols. pp. 194 and 254. Translated by Thérèse Aubray. With Aldous Huxley's introduction translated by Henri Fluchère.

D57...MORT DE SIEGMUND...Paris, Gallimard, 1934. pp. 276. A translation of *The Trespasser* by Hervé Southwell.

D58...LA VIERGE ET LE BOHÉMIEN...Paris, Plon, 1934. Feux Croisés. pp. 207. A translation of *The Virgin and the Gipsy* by E. Frédéric-Moreau.

D59...LA DAME EXQUISE...Paris, Calman-Levy, 1935. pp. 227. A translation of the *The Lovely Lady* by Jeanne Fournier-Pargoire.

D60...MATINÉES MEXICAINES SUIVIES DE PENSÉES...Paris, Librairie Stock, 1935. pp. 224. A translation of *Mornings in Mexico* and *Pansies* by Thérèse Aubray.

D61...LA VERGE D'AARON...Paris, Gallimard, 1935. pp. 371. A translation of *Aaron's Rod* by Roger Cornaz.

D62...L'AMAZONE FUGITIVE...Paris, Librairie Stock, 1936. Le Cabinet Cosmopolite 82. pp. 292. A translation by Jeanne Fournier-Pargoire of "The Woman Who Rode Away," "Two Blue Birds," "Sun," "Smile," "The Border Line," "Jimmy and the Desperate Woman," "The Last Laugh," "In Love," "Glad Ghosts" and "None of That." With an introduction by Jeanne Fournier-Pargoire.

D63...JACK DANS LA BROUSSE...Paris, Gallimard, 1938. pp. 375. A translation by Lilian Brach of *The Boy in the Bush*. With a preface by Francçois Mauriac.

D64...L'ARC-EN-CIEL...Paris, Gallimard, 1939. pp. 397. A translation by Albine Loisy of *The Rainbow*.

D65...RÉFLEXIONS SUR LA MORT D'UN PORC-ÉPIC ET AUTRES ESSAIS...Lyon, Confluences, 1945. Littérature Étrangère. pp. 177. A translation by Thérèse Aubray of "Reflections on the Death of a Porcupine," "The Novel," "Him With His Tail in His Mouth," "Blessed are the Powerful," "Love Was Once a Little Boy" and "Aristocracy." With a preface by Thérèse Aubray.

D66...L'AMANT DE LADY CHATTERLEY...Paris, Deux-Rives, 1946. pp. 332. A translation by Annie Brierre of *The First Lady Chatterley*, including the preface by Frieda Lawrence and the note on the manuscript by Esther Forbes. With illustrations in colour by André Collot.

D67...APOCALYPSE...Lyon, Confluences, 1946. Littérature Étrangère. pp. 200. A translation by Thérèse Aubray of *Apocalypse*.

D68...SARDAIGNE ET MÉDITERRANÉE...Paris, Charlot, 1946. pp. 350. A translation by André Bélamich of *Sea and Sardinia*.

D69...ETUDES SUR LA LITTÉRATURE CLASSIQUE AMÉRICAINE... Paris, Editions du Seuil, 1948. Collection Pierres Vives. pp. 223. A translation by Thérèse Aubray of *Studies in Classic American Literature*.

D70...PROMENADES ÉTRUSQUES...Paris, Gallimard, 1949. pp. 239. A translation by Thérèse Aubray of *Etruscan Places*.

D71...PENSÉES...Paris, Seghers, 1951. Collection Pierre Seghers 69. pp. 32. A translation by Thérèse Aubray of *Pansies*.

D72...CRÉPUSCULE SUR L'ITALIE...Paris, Gallimard, 1954. pp. 263. A translation by André Bélamich of *Twilight in Italy*.

D72.4...ÎLE MON ÎLE ... Paris, Stock, 1969. pp. 443. A translation by Léo Dilé of "England, My England" and other stories.

D72.41...HOMME D'ABORD...Paris, Union Générale d'Editions, 1969. A translation by Thérèse Aubray of a selection of essays, edited with an introduction by M. Marnat.

D72.42...EROS ET LES CHIENS...Paris, Christian Bourgois, 1969. pp. 317. A translation by Thérèse Lauriol of a selection of essays, edited with an introduction by M. Marnat.

D72.5...D. H. LAWRENCE: POÈMES... Paris, Aubier, 1976. A bilingual selection of poems, translated with a preface by J. J. Mayoux.

GERMAN

D73...DER REGENBOGEN... Leipzig, Insel-Verlag, 1922. pp. 663. A translation by Franz Franzius of *The Rainbow*.

D74...JACK IM BUSCHLAND... Struttgart, Deutsche Verlags-Anstalt, 1925. pp. 492. A translation by Else Jaffe-Richthofen of *The Boy in the Bush*.

D75...SÖHNE UND LIEBHABER... Leipzig, Insel-Verlag, 1925. pp. 633. A translation by Franz Franzius of *Sons and Lovers*.

D76...DER FUCHS... Leipzig, Insel-Verlag, 1926. Insel-Bucherei 384. pp. 86. A translation by Else Jaffe-Richthofen of "The Fox."

D77...LIEBENDE FRAUEN... Leipzig, Insel-Verlag, 1927. pp. 638. A translation by Thesi Mutzenbecher of *Women in Love*.

D78...DIE FRAU DIE DAVONRITT... Leipzig, Insel-Verlag, 1928. pp. 382. A translation by Else Jaffe-Richthofen of *The Woman Who Rode Away*.

D79...SPIEL DES UNBEWUSSTEN... Munich, Dornverlag G. Ullman, 1929. A translation by Walter Osborne of *Fantasia of the Unconscious*.

D80...LADY CHATTERLEY UND IHR LIEBHABER... Vienna, E. P. Tal, 1930. pp. 453. A translation by Herberth E. Herlitschka of *Lady Chatterley's Lover*. Published for subscribers only.

D81...A-PROPOS LADY CHATTERLEY... Leipzig and Vienna, Tal, 1931. pp. 114. A translation by Herberth E. Herlitschka of *A Propos of Lady Chatterley's Lover*.

D82...DIE FRAU DIE DAVONRITT... Leipzig, Insel-Verlag, 1931, Insel-Bucherei 419. pp. 71. A translation by Herberth E. Herlitschka of *The Woman Who Rode Away*.

D83...DER HENGST ST. MAWR... Leipzig, Insel-Verlag, 1931. pp. 240. A translation by Herberth E. Herlitschka of *St. Mawr*.

D84...APOKALYPSE...Leipzig, Insel-Verlag, 1932. pp. 292. A translation by Georg Goyert of *Apocalypse*.

D85...FROHE GEISTER...Leipzig, Insel-Verlag, 1932. Insel-Bucherei 428. pp. 95. A translation by Georg Goyert of *Glad Ghosts*.

D86...DIE GEFIEDERTE SCHLANGE...Leipzig, Insel-Verlag, 1932. pp. 480. A translation by Georg Goyert of *The Plumed Serpent*.

D87...LIEBENDE FRAUEN...Leipzig, Insel-Verlag, 1932. pp. 479. A translation by Herberth E. Herlitschka of *Women in Love*.

D88..SÖHE UND LIEBHABER...Leipzig, Insel-Verlag, 1932. pp. 570. A translation by Georg Goyert of *Sons and Lovers*.

D89...DER ZIGEUNER UND JUNGFRAU...Leipzig, Insel-Verlag, 1933. pp. 329. A translation by Karl Lerbs of *The Virgin and the Gipsy*.

D90...DER MARIENKÄFER...Leipzig, Insel-Verlag, 1934. pp. 282. A translation by Karl Lerbs of *The Ladybird*.

D91...DER WEISSE PFAU...Vienna and Leipzig, R. A. Höger Verlag, 1936. pp. 371. A translation by Herberth E. Herlitschka of *The White Peacock*.

D92...TODGEWEIHTES HERZ...Vienna, R. A. Höger-Verlag, 1937. pp. 306. A translation of *The Trespasser* by Herberth E. Herlitschka.

D93...BRIEFE AN FRAUEN UND FREUNDE...Berlin, Die Rabenpresse, 1938. pp. 327. A translation of *The Letters of D. H. Lawrence* by Richard Kraushaar. With an introduction by Wilhelm Emanuel Süskind.

D94...DAS VERLORENE MÄDCHEN...Vienna and Leipzig, A. Ibach, 1939. pp. 355. A translation by Christine Maurer of *The Lost Girl*.

D95...DIE ERSTE LADY CHATTERLEY...Bern, A. Scherz, 1946. pp. 331. A translation by Ursula von Wiese of *The First Lady Chatterley*.

D96...MEISTERNOVELLEN...Zurich, Manesse-Verlag, 1953. Manesse Bibliothek der Weltliteratur. pp. 485. A translation by Elisabeth

Schnack, Else Jaffe-Richthofen, Ursula Müller and Karl Lerbs of "Love Among the Haystacks," "The Shades of Spring," "The Rocking-Horse Winner," "The Princess," "The Man Who Loved Islands," "Sun" and "The Virgin and the Gipsy." With a foreword by Herbert Read and an introduction by Elisabeth Schnack.

D97...LANDSCHAFT UND GEHEIMNIS DER ETRUSKER...Zürich, Verlag der Arche, 1955. pp. 197. A translation by Oswalt von Nostitz of *Etruscan Places*. With a foreword by Richard Aldington.

D98...TODGEWEIHTES HERZ...Vienna, Munich and Basel, Desch, 1957. pp. 319. A translation of the *The Trespasser* by Georg Goyert.

D99...MEXIKANISCHE TAGE...Zürich, Verlag der Arche, 1958. pp. 167. A translation by Alfred Kuoni of *Mornings in Mexico*.

D99.1...DIE BLAUEN MOKASSINS UND ANDERE ERZÄHLUNGEN... Reinbeck bei Hamburg, Rowohlt, 1960 pp. 341. A translation by Martin Beheim-Schwarzbach and Elizabeth Schnack of "The Blue Moccasins" and other stories.

D99.12...LADY CHATTERLEY...Reinbeck bei Hamburg, Rowohlt, 1960. pp. 456. A translation of *Lady Chatterley's Lover*.

D99.13..DER HENGST ST. MAWR..Reinbeck bei Hamburg, Rowohlt, 1960. A translation by Gerda v. Uslar of *St. Mawr*.

D99.14...MEXIKANISCHER MORGEN, ITALIENISCHE DÄMMERUNG, DAS MEER UND SARDINIEN, ETRUSKISCHE STÄTTEN... Reinbeck bei Hamburg, Rowohlt, 1963. pp. 559. A translation by Alfred Kuoni and Georg Goyert of *Mornings in Mexico, Twilight in Italy, Sea and Sardinia, Etruscan Places*.

D99.15...DER REGENBOGEN...Reinbeck bei Hamburg, Rowohlt, 1964. pp. 422. A translation by Gisela Günther of *The Rainbow*.

D99.16...ZWEI BLAUE VÖGEL UND ANDERE ERZÄHLUNGEN... Zurich, Diogenes-Verlag, 1965. pp. 367. A translation by Elizabeth Schnack and Martin Beheim-Schwarzbach of "Two Blue Birds" and other stories.

D99.17...LADY CHATTERLEY...Berlin and Darmstadt, Deutsche Buchgemeinschaft, 1966. pp. 379. A translation of *Lady Chatterley's Lover*.

D99.18...GESAMMELTE ERZÄHLUNGEN...Reinbeck bei Hamburg, Rowohlt, 1968. pp. 432. A translation by Martin Beheim-Schwarzbach of "The Thorn in the Flesh," "A Fragment of Stained Glass," "Samson and Delilah," "The Fox," "The Princess," "Sun," "The Rocking-Horse Winner," "The Lovely Lady," "None of That," "Rawdon's Roof," "In Love," "Jimmy and the Desperate Woman," "The Woman Who Rode Away," "The Man Who Loved Islands," "The Virgin and the Gipsy," "The Blue Moccasins," "Things," "Mother and Daughter," "The Old Adam," "New Eve and Old Adam."

D99.19...DAS MÄDCHEN UND DER ZIGEUNER...Stuttgart, Reclam, 1970. pp. 87. A translation by Martin Geheim-Schwarzbach of *The Virgin and the Gipsy* with an afterword by Gerhard Marx-Mechler.

D99.2..LADY CHATTERLEY...Vienna, Buchgemeinschaft Donauland, 1971, pp. 383. A translation by Franz Maier-Bruck of *Lady Chatterley's Lover*.

D99.21... PORNOGRAPHIE UND OBSZONTAT UND ANDERE ESSAYS UBER LIEBE, SEX UND EMANZIPATION...Zurich, Diogenes-Verlag, 1971. pp. 127. A translation by Elizabeth Schnack of "Pornography and Obscenity" and other essays on sex and love.

D99.22...JOHN THOMAS AND LADY JANE...Zürich, Diogenes-Verlag, 1975. pp. 499. A translation by Susanna Rademacher of *John Thomas and Lady Jane* with an afterword by Roland Gant.

D99.23...SÄMTLICHE ERZÄHLUNGEN UND KURZROMANE... Zurich, Diogenes-Verlag, 1975. A translation by Martin Beheim-Schwarzbach, Georg Goyert, Marta Hackel, Karl Lerbs, Elizabeth Schnack and Gerda v. Uslar of the complete tales and short novels. 8 vols.
Vol. 1: "The Prussian Officer," "The Thorn in the Flesh," "The Mortal Coil," "The Thimble," "Daughters of the Vicar," "A Fragment of Stained Glass," "The Shades of Spring," "Second Best," "The Shadow in the Rose Garden," "Goose Fair," "The White Stocking," "Odour of Chrysanthemums."

Vol. 2: "England, My England," "Tickets Please," "The Blind Man," "Monkey Nuts," "Wintry Peacock," "You Touched Me," "Samson and Delilah," "The Primrose Path," "The Horse-Dealer's Daughter," "Fanny and Annie," "The Princess."

Vol. 3: "Two Blue Birds," "Sun," "The Woman Who Rode Away," "Smile," "The Border Line," "Jimmy and the Desperate Woman," "The Last Laugh," "In Love," "Glad Ghosts," "None of That."

Vol. 4: "The Lovely Lady," "Rawdon's Roof," "The Rocking-Horse Winner," "Mother and Daughter," "The Blue Moccasins," "Things," "A Modern Lover," "The Old Adam," "Witch à la Mode," "New Eve and Old Adam," "The Man Who Loved Islands."

Vol. 5: "Introduction" to *Memoirs of the Foreign Legion*, "Autobiographical Sketch," "Adolf," "Rex," "Mercury," "A Chapel Among the Mountains," "A Hay Hut Among the Mountains," "The Flying Fish," "Autobiographical Sketch II."

Vol. 6: "The Fox," "The Ladybird," "The Captain's Doll."

Vol. 7: "St. Mawr."

Vol. 8: "Love Among the Haystacks," "The Virgin and the Gipsy," "The Man Who Died," "The Risen Lord."

GREEK

D100...I YINAIKA POU EPHIYE ME T'ALOGO...Athens, Ekdosis Gobosti, 1944. pp. 156. A translation by Ari Alexandrou of *The Woman Who Rode Away*.

D101...O ERASTIS TIS LAIDIS TSATERLY...Athens, Logotechniki Morphotiki Etairia, 1954. pp. 320. A translation by Mando Anastassiadi of *Lady Chatterley's Lover*.

D102...O ERASTIS TIS LAIDIS TSATERLY...Athens, Enomenoi Ekdotes, 1956. pp. 255. A translation by Popi Stratiki of *Lady Chatterley's Lover*.

D103...TO KORITZI POU EPHIYE ME T'ALOGO... Athens, Ekdosis Gianni Zerba, 1957. pp. 151. A translation by Memou Panagiotopoulou of *The Woman Who Rode Away*.

D103.2...GHIDI KAI ERASTES...Athens, Enomenoi Ekdotes, 1962. pp. 304. A translation by Potes Stratikes of *Sons and Lovers*.

D103.3...ē ALEPOU...∴Thessalonike, Sfaira, 1970. pp. 110. A translation by Tanias Tsitselē of "The Fox."

D103.31...ē PARTHENA KAIO TSINGANOS...Athens, Angyra, 1971. pp. 131. A translation by Elē Iatridous of *The Virgin and the Gipsy*.

D103.32...O ERASTĒS TĒS LAIDĒS TSATERLY...Athens, Angyra, 1972. pp. 288. A translation by Lilika Tsoukala of *Lady Chatterley's Lover*.

HEBREW

D104...BANIN WE-OHAVIM...Tel-Aviv, Mizpeh, 1934. 2 vols. A translation by Shimón Ginsburg of *Sons and Lovers*.

D105...ME-AHAVAH SHEL LEDY CHATERLY...Tel-Aviv, Mizpeh, 1938. 2 vols. A translation by Baruch Krupnik of *Lady Chatterley's Lover*.

D106...HA-ISHAH SHE-NISTALKAH...Jerusalem, Shoken, 1947. pp. 99. A translation by Moshe Kaner, Elijahu Keshek and Carmela Sukenik of "The Woman Who Rode Away," "Jimmy and the Desperate Woman" and "Sun."

HINDI

D107...CONNIE...Allahabad, Kitab Mahal. pp. 148. A translation by Radhanath Chaturvedi of *Lady Chatterley's Lover*.

D108...DO DILOM KE BICH...Banaras, Visva Sahitya Sadan. pp. 316. A translation by Sajal Kumar of *Lady Chatterley's Lover*.

D108.5...LADY CHATTERLEY KA PREMI...Delhi, Anupam Prakasan, 1967. pp. 187. A translation by Narendranath of *Lady Chatterley's Lover*.

HUNGARIAN

D109...A TOLLAS KIGYÓ...Budapest, Révai, 1929. 2 vols. A translation by Gál Andor of *The Plumed Serpent*. With prefatory material by Juhász Andor.

D110...LADY CHATTERLEY ÉS A KEDVESE...Budapest, Cegléd, 1933. pp. 320. A translation by Braun Soma of *Lady Chatterley's Lover*.

D111...SZÉNABOGLYÁK KÖZÖTT...Budapest, Révai, 1947. pp. 144. A translation by Vajda Ernő of *Love Among the Haystacks*. With a preface by David Garnett.

D111.3...AKI A SZIGETEKET SZERETTE...Budapest, Európa, 1965. pp. 459. A translation by various persons of a collection of tales including "The Man Who Loved Islands," "The Fox," "The Woman Who Rode Away," "The Man Who Died," and others, with a postscript by Lengyel Balázs.

D111.31...SZERELEM A KAZLAK KÖZT...Budapest, Magyar Helikon Kiadó, 1967. pp. 65. A translation by Árpád Göncz of "The Woman Who Rode Away."

D111.32...SZÜLŐK ÉS SZERETŐK...Budapest, Europa, 1968. pp. 580. A translation by Róna Ilona of *Sons and Lovers*.

D111.4...SZIVÁRVÁNY...Budapest, Európa, 1974. pp. 549. A translation by Róna Ilona of *The Rainbow* with a postscript by Kéry László.

D111.41...SZERELMES ASSZONYOK...Budapest, Európa, 1975. pp. 530. A translation by Róna Ilona of *Women in Love*.

ITALIAN

D112...LA VOLPE, LA COCCINELLA...Milano, Treves, 1929. pp. 253. A translation by Carlo Linati of *The Fox* and *The Ladybird*. See (C253).

D113...DI CONTRABBANDO...Milano, Corbaccio, 1933. pp. 303. A translation by C. V. Lodovici of *The Trespasser*.

D114...IL PAVONE BIANCO...Milano, Corbaccio, 1933. pp. 379. A translation by Maria De Sanna of *The White Peacock*.

D115...FIGLI E AMANTI...Milano, Corbaccio, 1933. pp. 640. A translation by Alessandra Scalero of *Sons and Lovers*.

D116...IL PUROSANGUE...Milano and Verona, Mondadori, 1933. pp. 230. A translation by Elio Vittorini of *St. Mawr*.

D117...LA FANCIULLA PERDUTA...Milano, Corbaccio, 1933. pp. 447. A translation by Alessandra Scalero of *The Lost Girl*.

D118...DONNE INNAMORATE...Milano, Elettra, 1935. pp. 635. A translation by Rosa Adler, Maria Ricolli and Giuseppe Pulvirente Dottori of *Women in Love*. With a preface by Giuseppe Pulvirente Dottori.

D119...LA VERGINE E LO ZINGARO...Milano and Verona, Mondadori, 1935. pp. 472. A translation by Elio Vittorini of *The Virgin and the Gipsy*.

D120...IL SERPENTE PIUMATO...Milano and Verona, Mondadori, 1935. pp. 523. A translation by Elio Vittorini of *The Plumed Serpent*.

D121...IL SERPENTE PIUMATO...Milano, Mondadori, 1936. pp. 222. A translation by Giorgio Grempolini of *The Plumed Serpent*.

D122...L'ARCOBALÉNO...Milano, Elettra, 1937. pp. 402. A translation by Mario Benzi of *The Rainbow*.

D123...PAGINE DI VIAGGIO...Milano and Verona, Mondadori, 1938. pp. 339. A translation by Elio Vittorini of *Twilight in Italy, Mornings in Mexico, Sea and Sardinia, Etruscan Places*, the introduction to *Memoirs of the Foreign Legion* and "Section II" of *Phoenix* (A76), "People, Countries, Races."

D124...FIGLI E AMANTI...Roma, S. de Carlo, 1945. pp. 459. A translation by Italo Toscani of *Sons and Lovers*.

D125...L'AMANTE MODERNO...Roma, Jandi Sapi, 1945. pp. 175. A translation by Eugenio Giovannetti of *A Modern Lover*. With a preface by the translator.

D125.1...L'AMANTE DI LADY CHATTERLEY...Roma, De Luigi, 1945. pp. 479. A translation by Manlio Lo Vecchio Musti of *Lady Chatterley's Lover*.

D126...L'AMANTE DI LADY CHATTERLEY...Milano and Verona, Mondadori, 1946. pp. 434. A translation by Giulio Monteleone of *Lady Chatterley's Lover*. Illustrated by Luigi Broggni.

D127...APOCALISSE...Milano and Verona, Mondadori, 1947. pp. 219. A translation by Ernesto Ayassot of *Apocalypse*.

D128...L'UFFICIALE PRUSSIANO...Firenze, Edizioni d'arte, 1948. A translation by Eugenio Vaquer of *The Prussian Officer*. Illustrated by Emanuele Covalli and with a cover done in copper-plate especially for the book by Enrico Michelassi.

D129...LA RAGAZZA PERDUTA...Milano and Verona, Mondadori, 1948. pp. 392. A translation by Carlo Izzo of *The Lost Girl*.

D130...CLASSICI AMERICANI...Milano, Bompiani, 1948. pp. 336. A translation by Attilio Bertolucci of *Studies in Classic American Literature*.

D131...FIGLI E AMANTI...Torino, G. Einaudi, 1948. pp. 453. A translation by Franca Cancogni of *Sons and Lovers*.

D132...LA VERGA D'ARONNE...Milano and Verona, Mondadori, 1949. pp. 373. A translation by Carlo Izzo of *Aaron's Rod*.

D133...ROMANZI BREVI E FRAMMENTI DI ROMANZO...Milano and Verona, Mondadori, 1950. pp. 797. A translation by Carlo Izzo, Carlo Linati, Maria Massa, Elio Vittorini and Giorgio Monicelli of "Love Among the Haystacks," "Mister Noon," "The Fox," "The Captain's Doll," "The Ladybird," "St. Mawr," "The Princess," "The Flying Fish," "The Virgin and the Gipsy," "The Man Who Loved Islands" and "The Man Who Died." Edited with an introduction and notes by Piero Nardi. *Vol. VIII* of Mondadori's *Tutti Gli Scritti Di D. H. Lawrence*.

D134...RACCONTI...Milano and Verona, Mondadori, 1952. pp. 1054. A translation by Aldo Camerino, Milli Dandolo, Carlo Izzo, Maria Massa, Puccio Russo and Elio Vittorini of "A Prelude," "The Fly in the Ointment," "A Modern Lover," "The Old Adam," "The Witch à la Mode," "New Eve and Old Adam," "Strike Pay: Her Turn,"

"Strike Pay: Ephraim's Half-Sovereign," "The Miner at Home," "A Chapel Among the Mountains," "A Hay Hut Among the Mountains," "Once," "Adolf," "Rex" and the contents of *England, My England, The Woman Who Rode Away* and *The Lovely Lady. Vol. IX* of Mondadori's *Tutti Gli Scritti Di D. H. Lawrence.*

D135...FIGLI E AMANTI...Milano, Rizzoli, 1954. pp. 273. A translation by Ugo Dèttore of *Sons and Lovers.*

D136...LE TRE LADY CHATTERLEY...Milano and Verona, Mondadori, 1954. pp. 1052. A translation by Carlo Izzo of *Lady Chatterley's Lover, The First Lady Chatterley, The Second Lady Chatterley* (the second manuscript version) and *A Propos of Lady Chatterley's Lover.* See (A42h). With an introduction and notes by Piero Nardi. *Vol. VII* of Mondadori's *Tutti Gli Scritti Di D. H. Lawrence.*

D137...ELENA E SIEGMUND AMANTI...Eli, Italiane, 1956. pp. 287. A translation by Antonietta Bruno of *The Trespasser.*

D137.1...DONNE INNAMORATE...Torino, Einaudi, 1957. pp. 568. A translation by Lidia Storoni Mazzolani of *Women in Love.*

D137.12...LA RAGAZZA PERDUTA, LA VERGA D'ARONNE...Milano and Verona, Mondadori, 1957. A translation by Carlo Izzo of *The Lost Girl* and *Aaron's Rod.* With an introduction by Piero Nardi. *Vol. V* of Mondadori's *Tutti Gli Scritti Di D. H. Lawrence.*

D137.2...LIBRI DI VIAGGIO E PAGINE DI PAESE...Milano and Verona, Mondadori, 1961. A translation by Aldo Camerino, Giuliana De Carlo, Lorenzo Gigli, Maria Massa and Elio Vittorini of *Twilight in Italy, Sea and Sardinia,* "Introduction" to *Memoirs of the Foreign Legion, Mornings in Mexico, Etruscan Places,* and "Peoples, Countries, Races" from *Phoenix.* Edited with an introduction by Piero Nardi. *Vol. X* of Mondadori's *Tutti Gli Scritti Di D. H. Lawrence.*

D137.21...CANGURO, IL RAGAZZO NELLA BOSCAGLIA, IL SERPENTE PIUMATO...Milano and Verona, Mondadori, 1962. pp. 1471. A translation by Stefano Rossi-Mazzinghi, Tecla Starace and Elio Vittorini of *Kangaroo, The Boy in the Bush* and *The Plumed Serpent.* With an introduction by Piero Nardi. *Vol. VI* of Mondadori's *Tutti Gli Scritti Di D. H. Lawrence.*

D137.22...L'ARCOBALENO, DONNE INAMORATE...Milano and Verona, Mondadori, 1964. pp. 1241. A translation by Lidia Storoni Mazzolani of *The Rainbow* and *Women in Love*. Edited with an introduction by Piero Nardi. *Vol. IV* of Mondadori's *Tutti Gli Scritti Di D. H. Lawrence*.

D137.23...L'UFFICIALE PRUSSIANO E ALTRI RACCONTI...Milano, Feltrinelli, 1965. A translation by Camilla Salvago Raggi of "The Prussian Officer," "The Thorn in the Flesh," "Daughters of the Vicar," "A Fragment of Stained Glass," "The Shades of Spring," "Second Best," "The Shadow in the Rose Garden," "Goose Fair," "The White Stocking," "A Sick Collier," "The Christening" and "Odour of Chrysanthemums."

D137.24...IL PECCATORE...Rome, Casini, 1966. pp. 328. A translation by Ada Bonfirraro of *The Trespasser*.

D137.25...IL TRASGRESSORE...Milan, Zebetti, 1966. pp. 208. A translation by Ivar Colli of *The Trespasser*.

D137.26...FIGLI E AMANTE...Milano, Garzanti, 1968. pp. 516. A translation by Paola Francioli of *Sons and Lovers*. With an introduction by Piero Gelli.

D137.27...LA DONNA CHE FUGGÌ A CAVALLO...Milano, Il Saggiatore, 1969. pp. 72. A translation by Puccio Russo of "The Woman Who Rode Away."

D137.28...IL PAVONE BIANCO, IL TRASGRESSORE, FIGLI E AMANTI...Milano and Verona, Mondadori, 1970. pp. 1287. A translation by Attilio Landi, Maria Teresa Gradenigo Cipollato and Franca Cancogni of *The White Peacock*, *The Trespasser* and *Sons and Lovers*. With an introduction by Piero Nardi. *Vol. III* of Mondadori's *Tutti Gli Scritti Di D. H. Lawrence*.

D137.3...POESIE D'AMORE...Roma, Newton Compton Italiana, 1974. pp. 416. A translation by Paolo Patroni of *Love Poems, Amores, New Poems* and *Bay*.

D137.31...IL PAVONE BIANCO...Milano, Rizzoli, 1974. pp. 418. A translation by Evelina Grassi of *The White Peacock*. With an introduction by Giuseppe Calda.

D137.32...IL PAVONE BIANCO...Roma, Newton Compton Italiana, 1974. pp. 382. A translation by Anna Cecchi of *The White Peacock*. With an introduction by Elio Chinol.

D137.33...DONNE IN AMORE...Roma, Newton Compton Italiana, 1975. pp. 478. A translation by Delia Agozzonio of *Women in Love*.

D137.34...TEATRO E PROSE VARIE...Milano and Verona, Mondadori, 1975. pp. 1007. A translation by Stefano Rossi-Mazzinghi, Maria Stella Labroca, Remo Ceserani and Paola Ojetti of *The Widowing of Mrs. Holroyd, Touch and Go, David, A Collier's Friday Night, The Married Man, The Merry-Go-Round, The Fight for Barbara, The Daughter-in-Law, Noah's Flood, Altitude, Assorted Articles*, "Nature and Poetical Pieces" from *Phoenix*, "Reflections on the Death of a Porcupine" and "Introduction to These Paintings." Edited with an introduction by Piero Nardi. *Vol. XI* of Mondadori's *Tutti Gli Scritti Di D. H. Lawrence*.

D137.35...LA VERGINE E LO ZINGARO...Milano and Verona, Mondadori, 1975. pp. 228. A translation by Elio Vittorini of "The Princess," *The Virgin and the Gipsy* and "The Man Who Died."

D137.36...IL TRASGRESSORE...Milano and Verona, Mondadori, 1976. pp. 246. A translation by Maria Teresa Gradenigo Cipollato of *The Trespasser*. With an introduction by Claudio Gorlier.

JAPANESE

D138...KOISURU ONNA NO MURE...Tokyo, Ten'yu-sha, 1923. A translation by Tatsu Yaguchi of *Women in Love*.

D139...APOKARIPUSU...Tokyo, Shôwa-shobô, 1934. pp. 229. A translation by Masao Tô and Tatsuhiko Arakawa of *Apocalypse*.

D140...NIJI...Tokyo, Shinchô-sha, 1924. pp. 843. A translation by Shinzaburô Miyajima and Izumi Yanagida of *The Rainbow*.

D141...TAII NO NINGYÔ...Tokyo, Shûhôkaku, 1924. pp. 210. A translation by Tokuya Kojima of *The Captain's Doll*.

D142...LAWRENCE SHÔSETSU SHÛ...Tokyo, Kinsei-dô, 1933. pp. 116. A translation by Gyôma Ebata of "The Blind Man,"

"Sun," "Smile," "Corasmin and the Parrots" and "Autobiographical Sketch."

D143...D. H. LAWRENCE NO TEGAMI...Tokyo, Kinokunishoten, 1934. pp. 235. A translation by Masanobu Oda of *The Letters of D. H. Lawrence*.

D144 See D139.

D145...SHIMA O AISHITA OTOKO...Tokyo, Kenbun-sha, 1934. pp. 339. A translation by Toyoitsu Anzai of "The Man Who Loved Islands" and other pieces.

D146...CHATTERLEY FUJIN NO KOIBITO...Tokyo, Kenbun-sha. 1935. pp. 595. A translation by Sei Itô of *Lady Chatterley's Lover*.

D147...SHOJO TO JIPUSHII...Tokyo, Kenbun-sha, 1935. pp. 170. A translation by Tsunetarô Kinoshita of *The Virgin and the Gipsy*.

D148...UMA DE SATTA ONNA...Tokyo, Gyûzan-dô, 1935. pp. 269. A translation by Hôitsu Miyanishi of *The Woman Who Rode Away*.

D149...ATARASHII EVE TO FURUI ADAM...Tokyo, Yamamoto Shoten, 1936. A translation by Momoyo Hora of "New Eve and Old Adam."

D150...KOI SURU ONNA...Tokyo, Mikasa-shobô, 1936. pp. 374. A translation by Sei Itô and Momyo Hora of *Women in Love*.

D151...MUSUKO TO KOIBITO...Tokyo, Mikasa-shobô, 1936. 2 vols. pp. 534 and 408. A translation by Ikusaburô Miyake and Yôichirô Kiyono of *Sons and Lovers*.

D152...REN' AI SHISHÛ...Tokyo, Mikasa-shobô, 1936. pp. 235. A translation by Jû Adachi of a selection of love poems.

D153...SHINDA OTOKO...Tokyo, Shôkyû-shobô, 1936. pp. 123. A translation by Masanobu Oda of *The Man Who Died*.

D154...TAIYÔ...Tokyo, Sakuhin-sha, 1936. pp. 193. A translation by Tomoe Iwakura of *Sun*.

D155...TSUBASA NO ARU HEBI...Tokyo, Mikasa-shobô, 1936. pp. 289. A translation by Kôji Nishimura of *The Plumed Serpent*.

D156...TSUBASA NO ARU HEBI...Tokyo, Kôshin-sha, 1936. A translation by Tsunezô Kamei and Tatsuma Ôishi of *The Plumed Serpent*.

D157...ARON NO TSUE...Tokyo, Mikasa-shobô, 1937. pp. 475. A translation by Gisaburô Jûichiya and Masatake Sakiyama of *Aaron's Rod*.

D158...BUNGAKURON...Tokyo, Shôshin-sha, 1937. pp. 315. A translation by Sei Itô and Sadashi Nagamatsu of a selection of literary criticism.

D159...ITALY NO HAKUMEI...Tokyo, Fuzan-bô, 1939. pp. 221. A translation by Sadao Sotoyama of *Twilight in Italy*.

D160...MUISHIKI NO GENSÔ...Tokyo, Aoki-shoten, 1940. A translation by Kazuo Ogawa of *Fantasia of the Unconscious*.

D161...MUSUKO TO KOIBITO TACHI...Tokyo, Iwanamishoten, 1940. 3 vols. A translation by Kenshô Honda of *Sons and Lovers*.

D162...MEKISHIKO NO ASHITA...Tokyo, Ikuseisha-Kôdôka-ku, 1942. pp. 232. A translation by Sei Itô of *Mornings in Mexico*.

D163..HOSHIGUSA NO NAKA NO KOI..Tokyo, Hanawa-shobô, 1946. A translation by Kenkichi Hagawa of *Love Among the Haystacks*.

164..KOI SURU ONNA TACHI..Tokyo, Koyama-shoten, 1950. 2 vols. pp. 261 and 289. A translation by Tsuneari Fukuda of *Women in Love*.

D165...MUSUKO TO KOIBITO...Tokyo, Koyama-shoten, 1950. 3 vols. pp. 229, 230 and 241. A translation by Kenichi Yoshida of *Sons and Lovers*.

D166...CHATTERLEY FUJIN NO KOIBITO NI TSUITE...Tokyo, Aoki-Shoten, 1951. pp. 177. A translation by Yoshihide Iijima of *A Propos of Lady Chatterley's Lover* and *Pornography and Obscenity*.

D167...CHATTERLEY FUJIN...Tokyo, Rogosu-sha, 1952. pp. 296. A translation by Tarô Kiya of *Lady Chatterley's Lover*.

D168...CHATTERLEY FUJIN NO KOBITO...Kamakura, Keimei-sha, 1953. A translation by Momoyo Hara of *Lady Chatterley's Lover*.

D169...CHATTERLEY FUJIN NO KOIBITO...Tokyo, Sakuhin-sha, 1953. A translation by Yuzuru Jinzai of *Lady Chatterley's Lover*.

D170...NIJI...Tokyo, Shinchô-sha, 1954. pp. 600. A translation by Yoshio Nakano of *The Rainbow*.

D171...AI NO SHISHÛ...Koyto, Jinbun-shoin, 1955. pp. 235. A translation by Masaru Shiga of *Look! We Have Come Through!*

D172...BARAZONO NI TATSU KAGE...Kyoto, Sanwa-shobô, 1955. pp. 287. A translation by Tomohide Iwakura of "The Shadow in the Rose Garden" and other pieces.

D173...CHATTERLEY FUJIN NO KOIBITO...Tokyo, Taihei-shoin, 1955. pp. 450. A translation by Yûzan Nakano of *Lady Chatterley's Lover*.

D174...NIWA NO AOI TORI...Tokyo, Mikasa-shobô, 1955. pp. 190. A translation by Hirosaburô Nabara of *The Prussian Officer and Other Stories*.

D175...SHI NO FUNE SHISHU...Tokyo, Kokubun-sha, 1955. pp. 78. A translation by Shigehisa Narita of *The Ship of Death and Other Poems*.

D176...CHATTERLEY FUJIN NO KOIBITO...Tokyo, Kôfû-kan, 1956. pp. 354. A translation by Shinroku Saidô of *Lady Chatterley's Lover*.

D177...HADAKA NO KAMISAMA...Koyto, Sanwa-shobô, 1956. pp. 269. A translation by Tomohide Iwakura of "The Man Who Died," "The Woman Who Rode Away," "Smile," "Sun" and "The Crucifix Across the Mountains."

D178...HOSHIKUSA NO KOI...Tokyo, Nippon-Fukusôshinbun-sha Shuppan Kyoku, 1956. pp. 210. A translation by Takashi Ogura of *Love Among the Haystacks*.

D179...LAWRENCE NO TEGAMI...Tokyo, Yayoi-shobô, 1956 and 1957. 2 vols. pp. 291 and 276. A translation by Sei Itô and Sadamu Nagamatsu of *The Letters of D. H. Lawrence*.

D180..SEI BUNG AKU KENETSU.. Tokyo, Shinchô-sha, 1956. pp. 222. A translation by Tsuneari Fukuda of *Sex, Literature and Censorship*.

D181...AI TO SHI NO SHISHÛ...Tokyo, Kadokawa-shoten, 1957. pp. 188. A translation by Ichirô Andô of a selection of poems about love and death.

D182... EIKOKUYO WAGA EIKOKUYO...Tokyo, Eihô-sha, 1957. pp. 212. A translation by Isamu Muraoka and Hachirô Hidaka of *England, My England*.

D183...LAWRENCE TANPEN SHÛ...Tokyo, Shinchô-sha, 1957. pp. 200. A translation of a selection of short stories.

D184...SHINDA OTOKO...Tokyo, Shinchô-sha, 1957. pp. 224. A translation by Tsuneari Fukuda of "The Man Who Died" and "The Ladybird."

D185...D. H. LAWRENCE BUNGAKU RONSHÛ...Tokyo, Shuppan-shoin Patoria, 1958. pp. 312. A translation by Kenichi Haya of a selection of literary criticism.

D185.1...TORI KEMONO HANA...Tokyo, Heibon-sha, 1959. pp. 21. A translation by Ichirô Andô of a selection from *Birds, Beasts and Flowers*.

D185.11...DAPHNE-FUJIN NO KOI...Tokyo, Jijitsûshin-sha, 1959. pp. 160. A translation by Tomoe Iwakura of "The Ladybird" and "The Sick Collier."

D185.12...ÔIN SHISHÛ I...Tokyo, Kokubun-sha, 1960. pp. 255. A translation by Seitarô Tanaka of *Love Poems, Amores, New Poems* and *Bay*.

D185.13...MUSUKO TO KOIBITO...Tokyo, Kawadeshobô-shinsha, 1960. pp. 500. A translation by Sei Itô of *Sons and Lovers*.

D185.14...DÔDA BOKURA WA IKINUITE KITA...Tokyo, Kokubun-sha, 1960. pp. 302. A translation by Tamotsu Ueda and Atsushi Unno of *Look! We Have Come Through!*

D185.15...TSUBASA ARU HEBI...Tokyo, Kadokawa-shoten, 1963. 2 vols. pp. 410 and 352. A translation by Hôitsu Miyanishi of *The Plumed Serpent.*

D185.16...JYÔSHAKEN O DÔZO...Tokyo, Shûei-sha, 1963. A translation by Kazuo Ueda of "Tickets, Please."

D185.17...SHINNYÛSHA...Tokyo, Yashio-shuppen-sha, 1964. pp. 257. A translation by Kôji Nishimura of *The Trespasser.*

D185.18...KOI SURU ONNA TACHI...Tokyo, Kadokawa-shoten, 1964. 2 vols. pp. 372 and 385. A translation by Sakiko Nakamura of *Women in Love.*

D185.19...D. H. LAWRENCE SHISHÛ...Tokyo, Yayoi-shobô, 1965. pp. 146. A translation by Kazuo Ueda of a selection of poems by D. H. Lawrence.

D185.2...ITALIYA NO HAKUMEI...Tokyo, Shûei-sha, 1965. A translation by Jyunzaburô Nishiwaki of *Twilight in Italy.*

D185.21...CHATTERLEY-KYÔ FUJIN NO KOIBITO...Tokyo, Yashio-shuppan-sha, 1965. 2 vols. pp. 230 and 250. A translation by Kôji Nishimura of *Lady Chatterley's Lover.*

D185.22...GENDAIJIN WA AISHIURU KA...Tokyo, Chikuma-shobô, 1965. pp. 267. A translation by Tsuneari Fukuda of *Apocalypse.*

D185.23...D. H. LAWRENCE TANPEN SHÛ...Osaka, Aoyama-shoten, 1966. pp. 308. A translation by Eiichirô Yamamoto and Akira Yasukawa of "The Lovely Lady" and other stories.

D185.24...SAIGO SHISHÛ...Tokyo, Kokubun-sha, 1966. pp. 402. A translation by Shigehisa Narita of *Last Poems.*

D185.25...SHIRO KUJYAKU...Tokyo, Chûôkôron-sha, 1966. A translation by Rei Itô of *The White Peacock.*

D185.26...MUISHIKI NO GENSÔ...Tokyo, Nan'un-dô, 1966. pp. 283. A translation by Kazuo Ogawa of *Fantasia of the Unconscious.*

D185.27...GENDAIJIN NO AI NI TSUITE...Tokyo, Shakaishisô-sha, 1966. A translation by Ken'ichi Haya of a selection of D. H. Lawrence's essays.

D185.28...TORI TO KEMONO TO HANA...Tokyo, Kokubun-sha, 1969. pp. 371. A translation by Ken'ichi Haya and Masazumi Toraiwa of *Birds, Beasts and Flowers*.

D185.29...SANSHIKI SUMIRE IRAKUSA...Tokyo, Kokubun-sha, 1969. pp. 428. A translation by Rikutarô Fukuda and Saburô Kuramochi of a selection of D. H. Lawrence's poetry including *Pansies* and *Nettles*.

D185.3...ETORURIA ISEKI...Tokyo, Fushichô-sha, 1969. A translation by Shin'ichirô Suzuki of *Etruscan Places*.

D185.31...KOI SURU ONNA TACHI...Tokyo, Shûei-sha, 1970. A translation by Kazuo Ogawa and Tatsuo Izawa of *Women in Love*.

D185.32...MEXICO NO ASA...Tokyo, Fushichô-sha, 1970. pp. 92. A translation by Shin'ichirô Suzuki of *Mornings in Mexico*.

D185.33...REN'AI NI TSUITE...Tokyo, Kadokawa-shoten, 1970. pp. 150. A translation by Sei Itô of *Assorted Articles*.

D185.34...CHATTERLEY-FUJIN NO KOIBITO, KITSUNE, ETORURIA KIKÔ HOKA...Tokyo, Kawade-shobô-shinsha, 1970. A translation by Sei and Rei Itô of *Lady Chatterley's Lover*, "The Fox," *Etruscan Places* and *A Propos of Lady Chatterley's Lover*.

D185.341...SHOCHO NO IMI...Tokyo, 1972. pp. 349. A translation by Unno Atsushi of *The Symbolic Meaning*.

D185.342...UMI TO SARDINIA...Shirakawa, Fujicho, 1972. pp. 218. A translation by Suzuki Shin'ichiro of *Sea and Sardinia*.

D185.35...LAWRENCE...Tokyo, Chikuma-shobô, 1973. pp. 426. A translation by Takeshi Onodera and Hiroshi Ikuno of *Sons and Lovers*, "The Fox," "The Man Who Died," "Glad Ghosts" and "The Lovely Lady."

D185.36...CHATTERLEY-FUJIN NO KOIBITO...Tokyo, Kôdan-sha, 1973. pp. 627. A translation by Ken'ichi Haya of *Lady Chatterley's Lover*.

D185.37...SHOJO TO JIPUSHÎ, TAIYÔ MOJIN...Osaka, Osaka-kyôiku-tosho, 1973. pp. 275. A translation by Susumu Yamasaki of *The Virgin and the Gipsy*, "Sun" and "The Blind Man."

D185.38...ETORURIA NO ISEKI...Tokyo, Bijutsu-shuppan-sha, 1973. pp. 224. A translation by Tei-ichi Hijikata and Katsuo Matsu-ura of *Etruscan Places*.

D185.39...AMERICA BUNGAKU RON...Tokyo, Yayoi-shobô, 1974. pp. 260. A translation by Sadamu Nagamatsu of *Studies in Classic American Literature*.

D185.4...AMERICA KOTEN BUNGAKU KENKÛ...Tokyo, Kenkyû-sha, 1974. pp. 320. A translation by Masayuki Sakamoto of *Studies in Classic American Literature*.

D185.41...JOHN THOMAS TO LADY JANE...Tokyo, Shûei-sha, 1975. pp. 622. A translation by Masayoshi Ôsawa of *John Thomas and Lady Jane*.

D185.42...LAWRENCE TANPEN SHÛ...Sagamihara, Taiyô-sha, 1975. pp. 499. A translation by Tetsuhiko and others of a selection of D. H. Lawrence's essays and short stories.

D185.43...LAWRENCE TANPEN SHÛ...Tokyo, Yashio-shuppan-sha, 1976. pp. 290. A translation by Ken'ichi Haya of "A Prelude" and other stories.

D185.44..LAWRENCE TANPEN KESSAKU SHÛ..Kyoto, Apollon-sha, 1976. pp. 361. A translation by Tohru Okumura of *The Prussian Officer and Other Stories*.

KOREAN

D186...LORENSE SUGAN-JIP...Seoul, Minjoon SuKwan, 1954. A translation of a selection of Lawrence's letters by Wondal Yang.

D186.1 ... ADUL-GWA-YONIN ... Seoul, Dongguk, 1958. A translation of *Sons and Lovers* by Jai-nam Kim.

D186.11 ... MOOJIGAI ... Seoul, Jungum, 1958. A translation of *The Rainbow* by Jai-nam Kim.

D186.2 ... MIGUK-GOJUN-MOONHAK-YONKU ... Seoul, Shinyang, 1959. A translation of *Studies in Classic American Literature* by Byung-chul Kim.

D186.21 ... LORENSE-MOONHAK-RON ... Seoul, Yangmoon, 1960. A translation of a selection of Lawrence's essays by Byung-chul Kim.

D186.22 ... SUNG-GWA-MOONHAK ... Seoul, Jungum, 1964. A revision of (D186.21) with additions by Byung-chul Kim.

D186.3 ... NALGAI-DOTCHIN-BAIM ... Seoul, Ulyu, 1965. A translation of *The Plumed Serpent* by Jai-nam Kim.

D186.31 ... CHATALI-BUIN-UI-SARANG ... Seoul, Jungum, 1968. A translation of *Lady Chatterley's Lover* by Byung-taik Yang.

D186.32 ... CHATALI-BUIN-UI-SARANG ... Seoul, Mirim, 1972. A translation of *Lady Chatterley's Lover* by Jung-whan O.

D186.33 ... ADUL-GWA-YONIN ... Seoul, Moonwha, 1973. A translation of *Sons and Lovers* by Ryung Yu.

D186.4 ... JUGUM-UI-BAI ... Seoul, Minum, 1973. A translation of a selection of Lawrence's poems by Chong-wha Chung.

D186.41 ... CHATALI-BUIN-UI-SARANG ... Seoul, Samjin, 1976. A translation of *Lady Chatterley's Lover* by Nam-suk Kim.

D186.42 ... ADUL-GWA-YONIN ... Seoul, Samsung, 1977. A translation of *Sons and Lovers* by Byung-taik Yang.

D186.43 ... ADUL-GWA-YONIN ... Seoul, Kumsung, 1977. A translation of *Sons and Lovers* by Gook-kun O.

D186.44 ... CHATALI-BUIN-UI-SARANG ... Seoul, Jubu Sainghwal, 1977. A translation of *Lady Chatterley's Lover*, "The Woman Who Rode Away" and "The Man Who Loved Islands."

D186.5...MALUL-TAGO-DOMANGGAN-YOJA...Seoul,   Pyungmin,
1978. A translation of "The Woman Who Rode Away" by Taeju
Lee.

D186.51...LORENSE-DANPYUN-SUN...Seoul, Somoon, 1978. A translation of a selection of Lawrence's short stories by Yon-ki Hong.

D186.52...CHATALI-BUIN-UI-SARANG...Seoul, Woorim Moonwha,
1978. A translation of *Lady Chatterley's Lover* by Kyung-shik Lee.

NORWEGIAN

D187...DEN FALNE PAN...Oslo, Aschehoug, 1935. pp. 213. A translation by C. V. Holst of *St. Mawr*.

D188...SØNNER OG ELSKERE...Oslo, Aschehoug, 1935. pp. 502. A
translation by Johan Borgen of *Sons and Lovers*. With a foreword by
Sigrid Undset.

D189...MANNAN SOM ELSKET ØER...Oslo, Aschehoug, 1936. pp.
179. A translation by Helge Krog of "England, My England,"
"The Blind Man," "Wintry Peacock," "The Man Who Loved
Islands," "The Blue Moccasins" and "Things."

D190..DEN FØRSTE LADY CHATTERLEY...Theim, Holbaek Eriksen,
1950. pp. 326. A translation by Søren Riis of *The First Lady Chatterley*.
With a foreword by Frieda Lawrence.

D191...LADY CHATTERLEYS ELSKER...Oslo, Cappelan, 1952.
pp. 435. A translation by Leo Strøm of *Lady Chatterley's Lover*. With a
foreword by Hans Heiberg.

D191.5...D. H. LAWRENCE NOVELLER...Oslo, Gyldendal, 1973. pp.
311. A translation by Helge Hagerup of a collection of short
stories.

PERSIAN

D191.8...ASHEGH-E LIDI CHATERLI...Tehran, 1960. pp. 195. A
translation by Ali Pakbin of *Lady Chatterley's Lover*.

POLISH

D192...KOBIETA I PAW...Warszawa, Biblioteka Croszowa, 1931. pp. 292. A translation by Janiny Sujkowskiej of "Wintry Peacock," "Tickets Please," "The Blind Man," "Monkey Nuts," "England, My England," "You Touched Me," "Samson and Delilah," "The Primrose Path," "The Horse Dealer's Daughter" and "Fanny and Annie."

D193...KOCHANEK LADY CHATTERLY...Krakow and Warszawa, Panteon, 1932. pp. 491. A translation by Marcelego Tarnowskiego of *Lady Chatterley's Lover*.

D194...OBRONA LADY CHATTERLY...Warszawa, Księgarnia M. Fruchtmana, 1933. pp. 144. A translation by Marcelego Tarnowskiego of *A Propos of Lady Chatterley's Lover*.

D195...DOTEKNĘLAŚ MNIE...Warszawa, Biblioteka Echa Polskiego, 1936. A translation by Janiny Sujkowskiej of "You Touched Me," "Samson and Delilah," "The Primrose Path," "The Horse Dealer's Daughter" and "Fanny and Annie."

D195.3...SYNOWIE I KOCHANKOWIE...Warszawa, Czytelnik, 1960. A translation by Z. Sroczynska of *Sons and Lovers*.

D195.5...POEZJE WYBRANE...Krakow, Wydawnictwo Literackie, 1976. A translation by L. Elektorowicz of a selection from *Complete Poems*.

PORTUGUESE

D196...O AMANTE DE LADY CHATTERLEY...São Paulo, Editorial Minerva, 1938. pp. 452. A translation of *Lady Chatterley's Lover*.

D197...UMA MULHER FUGIU A CAVALO...Lisboa, Editorial Inquérito, 1941. pp. 75. A translation by Alberto Candeias of *The Woman Who Rode Away*.

D198...FILHOS E AMANTES...Lisboa, Portugália Editora, 1943. pp. 442. A translation by Cabral do Nascimento of *Sons and Lovers*. With an introduction by João Gaspar Simões.

D199...O AMANTE DE LADY CHATTERLEY...São Paulo, Editorial Minerva, 1945. pp. 365. A translation of *Lady Chatterley's Lover* and *A Propos of Lady Chatterley's Lover*.

D200...CONTOS...Coimbra, Atlantida Livraria Editora, 1952. pp. 219. A translation by Manuel Barbosa of "The Rocking-Horse Winner," "Tickets Please," "The Lovely Lady" and "Things." With a preface by the translator.

ROUMANIAN

D201...FII SI AMANTI...Bucharest, Alcalay and Co., n.d. 2 vols. A translation by Camil Balthazar of *Sons and Lovers*.

D202...FECIOARA ŞI ŢIGANUL...Bucharest, Alcalay and Co., n.d. pp. 205. A translation of *The Virgin and the Gipsy* and "The Fox."

D203...IN FAŢA FRONTULUI VIEŢII...Bucharest, Adevĕrul, 1930. Floarea Literaturilor Străine 281. pp. 31. A translation by Filip Rareş.

D204...ARMĂSARUL DOAMNEI LOU...Bucharest, Alcalay and Co., 1933. pp. 179. A translation of *St. Mawr*.

D205...A ŞA CEVA-NU...Bucharest, Adevĕrul, 1934. Floarea Literaturilor Străine 482. pp. 31. A translation by A. Marincu of "None of That" and other stories.

D206...FEMEI ÎN DRAGOSTE...Bucharest, Alcalay and Co., 1934. pp. 455. A translation by Z. Stancu of *Women in Love*.

D207...AMANTUL DOAMNEI CHATTERLEY...Bucharest, Ocneanu, 1935. pp. 369. A translation of *Lady Chatterley's Lover*. With an introduction by Petru Manoliu.

D208...ŞARPELE CU PENE...Bucharest, Cultura Romînească 1943. pp. 573. A translation by Julian Vesper of *The Plumed Serpent*.

D208.5...PARFUM DE CRIZANTEME...Bucharest, Editura Pentru Literatură Universală, 1967. pp. 514. A translation by Catinea Ralea of "Odour of Chrysanthemums."

D208.6...FII ŞI ÎNDRĂGOSTIŢI...Bucharest, Universala, 1971. pp. 528. A translation by Antoaneta Ralian of *Sons and Lovers*.

RUSSIAN

D209...PHLEITA AARONA...Moscow, Izd-Bo Nedra, 1925. pp. 400. A translation by M. Shik of *Aaron's Rod*.

D210..SEM'YA BRENGUENOV RADUGA..Moscow, Izd-Bo Nedra. 1925. pp. 365. A translation by V. Minina of *The Rainbow*.

D211...SYNOV'YA I LYUBOVNIKI...Leningrad, Knizhnye Novinki, 1927. pp. 287. A translation by N. Chukovskii of *Sons and Lovers*.

D212...DZHEK V DEBRYAKH AVSTRALII...Leningrad, Mysl, n.d. pp. 278. A translation by I. P. Martynova of *The Boy in the Bush*.

SINHALESE

D212.8...KANYĀVA SAHA JIPSI MINISĀ...Nugegoda, Viduruwana Press, 1962. pp. 118. A translation by Walter D. Costa and Siripāla Pādukka of *The Virgin and the Gipsy*.

SPANISH

D213..EL AMANTE DE LADY CHATTERLEY..Buenos Aires, Editorial Luz, 1932. pp. 239. A translation by Luis Klappenbach of *Lady Chatterley's Lover*.

D214...LA DEFENSA DE LADY CHATTERLEY...Buenos Aires, Editorial Luz, 1932. pp. 127. A translation by Natal A. Rufino of *A Propos of Lady Chatterley's Lover*. With prefatory material by Charles Duff and J. Benoist Mechin.

D215...PRINCESA...Santiago, Editorial Zig-Zag, 1932. pp. 51. A translation by R. R. of "The Princess." With a preface and biographical notes by R. R.

D216...CANGURO...Buenos Aires, Editoria Espasa-Calpe, 1933. pp. 509. A translation by Lino Novás Calvo of *Kangaroo*.

D217...HIJOS Y AMANTES...Buenos Aires, Editorial Luz, 1933. 3 vols. A translation by Luis Klappenbach of *Sons and Lovers*.

D218...ISLA, MI ISLA...Santiago, Editorial Ercilla, 1933. pp. 63. A translation by Carlos Vattier B. of "England, My England." With a study of Lawrence by Oscar Vera L. and an introduction by Carlos Vattier B.

D219...UNA MUJER PARTITÓ A CABALLO...Santiago, Editorial Zig-Zag, 1933. pp. 96. A translation by Xul Ventura and O. Torricelli of "The Woman Who Rode Away" and "Sun."

D220...LA MUJER Y LA BESTIA...Buenos Aires, Editorial El Ombú, 1933. Biblioteca de Autores Extranjeros Contemporáneos 5. pp. 175. A translation by Luis Klappenbach of *St. Mawr*.

D221...EL ZORRO...Santiago, Editorial Cultura, 1933. pp. 139. A translation by Oscar Vera L. of "The Fox." With a preface by the translator.

D222...EL AMANTE DE LADY CHATTERLEY...Santiago, Editorial Ercilla, 1934. pp. 324. A translation of *Lady Chatterley's Lover* with an essay on Lawrence by André Malraux.

D223..LA VIRGEN Y EL GITANO..Buenos Aires, Editorial Sur, 1934. pp. 272. A translation by Eduardo Uribe of *The Virgin and the Gipsy*.

D224..EL HOMBRE Y EL MUÑECO..Santiago, Editorial Ercilla, 1935. pp. 127. A translation by Carlos E. Morván of "The Captain's Doll" and "Goose Fair."

D225...LA SOMBRA EN EL ROSEDAL...Santiago, Editorial Ercilla, 1935. pp. 145. A translation by Carlos E. Morván of "The Shadow in the Rose Garden," "A Fragment of Stained Glass," "A Sick Collier," "Second Best" and "The Ladybird."

D226...SEXO, BELLEZA Y OTROS ENSAYOS...Santiago Editorial Zig-Zag, 1938. pp. 277. A translation by Ernesto Montenegro of *Assorted Articles*.

D227...LA VARA DE AARÓN...Santiago, Editorial Zig-Zag, 1938. pp. 333. A translation by Angel Cruchaga Santa María of *Aaron's Rod*.

D228...LA MUJER QUE SE FUÉ A CABALLO...Buenos Aires, Editorial Losada, 1939. pp. 209. A translation by Leonor de Acevedo of *The Woman Who Rode Away*.

D229...EL AMANTE DE LADY CHATTERLEY...Buenos Aires, Editorial Tor, 1939. pp. 318. A translation by Natal A. Rufino of *Lady Chatterley's Lover*.

D230...EL PAVO REAL BLANCO...Buenos Aires, Editorial Poseidón, 1940. pp. 407. A translation by León Mirlas of *The White Peacock*.

D231...LA SERPIENTE EMPLUMADA...Buenos Aires, Editorial Losada, 1940. pp. 444. A translation by Carmen Gallardo de Mesa of *The Plumed Serpent*.

D232...MAÑANAS EN MÉXICO...México, Letras de México, 1942. pp. 157. A translation by Octavio G. Barreda of *Mornings in Mexico*.

D233...LA MUJER PERDIDA...Buenos Aires, Editorial Santiago Rueda, 1943. pp. 373. A translation by Max Dickmann and Ricardo Atwell de Veyga of *The Lost Girl*.

D234...ARCO IRIS...Buenos Aires, Editorial Santiago Rueda, 1944. pp. 452. A translation by Anne Berlioz of *The Rainbow*.

D235...EL HOMBRE QUE MURIÓ...Buenos Aires, Editorial Losada, 1944. pp. 167. A translation by Patricio Cantó of *The Man Who Died*. Illustrated by Atilio Rossi.

D236...CARTAS...Buenos Aires, Editorial Imán, 1945. 2 vols. A translation of *The Letters of D. H. Lawrence* with an introduction by Aldous Huxley.

D237...ESTUDIOS SOBRE LITERATURA CLÁSICA NORTE-AMERI-CANA...Buenos Aires, Editorial Emecé, 1946. Grandes Ensayistas 15. pp. 270. A translation by Carlos María Reyes of *Studies in Classic American Literature*.

D238...LA PRIMERA LADY CHATTERLEY...Buenos Aires, Santiago, Rueda, 1946. A translation by Federico López Cruz of *The First Lady Chatterley*.

D239...FANTASIA DEL INCONSCIENTE...Buenos Aires, Santiago Rueda, 1946. A translation by Irma P. Fontana of *Fantasia of the Unconscious*.

D240...APOCALIPSIS...Buenos Aires, Santiago Rueda, 1947. pp. 218. A translation by León Mirlas of *Apocalypse*.

D241...LA DAMA ENCANTADORA...Buenos Aires, Santiago Rueda, 1947. pp. 228. A translation by Federico López Cruz of "The Lovely Lady," "Rawdon's Roof," "The Rocking-Horse Winner," "Mother and Daughter," "The Blue Moccasins" and "Things."

D242...EL HOMBRE Y EL MUÑECO...Barcelona, Editorial Luis Caralt, 1947. pp. 205. A translation by Jesús Ruiz of *The Captain's Doll*.

D243...FENIX. NATURALEZA, PUEBLOS, PAÍSES Y RAZAS...Buenos Aires, Santiago Rueda, 1948. pp. 243. A translation by León Mirlas of selections from *Phoenix: The Posthumous Papers of D. H. Lawrence*.

D244...AMORES, AMOR, SEXO, HOMBRES Y MUJERES...Buenos Aires, Santiago Rueda, 1948. pp. 359. A translation by León Mirlas of a selection of essays.

D245...CREPÚSCULO EN ITALIA...Buenos Aires, Santiago Rueda, 1949. pp. 405. A translation by León Mirlas of *Twilight in Italy*.

D246...UN AMOR MODERNO...Barcelona, Editorial Luis Caralt, 1950. pp. 234. A translation by Jesús Ruiz of *A Modern Lover*.

D246.2...EL AMANTE DE LADY CHATTERLEY...Mexico, Diana, 1961. (5th ed.) A translation by Federico López Cruz of *Lady Chatterley's Lover*.

D246.3...ST. MAWR...Barcelona, Caralt, 1963. pp. 193. A translation by Ignacio Rived of *St. Mawr*.

D246.4...EN EL ERIAL...Barcelona, Caralt, 1975. pp. 362. A translation by Fabricio Valserra of *The Boy in the Bush*.

SWEDISH

D247...SÖNER OCH ÄLSKARE...Stockholm, Bonnier, 1925. pp. 545. A translation by Gabriel Sanden of *Sons and Lovers*. With an introduction by Anders Österling.

D248...KVINNAN SOM RED BORT OCH ANDRA BERÄTTELSER ...Stockholm, H. Geber, 1930. pp. 340. A translation by Sigfrid Lindström and Siri Thorngren Olin of *The Woman Who Rode Away*.

D249...DU RÖRDE VID MIG...Stockholm, Tiden, 1931. pp. 302. A translation by Louis Renner of *England, My England*.

D250...AARONS STAV...Stockholm, Tiden, 1932. pp. 376. A translation by Barbro Linder of *Aaron's Rod*.

D251...DIKTER...Stockholm, Tiden, 1934. pp. 95. A translation by Erik Blomberg of a selection of poems.

D252...FLICKAN SOM SJÖNK...Stockholm, Tiden, 1934. pp. 423. A translation by Tore Ekman of *The Lost Girl*.

D253...KVINNOR SOM ÄLSKA...Stockholm, Tiden, 1936. pp. 574. A translation by Artur Lundkvist of *Women in Love*.

D254...DEN BEFJÄDRADE ORMEN...Stockholm, Tiden, 1938. pp. 518. A translation by Artur Lundkvist of *The Plumed Serpent*.

D255...MANNEN SOM DOG OCH ANDRA NOVELLER...Stockholm, Tiden, 1939. pp. 336. A translation by Artur Lundkvist of "The Man Who Died" and other stories.

D256...LADY CHATTERLEYS ÄLSKARE...Stockholm, C. E. Fritze, 1941. pp. 411. A translation by Elsa af Trolle of *Lady Chatterley's Lover*. With an introduction by Fredrik Böök.

D257...REGNBÅGEN...Stockholm, C. E. Fritze, 1942. pp. 645. A translation by Elsa af Trolle of *The Rainbow*. With an introduction by Fredrik Böök.

D258...KÄRLEK BLAND HÖSTACKAR...Stockholm, C. E. Fritze, 1943. pp. 119. A translation by Elsa af Trolle of *Love Among the Haystacks*. With an introduction by David Garnett.

D259...BREV...Stockholm, Wahlström and Widstand, 1950. pp. 217. A translation by Teddy Brunius and Göran B. Johansson of *The Letters of D. H. Lawrence.*

D260...RESA I ETRUSKERNAS LAND...Stockholm, Tiden, 1954. pp. 134. A translation by Gerd Mellvig-Ahlström of *Etruscan Places.* With a foreword by Gösta Säflund.

D261...BLOMMOR OCH MÄNNISKOR...Stockholm, FIB:s Lyrikklubb, 1957. FIB:s Lyrikklubb Bibliotek 33. pp. 77. A translation by Erik Blomberg of a selection of poems.

D261.1...LAWRENCE EN SAMLINGSVOLYM...Stockholm, Rabén and Sjögren, 1959. pp. 389. A translation by various persons of a collection of prose works by D. H. Lawrence, edited with an introduction by Knut Jaensson.

D261.11..LADY CHATTERLEYS ÄLSKARE...Stockholm, Fritze, 1961. pp. 342. A translation by Ingmar Forsström of *Lady Chatterley's Lover.*

D261.12...STUDIER I KLASSISK AMERIKANSK LITTERATUR... Malmö, Cavefors, 1964. A translation by Harry Järv of *Studies in Classic American Literature* with an introduction by the translator.

D261.13...MANNEN SOM DOG...Stockholm, Termac, 1965. pp. 100. A translation by Axel Österberg of *The Man Who Died.*

D261.14...MANNEN SOM ÄLSKADE ÖAR ANDRA NOVELLER ...Stockholm, Prisma, 1965. pp. 218. A translation by Artur Lundkvist of "The Man Who Loved Islands" and other stories. A reprint under a different title of (D255).

D261.15...SÖNER OCH ÄLSKANDE...Stockholm, Bonnier, 1970. pp. 453. A translation by Reider Ekner of *Sons and Lovers.*

TURKISH

D262...TILKI...Istanbul, Inkilap Kitabevi, 1942. pp. 128. A translation by Ferid N. Hansoy of *The Fox.*

D263...LADY CHATTERLEY'IN AŞÍĞI...Istanbul, Insel Kitabevi, 1943. pp. 188. A translation by Avni İnsel of *Lady Chatterley's Lover.*

D264

D264...ÇINGENE VE BAKIRE...Istanbul, Devrim Kitabevi, 1944. pp. 91. A translation by İnci Alev of *The Virgin and the Gipsy*.

D265...ERKEĞIM KIM...Ankara, Sakarya Basimevi, 1948. pp. 15. A translation by G. Demirkaya of *Love Among the Haystacks*.

D265.4...KANATLI YILAN...Istanbul, Türkiye Yayinevi, 1959. pp. 336. A translation by Sahire Sağman and Günseli Arda of *The Plumed Serpent*.

D265.41...OĞULLAR VE SEVGILILER...Istanbul, Güven Basim ve Yayinevi, 1959. pp. 381. A translation by Nihal Yeğinobali of *Sons and Lovers*.

D265.42...GÜNARKÂR...Istanbul, Güven Basim ve Yayinevi, 1961. pp. 300. A translation by Vahdet Gullekin of *The Trespasser*.

D265.43...ÖLEN ADAM...Istanbul, Ataç Kitabevi, 1962. pp. 76. A translation by Bilge Karasu of "The Man Who Died."

D265.5...ANKA KUŞU...Ankara, Bilgi Yayinevi, 1966. pp. 171. A translation by Akşit Göktürk.

D265.51...URSULA...Istanbul, Halk Kitabevi, 1967. pp. 430. A translation by Okşan Okandan.

D265.52...LAYD CHATTERLEY'IN SEVGILISI...Istanbul, Çeltüt Matbaasi, 1968. pp. 463. A translation by Akşit Göktürk of *Lady Chatterley's Lover*.

D265.53...AŞIKKADINLAR...Istanbul, Altin Kitaplar Yayinevi, 1970. pp. 459. A translation by Nihal Yeğinobali of *Women in Love*.

D265.54...SAMAN LIKTA AŞK...Istanbul, Habora Kitabevi, 1973. pp. 231. A translation by S. Ateş and Serap Ongun of "Love Among the Haystacks."

YIDDISH

D266...DER GELIBTER FUN LEJDI CZATERLEJ...Warsze, Jidisze Uniwersal Bibliotek, 1939. pp. 479. A translation by Awrohem Cimerman of *Lady Chatterley's Lover*.

The Captain's Doll, the American edition (A24b) with dust-jacket designed by Knud Merrild; *Birds, Beasts and Flowers*, first edition (A27a) with dust-jacket designed by Lawrence; *The Boy in the Bush*, with dust-jacket designed by Dorothy Brett; *The Plumed Serpent*, Alfred Knopf edition, with dust-jacket designed by Dorothy Brett

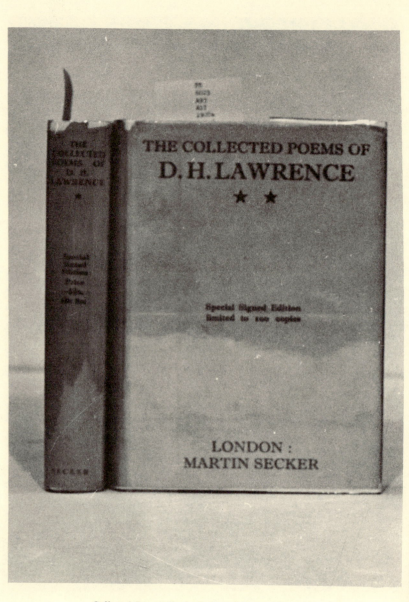

Collected Poems, limited signed issue (A43b)

Pansies, title page of copies issued in blue leather (A47d)

Fontana Vecchia
Taormina
Sicily :   9 Dec. 1920

When you come to Europe, sail to Naples & so come here.

Dear M.

Your dateless telling me about The Blind Man story in The Living Age Pinker's doing : and no word to me, and no cheque : sharp letter to him :

Had your cable on 3rd, about Lost Girl selling New York. Cabled Secker & wrote him pepper. He'll be offended for life. Tant mieux pour lui. Forbade him to issue W. in Love till May 1st — & altogether went it I was, & am, furious with the little moneygrub : he is no better. But his W. in Love won't be ready till May, I'm sure.

No further news of Lost Girl in London. Post very bad here.

Had your proofs of Rex from Dial. Do capture a copy of The Dial containing Rex, & Adolf which appears earlier : should be glad if you kept a copy, in print, of everything of mine that appears in America.

I am sending you Birds Beasts & Flowers poems — under registered manuscript cover. Sell as much as possible to periodicals first — also Harriett Monroe she likes me — or did. I've neglected her — I promised to let Amy Lowell see the MS. You might mail it to her & ask her for it back quick — Miss Amy Lowell, Heath Street, Brookline, Mass : & say who you are — But don't bother if you don't want.

Letter from D. H. Lawrence to Robert Mountsier, dated 9 December 1920 from Taormina about various works being placed in the United States and England.
The Smith Collection

E. MANUSCRIPTS

Compiled by Lindeth Vasey

Note: Manuscripts have been identified with an entry number from Powell (B46) or a page number from Tedlock (B51), although the specific manuscript listed here may not be identical with the one described by Powell or Tedlock.

COLLECTIONS

Bucknell University	PLeB
Columbia University	NNC
Cornell University	NIC
Dartmouth College	NhD
Various dealers	Dealer
Duke University	NcD
W. Forster	Forster
Harvard University	MH
William Heinemann, Ltd.	Heinemann
Henry E. Huntington Library and Art Gallery	CSmH
Indiana University	InU
Iowa State Education Association	IaE
George Lazarus	Lazarus
Mills College	COMC
New York Public Library	NN
Newberry Library	ICN
Northwestern University	IEN
Nottingham County Record Office	NCRecord
Nottinghamshire County Libraries	NCL
Pierpont Morgan Library	NNPM
Princeton University	NjP
Privately owned	Private
Philip H. & A. S. W. Rosenbach Foundation	PPRF
Harold Smith	Smith
Southern Illinois University	ICSo
Stanford University	CSt
State University of New York at Buffalo	NBuU
University of California at Berkeley	CU
University of California at Los Angeles	CLU
University of Chicago	ICU
University of Cincinnati	OCU
University of Illinois	IU
University of Liverpool	ULiv
University of New Mexico	NmU
University of Nottingham	N
University of Salford	USal
University of Texas at Austin	TxU
University of Toronto	CaOTU
University of Tulsa	OkTU
University of Virginia	ViU
Yale University	CtY

E. MANUSCRIPTS

E1 *À la Manière de D. H. Lawrence*

    Holograph manuscript, 1 p.   NjP

E1.5 *A Propos of Lady Chatterley's Lover*

    a. Holograph manuscript, 13 pp.   ICSo
          MS titled: *Introd. to Lady C.*
          Published as *My Skirmish with Jolly Roger*
    b. Corrected carbon typescript, 8 pp.   NmU
          MS titled: *Intro. to French ed. Lady Chatterley*
    c. Holograph manuscript, 42 pp.   TxU
          MS titled: *Continuation of Jolly Roger article*
          Powell 9

E1.7 *A woman of about thirty-five, beautiful, a little overwrought...*

    Holograph manuscript, 4 pp.   CtY
    Outline for a joint novel with Catherine Carswell

E2 *Aaron's Rod*

    a. Corrected original and carbon typescript, 479 pp. TxU
    b. Carbon typescript, 31 pp.   NNC
          Chapter XIII only (pp. 171–202)

E2.1 *Aaron's Rod, Foreword to*

    Holograph manuscript, 1 p.   Unlocated
    With letter of 15 August 1921 to Thomas Seltzer
    American Art Association catalogue (29–30 January 1936)
    item no. 378

E2.2 *Aaron's Rod, Introduction to*

    Holograph manuscript   Unlocated
    With letter of 22 October 1921 to Thomas Seltzer

E3 *Accumulated Mail*

    a. Holograph manuscript, 10 pp.   InU
    b. Corrected carbon typescript, 8 pp.   NmU
    c. Typescript, 8 pp.   TxU
    d. Carbon typescript, 12 pp.   CU

E3.3 *Adolf*

    a. Typescript, 10 pp.   TxU

b. Typescript and carbon copy, 12 pp., 12 pp.   TxU
c. Typescript, 7 pp.   CtY

E3.6 *After All Saints' Day*
Holograph manuscript, 1 p.   TxU
In Frieda Lawrence's hand

E3.8 *After Many Days*
Holograph manuscript   See E320.1

E4 *After School*
Holograph manuscript, 1 p.   See E317

E5 *After the Opera*
Holograph manuscript   See E319

E6 *After the Theatre.* See *Embankment at Night, Before the War: Outcasts*

E7 *Afterwards.* See *Firelight and Nightfall* and *Grey Evening*

E8 *Ah, Muriel!*
a. Holograph manuscript   See E320.1
b. Holograph manuscript, 1 p.   TxU
c. Holograph manuscript, 1 p.   See E320.4

E9 *All of Roses.* See *River Roses, Gloire de Dijon, Roses on the Breakfast Table* and *All of Roses: IV*

E9.1 *All of Roses: IV*
a. Holograph manuscript   See E318
b. Typescript   See E319.7

E9.5 *All Souls' Day*
Holograph manuscript, 1 p.   TxU
In Frieda Lawrence's hand

E10 *All There*
a. Holograph manuscript, 1 pp.   CU
    Tedlock p. 211, Powell 84A
b. Typescript, 4 pp.   CU

E11 *All Things Are Possible*
a. Holograph manuscript, 157 pp.   Lazarus
    Includes *Foreword*, 4 pp.
b. Corrected page proofs   Unlocated
    First 16 pp. are present in two states
    Parke-Bernet Galleries catalogue (19 February 1963)
    item no. 130

E12 *Almond Blossom*
a. Typescript, 5 pp.   CU

   b. Proof   Unlocated
       With letter of 26 January 1922 to Curtis Brown

E12.5 *Aloof in Gaiety*
   a. Holograph manuscript   See E320.1
       See also *Coldness in Love*
   b. Holograph manuscript, 1 p.   See E320.4

E12.7 *Altercation*
   a. Holograph manuscript, 1 p.   ICSo
   b. Holograph manuscript   See E302

E13 *Altitude* (An unfinished play)
   a. Holograph manuscript, 28 pp.   CU
       Tedlock pp. 121–3, Powell 68
   b. Carbon typescript, 26 pp.   CU
   c. Carbon typescript, 26 pp.   TxU
   d. Typescript, 14 pp.   TxU
       Revisions in Spud Johnson's hand
   e. Carbon typescript, 14 pp.   CU

E14 *American Eagle, The*
   a. Holograph manuscript   See E47
   b. Holograph manuscript, 1 p.   IaE
       Incomplete, begins: The new, full-fledged Republic...
   c. Holograph manuscript, 2 pp.   Unlocated
       Scriptorium catalogue (1976)

E14.3 *Americans, Review of*
    Corrected typescript, 9 pp.   CtY
    MS titled: *Model Americans*

E14.5 *Amores*
   a. Holograph ms or typescript   Destroyed: Duckworth fire
   b. Carbon typescript, 100 pp.
   c. Proofs, c.137 pp.
       Duckworth proofs sent to Huebsch for (A9b)
   d. Author's copy with holograph corrections, 138 pp.   Lazarus

E15 *Amour.* See *Autumn Sunshine*

E16 *And what do I care...*
   a. Holograph manuscript, 3 pp.   CU
       Powell 63C
   b. Typescript, 3 pp.   NmU
   c. Two carbon typescripts, 3 pp., 3 pp.   See E315
       See also *Blueness* and *Shadow of Death, The*

E17 *Apocalypse*
 a. Holograph manuscript, 102 pp.   TxU
  Five fragments in a notebook, pp. 11–53,
  23–58[57], 27–32, 43–56, 13–4
  Tedlock pp. 146–8, Powell 110B
 b. Holograph manuscript, 11 pp.   TxU
  A fragment, pp. 33, 34, 34–42
  MS titled: *Apocalypsis II: DHL*
  Tedlock p. 149, Powell 110B
 c. Holograph manuscript, 160 pp.   TxU
  Tedlock pp. 143–4, Powell 110A
 d. Corrected carbon typescript, 121 pp.   TxU
  Tedlock pp. 144–5, Powell 110C
 e. Galley proofs   Dealer
 f. Proof sheets, 155 pp.   Lazarus
 g. Proof copy   Dealer
  Orioli, 1931 (A57a)
 h. Proof copy   Dealer
  Orioli, 1931 (A57a)

E18 *Apocalypse, Outline for*
 a. Holograph manuscript, 7 pp.   CU
  p. 2 is missing
  Tedlock pp. 148–9, Powell 84A
 b. Holograph manuscript, 1 p.   TxU
  p. 2 only in *Apocalypse* fragments notebook
  Tedlock p. 148

E19 *Apostrophe of a Buddhist Monk*
 Holograph manuscript, 1 p.   TxU
 Published as *Apostrophe to a Buddhist Monk*

E20 *Appeal, The*
 a. Holograph manuscript   See E213
 b. Holograph manuscript   See E320.1
  See also *Under the Oak*

E21 *Apropos of Lady Chatterley's Lover*. See *A Propos of Lady Chatterley's Lover*

E22 *Are You Pining?*
 Holograph manuscript, 1 p.   CSt
 Untitled, begins: Are you pining to be superior?...
 Powell 61

E23 *Aristocracy*
    a. Holograph manuscript, 16 pp.   CU
        Tedlock p. 140, Powell 84A
    b. Corrected carbon typescript, 12 pp.   CU
        Tedlock p. 141
    c. Carbon typescript, 18 pp.   CU
    d. Carbon typescript, 18 pp.   NmU
    e. Carbon typescript, 18 pp.   TxU

E23.1 *Aristocracy, German translation*
    Holograph manuscript, 7 pp.   TxU
    Incomplete
    MS titled: *Aristokratie*
    In Frieda Lawrence's hand

E24 *Art and Morality*
    a. Holograph manuscript, 1 p.   Lazarus
        An early version of the first paragraph only
        Tedlock p. 164
    b. Holograph manuscript, 9 pp.   TxU
        An early version
        Tedlock pp. 165–6, Powell 116
    c. Typescript, 8 pp.   CU
    d. Typescript and carbon copy, 8 pp., 8 pp.   TxU
    e. Holograph manuscript, 10 pp.   TxU
        A later version
        Tedlock pp. 165–6, Powell 116
    f. Corrected carbon typescript, 11 pp.   CU
        Tedlock p. 166
    g. Typescript, 10 pp.   CU
    h. Typescript, 8 pp.   TxU
    i. Carbon typescript, 10 pp.   TxU

E24.3 *Art and the Individual*
    a. Holograph manuscript, 9 pp.   Private
    b. Holograph manuscript, 6 pp.   Private
        Comments for expansion of essay

E24.5 *Art Nonsense and Other Essays, Review of*
    a. Holograph manuscript, 7 pp.   Unlocated
        Tedlock p. 263, Powell 105
    b. Carbon typescript, 8 pp.   TxU

E24.7 *As for Me, I'm a Patriot*
    Holograph manuscript, 1 p.   TxU

E25 *As I*...See [*Fragments*] *An*...

E26 *Ass, The*
    a. Holograph manuscript   See E47
    b. Holograph manuscript, 2 pp.   IaE
    c. Typescript   See E314.5

E27 *Assorted Articles*   TxU
    Corrected and uncorrected original and carbon typescripts, 112 pp.
    Tedlock pp. 217–9, 221–3, 225–6, 228–33, 235–8, Powell 84B

Men Must Work and Women As Well	18 pp.
Enslaved by Civilization	8 pp.
The Risen Lord	12 pp.
The State of Funk	9 pp.
Red Trousers	5 pp.
Dull London	4 pp.
Insouciance	5 pp.
Give Her a Pattern	7 pp.
Do Women Change?	8 pp.
Ownership	5 pp.
Master in His Own House	5 pp.
Matriarchy	7 pp.
Cocksure Women and Hensure Men	5 pp.
On Human Destiny	8 pp.
On Being a Man	7 pp.

E27.2 *Assuming the Burden*
    Holograph manuscript, 2 pp.   See E319.2

E27.3 *At a Loose End*
    a. Holograph manuscript   See E320.1
        See also *Troth with the Dead* and *Enkindled Spring, The*
    b. Holograph manuscript   See E320.2

E27.5 *At the Cearne*
    Holograph manuscript, 2 pp.   See E319.2

E27.7 *At the Front*
    a. Holograph manuscript   See E317
        A fragment
        See also *In Church* and *North Country, The*
        Includes: Far off the lily statues stand tall...
    b. Holograph manuscript   See E320.2
    c. Holograph manuscript, 1 p.   See E269.5

E28 *At the Window*
    a. Holograph manuscript, 2 pp.   See E317

b. Holograph manuscript, 1 p.   See E320.4

c. Typescript   See E314.3

E28.5 *Attila*

Galley proof   See E319.6

E29 *August Holidays*

Holograph manuscript, 3 pp.   TxU

E30 *Autobiographical Fragment*

a. Holograph manuscript, 42 pp.   CU

     MS untitled, begins: Nothing depresses me more...

     MS titled by Powell: *Newthorpe in 2927*

     Tedlock pp. 64–5, Powell 50

b. Carbon typescript, 34 pp.   CU

Published in *Phoenix* (A76) as *Autobiographical Fragment*
and in *The Princess* (A114) as *A Dream of Life*

E31 *Autobiographical Sketch*

Holograph manuscript, 20 pp.   OCU

Published in *Phoenix II* (A107) as [*Return to Bestwood*]

E31.3 *Autobiography*

Holograph manuscript, 4 pp.   TxU

Published in *Nehls* (B60) and *Phoenix II* (A107) with title
Autobiographical Sketch

With letter of 18 July 1928 to Jean Watson

E31.5 *Autumn at Taos*

Corrected typescript, 1 p.   TxU

E31.7 *Autumn Sunshine*

a. Holograph manuscript, 2 pp.   See E317

b. Holograph manuscript   See E320.2

     Five drafts, four incomplete

c. Holograph manuscript, 1 p.   See E269.5

E32 *Aware*

Holograph manuscript, 1 p.   See E213

E33 *Baby Asleep After Pain, A*

a. Holograph manuscript, 1 p.   See E317

b. Holograph manuscript   See E320.1

c. Holograph manuscript, 2 pp.   TxU

     Tedlock pp. 77–9, Powell 52

d. Holograph manuscript   See E320.4

e. Holograph manuscript   See E320.2

E34 *Baby Movements.* See *Baby Asleep After Pain, A* and *Baby
Running Barefoot*

439

E34.5 *Baby Running Barefoot*
    a. Holograph manuscript, 1 p.   See E317
    b. Holograph manuscript   See E320.1
    c. Holograph manuscript, 2 pp.   TxU
        Tedlock pp. 77–9, Powell 52
    d. Holograph manuscript   See E320.4
    e. Holograph manuscript   See E320.2

E35 *Baby Songs: Ten Months Old*. See *Ten Months Old*

E36 *Bad Side of Books, The*
    a. Holograph manuscript, 4 pp.   TxU
        MS titled: *Introduction to Bibliography*
        Tedlock p. 243, Powell 90
    b. Corrected typescript, 5 pp.   TxU
        MS titled: *Introduction to Bibliography*
    c. Carbon typescript, 5 pp.   OkTU
        Untitled

E37 *Ballad of a Wilful Woman*
    Holograph manuscript, 5 pp.   See E320.6

E38 *Ballad of Another Ophelia*
    a. Holograph manuscript   See E320.1
        Two drafts
    b. Holograph manuscript   Private
        MS on verso of *A Fragment of Stained Glass*
    c. Holograph manuscript, 3 pp.   See E320.4
    d. Holograph manuscript, 1 p.   ICU
    e. Holograph manuscript or typescript   See E314.2

E39 *Bare Fig-Trees*
    Typescript, 3 pp.   CU

E40 *Bathing Resort*
    Holograph manuscript, 1 p.   TxU
    Incomplete

E40.5 *Bay*
    a. Holograph manuscript   Unlocated
        With letter of 11 December 1916 to Lady C. Asquith
    b. Holograph manuscript   Unlocated
        With letter of 11 December 1916 to J. B. Pinker
    c. Holograph manuscript, 1 p.   Lazarus
         Dedication page
    d. Printer's pulls, 23 pp.   Lazarus
         Includes one extra sheet printed on one side only

e. Sheet proofs, 5 pp.   TxU
    Unfolded gatherings, complete
f. Corrected rough proofs, 16 pp.   OCU
    pp. 9–24
g. Corrected rough proofs, 28 pp.   ICSo
    pp. 9–24, 32–43
h. Corrected page proofs, 8 pp.   TxU
    pp. 25–32
i. Proof pages, 23 pp.   Lazarus

E40.7 *Be a Demon*
Holograph manuscript, 1 p.   See E302

E41 *Be men—be individual men*...
a. Holograph manuscript, 2 pp.   TxU
b. Holograph manuscript, 2 pp.   Lazarus
    MS untitled, begins: to all men who are men:
    Be men, be individual men...
    With letter of 28 December 1928 to Charles Wilson

E42 *Bei Hennef*
a. Holograph manuscript,   See E213
b. Corrected carbon typescript, 1 p.   See E205.8

E43 *Bells*
a. Holograph manuscript   See E314
b. Typescript and carbon copy, 1 p., 1 p.   TxU

E44 *Bereavement*
Holograph manuscript   See E317
Two drafts

E44.5 *Best of School, The*
Holograph manuscript   See E205.8

E45 *Beyond the Rockies*
a. Holograph manuscript, 2 pp.   TxU
    Tedlock p. 101, Powell 118
b. Typescript and carbon copy, 2 pp., 2 pp.   TxU
c. Carbon typescript, 2 pp.   CU

E45.5 *Bibbles*
Holograph manuscript   See E47

E46 *Bibliography, Introduction to.* See *Bad Side of Books, The*

E46.5 *Birdcage Walk*
a. Holograph manuscript, 1 p.   See E317
b. Holograph manuscript   See E320.2
c. Holograph manuscript, 1 p.   See E269.5

E47 *Birds, Beasts and Flowers*
    a. Holograph manuscript, 22 pp.   CU
        Tedlock pp. 87–101, Powell 56

Tropic	*Purple Anemones*
Peace	*The Ass*
Southern Night	*Eagle in New Mexico*
Sicilian Cyclamens	*The American Eagle*
Hibiscus and Salvia Flowers	

    b. Typescript   Unlocated
        12 poems sent to Harriet Monroe by Robert
        Mountsier, his letter of 6 September 1922
        to Monroe, her letter of 16 September 1922
        to Mountsier, including:
        Turkey Cock (*Turkey-Cock*)
        The Evening Land
        St. Matthew
        9 unidentified

    c. Holograph manuscript and typescript, 128 pp.   Lazarus
        Follows closely the English edition.
        Includes in holograph *Figs, Tropic,*
        Snake, Eagle in New Mexico, The Blue
        Jay, Elephant, Kangaroo, Bibbles, Mountain
        Lion; lacks *Tortoises* poems and *The*
        American Eagle; *Almond Blossom* is
        supplied from printed source

    d. Corrected typescript, 125 pp.   NIC
        Printer's copy for American edition (A27a)

    e. Corrected carbon typescript, 124 pp.   CaOTU
        Lacks title page and *The American Eagle*; *Tortoises*
        poems supplied from printed source

    f. Corrected galley proofs, 95 pp.   IaE
    g. Proofs, 207 pp.   TxU
        Secker, 1923 (A27b)

    h. Author's copy with holograph corrections   TxU
        Secker, 1923 (A27b)

E47.1 *Birds, Beasts and Flowers, French translation*
    a. Carbon typescript, 99 pp.   TxU
    b. Typescript, 11 pp.   CU
        Grenade (*Pomegranate*)
        Nefles et Sorbes (*Medlars and Sorb-Apples*)
        Tropique (*Tropic*)

Le Colibri (*Humming-Bird*)
Nuit du Sud (*Southern Night*)
Fleur d'Amandier (*Almond Blossom*)
Anemones Pourpres (*Purple Anemones*)
These two typescripts make a complete copy, including
Tortoises poems

E47.2 *Birds, Beasts and Flowers, Section Introductions*
    Holograph manuscript, 3 pp.   TxU
    With letter of 12 November [1929] to Blair Hughes-Stanton

E48 *Birthday.* See *On That Day*

E49 *Bits*
    a. Holograph manuscript, 6 pp.   ICU
        The Last Minute
        Vicar's Son
        Drill in the Heat
        Mother's Son in Salonika
        Casualty
        Maiden's Prayer
        Man Hauling a Wagon
        Sighs
        Daughter of the Great Man
        The Child and the Soldier
        Pietà
        The Grey Nurse
        Litany of Grey Nurses
        Message to a Perfidious Soldier
        Dust in the East
        The Girl in Cairo
        The Jewess and the V. C.
        Zeppelin Nights
        Munitions
        Land-Worker
        Mourning
        Mesopotamia
        Tales (*The Gazelle Calf*)
        Foreign Sunset
        Prisoner at Work in a Turkish Garden
        Response From the Harem
        Swing Song of a Girl and a Soldier
        Prisoners at Work in the Rain

> *The Well in Africa*
> *Neither Moth nor Rust*

b. Corrected carbon typescript, 34 pp.   Lazarus

> *Farewell and Adieu (The Last Minute)*
>
> *Star Sentinel: A young woman muses on her betrothed, who is in Mesopotamia (Mother's Son in Salonika)*
>
> *Near the Mark: A timid girl sighs her unconfessed love for the man in Flanders (Sighs)*
>
> *Man Hauling a Waggon*
>
> *The Well of Kilossa: A thirsty soldier in East Africa praises the well at which he drank (The Well in Africa)*
>
> *Straying Thoughts: A girl goes to the cathedral church, to pray for her beloved (Maiden's Prayer)*
>
> *Twofold: A young lady hears that her lover is wounded (Casualty)*
>
> *Fragile Jewels: A child speaks to his brother, who is a soldier (The Child and the Soldier)*
>
> *Benediction: An old father kisses his son, who is a soldier (Vicar's Son)*
>
> *Supplication: A young lieutenant who joined the Roman Catholic Church whilst at Oxford, prays on the battle-field (Pietà)*
>
> *The Grey Nurse*
>
> *The Saint: Litany of Grey Nurses (Litany of Grey Nurses)*
>
> *The Wind, the Rascal: A girl, sitting alone at night, starts at the sound of the wind (The Wind, the Rascal)*
>
> *Rose, Look Out Upon Me: A soldier catches sight of a young lady at her window in Salonika*
>
> *Unrelenting: Message from a pious mistress to a soldier (Message to a Perfidious Soldier)*
>
> *Dust: Drought in the Near East (Dust in the East)*
>
> *A Powerful Ally: A young lady speaks to the colonel of her lover's regiment (The Girl in Cairo)*
>
> *The Daughter of the Great Man: A wounded captain is entertained by a young lady (Daughter of the Great Man)*
>
> *Drill on Salisbury Plain in Summer Time (Drill in the Heat)*
>
> *An Elixir: A woman of the East encourages her young man, who is home on leave (The Jewess and the V. C.)*
>
> *Night-Fall in the Suburbs (Zeppelin Nights)*
>
> *Munitions Factory (Munitions)*
>
> *Forlorn: A maiden weeps for her dead husband (Land-Worker)*
>
> *Needless Worry: A poor girl thinks of the dead (Mourning)*
>
> *The Gazelle Calf: A blind soldier tells his children about Arabia (The Gazelle Calf)*

Foreign Sunset : Coloured labourers behind the fighting-line complain that they are done up (Foreign Sunset)
Too Late : A straggler in Mesopotamia finds himself lost (Mesopotamia)
Antiphony : A British sailor, prisoner of war, works in a garden in Turkey (Prisoner at Work in a Turkish Garden)
Swing Song : A girl in a swing, and a soldier swinging her (Swing Song of a Girl and a Soldier)
Prisoners at Work in the Rain
Neither Moth Nor Rust
MS titled: *All of Us*

E49.5 *Black Swans, Preface to*
  Holograph manuscript, 4 pp.   TxU
  Tedlock pp. 243–4, Powell 118

E49.6 *Blessed Are the Powerful*
  Holograph manuscript, 12 pp.   Unlocated
  MS titled: *Power*
  Harry Levinson (Beverly Hills) catalogue (5 June 1951) item no. 31

E49.9 *Blue Jay, The*
  Holograph manuscript   See E47

E50 *Blue Moccasins*
  a. Holograph manuscript, 7 pp.   TxU
     An early version, incomplete
     Tedlock p. 71, Powell 48B
  b. Holograph manuscript, 32 pp.   TxU
     Tedlock pp. 69–71, Powell 48A
  c. Carbon typescript, 27 pp.   CU

E50.5 *Blueness*
  a. Holograph manuscript   See E320.1
     Two drafts
  b. Holograph manuscript   See E320.4
  See also *Shadow of Death, The* and *And what do I care . . .*

E51 *Body Awake, The.* See *Virgin Youth*

E51.5 *Bombardment*
  a. Holograph manuscript   See E320.1
  b. Holograph manuscript   See E320.2

E52 *Books*
  a. Holograph manuscript, 8 pp.   CU
     Tedlock pp. 160–1, Powell 84A
  b. Carbon typescript, 7 pp.   CU

    c. Carbon typescript, 7 pp.   NmU
    d. Carbon typescript, 7 pp.   TxU

E53 *Border Line, The*
    a. Holograph manuscript, 16 pp.   Lazarus
        An early version
        Powell 36B
    b. Holograph manuscript, 25 pp.   Lazarus
        Another early version, follows printed version
        through p. 17 and then entirely different
        Powell 36A

E54 *Bottom Dogs, Introduction to*
    a. Holograph manuscript, 8 pp.   CU
        Tedlock pp. 249–50, Powell 93
    b. Carbon typescript, 11 pp.   CU
    c. Carbon typescript, 11 pp.   NmU
        MS titled: *Introduction to Edward Dahlberg's novel*
    d. Carbon typescript, 11 pp.   TxU
        MS also titled: *Introduction to Edward Dahlberg's*
        novel, for Putnams

E55 *Boy in the Bush, The*
    a. Holograph manuscript, 580 pp.   CU
        Chapters I–XXV (lacking Chapter XXVI)
    b. Holograph manuscript, 10 pp.   IaE
        Chapter XXVI only
    c. Holograph notes, 1 p.   Unlocated
        List of characters
        Tedlock p. 134
    d. Holograph notes, 2 pp.   IaE
        Alterations requested by Mollie Skinner for publication
    e. Corrected original and carbon typescript, 543 pp.   TxU
    f. Corrected typescript, 543 pp.   NNC
    g. Secker, 1924 edition (A29) marked by Mollie Skinner   TxU

E56 *Bread Upon the Waters*
    Holograph manuscript, 1 p.   See E319

E56.3 *Bride, The*
    a. Holograph manuscript   See E320.1
    b. Holograph manuscript   See E320.2

E56.5 *Britannia's Baby*
    a. Holograph manuscript, 1 p.   See E266

b. Carbon typescript	See E266

E56.7 *British Boy, The*
Carbon typescript | See E266

E57 *British Sincerity*
Carbon typescript | See E266

E57.3 *British Workman and the Government, The*
a. Holograph manuscript | See E266
b. Carbon typescript | See E266

E57.5 *Britisher Has a Word with an Editor, A*
Holograph manuscript, 1 p. | TxU
MS titled: *A Britisher Has a Word with Harriett Monroe*

E58 *Brooding Grief*
a. Holograph manuscript | See E317
b. Holograph manuscript | See E320.2
c. Typescript | See E314.3

E58.5 *Brother and Sister*
a. Holograph manuscript | See E320.1
b. Holograph manuscript | See E320.2

E59 *Brotherhood.* See *Embankment at Night, Before the War : Charity*

E59.3 *[Burns Novel]*
Holograph manuscript, 13 pp. | TxU
Two fragments, pp. 1–12, 1

E59.5 *But the Captains brow was sad...*
Holograph manuscript, 1 p. | N
With letter of 2 September 1908 to Louie Burrows

E60 *Campions*
Holograph manuscript | See E317

E60.3 *Canvassing for the Election*
Holograph manuscript | See E302

E60.5 *Captain's Doll, The*
a. Holograph manuscript, 77 pp. | OkTU
    Tedlock pp. 49–50, Powell 12
b. Corrected typescript, 85 pp. | PLeB

E61 *Casualty*
a. Holograph manuscript, 1 p. | See E319.5
b. Holograph manuscript | See E49
c. Corrected carbon typescript, 1 p. | See E49

E62 *Cavalleria Rusticana and Other Stories*
 Holograph manuscript, 60 pp.   CU
 Tedlock pp. 272–3, Powell 108

Cavalleria Rusticana	10 pp.
The She-Wolf (La Lupa)	7 pp.
Fantasticalities (Caprice)	10 pp.
Jeli the Shepherd (Jeli the Herdsman)	33 pp.

E63 *Cavalleria Rusticana and Other Stories, Translator's Preface*
 a. Holograph manuscript, 11 pp.   CU
  Tedlock pp. 273–4, Powell 108
 b. Corrected typescript, 28 pp.   Unlocated
  Argus Book Shop catalogue no. 827 (1943) item 26
 c. Corrected carbon typescript, 23 pp.   TxU
  Includes title page and table of contents

E63.2 *Censors*
 Galley proof   See E319.6

E63.3 *Certain Americans and an Englishman*
 Typescript, 13 pp.   TxU

E63.7 *Change of Government*
 a. Holograph manuscript, 1 p.   See E266
 b. Carbon typescript   See E266

E64 *Change of Life*
 a. Holograph manuscript, 8 pp.   Unlocated
  Powell 63F
 b. Two carbon typescripts, 9 pp., 9 pp.   See E315

E65 *Chaos in Poetry*
 a. Holograph manuscript, 9 pp.   TxU
  MS titled: *Introduction to Chariot of the Sun*
 b. Corrected typescript, 10 pp.   TxU
  Tedlock pp. 247–9, Powell 92
 c. Carbon typescript, 14 pp.   TxU

E66 *Chapel Among the Mountains, A*
 a. Holograph manuscript, 16 pp.   CtY
  Tedlock p. 177, Powell 28
 b. Typescript partly carbon, 15 pp.   CU
  Tedlock p. 178

E67 *Cherry Robbers*
 a. Holograph manuscript, 1 p.   See E317
 b. Holograph manuscript, 1 p.   ULiv
  With letter of 20 January 1909 to Blanche Jennings

c. Holograph manuscript, 2 pp.   See E320.3
     A draft and a fragment
d. Holograph manuscript, 1 p.   See E213
e. Holograph manuscript, 1 p.   Private
     MS titled: *Throstles in the Cherry Tree*

E67.5 *Chief Mystery, The*
     Holograph manuscript, 3 pp.   See E319.2

E68 *Child and the Soldier, The*
     a. Holograph manuscript   See E49
     b. Corrected carbon typescript, 1 p.   See E49

E68.2 *Christening, The*
     Holograph manuscript, 9 pp.   TxU
     Powell 33

E68.5 *Climbing Down Pisgah*
     a. Holograph manuscript, 6 pp.   TxU
         Tedlock pp. 161–2, Powell 118
     b. Corrected typescript and corrected carbon copy,
         7 pp., 7 pp.   TxU

E68.6 *Climbing Up*
     Holograph manuscript   See E302

E68.7 *Clouds*
     Holograph manuscript, 12 pp.   CtY

E68.8 *Clydesider*
     a. Holograph manuscript   See E266
     b. Carbon typescript   See E266

E69 *Coast of Illusion.* See *Gifts of Fortune, Review of*

E70 *Cocksure Women and Hensure Men*
     a. Holograph manuscript, 3 pp.   CU
         Tedlock pp. 223–4, Powell 84A
     b. Carbon typescript, 5 pp.   See E27

E71 *Coldness in Love*
     a. Holograph manuscript   See E320.1
         See also *Aloof in Gaiety*
     b. Holograph manuscript   See E213

E72 *Collected Poems Volume I*
     Corrected original and carbon typescript, 193 pp.   TxU
     Tedlock pp. 102–3, Powell 57

E73 *Collected Poems, Foreword to*
     a. Holograph manuscript, 8 pp.   CLU

Published in introduction section of *Phoenix* (A76) and
as *Foreword* in *Complete Poems* (A104)
Powell 58
b. Carbon typescript, 7 pp.   TxU

E73.1 *Collected Poems, Note to*
Holograph manuscript, 4 pp.   IaE

E74 *Collier's Friday Night, A*
a. Holograph manuscript, 134 pp.   TxU
b. Carbon typescript, 95 pp.   CU

E74.3 *Collier's Wife, The*
Holograph manuscript   See E213

E74.5 *Come Spring, Come Sorrow*
a. Holograph manuscript   See E320.1
b. Holograph manuscript, 3 pp.   See E320.4

E75 *Comfortless Memory, Ashenden or the British Agent, England and the Octopus
and The Station, Review of.* See *Station: Athos, Treasures and Men, The;
England and the Octopus; Comfortless Memory; and Ashenden, or The
British Agent; Review of*

E75.2 *Coming Awake*
Carbon typescript, 1 p.   See E205.8

E75.5 *Complaint of the Soul of a Worker, The*
Holograph manuscript   See E320.1

E76 *Corasmin and the Parrots*
a. Holograph manuscript, 8 pp.   TxU
MS titled: *Mornings in Mexico. Friday Morning*
Tedlock pp. 186–7, Powell 76
b. Corrected carbon typescript, 9 pp.   TxU
MS titled: *Mornings in Mexico. Corasmin and the Parrots*
Tedlock pp. 187–8, Powell 76
c. Page proofs   See E246.2

E77 *Corot*
a. Holograph manuscript   See E320.1
b. Holograph manuscript   See E213

E77.5 *Craving for Spring*
Typescript   See E319.8

E78 *Crow, The.* See *In Church, At the Front* and *North Country, The*
E79 *Crowd Watches, The.* See *Guards*

E80 *Crown, The*
    a. Holograph manuscript, 48 pp.   TxU
        Chapters IV–VI
    b. Typescript, 35 pp.   TxU
        Chapters I–III
    c. Carbon typescript, 11 pp.   CU
        Chapter II
    d. Carbon typescript, 6 pp.   NmU
        Chapter III, incomplete, pp. 6–11 only
    e. Carbon typescript, 13 pp.   Smith
        Chapter I

E81 *Crown, Note to The*
    a. Holograph manuscript, 2 pp.   TxU
        MS titled: *Note to the Crown*
        Tedlock pp. 244–5
    b. Corrected typescript, 2 pp.   CU
        Tedlock p. 245

E81.5 *Crucifix Across the Mountains, The*
    a. Holograph manuscript, 6 pp.   TxU
        Tedlock pp. 179–80, Powell 70
    b. Carbon typescript, 8 pp.   TxU
    MSS titled: *Christs in the Tirol*

E82 *Cruelty and Love.* See *Love on the Farm*

E82.3 *Cry of the Masses*
    Carbon typescript   See E266

E83 *Daddy-Do-Nothing*
    Carbon typescript   See E266

E83.5 *Dance of the Sprouting Corn, The*
    a. Holograph manuscript, 6 pp.   Private
        Tedlock pp. 182–3, Powell 73
    b. Page proofs   See E246.2

E84 *Daughter-in-Law, The*
    a. Holograph manuscript, 63 pp.   NN
    b. Typescript, 105 pp.   TxU
    c. Carbon typescript, 106 pp.   CU
    d. Typescript prompt copy, 164 pp.   USal
        MS titled: *My Son's My Son*
        Adapted by Walter Greenwood for his production
        at Playhouse Theatre, London, 1936

E85 *Daughter of the Great Man*
    a. Holograph manuscript   See E49
    b. Corrected carbon typescript, 1 p.   See E49

E86 *Daughters of the Vicar*
    a. Holograph manuscript, 1 p.   Lazarus
       A fragment (p. 23) from an early version
    b. Holograph manuscript, 67 pp.   Lazarus
       A complete draft, heavily revised with substantial excisions:
       pp. 1–23, 14 [24], 24–6 [25–7], 17–22 [28–33],–[34],–[35],
       24–31 [36–43], 31 [44], 33–49 [45–61], 49–54 [62–7]
       First 45 pp. are close to *Time and Tide* version of
       Two Marriages (C214)
       MS titled: *Two Marriages*
    c. Two carbon typescripts, 44 pp., 44 pp.   CU
       Revision of second version, incomplete
       Equivalent to first IX and a half sections of *The*
       Prussian Officer and Other Stories version
       Published in *Time and Tide* as *Two Marriages* (C214)
       MS titled: *Two Marriages*
    d. Holograph ms and corrected typescript, 59 pp.   Lazarus
       MS: 1–14, 14A [15], 15–24 [16–25], TS: 19–23 (also num-
       bered 24–28), [26–30], MS: 24 (29) [31], TS: 25 (30) [32],
       MS: 26 (31) [33], TS: 29–52 (32–50, 50A, 51–4) [34–57], MS:
       53–4 (55–6) [58–9]
       A complete later version
       The 30 pp. of heavily corrected typescript are
       from an earlier version
       Unpublished in this version

E87 *David* (A play)
    a. Holograph manuscript, 191 pp.   Lazarus
       pp. 1–70, 80–94, 94B, 95–121, 121B, 122–48, 150–5, 155B,
       156–7, 170,157–71, 170–3, 173B, 174–8, 178B, 180–6, 172–4,
       174B, 175–8
       Two versions of last two scenes, many pages crossed out
       Tedlock pp. 123–4, Powell 69A
    b. Corrected typescript, 118 pp.   TxU
    c. Corrected page proofs, 123 pp.   TxU
    d. Author's proof copy with holograph corrections   Unlocated
       Melvin Rare Book Catalogue (1949) item no. 32 (F53)

E87.1 *David, German translation* (A play)
    a. Holograph manuscript, 254 pp.   CU
        Translated by Lawrence and Frieda Lawrence
    b. Corrected typescript, 104 pp.   CU
        MS titled: *David, ein Schauspiel*
        Tedlock pp. 124–5, Powell 69B

E87.2 *David, Music for* (A play)
    a. Holograph manuscript, 4 pp.   NhD
        Lyrics and notes
        With letter of 16 October 1926 to Robert Atkins
    b. Holograph manuscript, 6 pp.   TxU
        Tedlock p. 20

E88 *David* (An essay)
    a. Corrected carbon typescript, 7 pp.   CU
        Tedlock pp. 180–1, Powell 82
    b. Carbon typescript, 8 pp.   TxU

E89 *Death of the Baron, The*
    Holograph manuscript, 4 pp.   See E317

E90 *Decision, A*
    a. Holograph manuscript, 1 p.   See E317

E90.5 *Delilah and Mr. Bircumshaw*
    a. Holograph manuscript, 11 pp.   CU
        An early version, incomplete, pp. 9–19 only
        MS untitled, begins: Then "Come into the
        kitchen," said Mrs. Bircumshaw...
        Tedlock p. 41, Powell 51D
    b. Typescript, 13 pp.   TxU

E91 *Democracy*
    a. Corrected carbon typescript, 29 pp.   CU
        Tedlock pp. 132–3, Powell 112
    b. Carbon typescript, 28 pp.   Smith
    c. Carbon typescript, 36 pp.   NmU
    d. Carbon typescript, 36 pp.   TxU

E92 *Demon Justice*
    a. Holograph manuscript   See E302
    b. Carbon typescript, 1 p.   See E319.1

E93 *Diary*
    Holograph manuscript, 13 pp.   CU
    In Notebook with *Birds, Beasts and Flowers*
    Tedlock pp. 87–101, Powell 56

E94 *Dim Recollections.* See *Narcissus*

E94.5 *Disagreeable Advice*
    a. Holograph manuscript   See E320.1
    b. Holograph manuscript   See E320.2

E95 *Discipline*
    a. Holograph manuscript, 2 pp.   See E317
    b. Holograph manuscript   See E320.1
        Two drafts
        See also *Prophet*
    c. Holograph manuscript, 1 p.   TxU
        A three-stanza fragment
        Tedlock pp. 79–81
    d. Holograph manuscript, 3 pp.   TxU
        Tedlock pp. 77–9, Powell 52
        See also *Prophet*
    e. Holograph manuscript   See E320.2

E95.5 *Discord in Childhood*
    a. Holograph manuscript   See E320.1
    b. Holograph manuscript   See E320.2

E96 *Do Women Change?*
    a. Holograph manuscript, 4 pp.   TxU
        Tedlock p. 232, Powell 84A
    b. Corrected typescript, 7 pp.   CSt
    c. Corrected carbon typescript, 8 pp.   See E27

E97 *Doe at Evening, A*
    Typescript, 1 p.   ICU

E98 *Dog-Tired*
    a. Holograph manuscript   See E213
    b. Holograph manuscript, 2 pp.   See E317

E98.5 *Dolour of Autumn*
    a. Holograph manuscript   See E320.1
    b. Holograph manuscript, 2 pp.   MH
    c. Holograph manuscript   See E320.2
    MSS titled: *Dolor of Autumn*

E99 *Don Juan*
    Holograph manuscript, 1 p.   See E320.6

E99.5 *Don't Look at Me*
    Holograph manuscript, 1 p.   See E302

E100 *Dostoevsky*
    a. Holograph manuscript, 8 pp.   NN
        Titled by Murry: *On Tragedy* (c202)
    b. Typescript, 4 pp.   TxU
    c. Typescript, 5 pp.   N
    d. Typescript and carbon typescript, 6 pp., 6 pp.   N

E101 *Dragon of the Apocalypse, Introduction to*
    a. Holograph manuscript, 21 pp.   CU
        Tedlock pp. 141–3, Powell 95
    b. Carbon typescript, 24 pp.   CU
    c. Carbon typescript, 20 pp.   CU
    d. Carbon typescript, 13 pp.   CU

E101.3 *Drained Cup, The*
    Holograph manuscript   See E213

E101.5 *Drama, A*
    a. Holograph manuscript   See E320.1
    b. Holograph manuscript, 9 pp.   See E320.4

E102 *Dream.* See *Dream-Confused*

E103 *Dream-Confused*
    a. Holograph manuscript   See E317
        Two drafts
    b. Holograph manuscript   See E213

E104 *Dreams Old and Nascent*
    a. Holograph manuscript, 9 pp.   See E317
        Two drafts
    b. Holograph manuscript   See E320.1
    c. Holograph manuscript, 5 pp.   TxU
        Dreams Old and Nascent: Old, incomplete
        Includes *Prophet*
        Tedlock pp. 77–9, Powell 52
    d. Holograph manuscript, 5 pp.   See E320.4
    e. Holograph manuscript   See E320.2

E105 *Drill in the Heat*
    a. Holograph manuscript   See E49
    b. Corrected manuscript   See E49

E105.5 *Drunk*
    a. Holograph manuscript   See E320.1
    b. Holograph manuscript, 4 pp.   See E320.4
    c. Typescript, 3 pp.   See E320.5

E106 *Duc de Lauzun, The*
    a. Holograph manuscript, 8 pp.   CU
       First version
       Tedlock pp. 245–7, Powell 89
    b. Carbon typescript, 8 pp.   TxU
    c. Two carbon typescripts, 8 pp., 8 pp.   CU
    d. Holograph manuscript, 9 pp.   CU
       Second version
       Title *The Duc de Lauzun* struck out, begins: There is something
       depressing about French eighteenth-century literature...
       Published as *The Good Man*
       Tedlock pp. 245–7, Powell 89
    e. Carbon typescript, 9 pp.   CU
    f. Carbon typescript, 9 pp.   TxU

E107 *Dull London*
    a. Holograph manuscript, 4 pp.   TxU
       MS titled: *Why I Don't Like Living in London*
       Tedlock p. 222, Powell 84A
    b. Corrected carbon typescript, 4 pp.   See E27
    c. Carbon typescript, 4 pp.   CU
       MS titled: *Why I Don't Like Living in London*

E107.5 *Dusk-flower, look hither...*
    Holograph manuscript, 1 p.   N
    With letter of 15 December 1910 to Louie Burrows

E108 *Dust in the East*
    a. Holograph manuscript   See E49
    b. Corrected carbon typescript, 1 p.   See E49

E109 *Eagle in New Mexico*
    a. Holograph manuscript   See E47
    b. Holograph manuscript   See E47
    b. Holograph manuscript, 5 pp.   TxU
    c. Holograph manuscript, 3 pp.   CSmH
       Powell 63A
    d. Corrected typescript, 3 pp.   TxU

E110 *Eastwood* or *Eastwood—Evening*. See *Little Town at Evening, The*

E110.5 *Editorial Office*
    a. Holograph manuscript   See E266
    b. Carbon typescript   See E266

E111 *Education and Sex*. See *Fantasia of the Unconscious*

E112 *Education of the People*
    a. Holograph manuscript, 116 pp.   TxU
        Tedlock pp. 131–2, Powell 111
    b. Two carbon typescripts, 143 pp., 143 pp.   CU
    c. Carbon typescript, 142 pp.   TxU
        Lacking p. 141

E112.3 *Ego Bound Women*
    Holograph manuscript   See E302

E112.5 *Elephant*
    a. Holograph manuscript or typescript   See E314.6
    b. Holograph manuscript   See E47

E113 *Elephants of Dionysus, The*
    a. Holograph manuscript, 1 p.   CU
        Tedlock pp. 212–3, Powell 84A
    b. Two carbon typescripts, 2 pp., 2 pp.   CU
    c. Carbon typescript, 2 pp.   TxU

E113.2 *Eloi, Eloi Lama Sabachthani?*
    a. Holograph manuscript, 3 pp.   PLeB
        An early version, incomplete
    b. Holograph manuscript, 3 pp.   ICU
        Extracts of another early version, incomplete
        In Harriet Monroe's hand
        MS titled: *Passages from Ecce Homo*
    c. Holograph manuscript, 4 pp.   NNPM

E113.3 *Elysium*
    Holograph manuscript, 1 p.   TxU
    In *Women in Love* notebook
    MS titled: *The Blind*

E113.4 *Emasculation*
    Holograph manuscript, 1 p.   See E266

E113.5 *Embankment at Night, Before the War: Charity*
    a. Holograph manuscript, 4 pp.   See E317
        Two drafts
    b. Holograph manuscript   See E320.3
        A fragment
    c. Holograph manuscript, 1 p.   See E320.4
    d. Holograph manuscript   See E320.2
    e. Holograph manuscript, 1 p.   See E269.5

E113.6 *Embankment at Night, Before the War: Outcasts*
    a. Holograph manuscript, 3 pp.   See E317

b. Holograph manuscript   See E320.2
    Two drafts
c. Holograph manuscript, 4 pp.   See E269.5

E 1 1 3.9 *End, The*
a. Holograph manuscript   See E320.1
b. Holograph manuscript   See E320.2

E 1 1 4 *End of Another Home Holiday*
a. Holograph manuscript, 5 pp.   See E317
    Two drafts
b. Holograph manuscript   See E320.3
    Two drafts and two fragments
c. Holograph manuscript, 3 pp.   See E213

E 1 1 4.3 *Endless Anxiety*
a. Holograph manuscript   See E320.1
b. Holograph manuscript   See E320.2

E 1 1 4.5 *England, My England*
Corrected galley proofs, 5 pp.   NCL

E 1 1 4.8 *Enkindled Spring, The*
a. Holograph manuscript   See E320.1
    See also *Troth with the Dead* and *At a Loose End*
b. Holograph manuscript   See E320.2

E 1 1 5 *Enslaved by Civilization*
a. Holograph manuscript, 4 pp.   TxU
    Tedlock pp. 234–5, Powell 84A
b. Carbon typescript, 8 pp.   See E27

E 1 1 5.6 *Epistle from Thelma, An*
Holograph manuscript   See E320.1

1 1 5.7 *Erinnyes*
Holograph manuscript, 4 pp.   MH

E 1 1 5.9 *Erotic*
Holograph manuscript, 1 p.   See E320.4

E 1 1 6 *Escaped Cock, The*
Part I
a. Holograph manuscript, 22 pp.   IaE
    An early version
b. Corrected original and carbon typescript, 25 pp.   OkTU
    pp. 1–14, 14a [15], 15–24 [16–25]
    Tedlock pp. 65–6, Powell 19A
c. Corrected typescript, 23 pp.   TxU
    A later version

d. Corrected typescript, 32 pp.   TxU
    Final version
e. Corrected carbon typescript, 32 pp.   TxU
Part II
f. Holograph manuscript, 32 pp.   Lazarus
    An early version, incomplete
    Tedlock pp. 66–9, Powell 19B
g. Two typescripts, 10 pp., 10 pp.   CU
    Copies of early version of *Part II*, incomplete
h. Holograph manuscript, 49 pp.   IaE
i. Corrected typescript, 39 pp.   TxU
Parts I and II
j. Corrected carbon typescript, 52 pp.   NmU
    Corrections in another hand (Frieda Lawrence?)
k. Corrected page proofs, 102 pp.   CLU
    Black Sun Press, 1929 (A50a)
l. Corrected page proofs, 94 pp.   TxU
    Black Sun Press, 1929 (A50a)

E117 *Etruscan Places*
a. Holograph manuscript, 192 pp.   TxU

I.	*Cerveteri*	27 pp.
II.	*Tarquinia*	25 pp.
III.	*The Painted Tombs of Tarquinia (I)*	26 pp.
IV.	*The Painted Tombs of Tarquinia (II)*	34 pp.
V.	*Vulci*	33 pp.
VI.	*Volterra*	38 pp.
VII.	*The Florence Museum*	9 pp.

    MS titled: *Sketches of Etruscan Places*
b. Corrected typescript, 160 pp.   TxU
    Tedlock pp. 195–7, Powell 83A
c. Corrected carbon typescript, 56 pp.   TxU
    MS titled: *Sketches of Etruscan Places*
    Painted Tombs of Tarquinia II, The and *Vulci* only
d. Corrected original and carbon typescript, 56 pp.   TxU
    MS titled: *Sketches of Etruscan Places*
    Painted Tombs of Tarquinia II, The and *Vulci* only
e. Corrected carbon and original typescript, 84 pp.   OkTU
    Tarquinia, Painted Tombs of Tarquinia, The and *Volterra* only
f. Page proofs, 200 pp.   OkTU
    Secker, 1932 (A60)

E118 *Etruscan Places, Notes for*
    Holograph manuscript, 1 p.   CU
    Tedlock pp. 62–3

E118.5 *Etruscan Places, Photographs for*
    47 photographs of places and relics with Lawrence's
    titles and notes on 44   CU
    Tedlock p. 197, Powell 83B

E119 *Eve*
    Holograph manuscript, 2 pp.   See E317

E119.5 *Evening Land, The*
    Typescript   See E47

E120 *Evening of a Week-day*. See *Twilight*

E120.5 *Everlasting Flowers: For a Dead Mother*
    a. Holograph manuscript   See E320.2
    b. Holograph manuscript, 2 pp.   See E269.5
    c. Corrected carbon typescript, 2 pp.   See E205.8

E121 *Evolutions of Soldiers*. See *Guards*

E121.5 *Excursion Train*
    Holograph manuscript   See E317
    Two drafts

E121.7 *Factory Cities, The*
    Carbon typescript   See E266

E122 *Failure, A*
    Holograph manuscript, 1 p.   See E317

E123 *Fall of Day, The*
    Holograph manuscript, 1 p.   See E317

E124 *Fallen Leaves, Review of*
    a. Holograph manuscript, 8 pp.   TxU
        Tedlock p. 262, Powell 104
    b. Carbon typescript, 7 pp.   CU
    c. Carbon typescript, 8 pp.   CU
    d. Carbon typescript, 6 pp.   NmU
        Incomplete
    e. Carbon typescript, 8 pp.   TxU

E125 *Fantasia of the Unconscious*
    a. Corrected typescript and holograph manuscript, 126 pp.   Cu
    b. Corrected typescript and holograph manuscript, 138 pp.   TxU
    c. Corrected carbon typescript, 10 pp.   NmU
        From Chapter VIII

MS titled: *Education and Sex*
d. Carbon typescript, 7 pp.   NmU
   From Chapter XI
   MS titled: *On Love and Marriage*

E126 *Fantasia of the Unconscious, Foreword to*
a. Holograph manuscript, 16 pp.   TxU
b. Corrected typescript, 19 pp.   TxU
   MS titled: *Foreword. An Answer to Some Critics*
c. Carbon typescript, 13 pp.   TxU
   Incomplete
   MS titled: *Foreword Answer to Some Critics*

E127 *Fantasticalities.* See *Cavalleria Rusticana*

E128 *Far off the lily statues stand tall . . .* See *At the Front*

E128.7 *Fate and the Younger Generation*
   Holograph manuscript   See E302
   Two copies

E129 *Father Neptune's Little Affair with Freedom.* See *Neptune's
   Little Affair with Freedom*

E130 *Fight for Barbara, The*
a. Holograph manuscript, 56 pp.   TxU
   Tedlock pp. 119–21, Powell 67
b. Three typescripts, 92 pp., 92 pp., 92 pp.   CU
c. Carbon typescript, 92 pp.   TxU
d. Holograph manuscript, 4 pp.   TxU
   A fragment in Frieda Lawrence's hand
e. Carbon typescript, 1 p.   TxU
   A fragment, beginning of Act IV

E130.5 *Figs*
a. Holograph manuscript, 2 pp.   IaE
   MS titled: *Fig*
b. Holograph manuscript   See E47

E130.7 *Finding Your Level*
   Holograph manuscript   See E302

E131 *Fire*
a. Holograph manuscript, 1 p.   Unlocated
   Powell 63D
b. Two carbon typescripts, 2 pp., 2 pp.   See E315

E132 *Fire: did you ever warm your hands . . .*
   Holograph manuscript, 2 pp.   CU

MS titled by Powell: *Invocation to Fire*; published as *Fire* (A116)
Tedlock pp. 213–4, Powell 84A

E133 *Fireflies in the Corn*
  a. Holograph manuscript   See E318
  b. Typescript, 1 p.   See E316

E133.5 *Firelight and Nightfall*
  a. Holograph manuscript   See E320.6
    Second stanza only
  b. Holograph manuscript   NN
    First and second stanzas only
    MS titled: *Grief*
    With letter of 17 December 1913 to Edward Marsh
  See also *Grey Evening*

E134 *Fireworks in Florence*
  Holograph manuscript, 8 pp.   TxU
  MS titled: *Fireworks*
  Tedlock pp. 192–3, Powell 80

E134.1 *First Story*
  Holograph manuscript, 15 pp.   Lazarus

E134.2 *Flapper*
  a. Holograph manuscript, 1 p.   See E317
  b. Holograph manuscript   See E320.3
    A draft and a fragment
  c. Holograph manuscript, 1 p.   See E320.4
  d. Holograph manuscript   See E320.2
  e. Holograph manuscript, 1 p.   TxU
    MS titled: *Song*
    With letter of 23 December 1909 to Grace Crawford
  f. Holograph manuscript, 1 p.   See E269.5

E134.3 *Flapper Vote*
  a. Holograph manuscript   See E266
  b. Carbon typescript   See E266

E134.5 *Flat Suburbs, S. W., in the Morning*
  a. Holograph manuscript   See E320.1
  b. Holograph manuscript   See E320.2
  c. Holograph manuscript, 1 p.   See E269.5

E134.7 [*Flat-Foot's Song*]
  Holograph manuscript, 1 p.   TxU
  Included in *Him With His Tail in His Mouth* (An essay) and later published separately as a poem

E135 *Flowery Tuscany*
    a. Holograph manuscript, 31 pp.   Lazarus
         In three sections, each titled and numbered
            separately: 1–10, 1–10, 1–11
    b. Typescript, partly carbon, 33 pp.   CU
    c. Carbon typescript, 8 pp.   CU
         Part IV only
E135.5 *Fly in the Ointment, The*
    a. Holograph manuscript, 8 pp.   Private
    b. Corrected typescript, 8 pp.   TxU
    c. Typescript, 6 pp.   TxU
E136 *Flying Fish, The* (An unfinished story)
    a. Holograph manuscript, 40 pp.   Unlocated
         Tedlock pp. 55–6, Powell 17
    b. Corrected carbon typescript, 34 pp.   TxU
    c. Carbon typescript, 34 pp.   CU
E137 *Fooled* or *Fooled!* See *Rebuked*
E137.5 *Forecast*
    a. Holograph manuscript   See E320.1
    b. Holograph manuscript   See E320.2
E138 *Foreign Sunset*
    a. Holograph manuscript   See E49
    b. Corrected carbon typescript, 1 p.   See E49
E139 *Fox, The*
    a. Holograph manuscript, 22 pp.   Lazarus
         An early version
    b. Corrected galley sheets, 8 pp.   Dealer
         For *Hutchinson's Story Magazine* (C73.5)
    c. Holograph manuscript and corrected carbon
         typescript, 68 pp.   TxU
         Includes 30 pp. of typescript
         Powell 11
E140 *Fragment of Stained Glass, A*
    a. Holograph manuscript, 6 pp.   Private
         An early version, incomplete
         MS titled: *Legend* and *Legend: Ruby-Glass*
         MS on verso: *Ballad of Another Ophelia*
    b. Holograph manuscript, 8 pp.   TxU
         Another early version
         MS titled: *Legend*
         Tedlock pp. 31–2, Powell 20

E140.5
- c. Holograph manuscript, 26 pp. — N
- d. Carbon typescript, 10 pp. — CU
- e. Carbon typescript, 10 pp. — NmU

E140.5 *[Fragments]*
- a. *An . . .* — See E317
  Holograph manuscript, 2 pp.
  Second line begins: Never . . .
  MS untitled
- b. *Letters f . . . Unde[r]* — See E317
  Holograph manuscript, 2 pp.
- c. *. . . that where . . . three men went from Daniel . . .* — N
  Holograph manuscript, 1 p.
  MS untitled
  In the Louie Burrows collection

E141 *From a College Window*
- a. Holograph manuscript — See E317
- b. Holograph manuscript — See E320.2
- c. Holograph manuscript, 1 p. — See E269.5

E142 *Frost Flowers*
  Typescript 2 pp. — ICU

E143 *Gazelle Calf, The*
- a. Holograph manuscript — See E49
  MS titled: *Tales*
- b. Corrected carbon typescript, 1 p. — See E49
- c. Holograph manuscript — See E266

E143.3 *Gentleman from San Francisco, The*
  Corrected typescript, 32 pp. — TxU
  Corrections in Leonard Woolf's hand

E143.7 *Germans and Latins*
- a. Holograph manuscript, 10 pp. — Unlocated
  MS titled: *Summer in Tuscany, or, Germans and Latins*
  Powell 81
- b. Carbon typescript, 8 pp. — TxU
- c. Typescript and two carbon copies, 10 pp., 10 pp., 10 pp. — TxU
  Another version
  Published as *Germans and English* in *Phoenix II* (A107)

E144 *Getting On*
  Holograph manuscript, 8 pp. — OCU
  Early version of *Autobiographical Sketch* in *Assorted Articles* (A53)

E145 *Gifts of Fortune, Review of*
    a. Holograph manuscript, 8 pp.   TxU
        Tedlock pp. 256–7, Powell 98
    b. Carbon typescript, 7 pp.   TxU

E145.5 *Gipsy*
    a. Holograph manuscript, 1 p.   N
        MS titled: *Self-contempt*
        With letter of 6 December 1910 to Louie Burrows
    b. Holograph manuscript, 1 p.   TxU
    c. Holograph manuscript, 1 p.   See E269.5

E146 *Girl in Cairo, The*
    a. Holograph manuscript   See E49
    b. Corrected carbon typescript, 1 p.   See E49

E147 *Give Her a Pattern*
    a. Holograph manuscript, 6 pp.   CU
        MS titled: *Oh These Women!*
        Tedlock pp. 225–6, Powell 84A
    b. Carbon typescript, 7 pp.   CU
        MS titled: *Oh These Women!*
    c. Carbon typescript, 7 pp.   TxU
        MS titled: *Oh These Women!*
    d. Carbon typescript, 7 pp.   See E27

E147.5 *Give Me a Sponge*
    Carbon typescript   See E266

E148 *Glad Ghosts*
    a. Holograph manuscript, 9 pp.   Lazarus
        An early version, incomplete
        Powell 39B
    b. Holograph manuscript, 78 pp.   Lazarus
        Incorrectly paginated
        Powell 39A
    c. Corrected typescript, 48 pp.   CtY
        Lacking 1 p.
    d. Advance proof copy, 84 pp.   Dealer
        Ernest Benn, 1926 (A36)

E148.5 *Gloire de Dijon*
    a. Holograph manuscript   See E318
    b. Typescript   See E319.7

E149 *Going Back*
    Holograph manuscript   See E320

E150 *Good Man, The.* See *Duc de Lauzun, The*

E150.5 *Good Night*
    Holograph manuscript   See E319.3

E150.7 *Goose Fair*
    a. Holograph manuscript, 12 pp.   N
    b. Holograph manuscript, 13 pp.   Unlocated
        Powell 21

E151 *Grand Inquisitor, Introduction to The*
    a. Holograph manuscript, 14 pp.   CU
        Tedlock pp. 250–1, Powell 94
    b. Typescript, 13 pp.   CU
    c. Two carbon typescripts, 14 pp., 14 pp.   TxU

E151.7 *Great Newspaper Editor to His Subordinate, The*
    a. Holograph manuscript   See E266
        MS titled: *The Great Newspaper Editor and his Subordinate*
    b. Carbon typescript   See E266

E152 *Green*
    a. Holograph manuscript   See E318
    b. Typescript, 1 p.   See E316
    c. Typescript   See E319.7
    d. Typescript, 1 p.   CtY

E152.5 *Grey Evening*
    a. Holograph manuscript   NN
        Third stanza only
        MS titled: *Grief*
        With letter of 17 December 1913 to Edward Marsh
    b. Holograph manuscript   See E320.6
        First and third stanzas only
    See also *Firelight and Nightfall*

E153 *Grey Nurse, The*
    a. Holograph manuscript   See E319.5
    b. Holograph manuscript   See E49
    c. Corrected carbon typescript, 1 p.   See E49

E154 *Grief*
    Holograph manuscript   See E317

E154.7 *"Gross, Coarse, Hideous"*
    Holograph manuscript, 1 p.   CSt
    Untitled, begins: Lately I saw a sight most quaint...
    With letter of Saturday [14 September 1929] to Charles Lahr

E155 *Guards*
    a. Holograph manuscript, 3 pp.   See E317
    b. Holograph manuscript   See E320.2
    c. Holograph manuscript, 1 p.   CSt
        MS titled: *Guards! A Review in Hyde Park, 1913*
        MS subtitled: *The Crowd Watches, Evolutions of Soldiers*
    d. Holograph manuscript, 2 pp.   TxU
        MS titled: *Guards A Review in Hyde Park, before the War*
        MS subtitled: *The Crowd Watches, Evolutions of Soldiers,*
        Potency of Men

E156 *Guelder Roses*
    Holograph manuscript   See E317

E156.7 *Hands of the Betrothed, The*
    a. Holograph manuscript   See E320.1
    b. Holograph manuscript, 3 pp.   See E320.4

E157 *Hay Hut Among the Mountains, A*
    Carbon typescript, 13 pp.   CU
    Includes an erased ending, pp. 61–2
    MS titled: *A Hay-Hut Among the Mountains*
    Tedlock pp. 178–9

E158 *Heat, Review of*
    a. Holograph manuscript, 8 pp.   CU
        Tedlock p. 256, Powell 97
    b. Carbon typescript, 6 pp.   CU
        Incomplete

E159 *"Henry," she said, "I want to disappear for a year."* ...
    Holograph manuscript, 5 pp.   CU

E159.5 *Her Turn*
    Holograph manuscript, 10 pp.   Unlocated
    Powell 26

E160 *Hibiscus and Salvia Flowers*
    a. Holograph manuscript   See E47
    b. Holograph manuscript   See E314.4
    c. Typescript   See E314.5

E161 *Him With His Tail in His Mouth* (An essay)
    a. Holograph manuscript, 10 pp.   TxU
        Tedlock p. 139
    b. Corrected carbon typescript, 11 pp.   CU
        Tedlock pp. 139–40

Includes poems later published separately as *Him
With His Tail in His Mouth* and [*Flat-Foot's Song*]

E161.1 *Him With His Tail in His Mouth* (A poem)
    Holograph manuscript, 1 p.   TxU
    Included in *Him With His Tail in His Mouth* (An essay)
    and later published separately as a poem

E162 *Honeymoon*. See *Excursion Train*

E163 *Honour and Arms*. See *Prussian Officer, The*

E164 *Hopi Snake Dance, The*
    a. Holograph manuscript, 18 pp.   TxU
        Tedlock pp. 184–6, Powell 72
    b. Corrected carbon typescript, 19 pp.   CU
        Tedlock p. 186
    c. Page proofs   See E246.2

E164.5 *Hyde Park at Night, Before the War: Clerks*
    a. Holograph manuscript, 2 pp.   See E317
    b. Holograph manuscript, 1 p.   See E320.4
    c. Holograph manuscript   See E320.2
    d. Holograph manuscript, 1 p.   See E269.5

E164.9 *Hymn to Nothingness*
    Holograph manuscript, 3 pp.   TxU

E165 *Hymns in a Man's Life*
    Holograph manuscript, 6 pp.   N

E166.5 *I Am in a Novel*
    Holograph manuscript   See E319.4

E167 *If you are a woman, and if ever you can pray . . .*
    Holograph manuscript, 9 pp.   CU
    Tedlock pp. 73–4, Powell 51F

E168 *Illicit*. See *On the Balcony*

E169 *Image-Making Love*
    Holograph manuscript   See E319.1

E170 *In a Boat*
    a. Holograph manuscript, 2 pp.   See E317
    b. Holograph manuscript, 2 pp.   See E320.4
    c. Holograph manuscript   MH
        MS titled: *Tired of the Boat*
    d. Holograph manuscript   See E320.2
    e. Typescript, 1 p.   See E320.5

E170.2 *In Church*
    a. Holograph manuscript   See E317
        See also *At the Front* and *North Country, The* .
    b. Holograph manuscript   See E320.2
    c. Holograph manuscript, 1 p.   See E269.5

E170.3 *In Love*
    a. Holograph manuscript, 20 pp.   TxU
        MS titled: *More Modern Love*
        Tedlock pp. 63–4, Powell 41
    b. Typescript, 17 pp.   CtY
        MS titled: *Modern Love*

E170.7 *In Trouble and Shame*
    a. Holograph manuscript   See E320.2
    b. Typescript   See E314.3

E170.8 *Indians and an Englishman*
    a. Corrected typescript, 12 pp.   CtY
    b. Carbon typescript, 14 pp.   TxU

E171 *Indians and Entertainment*
    a. Holograph manuscript, 13 pp.   CU
        Tedlock p. 183, Powell 74
    b. Carbon typescript, 18 pp.   CU
    c. Carbon typescript, 18 pp.   TxU
    d. Page proofs   See E246.2

E172 [*Individual Consciousness v. the Social Consciousness, The*]
    a. Holograph manuscript, 6 pp.   TxU
        MS untitled, begins: The more one reads of modern novels ...
        Tedlock pp. 170–1, Powell 84A
    b. Carbon typescript, 6 pp.   CU
    c. Carbon typescript, 6 pp.   TxU

E173 *Inheritance, The*
    a. Holograph manuscript   See E320.1
        See also *Noise of Battle*
    b. Holograph manuscript   See E320.6
        See also *Noise of Battle*
    c. Holograph manuscript   See E320.2

E173.5 *Innocent England*
    Carbon typescript   See E266

E174 *Insouciance*
    a. Holograph manuscript, 4 pp.   TxU
        Tedlock pp. 220–1, Powell 84A

b. Carbon typescript, 5 pp.   See E27

E175 *Intimates*

  Holograph manuscript   See E319.1

E176 *Into a deep pond, an old sheep dip,* ... See *Wild Common, The*

E177 *Is England Still a Man's Country?*

  a. Holograph manuscript, 6 pp.   TxU

    Tedlock p. 226, Powell 84A

  b. Two corrected carbon typescripts, 4 pp., 4 pp.   CU

    Tedlock p. 227, Powell 84B

E177.3 *Island Pharisees, Review of*

  Holograph manuscript, 2 pp.   Unlocated

  Argus Book Shop catalogue no. 827 (1943) item no. 34

E177.4 *It depends! And that is always the disconcerting answer!* ...

  Holograph manuscript, 1 p.   Lazarus

  Tedlock pp. 163–4

E177.7 *It's Either You Fight or You Die*

  Holograph manuscript   See E319.4

E178 *Jeli the Shepherd.* See *Cavalleria Rusticana*

E179 *"Jeune Fille" Wants to Know, The*

  a. Holograph manuscript, 4 pp.   TxU

    Tedlock p. 220, Powell 84A

  b. Holograph manuscript, 1 p.   Lazarus

    A fragment, the final paragraph is written on a scrap torn from the foot of the last galley sheet for (A53)

E179.5 *Jeune Fille, The*

  Holograph manuscript, 1 p.   See E302

E180 *Jewess and the V. C., The*

  a. Holograph manuscript, 1 p.   See E319.3

  b. Holograph manuscript   See E49

  c. Corrected carbon typescript, 1 p.   See E49

E181 *Jimmy and the Desperate Woman*

  a. Holograph manuscript, 32 pp.   Lazarus

    Powell 37A

  b. Corrected typescript, 25 pp.   Lazarus

    Powell 37B

E181.3 *John Galsworthy*

  a. Holograph notes, 1 p.   TxU

    MS untitled, begins: The moon at her curve's summit floated at peace ...

Tedlock pp. 169–70
   b. Holograph manuscript, 16 pp.   TxU
     MS titled: *A Scrutiny of the Work of John Galsworthy*
     Tedlock pp. 171–2, Powell 87

E181.9 *Just Back from Snake Dance*
   a. Holograph manuscript, 2 pp.   CtY
   b. Typescript, 4 pp.   IEN

E182 *Kangaroo*
   a. Holograph manuscript, 572 pp.   TxU
     Chapters I–XVII (lacking Chapter XVIII)
     Tedlock pp. 16–8, Powell 6
   b. Holograph manuscript, 20 pp.   Private
     Chapter XVIII only
   c. Corrected typescript, 331 pp.   NN
     An early version, incomplete
   d. Corrected carbon typescript, 313 pp.   NN
     Carbon of above, incomplete
   e. Corrected carbon typescript, 569 pp.   NN
     Printer's copy

E182.3 *Kangaroo* (A poem)
   Holograph manuscript   See E47

E183 *Kiss, A*
   a. Holograph manuscript   See E320.1
     A draft and a fragment
   b. Holograph manuscript, 1 p.   See E320.6

E184 *Kisses in the Train*
   Holograph manuscript   See E213

E185 *Labour Battalion*
   Corrected galley proof, 1 p.   TxU

E186 *Lady Chatterley's Lover*
   a. Holograph manuscript, 398 pp.   TxU
     First version
     Tedlock pp. 20–1
   b. Holograph manuscript, 580 pp.   TxU
     Second version
     Tedlock pp. 23–4
   c. Holograph manuscript, 728 pp.   TxU
     Third version
     MS titled: *My Lady's Keeper*
     Tedlock pp. 24–7

    d. Holograph manuscript, 6 pp.   ICSo
        MS titled: *The Grange Farm*
        An early form of concluding letter, third version
    e. Corrected typescript, 3 pp.   TxU
        A fragment, conclusion of Chapter ɪx (i.e., xɪɪ)
        of the third version
    f. Corrected original and carbon typescript, 423 pp.   TxU
        Third version
        MS titled: *John Thomas and Lady Jane*
        Powell 8
    g. Corrected proof of title page, 1 p.   Dealer
        Argus Book Shop catalogue 827 (1943) item 40f

E187 *Ladybird, The*
    Holograph manuscript, 108 pp.   NN
        pp. [1]–15, 15–22 [16–23],—[24], 22–96 [25–99],
        95–103 [100–8] plus 6 blank pages

E188 *Land-Worker*
    a. Holograph manuscript   See E319.5
    b. Holograph manuscript   See E49
    c. Corrected carbon typescript, 1 p.   See E49

E189 *Last Hours*
    a. Holograph manuscript, 2 pp.   See E317
    b. Corrected typescript, 1 p.   CtY

E190 *Last Laugh, The*
    a. Holograph manuscript, 24 pp.   Lazarus
        Powell 38A
    b. Corrected typescript, 21 pp.   Lazarus
        Powell 38B

E190.5 *Last Lesson of the Afternoon*
    a. Holograph manuscript   See E320.1
    b. Holograph manuscript   See E213

E191 *Last Minute, The*
    a. Holograph manuscript   See E49
    b. Corrected carbon typescript, 1 p.   See E49

E192 *Last Poems*
    a. Holograph manuscript, 195 pp.   TxU
        In two notebooks
    b. Typescript and page proofs, 192 pp.   TxU
        Incomplete

E193 *Last Words to Miriam*
    a. Holograph manuscript   See E317
    b. Holograph manuscript   See E320.2
    c. Typescript, 1 p.   See E320.5

E193.3 *Late at Night*
    a. Holograph manuscript   See E320.1
    b. Holograph manuscript   See E320.2
    c. Holograph manuscript, 1 p.   See E269.5

E193.5 *Late at Night Along the Home Road*
    a. Holograph manuscript   See E320.1
    b. Holograph manuscript, 2 pp.   MH

E193.7 *Late in Life*
    a. Holograph manuscript, 2 pp.   See E317
    b. Holograph manuscript   See E320.2
    c. Holograph manuscript, 1 p.   See E269.5
    d. Corrected proof copy, 1p.   Private

E194 *Laura Philippine*
    a. Holograph manuscript   Unlocated
        Bumpus case no. 5 (F28.5)
    b. Corrected typescript, 7 pp.   CU

E194.1 *Laura Philippine, French translation*
    Carbon typescript, 7 pp.   CU
    Corrections in an unknown hand

E195 *Le Gai Savaire.* See *Study of Thomas Hardy*

E195.5 *Leaves of Grass, Flowers of Grass*
    Carbon typescript   See E266

E196 *Legend.* See *Fragment of Stained Glass, A*

E196.4 *Lessford's Rabbits*
    a. Holograph manuscript, 10 pp.   Heinemann
    b. Typescript   Unlocated
        Phoenix II (A107), p. 630

E196.5 *Lesson on a Tortoise, A*
    a. Holograph manuscript, 8 pp.   Heinemann
    b. Typescript   Unlocated
        Phoenix II (A107), p. 630

E196.6 *Let the flood rise and cover me . . .*
    Holograph manuscript, 1 p.   TxU
    Last two lines are an early version of *Grasshopper is a Burden*

E196.7 *Let Us Be Men*
  Holograph manuscript   See E319.4
E197*Letter from Germany*
  a. Holograph manuscript, 6 pp.   TxU
      Tedlock pp. 181–2, Powell 78
  b. Two carbon typescripts, 7 pp., 7 pp.   CU
E197.7 *Letter from Town: On a Grey Morning in March*
  a. Holograph manuscript, 2 pp.   See E317
  b. Holograph manuscript   See E320.2
  c. Holograph manuscript, 1 p.   See E269.5
E198 *Letter from Town: The Almond-Tree*
  a. Holograph manuscript, 2 pp.   See E317
  b. Holograph manuscript   See E320.3
      A draft and a fragment
  c. Holograph manuscript   See E320.2
  d. Holograph manuscript, 1 p.   See E269.5
E199 *Letter from Town The City.* See *Letter from Town: On a Grey
    Morning in March*
E200 *Life*
  a. Corrected typescript, 5 pp.   CU
      Tedlock p. 203
  b. Carbon typescript, 7 pp.   CU
E200.5 *Life History In Harmonies and Discords, A*
  Holograph manuscript   See E320.1
E201 *Lightning*
  a. Holograph manuscript, 2 pp.   See E317
  b. Printed copy   See E213
E202 *Lilies in the Fire*
  Holograph manuscript   See E213
E202.5 *Listening*
  a. Holograph manuscript   See E320.1
      Two drafts
  b. Holograph manuscript   See E320.2
      A draft and a stanza
  See also *Silence*
E203 *Litany of Grey Nurses*
  a. Holograph manuscript   See E49
  b. Corrected carbon typescript, 1 p.   See E49

E203.5 *Little Moonshine with Lemon, A*
    a. Holograph manuscript, 6 pp.   Unlocated
       Powell 75
    b. Typescript and two carbon copies, 5 pp., 5 pp., 5 pp.   TxU
       MS titled: "*Ye Gods, He Doth Bestride the Narrow*
       World Like a Colosses—!"
    c. Carbon typescript, 4 pp.   TxU
       MS titled: "*Ye Gods, He Doth Bestride the Narrow*
       World Like a Collosus—!"
    d. Page proofs   See E246.2

E204 *Little Novels of Sicily*
    Holograph manuscript, 181 pp.   TxU
    Tedlock pp. 270–2, Powell 107

E204.5 *Little Town at Evening, The*
    a. Holograph manuscript, 1 p.   See E317
    b. Holograph manuscript   See E320.2
       A fragment
    c. Holograph manuscript, 1 p.   IaE

E205 *Little Wowser, The*
    a. Holograph manuscript   See E319.4
    b. Holograph manuscript, 1 p.   See E302
    c. Carbon typescript   See E319.1

E205.2 *Lizard*
    Galley proof   See E319.6

E205.3 *London Mercury*
    a. Holograph manuscript   See E266
    b. Carbon typescript   See E266

E205.8 *Look! We Have Come Through!*
    a. Holograph manuscript   Unlocated
       With letter of 18 February 1917 to C. Carswell
    b. Corrected proofs, 163 pp.   Lazarus
    c. Author's copy with holograph corrections, 168 pp.   TxU
       Chatto and Windus, 1917 (A17), for (A43)
       Includes corrected and uncorrected carbon typescripts of
       Bei Hennef   1p.
       Everlasting Flowers (*Everlasting Flowers:*
         For a Dead Mother)   2 pp.
       Coming Awake   1 p.
       Song of a Man Who is Loved   1 p.

E206 *Looking Down on the City*
    Corrected typescript, 5 pp.   CLU

E207 *Loss*
    Holograph manuscript   See E317

E208 *Lost.* See *Turned Down*

E209 *Lost Girl, The*
    a. Holograph manuscript, 20 pp.   ICSo
        An early version, incomplete
        Untitled, begins: My mother made a failure of her life...
        Published in Cambridge edition of *The Lost Girl* as
        Elsa Culverwell
        Tedlock pp. 44–6, Powell 51A
    b. Holograph manuscript, 450 pp.   TxU
    c. Typescript, 486 pp.   Smith
        Incomplete, pp. 1–42, 42A, 43–127, 151–217,
        219–403, 405–510
    d. Corrected page proofs, 122 pp.   Unlocated
        City Book Auction catalogue no. 247 (18
        September 1943) item no. 175

E209.5 *Lotus and Frost*
    a. Holograph manuscript   See E320.2
    b. Typescript, 1 p.   See E320.5

E210 *Love* (An essay)
    a. Corrected typescript, 7 pp.   CU
        Tedlock p. 202
    b. Carbon typescript, 10 pp.   CU

E211 *Love Among the Haystacks*
    Carbon typescript, 60 pp.   CU
    Tedlock pp. 42–3

E212 *Love Comes Late.* See *Late in Life*

E212.5 *Love on the Farm*
    a. Holograph manuscript   See E320.1
    b. Holograph manuscript   See E213

E212.7 *Love-Passage, A*
    a. Holograph manuscript   See E320.1
        Two drafts
    b. Holograph manuscript, 2 pp.   See E320.4

E213 *Love Poems*
    a. Holograph manuscript, 37 pp.   TxU

Kisses in the Train
Cruelty and Love (*Love on the Farm*)
Lilies in the Fire
Coldness in Love
Reminder
Bei Hennef
Lightning
Song-Day in Autumn
A Pang of Reminiscence
A White Blossom
Red Moon-Rise
Return
The Appeal
Repulsed
Dream-Confused
Corot
Morning Work
Transformations
Renascence
Dog-Tired

b. Holograph manuscript, 8 pp.   N

Wedding Morn	3 pp.
Cherry Robbers	1 p.
End of Another Home-Holiday (*End of Another Home Holiday*)	3 pp.
Aware	1 p.

Both were originally one manuscript; *Lightning* supplied
from a printed source
    Tedlock pp. 82–5, Powell 53

c. Holograph manuscript   Unlocated

Michael-Angelo
Violets
Whether or Not
A Collier's Wife (*The Collier's Wife*)
The Drained Cup
The Schoolmaster
  I. *A Snowy Day in School*
  II. *The Best of School*
  III. *Afternoon in School* (*The Last Lesson of the Afternoon*)

477

E214 *Love Poems and Others*
    a. Corrected page proofs, 72 pp.   TxU
        Powell 54
    b. Author's copy with holograph corrections   NBuU
        Duckworth, 1913 (A3)

E214.3 *Love Song, A*
    a. Holograph manuscript   N
        A four-line fragment, published as [*To Toss
        the Troubled Night Long*] in (A104)
        In the Louie Burrows collection
    b. Holograph manuscript   See E320.1
    c. Holograph manuscript, 1 p.   See E320.4

E214.7 *Love Storm*
    Holograph manuscript, 2 pp.   See E320.6

E215 ... *Love Was Once a Little Boy*
    a. Holograph manuscript, 17 pp.   TxU
        MS titled: *Love*
    b. Corrected carbon typescript, 21 pp.   CU
        Tedlock pp. 208–9

E216 *Lovely Lady, The* (story)
    a. Holograph manuscript, 32 pp.   Lazarus
    b. Corrected typescript, 42 pp.   CtY
        Original version
    c. Carbon typescript, 20 pp.   CU
        Condensed version for *The Black Cap* (B23)
    d. Carbon typescript, 2 pp.   NmU
        Incomplete, pp. 19–20 only

E216.5 *Lovely Lady, The* (book)
    Proof copy, 208 pp.   TxU
    Spacing between lines was adjusted and the number
    of pp. increased before publication
    Secker, 1933 (A63)

E217 *Lucifer*
    Holograph manuscript   See E319.1

E218 *Luhan Story.* See *Wilful Woman, The*

E219 *Luhan Story, Notes for.* See *Wilful Woman, Notes for The*

E219.5 *Magnificent Democracy*
    Carbon typescript   See E266

E220 *Maiden's Prayer*
    a. Holograph manuscript   See E319.5

b. Holograph manuscript	See E49
c. Corrected carbon typescript, 1 p.	See E49

E221 *Making Love to Music*
a. Holograph manuscript, 13 pp.	CtY
Tedlock p. 210, Powell 84A	
b. Two carbon typescripts, 11 pp., 11 pp.	CU
c. Carbon typescript, 11 pp.	TxU

E222 *Making Pictures*
a. Holograph manuscript, 6 pp.	TxU
Tedlock pp. 233–4, Powell 114	
b. Corrected carbon typescript, 9 pp.	TxU
Tedlock p. 234, Powell 114	

E222.5 *Malade*
a. Holograph manuscript	See E320.1
In prose	
b. Holograph manuscript	See E320.2
In prose	

E223 *Man at Play on the River, A.* See *Movements: 4. A Man at Play on the River*

E224 *Man Hauling a Wagon*
a. Holograph manuscript	See E49
b. Corrected carbon typescript, 1 p.	See E49

E225 *Man in the Street, The*
a. Holograph manuscript, 1 p.	See E314
b. Holograph manuscript	See E266
c. Two carbon typescripts, 1 p., 1 p.	See E315
d. Typescript and carbon copy, 1 p., 1 p.	CLU
Tedlock p. 114, Powell 62	

E226 *Man is a Hunter*
a. Holograph manuscript, 4 pp.	TxU
Tedlock pp. 191–2	
b. Carbon typescript, 3 pp.	NmU
c. Carbon typescript, 5 pp.	TxU

E226.5 *Man is essentially a soul…*
Holograph manuscript, 4 pp.	TxU
A philosophical fragment	
Tedlock p. 138, Powell 118	

E227 *Man Who Died, A*
a. Holograph manuscript, 2 pp.	N

MS untitled, begins: Ah stern, cold man . . .
In the Louie Burrows collection

b. Holograph manuscript	See E320.1
c. Holograph manuscript	See E318
d. Holograph manuscript, 3 pp.	See E320.4
e. Holograph manuscript	See E320.2
f. Holograph manuscript, 3 pp.	See E269.5
g. Holograph manuscript	See E314.1
h. Typescript 1 p.	See E316

E227.3 *Man Who Loved Islands, The*

a. Holograph manuscript, 44 pp.	PLeB
b. Corrected typescript, 30 pp.	CtY

E227.4 *Man Who Was Through with the World, The* (An unfinished story)

a. Holograph manuscript, 10 pp.	CU

Untitled, begins: There was a man not long ago,
who felt he was through with the world . . .
Tedlock pp. 62–3, Powell 51E

b. Typescript, 7 pp.	TxU
c. Carbon typescript, 7 pp.	CU

E227.5 *Man's Image*

Holograph manuscript	See E302

E227.7 *Market Day*

a. Holograph manuscript, 9 pp.	TxU

MS titled: *Mornings in Mexico. Saturday Morning*
Tedlock pp. 186–7, Powell 76

b. Page proofs	See E246.2

E228 *Married in June*

a. Holograph manuscript, 1 p.	See E317
b. Holograph manuscript	See E320.2

A fragment

E229 *Married Man, The*

a. Holograph manuscript, 67 pp.	CU

Tedlock pp. 118–9, Powell 66

b. Typescript, 84 pp.	CU
c. Typescript, 84 pp.	TxU
d. Two typescripts, 62 pp., 62 pp.	CU
e. Typescript, mostly carbon, 63 pp.	OkTU

Incomplete, all MSS lacking pp. 1–5

E229.5 *Martyr a la Mode*

a. Holograph manuscript, 2 pp.	N

MS untitled, begins: Ah Life, God, Law, whatever
name you have...
Published as [*Two Fragments on Sleep*] (A104b)
In the Louie Burrows collection
b. Holograph manuscript See E320.2

E230 *Master in His Own House*
a. Holograph manuscript, 4 pp. TxU
 MS titled: *Men Must Rule*
 Tedlock pp. 220–1, Powell 84A
b. Carbon typescript, 5 pp. See E27

E230.9 *Mastro-don Gesualdo*
a. Holograph manuscript, 582 pp. TxU
 Tedlock pp. 267–9, Powell 106
b. Typescript, 401 pp. TxU
c. Corrected galley proofs, 128 pp. TxU

E231 *Mastro-don Gesualdo, Introductions to*
a. Holograph manuscript, 6 pp. TxU
 First version, unpublished
 MS titled: *Introductory Note*
 Tedlock p. 269, Powell 106
b. Corrected typescript, 4 pp. TxU
c. Holograph manuscript, 6 pp. TxU
 Second version, published as *Biographical Note* in
 Mastro-don Gesualdo (A28a)
 MS titled: *Introductory Note*
 Includes also principal characters, bibliography
d. Two carbon typescripts, 5 pp., 5 pp. TxU
 MS titled: *Introductory Note*
e. Holograph manuscript, 17 pp. TxU
 Third version, published in *Phoenix* (A76)
 MS titled: *Introduction to Mastro don Gesueldo—Translation
 from Verga* (written in unknown hand)
 Tedlock pp. 269–70, Powell 106
f. Carbon typescript, 15 pp. CU
 Third version
 Untitled, begins: It seems curious that modern Italian
 literature...
g. Corrected typescript, 10 pp. Lazarus
 Another version, substantially unpublished

E232 *Matriarchy*
    a. Holograph manuscript, 6 pp.   TxU
          Tedlock p. 230, Powell 84A
    b. Typescript, 7 pp.   See E27
    c. Typescript, 7 pp.   MH

E233 *Mediterranean in January*
    a. Holograph manuscript, 2 pp.   TxU
          Tedlock p. 101, Powell 118
    b. Carbon typescript, 3 pp.   CU
    c. Carbon typescript, 3 pp.   TxU

E233.5 *Meeting Among the Mountains*
    Carbon typescript, 2 pp.   TxU

E233.7 *Memoirs of the Foreign Legion, Introduction to*
    Holograph manuscript, 59 pp.   Smith
    MS titled: *Memoir of Maurice Magnus*
    pp. 1–31, 31, 32–47, 47a, 48, 49, 51–8

E234 *Men and Women.* See *Men Must Work and Women As Well*

E234.5 *Men in New Mexico*
    a. Corrected typescript, 2 pp.   TxU
    b. Typescript, 2 pp.   TxU

E235 *Men Must Work and Women As Well*
    a. Holograph manuscript, 12 pp.   TxU
          MS titled: *Men and Women*
          Tedlock p. 237, Powell 84A
    b. Carbon typescript, 18 pp.   CU
          MS titled: *Men and Women*
    c. Carbon typescript, 18 pp.   See E27

E236 *Mercury*
    a. Holograph manuscript, 9 pp.   CU
          Tedlock pp. 193–4, Powell 79
    b. Carbon typescript, 8 pp.   CU
    c. Carbon typescript, 8 pp.   TxU

E237 *Merry-Go-Round, The*
    a. Holograph manuscript, 152 pp.   CU
          Tedlock p. 117, Powell 65
    b. Typescript, 146 pp.   CU
    c. Carbon typescript, 146 pp.   TxU
    d. Two typescripts, 110 pp., 110 pp.   CU
    e. Carbon typescript, 110 pp.   OkTU
          Two pages are original typescript

E238 *Mesopotamia*
    a. Holograph manuscript   See E49
    b. Corrected carbon typescript, 1 p.   See E49
E239 *Message to a Perfidious Soldier*
    a. Holograph manuscript   See E319.3
    b. Holograph manuscript   See E49
    c. Corrected carbon typescript, 1 p.   See E49
E239.3 *Michael Angelo*
    a. Holograph manuscript   See E320.1
    b. Holograph manuscript, 1 p.   See E320.4
    c. Holograph manuscript   See E213
E240 *Mr Noon*
    a. Holograph manuscript, 450 pp.   TxU
    b. Corrected typescript, 407 pp.   TxU
    c. Corrected carbon typescript, 143 pp.   TxU
        Tedlock pp. 48–9, Powell 13
    d. Carbon typescript, 156 pp.   CU
E240.7 *Modern Lover, A*
    Holograph manuscript, 56 pp.   NN
E241 *Modern Novel, The.* See *Novel, The*
E241.5 *Modern Prayer*
    Carbon typescript   See E266
E242 *Money-Madness*
    Carbon typescript   See E319.1
E242.3 *Monologue of a Mother*
    a. Holograph manuscript   See E320.1
    b. Holograph manuscript   See E318
    c. Holograph manuscript   See E320.2
E242.4 *Moon Memory*
    Holograph manuscript   See E302
E242.5 *Moon New-Risen*
    Holograph manuscript, 1 p.   See E320.4
E242.7 *Moonrise*
    a. Holograph manuscript   See E320.4
        See also *Sea, The*
    b. Typescript   See E319.8
E243 *Morality.* See *Man's Image*
E244 *Morality and the Novel*
    a. Holograph manuscript, 9 pp.   TxU

First version
Tedlock pp. 166–7, Powell 85D
b. Typescript and carbon copy, 8 pp., 8 pp.   TxU
c. Carbon typescript, 8 pp.   CU
d. Holograph manuscript, 10 pp.   TxU
Second version
Tedlock pp. 166–7, Powell 85D
e. Carbon typescript, 10 pp.   CU
Tedlock p. 168
f. Carbon typescript, 9 pp.   CU
g. Carbon typescript, 9 pp.   TxU
h. Typescript, 7 pp.   TxU

E245 *More Modern Love.* See *In Love*

E246 *Morning Work*
a. Holograph manuscript   See E320.1
b. Holograph manuscript, 1 p.   TxU
c. Holograph manuscript   See E213

E246.2 *Mornings in Mexico*
Page proofs   Unlocated
Union Square Book Shop catalogue (30 September 1930)
item no. 68

E246.8 *Mortal Coil, The*
Typescript, 8 pp.   TxU
Incomplete

E247 *Mosquito, The.* See *Mosquito Knows, The*

E247.3 *Mosquito Knows, The*
Holograph manuscript   See E302

E249 *Mother and Daughter*
a. Holograph manuscript, 44 pp.   TxU
Tedlock pp. 72–3, Powell 46
b. Carbon typescript, 34 pp.   CU
c. Corrected galley proofs, 8 pp.   TxU

E249.5 *Mother, Introduction to The*
a. Holograph manuscript, 7 pp.   CU
Tedlock p. 249, Powell 91
b. Carbon typescript, 6 pp.   CU
c. Carbon typescript, 6 pp.   TxU

E250 *Mother of Sons, The.* See *Monologue of a Mother*

E251 *Mother's Son in Salonika*
a. Holograph manuscript   See E319.5

b. Holograph manuscript   See E49
c. Corrected carbon typescript, 1 p.   See E49

E251.5 *Mountain Lion*
Holograph manuscript   See E47

E252 *Mournful Young Man*
Carbon typescript   See E319.1

E253 *Mourning*
a. Holograph manuscript   See E49
b. Corrected carbon typescript, 1 p.   See E49

E254 *Movements*. See *Baby Running Barefoot, Baby Asleep After Pain, A, Virgin Youth, Movements: 4. A Man at Play on the River* and *Guards*

E254.5 *Movements: 4. A Man at Play on the River*
Holograph manuscript, 2 pp.   See E317

E255 *Movements in European History*
a. Holograph manuscript, 134 pp.   Lazarus
    Incomplete, Chapters I–VIII and 6 pp. of Chapter IX
    MS titled: *Landmarks in European History*
b. Author's copy with holograph corrections   IaE
    Oxford, 1921 (A17)

E256 *Movements in European History, Epilogue to*
Carbon typescript, 24 pp.   CLU

E257 *Mowers, The*. See *Youth Mowing, A*

E258 *Mozo, The*
a. Holograph manuscript, 13 pp.   TxU
    MS titled: *Mornings in Mexico. Monday Morning*
    Tedlock pp. 186–7, Powell 76
b. Corrected carbon typescript, 14 pp.   TxU
    MS titled: *Mornings in Mexico. The Mozo*
    Tedlock p. 188, Powell 76
c. Page proofs   See E246.2

E259 *Munitions*
a. Holograph manuscript   See E49
b. Corrected carbon typescript, 1 p.   See E49

E260 *Mushrooms*
Holograph manuscript, 1 p.   OCU
An unfinished autobiographical sketch

E261 *Music for David*. See *David, Music for* (A play)

E261.4 *My Little Critics*
a. Holograph manuscript   See E266

b. Carbon typescript   See E266

E261.8 *My Native Land*
Carbon typescript   See E266

E262 *My Naughty Book*
a. Holograph manuscript, 1 p.   See E319.4
b. Carbon typescript, 1 p.   See E319.1

E263 *My Skirmish with Jolly Roger.* See *A Propos of Lady Chatterley's Lover*

E264 *Mystery*
a. Holograph manuscript, 1 p.   See E320.6
b. Holograph manuscript   See E320.2
    Two drafts
c. Typescript, 1 p.   See E320.5

E264.3 *Narcissus*
a. Holograph manuscript, 2 pp.   See E317
b. Holograph manuscript   See E320.2
c. Holograph manuscript, 1 p.   See E269.5

E264.7 *Near the Mark*
Holograph manuscript, 1 p.   N
With letter of 6 December 1910 to Louie Burrows

E265 *Neither Moth nor Rust*
a. Holograph manuscript   See E319.5
b. Holograph manuscript   See E49
c. Corrected carbon typescript, 1 p.   See E49

E265.5 *Neptune's Little Affair with Freedom*
a. Holograph manuscript, 1 p.   See E314
b. Holograph manuscript, 1 p.   See E266
c. Carbon typescript   See E266

E266 *Nettles*
a. Holograph manuscript, 6 pp.   TxU
    A Rose is not a Cabbage   1 p.
    The Man in the Street
    Britannia's baby   1 p.
    Change of Government   1 p.
    The British Workman And the Government   1 p.
    Clydesider
    Flapper Vote   1 p.
    Neptune's little affair with Freedom   1 p.
b. Holograph manuscript, 5 pp.   Lazarus
    Puss-Puss!   1 p.

London Mercury
My Little Critics
Never had a Daddy (*Emasculation*)   1 p.
Editorial Office   3 pp.
The Great Newspaper Editor and His
    Subordinate (*The Great Newspaper*
    Editor to His Subordinate)
With letter of 23 August [1929] to Charles Lahr

c. Carbon typescript, 18 pp.   CU

A Rose is not a Cabbage
Britannia's Baby
Change of Government
The British Workman and the Government
Clydesider
Flapper Vote
Neptune's little affair with freedom
My Native Land
The British Boy
13000 People
Innocent England
Give me a sponge
Puss-Puss!
London Mercury
My little critics
Daddy-Do-Nothing
Question
Editorial Office
British Sincerity
The Great Newspaper Editor to his subordinate
Modern Prayer
Cry of the Masses
What have they done to you—?
The People
The factory cities
Leaves of grass, flowers of grass
Magnificent democracy

E267 *Never*...See [*Fragments*] *An*...

E268 *New Eve and Old Adam*
    a. Holograph manuscript, 14 pp.   OkTU
      Powell 27

E269

b. Two carbon typescripts, 38 pp., 38 pp.   CU

E269 *New Mexico*

a. Holograph manuscript, 8 pp.   Unlocated
     Tedlock pp. 194–5, Powell 71

b. Typescript, 12 pp.   TxU

c. Carbon typescript, 12 pp.   CU

E269.5 *New Poems*

Holograph manuscript, 47 pp.   TxU

From a College Window	1 p.
Flapper	1 p.
In the Street (Birdcage Walk)	1 p.
Letter from Town: The Almond Tree (Letter from Town: The Almond-Tree)	1 p.
Flat Suburbs S. W., in the Morning (Flat Suburbs, S. W., in the Morning)	1 p.
Thief in the Night	1 p.
Letter from Town: On a Grey Evening in March (Letter from Town: On a Grey Evening in March)	1 p.
Suburbs on a Hazy Day	1 p.
Hyde Park at Night—Clerks (Hyde Park at Night, Before the War: Clerks)	1 p.
Gipsy	1 p.
Two-Fold (Twofold)	1 p.
Under the Oak	1 p.
Sigh No More	1 p.
Suburbs on the Hills in the Evening (Parliament Hill in the Evening)	1 p.
Piccadilly Circus at Night—Street Walkers (Piccadilly Circus at Night: Street-Walkers)	1 p.
Tarantella	1 p.
In Church	1 p.
Piano	1 p.
Embankment at Night—Charity (Embankment at Night, Before the War: Charity)	1 p.
Phantasmagoria (Late at Night)	1 p.
Next Morning	1 p.
Palimpsest of Twilight (Twilight)	1 p.
Embankment at Night—Outcasts (Embankment at Night, Before the War: Outcasts)	4 pp.
Winter in the Boulevard	1 p.
School on the Outskirts	1 p.

Sickness	1 p.
Everlasting Flowers (*Everlasting Flowers: For a Dead Mother*)	2 pp.
The North Country	1 p.
Bitterness of Death (*A Man Who Died*)	3 pp.
Late in Life	1 p.
Reading a Letter	1 p.
Apprehension (*Noise of Battle*)	1 p.
Twenty Years Ago	1 p.
Heimweh (*At the Front*)	1 p.
Débâcle (*Reality of Peace, 1916*)	1 p.
Narcissus	1 p.
Spring Sunshine (*Autumn Sunshine*)	1 p.
On That Day	1 p.

Includes title page, dedication and table of contents, 3 pp.

b. Proofs   Unlocated
    With letter of 23 September 1918 to Amy Lowell

E269.6 *New Poems, Preface to*
  a. Holograph manuscript, 3 pp.   TxU
  b. Holograph manuscript, 3 pp.   Dealer
    MS titled: *Verse Free and Unfree*
    With letter of 29 August 1919 to Thomas Moult

E270 *Newthorpe in 2927.* See *Autobiographical Fragment*

E270.5 *Next Morning*
  a. Holograph manuscript   See E320.1
    Incomplete
  b. Holograph manuscript   See E320.2
    Two drafts
  c. Holograph manuscript, 1 p.   See E269.5

E271 *Nigger Heaven, Flight, Manhattan Transfer and In Our Time, Review of*
  a. Holograph manuscript, 10 pp.   CLU
    MS titled: *Four Reviews: Nigger Heaven, Flight, Manhattan Transfer, In Our Time*
    Powell 99
  b. Carbon typescript, 11 pp.   CU
    MS titled: *Reviews of Books*
  c. Carbon typescript, 11 pp.   TxU
    MS titled: *Reviews of Books*

E272 *Nightingale, The*
    a. Holograph manuscript, 8 pp.   CtY
    b. Corrected typescript, 5 pp.   CU
    c. Typescript, 7 pp.   TxU
    d. Typescript and carbon copy, 8 pp., 8 pp.   TxU
    e. Holograph manuscript, 8 pp.   Lazarus
        Incomplete; published in (B40)
        In the hands of Frieda Lawrence and an
        unidentified person

E272.5 *No News*
    Corrected proof, 1 p.   Lazarus

E273 *Noah's Flood*
    a. Holograph manuscript, 11 pp.   TxU
        A longer early version
        Tedlock pp. 125–6, Powell 118
    b. Holograph manuscript, 10 pp.   CU
        A later version
        Tedlock pp. 127–8, Powell 84
    c. Carbon typescript, 8 pp.   CU
    d. Carbon typescript, 8 pp.   NmU
    e. Carbon typescript, 8 pp.   TxU

E273.5 *Noble Englishman, The*
    Holograph manuscript, 1 p.   See E302

E274 *Nobody Loves Me*
    a. Holograph manuscript, 12 pp.   CtY
        Notebook cover titled: *Three Essays for Vanity Fair*
        Powell 117
    b. Carbon typescript, 12 pp.   TxU
    c. Typescript, 13 pp.   TxU
    d. Carbon typescript, 13 pp.   CU

E274.7 *Noise of Battle*
    a. Holograph manuscript   See E320.1
        See also *Inheritance, The*
    b. Holograph manuscript   See E320.6
        See also *Inheritance, The*
    c. Holograph manuscript   See E320.2
    d. Holograph manuscript, 1 p.   See E269.5

E275 *None of That!*
    a. Holograph manuscript, 33 pp.   PPRF
    b. Typescript, 33 pp.   CU

E275.5 *North Country, The*
    a. Holograph manuscript   See E317
      See also *In Church* and *At the Front*
    b. Holograph manuscript   See E320.2
    c. Holograph manuscript, 1 p.   See E269.5

E276 *Nostalgia*
    a. Holograph manuscript, 1 p.   See E319
    b. Holograph manuscript, 1 p.   Lazarus

E277 *Notes concerning "The Hand of Man"*
    Holograph manuscript, 2 pp.   TxU
    Written to Earl H. Brewster

E278 *Nothing depresses me more* ... See *Autobiographical Fragment*

E279 *Nottingham and the Mining Countryside*
    a. Holograph manuscript, 9 pp.   CU
    b. Carbon typescript, 13 pp.   CU
    c. Carbon typescript, 14 pp.   NmU

E280 *Novel, The*
    a. Holograph manuscript, 13 pp.   TxU
      A shorter early version
      MS titled: *The Modern Novel*
      Tedlock p. 162, Powell 85B
    b. Corrected typescript, 7 pp.   TxU
      Tedlock p. 163
    c. Holograph manuscript and corrected typescript, 12 pp.   CtY
      pp. 1–5 typescript, pp. 6–12 holograph manuscript

E281 *Novel and the Feelings, The*
    a. Holograph manuscript, 12 pp.   TxU
      Tedlock p. 169, Powell 85C
    b. Typescript, 9 pp.   TxU
    c. Two carbon typescripts, 9 pp., 9 pp.   CU

E281.3 *November by the Sea*
    Galley proof   See E319.6

E281.7 *Now It's Happened*
    Holograph manuscript, 2 pp.   TxU
    MS untitled, begins: One cannot now help thinking...

E282 *O! Americans*
    a. Holograph manuscript, 8 pp.   COMC
      Powell 64E
    b. Two carbon typescripts, 9 pp., 9 pp.   See E315

E282.5 *O! Start a Revolution*
    a. Holograph manuscript   See E319.4
    b. Holograph manuscript   See E302

E283 *Obsequial Ode*
    a. Holograph manuscript, 1 p.   ICN
       MS titled: *Obsequial Chant*
    b. Holograph manuscript, 2 pp.   Lazarus
    c. Corrected typescript, 2 pp.   Lazarus
    d. Typescript, 1 p.   TxU

E284 *Odour of Chrysanthemums*
    a. Holograph manuscript, 6 pp.   TxU
       A fragment from an early version
       Tedlock pp. 33–7, Powell 22
    b. Holograph manuscript, 39 pp.   TxU
       A later version
       In Louie Burrows' hand
       Tedlock pp. 33–7, Powell 22
    c. Corrected proof sheets, 35 pp.   N
       Includes 8 pp. of holograph corrections
       For *English Review*

E285 *Oh These Women!* See *Give Her a Pattern*

E286 *Old Adam, The*
    Holograph manuscript, 27 pp.   Lazarus
    Powell 23

E287 *Old Orchard, The*
    Holograph manuscript, 2 pp.   OCU

E288 *On Being a Man*
    Corrected typescript, 7 pp.   See E27

E288.5 *On Being in Love*
    Holograph notes, 1 p.   Private
    Tedlock pp. 203–4

E289 *On Being Religious*
    a. Holograph manuscript, 2 pp.   Private
       A fragment
       MS untitled, begins: There is no real battle between me
       and Christianity...
       Tedlock pp. 134–6, Powell 84A
    b. Corrected typescript, 7 pp.   NmU
    c. Carbon typescript, 7 pp.   TxU
    d. Carbon typescript, 11 pp.   CU

E290 *On Coming Home*
    a. Holograph manuscript, 11 pp.   TxU
    b. Corrected typescript, 11 pp.   CU
        Tedlock pp. 206–8
    c. Typescript, 8 pp.   TxU
        A shorter and possibly earlier version

E291 *On Human Destiny*
    Corrected typescript, 8 pp.   See E27

E292 *On Love and Marriage.* See *Fantasia of the Unconscious*

E292.5 *On Taking the Next Step*
    Holograph manuscript, 3 pp.   Private
    Incomplete
    Tedlock pp. 205–6, Powell 84

E293 *On That Day*
    a. Holograph manuscript   See E320.1
    b. Holograph manuscript   See E318
    c. Holograph manuscript, 1 p.   See E269.5
    d. Typescript, 1 p.   See E316

E294 *On the Balcony*
    a. Holograph manuscript   See E318
    b. Holograph manuscript, 1 p.   See E320.6
    c. Typescript   See E319.7
    d. Typescript, 1 p.   See E316

E294.5 *On the Lago di Garda*
    a. Holograph manuscript, 26 pp.   TxU
        The Spinner and the Monks   8 pp.
        The Lemon Garden of the Signor di P.—
            (*The Lemon Gardens*)   10 pp.
        The Theatre   8 pp.
        MS titled: *By the Lago di Garda*
        MS titled in other hand: *Italian Studies*
    b. Corrected typescript, 2 pp.   NCRecord
        A fragment, pp. 15–16 of *The Lemon Gardens*

E295 *On the March*
    a. Holograph manuscript, 2 pp.   See E317
    b. Corrected typescript, 2 pp.   CtY

E296 *Once*
    a. Holograph manuscript, 13 pp.   TxU
    b. Carbon typescript, 14 pp.   CU
        Tedlock pp. 43–4

E297 *Origins of Prohibition, Review of The*
    a. Holograph manuscript, 7 pp.   TxU
        Tedlock p. 255, Powell 96
    b. Carbon typescript, 5 pp.   CU
    c. Carbon typescript, 5 pp.   TxU

E297.5 *Other women have reared in me* . . .
    Holograph manuscript, 1 p.   See E319.2

E298 *Overtone, The*
    a. Holograph manuscript, 12 pp.   TxU
    b. Corrected carbon typescript, 21 pp.   NmU

E299 *Ownership*
    a. Holograph manuscript, 4 pp.   CU
        Tedlock p. 227, Powell 84A
    b. Typescript, 5 pp.   See E27
    c. Carbon typescript, 5 pp.   CU

E300 *Paintings, Introduction to These*
    a. Holograph manuscript, 37 pp.   TxU
        Powell 113
    b. Typescript and carbon copy, 58 pp., 58 pp.   CU
    c. Carbon typescript, 58 pp.   CLU
    d. Carbon typescript, 58 pp.   TxU
    e. Carbon typescript, 58 pp.   NNC
    MSS titled: *Introduction to Painting*

E300.5 *Pan in America*
    a. Holograph manuscript, 7 pp.   TxU
        An early version
        Tedlock pp. 136–7
    b. Holograph manuscript, 12 pp.   NcD
    c. Carbon typescript, 18 pp.   TxU

E301 *Pang of Reminiscence, A*
    Holograph manuscript   See E213

E302 *Pansies*
    a. Holograph manuscript, 10 pp.   Unlocated
        Powell 60
        Finding Your Level
        Altercation
        What is Man Without an Income?
        Climbing Up
        Canvassing for the Election
        A Rise in the World

b. Holograph manuscript, 2 pp.   TxU
    Morality (*Man's Image*)   1 p.
    Roses
    The Gazelle Calf
    The Mosquito (*The Mosquito Knows*)   1 p.
    Self Pity (*Self-Pity*)
    Seaweed (*Sea-Weed*)
    MS titled: *Pensées for Achsah* [Brewster] *from D. H. L.*
c. Holograph manuscript notes, 1 p.   TxU
    A list of 9 titles and first lines
    Tedlock p. 71
d. Holograph manuscript, 99 pp.   TxU
    An early version
    Includes a list of titles of poems
    Tedlock pp. 104–12, Powell 59
e. Holograph manuscript, 14 pp.   Forster
    In unidentified hand
    Don't look at me! (*Don't Look at Me*)   1 p.
    When I read Shakespeare (*When I*   1 p.
       Read Shakespeare)
    Salt of the earth— (*Salt of the Earth*)
    The Little Wowser   1 p.
    The Jeune Fille   1 p.
    Fate and the Younger Generation   1 p.
    What Matters   2 pp.
    Women want Fighters for their   1 p.
       lovers— (*Women Want Fighters for*
       Their Lovers)
    Ego-bound Women— (*Ego Bound Women*)
    Moon Memory   1 p.
    O Start a revolution— (*O! Start a Revolution*)
    There is rain in me— (*There is Rain in me*)
    Why—? (*Why?*)   1 p.
    What is he? (*What is He?*)
    The Noble Englishman   1 p.
    Be a Demon   1 p.
    Demon Justice   1 p.

What does She Want? (*What Does*　　　1 p.
　　She Want?)
Fate and the Younger Generation
f. Corrected typescript, 102 pp.　　　　　Lazarus
　An early version
g. Typescript, 108 pp.　　　　　　　　　Forster
　pp. [i]–[iii] contents, [1]–2 Foreword, 1–65, 69,
　66–8, 70–103; sent to Guy Aldred to consider for
　publication; with a few minor corrections in an
　unidentified hand
h. Galley proofs, 98 pp.　　　　　　　　Unlocated
　Union Square Book Shop Catalogue (30
　September 1930) item no. 67

E302.5 *Pansies, Foreword to*
Holograph manuscript, 2 pp.　　　　　　　TxU
With letter of 27 April 1929 to Laurence Pollinger

E303 *Pansies, Introduction to*
a. Holograph manuscript, 2 pp.　　　　　　CU
b. Holograph manuscript, 3 pp.　　　　　　TxU
　Another version
　Tedlock p. 103, Powell 59

E303.3 *Paradise Re-Entered*
Holograph manuscript, 2 pp.　　　　　See E320.6

E303.5 *Parliament Hill in the Evening*
a. Holograph manuscript　　　　　　　See E320.1
b. Holograph manuscript　　　　　　　See E320.2
c. Holograph manuscript, 1 p.　　　　　See E269.5

E304 *Passing-Bell, A*
a. Holograph manuscript, 2 pp.　　　　　See E317
b. Holograph manuscript　　　　　　　See E320.3
　A fragment
c. Holograph manuscript, 2 pp.　　　　　See E320.4
d. Holograph manuscript　　　　　　　See E320.2

E304.3 *Passing Visit to Helen*
Holograph manuscript, 2 pp.　　　　　See E320.4

E305 *Peace*
a. Holograph manuscript　　　　　　　　See E47
b. Holograph manuscript, 1 p.　　　　　　ViU
　MS titled: *Slopes of Etna*

With letter of 1 December 1920 to Professors John
Calvin Metcalf and James Southall Wilson

E305.5 *Pear-Blossom*
    Holograph manuscript, 2 pp.   See E319.2

E306 *Pedro De Valdivia, Review of*
    Corrected typescript, 7 pp.   CU
    Tedlock p. 257

E307 *Peep Show, Review of*
    a. Holograph manuscript, 6 pp.   CU
        An early version, incomplete, pp. 3–8 only
        MS titled in unknown hand: *Review of Puppet Show*
        Tedlock pp. 258–9, Powell 101
    b. Two carbon typescripts, 5 pp., 5 pp.   TxU
        MS titled: *Review of Puppet Show*
    c. Holograph manuscript, 10 pp.   CU

E308 *Pentecostal.* See *Shades*

E308.2 *People*
    a. Holograph manuscript   See E320.1
    b. Holograph manuscript   See E320.4
        See also *Street Lamps*

E308.3 *People, The*
    Carbon typescript   See E266

E308.8 *Physician, The*
    Holograph manuscript, 1 p.   N
    With letter of 15 December 1910 to Louie Burrows

E309 *Piano*
    a. Holograph manuscript, 2 pp.   See E317
    b. Holograph manuscript   See E320.2
        Two drafts
    c. Holograph manuscript, 1 p.   See E269.5

E309.5 *Piccadilly Circus at Night: Street-Walkers*
    a. Holograph manuscript, 1 p.   See E317
    b. Holograph manuscript, 1 p.   See E320.4
    c. Holograph manuscript   See E320.2
    d. Holograph manuscript, 1 p.   See E269.5

E310 *Pictures, Introduction to*
    a. Holograph manuscript, 17 pp.   TxU
        Tedlock pp. 172–3, Powell 109
    b. Carbon typescript, 13 pp.   CU

E311 *Pictures on the Walls*
- a. Holograph manuscript, 9 pp.   Unlocated
  - MS titled: *Pictures on the Wall*
  - Tedlock p. 238, Powell 115
- b. Carbon typescript, 14 pp.   TxU
  - Tedlock pp. 238–9, Powell 115

E312 *Pietà*
- a. Holograph manuscript   See E47
- b. Corrected carbon typescript, 1 p.   See E47

E313 *Plumed Serpent, The*
- a. Holograph manuscript, 594 pp.   TxU
  - First version
  - MS titled: *Quetzalcoatl*
- b. Corrected typescript, 360 pp.   MH
- c. Holograph manuscript, 806 pp.   TxU
  - Second version
  - MS titled: *Quetzalcoatl*
- d. Corrected original and carbon typescript, 743 pp.   TxU
  - Powell 7
- e. Corrected typescript, 18 pp.   CLU
  - Chapter VI only
- f. Corrected typescript, 5 pp.   CU
  - Chapter VII, incomplete
  - Tedlock pp. 18–20
- g. Corrected carbon typescript, 24 pp.   CU
  - Chapters VI and VII, latter is incomplete
  - Tedlock pp. 18–20
- h. Two sets of galley proofs, 156 pp., 160 pp.   TxU
  - One set lacks sheet 156; the other has 3 duplicate sheets

E314 *Poems*
- Holograph manuscript, 4 pp.   CLU
  - Tedlock pp. 112–4, Powell 62
  - *Bells*   1 p.
  - *The Triumph of the Machine*   1 p.
  - *Father Neptune's Little Affair with Freedom*   1 p.
    - (*Neptune's Little Affair with Freedom*)
  - *The Man in the Street*   1 p.

E314.1 *Poems*
- Holograph manuscript   Unlocated
  - Three poems sent to Austin Harrison, his letter of 6 April
  - 1911 to Lawrence

Sorrow
A Husband Dead (A Man Who Died)
1 unidentified

E314.2 *Poems*

Holograph manuscript or typescript   Unlocated
Four poems with letter of 27 February 1914 to Harold Monro
Ballad of Another Ophelia
3 unidentified

E314.3 *Poems*

Typescript   Unlocated
Two batches of poems sent to Amy Lowell, her letter of
15 February 1916 to Lawrence, including:
At the Window
Brooding Grief
In Trouble and Shame
Perfidy (Turned Down)

E314.4 *Poems*

Holograph manuscript   Unlocated
Three poems with letter of 7 March 1921 to J. C. Squire,
see also letter of 4 April 1921 to Curtis Brown and *Diary*
entry for 7 March 1921
Hibiscus and Salvia Flowers
Purple Anemones
Pomegranate

E314.5 *Poems*

Typescript   Unlocated
Three poems sent to Robert Mountsier, letter of 4 April 1921
to Curtis Brown
Hibiscus and Salvia Flowers
Purple Anemones
The Ass

E314.6 *Poems*

Holograph manuscript or typescript   Unlocated
Two poems sent to Austin Harrison, letter of 10 February 1923
to Curtis Brown
Elephant
1 unidentified

E315 *Poems*

a. Two carbon typescripts, 30 pp., 30 pp.   CU
Restlessness   1 p.

499

Traitors, oh, liars . . .	1 p.
Softly, then, softly . . .	2 pp.
Fire	2 pp.
And what do I care . . .	3 pp.
Change of Life	9 pp.
O! Americans	9 pp.
The Man in the Street	1 p.
Rainbow	2 pp.

   b. Carbon typescript, 30 pp.   TxU

     A copy of each poem as above, except: *Fire* (two different copies), *Change of Life* (two copies)

E316 *Poems*

   Typescript, 7 pp.   CU

   Tedlock pp. 85–6

The Mowers (*A Youth Mowing*)	1 p.
Green	1 p.
Fireflies in the Corn	1 p.
A Woman and Her Dead Husband (*A Man Who Died*)	1 p.
Illicit (*On the Balcony*)	1 p.
Birthday (*On That Day*)	1 p.

E317 *Poems*

   Holograph manuscript, 84 pp.   N

   A Nottingham University College Notebook, also containing Latin notes. Includes three torn pages and two inside covers. The numbering given for some poems is that of the notebook

   The Crow (*In Church, At the Front, The North Country*)

   Honeymoon (second draft, *Excursion Train*)

   Sorrow (second draft)

   Last Words to Muriel (*Last Words to Miriam*)

    1 *Campions*

    2 *Guelder Roses*

    3 *From a College Window*

    4 *Study*, 2 pp.

    5 *The last hours of a holiday* (*Last Hours*), 2 pp.

    6 *The Fall of Day*, 1 p.

    7 *Evening of a Week-day* (*Twilight*), 1 p.

    8 *Eastwood—Evening* (*The Little Town at Evening*), 1 p.

    9 *The Piano* (*Piano*), 2 pp.

   10 *Lightning*, 2 pp.

   11 *Married in June*, 1 p.

[Untitled], *Into a deep pond, an old sheep dip,...* (*The Wild Common*), 2 pp.

14 *The Worm Turns*, 1 p.

15 *On the Road* (*On the March*), 2 pp.

16 *The Death of the Baron*, 4 pp.

17 *Song* (*Flapper*), 1 p.

18 *Love comes late* (*Late in Life*), 2 pp.

19 *A Tarantella* (*Tarantella*), 2 pp.

20 *Song* (*Song: Wind Among the Cherries*), 2 pp.

[Fragment, page torn], *An...*, *2* pp.

22 *Cherry-Robbers* (*Cherry Robbers*), 1 p.

23 *In a Boat*, 2 pp.

24 *Dim Recollections* (*Narcissus*), 2 pp.

Renaissance (*Renascence*), 2 pp.

A Failure, 1 p.

A Winter's Tale, 1 p.

A Decision, 1 p.

Dog-tired (*Dog-Tired*), 2 pp.

A Train at Night, 1 p.

Violets for the Dead (*Violets*), 2 pp.

Baby Songs Ten Months Old (*Ten Months Old*), 1 p.

Trailing Clouds, 1 p.

Triolet (*Birdcage Walk*), 1 p.

Coming Home From School Rondeau Redoublé [*Rondeau of a Conscientious Objector*), 2 pp.

Eve, 2 pp.

After School, 1 p.

School (*A Snowy Day in School*), 1 p.

A Snowy Day at School, 3 pp.

Letters from Town The Almond Tree (*Letter from Town: The Almond-Tree*), 2 pp.

Letter from Town The City (*Letter from Town: On a Grey Morning in March*), 2 pp.

[Fragment, page torn], *Letters f...Unde[r]*, 2 pp.

Discipline, 2 pp.

A Still Afternoon in School (first draft, *Dreams Old and Nascent*), 4 pp.

A Still Afternoon in School (second draft, *Dreams Old and Nascent*), 5 pp.

Reading in the Evening (*Reading a Letter*), 1 p.

Movements 1. *A Baby Running Barefoot* (*Baby Running Barefoot*), 1 p.

    2. *A Baby Asleep After Pain*, 1 p.

    3. *The Body Awake* (*Virgin Youth*), 1 p.

    4. *A Man at Play on the River*, 2 pp.

    5. *The Review of the Scots Guards* (*Guards*), 3 pp.

Restlessness, 3 pp.

A Passing Bell (*A Passing-Bell*), 2 pp.

Lost (*Turned Down*), 2 pp.

After the Theatre (*Embankment at Night, Before the War: Outcasts*), 3 pp.

Brotherhood (first draft, *Embankment at Night, Before the War: Charity*), 2 pp.

The end of another Home-holiday (first draft, *End of Another Home Holiday*), 2 pp.

Brotherhood (second draft, *Embankment at Night, Before the War: Charity*), 2 pp.

End of another Home-holiday (second draft, *End of Another Home Holiday*), 3 pp.

The Songless 1. *Today* (*Hyde Park at Night, Before the War: Clerks*), 2 pp.

    2. *Tomorrow* (*Piccadilly Circus at Night: Street-Walkers*), 1 p.

[Untitled], *When on the autumn roses . . .* (*Song-Day in Autumn*), 2 pp.

Amour (*Autumn Sunshine*), 2 pp.

At the Window, 2 pp.

Weeknight Service, 2 pp.

Fooled (*Rebuked*), 1 p.

Dream (first draft, *Dream-Confused*)

Dream (second draft, *Dream-Confused*), 1 p.

Bereavement (two drafts)

Loss

Brooding (*Brooding Grief*)

Grief

Sorrow (first draft)

Honeymoon (first draft, *Excursion Train*)

E318 *Poems*

    Holograph manuscript, 9 pp.   CSt

    The Mowers (*A Youth Mowing*)

    Green

    All of Roses (*River Roses, Gloire de Dijon, Roses on the Breakfast Table, All of Roses: IV*)

    Fireflies in the Corn

    A Woman and Her Dead Husband (*A Man Who Died*)

    The Wind, the Rascal

    Illicit (*On the Balcony*)
    Birthday (*On That Day*)
    The Mother of Sons (*Monologue of a Mother*)

E319 *Poems*

Holograph manuscript, 4 pp.   ICU

Tommies in the Train	1 p.
After the Opera	1 p.
War-Baby	
Bread Upon the Waters	1 p.
Nostalgia	1 p.

E319.1 *Poems*

a. Holograph manuscript, 3 pp.   NBuU

True love at last! (*True Love at Last*)	1 p.
Lucifer	
Sphinx	1 p.
Intimates	
Image-making love (*Image-making Love*)	1 p.
Ultimate Reality	

b. Corrected carbon typescript, 5 pp.   NBuU

Mournful young man (*Mournful Young Man*)	1 p.
There is no way out (*There is no Way Out*)	
Money-madness (*Money-Madness*)	
My naughty book (*My Naughty Book*)	1 p.
The little wowser (*The Little Wowser*)	1 p.
The young and their moral guardians (*The Young and their Moral Guardians*)	
Volcanic Venus	1 p.
What does she want? (*What Does She Want?*)	
Wonderful spiritual women (*Wonderful Spiritual Women*)	
Poor bit of a wench! (*Poor Bit of a Wench!*)	
Demon justice (*Demon Justice*)	1 p.

With a letter of 10 August 1929 to Hilda Doolittle

E319.2 *Poems*

Holograph manuscript, 11 pp.   NN

The Chief Mystery	3 pp.
At the Cearne	2 pp.
Pear-Blossom	2 pp.
Assuming the Burden	2 pp.

She Was a Good Little Wife   1 p.

[Untitled], *Other women have reared in me* . . . 1 p.

E319.3 *Poems*

Holograph manuscript, 4 pp.   N

Elixir (The Jewess and the V. C.)   1 p.

Good Night   1 p.

Sympathy

Love Message (Message to a Perfidious Soldier) 1 p.

The Witch: I

The Witch: II   1 p.

In the Louie Burrows collection

E319.4 *Poems*

Holograph manuscript, 3 pp.   Lazarus

   For God's Sake (Let Us Be Men)   1 p.

   O! Start a revolution! (O! Start a Revolution)

   It's either you fight or you die (It's Either You Fight or You Die)

   My naughty book (My Naughty Book)   1 p.

   An old acquaintance (The Little Wowser)   1 p.

   Character in a novel (I Am in a Novel)

With letter of 28 December 1928 to Charles Wilson

E319.5 *Poems*

Holograph manuscript, 3 pp.   N

   At Midnight (Mother's Son in Salonika)   1 p.

   Beloved (Land-Worker)

   Moth and Rust (Neither Moth nor Rust)   1 p.

   Irreverent Thoughts (Maiden's Prayer)

   The Prophet in the Rose Garden (The Grey Nurse)

   Two-fold (Casualty)   1 p.

In the Louie Burrows collection

E319.6 *Poems*

Galley proofs, 3 pp.   CtY

   To Let Go or to Hold On—? (To Let Go or to Hold On?)

   Things Men Have Made

   Whatever Man Makes— (Whatever Man Makes)

   Work

   What Would You Fight For?

Attila
Sea-Weed
Lizard
Censors
November by the Sea
MS titled: *Ten Poems*

E319.7 *Poems*
    Typescript, 5 pp.   NN
       All of Roses (River Roses, Gloire de Dijon, Roses on
          the Breakfast Table, All of Roses: IV)
       Green
       Illicit (On the Balcony)
       The Wind, the Rascal

E319.8 *Poems*
    Typescript   Unlocated
    Three poems sent to Harriet Monroe, letter of
    29 August 1917 from J. B. Pinker
    Moonrise   1 unidentified
    Craving for Spring

E320 *Poems*
    Holograph manuscript, 3 pp.   ICU
       Town (Town in 1917)
       Going Back
       Winter-Lull

E320.1 *Poems*
    Holograph manuscript notebook   Private
    A Nottingham University College Notebook
       Discipline (two drafts, *Discipline, Prophet*)
       A Still Afternoon Dreams Old and Nascent (Dreams Old and Nascent)
       BABY MOVEMENTS 1. *Running Barefoot (Baby Running Barefoot)*
            2. "*Trailing Clouds*" (*A Baby Asleep After Pain*)
       Restlessness
       A Beloved (Love on the Farm)
       The Punisher
       An Epistle from Thelma
       An Epistle from Arthur (Disagreeable Advice)
       Epilogue from Thelma (Forecast)
       Sickness
       A Day in November (Next Morning)
       A LIFE HISTORY IN HARMONIES AND DISCORDS

First Harmony
Discord
Second Harmony
Discord
Third Harmony (Twenty Years Ago)
Discord (Discord in Childhood)
Fourth Harmony
Baiser (A Kiss)
Discord
Last Harmony
Kiss (A Kiss)
The Street-Lamps (People, Street Lamps)
The Complaint of the Soul of a Worker
Monologue of a Mother
SCHOOL 1. *Morning The Waste Lands (Ruination)*
                          The Street
                          Scripture (The Schoolmaster)
              Afternoon (Last Lesson of the Afternoon)
Malade (in prose)
A Love-Passage A Rift in the Lute (first draft, *A Love-Passage*)
[Title crossed out: *Spring in the City*] (*Bombardment*)
Infidelity (Ah, Muriel!)
Scent of Irises
Sigh No More
Late at Night Along the Home Road
New Wine (Late at Night)
Ophelia (first draft, *Ballad of Another Ophelia*)
Liaison (first draft, *The Yew-Tree on the Downs*)
Liaison (second draft, *The Yew-Tree on the Downs*)
Dolor of Autumn (Dolour of Autumn)
Unwitting (Reality of Peace, 1916)
[Fragment], *Nocturne (Repulsed)*
Nocturne (Repulsed)
The Appeal (Under the Oak, The Appeal)
Reproach (Release)
Nils Lykke Dead (A Man Who Died)
Submergence
Reminder
A Wise Man (Tease)
A Plaintive Confession (Coldness in Love, Aloof in Gaiety)
To Lettice, My Sister (Brother and Sister)
Anxiety (Endless Anxiety)
Patience (Suspense)

[Fragment], *Winter* (*Winter in the Boulevard*)
Winter (*Winter in the Boulevard*)
Another Ophelia (second draft, *Ballad of Another Ophelia*)
To My Mother—Dead (*The End*)
The Dead Mother (*The Bride*)
My Love, My Mother (*The Virgin Mother*)
TRANSFORMATIONS 1. *Evening* (*Parliament Hill in the Evening*)
        2. *Morning* (*Flat Suburbs, S. W., in the Morning*)
        3. *Men in the Morning* (*Morning Work*)
        4. *The Inanimate that Changes Not in Shape*
         Oh stiffly shapen houses that change not . . . (*Suburbs on a Hazy Day*)
          The Town (*Transformations: I. The Town*)
          The Earth (*Transformations: II. The Earth*)
        5. *The Changeful Animate Men: Whose Shape is Multiform*
          (*Transformations: III. Men*)
        6. *Corot*
        7. *Raphael* (*Michael Angelo*)
Blue (first draft, *The Shadow of Death, Blueness*)
Blue (second draft, *The Shadow of Death, Blueness*)
II. Red Passion and Death (*Red*)
Silence (first draft, *Silence, Listening*)
Silence (second draft, *Silence, Listening*)
The Inheritance (with interlined, *Noise of Battle*)
A Drama
Mating (*Come Spring, Come Sorrow*)
Meeting (*After Many Days*)
Return
Separated
Troth With the Dead (*Troth With the Dead, The Enkindled Spring, At a Loose End*)
A Love-Song (*A Love Song*)
Her Birthday (*On That Day*)
Hands (*The Hands of the Betrothed*)
Drunk
[Untitled], *Do not hold me Siegmund . . .* (second draft, *A Love-Passage*)

E320.2 *Poems*
Holograph manuscript, 66 pp.   Private

A notebook also containing *Accounts at Porthcothan*
Includes three trial dedications and an untitled joking poem,
Two, there are two words only...
The numbering given for some of the poems is that of the notebook
  Apprehension (Noise of Battle)
  Suburb in the Morning (Flat Suburbs, S. W., in the Morning)
  Suburb in the Evening (Parliament Hill in the Evening)
  Premonition (first draft, *Under the Oak*)
  Suburbs on the Hills (Suburbs on a Hazy Day)
  Winter in the Boulevard
  Under the Oak (second draft)
  The Interim (Reality of Peace, 1916)
  Voice of a Woman (A Man Who Died)
  Reading a Letter
  Sigh No More
  Ruination
  Bombardment
  Hyde Park, Years Ago. A Review of the Scots Guards (Guards)
  Twenty Years Ago
  Groping (Sickness)
  Next Morning (two drafts)
  On that Day (On That Day)
  From the Italian Lakes (Everlasting Flowers: For a Dead Mother)
  Phantasmagoria (Late at Night)
  From a College Window
  Palimpsest of Twilight (first draft, *Twilight*)
  The Piano (second draft, *Piano*)
  In Church
  Engulphed (At the Front)
  Indoors and Out (Twofold)
  Tarantella
  Late in Life
  Flapper
  In the Park (Birdcage Walk)
  Sentimental Correspondence 1. *The Almond Tree (Letter from
    Town: The Almond-Tree)*
  Letter to the North (Letter from Town: On a Grey Morning in March)
  The North Countrie (The North Country)
  The School on the Waste Lands (School on the Outskirts)
  Neckar (Narcissus)

LONDON NIGHT Year 1910 (first draft, *Embankment at Night, Before the War: Outcasts*)
LONDON NIGHT Year 1910: Charing Cross Railway Bridge (second draft, *Embankment at Night, Before the War: Outcasts*)
LONDON NIGHTS Year 1910 Clerks in the Parks (*Hyde Park at Night, Before the War: Clerks*)
LONDON NIGHTS Embankment 1910 (*Embankment at Night, Before the War: Charity*)
LONDON NIGHTS Piccadilly Circus (*Piccadilly Circus at Night: Street-Walkers*)
Spring-Fire (*Autumn Sunshine*)
1 *Martyr* (*Martyr à la Mode*)
2 *In Trouble and Shame*
3 *Brooding Grief*
4 *Lotus Hurt by the Cold* (*Lotus and Frost*)
5 *Mystery* (two drafts)
6 *Last Words to Miriam*
7 *Study*
  Evening of a Week-day (second draft, *Twilight*)
  [Fragment], *Eastwood* (*The Little Town at Evening*)
8 *Piano* (first draft)
  [Fragment], *Married in June*
9 *In a Boat*
10 *A Winter's Tale*
11 *A Baby Asleep After Pain*
12 *Perfidy* (*Turned Down*)
  Amour (*Autumn Sunshine*)
  The End
  The Bride
15 *The Virgin Mother*
  Silence (first draft, *Silence, Listening*)
16 *The Inheritance*
17 *Troth with the Dead*
18 *The World after her Death* (*The Enkindled Spring*)
19 *Bitterness* (*At a Loose End*)
20 *Silence* (second draft, *Silence*)
21 *Listening*
22 *Sorrow*
23 *Brother and Sister*
24 *Anxiety* (*Endless Anxiety*)

25 *Patience* (*Suspense*)
26 *Passing Bell* (*A Passing-Bell*)
27 *Discipline*
28 *Dreams Old and Nascent: Old*
29 *Dreams Old and Nascent: Nascent*
30 *A Baby Running Barefoot* (*Baby Running Barefoot*)
31 *Virgin Youth*
32 *Restlessness*
33 *The Punisher*
34 *Irony* (*Disagreeable Advice*)
35 *Epilogue* (*Forecast*)
36 *Discord in Childhood*
37 *Monologue of a Mother*
38 *Malade* (in prose)
39 *Liaison* (*The Yew-Tree on the Downs*)
40 *Dolor of Autumn* (*Dolour of Autumn*)
41 *Reproach* (*Release*)
  [Fragment], *Blue* (*The Shadow of Death*)
  [Fragments, three untitled] (*Autumn Sunshine*)

E320.3 *Poems*
Holograph manuscript, 25 pp.   CU
The numbering given is that of the manuscript pages
Tedlock pp. 81–2, Powell 55
  1–7 *Restlessness*
  9 *Violets for the Dead* (*Violets*)
  13 *Song* (*Flapper*)
  15 *Song Wind Among the Cherries*
  17 *Cherry-stealers* (*Cherry Robbers*)
  19 *A Letter from Town The Almond Tree* (*Letter from
        Town: The Almond-Tree*)
  21 *Lost* (*Turned Down*)
  25 [Fragment], *A Bell* (*A Passing-Bell*)
  27 *The End of Another Home-Holiday* (two drafts and a
        fragment, *End of Another Home Holiday*)
    [Fragment, untitled] (*Embankment at Night, Before the
        War: Charity*)
  35 [Fragment, untitled] (*Restlessness*)
  38 [Fragment], *Lost* (*Turned Down*)
  39 [Fragment, untitled] (*Letter from Town: The Almond-Tree*)
  42 [Fragment, untitled] (*Flapper*)
    [Fragment, untitled] (*Cherry Robbers*)

44 [Second fragment, untitled] (*Restlessness*)
48–50 [Second fragment, untitled] (*End of Another Home Holiday*)

E320.4 *Poems*

Holograph manuscript, 95 pp.   NN

Ah with his blessing bright on thy mouth and thy brow . . . (Michael Angelo)	1 p.
Moon New-Risen	1 p.
Erotic	1 p.
Separated	1 p.
Aloof in Gaiety	1 p.
A Love-Passage	2 pp.
A Drama	9 pp.
Red	2 pp.
Fooled! (Rebuked)	1 p.
Infidelity (Ah, Muriel!)	1 p.
Teasing (Tease)	2 pp.
In a Boat	2 pp.
Weeknight Service	2 pp.
A STILL AFTERNOON IN SCHOOL 1. *The Old Dream . . . 2. The Nascent (Dreams Old and Nascent)*	5 pp.
BABY-MOVEMENTS 1. *Running Barefoot Baby Running Barefoot)*	2 pp.
Another Ophelia (Ballad of Another Ophelia)	3 pp.
BABY-MOVEMENTS 2. *Trailing Clouds (A Baby Asleep After Pain*, written with *Baby Running Barefoot)*	
At the Window	1 p.
Intoxicated (Drunk)	4 pp.
Beneath the Yew Tree (The Yew-Tree on the Downs)	3 pp.
Reproach (Release)	3 pp.
Her Hands (The Hands of the Betrothed)	3 pp.
Mating (Come Spring, Come Sorrow)	3 pp.
A Love Song in Actuality (A Love Song)	1 p.
Snap-Dragon	6 pp.
A Bell (A Passing-Bell)	2 pp.
Blue (Blueness, The Shadow of Death)	4 pp.
An Address to the Sea (The Sea, Moonrise)	3 pp.
Street-Lamps (People, Street Lamps)	2 pp.
Song (Flapper)	1 p.

SONGS OF WORK PEOPLE AT NIGHT

1. *Tired* (*Hyde Park at Night, Before the War:*
   Clerks)   1 p.
2. *Tired But Dissatisfied* (*Piccadilly Circus*
   at Night: Street-Walkers)   1 p.

And Jude the Obscure and his Beloved (*Passing*
   Visit to Helen)   2 pp.
Cuckoo and Wood-Dove (*Sigh No More*)   1 p.
Tarantella   2 pp.
Brotherhood (*Embankment at Night, Before the*
   War: Charity)   1 p.
Nils Lykke Dead (*A Man Who Died*)   3 pp.
White (*Two Wives*)   9 pp.

E320.5 *Poems*

Typescript, 11 pp.   MH

Drunk   3 pp.
In a Boat   1 p.
Tease   1 p.
Mystery   1 p.
Study   1 p.
Submergence   1 p.
Last Words to Miriam   1 p.
A Winter's Tale   1 p.
Lotus Hurt by the Cold (*Lotus and Frost*)   1 p.

E320.6 *Poems*

Holograph manuscript, 17 pp.   NN

Song of a Man Who is Loved   1 p.
Afterwards (*Grey Evening, Firelight and*
   Nightfall)   1 p.
Don Juan   1 p.
Storm in Rose-Time (*Love Storm*)   2 pp.
Purity (*Paradise Re-Entered*)   2 pp.
Mystery   1 p.
Illicit (*On the Balcony*)   1 p.
A Kiss   1 p.
The Wind, the Rascal   1 p.
The Inheritance (*The Inheritance, Noise of Battle*) 1 p.
Ballad of a Wayward Woman (*Ballad of a Wilful*
   Woman)   5 pp.

E320.8 *...polite to one another—through the glass partitions...*

Holograph manuscript, 6 pp.   Private

A fragment
Tedlock pp. 204–5, Powell 84A

E320.9 *Pomegranate*
  a. Holograph manuscript   See E314.4
  b. Typescript, 1 p.   CtY

E321 *Poor Bit of a Wench!*
  Carbon typescript   See E319.1

E322 *Pornography and Obscenity*
  a. Holograph manuscript, 32 pp.   TxU
    Powell 10
  b. Typescript, 38 pp.   CU
    Tedlock pp. 173–4
  c. Carbon typescript, 19 pp.   CU

E322.2 *Prelude, A*
  Typescript, 13 pp.   TxU
  MS titled: *An Enjoyable Christmas. A Prelude*

E322.5 *Prestige*
  Holograph manuscript, 1 p.   ICSo
  A fragment

E322.7 *Primrose Path, The*
  a. Holograph manuscript, 21 pp.   N
  b. Corrected typescript, 21 pp.   TxU
  c. Corrected typescript and carbon copy, 25 pp., 25 pp.   TxU
  d. Typescript, 10 pp.   N

E322.8 *Princess, The*
  Holograph manuscript, 51 pp.   TxU
  Tedlock pp. 54–5, Powell 16

E323 *Prisoner at Work in a Turkish Garden*
  a. Holograph manuscript   See E49
  b. Corrected carbon typescript, 1 p.   See E49

E324 *Prisoners at Work in the Rain*
  a. Holograph manuscript   See E49
  b. Corrected carbon typescript, 1 p.   See E49

E325 *Prodigal Husband, The*. See *Samson and Delilah*

E326 *Proper Study, The*
  a. Holograph manuscript, 10 pp.   TxU
  b. Carbon typescript, 6 pp.   TxU
  c. Carbon typescript, 6 pp.   OkTU
  d. Three carbon typescripts, 9 pp., 9 pp., 9 pp.   CU
  e. Carbon typescript, 9 pp.   TxU

E326.2 *Prophet*
    a. Holograph manuscript   See E320.1
    b. Holograph manuscript   TxU
         Included with *Dreams Old and Nascent*
         Tedlock pp. 77–9, Powell 52
     See also *Discipline*

E326.5 *Prussian Officer, The*
     Holograph manuscript, 16 pp.   TxU
     MS titled: *Honour and Arms*
     Tedlock pp. 46–8, Powell 30

E326.6 *Prussian Officer and Other Stories, The*
     Corrected page proofs, 310 pp.   NCL

E326.7 *Psychoanalysis and the Unconscious*
    a. Corrected typescript, 29 pp.   Unlocated
         Chicago Book and Art Auctions catalogue
         (27–28 October 1931) item no. 286
    b. Author's copy with holograph corrections   TxU
         Seltzer, 1921 (A18)

E326.8 *Punisher, The*
    a. Holograph manuscript   See E320.1
    b. Holograph manuscript, 2 pp.   MH
    c. Holograph manuscript   See E320.2

E327 *Purity.* See *Paradise Re-Entered*

E328 *Purple Anemones*
    a. Holograph manuscript   See E47
    b. Holograph manuscript, 2 pp.   IaE
    c. Holograph manuscript   See E314.4
    d. Typescript   See E314.5

E328.5 *Puss-Puss!*
    a. Holograph manuscript   See E266
    b. Carbon typescript   See E266

E329 *Question*
     Carbon typescript   See E266

E330 *Rabbit Snared in the Night*
     Typescript, 2 pp.   ICU

E330.5 *Rachel Annand Taylor*
     Holograph manuscript, 8 pp.   Private

E331 *Rainbow, The* (A novel)
    a. Holograph manuscript and corrected typescript, 811 pp.   TxU
         Tedlock pp. 12–6, Powell 4

b. Corrected typescript and holograph manuscript, 732 pp. TxU

E332 *Rainbow* (A poem)
    a. Holograph manuscript, 1 p.   TxU
        Untitled poem on verso, begins: There's no immortal heaven...
    b. Typescript, 2 pp.   Unlocated
        Powell 63B
    c. Two carbon typescripts, 2 pp., 2 pp.   See E315

E333 *Rascal, The.* See *Wind, the Rascal, The*

E334 *Rawdon's Roof*
    a. Holograph manuscript, 21 pp.   Lazarus
        Version published in *The Lovely Lady* (A63)
        Powell 44A
    b. Corrected typescript, 20 pp.   Lazarus
        Follows closely Elkin Mathews, 1928 (A40); pp.
        1–11 are almost the same as the holograph manu-
        script; pp. 12–20 differ from it
        Powell 44B
    c. Corrected typescript, 21 pp.   CU

E335 *Reach Over*
    Holograph manuscript, 1 p.   CSt
    Untitled, begins: Reach over, then, reach over across the chasm...
    Powell 61

E336 *Reading a Letter*
    a. Holograph manuscript, 1 p.   See E317
    b. Holograph manuscript   See E320.2
    c. Holograph manuscript, 1 p.   See E269.5

E337 *Real Thing, The*
    a. Holograph manuscript, 10 pp.   CtY
        Notebook cover titled: *Three Essays for Vanity Fair*
        Powell 117
    b. Carbon typescript, 12 pp.   CU
    c. Carbon typescript, 12 pp.   TxU

E337.5 *Reality of Peace, 1916*
    a. Holograph manuscript   See E320.1
    b. Holograph manuscript   See E320.2
    c. Holograph manuscript, 1 p.   See E269.5

E338 *Reality of Peace, The*
    a. Typescript, 30 pp.   CU
        Tedlock pp. 201–2
    b. Carbon typescript, 45 pp.   CU

    c. Carbon typescript, 45 pp.   TxU

E338.5 *Rebuked*
    a. Holograph manuscript, 1 p.   See E317
    b. Holograph manuscript, 1 p.   See E320.4

E338.7 *Red*
    a. Holograph manuscript   See E320.1
    b. Holograph manuscript, 2 pp.   See E320.4

E339 *Red Moon-Rise*
    Holograph manuscript   See E213

E340 *Red Trousers*
    a. Holograph manuscript, 4 pp.   Private
        Tedlock p. 229, Powell 84A
    b. Corrected carbon typescript, 5 pp.   See E27
    c. Typescript, 5 pp.   MH

E340.3 *Red Wolf, The*
    Corrected typescript, 3 pp.   TxU

E340.4 *Reflections on the Death of a Porcupine*
    Corrected carbon typescript, 20 pp.   TxU
    Tedlock pp. 209–10

E340.5 *Reflections on the Death of a Porcupine, German translation*
    Holograph manuscript, 15 pp.   TxU
    Incomplete
    In Frieda Lawrence's hand
    MS titled: *Betrachtungen über den Tod eines Stachelschweins von D. H. Lawrence*

E340.6 *Reflections on the Death of a Porcupine and Other Essays*
    Corrected carbon typescript, 151 pp.   OkTU
    Includes title page and table of contents

E340.8 *Release*
    a. Holograph manuscript   See E320.1
    b. Holograph manuscript, 3 pp.   See E320.4
    c. Holograph manuscript   See E320.2

E341 *Reminder*
    a. Holograph manuscript   See E320.1
    b. Holograph manuscript   See E213

E342 *Renascence*
    a. Holograph manuscript, 2 pp.   See E317
    b. Holograph manuscript, 1 p.   ULiv
        MS titled: *Renaissance*
        With letter of 20 January 1909 to Blanche Jennings

c. Holograph manuscript	See E213

E343 *Repulsed*
    a. Holograph manuscript   See E320.1
        A draft and a fragment
    b. Holograph manuscript   See E213

E344 *Response from the Harem*
    Holograph manuscript   See E49

E345 *Restlessness*
    a. Holograph manuscript, 3 pp.   See E317
    b. Holograph manuscript   See E320.1
    c. Holograph manuscript   See E320.3
        A draft and two fragments
    d. Holograph manuscript   See E320.2
    e. Two carbon typescripts, 1 p., 1 p.   See E315

E346 *Resurrection* (A poem)
    a. Holograph manuscript, 4 pp.   MH
    b. Holograph manuscript, 4 pp.   ICU
    c. Holograph manuscript, 5 pp.   TxU
    d. Holograph manuscript, 1 p.   TxU
        A six-line fragment
        With letter of 28 November 1915 to Lady C. Asquith
    e. Typescript, 3 pp.   ICU
    f. Proof, 1 p.   ICU
        A six-line fragment

E346.1 *Resurrection* (An essay)
    a. Holograph manuscript, 4 pp.   TxU
        Tedlock p. 137, Powell 118
    b. Typescript and carbon copy, 4 pp., 4 pp.   CU
        Tedlock pp. 137–8
    c. Carbon typescript, 5 pp.   TxU
    d. Carbon typescript, 5 pp.   CU
    e. Carbon typescript, 5 pp.   NmU

E346.5 *Resurrection of the Flesh*
    Holograph manuscript, 2 pp.   Unlocated
    Argus Book Shop catalogue no. 827 (1943) item no. 29

E347 *Return*
    a. Holograph manuscript   See E320.1
    b. Holograph manuscript   See E49

E348 *Review in Hyde Park, 1913, A.* See *Guards*

E349 *Review of the Scots Guards, The.* See *Guards*

E349.5 *Rex*
    a. Holograph manuscript, 7 pp.   CtY
        With letter of 30 May [1920] to Richard Aldington
    b. Carbon typescript, 11 pp.   Private

E349.7 *Rise in the World, A*
    Holograph manuscript   See E302

E350 *Risen Lord, The*
    a. Holograph manuscript, 6 pp.   CU
        Tedlock pp. 235–6, Powell 84A
    b. Carbon typescript, 12 pp.   See E27
    c. Carbon typescript, 12 pp.   CU

E350.5 *River Roses*
    a. Holograph manuscript   See E318
    b. Typescript   See E319.7

E351 *Rocking-Horse Winner, The*
    a. Holograph manuscript, 30 pp.   Lazarus
        Powell 45
    b. Carbon typescript, 24 pp.   CU

E351.3 *Rondeau of a Conscientious Objector*
    a. Holograph manuscript, 2 pp.   See E317
    b. Holograph manuscript, 1 p.   Dealer
    c. Corrected typescript, 1 p.   CtY

E351.5 *Rose is not a Cabbage, A*
    a. Holograph manuscript   See E266
    b. Carbon typescript   See E266

E351.7 *Rose, Look Out Upon Me: A soldier catches sight of a young lady at her window in Salonika*
    Corrected carbon typescript, 1 p.   See E49

E352 *Roses*
    Holograph manuscript   See E302

E352.1 *Roses on the Breakfast Table*
    a. Holograph manuscript   See E318
    b. Typescript   See E319.7

E352.3 *Ruination*
    a. Holograph manuscript   See E320.1
    b. Holograph manuscript   See E320.2
    c. Holograph manuscript, 1 p.   CtY

E352.5 *St. John*
    Typescript, 3 pp.   CtY
    MS also titled: *The Apostolic Beasts*

E352.53 *St. Luke*
　Typescript, 3 pp.　　　　　　　　　　　　　　　CtY
　MS also titled: *The Apostolic Beasts*

E352.55 *St. Mark*
　Typescript, 3 pp.　　　　　　　　　　　　　　　CtY
　MS also titled: *The Apostolic Beasts*

E352.57 *St. Matthew*
　Typescript　　　　　　　　　　　　　　　See E47

E352.6 *St. Mawr*
　a. Holograph manuscript, 41 pp.　　　　Destroyed: Huxley fire
　　An early version, incomplete, pp. 17–58 only
　　Powell 14A
　b. Holograph manuscript, 129 pp.　　　Destroyed: Huxley fire
　　Powell 14A
　c. Corrected typescript, 183 pp.　　　　　　　Lazarus
　　pp. 1–178 and 38A, 125A, 128A, 138A and
　　19 & 20 (one page)
　　Powell 14B

E352.65 *Salt of the Earth*
　Holograph manuscript　　　　　　　　　See E302

E352.7 *Samson and Delilah*
　Holograph manuscript, 34 pp.　　　　　　　　TxU
　Incomplete by several paragraphs
　MS titled: *The Prodigal Husband*

E352.9 *Scent of Irises*
　a. Holograph manuscript　　　　　　　　See E320.1
　b. Holograph manuscript, 3 pp.　　　　　　　　MH

E353 *School.* See *Snowy Day in School, A*

E353.3 *School: 1. Morning, The Street*
　Holograph manuscript　　　　　　　　　See E320.1

E353.5 *School on the Outskirts*
　a. Holograph manuscript　　　　　　　　See E320.2
　b. Holograph manuscript, 1 p.　　　　　　See E269.5

E353.8 *Schoolmaster, The*
　a. Holograph manuscript　　　　　　　　See E320.1
　b. Holograph manuscript　　　　　　　　See E213

E354 *Scrutiny of the Work of John Galsworthy, A.* See *John Galsworthy*

E355 *Sea and Sardinia*
　a. Corrected typescript, 307 pp.　　　　　　　TxU
　　MS titled: *Diary of a Trip to Sardinia*
　　Powell 77

    b. Corrected typescript, 305 pp.   NNC
    c. Corrected carbon typescript, 305 pp.   CtY
    d. Typescript, 32 pp.   CtY

        As Far as Palermo   14 pp.
        Cagliari   18 pp.

E355.5 *Sea, The*
    Holograph manuscript   See E320.4
    See also *Moonrise*

E356 *Sea-Weed*
    a. Holograph manuscript   See E302
    b. Galley proof   See E319.6

E356.5 *Second Best*
    Holograph manuscript, 14 pp.   N

E356.7 *Second Supper*
    Holograph manuscript, 16 pp.   Lazarus
    Includes *Introduction*, 2 pp.

E357 *See Mexico After, by Luis Q.*
    a. Holograph manuscript, 8 pp.   Private
        Lawrence has apparently rewritten the essay on
        Quintanilla's typescript titled *Mexico, Why Not?*
    b. Holograph manuscript, 1 p.   CU
        A twenty-line fragment
        Tedlock p. 189
    c. Holograph manuscript, 8 pp.   TxU
        Tedlock pp. 189–90, Powell 118
    d. Typescript, 7 pp.   Private
    e. Corrected, mostly carbon, typescript, 7 pp.   CU
        Tedlock pp. 190–1
    f. Two carbon typescripts, 10 pp., 10 pp.   CU
    g. Carbon typescript, 10 pp.   TxU

E358 *Self-Pity*
    Holograph manuscript   See E302

E358.7 *Separated*
    a. Holograph manuscript   See E320.1
    b. Holograph manuscript, 1 p.   See E320.4

E359 *Sex Appeal*. See *Sex Versus Loveliness*

E359.1 *Sex Versus Loveliness*
    a. Holograph manuscript, 10 pp.   TxU
        MS titled: *Sex Appeal*
        Tedlock pp. 231–2, Powell 84A
    b. Holograph manuscript, 1 p.   TxU

A two-line fragment; Tedlock p. 231

E359.3 *Shades*
    a. Holograph manuscript, 1 p.   ICN
       MS titled: *Pentecostal*
    b. Corrected typescript, 1 p.   Lazarus

E359.4 *Shades of Spring, The*
    a. Holograph manuscript, 24 pp.   MH
       MS titled: *The Right Thing to Do* and *The Only Thing to Be Done*; deleted title: *The Harassed Angel*
    b. Corrected typescript, 27 pp.   NN
       MS titled: *The Soiled Rose*
    c. Corrected page proofs   NCL
       MS titled: *The Dead Rose*

E359.5 *Shadow in the Rose Garden, The*
    a. Holograph manuscript, 7 pp.   TxU
       Tedlock pp. 32–3, Powell 29
    b. Two carbon typescripts, 6 pp., 6 pp.   CU
    MSS titled: *The Vicar's Garden*

E359.7 *Shadow of Death, The*
    a. Holograph manuscript   See E320.1
       Two drafts
    b. Holograph manuscript   See E320.4
    c. Holograph manuscript   See E320.2
    See also *Blueness* and *And what do I care...*

E359.8 *She was a Good Little Wife*
    Holograph manuscript, 1 p.   See E319.2

E360 *She-Wolf, The.* See *Cavalleria Rusticana*

E360.5 *Ship of Death, The*
    Corrected typescript   Unlocated
    Argus Book Shop catalogue no. 827 (1943) item no. 37

E361 *Sicilian Cyclamens*
    Holograph manuscript   See E47

E361.3 *Sick Collier, A*
    a. Holograph manuscript, 11 pp.   Lazarus
       Powell 34
    b. Corrected galley proofs, 2 pp.   Private
       For *New Statesman* (C25)

E361.5 *Sickness*
    a. Holograph manuscript   See E320.1
    b. Holograph manuscript   See E320.2

c. Holograph manuscript, 1 p.   See E269.5

E361.7 *Sigh No More*
a. Holograph manuscript   See E320.1
b. Holograph manuscript, 1 p.   See E320.4
c. Holograph manuscript   See E320.2
d. Holograph manuscript, 1 p.   See E269.5

E362 *Sighs*
a. Holograph manuscript   See E49
b. Corrected carbon typescript, 1 p.   See E49

E362.2 *Silence*
a. Holograph manuscript   See E320.1
    Two drafts
b. Holograph manuscript   See E320.2
    A draft and a stanza
    See also *Listening*

E362.6 *Smile*
Holograph manuscript, 9 pp.   Unlocated
Powell 43

E362.7 *Snake*
a. Holograph manuscript   See E47
b. Typescript, 2 pp.   CtY

E362.8 *Snap-Dragon*
Holograph manuscript, 6 pp.   See E320.4

E363 *Snow* ... See *Snowy Day at School, A*

E364 *Snowy Afternoon at School, A.* See *Snowy Day in School, A*

E365 *Snowy Day at School, A*
Holograph manuscript, 3 pp.   See E317

E365.1 *Snowy Day in School, A*
a. Holograph manuscript, 1 p.   See E317
b. Holograph manuscript, 1 p.   TxU
    Two fragments, probably the poem called *A
    Snowy Afternoon at School* (E364)
    In the Helen Corke collection
c. Holograph manuscript   See E213

E365.5 *So vivid a vision, everything so visually poignant* ...
Holograph manuscript, 8 pp.   TxU
Published as a letter of 1 December 1915 to Lady
Ottoline Morrell in *Letters* (A61)

E366 *Social Basis of Consciousness, Review of The*
    a. Holograph manuscript, 12 pp.   TxU
        Tedlock pp. 259–60, Powell 102
    b. Carbon typescript, 11 pp.   CU
E367 *Softly, Then, Softly!*
    a. Holograph manuscript   Unlocated
        Powell 61 untitled, begins: Softly, then, softly...
    b. Typescript, 2 pp.   NmU
    c. Two carbon typescripts, 2 pp., 2 pp.   See E315
E368 *Solitaria and The Apocalypse of Our Times, Review of*
    a. Holograph manuscript, 10 pp.   TxU
        Tedlock p. 259, Powell 100
    b. Carbon typescript, 8 pp.   CU
    c. Carbon typescript, 8 pp.   TxU
E369 *Song* (A poem). See *Flapper*
E369.1 *Song* (Another poem). See *Song: Wind Among the Cherries*
E370 *Song-Day in Autumn*
    a. Holograph manuscript, 2 pp.   See E317
    b. Holograph manuscript   See E213
E371 *Song of a Man Who is Loved*
    a. Holograph manuscript, 1 p.   See E320.6
    b. Holograph manuscript   Unlocated
        Another version
        Argus Book Shop catalogue 827 (1943) item 30
    c. Corrected carbon typescript, 1 p.   See E205.8
E371.5 *Song of Death*
    Holograph manuscript, 1 p.   TxU
    In Frieda Lawrence's hand
E371.7 *Song: Wind Among the Cherries*
    a. Holograph manuscript, 2 pp.   See E317
    b. Holograph manuscript   See E320.3
E372 *Songless, The.* See *Hyde Park at Night, Before the War: Clerks* and *Piccadilly Circus at Night: Street-Walkers*
E373 *Sons and Lovers*
    a. Holograph manuscript, 58 pp.   CU
        An early draft, incomplete
    b. Holograph manuscript, 23 pp.   TxU
        A fragment, pp. 204–26
        Known as *The Miriam Papers*
        In Lawrence's hand with Jessie Chambers' comments

   c. Holograph manuscript, 17 pp.   TxU
      Five fragments; in Jessie Chambers' hand
      On Saturday afternoon Agatha and
         Miriam were upstairs dressing...   3 pp.
      Easter Monday   4 pp.
      [Flower sequence] Miriam had discontinued
         the habit of going each Thursday
         evening...   2 pp.
      Again, the first time that Miriam saw
         Paul to perceive him...   4 pp.
      Chapter ix   4 pp.
   d. Holograph manuscript, 271 pp.   TxU
      An early draft, incomplete
      MS titled: *Paul Morel*
      Powell 3
   e. Holograph manuscript, 530 pp.   CU
      Final version used for Duckworth, 1913 (A4)
   f. Corrected galley proofs,   N
      Incomplete, galleys 175–83, 198–209
   g. Page proofs, 423 pp.   TxU
      Duckworth, 1913 (A4); two extra sets of pp. 357–52

E373.1 *Sons and Lovers, Foreword to*
  Holograph manuscript, 7 pp.   TxU

E374 *Sorrow*
   a. Holograph manuscript   See E317
      Two drafts
   b. Holograph manuscript   See E320.2
   c. Holograph manuscript   See E314.1

E375 *Southern Night*
  Holograph manuscript   See E47

E376 *Sphinx*
  Holograph manuscript   See E319.1

E376.4 *Spirits Summoned West*
  Corrected typescript, 3 pp.   TxU

E377 *State of Funk, The*
   a. Holograph manuscript, 6 pp.   TxU
      Tedlock p. 228, Powell 84A
   b. Carbon typescript, 9 pp.   See E27
   c. Carbon typescript, 4 pp.   CU

d. Carbon typescript, 1 p.   NmU
   Incomplete, p. 6 only

E377.5 *Station: Athos, Treasures and Men, The; England and the Octopus;*
   Comfortless Memory; and Ashenden, or The British Agent; Review of
   a. Holograph manuscript, 4 pp.   TxU
      An early version
      MS titled: *Review for Vogue*
      Tedlock pp. 261–2, Powell 103B
   b. Holograph manuscript, 1 p.   TxU
      An eight-line fragment
      Tedlock pp. 260–1
   c. Holograph manuscript, 8 pp.   TxU
      MS titled: *Review for Vogue*
      Tedlock pp. 261–2, Powell 103A

E378 *Still Afternoon in School, A.* See *Dreams Old and Nascent*

E379 *Storm in Rose-Time.* See *Love Storm*

E379.9 *Story of Doctor Manente, The*
   a. Holograph manuscript, 1 p.   TxU
      Introductory synopsis
      MS titled: *Third Supper*
   b. Holograph manuscript, 69 pp.   TxU
      MS titled: *Tenth Story and Last*
      Tedlock pp. 274–5, Powell 109
   c. Holograph notes, 2 pp.   Lazarus
      Not used in published version
   d. Holograph manuscript, 9 pp.   Lazarus
      Notes to the text
   e. Corrected galley proofs, 30 pp.   Lazarus
      Orioli, 1929 (A45)

E380 *Story of Doctor Manente, Foreword to The*
   a. Holograph manuscript, 7 pp.   Lazarus
   b. Corrected galley sheets, 8 pp.   CLU
      Orioli, 1929 (A45)

E380.1 *Story of Doctor Manente, Prospectus for The*
   Holograph manuscript, 4 pp.   Lazarus
   Leaflet to promote this work and Lungarno series

E380.7 *Street Lamps*
   a. Holograph manuscript   See E320.1
   b. Holograph manuscript   See E320.4
   See also *People*

E381 *Strike Pay*
    Holograph manuscript, 15 pp.   Lazarus
    Powell 25
E382 *Studies in Classic American Literature*
    a. Holograph manuscript, 7 pp.   NNPM
       Whitman
    b. Holograph manuscript, 20 pp.   Smith
       MS titled: *Studies in Classic American Literature* (*XIII*) *Whitman*
    c. Typescript, 9 pp.   OkTU
       Incomplete, begins: Whitman the great poet,
       has meant so much to me...
       Whitman
    d. Carbon typescript, 8 pp.   Smith
       Whitman
    e. Holograph notes, 9 pp.   PLeB
       Early notes for *Nathaniel Hawthorne and "The Scarlet Letter"*
       MS titled: *A Study of Sin*
    f. Holograph manuscript, 13 pp.   Smith
       MS titled: *Studies in Classic American Literature* (*VIII*)
       Nathaniel Hawthorne (*II.*)
       pp. 10–13 are page proofs with revisions by Lawrence
    g. Holograph manuscript and corrected typescript, 28 pp.   TxU
       MS titled: *Studies in Classic American Literature* (*VII*)
       by D. H. Lawrence, *Nathaniel Hawthorne*
       Published as *Nathaniel Hawthorne and "The Scarlet Letter"*
       Tedlock pp. 153–6, Powell 88A
    h. Corrected typescript, 12 pp.   TxU
       MS titled: *The Scarlet Letter*
       Published as *Hawthorne's "Blithedale Romance"*
       Tedlock pp. 157–8, Powell 88B
    i. Holograph manuscript, 26 pp.   Smith
       MS titled: *Studies in Classic American Literature* (*XII*)
       Herman Melville (*2*)
       Published as *Herman Melville's "Moby Dick"*
    j. Corrected typescript, 19 pp.   TxU
       Herman Melville's "Moby Dick"
       Tedlock pp. 159–60, Powell 88D
    k. Corrected typescript, 23 pp.   NmU
       MS titled: *Studies in Classic American Literature* (*XII*)
       Herman Melville's "Moby Dick"
    l. Holograph manuscript, 14 pp.   Smith

MS titled: *Studies in Classic American Literature* (*XI*)
Herman Melville (1)
Published as *Herman Melville's "Typee" and "Omoo"*
m. Corrected typescript, 13 pp.   TxU
   MS titled: *Studies in Classic American Literature* (*XI*)
   Herman Melville's "Typee" and "Omoo"
   Tedlock p. 159, Powell 88C
n. Holograph manuscript, 22 pp.   Smith
   MS titled: *Studies in Classic American Literature* (*X*) *Dana*
   pp. 1–7, 9–23
o. Corrected typescript, 23 pp.   Unlocated
   American Art Association catalogue (29–30
   January 1936) item no. 379
   Foreword
   The Spirit of Place
   Benjamin Franklin
p. Typescript, 237 pp.   Smith
   TS titled: *Studies in Classic American Literature*
   With minor corrections in the hand of Robert Mountsier
     I *The Spirit of Place*, 19 pp.
     II *Benjamin Franklin*, 16 pp.
     III *Henry St. John de Crevecoeur* (*Hector St. John
       Crevecoeur*), 19 pp.
     IV *Fenimore Cooper's Anglo-American Novels*, 17 pp.
     V *Fenimore Cooper's Leatherstocking Novels*, 21 pp.
     VI *Edgar Allan Poe*, 18 pp.
     VII *Nathaniel Hawthorne*, 17 pp.
     VIII *Nathaniel Hawthorne's "Blithedale Romance,"* 12 pp.
     IX *The Two Principles*, 17 pp.
     X *Dana's "Two Years Before the Mast,"* 24 pp.
     XI *Herman Melville's "Typee" and "Omoo,"* 13 pp.
     XII *Herman Melville's "Moby Dick,"* 22 pp.
     XIII *Whitman*, 22 pp.
q. Combination holograph manuscript and corrected   Smith
   typescript, 161 pp.
   MS titled: *Studies in Classic American Literature*
     I *The Spirit of Place*, corrected typescript, 8 pp.
     II *Benjamin Franklin*, corrected typescript, 13 pp.
     III *Henry St. John de Crevecoeur* (*Hector St. John Crevecoeur*),
       corrected typescript, 13 pp.

  IV *Fenimore Cooper's White Novels*, holograph manuscript and corrected typescript, 11 pp.

  V *Fenimore Cooper's Leatherstocking Novels*, holograph manuscript, 13 pp.

  VI *Edgar Alan Poe*, holograph manuscript and corrected typescript, 16 pp.

  VII *Nathaniel Hawthorne and "The Scarlet Letter,"* holograph manuscript, 14 pp.

  VIII *Hawthorne's "Blithedale Romance,"* holograph manuscript, 9 pp.

  IX *Dana's "Two Years Before the Mast,"* holograph manuscript and corrected typescript, 22 pp.

  X *Herman Melville's "Typee" and "Omoo,"* holograph manuscript, 13 pp.

  XI *Herman Melville's "Moby Dick,"* holograph manuscript and corrected typescript, 19 pp.

  XII *Whitman*, holograph manuscript, 10 pp.

E382.5 *Studies in Classic American Literature, Foreword to*

a. Holograph manuscript, 6 pp.	Smith
b. Corrected typescript, 2 pp.	Smith
c. Corrected typescript, 6 pp.	Smith

E383 *Study*

a. Holograph manuscript, 2 pp.	See E317
b. Holograph manuscript	See E320.2
c. Typescript, 1 p.	See E320.5

E384 *Study of Thomas Hardy*

a. Typescript, partly carbon, 186 pp.	CU

  MS titled: *Le Gai Savaire*
  Powell 86

b. Carbon typescript, 215 pp.	TxU
c. Typescript, 244 pp.	TxU
d. Carbon typescript, 244 pp.	TxU

E384.1 *Submergence*

a. Holograph manuscript	See E320.1
b. Typescript, 1 p.	See E320.5

E384.4 *Suburbs on a Hazy Day*

a. Holograph manuscript	See E320.1
b. Holograph manuscript	See E320.2
c. Holograph manuscript, 1 p.	See E269.5

E384.8 *Suggestions for Stories—never carried out! D. H. L.*
    Holograph notes, 2 pp.   TxU
    Tedlock pp. 56–8, Powell 118

E385 *Sun*
    a. Holograph manuscript, 44 pp.   TxU
    b. Corrected typescript, 21 pp.   Lazarus
      Altered version
    c. Corrected typescript, 21 pp.   TxU
      Altered version
      Tedlock pp. 58–9, Powell 40

E385.5 *Surgery for the Novel—Or a Bomb*
    a. Holograph manuscript, 11 pp.   NNC
    b. Corrected typescript, 6 pp.   NNC
    c. Carbon typescript, 6 pp.   OkTU
    MSS titled: *The Future of the Novel*

E385.7 *Suspense*
    a. Holograph manuscript   See E320.1
    b. Holograph manuscript   See E320.2

E386 *Swing Song of a Girl and a Soldier*
    a. Holograph manuscript   See E49
    b. Corrected carbon typescript, 1 p.   See E49

E386.5 *Sympathy*
    Holograph manuscript   See E319.3

E387 *Tales.* See *Gazelle Calf, The*

E388 *Taos*
    a. Carbon typescript, 4 pp.   CU
      Tedlock p. 181
    b. Carbon typescript, 6 pp.   CU

E389 *Tarantella*
    a. Holograph manuscript, 2 pp.   See E317
    b. Holograph manuscript, 2 pp.   See E320.4
    c. Holograph manuscript   See E320.2
    d. Holograph manuscript, 1 p.   See E269.5

E389.4 *Tease*
    a. Holograph manuscript, 1 p.   N
      A two-stanza fragment
      With letter of 29 March 1911 to Louie Burrows
    b. Holograph manuscript   See E320.1
    c. Holograph manuscript, 2 pp.   See E320.4
    d. Typescript, 1 p.   See E320.5

e. Typescript, 2 pp.   Lazarus
 MS titled: *Teasing*

E389.6 *Ten Months Old*
 a. Holograph manuscript, 1 p.   See E317
 b. Holograph manuscript, 1 p.   ULiv
  With letter of 20 January 1909 to Blanche Jennings

E390 *That Women Know Best*
 Holograph manuscript, 5 pp.   CU

E391 *Then "Come into the kitchen," said Mrs. Bircumshaw* ... See
Delilah and Mr. Bircumshaw

E392 *There is a small cottage off the Addiscombe Road about a mile from East
Croydon station....* (An unfinished story)
 a. Holograph manuscript, 48 pp.   CU
  Tedlock pp. 37–9, Powell 51C
 b. Typescript and carbon copy, 29 pp., 29 pp. TxU
 c. Two carbon typescripts, 29 pp., 29 pp.   CU
 d. Typescript, 22 pp.   TxU

E393 *There is no Way Out*
 Corrected carbon typescript   See E319.1

E393.5 *There is Rain in Me*
 Holograph manuscript   See E302

E394 *There is something depressing about French eighteenth-century literature* ...
See *Duc de Lauzun, The*

E394.5 *There Was a Gay Bird Named Christine*
 Holograph manuscript, 1 p.   TxU
 Untitled, begins: There was a gray bird named Christine ...

E395 *There was a man not long ago, who felt he was through with the world* ...
See *Man Who Was Through with the World, The*

E395.5 *There was a young man in the corridor* ...
 Holograph manuscript   Unlocated
 MS on title page of *The Rainbow*, Methuen, 1915 (A7)
 Myers & Co. Autumn Catalogue of Modern Books
 ...no. 297 (1933) item no. 31

E396 *There were, three years back, two schools in the mining village of High
Park* ... (An unfinished story)
 Holograph manuscript, 7 pp.   CU
 Tedlock pp. 40–1, Powell 51B

E396.3 *There's no immortal heaven* ...
 Holograph manuscript, 1 p.   TxU
 Poem on verso: *Rainbow*

E396.5 *Thief in the Night*
  Holograph manuscript, 1 p.   See E269.5

E396.7 *Thimble, The*
  a. Holograph manuscript, 24 pp.   CSt
  b. Typescript, 14 pp.   TxU

E397 *Things*
  a. Holograph manuscript, 19 pp.   TxU
       Tedlock p. 72, Powell 47
  b. Carbon typescript, 16 pp.   CU
  c. Typescript and two carbon copies, 19 pp., 19 pp., 19 pp.   TxU
  d. Corrected proof sheets, 8 pp.   NmU

E397.5 *Things Men Have Made*
  Galley proof   See E319.6

E398 *Thinking About Oneself*
  a. Holograph manuscript, 4 pp.   TxU
       Tedlock p. 211, Powell 84A
  b. Carbon typescript, 4 pp.   CU
  c. Two carbon typescripts, 4 pp., 4 pp.   CU
       Another typing
  d. Carbon typescript, 4 pp.   TxU

E399 *Third Supper, The.* See *Story of Doctor Manente, The*

E399.2 *13000 People*
  Carbon typescript   See E266

E399.7 *To Let Go or to Hold On?*
  Galley proof   See E319.6

E400 *Tommies in the Train*
  a. Holograph manuscript, 1 p.   See E319
  b. Corrected typescript, 2 pp.   CtY

E401 *Tomorrow.* See *Piccadilly Circus at Night: Street-Walkers*

E401.5 *Tortoises*
  Corrected page proofs, 30 pp.   NjP
  Text pages without half-titles, duplicates for pp. 23–4

E401.6 *Touch and Go*
  Holograph manuscript   Unlocated
  Frieda Lawrence wrote to Willie Hopkin on 9 November
  1936 that she will give him the MS if she can get it
  from a woman who says Lawrence gave it to her

E402 *Town in 1917*
  Holograph manuscript   See E320

E403 *Trailing Clouds* (A poem)
    Holograph manuscript, 1 p.   See E317

E404 *Train at Night, A*
    Holograph manuscript, 1 p.   See E317

E404.5 *Train, The*
    Holograph manuscript, 1 p.   N
    An untitled fragment, beginning: Train, with your
    smoke flag waving...
    In the Louie Burrows collection

E405 *Traitors*
    a. Holograph manuscript, 1 p.   CSt
        Untitled, begins: Traitors, oh, liars...
        Powell 61
    b. Two carbon typescripts, 1 p., 1 p.   See E315

E406 *Transformations*
    a. Holograph manuscript   See E320.1
    b. Holograph manuscript   See E213
        I. *The Town*
        II. *The Earth*
        III. *Men*

E407 *Trespasser, The*
    a. Holograph manuscript, 182 pp.   CU
        Fragments of an early version, pp. 13–207
        Tedlock pp. 11–2, Powell 2B
    b. Holograph manuscript, 485 pp.   CU
        Tedlock pp. 7–11, Powell 2A
    c. Page proofs, 292 pp.   NCL
        Duckworth, 1912 (A2)

E408 *Triolet.* See *Birdcage Walk*

E409 *Triumph of the Machine, The*
    a. Holograph manuscript, 1 p.   See E314
    b. Carbon typescript, 1 p.   TxU

E409.5 *Tropic*
    a. Holograph manuscript   See E47
    b. Holograph manuscript   See E47
    c. Holograph manuscript, 1 p.   ViU
        With letter of 1 December 1920 to Professors
        John Calvin Metcalf and James Southall Wilson

E409.7 *Troth with the Dead*
    a. Holograph manuscript   See E320.1

E413.7 *Twofold*
    a. Holograph manuscript   See E320.2
    b. Holograph manuscript, 1 p.   See E269.5
E414 *Ultimate Reality*
    Holograph manuscript   See E319.1
E414.5 *Under the Oak*
    a. Holograph manuscript   See E320.1
        First three stanzas only
        See also *Appeal, The*
    b. Holograph manuscript   See E320.2
        Two drafts
    c. Holograph manuscript, 1 p.   See E269.5
E415 *Undying Man, The* (An unfinished folk-tale)
    a. Holograph manuscript, 8 pp.   Unlocated
        Powell 49
    b. Typescript and carbon copy, 6 pp., 6 pp.   TxU
    c. Carbon typescript, 6 pp.   TxU
        Another typing
    d. Two carbon typescripts, 6 pp., 6 pp.   CU
E416 *Verism, naturalism, realism—these names seem big with meaning...*
    Holograph manuscript copy, 4 pp.   TxU
    An introduction to the novels and tales of Giovanni Verga
    Written in another hand
E417 *Vicar's Garden, The.* See *Shadow in the Rose Garden, The*
E418 *Vicar's Son*
    a. Holograph manuscript   See E49
    b. Corrected carbon typescript, 1 p.   See E49
E419 *Violets*
    a. Holograph manuscript, 2 pp.   See E317
    b. Holograph manuscript   See E320.3
    c. Holograph manuscript   See E213
E420 *Virgin and the Gipsy, The*
    a. Holograph manuscript, 160 pp.   TxU
        Tedlock pp. 59–60, Powell 18
    b. Galley proofs, 98 pp.   TxU
E420.3 *Virgin Mother, The*
    a. Holograph manuscript   See E320.1
    b. Holograph manuscript   See E320.2
E420.5 *Virgin Youth*
    a. Holograph manuscript, 1 p.   See E317

b. Holograph manuscript	See E320.2
E421 *Volcanic Venus*	
Carbon typescript	See E319.1
E421.7 *Walk to Huayapa*	
a. Holograph manuscript, 14 pp.	TxU
MS titled: *Mornings in Mexico. Sunday Morning*	
Tedlock pp. 186–7, Powell 76	
b. Corrected typescript, 16 pp.	IU
MS titled in another hand: *Sunday Stroll*	
c. Page proofs	See E246.2
E422 *War-Baby*	
Holograph manuscript	See E319
E422.5 *Was feeling for a new rhythm—* ...	
Holograph manuscript, 1 p.	TxU
A fifteen-line fragment	
E422.7 *We Need One Another*	
Holograph manuscript, 11 pp.	CtY
Notebook cover titled: *Three Essays for Vanity Fair*	
Powell 117	
E423 *Wedding Morn*	
Holograph manuscript, 3 pp.	See E213
E424 *Weeknight Service*	
a. Holograph manuscript, 2 pp.	See E317
b. Holograph manuscript, 2 pp.	See E320.4
c. Holograph manuscript, 2 pp.	MH
E425 *Well in Africa, The*	
a. Holograph manuscript	See E49
b. Corrected carbon typescript, 1 p.	See E49
E426 *What Does She Want?*	
a. Holograph manuscript	See E302
b. Corrected carbon typescript	See E319.1
E426.3 *What Have They Done to You?*	
Carbon typescript	See E266
E426.4 *What is He?*	
Holograph manuscript	See E302
E426.5 *What Is Man Without an Income?*	
a. Holograph manuscript, 1 p.	ICSo
b. Holograph manuscript	See E302

E426.55 *What Matters*
   Holograph manuscript, 2 pp.   See E302
E426.6 *What Would You Fight For?*
   Galley proof   See E319.6
E426.7 *Whatever Man Makes*
   Galley proof   See E319.6
E426.8 *When I Read Shakespeare*
   Holograph manuscript   See E302
E427 *When on the autumn roses* ... See *Song-Day in Autumn*
E427.5 *Whether or Not*
   Holograph manuscript   See E213
E428 *Which Class I Belong To*
   Holograph manuscript, 10 pp.   OCU
   Includes some autobiographical material
E429 *White Blossom, A*
   Holograph manuscript   See E213
E430 *White Peacock, The*
   a. Holograph manuscript, 58 pp.   CU
      Two fragments of an early version
      Tedlock pp. 3–6, Powell 1A
   b. Holograph manuscript, 1 p.   TxU
      A fragment, left half of one page
   c. Holograph manuscript, 1 p.   Private
      A fragment, left half of one page
   d. Holograph manuscript, 802 pp.   Lazarus
      645 pp. in Lawrence's hand; 157 pp. in the hands
      of Agnes Holt, Agnes Mason and Helen Corke
   e. Corrected galley sheets, 123 pp.   CLU
      Lacking no. 59
      Tedlock pp. 6–7, Powell 1B
   f. Review copy   Unlocated
      Notes by Edward Garnett
      Elkin Mathews catalogue (December 1930) item no. 494
E430.3 *White Stocking, The*
   Holograph manuscript, 18 pp.   Private
   MS also titled: *Amusing*
E430.9 *Why?*
   Holograph manuscript   See E302

E432 *Why the Novel Matters*
    a. Holograph manuscript, 14 pp.   TxU
        Tedlock p. 168, Powell 85A
    b. Typescript, 10 pp.   TxU
    c. Carbon typescript, 10 pp.   CU
    d. Carbon typescript, 10 pp.   CU
        Another typing

E432.3 *Wild Common, The*
    Holograph manuscript, 2 pp.   See E317
    Incomplete, first twelve lines missing

E432.6 *Wilful Woman, The*
    Holograph manuscript, 7 pp.   CU
    MS untitled, begins: November of the year 1916. A woman
    travelling from New York to the South West...
    MS titled by Powell: *Journey to the Southwest*
    Tedlock pp. 50–2, Powell 108
    MS titled by Roberts: *Luhan Story*
    Published in (A114) as *The Wilful Woman*

E432.7 *Wilful Woman, Notes for The*
    Holograph manuscript, 1 p.   CU
    Notes for a novel about Mabel Dodge Luhan
    Tedlock pp. 52–3

E433 *Wind, the Rascal, The*
    a. Holograph manuscript   N
        With letter of 15 December 1910 to Louie Burrows
    b. Holograph manuscript, 1 p.   TxU
    c. Holograph manuscript   See E318
    d. Holograph manuscript, 1 p.   See E320.6
    e. Holograph manuscript, 1 p.   Private
    f. Corrected carbon typescript, 1 p.   See E49
    g. Typescript   See E319.7

E434.5 *Winter in the Boulevard*
    a. Holograph manuscript   See E320.1
        A fragment and a draft
    b. Holograph manuscript   See E320.2
    c. Holograph manuscript, 1 p.   See E269.5

E435 *Winter-Lull*
    Holograph manuscript   See E320

E436 *Winter's Tale, A*
    a. Holograph manuscript, 1 p.   See E317

b. Holograph manuscript, 1 p.   ULiv
    With letter of 20 January 1909 to Blanche Jennings
c. Holograph manuscript   See E320.2
d. Typescript, 1 p.   See E320.5

E437 *Wintry Peacock*
a. Holograph manuscript, 16 pp.   Lazarus
b. Corrected typescript, 26 pp.   Unlocated
    Powell 35
c. Corrected proof sheets, 4 pp.   TxU
    Metropolitan sheets (c84) revised for (B10)
    MS also titled: *The Poet's Tale*

E438 *Witch à la Mode, The*
a. Holograph manuscript, 36 pp.   PLeB
    MS titled: *Intimacy*
    Powell 24A
b. Holograph manuscript, 29 pp.   PLeB
    MS titled: *The White Woman*
    Powell 24B
c. Corrected typescript, 26 pp.   PLeB
    Powell 24C
d. Carbon typescript, 27 pp.   CU

E438.3 *Witch: I, The*
Holograph manuscript   See E319.3

E438.5 *Witch: II, The*
Holograph manuscript, 1 p.   See E319.3

E439 *Woman and Her Dead Husband, A.* See *Man Who Died, A*

E439.5 *Woman Who Rode Away, The*
a. Holograph manuscript, 45 pp.   Unlocated
    Tedlock pp. 53–4, Powell 15
b. Corrected typescript, 48 pp.   CtY

E440 *Women Are So Cocksure*
a. Holograph manuscript, 4 pp.   CU
    Tedlock p. 212, Powell 84A
b. Holograph manuscript, 7 pp.   TxU
    Fair copy in Frieda Lawrence's hand
c. Carbon typescript, 4 pp.   TxU
d. Two carbon typescripts, 4 pp., 4 pp.   CU

E440.5 *Women aren't fools, but men are . . .*
Holograph manuscript, 1 p.   TxU
A seventy-word fragment

E441 *Women in Love*
    a. Holograph manuscript, 14 pp.   TxU
       Two fragments, pp. 291–6, 373–80
    b. Holograph manuscript, 55 pp.   TxU
       Chapter 1 Prologue and *Chapter 11 The Wedding* only
    c. Holograph manuscript, 436 pp.   TxU
       In ten exercise books
       Chapters XXIII–XXXI only
    d. Corrected original and carbon typescript, 665 pp.   TxU
    e. Corrected, mostly carbon, typescript, 666 pp.   CaOTU
    f. Corrected typescript, 766 pp.   TxU
    g. Corrected proof copy, 508 pp.   TxU
       Secker trade edition, 1921 (A15c)
       Powell 5

E442 *Women in Love, Foreword to*
    a. Holograph manuscript, 1 p.   Missing from CSt
    b. Page proofs, 4 pp.   CSt
    c. Final proofs, 4 pp.   CSt

E442.5 *Women Want Fighters for Their Lovers*
     Holograph manuscript   See E302

E443 *Wonderful Spiritual Women*
     Carbon typescript   See E319.1

E443.5 *Work*
     Galley proof   See E319.6

E444 *Workdays*. See *Rondeau of a Conscientious Objector*

E445 *Worm Turns, The*
     Holograph manuscript, 1 p.   See E317

E445.5 *Yew-Tree on the Downs, The*
    a. Holograph manuscript   See E320.1
       Two drafts
    b. Holograph manuscript, 3 pp.   See E320.4
    c. Holograph manuscript, 2 pp.   MH
       MS titled: *Affaire d'Amour*
    d. Holograph manuscript   See E320.2

E446 *Young and Their Moral Guardians, The*
     Carbon typescript   See E319.1

E446.5 *Young Soldier with Bloody Spurs, The*
     Holograph manuscript, 4 pp.   NN

E446.7 *Youth Mowing, A*
    a. Holograph manuscript   See E318
    b. Typescript, 1 p.   See E316

E447 *Zeppelin Nights*
    a. Holograph manuscript   See E49
    b. Corrected carbon typescript, 1 p.   See E49

F. BOOKS AND PAMPHLETS ABOUT D. H. LAWRENCE

F. BOOKS AND PAMPHLETS
ABOUT D. H. LAWRENCE

F0.5 *D. H. Lawrence, The Man and His Work*, Adele Seltzer. Thomas Seltzer, New York. 1922.

F1 *D. H. Lawrence, An American Interpretation*, Herbert J. Seligmann. Thomas Seltzer, New York. 1924.

F2 *D. H. Lawrence and Maurice Magnus, A Plea for Better Manners*, Norman Douglas. Privately Printed. 1924.

F3 *A Bibliography of the Writings of D. H. Lawrence*, Edward D. McDonald. The Centaur Bookshop, Philadelphia. 1925. See B16.

F4a. *D. H. Lawrence, An Indiscretion*, Richard Aldington. The University of Washington Book Store, Seattle. 1927.

b. *D. H. Lawrence*, Richard Aldington. Chatto and Windus, London. 1930.

c. *D. H. Lawrence, An Appreciation*, Richard Aldington. Penguin Books, Harmondsworth. [1950].

F5 *D. H. Lawrence, A First Study*, Stephen Potter. Jonathan Cape, London. 1930.

F6 *J. C. Squire v. D. H. Lawrence*, John Arrow. E. Lahr, London. [1930].

F7a. *Elegy*, Rebecca West. Phoenix Book Shop, New York. 1930.

b. *D. H. Lawrence*, Rebecca West. Martin Secker, London. 1930.

F8 *Sing a Song of Sixpence, D. H. Lawrence and the Press*, [Catherine Carswell]. The Broadsheet Press, London. 1930.

F9 *D. H. Lawrence*, John Middleton Murry. The Minority Press, Cambridge. 1930.

F10 *D. H. Lawrence*, F. R. Leavis. The Minority Press, Cambridge. 1930.

F11 *Son of Woman*, John Middleton Murry. Jonathan Cape, London. [1931]. See B30.

F12 *Der Pessimismus bei D. H. Lawrence,* Werner Wesslau. Hans Adler, Griefswald. 1931.

F13 *The Writings of D. H. Lawrence 1925–1930, A Bibliographical Supplement,* Edward D. McDonald. The Centaur Book Shop, Philadelphia. 1931. See B31.

F14 *Young Lorenzo, Early Life of D. H. Lawrence,* Ada Lawrence and G. Stuart Gelder. G. Orioli, Florence. [1932]. See B34.

F15 *Lorenzo in Taos,* Mabel Dodge Luhan. Alfred Knopf, New York. 1932. See B35.

F16 *D. H. Lawrence, An Unprofessional Study,* Anaïs Nin. Edward W. Titus, Paris. [1932]. See B36.

F17a. *The Savage Pilgrimage,* Catherine Carswell. Chatto and Windus, London. 1932. See B37.

   b. *The Savage Pilgrimage,* Catherine Carswell. Martin Secker, London. 1932. (Revised edition).

F18 *Footnote to Lawrence,* Richard Goodman. The White Owl Press, London. 1932.

F19 *D. H. Lawrence and the Body Mystical,* Frederick Carter. Denis Archer, London. 1932.

F20 *A Catalogue of English and American First Editions 1911–1932 of D. H. Lawrence,* Harold Jay Snyder. Published by the author, New York. 1932.

F21 *Elegy in the Manner of a Requiem in Memory of D. H. Lawrence,* Walter Lowenfels. Carrefour, Paris. 1932.

F22 *Naturalisme et Mysticisme Chez D. H. Lawrence,* Saul Cohn. Librairie Lipschutz, Paris. 1932.

F23 *Further Reflections on the Death of a Porcupine,* Olive Moore. Blue Moon Press, London. 1932.

F24 *Reminiscences of D. H. Lawrence,* John Middleton Murry. Jonathan Cape, London. [1933]. See B38.

F25 *D. H. Lawrence, His First Editions, Points and Values,* Gilbert H. Fabes. W. and G. Foyle, London. [1933].

F26a. *Lawrence and Brett, A Friendship,* Dorothy Brett. J. B. Lippincott, Philadelphia. [1933].

b. *Lawrence and Brett, A Friendship*, Dorothy Brett. Sunstone Press, Santa Fe. 1974. (with introduction, prologue and epilogue by John Manchester).

F27 *Lawrence and Apocalypse*, Helen Corke. William Heinemann, London. [1933].

F28 *Pilgrim of the Apocalypse*, Horace Gregory. Viking Press, New York. 1933.

F28.5 *D. H. Lawrence: An Exhibition of Original Manuscripts, Corrected Typescripts, Sketches*, etc., J. and E. Bumpus, Ltd. London. 1933.

F29 *D. H. Lawrence, Reminiscences and Correspondence*, Earl and Achsah Brewster. Martin Secker, London. [1934]. See B39.

F30 *Not I, But the Wind*, Frieda Lawrence. Rydal Press, Santa Fe. [1934]. See B40.

F31 *D. H. Lawrence*, Knut Jaensson. Tidens, Stockholm. 1934.

F32 *Liebe und Ärgernis des D. H. Lawrence*, René Schickele. Albert de Lange, Amsterdam. [1934].

F33 *Studien über die Personlichkeit und die Kunstform von D. H. Lawrence*, Irmgard Reuter. Pöppinghaus, Marburg. 1934.

F34 *D. H. Lawrence, A Personal Record*, E. T. Jonathan Cape, London. [1935]. See B43.

F35 *D. H. Lawrence, A Complete List of His Works with a Critical Appreciation*, Richard Aldington. William Heinemann, London. [1935].

F36 *La Vie de D. H. Lawrence*, Alfred Fabre-Luce. Grasset, Paris. [1935].

F37 *David Herbert Lawrence et les Récentes Idéologies Allemandes*, Ernest Seillière. Boivin, Paris 1936.

F38 *D. H. Lawrence, Essai sur la Formation et le Développement de sa Pensée d'après son Oeuvre en Prose*, Maurice Couaillac. Imprimerie du Commerce, Toulouse. 1937.

F39 *D. H. Lawrence e Outros*, Eugênio Gomes. Globo, Pôrto Alegre. 1937.

F40 *D. H. Lawrence et Forsøg paa en Politsk Analyse*, Elias Bredsdorff. Munksgaard, Copenhagen. 1937.

F41 *D. H. Lawrence fra Nottinghamshire*, Fredrik Wulfsberg. Francis Bull, Oslo. 1937.

F42 *The Manuscripts of D. H. Lawrence*, Lawrence Clark Powell. The Public Library, Los Angeles. 1937. See B46.

F43 *L'Oeuvre de D. H. Lawrence*, Paul de Reul. Vrin, Paris. 1937.

F44 *A Poet and Two Painters*, Knud Merrild. Routledge, London. [1938]. See B47.

F45 *D. H. Lawrence*, Hugh Kingsmill. Methuen, London. [1938].

F46 *Botschaftsverkündigung und Selbstausdruck im Prosawerk von D. H. Lawrence*, Ingeborg Weidner. Forst, Berlin. 1938.

F47 *D. H. Lawrence and Susan His Cow*, William York Tindall. Columbia University, New York. 1939.

F48 *D. H. Lawrence ett Modernt Tankeäventyr*, Melker Johnsson. Bonniers, Stockholm. [1939].

F49 *La Vita di D. H. Lawrence*, Piero Nardi. Mondadori, Milano. [1947].

F50 *The Frieda Lawrence Collection of D. H. Lawrence Manuscripts*, E. W. Tedlock, Jr. University of New Mexico, Albuquerque. 1948. See B51.

F51 *"L'Amante de Lady Chatterley" o del Pudore*, Giovanni Napolitano. Miccoli, Napoli. [1948].

F52 *Portrait of a Genius, But . . .*, Richard Aldington. William Heinemann, London. [1950].

F53 *A Catalogue of Valuable Books by D. H. Lawrence*. Melvin Rare Books, Edinburgh. [1948]. See B54.

F54 *D. H. Lawrence, A Checklist*, William White. Wayne University, Detroit. 1950.

F55 *D. H. Lawrence*, Anthony West. Arthur Barker, London. [1950].

F56 *Taos Quartet in Three Movements*, Merle Armitage. Privately printed, New York. 1950.

F57 *The Life and Works of D. H. Lawrence*, Harry T. Moore. Twayne, New York. [1951].

F58 *D. H. Lawrence and Human Existence*, Father William Tiverton [Martin Jarrett-Kerr.] Rockliff, London. [1951].

F59 *D. H. Lawrence's Princess, A Memory of Jessie Chambers*, Helen Corke. The Merle Press, Thames Ditton. 1951.

F60 *Fire-Bird, A Study of D. H. Lawrence*, Dallas Kenmare. Barrie, London. 1951.

F61 *Journey With Genius, Recollections and Reflections Concerning the D. H. Lawrences*, Witter Bynner. Day, New York. [1951]. See B55.

F62 *"A Proposito di L'Amante di Lady Chatterley" di D. H. Lawrence*, Dino De Lucia. Motemurro, Matera. 1951.

F63 *The Mysticism of D. H. Lawrence*, Martin Wickramasinghe. Published for the author, Colombo. 1951.

F64 *D. H. Lawrence, Prophet of the Midlands*, Vivian de Sola Pinto. University of Nottingham, Nottingham. 1951.

F65 *D. H. Lawrence*, Kenneth Young. Longmans, Green, London. [1952].

F66 *Lorenzo in Search of the Sun*, Eliot Fay. Bookman Associates, New York. [1953].

F67 *The Achievement of D. H. Lawrence*, Frederick J. Hoffman and Harry T. Moore, editors. University of Oklahoma, Norman. [1953].

F68 *The Intelligent Heart*, Harry T. Moore. Farrar, Straus and Young, New York. [1954]. See B57.

F69 *The Love Ethic of D. H. Lawrence*, Mark Spilka. Indiana University, Bloomington. 1955.

F70 *D. H. Lawrence, A Basic Study of His Ideas*, Mary Freeman. University of Florida, Gainesville. 1955.

F71 *D. H. Lawrence, Novelist*, F. R. Leavis. Chatto and Windus, London. 1955.

F72 *Two Exiles, Lord Byron and D. H. Lawrence*, Graham Hough. University of Nottingham, Nottingham. 1956.

F73 *Poste Restante, A Lawrence Travel Calendar*, Harry T. Moore. University of California, Berkeley and Los Angeles. 1956.

F74 *The Spiral Flame, A Study in the Meaning of D. H. Lawrence*, David Boadella. Ritter, Nottingham. 1956.

F75 *The Dark Sun, A Study of D. H. Lawrence*, Graham Hough. Duckworth, London. [1956].

F75.1 *Deutschland in der Sicht von D. H. Lawrence und T. S. Eliot*, Hans Galinsky. Akademie der Wissenschaften und der Literatur in Mainz, Wiesbaden. 1956.

F76 *Die Naturbetrachtung im Prosawerk von D. H. Lawrence*, Elizabeth Hess. Bern. [1957].

F77 *D. H. Lawrence, A Composite Biography*, Edward Nehls. 3 vols. The University of Wisconsin, Madison. 1957, 1958, 1959. See B60.

F78 *Love, Freedom and Society*, John Middleton Murry. Jonathan Cape, London. [1957].

F79 *D. H. Lawrence, An Exhibition of First Editions, Manuscripts, etc.*, Earl Tannenbaum. Southern Illinois University, Carbondale. 1958. See B61.

F80 *D. H. Lawrence and America*, Armin Arnold. Linden, London. 1958.

F81 *Brave Men, A Study of D. H. Lawrence and Simone Weil*, Richard Rees. Gollancz, London. 1958.

F82 *A D. H. Lawrence Miscellany*, Harry T. Moore, editor. Southern Illinois University Press, Carbondale. 1959. See B63.

F82.1 *Opinion, Grove Press, Inc. and Readers' Subscription, Inc., Plaintiffs, against Robert K. Christenberry, Defendent, United States District Court Southern District of New York*, Civil 147–87. The Readers' Subscription, New York. 1959.

F83 *D. H. Lawrence, The Failure and the Triumph of Art*, Eliseo Vivas. Northwestern University Press. [1960].

F84 *D. H. Lawrence After Thirty Years, 1930–1960 Catalogue of an Exhibition held in the Art Gallery of the University of Nottingham 17 June–30 July 1960*, Vivian de S. Pinto, editor. University of Nottingham. 1960. See B64.

F84.1 *David Herbert Lawrence, L'Oeuvre et la Vie*, F. J. Temple. Pierre Seghers, Paris. 1960. See B65.

F84.2 *The University of New Mexico D. H. Lawrence Fellowship Fund Manuscript Collection*, [Warren Roberts]. Humanities Research Center, Austin. 1960. See B63.5.

F84.3 *Tradition and D. H. Lawrence, Inaugural Lecture*, R. L. Drain. J. B. Wolters, Groningen. 1960.

F85 *Frieda Lawrence, The Memoirs and Correspondence*, E. W. Tedlock, editor. Heinemann, London. [1961]. See B68.

F86 *D. H. Lawrence*, Anthony Beal. Oliver and Boyd, Edinburgh and London. 1961.

F87 *The Trial of Lady Chatterley*, C. H. Rolph, editor. Penguin Books, Harmondsworth. 1961.

F88 *David Herbert Lawrence in Selbstzeugnissen und Bilddokumenten*, Richard Aldington. Rowohlt, Reinbek. 1961.

F89 *Books by and about D. H. Lawrence*, A Bookseller's Catalogue. The Gotham Book Mart, New York. 1961.

F90 *Oedipus in Nottingham: D. H. Lawrence*, Daniel A. Weiss. University of Washington Press, Seattle. 1962.

F91 *The Art of Perversity, D. H. Lawrence's Shorter Fiction*, Kingsley Widner. University of Washington Press, Seattle. 1962.

F92 *A Bibliography of D. H. Lawrence*, Warren Roberts. Rupert Hart-Davis, London. 1963.

F93 *D. H. Lawrence, A Collection of Critical Essays*, Ed. Mark Spilka. Prentice Hall Inc., Englewood Cliffs, N. J. 1963.

F94 *The Deed of Life, The Novels and Tales of D. H. Lawrence*, Julian Moynahan. Princeton University Press, Princeton. 1963.

F95 *D. H. Lawrence*, David Daiches. Privately printed, Brighton. 1963.

F96 *The Utopian Vision of D. H. Lawrence*, Eugene Goodheart. University of Chicago Press, Chicago. 1963.

F97 *D. H. Lawrence, Artist and Rebel, A Study of Lawrence's Fiction*, E. W. Tedlock, Jr. University of New Mexico Press, Albuquerque. 1963.

F98 *D. H. Lawrence and German Literature*, Armin Arnold. Mansfield Book Mart: H. Heinemann, Montreal. 1963. See B69.

F99 *D. H. Lawrence, ou le Puritain Scandaleux*, Daniel Gillès. Rene Julliard, Paris. 1964.

F100 *Adventure in Consciousness, The Meaning of D. H. Lawrence's Religious Quest*, George Panichas. Mouton, The Hague. 1964.

F101 *The Geographical Background of the Early Works of D. H. Lawrence*, Claude M. Sinzelle. Didier, Paris. 1964.

F102 *Dark Night of the Body*, L. D. Clark. University of Texas Press, Austin. 1964.

F103 *D. H. Lawrence*, R. P. Draper. Twayne Publishers, Inc., New York. 1964.

F104 *Paintings of D. H. Lawrence*, Ed. Mervyn Levy. Copy, Adams and Mackay, London. 1964. See B70.

F105 *D. H. Lawrence and Sons and Lovers: Sources and Criticism.* E. W. Tedlock, Jr. New York University Press, 1965.

F106 *D. H. Lawrence, The Croydon Years*, Helen Corke. University of Texas Press, Austin. 1965.

F107 *The Forked Flame, A Study of D. H. Lawrence*, H. M. Daleski. Faber and Faber, London. 1965.

F108 *Double Measure, A Study of the Novels and Stories of D. H. Lawrence*, George H. Ford. Holt, Rinehart and Winston, New York. 1965.

F109 *D. H. Lawrence: Sons and Lovers*, Henry A. Talon. Lettres Modernes, Paris. 1965.

F110 *D. H. Lawrence e l'Italia*, Mary Corsani. U. Mursia, Milan. 1965.

F111 *The Influence of D. H. Lawrence on Tennessee Williams*, Norman J. Fedder. Mouton, The Hague. 1966.

F112 *D. H. Lawrence and His World*, Harry T. Moore and Warren Roberts. Thames and Hudson, London. 1966.

F113 *The Art of D. H. Lawrence*, Keith Sagar. Cambridge University Press, Cambridge. 1966.

F114 *D. H. Lawrence as a Literary Critic*, David J. Gordon. Yale University Press, New Haven. 1966.

F115 *D. H. Lawrence: Sons and Lovers*, Gãmini Salgãdo. Edward Arnold, London. 1966.

F116 *Notes on D. H. Lawrence: Sons and Lovers*, Graham Handley. James Brodie, Bath. 1967.

F117 *The Phoenix is My Badge and Sign, Lawrence in the War Years*, Mark Schorer. Stanford University Library, Stanford University. 1968.

F118 *Lawrence and Education*, R. H. Poole. University of Nottingham Institute of Education, Nottingham. 1968.

F119 *D. H. Lawrence: A Finding List*, Lucy Edwards. Nottingham City Library, Nottingham. 1968. See B73.

F120 *D. H. Lawrence, Sons and Lovers*, Raghukul Tilak. Aarti Book Centre, New Delhi. 1968.

F121 *D. H. Lawrence's Sons and Lovers, Self- Encounter and the Unknown Self*, John E. Stoll. Ball State University, Muncie, Indiana. 1968.

F122 *D. H. Lawrence*, Mark Schorer. Dell Publishing Co. Inc., New York. 1968.

F123 *D. H. Lawrence: A Season of Plays*. Royal Court Theatre, London. 1968.

F124 *D. H. Lawrence, Die Charaktere in der Handlung und Spannung Seiner Kurzgeschichten*, Adrian Hsia. H. Bouvier, Bonn. 1968.

F125 *Conflict in the Novels of D. H. Lawrence*, Yudhishtar. Barnes and Noble, New York. 1969.

F126 *D. H. Lawrence, Sons and Lovers, A Casebook*, Ed. Gãmini Salgãdo. Macmillan, London. 1969.

F127 *D. H. Lawrence: L'Homme et la Genèse de Son Oeuvre, Les Années de Formation: 1885–1919*, Emile Delavenay. Librairie C. Klincksieck, Paris. 1969. 2 vols. See B74, F173.

F128 *River of Dissolution: D. H. Lawrence and English Romanticism*, Colin Clarke. Routledge and Kegan Paul, London. 1969.

F129 *D. H. Lawrence*, Tony Slade. Evans Brothers, London. 1969.

F130 *D. H. Lawrence, Sea and Sardinia. The Rainbow: Notes on Literature No. 100*, Gãmini Salgãdo. The British Council, London. 1969.

F131 *D. H. Lawrence, The Rocking-Horse Winner*, Ed. Dominick P. Consolo. Charles E. Merrill Publishing Company, Columbus, Ohio. 1969.

F132 *D. H. Lawrence as Critic*, Illeana Čure-Sazdanic. Munshiram Manoharlal, Delhi. 1969.

F133 *D. H. Lawrence, The Rainbow and Women in Love, A Casebook*, Ed. Colin Clarke. Macmillan, London. 1969.

F134 *D. H. Lawrence and the New World*, David Cavitch. Oxford University Press, New York. 1969.

F135 *Twentieth Century Interpretations of Women in Love, A Collection of Critical Essays*, Ed. Stephen J. Miko. Prentice-Hall, Englewood Cliffs, N. J. 1969.

F136 *Profiles in Literature*, R. P. Draper. Routledge and Kegan Paul, London. 1969.

F137 *A Critical Study of Sons and Lovers*, Som Deva. Literary Publication Bureau, Beharipur, Bareilly. 1969. Second Edition.

F138 *Notes for an Exhibition at the Lawrence Ranch*. Humanities Research Center, Austin. 1970.

F139 *Another Ego, The Changing View of Self and Society in the Work of D. H. Lawrence*, Baruch Hochman. University of South Carolina Press, Columbia. 1970.

F140 *D. H. Lawrence and the Dominant Male*, Derek Patmore. The Covent Garden Press, London. 1970.

F141 *D. H. Lawrence, The Critical Heritage*, Ed. R. P. Draper. Routledge and Kegan Paul, London. 1970.

F142 *D. H. Lawrence and the Dial*, Nicholas Joost and Alvin Sullivan. Southern Illinois University Press, Carbondale. 1970. See B76.

F143 *D. H. Lawrence's American Journey, A Study in Literature and Myth*, James C. Cowan. Case Western Reserve University Press, Cleveland. 1970.

F144 *D. H. Lawrence: An Eastern View*, Chaman Nahal. A. S. Barnes, New York. 1970.

F145 *Letters from a Publisher, Martin Secker to D. H. Lawrence and Others 1911–1929*, Martin Secker. Enitharmon Press, London. 1970.

F146 *Two Tributes, The Death of Lawrence*, Fred B. Millett and *I call on Frieda*, Frederic A. Fisher, Jr. The Washington Street Press, Whitman, Massachusetts. 1970.

F147 *D. H. Lawrence and His World*, Koji Nishimura. Chuo Kovon Sha, Tokyo. 1970.

F148 *The Psychic Mariner, A Reading of the Poems of D. H. Lawrence*, Tom Marshall. The Viking Press, New York. 1970.

F149 *A Concordance to the Poetry of D. H. Lawrence*, Ed. Reloy Garcia and James Karabatsos. University of Nebraska Press, Lincoln. 1970.

F150 *Réflexions et Directives pour L'Etude de D. H. Lawrence, Women in Love*, Anne-Marie Fraisse. Lettres Modernes, Paris. 1970.

F151 *Twentieth Century Interpretations of Sons and Lovers, A Collection of Critical Essays*, Ed. Judith Farr. Prentice-Hall, Englewood Cliffs, N. J. 1970.

F152 *D. H. Lawrence's Rainbow*, Graham Martin. The Open University, Bletchley. 1971.

F153 *D. H. Lawrence's Bestiary*, Kenneth Inniss. Mouton, The Hague. 1971.

F154 *The Visual Imagination of D. H. Lawrence*, Keith Alldritt. Edward Arnold, London. 1971.

F155 *D. H. Lawrence's Response to Russian Literature*, George J. Zytaruk. Mouton, The Hague. 1971.

F156 *D. H. Lawrence: Body of Darkness*, R. E. Pritchard. Hutchinson University Library, London. 1971.

F157 *Toward Women in Love, The Emergence of a Laurentian Aesthetic*, Stephen J. Miko. Yale University Press, New Haven. 1971.

F158 *D. H. Lawrence and Edward Carpenter, A Study in Edwardian Transition*, Emile Delavenay. William Heinemann, London. 1971.

F159 *Twentieth Century Interpretations of The Rainbow, A Collection of Critical Essays*, Ed. Mark Kinkead-Weekes. Prentice-Hall, Englewood Cliffs, N. J. 1971.

F160 *D. H. Lawrence, The Rainbow*, Raghukul Tilak. Aarti Book Centre, New Delhi. 1971.

F161 *D. H. Lawrence: The Rainbow*, Frank Glover Smith. Edward Arnold, London. 1971.

F162 *Critics on D. H. Lawrence, Readings in Literary Criticism*, Ed. W. T. Andrews. George Allen and Unwin, London. 1971.

F163 *D. H. Lawrence, Guide to 20th Century English and American Literature*, Vol. 5, Koji Nishimura. Kenkyusha, Tokyo. 1971.

F164 *D. H. Lawrence in Taos*, Joseph Foster. University of New Mexico Press, Albuquerque. 1972.

F165 *The Country of My Heart, A Local Guide to D. H. Lawrence*, Bridget Pugh. Nottinghamshire Local History Council, Nottingham. 1972.

F166 *Lawrence, Hardy and American Literature*, Richard Swigg. Oxford University Press, New York. 1972.

F167 *Steinbeck and D. H. Lawrence: Fictive Voices and the Ethical Imperative*, Reloy Garcia. The John Steinbeck Society of America, Ball State University, Muncie, Indiana. 1972.

F168 *Young Bert, An Exhibition of the Early Years of D. H. Lawrence*, Lucy I.

Edwards, David Phillips, Arnold Rattenbury, Jo Barnes. Castle Museum, Nottingham. 1972. See B79.

F169 *D. H. Lawrence, Sons and Lovers, A Critical Study*, Ravendra Prakash. Lakshmi Narain Agarwal, Agra. 1972.

F170 *Sons and Lovers, A Critical Study*, Om Prakash. Prakash Book Depot, Bareilly. 1972.

F171 *Acts of Attention, The Poems of D. H. Lawrence*, Sandra M. Gilbert. Cornell University Press, Ithaca. 1972.

F172a. *Frieda von Richthofen, Ihr Leben mit D. H. Lawrence dem Dichter der Lady Chatterley*, Robert Lucas. Kindler Verlag, Munich. 1972.

b. *Frieda Lawrence, The Story of Frieda von Richthofen and D. H. Lawrence*. Robert Lucas. Secker and Warburg, London. 1973.

F173 *D. H. Lawrence: The Man and His Work, The Formative Years: 1885–1919*, Emile Delavenay. William Heinemann, London. 1972. Revised Edition. See F127.

F174 *A Concordance to the Short Fiction of D. H. Lawrence*, Ed. Reloy Garcia and James Karabatsos. U. of Nebraska Press, Lincoln. 1972.

F175 *A Visitor's Guide to Eastwood and the Countryside of D. H. Lawrence*, Michael Bennett. Nottinghamshire County Council, Nottingham. 1972.

F176 *Lawrence*, Frank Kermode. Fontana–Collins, London. 1973.

F177 *D. H. Lawrence, A Critical Anthology*, Ed. H. Coombes. Penguin Books, Harmondsworth. 1973.

F178 *An Exhibition of First Editions and Manuscripts from the D. H. Lawrence Collection of John E. Baker, Jr.*, Keith Cushman. Joseph Regenstein Library, The University of Chicago, Chicago. 1973.

F179 *D. H. Lawrence, The World of the Five Major Novels*, Scott Sanders. The Viking Press, New York. 1973.

F180 *D. H. Lawrence, Novelist, Poet, Prophet*, Ed. Stephen Spender Weidenfeld and Nicolson, London. 1973.

F181 *The Hostile Sun, The Poetry of D. H. Lawrence*, Joyce Carol Oates. Black Sparrow Press, Los Angeles. 1973.

F182 *The Fox*, Kenneth Mackenzie. The Open University, Milton Keynes. 1973.

F183 *D. H. Lawrence: A Collection of Criticism*, Leo Hamalian. McGraw-Hill, New York. 1973.

F184 *Prospectus and Notes for Volume Editors, The Letters of D. H. Lawrence*, James T. Boulton, General Editor. Cambridge University Press, Cambridge. 1973. See B80.

F185 *D. H. Lawrence, The Phoenix and the Flame*, Geoffrey Trease. Macmillan, London. 1973.

F186 *The Priest of Love, A Life of D. H. Lawrence*, Harry T. Moore. Farrar, Straus and Giroux, New York. 1974. Originally published as *The Intelligent Heart*. See B57.

F187 *The von Richthofen Sisters, The Triumphant and the Tragic Modes of Love, Else and Frieda von Richthofen, Otto Gross, Max Weber, and D. H. Lawrence, in the Years 1870–1970*, Martin Green. Basic Books, New York. 1974.

F188 *Boarding the Ship of Death, D. H. Lawrence's Quester Heroes*, Samuel A. Eisenstein. Mouton, The Hague. 1974.

F189 *A Conversation on D. H. Lawrence by Aldous Huxley, Frieda Lawrence Ravagli, Majl Ewing, Lawrence Powell, Dorothy Mitchell Conway*, Ed. Haruhide Mori. Friends of the UCLA Library, Los Angeles. 1974.

F190 *D. H. Lawrence and the Psychology of Rhythm*, Peter Balbert. Mouton, The Hague. 1974.

F191 *D. H. Lawrence and the Way of the Dandelion*, Michael Adam. The Ark Press, Penzance, Cornwall. 1975.

F192 *Son and Lover, The Young Lawrence*, Philip Callow. The Bodley Head, London. 1975.

F193 *The Plays of D. H. Lawrence, A Biographical and Critical Study*, Sylvia Sklar. Vision Press, London. 1975.

F194 *Lorenzo, D. H. Lawrence and the Women Who Loved Him*, Emily Hahn. J. B. Lippincott, Philadelphia. 1975.

F195 *D. H. Lawrence: A Critical Study*, Wagdy Feshawy. Dar-al-Sakata, Cairo. 1975.

F196 *Thought, Words and Creativity, Art and Thought in Lawrence*, F. R. Leavis. Chatto and Windus, London. 1976.

F197 *Who's Who in D. H. Lawrence*, Graham Holderness. Hamish Hamilton, London. 1976.

F198 *D. H. Lawrence: The Polarity of North and South, Germany and Italy in his Prose Works*, Jennifer Michaels-Tonks. Bouvier, Bonn. 1976.

F199 *D. H. Lawrence I: 1885–1914*, J. C. F. Littlewood. Longman for the British Council, Harlow, 1976.

F200 *D. H. Lawrence, Sons and Lovers: Notes on Literature 161*, Rodney Hillman. The British Council, London. 1976.

F201 *D. H. Lawrence, The Rainbow: Notes on Literature 162*, Gãmini Salgãdo. The British Council, London. 1976.

F202 *D. H. Lawrence, Women in Love: Notes on Literature 163*, Damian Grant. The British Council, London. 1976.

F203 *D. H. Lawrence, The Plumed Serpent: Notes on Literature 164*, Alastair Niven. The British Council, London. 1976.

F204 *D. H. Lawrence, Lady Chatterley's Lover: Notes on Literature 165*, Richard Gravil. The British Council, London. 1976.

F205 *D. H. Lawrence, A Bibliography 1911–1975*, John E. Stoll. Whitson Publishing Company, Troy, New York. 1977.

F206 *The Art of the Self in D. H. Lawrence*, Marguerite Beede Howe. Ohio University Press, Athens. 1977.

F207 *D. H. Lawrence, The Novels*, Alastair Niven. Cambridge University Press, Cambridge. 1978.

F208 *The Cambridge Edition of the Works of D. H. Lawrence, Prospectus and Notes for Volume Editors*, James T. Boulton, Warren Roberts. Cambridge University Press, Cambridge. 1978. See B84.

F209 *D. H. Lawrence, Supplement to Catalogue 38*, J. Stephan Lawrence. Rare Books, Chicago. 1978.

F210 *Lawrence and Women*, Ed. Anne Smith. Vision Press, London. 1978.

F211 *D. H. Lawrence's Nightmare*, Paul Delany. Basic Books, New York. 1978.

F212 *D. H. Lawrence at Work*, Keith Cushman. University of Virginia Press, Charlottesville. 1978.

F213 *A D. H. Lawrence Companion*, Frank Pinion. Macmillan, London. 1978.

F214 *D. H. Lawrence: A Critical Study of the Major Novels and Other Writings*, A. H. Gomme. Harvester Press, Sussex. 1978.

F215 *Brodie's Notes on D. H. Lawrence's "The Rainbow,"* W. S. Bunnell. Pan Books, London. 1978.

F216 *D. H. Lawrence: A Calendar of His Works,* Keith Sagar. Manchester University Press, Manchester. 1979.

F217 *D. H. Lawrence Collection: A Catalogue,* University of Nottingham Department of Manuscripts. University of Nottingham, Nottingham. 1979.

F218 *D. H. Lawrence: An Exhibit,* Richard F. Peterson and Alan M. Cohn. Morris Library, Southern Illinois University, Carbondale. 1979.

F219 *D. H. Lawrence and the Idea of the Novel,* John Worthen. The Macmillan Press, Ltd., London. 1979.

F220 *D. H. Lawrence Country: A Portrait of His Early Life and Background,* Roy Spencer. Cecil Woolf, London. 1979. See B85.

F221 *Bibliography of the D. H. Lawrence Collection at Illinois State University,* Roger Tarr and Robert Sokan. Scarlet Ibis Press, Bloomington. 1979.

F222 *The Composition of "The Rainbow" and "Women in Love,"* Charles Ross. University of Virginia Press, Charlottesville. 1979.

F223 *D. H. Lawrence and the High Temptation of the Mind,* Charles Olson. Black Sparrow Press, Santa Barbara. 1980.

F224 *Notes on "Aaron's Rod,"* Henry Miller. Black Sparrow Press, Santa Barbara. 1980.

F225 *D. H. Lawrence and Women,* Carol Dix. The Macmillan Press, Ltd., London. 1980.

F226 *The Life of D. H. Lawrence,* Keith Sagar. Eyre Methuen, London. 1980.

F227 *The World of Lawrence,* Henry Miller. Capra Press, Santa Barbara. 1980.

F228 *D. H. Lawrence: A Phoenix in Flight, Notes to Accompany an Exhibition.* Nottingham University Library, Nottingham. 1980.

F229 *D. H. Lawrence: The Writer and His Work,* Alastair Niven. The British Council, London. 1980.

F230 *D. H. Lawrence and Nottinghamshire 1885–1910,* Sheila M. Cooke. Nottingham County Council, Nottingham. 1980.

F231 *D. H. Lawrence: "Sons and Lovers"* (York Notes), Lance St John Butler. Longmans, London. 1980.

F232 *The Novels of D. H. Lawrence: A Search for Integrity*, John E. Stoll. University of Missouri Press, Columbia. 1980.

F233 *The Minoan Distance: The Symbolism of Travel in D. H. Lawrence.* L. D. Clark. University of Arizona Press, Tucson. 1980.

F234 *Lapsing Out: Embodiments of Death and Rebirth in the Last Writings of D. H. Lawrence*, Donald Gutierrez. Farleigh Dickinson University Press, Rutherford. 1980.

F235 *D. H. Lawrence: The Man Who Lived.* Southern Illinois University Press, Carbondale. 1980.

F236 *Nature and Culture in D. H. Lawrence*, Aidan Burns. Macmillan Press, Ltd., London. 1980.

F237 *D. H. Lawrence and the Art of Translation*, G. M. Hyde. Macmillan Press, Ltd., London. 1981.

F238 *D. H. Lawrence: Interviews and Recollections*, Ed. Norman Page. 2 vols. Macmillan Press, Ltd., London. 1981.

F239 *A Memoir of D. H. Lawrence, The Betrayal*, by G. H. Neville, Ed. Carl Baron. Cambridge University Press, Cambridge. 1981.

F240 *A Reader's Guide to D. H. Lawrence*, Philip Hobsbaum. Thames and Hudson, London. 1981.

F241 *D. H. Lawrence in Australia*, Robert Darroch. Macmillan Company of Australia. Pty, Ltd., Melbourne. 1981.

F242 *D. H. Lawrence: An Annotated Bibliography*, Ed. James C. Cowan. Northern Illinois University Press, De Kalb. 1981.

APPENDIXES

APPENDIX I

A. PARODIES OF
LADY CHATTERLEY'S LOVER

I. ROBERT LEICESTER | [*decorative rule*] | SADIE | CATTERLEY'S | COVER | A LEG-PULL | 1933 | CRANLEY & DAY

Blue cloth boards, printed in dark-blue on upper cover. All edges trimmed, $7\frac{5}{16}'' \times 4\frac{7}{8}''$. Robert Leicester is the pseudonym for William S. Scott.

II. LADY LOVERLEY'S | chatter | [*drawing*] | *by* | MART REB | WITH DESIGNS AND DECORATIONS | BY | FRITZ WILLIS | FOR THE ARTHUR YEOMAN PRESS

Green cloth boards, printed in black on upper cover. All edges trimmed, $5\frac{5}{16}'' \times 4''$.

III. [*single rule*] | THE ARDENT CLASSICS NUMBER TWO | [*single rule*] | LADY | CHATTERLEY'S | LOVER | A Dramatization of his Version | of D. H. LAWRENCE'S Novel | by | SAMUEL ROTH | [*single rule*] | 1931 WILLIAM FARO, INC. New York 1931 | [*single rule*]

Black cloth boards, cream paper label on spine printed in black. All edges trimmed, $7\frac{5}{16}'' \times 4\frac{3}{4}''$.

IV. LADY | CHATTERLEY'S | HUSBANDS | AN ANONYMOUS SEQUEL TO | THE CELEBRATED NOVEL | LADY CHATTER-LEY'S | LOVER | PUBLISHED BY WILLIAM FARO, INC. | IN NEW YORK CITY, THE YEAR 1931

Black cloth boards, cream paper label on spine printed in black. All edges trimmed, $7\frac{9}{16}'' \times 5\frac{1}{4}''$. The author of this book was Samuel Roth.

V. JEHANNE D'ORLIAC | *Lady Chatterley's* | *Second Husband* | *Translated from the French by* | WARRE BRADLEY WELLS | *Robert M. McBride & Company, New York*

Orange cloth boards, stamped in silver on upper cover. All edges trimmed, top edges stained red, $7\frac{7}{8}'' \times 5''$. The original edition of this book, *Le Deuxième Mari de Lady Chatterley*, was published in Paris by Albin Michel in 1934 with a note by André Malraux.

VI. LADY | CHATTERLEY'S | FRIENDS | [*dot*] | *A New Sequel to* | LADY CHATTERLEY'S | LOVER *and* LADY CHATTERLEY'S | HUSBANDS | [*dot*] | 1932 | WILLIAM FARO, INC. | NEW YORK

Dark green cloth boards, cream paper label on spine printed in black. All edges trimmed, $7\frac{13}{16}'' \times 5\frac{1}{8}''$.

VII. *Lady* | *Loverley's* | *Chatter* | EDITED AND COMPILED BY | *Warren Watwood* | [*publisher's device*] | W.H.ALLEN | LONDON | 1960

Yellow paper covers printed in red, black and white. All edges trimmed, $8\frac{9}{16}'' \times 5\frac{5}{8}''$. This booklet is made up of still photographs from silent movies with humorous captions by Warren Watwood.

VIII. STAVROS MELISSINOS | THE LADY | AND THE GAMEKEEPER | A stage play based on the story | LADY CHATTERLEY'S LOVER | By | D. H. LAWRENCE | ATHENS | 1969

White paper covers printed in black and red. All edges trimmed, $8\frac{3}{16}'' \times 5\frac{9}{16}''$.

B. PIRACIES AND FORGERIES OF
LADY CHATTERLEY'S LOVER

I. LADY CHATTERLEY'S LOVER | BY | D. H. LAWRENCE | PRIVATELY PRINTED | 1928

Mulberry-coloured paper boards, cream paper label on spine printed in black. Top edges rough-trimmed, fore and bottom edges untrimmed, 9″ × 6¼″. This forgery is reported to have been done in England; it is a photographic facsimile of the genuine first edition (A42a), but differs in several important details. The genuine first edition measures one inch thick inside the covers, while the forgery measures one and one-fourth inches. The statement of limitation in the forgery reads, "limited to 1500 copies."

II. LADY CHATTERLEY'S | LOVER | BY | D. H. LAWRENCE | PRIVATELY PRINTED | 1929

Red-brown cloth boards, printed in black on upper cover. All edges trimmed, 8½″ × 5⁷⁄₁₆″. The frontispiece consists of a photographic reproduction of Jo Davidson's bust of D. H. Lawrence which was not done until March of 1930, hence if the frontispiece occurs in all copies, its presence would seem to indicate that the book was actually made later than the date on the title page. Although the printer's imprint states that the book was printed by the Tipografia Giuntina at Florence, there is no evidence to indicate that the Tipografia Giuntina ever printed any editions of *Lady Chatterley's Lover* other than those described in (A42a) and (A42b). Only one copy of this book was examined, and it was not numbered. The statement of limitation claims the book to be the third edition, limited to 500 copies.

III. LADY CHATTERLEY'S [*in red*] | LOVER [*in red*] | BY | D. H. LAWRENCE | *Florence* | PRIVATELY PRINTED [*in red*] | 1928

Red paper boards, grey paper label on spine printed in black. Top and bottom edges trimmed, fore edges untrimmed, 8⅞″ × 6⅜″. The text of this piracy follows that of the first edition, but at least a portion of the typographical errors have been corrected. The statement of limitation says that 1000 copies were printed.

IVa. BY D. H. LAWRENCE | [*double rule in red*] | L [*in red*] ADY | C [*in red*] HATTERLEY'S | L [*in red*] OVER | [*short double rule in red*] 1930 [*short double rule in red*] | WILLIAM FARO, INC.

Black cloth boards, cream paper label on spine printed in black. Top edges trimmed, fore edges untrimmed, bottom edges rough-trimmed, $9\frac{3}{8}'' \times 6\frac{3}{8}''$.

b. LADY | CHATTERLEY'S | LOVER [*preceding three lines in red*] | BY | D. H. LAWRENCE | THE SAMUEL ROTH EDITION AS ORI- | GINALLY PUBLISHED BY WILLIAM | FARO, INC., NEW YORK CITY. 1931 [*preceding three lines in red*]

Black cloth boards, $8\frac{1}{2}'' \times 5\frac{9}{16}''$.

c. LADY | CHATTERLEY'S | LOVER | *By* | D. H. LAWRENCE | [*printer's ornaments*] | The Samuel Roth Edition as Originally | Published by William Faro, Inc.; New York City, 1932

Grey cloth boards, $8\frac{15}{16}'' \times 5\frac{15}{16}''$.

All three of the Faro piracies were printed from the same plates; the first two have a frontispiece consisting of a portrait of Lady Chatterley with the industrial Midlands in the background. The illustration is signed by A. K. Skillin, 1930. The Faro text is expurgated and consequently unreliable.

Va. LADY | CHATTERLEY'S | LOVER | BY | D. H. LAWRENCE | [*emblem of sun with rays*] | Published by | NESOR PUBLISHING CO.

Green cloth boards, printed on the spine in red. All edges trimmed, $8\frac{15}{16}'' \times 5\frac{3}{4}''$.

b. LADY | CHATTERLEY'S | LOVER | BY | D. H. LAWRENCE | [*emblem of sun with rays*] | Published by | NESOR PUBLISHING CO.

Blue cloth boards, otherwise the same as Va. The Nesor text is the same as that for the Faro piracies.

VI. *AN EXCERPT FROM* | LADY CHATTERLEY'S LOVER | *BY D. H. LAWRENCE.*

This is a two leaf, four page folio measuring $11\frac{5}{8}'' \times 9\frac{1}{4}''$. Page [1] serves as the title page as above. Page [2] begins with an illustration by R. K., presumably Rockwell Kent. The excerpt is on page [2] and [3] and is taken from Chapter X of *Lady Chatterley*. Page [4] reads: *50 copies of this selection were handset in Baskerville and printed on | Maidstone paper by A. L. & S. K. in February, 1930. The drawing is | also an excerpt and is from an unpublished illustration by R. K. This | printing is for private distribution and it is not for sale, Copy number | [hand-lettered number]*

APPENDIX II

OTHER SPURIOUS WORKS

I. SUN [*in red*] | [*single rule*] | BEING THE UNEXPURGATED | VERSION OF THIS STORY BY | D. H. LAWRENCE | [*single rule*] | [*ornamental device in red*] | [*single rule*] | PRIVATELY PRINTED | MCMXXIX | [*within an ornamental rule forming a border*]

Decorative paper boards with a red cloth backstrip, stamped in gold on spine. Top edges trimmed, fore and bottom edges untrimmed, $8\frac{7}{8}''$ × 6″.

II. DIRTY | WORDS

Green paper covers, printed in black on upper cover. All edges trimmed, 8″ × $5\frac{3}{8}''$. According to McDonald (B16), this pamphlet began to appear in the United States during the spring of 1931. Although Aldous Huxley's name is associated with the pamphlet because of the statement of limitation which reads, "One hundred and fifty copies printed for A. H.," apparently he had nothing to do with its publication, and there is no evidence to show that the essay was written by D. H. Lawrence.

III. D. H. LAWRENCE | AUTUMN IN NEW MEXICO [*in red*] | *& other poems* | [*publisher's device*] | NETHERMERE PRESS

Decorative paper boards, tan paper labels on upper cover and spine, printed in black. All edges untrimmed, $9\frac{5}{8}''$ × $6\frac{3}{8}''$.

Contains: An Epistle from Thelma—An Epistle from Arthur—The Complaint of the Soul of a Worker—Late at Night Along the Home Road—Transformations: Morning (preceding five poems reprinted from C259)—Amphibian—Salt-Licks—Widdershins—War—The Maleficent Triangle—Beauty and Truth—Fire (the preceding seven poems reprinted from C257)—Autumn in New Mexico (a variant of "Autumn at Taos" reprinted from *Palms* 1 : 4, Autumn 1923; see contents for *Birds, Beasts and Flowers* (A27)).

This publication was not authorized by the Lawrence estate.

IV. LITTLE BLUE BOOK NO. 1610 | Edited by E. Haldeman-Julius |
One Lover Among | Many | D. H. Lawrence | HALDEMAN-JULIUS
PUBLICATIONS | GIRARD, KANSAS

Cream paper covers, printed in black on upper cover as the title page
above. All edges trimmed, $5'' \times 3\frac{3}{8}''$. This little booklet contains
Lawrence's story "Once" under the title "One Lover Among
Many." The verso of the title page bears a copyright notice on behalf
of the Haldeman-Julius Company, but no date. See (A56).

V. Love Among The | Haystacks | D.H. LAWRENCE | HALDEMAN-
JULIUS PUBLICATIONS | GIRARD, KANSAS

Blue paper covers, printed in black on upper cover as the title page
above. All edges trimmed, $8\frac{7}{16}'' \times 5\frac{5}{16}''$. Contains Lawrence's story,
"Love Among the Haystacks." The verso of the title page bears a
copyright notice on behalf of E. Haldeman-Julius, but no date. See
(A56).

APPENDIX III

A PERIODICAL

THE PHOENIX | [*drawing of a stylized phoenix*] | vol. I, no. I, Spring 1938

Grey paper covers, printed in blue on the upper cover and spine. Top edges rough-trimmed, fore and bottom edges untrimmed, $7\frac{3}{4}''\times 5\frac{1}{8}''$. The first issue of *Phoenix*, published by Peter Cooney at Woodstock, New York, was the March–April–May number for 1938. Apparently Mr Cooney conceived his quarterly for the purpose of furthering the ideas of D. H. Lawrence. When it began, the magazine had for its European editor Henry Miller, later replaced by Derek Savage. Each issue carried a reprint of a piece by D. H. Lawrence.

INDEX

INDEX

INDEX

574

INDEX

INDEX

INDEX

FRESH WATER, A47
Freud, Sigmund, B49.7
Frieda Lawrence Collection of D. H. Lawrence Manuscripts, The, B51, F50
Frieda Lawrence, The Memoirs and Correspondence, B68, F85
Frieda Lawrence, The Story of Frieda von Richthofen and D. H. Lawrence, F172
Frieda von Richthofen, Ihr Leben mit D. H. Lawrence dem Dichter der Lady Chatterley, F172
FROHNLEICHNAM, A10, A43
FROM A COLLEGE WINDOW, A11, A43, E141
FROM THE ITALIAN LAKES, E320.2
FROST FLOWERS, A10, A43, C51, E142
FULL LIFE, A62
FULL SCORE, TWENTY TALES, A81
Fuller, H. B., A20
Furbank, P. N., A121
FURNITURE, A62
Furst, H., A46
Further Reflections on the Death of a Porcupine, F23
FUTURE OF THE NOVEL, THE, E385.5
FUTURE RELATIONSHIPS, A62
FUTURE RELIGION, A62, A101, A111
FUTURE STATE, A62
FUTURE WAR, A62
Fyfe, Hamilton, A16

G. K.'s Weekly, A31
G., W. N., A50
GAI SAVAIRE, LE, E384
Galinsky, Hans, F75.1
Gallup, Donald, C267
Galsworthy, John, E177.3, (*see* JOHN GALSWORTHY)
Garcia, Reloy, F149, F167, F174
Gardiner, Margaret, C225.5
Gardiner, Rolfe, C225.5
Garnett, Constance, B66
Garnett, David, A47, A56, A61, A63, A76, B53, B57, B59
Garnett, Edward, A2, A3, A4, A6, A16, A23, A28, A47, A69, A76, B66, C3, C34, C109, C207, C213, C226, C227, E430
Garnett Family, The, B66

Garvin, J. L., B67
Gass, W. H., A107
Gates, Barrington, A47
Gathorne-Hardy, Robert, B81
GAZELLE CALF: A BLIND SOLDIER TELLS HIS CHILDREN ABOUT ARABIA, THE, E49
GAZELLE CALF, THE, A47, A116, E143
Gelder, G. Stuart, B34, F14
GENTLE ART OF MARKETING IN MEXICO, THE (*see* MARKET DAY)
Gentleman from San Francisco and Other Stories, The, B9
GENTLEMAN FROM SAN FRANCISCO, THE, A107, B9, C88, E143.3
GENTLEMAN, THE, A104
Gentry, Curt, A102
GENTRY, THE, A30
Geographical Background of the Early Works of D. H. Lawrence, The, F101
Georgian Literary Scene, The, C21
Georgian Poetry 1911–1912, B1
Georgian Poetry 1913–1915, B3
Georgian Poetry 1920–1922, B11
GEORGIAN POETRY 1911–1912, A REVIEW OF, A76, A95, C19
GEORGIAN RENAISSANCE, THE (*see* GEORGIAN POETRY 1911–1912, A REVIEW OF)
Georgian Stories, C31
GERMAN BOOKS, THOMAS MANN, A76, A95, C21
GERMAN IMPRESSIONS, FRENCH SONS OF GERMANY, A76, C16
GERMAN IMPRESSIONS, HAIL IN THE RHINELAND, A76, C17
"German Letters of D. H. Lawrence, The," C247
[GERMANS AND ENGLISH], A197, C165.5, C217, E143.7
GERMANS AND LATINS, A76, (*see* [GERMANS AND ENGLISH])
Gertler, Mark, A9
GETTING ON, E144
Ghost Book, B19
Gibbon, Perceval, A4
GIFTS OF FORTUNE by H. M. Tomlinson, A REVIEW OF, A76, C150, E145

Roth, Samuel (*see* Appendix I)
Royal Court Theatre, F123
Rozanov, V. V., C156, C196
Rubenstein, H. F., A92b
RUINATION, A12, A43, E352.3
RUNNING BAREFOOT, E320.1, E320.4
Russ, Stephen, A115
Russell, Bertrand, A84, B81, C230

Sackbut, A46
Sackville-West, Edward, A32, A34
Sackville-West, Victoria, A54
SADDEST DAY, THE, A47
Sadie Catterley's Cover (*see* Appendix I)
Sagar, Keith, A114, A115, A116, C245, C250, F113, F216, F226
SAÏD THE FISHERMAN by Marmaduke Pickthall, A REVIEW OF, A76, C133.5, C148
ST. GEORGE AND THE DRAGON, A62
St. Irvine, Lyn, A45
ST. JOHN, A27, A43, A88, A116, C79, E352.5
ST. JOSEPH'S ASS (*see* STORY OF THE SAINT JOSEPH'S ASS)
SAINT: LITANY OF GREY NURSES, THE, E49
ST. LUKE, A27, A43, A88, A116, C79, E352.53
ST. MARK, A27, A43, A83, A88, A116, C79, E352.55
ST. MATTHEW, A27, A43, A88, A116, C79, C106, C111, E352.57
ST. MAWR, A31
ST. MAWR, A31, A67, A72, A91, A96, A112, D10.1, D10.2, D34.34, D39.31, D47, D83, D99.13, D99.23, D116, D133, D187, D204, D220, D246.3, E352.6
ST. MAWR TOGETHER WITH THE PRINCESS, A31
Salgādo, Gāmini, F115, F126, F130, F201
SALT, A62, A101
SALT-LICKS, C257, (*see* Appendix II)
SALT OF THE EARTH, A47, E352.65
SALVATION, A62
SAMSON AND DELILAH, A23, A67, A81, A94, C43, D20, D99.18, D99.23, D192, D195, E352.7

San Francisco Chronicle, A102
SAN GAUDENZIO (*see* ON THE LAGO DI GARDA)
Sanders, Norman, A121
Sanders, Scott, F179
SANE AND INSANE, A47
SANE REVOLUTION, A, A47, A88
SANE UNIVERSE, THE, A47
SATISFACTION, A62
Saturday Review, A1, A2, A4, A5, A6, A21, A24, A26, A29, A31, A33, A37, A41, A43, A53, A54, A57, A60, A62, A102
Saturday Review of Literature, A29, A30, A31, A33, A37, A41, A43, A50, A53, A54, A57, A61, A62, A63, A71, A76, A83, A91, C208
Saturday Westminster Gazette, C11, C12, C13, C15, C16, C17, C20, C24, C26
Savage, Derek (*see* Appendix III)
Savage, Henry, A1, C242, C260
Savage Pilgrimage, The, B37, F17
Scarlet Letter, The, by Nathaniel Hawthorne (*see* NATHANIEL HAWTHORNE AND "THE SCARLET LETTER")
SCENT OF IRISES, A9, A38, A43, A68, B2, E352.9
Schaffner, Halle, A37
Schickele, René, F32
Schneider, Isidor, A43, A62, A63
SCHOOL (a poem), E317
SCHOOL (another poem), E320.1
SCHOOL, AFTERNOON, E320.1
SCHOOL: I. MORNING, A104d, C259, E353.8
SCHOOL: I. MORNING, SCRIPTURE, E320.1
SCHOOL: I. MORNING, THE STREET, E353.3
SCHOOL: I. MORNING, THE WASTE LANDS, E320.1
SCHOOL ON THE OUTSKIRTS, A11, A43, E353.5
SCHOOL ON THE WASTE LANDS, THE, E320.2
SCHOOLGIRL, excerpt from THE RAINBOW, A117
SCHOOLMASTER, AFTERNOON IN

INDEX

INDEX